D0603637

A Legal Guide for Student Affairs Professionals

A Legal Guide for
Student Affairs Professionals

Adapted from
The Law of Higher Education,
Third Edition

William A. Kaplin
Barbara A. Lee

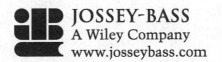

JOSSEY-BASS
A Wiley Company
www.josseybass.com

Published by

JOSSEY-BASS
A Wiley Company
989 Market Street
San Francisco, CA 94103-1741

www.josseybass.com

Copyright © 1997 by John Wiley & Sons, Inc.

Jossey-Bass is a registered trademark of John Wiley & Sons, Inc.

No part of this publication may be reproduced, stored in a retrieval system, or transmitted in any form or by any means, electronic, mechanical, photocopying, recording, scanning, or otherwise, except as permitted under Sections 107 or 108 of the 1976 United States Copyright Act, without either the prior written permission of the Publisher or authorization through payment of the appropriate per-copy fee to the Copyright Clearance Center, 222 Rosewood Drive, Danvers, MA 01923, (978) 750-8400, fax (978) 750-4744. Requests to the Publisher for permission should be addressed to the Permissions Department, John Wiley & Sons, Inc., 605 Third Avenue, New York, NY 10158-0012, (212) 850-6011, fax (212) 850-6008, e-mail: permreq@wiley.com.

Jossey-Bass books and products are available through most bookstores. To contact Jossey-Bass directly, call (888) 378-2537, fax to (800) 605-2665, or visit our website at www.josseybass.com.

Substantial discounts on bulk quantities of Jossey-Bass books are available to corporations, professional associations, and other organizations. For details and discount information, contact the special sales department at Jossey-Bass.

We at Jossey-Bass strive to use the most environmentally sensitive paper stocks available to us. Our publications are printed on acid-free recycled stock whenever possible, and our paper always meets or exceeds minimum GPO and EPA requirements.

Library of Congress Cataloging-in-Publication Data

Kaplin, William A.
   A legal guide for student affairs professionals / William A. Kaplin, Barbara A. Lee. — 1st ed.
      p. cm. — (The Jossey-Bass higher and adult education series)
   "Adapted from the Law of higher education, third edition."
   Includes index.
   ISBN 0–7879–0862–2 (cloth: acid-free paper)
   1. College students—Legal status, laws, etc.—United States.
2. Universities and colleges—Law and legislation—United States.
I. Lee, Barbara A. II. Kaplin, William A. Law of higher education.
III. Title. IV. Series.

KF4243.K36 1997
344.73'079—dc21   96–51218
                                                                          CIP

FIRST EDITION
HB Printing   10 9 8 7 6 5 4 3

The Jossey-Bass
Higher and Adult Education Series

CONTENTS

*W.K.: To Robert M. Kiebala (1943–1991), my college roommate,
fellow lawyer, and constant friend; and to Janet N. Gantt (1945–1994),
my special friend in a couples covenant group—both of whom died
during the time I was preparing the manuscript for* The Law of Higher
Education, *Third Edition. "Kuby"'s sense of humor and fun-loving laughter
and grin, and Janet's unwavering Christian faith, will always
be shining examples for me.*

*B.L.: To my late parents, Robert and Keren Dalrymple Lee,
whose love and encouragement have always inspired and motivated me,
and to Jim and Robby, without whose patience and forbearance
this project could not have been completed.*

PREFACE

Today's college campuses present a multitude of challenges for student affairs professionals. Often the issues they face involve institutional policy, but with increasing frequency they have legal implications as well. For example, a student religious organization may approach the dean of students seeking recognition or an allocation from the fund for student activities. How should the administration respond? Or perhaps a wealthy alumna calls the vice president for student affairs and offers to make a multi-million-dollar donation for scholarships—on the condition that they be awarded only to African American students from disadvantaged families. Can and should the vice president accept the donation and follow the potential donor's wishes? Or the director of admissions is asked whether the college should deny admission to an applicant who indicates that he has been imprisoned for assault and robbery. He has completed his prison term and wants to make a fresh start. Are there legal risks to admitting the student, or is there potential legal liability if he is denied admission?

Legal problems regarding students can arise even before students come to campus. Examples include admissions issues, or postadmission requests for information concerning accommodation for students with disabilities. And the problems continue even after students graduate; they include, for example, maintaining the privacy of education records, deciding whether to report defaults on the repayment of student loans, or determining whether to revoke a degree due to belatedly discovered academic misconduct. While students are enrolled, other difficult questions regarding disabilities, education records, and academic misconduct may arise, along with questions about disciplinary procedures, administration of federal financial aid programs, residence hall life, regulation of fraternities and student organizations, breaches of campus security, student protests, sexual harassment of students by faculty, hate speech, administrative authority over student newspapers, and a host of other matters. To handle such problems, student affairs professionals must have a sound knowledge of the legal landscape, a sensitivity to the relationship between law and institutional policy, and good working relationships with legal counsel.

This book is designed to help student affairs professionals—from vice presidents to deans to entry-level staff persons—develop the capacities they need to successfully meet the myriad legal challenges they face. Although certainly no substitute for the advice of a competent attorney, this book analyzes legal developments, identifies trends, and tracks their implications for academic institutions, sometimes pointing out how particular legal developments may clash with academic practices or values. It also suggests preventive law measures and otherwise facilitates effective working relationships between counsel and administrators.

RELATION TO *THE LAW OF HIGHER EDUCATION,* THIRD EDITION

This book is adapted from a longer work, *The Law of Higher Education,* Third Edition (*LHE* 3d). In preparing this special edition of *LHE* 3d, we retained all the core material that is of particular interest to student affairs professionals, as well as more general background information on matters such as the law of copyright, dealing with the federal government, working with counsel, and the litigation process. The material from *LHE* 3d is thoroughly reorganized and re-edited for focus and ease of use.

We have also added new material on developments that had not yet occurred when *LHE* 3d went to press, such as the *Hopwood* case on affirmative action in admissions, the *Rosenberger* case on student fee allocations to student religious organizations, the *Cohen* case on sexual harassment in the classroom, and *Goehring v. Brophy* on subsidizing abortion services from mandatory student fees. New material has also been added on developments that have become the focus of greater attention since the third edition. Examples are legal issues concerning campus computer networks and the Internet, and legal issues regarding athletes with disabilities. To produce the volume in a timely fashion, however, we did not update every section. Therefore, some sections remain current as of August 1994, the press deadline for *LHE* 3d. Updating for these sections will be provided by a supplement to *LHE* 3d that will be published in mid-1997 by the National Association of College and University Attorneys. The supplement will be keyed to this book, as well as to *LHE* 3d.

This special adaptation of *LHE* 3d contains material from all nine of its chapters. Almost all of the material from *LHE* Chapter One ("Overview of Post-secondary Education Law") and *LHE* Chapter Four ("The College and the Students") is included. The other *LHE* chapters are each represented by selected sections that we believe have particular relevance to student affairs (for example, the material on academic freedom in the classroom from *LHE* Chapter Three, which has particular relevance for staff investigating student harassment complaints).

OVERVIEW OF THE CONTENTS

This book is divided into twelve chapters and covers approximately two hundred topics. To serve its audience, the book organizes and conceptualizes the entire range of legal considerations pertinent to student affairs administration. As with *LHE* 3d, all of postsecondary education is included: the large state university and the small private, liberal arts college; the graduate and professional school as well as the community college and vocational and technical institution; the traditional campus-based program and the innovative off-campus or multistate program. The text avoids legal jargon and technicalities when possible and explains them when they are used.

This book also reflects the same perspective on the intersection of law and education as does *LHE* 3d:

> The law has arrived on the campus. Sometimes it has been a beacon, other
> times a blanket of ground fog. But even in its murkiness, the law has not come
> "on little cat feet," like Carl Sandburg's "Fog"; nor has it sat silently on its
> haunches; nor will it soon move on. It has come noisily and sometimes has
> stumbled. And even in its imperfections, the law has spoken forcefully and
> meaningfully to the higher education community and will continue to do
> so [Preface, *LHE* 1st, 2d, 3d].

CITATIONS AND REFERENCES

Each chapter ends with a selected annotated bibliography. Readers can use the listed books, articles, reports, and other sources to extend the discussion of particular issues presented in the chapter, to explore issues not treated in the chapter, to obtain additional practical guidance in dealing with the chapter's issues, to keep abreast of later developments, and to discover resources for research. Other sources pertaining to particular questions are cited in the text, and footnotes occasionally provide additional explanation of legal terms or additional background information. Court decisions, statutes, and administrative regulations are cited throughout the text. The citation form generally follows *The Bluebook: A Uniform System of Citation* (15th ed., Columbia Law Review Association, Harvard Law Review Association, *University of Pennsylvania Law Review,* and *Yale Law Journal,* 1991). The legal sources that these citations refer to are described in Chapter One, Section 1.3.3, of this edition.

RECOMMENDATIONS FOR USING THE BOOK AND KEEPING UP-TO-DATE

As noted in the prefaces for all three editions of *LHE,* some precautions on using this adaptation are in order:

> The legal analyses and suggestions, of necessity, are general; they are not adapted to the law of any particular state or to the circumstances prevailing at any particular postsecondary institution. Thus, the book is not a substitute for the advice of legal counsel, for further research into primary legal resources, or for individualized study of each legal problem's specific circumstances. Nor is the book necessarily the latest word on the law. There is a saying among lawyers that "the law must be stable and yet it cannot stand still" [R. Pound, *Interpretations of Legal History,* p. 1 (1923)], and the law is moving especially fast in its applications to postsecondary education. Thus, administrators and counsel will want to keep abreast of ongoing developments concerning the issues in this book. Various aids [described hereafter] exist for this purpose.

Keeping abreast of developments is just as much a necessity—and a challenge—as it was when the previous editions of *LHE* were published. In addition to the updates of *LHE* that will be published every other year, readers will find helpful the annual reviews of higher education cases ("The Law of Higher Education and the Courts") that are published in the National Association of College and University Attorneys' (NACUA) *Journal of College and University Law.* Also, reprints of court opinions and commentary on higher education law are published biweekly in *West's Education Law Reporter* by West Publishing Company (included in the selected annotated bibliography for Chapter One (Section 1.1)).

Also helpful are various periodicals that provide information on current legal developments. *Synthesis: Law and Policy in Higher Education,* published five times a year by College Administration Publications, Asheville, North Carolina, provides in-depth analysis and commentary on major contemporary issues. *Synfax Weekly Report* and *Synfax Bulletin,* published by Synfax, Crofton, Maryland, are fax newsletters that digest and critique current legal and policy developments. These resources are also included in the selected annotated bibliography for Chapter One (Sections 1.1 and 1.2). The *School Law News*—a biweekly publication of Capitol Publications, Alexandria, Virginia—provides journalistic coverage of legal events. The *College Law Digest,* published every four weeks for its members by NACUA in cooperation with West Publishing Company, reports on recent court decisions (unpublished as well as published), journal articles and other publications, and acquisitions by NACUA's Exchange of Legal Information service; it also contains original commentary on current topics. *Perspective: The Campus Legal Monthly,* published by Magna Publications, Madison, Wisconsin, provides analysis of recent cases and campus issues, along with preventive law suggestions. *Lex Collegii,* a newsletter published quarterly by College Legal Information, Nashville, Tennessee, analyzes selected legal issues and provides preventive law suggestions, especially for private institutions. The NASPA *Forum* also contains information on recent legal developments of significance to student affairs professionals.

For news reporting of current events in higher education generally, but particularly for substantial coverage of legal developments, readers may wish to consult the *Chronicle of Higher Education,* published weekly by Editorial Projects for Education, Washington, D.C.; or *Education Daily,* published every weekday by Capitol Publications.

For keeping abreast of conference papers, journal articles, and pertinent government and association reports, *Higher Education Abstracts* would be helpful; it is published four times a year by the Claremont Graduate School, Claremont, California. The ERIC (Educational Resources Information Center) database, sponsored by the U.S. Department of Education, performs a similar service encompassing books, monographs, research reports, conference papers and proceedings, bibliographies, legislative materials, dissertations, and journal articles on higher education.

For extended analytical commentary on recent developments, two journals should be especially helpful: the *Journal of College and University Law,* published quarterly by NACUA and focusing exclusively on postsecondary education, and the *Journal of Law and Education,* covering elementary and secondary as well as postsecondary education and published quarterly by Jefferson Lawbook Company, Cincinnati, Ohio.

Many of these resources are described, and their uses are examined, in R. Shaffer, *Legal Resources for Higher Education Law: A Review Essay,* Monograph 84–3 (Institute for Higher Education Law and Governance, University of Houston, 1984), reprinted in 7 *Review of Higher Education* 443 (1984) and in 12 *Journal of College and University Law* 83 (1985).

A final resource may be of interest to those who wish to use either *LHE* 3d or this book as a classroom or workshop text. An instructor's manual is available that includes edited versions of leading court opinions, illustrative statutes and regulations, notes and discussion questions, problems and sample examination questions (with outlines of suggested answers), and other useful materials. The manual, entitled *Cases, Problems, and Materials: An Instructional Supplement to* The Law of Higher Education, is available from the National Association of College and University Attorneys.

Overall, this book has the same goal for student affairs professionals as the previous *LHE* editions have had for all higher education administrators:

> The hope of this book is to provide a base for the debate concerning law's role on campus; for improved understanding between law and academia; and for effective relationships between administrators and counsel. The challenge of our age is not to get the law off campus; it is there to stay. The challenge is to make law more a beacon and less a fog. The challenge is for law and higher education to accommodate one another, preserving the best values of each for the mutual benefit of both. Just as academia benefits from the understanding and respect of the legal community, so law benefits from the understanding and respect of academia.

March 1997

WILLIAM A. KAPLIN
Washington, D.C.
BARBARA A. LEE
New Brunswick, N.J.

ACKNOWLEDGMENTS

Colleagues in and out of academia reviewed portions of the third edition manuscript, providing helpful feedback on matters within their expertise and good wishes for the project: Lou Barracato, Cliff Fishman, Bill Fox, George Garvey, Roger Hartley, Kathy Kelly, David Kempler, Lisa Lerman, Veryl Miles, Benjamin Mintz, Michael Noone, Shira Perlmutter, George Smith, Bill Wagner, and Harvey Zuckman, all professors at the Columbus School of Law, Catholic University of America; Craig Parker, general counsel for Catholic University of America; David Scott, Beckmann Rich, and Shirley Weitz of the University Counsel's office at Rutgers University; Frances Loren and John Wolf from the Employment and Labor Counsel's office at Rutgers; Claire M. Boccella, health, safety, and environment counsel for Rhone Poulenc; Ralph Brown, an emeritus professor at Yale University Law School; Peter Byrne, professor of law at Georgetown University; Sandra Mulay Casey, assistant counsel for the State University of New York; Richard B. Crockett, a private practitioner in New York; Rosalind Fink, a private practitioner in New York; Ann Franke, associate secretary and counsel, American Association of University Professors; John Garland, executive assistant to the president of the University of Virginia; Eileen Jennings, university counsel at Central Michigan University; Jordan Kurland, associate general secretary of the American Association of University Professors; Sandra McMullan, general counsel for North Harris Montgomery Community College Distrct; Marcus Mills, immigration specialist at the University of

Iowa; Michael Olivas, Bates professor and director, Institute for Higher Education Law and Governance, University of Houston; Steven G. Olswang, vice provost at the University of Washington; Gary Pavela, director of judicial programs at the University of Maryland; Benjamin Rawlins, special assistant to the chancellor and legal counsel at North Carolina A&T University; Bonita Sindelar, a private practitioner in New Jersey; Ted Sky, senior counsel and former associate general counsel at the U.S. Department of Education; and Joan Van Tol, corporate counsel and executive assistant to the president at the Law School Admission Service.

The work of research assistants for *The Law of Higher Education*, Third Edition also remains evident in this new volume. At Catholic University: Beth Andreozzi, George Hani, Lisa Mangan, Melanie Santos, Vytas Vergeer; and S. Dawn Robinson (summer research associate). At Wake Forest University: Barbara Allen, Jesse Bone, Kevin Lake, and Christopher Roshon. At the University of Houston: Albert Garcia. At Rutgers University: Celeste Campos and Norman Jimerson.

In addition, the assistance of Catholic University law librarians Patrick Petit, Diana Botluck, Mark Hammond, and James Roscher is still reflected in this new volume, as is the heroic service provided by Dorothy Conway, manuscript editor for both the second and third editions of *LHE*.

Other persons have made new contributions to our work on this new volume for student affairs professionals. Our special thanks go to Gabrielle Fenlon, member of the faculty support staff at Catholic University, who accurately prepared the manuscript and provided other valuable support services as well; Jennifer Orzechowski and Claire Milner, law student research assistants; and Barbara Kaplin, who assisted with proofreading.

W.A.K.
B.A.L.

THE AUTHORS

W ILLIAM A. KAPLIN is professor of law at the Columbus School of Law,
Catholic University of America, in Washington, D.C., where he is also
special counsel to the university general counsel. He has been a visiting professor at Cornell Law School and at Wake Forest University School of
Law; a distinguished visiting scholar at the Institute for Higher Education Law
and Governance, University of Houston; and a visiting scholar at the Institute
for Educational Leadership, George Washington University. A former editor of
the *Journal of College and University Law* and a former member of the Education Appeal Board at the U.S. Department of Education, he is the immediate
past Chair of the Education Law Section, Association of American Law Schools,
and is currently a contributing editor for *Synfax Weekly Report* and a member
of the advisory board for *Synthesis: Law and Policy in Higher Education.*

Kaplin received the American Council on Education's Borden Award, in
recognition of the first edition of *The Law of Higher Education,* and the Association for Student Judicial Affairs' D. Parker Young Award for research contributions. He has also been named a Fellow of the National Association of College
and University Attorneys.

Kaplin is the author of the first two editions of *The Law of Higher Education*
and coauthor of *LHE* 3d, as well as the companion volume *Cases, Problems, and
Materials: An Instructional Supplement to* The Law of Higher Education. He has
also coauthored *State, School, and Family: Cases and Materials on Law and Education* (2d ed., 1979) and has written *The Concepts and Methods of Constitutional*

Law (1992) as well as numerous articles, monographs, and reports on education law and policy and on constitutional law.

William Kaplin received his B.A. degree (1964) in political science from the University of Rochester and his J.D. degree (1967) from Cornell University, where he was editor-in-chief of the *Cornell Law Review*. He then worked with a Washington, D.C., law firm, served as a law clerk at the U.S. Court of Appeals for the District of Columbia Circuit, and was an attorney in the education division of the U.S. Department of Health, Education, and Welfare before joining the Catholic University law faculty.

BARBARA A. LEE is professor of human resource management at the School of Management and Labor Relations, Rutgers University, New Brunswick, New Jersey, where she teaches in the graduate program in human resource management and previously served as associate provost for the social sciences. She is cochair of the editorial board of the *Journal of College and University Law,* a former member of the board of directors of the National Association of College and University Attorneys, a member of the executive committee of the Human Resources Division of the Academy of Management, and a member of the executive committee of the Labor and Employment Law Section of the New Jersey Bar Association. She was also named a Fellow of the National Association of College and University Attorneys.

Lee is the coauthor of *LHE* 3d and the companion volume, *Cases, Problems, and Materials.* She is also the author of numerous books, chapters, and articles focusing on the legal aspects of academic employment, including the book *Academics in Court* (1987, with George LaNoue). Her work in the area of employment discrimination and labor relations in corporate settings has also been published extensively.

Barbara Lee received her B.A. degree (1971) in English and French from the University of Vermont and both her M.A. degree (1972) in English and her Ph.D. degree (1977) in higher education administration from the Ohio State University. She received her J.D. degree (1982) from Georgetown University. She has held professional positions with the U.S. Department of Education and the Carnegie Foundation for the Advancement of Teaching and has taught at Rutgers University since 1982.

A Legal Guide for Student Affairs Professionals

CHAPTER ONE

Overview of Postsecondary Education Law

SEC. 1.1. HOW FAR DOES THE LAW REACH AND HOW LOUD DOES IT SPEAK?

Law's presence on the campus and its impact on the daily affairs of post-secondary institutions have grown continuously since publication of the first edition of *The Law of Higher Education* in 1978. Whether one is responding to campus disputes, planning to avoid future disputes, or charting the institution's policies and priorities, law remains an indispensable consideration. Legal issues arising on campuses across America also continue to be aired not only within the groves of academia but also in external forums. Students, faculty members, staff members, and their institutions, for example, are still frequently litigants in the courts. As this trend continues, more and more questions of educational policy become converted into legal questions as well. Litigation has extended into every corner of campus activity. In some of the more striking cases, students have sued their universities for damages after being accused of plagiarism; a student has sued after being barred from the campus computer network; student athletes have sought injunctions ordering their institutions or athletic conferences to grant or reinstate eligibility for intercollegiate sports; disabled students have filed suits against their institutions or state rehabilitation agencies, seeking sign language interpreters or other auxiliary services to support their education; students who have been victims of violence have sued their institutions for alleged failures of campus security; and former students involved in bankruptcy proceedings have sought judicial discharge of student-loan debts owed to institutions. Disappointed students have sued over grades—and have even lodged challenges such as the remarkable 1980s lawsuit in which a student sued her institution for $125,000 after an instructor gave her a B + grade, which she claimed should have been an A–. Women and minority students have challenged the heavy reliance by scholarship selection panels and medical schools on standardized tests, and "truth-in-testing" proponents have sued to force disclosure of standardized test questions and answers. Students and others supporting animal rights have used lawsuits (and civil disobedience as well) to pressure research laboratories to reduce or eliminate the use of animals. And rejected female applicants have successfully sued two all-male bastions, Virginia Military Institute and The Citadel, seeking increased opportunities for women.

Faculty members have been similarly active. Professors have sought legal redress after their institutions have changed their laboratory or office space or increased the size of their classes. One group of faculty members in the 1980s challenged their institution's plan to build a new basketball arena, because they feared that construction costs would create a drain on funds available for academic programs. Female faculty members have increasingly brought sexual harassment claims to the courts. Across the country, suits brought by faculty members who have been denied tenure—once one of the most closely guarded and sacrosanct of all institutional judgments—are now commonplace.

Outside parties also have been increasingly involved in postsecondary education litigation. In the student athlete cases, athletic conferences were sometimes defendants. In the disabled student cases, state rehabilitation agencies were sometimes defendants. In the truth-in-testing litigation, testing organizations were defendants. Private student clubs have been in litigation regarding the exclusion or admission of women. Sporting goods companies have been sued by universities for trademark infringement because they allegedly appropriated university insignia and emblems for use on their products. Broadcasting companies have been in litigation over rights to control television broadcasts of intercollegiate athletic contests. Separate entities created by institutions, or with which institutions affiliate, have been involved in litigation with the institutions. Drug companies have sued and been sued in disputes over patent rights to discoveries. And increasingly, other commercial and industrial entities of various types have engaged in litigation with institutions regarding purchases, sales, and research ventures. Community groups, environmental organizations, taxpayers, and other outsiders have also gotten into the act, suing institutions for a wide variety of reasons, from curriculum to land use. Recipients of university services have also resorted to the courts. In one late-1980s suit, a couple sued a state university veterinary hospital after their llama died while being examined by a vet-

lawsuit, or it may issue a "preliminary injunction" prior to trial in order to preserve the status quo or otherwise protect the plaintiff's rights during the pendency of the lawsuit.

Preliminary injunctions raise a host of important tactical questions for both plaintiffs and defendants. In determining whether to grant a motion for such an injunction, the court will commonly balance the plaintiff's likelihood of success on the merits of the lawsuit, the likelihood that the plaintiff will suffer irreparable harm absent the injunction, the injury that the defendant would sustain as a result of the injunction, and the general public interest in the matter. In *Jones v. University of North Carolina,* 704 F.2d 713 (4th Cir. 1983), the court applied such a balancing test and granted the plaintiff's request for a preliminary injunction. The plaintiff was a nursing student who had been accused of cheating on an examination, found guilty after somewhat contorted proceedings on campus, and barred from taking courses during the spring semester. She then filed a Section 1983 suit (see Section 2.3.3), alleging that the university's disciplinary action violated her procedural due process rights. She requested and the court granted a preliminary injunction ordering the university to reinstate her as a student in good standing pending resolution of the suit. The university appealed the court's order, claiming it was an abuse of the court's discretion. The appellate court considered the hardships to both parties and the seriousness of the issues the plaintiff had raised. Regarding hardships, the court noted that, without the injunction, the plaintiff would have been barred from taking courses and delayed from graduating, denied the opportunity to graduate with her classmates, and forced to explain this educational gap throughout her professional career. On the other hand, according to the court, issuance of the injunction would not significantly harm the university's asserted interests:

> While we recognize the University's institutional interest in speedy resolution of disciplinary charges and in maintaining public confidence in the integrity of its processes, Jones will suffer far more substantial, concrete injury if the injunction is dissolved and she is ultimately vindicated than will the University if the injunction stands and its position is finally upheld [704 F.2d at 716].

Similarly, in *Cohen v. Brown University,* 991 F.2d 888 (1st Cir. 1993), a U.S. Court of Appeals upheld a district court's preliminary injunction ordering Brown University to reinstate its women's gymnastics and women's volleyball programs to full varsity status pending the trial of a Title IX claim. Both programs had been reduced to club status as a result of budget constraints. Although men's programs were also cut back, the plaintiffs alleged that the cuts discriminated against women at the school. The appellate court approved the district judge's determination that the plaintiffs would most likely prevail on the merits when the case was finally resolved. Further, the court observed that if the volleyball and gymnastics teams continued in their demoted state for any length of time, they would suffer irreparably because they would lose recruitment opportunities and coaches. The court found that these harms outweighed the small financial loss the university would sustain in keeping the teams at a varsity level until final resolution of the suit. (The *Cohen* case is further discussed in Section 10.3.)

1.4.5. Managing Litigation and the Threat of Litigation

Managing, settling, and conducting litigation, like planning its avoidance, requires the in-depth involvement of attorneys at all stages.[1] Institutions should place heavy emphasis on this aspect of institutional operations. Both administrators and counsel should cultivate conditions in which they can work together as a team in a treatment law mode (see Section 1.7.2). The administrator's basic understanding of the tactical and technical matters discussed in Sections 1.4.1 through 1.4.4, and counsel's mastery of these technicalities and the tactical options and difficulties they present, will greatly enhance the institution's capacity to engage in treatment law that successfully protects the institution's mission as well as its reputation and financial resources.

Litigation management is a two-way street. It may be employed either in a defensive posture when the institution or its employees are sued or threatened with suit, or in an offensive posture when the institution seeks access to the courts as the best means of protecting its interests in a conflict situation. Administrators, like counsel, will thus do well to consider treatment law from both perspectives and to view courts and litigation as a potential benefit in some circumstances, rather than only as a hindrance.

Although administrators and counsel must accord great attention and energy to lawsuits when they arise, and thus must emphasize the expert practice of treatment law, their primary and broader objective should be to avoid lawsuits or limit their scope whenever that can be accomplished consistent with the institutional mission. Once a lawsuit has been filed, they sometimes can achieve this objective by using summary judgment motions or (if the institution is a defendant) motions to dismiss, or by encouraging pretrial negotiation and settlement. Moreover, by agreement of the parties, the dispute may be diverted from the courts to a mediator or an arbitrator. Even better, they may be able to derail disputes from the litigation track before any suit is filed by providing for a suitable alternative mechanism for resolving the dispute. Mediation and arbitration are common and increasingly important examples of such ADR (alternative dispute-

---

[1]The suggestions in this section apply not only to litigation against the institution but also to suits against officers or *employees* of the institution when the institution is providing, or considering providing, legal representation or related assistance to the employee. In suits where both the institution and one or more named institutional officers or employees are defendants, questions may arise concerning possible conflicts of interest that should preclude the institution's legal staff from representing all or some of the officers or employees.

resolution) mechanisms (see Section 1.1), which are usable whether the institution is a defendant or a plaintiff, and whether the dispute is an internal campus dispute or an external dispute with a commercial vendor, construction contractor, or other outside entity. For internal campus disputes, internal grievance processes and hearing panels (see, for example, Section 7.1) are also important ADR mechanisms and may frequently constitute remedies that, under the exhaustion doctrine (Section 1.4.2), disputants must utilize before resorting to court.

Even before disputes arise, administrators and counsel should be actively engaging in preventive law (Section 1.7.2) as the most comprehensive and forward-looking means of avoiding and limiting lawsuits. Preventive law also has a useful role to play in the wake of a lawsuit, especially a major one in which the institution is sued and loses. In such a circumstance, administrators may engage in a postlitigation audit of the institutional offices and functions implicated in the lawsuit. The purpose would be to use the litigation constructively, as a kind of lens through which to view institutional shortcomings of the type that led to the lawsuit and the judgment against the institution, and to rectify such shortcomings so that lawsuits need not arise again in that area of concern.

SEC. 1.5. THE PUBLIC-PRIVATE DICHOTOMY

1.5.1. Background

Historically, higher education has roots in both the public and the private sectors, although the strength of each one's influence has varied over time (see generally F. Rudolph, *The American College and University: A History* (University of Georgia Press, 1990)). Sometimes following and sometimes leading this historical development, the law has tended to support and reflect the fundamental dichotomy between public and private education.

A forerunner of the present university was the Christian seminary. Yale was an early example. Dartmouth began as a school to teach Christianity to the Indians. Similar schools sprang up throughout the colonies. Though often established through private charitable trusts, they were also chartered by the colony, received some financial support from the colony, and were subject to its regulation. Thus, colonial colleges were often a mixture of public and private activity. The nineteenth century witnessed a gradual decline in governmental involvement with sectarian schools. As states began to establish their own institutions, the public-private dichotomy emerged. (See D. Tewksbury, *The Founding of American Colleges and Universities Before the Civil War* (Anchor Books, 1965).) In recent years, this dichotomy has again faded as state and federal governments have provided larger amounts of financial support to private institutions, many of which are now secular.

Although private institutions have always been more expensive to attend than public institutions, private higher education has been a vital and influential force in American intellectual history. The private school can cater to special interests that a public one often cannot serve because of legal or political constraints. Private education thus draws strength from "the very possibility of doing something different than government can do, of creating an institution free to make choices government cannot—even seemingly arbitrary ones— without having to provide a justification that will be examined in a court of law" (H. Friendly, *The Dartmouth College Case and the Public-Private Penumbra* (Humanities Research Center, University of Texas, 1969), 30).

Though modern-day private institutions are not always free from examination "in a court of law," the law often does treat public and private institutions differently. These differences will underlie much of the discussion in this book. They are critically important in assessing the law's impact on the roles of particular institutions and the duties of their administrators.

Whereas public institutions are usually subject to the plenary authority of the government that creates them, the law protects private institutions from such extensive governmental control. Government can usually alter, enlarge, or completely abolish its public institutions; private institutions, however, can obtain their own perpetual charters of incorporation, and, since the famous *Dartmouth College* case (*Trustees of Dartmouth College v. Woodward*, 17 U.S. 518 (1819)), government has been prohibited from impairing such charters. In that case, the U.S. Supreme Court turned back New Hampshire's attempt to assume control of Dartmouth by finding that such action would violate the Constitution's contracts clause. Subsequently, in three other landmark cases—*Meyer v. Nebraska*, 262 U.S. 390 (1923); *Pierce v. Society of Sisters*, 268 U.S. 510 (1925); and *Farmington v. Tokushige*, 273 U.S. 284 (1927)—the Supreme Court used the due process clause to strike down unreasonable governmental interference with teaching and learning in private schools.

Nonetheless, government does retain substantial authority to regulate private education. But—whether for legal, political, or policy reasons—state governments usually regulate private institutions less than they regulate public institutions. The federal government, on the other hand, has tended to apply its regulations comparably to both public and private institutions or, bowing to considerations of federalism, has regulated private institutions while leaving public institutions to the states.

In addition to these differences in regulatory patterns, the law makes a second and more pervasive distinction between public and private institutions: public institutions and their officers are fully subject to the constraints of the federal Constitution, whereas private institutions and their officers are not. Because the Constitution was designed to limit only the exercise of government power, it does not prohibit private individuals or corporations from impinging on such freedoms as free speech, equal protection, and due process. Thus, *insofar as the federal Constitution is concerned,* a private university can engage in private acts of discrimination, prohibit student protests, or expel a student without affording the procedural safeguards that a public university is constitutionally required to provide.

Indeed, this distinction can be crucial even within a single university. In *Powe v. Miles,* 407 F.2d 73 (2d Cir. 1968), seven Alfred University students had been suspended for engaging in protest activities that disrupted an ROTC ceremony. Four of the students attended Alfred's liberal arts college, while the remaining three were students at the ceramics college. The state of New York had contracted with Alfred to establish the ceramics college, and a New York statute specifically stated that the university's disciplinary acts with respect to students at the ceramics college were considered to be taken on behalf of the state. The court found that the dean's action in suspending the ceramics students was "state action," but the suspension of the liberal arts students was not. Thus, the court ruled that the dean was required to afford the ceramics students due process but was not required to follow any constitutional dictates in suspending the liberal arts students, even though both groups of students had engaged in the same course of conduct.

1.5.2. The State Action Doctrine

As *Powe* makes clear, before a court will apply constitutional guarantees of individual rights to a postsecondary institution, it must first determine that the institution's action is "state (governmental) action." Although this determination is essentially a matter of distinguishing public from private institutions, or the public part of an institution from the private part, these distinctions do not necessarily depend on traditional notions of public or private. Because of varying patterns of government assistance and involvement, a continuum exists, ranging from the obvious public school (such as the tax-supported state university) to the obvious private school (such as the religious seminary). The large gray area between these extremes provides a continuing source of debate about how far the government must be involved before a "private" institution may be considered "public" under the Constitution. Since the early 1970s, however, the trend of the U.S. Supreme Court's opinions has been to trim back the state action concept, making it less likely that courts will find state action to exist in particular cases. The leading case in this line involving educational institutions is *Rendell-Baker v. Kohn,* 457 U.S. 830 (1982), discussed below.

Though government funding is a relevant consideration, much more than money is involved in a state action determination. Courts and commentators have dissected the state action concept in many different ways, but at heart essentially three approaches have emerged for attributing state action to an ostensibly private entity. When the private entity (1) acts as an agent of government in performing a particular task delegated to it by government (the delegated power theory), or (2) performs a function that is generally considered the responsibility of government (the public function theory), or (3) obtains substantial resources, prestige, or encouragement from its involvement with government (the government contacts theory), its actions may become state action subject to constitutional constraints.

The first theory, delegated power, was relied on in the *Powe v. Miles* case (discussed in Section 1.5.1), where the court found that New York State had delegated authority to Alfred to operate a state ceramics school at the university. This same court also considered the delegated power theory in *Wahba v. New York University*, 492 F.2d 96 (2d Cir. 1974), in which a research professor had been fired from a government-funded research project. But here, the court refused to find that the firing was state action, since the government did not exercise any managerial control over the project. This focus on state involvement *in addition to funding* has assumed increasing importance in state action law. In *Greenya v. George Washington University*, 512 F.2d 556 (D.C. Cir. 1975), for instance, the university had a contract with the Navy to provide instruction at the U.S. Naval School of Hospital Administration. When the university fired a teacher assigned to teach in this program, he argued state action on the basis that he had been teaching government employees at government facilities— essentially a delegated power theory. But the court rejected the argument on grounds similar to those in Wahba:

> [Plaintiff] was always under the supervision and control of university officials, and . . . he maintained no contractual relations with the Navy. Nothing in the record indicates that the Navy had any right to say who would be hired to teach the English course. Neither does the record indicate that the Navy had anything whatsoever to do with the failure to renew appellant's contract. Appellant was merely the employee of an independent contractor who was providing educational services to the Navy [512 F.2d at 561–62].

The second theory, the public function theory, has generally not been a basis for finding state action in education cases. Though the issue has often been raised, courts have recognized that education has substantial roots in the private sector and cannot be considered a solely public function. In the *Greenya* case, for instance, the court simply remarked, "We have considered whether higher education constitutes 'state action' because it is a 'public function' as that term has been developed . . . and have concluded that it is not. . . . Education . . . has never been a state monopoly in the United States." In the later case of *State v. Schmid*, 423 A.2d 615 (N.J. 1980) (see Section 11.5.3), however, the court was unwilling to accord the public function theory such a summary rejection. The case concerned the applicability of the First Amendment to Princeton University's removal from campus of a nonstudent who was distributing political leaflets. After refusing to find state action under the government contacts theory, the court set out the most comprehensive analysis to date of the application of the public function theory to private college campuses. But because of the absence of decisional authority and "strong cross-currents of policy" regarding the question, the court deferred any final determination on the public function theory, deciding the case instead under the New Jersey state constitution.

It is the third theory, the government contacts theory, that has had the greatest workout in postsecondary education cases. Although this theory is closely related to the delegated power theory, it focuses on less formal and particularized relationships between government and private entities. As the U.S. Supreme Court noted in the landmark *Burton v. Wilmington Parking Authority* case, 365 U.S. 715, 722 (1961), "Only by sifting facts and weighing circumstances can the nonobvious involvement of the state in private conduct be attributed its true significance." The search focuses initially on state involvement in the particular activity that gives rise to the lawsuit: "[T]he inquiry must be whether there is a sufficiently close nexus between the State and the challenged action of the [private] entity so that the action of the latter may be fairly treated as that of the State itself" (*Jackson v. Metropolitan Edison Co.,* 419 U.S. 345, 351 (1974)).[2] Alternately, a state action finding may be based on the state's overall involvement with the private institution, if "the state has so far insinuated itself into a position of interdependence with . . . [the institution] that it must be recognized as a joint participant in the challenged activity" (*Burton,* 345 U.S. at 725, establishing the "joint venturer" or "symbiotic relationship" branch of the government contacts theory). When the state is so substantially involved in the whole of the private entity's activities, courts will not normally require proof that it was specifically involved in (or had a "nexus" with) the particular activity challenged in the lawsuit.

The *Greenya* case also illustrates the government contacts theory. In challenging his termination by George Washington University, the plaintiff sought to base state action not only on the government's contract with the university but also on the government's general support for the university. The court quickly affirmed that neither the grant of a corporate charter nor the grant of tax-exempt status is sufficient to constitute state action. It then reached the same conclusion regarding federal funding of certain university programs and capital

---

[2]In *Jackson,* the U.S. Supreme Court nailed down this point when it rejected the petitioner's state action argument because "there was no . . . [state] imprimature placed on the practice of . . . the private entity] about which petitioner complains," and the state "has not put its own weight on the side of the . . . practice by ordering it" (419 U.S. at 357). Such a showing of state involvement in the precise activity challenged may not be required, however, in race discrimination cases (see *Norwood v. Harrison,* 413 U.S. 455 (1973)), and the cases discussed later in this section.

expenditures. Government funding, in the court's view, would not amount to state action unless and until the conditions placed on such funding "become so all-pervasive that the government has become, in effect, a joint venturer in the recipient's enterprise" (*Greenya* at 561). In contrast, in *Benner v. Oswald,* 592 F.2d 174 (3d Cir. 1979), the court found state action by applying the government contacts theory. The plaintiffs in the case, students at Pennsylvania State University, challenged the process for selecting members of the university's board of trustees. Relying on numerous contacts between the university and the state, the court used the *Burton* joint venturer test to hold that selection of the trustees constituted state action.

Most state action cases, like those above, are concerned with whether government is so involved in the activities of a private institution as to render those activities state action. But state action issues may also arise with respect to public institutions. In that context, the basic question is whether the public institution is so involved with the activity of some private entity as to render that entity's activity state action. In *Shapiro v. Columbia Union National Bank and Trust Co.,* 576 S.W.2d 310 (Mo. 1978), for example, the question was whether the University of Missouri at Kansas City (a public institution) was so entwined with the administration of a private scholarship trust fund that the fund's activities became state action. The plaintiff, a female student, sued the school and the bank, which was the fund's trustee. The fund had been established as a trust by a private individual, who had stipulated that all scholarship recipients be male. Shapiro alleged that, although the Columbia Union National Bank was named as trustee, the university in fact administered the scholarship fund; that she was ineligible for the scholarship solely because of her sex; and that the university's conduct in administering the trust therefore was unconstitutional. She further claimed that the trust constituted three-fourths of the scholarship money available at the university and that the school's entire scholarship program was thereby discriminatory.

The trial court twice dismissed the complaint for failure to state a cause of action, reasoning that the trust was private and the plaintiff had not stated facts sufficient to demonstrate state action. On appeal the Supreme Court of Missouri reviewed the university's involvement in the administration of the trust, applying the government contacts theory:

> We cannot conclude that by sifting all the facts and circumstances there was
> state action involved here. Mr. Victor Wilson established a private trust for
> the benefit of deserving Kansas City "boys." He was a private individual; he
> established a trust with his private funds; he appointed a bank as trustee;
> he established a procedure by which recipients of the trust fund would be
> selected. The trustee was to approve the selections. Under the terms of the will,
> no public agency or state action is involved. Discrimination on the basis of sex
> results from Mr. Wilson's personal predilection. That is clearly not unlawful.

The dissemination of information by the university in a catalogue and by other means, the accepting and processing of applications by the financial aid office, the determining of academic standards and financial needs, the making of a tentative award or nomination and forwarding the names of qualified male students to the private trustee . . . does not in our opinion rise to the level of state action [576 S.W.2d at 320].

Disagreeing with this conclusion, one member of the appellate court wrote in a dissenting opinion:

The university accepts the applications, makes a tentative award, and in effect "selects" the male applicants who are to receive the benefits of the scholarship fund. The acts of the university are more than ministerial. The trust as it has been administered has shed its purely private character and has become a public one. The involvement of the public university is . . . of such a prevailing nature that there is governmental entwinement constituting state action [576 S.W.2d at 323].

Having declined to find state action, thus denying the plaintiff a basis for applying the Constitution to the trust fund, the appellate court majority affirmed the dismissal of the case. (For a discussion of the treatment of sex-restricted scholarships under Title IX, see Section 4.2.3.)

Four years after *Shapiro*, a major U.S. Supreme Court case added more firepower to the postsecondary arsenal for thwarting state action challenges. *Rendell-Baker v. Kohn*, 457 U.S. 830 (1982), was a suit brought by teachers at a private school who had been discharged as a result of their opposition to school policies. They sued the school and its director, Kohn, alleging that the discharges violated their federal constitutional rights to free speech and due process. The issue before the Court was whether the private school's discharge of the teachers was "state action," subjecting it to the constraints of the Constitution.

The defendant school specializes in dealing with students who have drug, alcohol, or behavioral problems or other special needs. Nearly all students are referred by local public schools or by the drug rehabilitation division of the state's department of health. The school receives funds for student tuition from the local public school boards and is reimbursed by the state department of health for services provided to students referred by the department. The school also receives funds from other state and federal agencies. Virtually all the school's income, therefore, is derived from government funding. The school is also subject to state regulations on various matters, such as record keeping and student-teacher ratios, and to requirements concerning services provided under its contracts with the local school boards and the state health department. Few of these requirements, however, relate to personnel policy.

Using an analysis based on the government contacts theory, the Supreme Court held that neither the government funding nor the government regulation was sufficient to make the school's discharge decisions state action. As to funding, the Court analogized the school's funding situation to that of a private corporation whose business depends heavily on government contracts to build "roads, bridges, dams, ships, or submarines" for the government. And as to regulation:

> Here the decisions to discharge the petitioners were not compelled or even influenced by any state regulation. Indeed, in contrast to the extensive regulation of the school generally, the various regulators showed relatively little interest in the school's personnel matters. The most intrusive personnel regulation promulgated by the various government agencies was the requirement that the Committee on Criminal Justice had the power to approve persons hired as vocational counselors. Such a regulation is not sufficient to make a decision to discharge made by private management, state action [457 U.S. at 841].

The Court also considered and rejected two other arguments of the teachers: that the school was engaged in state action because it performs a "public function" and that the school had a "symbiotic relationship" with—that is, was engaged in a "joint venture" with—government, which constitutes state action under *Burton v. Wilmington Parking Authority,* discussed above. As to the former argument, the Court reasoned:

> [T]he relevant question is not simply whether a private group is serving a "public function." We have held that the question is whether the function performed has been "traditionally the *exclusive* prerogative of the state" (*Jackson v. Metropolitan Edison Co.*, 419 U.S. at 353). There can be no doubt that the education of maladjusted high school students is a public function, but that is only the beginning of the inquiry. [Massachusetts law] demonstrates that the state intends to provide services for such students at public expense. That legislative policy choice in no way makes these services the exclusive province of the state. Indeed, the Court of Appeals noted that until recently the state had not undertaken to provide education for students who could not be served by traditional public schools (641 F.2d at 26). That a private entity performs a function which serves the public does not make its acts state action [457 U.S. at 842].

As to the latter argument, the Court concluded simply that "the school's fiscal relationship with the state is not different from that of many contractors performing services for the government. No symbiotic relationship such as existed in *Burton* exists here."

Having rejected all the teachers' arguments, the Court, by a 7–to–2 vote, concluded that the school's discharge decisions did not constitute state action, and it affirmed the lower court's dismissal of the lawsuit.

As part of the narrowing trend evident in the Court's state action opinions since the early 1970s, *Rendell-Baker* illustrates the trend's application to private education. The case serves to confirm the validity of many earlier cases where the court refused to find state action respecting activities of postsecondary institutions, and to cast doubt on some other cases where state action has been found. *Rendell-Baker* thus insulates postsecondary institutions further from state action findings and the resultant application of federal constitutional constraints to their activities.

Lower court cases subsequent to *Rendell-Baker* illustrate the constricting effect of that case on the state action doctrine. In an opinion relying on a companion case to *Rendell-Baker, Blum v. Yaretsky,* 457 U.S. 991 (1982), a federal appellate court, after protracted litigation, refused to extend the state action doctrine to the disciplinary actions of a private college (*Albert v. Carovano,* 824 F.2d 1333, *modified on rehearing,* 838 F.2d 871 (2d Cir. 1987), *panel opin. vacated,* 851 F.2d 561 (2d Cir. 1988) (*en banc*)). The suit was brought against Hamilton College by students whom the college had disciplined under authority of its policy guide on freedom of expression and maintenance of public order. The college had promulgated this guide in compliance with New York Education Law, Section 6450 (the Henderson Act), which requires colleges to adopt rules for maintaining public order on campus and file them with the state. The trial court dismissed the students' complaint on the grounds that they could not prove that the college's action was state action. After an appellate court panel reversed, the full court affirmed the pertinent part of the trial court's dismissal. The *en banc* court concluded:

> [A]ppellants' theory of state action suffers from a fatal flaw. That theory assumes that either Section 6450 or the rules Hamilton filed pursuant to that statute constitute "a rule of conduct imposed by the state." 457 U.S. at 937. Yet nothing in either the legislation or those rules required that these appellants be suspended for occupying Buttrick Hall. Moreover, it is undisputed that the state's role under the Henderson Act has been merely to keep on file rules submitted by colleges and universities. The state has never sought to compel schools to enforce these rules and has never even inquired about such enforcement [851 F.2d at 568].

Finding that the state had taken no action regarding the disciplinary policies of private colleges in the state, and that the administrators of Hamilton College did not believe that the Henderson Act required them to take particular disciplinary actions, the court refused to find state action.

In *Smith v. Duquesne University,* 612 F. Supp. 72 (W.D. Pa. 1985), *affirmed without opin.,* 787 F.2d 583 (3d Cir. 1985), a graduate student challenged his expulsion on due process and equal protection grounds, asserting that Duquesne's action constituted state action. The court used both the "joint venturer" and the "nexus" analyses to determine that Duquesne was not a state actor. Regarding the former, the court distinguished Duquesne's relationship with the state of Pennsylvania from that of Temple University and the University of Pittsburgh (which were viewed as state actors in *Krynicky v. University of Pittsburgh*, 742 F.2d 94 (3d Cir. 1984)), and held that the relationship with Duquesne was "so tenuous as to lead to no other conclusion but that Duquesne is a private institution and not a state actor" (612 F. Supp. at 77–78). There was no statutory relationship between the state and the university, the state did not review the university's expenditures, and the university was not required to submit the types of financial reports to the state that state-related institutions, such as Temple and Pitt, were required to submit. Regarding the latter (the nexus test), the court determined that the state could not "be deemed responsible for the specific act" complained of by the plaintiff:

> [T]his case requires no protracted analysis to determine that Duquesne's decision to dismiss Smith cannot fairly be attributable to the Commonwealth. . . . The decision to expel Smith, like the decision to matriculate him, turned on an academic judgment made by a purely private institution according to its official university policy. If indirect involvement is insufficient to establish state action, then certainly the lack of any involvement cannot suffice [612 F. Supp. at 78].

And in *Imperiale v. Hahnemann University*, 966 F.2d 125 (3d Cir. 1992), a federal appellate court rejected the plaintiff's claim that the university had engaged in unconstitutional state action when it revoked his medical degree. Considering both the joint venturer and the nexus tests, the court denied the contention that the state action doctrine should apply because the university was "state-aided."

Rendell-Baker and later cases, however, do not create an impenetrable protective barrier for postsecondary institutions. In particular, there may be situations in which government is directly involved in the challenged activity—in contrast to the absence of government involvement in the personnel actions challenged in *Rendell-Baker*. Such involvement may supply the "nexus" missing in the Supreme Court case (see *Milonas v. Williams*, 691 F.2d 931 (10th Cir. 1982)). Moreover, there may be situations, unlike *Rendell-Baker*, in which government officials by virtue of their offices sit on or nominate others for an institution's board of trustees. Such involvement, perhaps in combination with other "contacts," may create the "symbiotic relationship" that did not exist in the Supreme Court case (see *Krynicky v. University of Pittsburgh* and *Schier v. Temple University*, 742 F.2d 94 (3d Cir. 1984)). Because these and other such circumstances continue to pose complex issues, administrators in private institutions should keep the state action concept in mind in major dealings with government. They should also rely heavily on legal counsel for guidance in this technical area. And, most important, administrators should confront the question that the state action cases leave squarely on their doorsteps: When the law does not impose constitutional constraints on your action, to what extent and in what manner will your institution undertake on its own initiative to protect freedom of speech and press, equality of opportunity, due process, and other such values on your campus?

1.5.3. Other Bases for Legal Rights in Private Institutions

The inapplicability of the federal Constitution to private schools does not necessarily mean that students, faculty members, and other members of the private school community have no legal rights assertable against the school. There are other sources for individual rights, and these sources may resemble those found in the Constitution.

The federal government and, to a lesser extent, state governments have increasingly created statutory rights enforceable against private institutions, particularly in the discrimination area. The federal Title VII prohibition on employment discrimination (42 U.S.C. §2000e *et seq.*), applicable generally to public and private employment relationships, is a prominent example. Other major examples are the Title VI race discrimination law (42 U.S.C. §2000d *et seq.*) and the Title IX sex discrimination law (20 U.S.C. §1681 *et seq.*) (see Sections 12.4.2 and 12.4.3) applicable to federal aid recipients. Such sources provide a large body of nondiscrimination law, which parallels and in some ways is more protective than the equal protection principles derived from the Fourteenth Amendment.

Beyond such statutory rights, several common law theories for protecting individual rights in private, postsecondary institutions have been advanced. Most prominent by far is the contract theory, under which students and faculty members are said to have a contractual relationship with the private school. Express or implied contract terms establish legal rights that can be enforced in court if the contract is breached. Although the theory is a useful one that is often referred to in cases (see Section 3.2), most courts agree that the contract law of the commercial world cannot be imported wholesale into the academic environment. The theory must thus be applied with sensitivity to academic customs and usages. Moreover, the theory's usefulness is somewhat limited. The "terms" of the "contract" may be difficult to identify, particularly in the case of students. (To what extent, for instance, is the college catalogue a source of contract terms?) Some of the terms, once identified, may be too vague or ambiguous to enforce. Or the contract may be so barren of content or so one-sided in favor of the institution that it is an insignificant source of individual rights.

Despite its shortcomings, the contract theory has gained in importance. As it has become clear that the bulk of private institutions can escape the tentacles of the state action doctrine, alternative theories for establishing individual rights are increasingly used. Since the lowering of the age of majority, postsecondary students have had a capacity to contract under state law—a capacity that many previously did not have. In what has become the age of the consumer, students have been encouraged to import consumer rights into postsecondary education. And, in an age of collective negotiation, faculty and staff have often sought to rely on a contract model for ordering employment relationships on campus.

Such developments can affect both public and private institutions, although state law may place additional restrictions on contract authority in the public sphere. While contract concepts can of course limit the authority of the institution, they should not be seen only as a burr in the administrator's side. They can also be used creatively to provide order and fairness in institutional affairs and to create internal grievance procedures that encourage in-house rather than judicial resolution of problems. Administrators thus should be sensitive to both the problems and the potentials of contract concepts in the postsecondary environment.

State constitutions have also assumed critical importance as a source of legal rights for individuals to assert against private institutions. The key case is *Prune-Yard Shopping Center v. Robins*, 592 P.2d 341 (Cal. 1979), *affirmed*, 447 U.S. 74 (1980). In this case, a group of high school students who were distributing political material and soliciting petition signatures had been excluded from a private shopping center. The students sought an injunction in state court to prevent further exclusions. The California Supreme Court sided with the students, holding that they had a state constitutional right of access to the shopping center to engage in expressive activity. In the U.S. Supreme Court, the shopping center argued that the California court's ruling was inconsistent with an earlier U.S. Supreme Court precedent, *Lloyd v. Tanner*, 407 U.S. 551 (1972), which held that the First Amendment of the federal Constitution does not guarantee individuals a right to free expression on the premises of a private shopping center. The Court rejected the argument, emphasizing that the state had a "sovereign right to adopt in its own constitution individual liberties more expansive than those conferred by the federal Constitution."

The shopping center also argued that the California court's decision, in denying it the right to exclude others from its premises, violated its property rights under the Fifth and Fourteenth Amendments of the federal Constitution. The Supreme Court rejected this argument as well:

> It is true that one of the essential sticks in the bundle of property rights is the right to exclude others (*Kaiser Aetna v. United States*, 444 U.S. 164, 17980 (1979)). And here there has literally been a "taking" of that right to the extent that the California Supreme Court has interpreted the state constitution to entitle its citizens to exercise free expression and petition rights on shopping center property. But it is well established that "not every destruction or injury to property by governmental action has been held to be a 'taking' in the constitutional sense" (*Armstrong v. United States*, 364 U.S. 40, 48 (1960)). . . .
>
> Here the requirement that appellants permit appellees to exercise state-protected rights of free expression and petition on shopping center property clearly does not amount to an unconstitutional infringement of appellants'

property rights under the taking clause. There is nothing to suggest that preventing appellants from prohibiting this sort of activity will unreasonably impair the value or use of their property as a shopping center. The PruneYard is a large, commercial complex that covers several city blocks, contains numerous separate business establishments, and is open to the public at large. The decision of the California Supreme Court makes it clear that the PruneYard may restrict expressive activity by adopting time, place, and manner regulations that will minimize any interference with its commercial functions. Appellees were orderly, and they limited their activity to the common areas of the shopping center. In these circumstances, the fact that they may have "physically invaded" appellants' property cannot be viewed as determinative [447 U.S. at 82–84].

PruneYard has gained significance in educational settings with the New Jersey Supreme Court's decision in *State v. Schmid*, 423 A.2d 615 (N.J. 1980) (see Section 11.5.3). The defendant, who was not a student, had been charged with criminal trespass for distributing political material on the Princeton University campus in violation of Princeton regulations. The New Jersey court declined to rely on the federal First Amendment, instead deciding the case on state constitutional grounds. It held that, even without a finding of state action (a prerequisite to applying the federal First Amendment), Princeton had a state constitutional obligation to protect Schmid's expressional rights (N.J. Const. (1947), Art. I, para. 6 and para. 18). In justifying its authority to construe the state constitution in this expansive manner, the court relied on *PruneYard*. A subsequent case involving Muhlenberg College, *Pennsylvania v. Tate*, 432 A.2d 1382 (Pa. 1981), follows the *Schmid* reasoning in holding that the Pennsylvania state constitution protected the defendant's rights.

In contrast, a New York court refused to permit a student to rely on the state constitution in a challenge to her expulsion from a summer program for high school students at Cornell. In *Stone v. Cornell University*, 510 N.Y.S.2d 313 (N.Y. App. Div. 1987), the sixteen-year-old student was expelled after she admitted smoking marijuana and drinking alcohol while enrolled in the program and living on campus. No hearing was held. The student argued that the lack of a hearing violated her rights under New York's constitution (Art. I, §6). Disagreeing, the court invoked a "state action" doctrine similar to that used for the federal Constitution (see Section 1.5.2) and concluded that there was insufficient state involvement in Cornell's summer program to warrant constitutional due process protections.

SEC. 1.6. RELIGION AND THE PUBLIC-PRIVATE DICHOTOMY

Under the establishment clause of the First Amendment, public institutions must maintain a neutral stance regarding religious beliefs and activities; they must, in other words, maintain religious neutrality. Public institutions cannot favor or support one religion over another, and they cannot favor or support religion over nonreligion. Thus, for instance, public schools have been prohibited from using an official nondenominational prayer (*Engel v. Vitale*, 370 U.S. 421 (1962)) and from prescribing the reading of verses from the Bible at the opening of each school day (*Abington School District v. Schempp*, 374 U.S. 203 (1963)).

The First Amendment contains two "religion" clauses. The first prohibits government from "establishing" religion; the second protects individuals' "free exercise" of religion from governmental interference. Although the two clauses have a common objective of ensuring governmental "neutrality," they pursue it in different ways. As the U.S. Supreme Court explained in *Abington School District v. Schempp:*

> The wholesome "neutrality" of which this Court's cases speak thus stems from a recognition of the teaching of history that powerful sects or groups might bring about a fusion of governmental and religious functions or a concert or dependency of one upon the other to the end that official support of the state or federal government would be placed behind the tenets of one or of all orthodoxies. This the establishment clause prohibits. And a further reason for neutrality is found in the free exercise clause, which recognizes the value of religious training, teaching, and observance and, more particularly, the right of every person to freely choose his own course with reference thereto, free of any compulsion from the state. This the free exercise clause guarantees. . . . The distinction between the two clauses is apparent—a violation of the free exercise clause is predicated on coercion, whereas the establishment clause violation need not be so attended [374 U.S. at 222–23].

Neutrality, however, does not necessarily require a public institution to prohibit all religious activity on its campus or at off-campus events it sponsors. In some circumstances, the institution may have discretion to permit noncoercive religious activities (see *Lee v. Weisman*, 112 S. Ct. 2649 (1992) (finding indirect coercion in context of religious invocation at *high school* graduation)). Moreover, if a rigidly observed policy of neutrality would discriminate against campus organizations with religious purposes or could impinge on an individual's right to "free exercise" of religion or to freedom of speech, the institution may be required to allow some religion on campus. In *Keegan v. University of Delaware*, 349 A.2d 14 (Del. 1975), for example, the university had banned all religious worship services from campus facilities. The plaintiffs contended that this policy was unconstitutional as applied to students' religious services in the commons areas of campus dormitories. After determining that the university could permit religious worship in the commons area without violating the establishment clause, the court then held that the university was constitutionally *required* by the free exercise clause to make the commons area available for students' religious worship:

The only activity proscribed by the regulation is worship. . . . The commons area is already provided for student use and there is no request here that separate religious facilities be established. The area in question is a residence hall where students naturally assemble with their friends for many purposes. Religion, at least in part, is historically a communal exercise. . . .

It can be argued, as it has been, that the question is whether the university must permit the students to worship on university property. But, in terms of religious liberty, the question is better put, in our judgment, from the perspective of the individual student. Can the university prohibit student worship in a commons area of a university dormitory which is provided for student use and in which the university permits every other student activity? It is apparent to us that such a regulation impedes the observance of religion [349 A.2d at 17, 18].

In a later case that has now become a landmark decision, *Widmar v. Vincent,* 454 U.S. 263 (1981) (discussed in Section 9.1.4), the U.S. Supreme Court determined that student religious activities on public campuses are also protected by the First Amendment's free speech clause. The Court indicated a preference for using the free speech clause rather than the free exercise of religion clause, whenever the institution has created a "public forum" generally open for student use. The Court also concluded that the First Amendment's establishment clause would not be violated by an "open-forum" or "equal-access" policy permitting student use of campus facilities for both nonreligious and religious purposes. The U.S. Supreme Court subsequently affirmed and extended these principles in *Lamb's Chapel v. Center Moriches Union Free School District,* 113 S. Ct. 2141 (1993) and *Rosenberger v. Rector and Visitors of the University of Virginia,* 115 S. Ct. 2510 (1995) (discussed in Section 9.1.4).

A private institution's position under the establishment and free exercise clauses differs markedly from that of a public institution. Private institutions have no obligation of neutrality under these clauses. Moreover, these clauses affirmatively protect the religious beliefs and practices of private institutions from government interference. For example, establishment and free exercise considerations may restrict the judiciary's capacity to entertain lawsuits against religiously affiliated institutions. Such litigation may involve the court in the interpretation of religious doctrine or in the process of church governance, thus creating a danger that the court—an arm of government—would entangle itself in religious affairs in violation of the establishment clause. Or such litigation may invite the court to enforce discovery requests (such as subpoenas) or award injunctive relief that would interfere with the religious practices of the institution or its sponsoring body, thus creating dangers that the court's orders would violate the institution's rights under the free exercise clause. Sometimes such litigation may present both types of federal constitutional problems or, alternatively, may present parallel problems under the state constitution. When the judicial involvement requested by the plaintiff(s) would cause the court to intrude upon establishment or free exercise values, the court must decline to enforce certain discovery requests, or must modify the terms of any remedy or relief it orders, or must decline to exercise any jurisdiction over the dispute, thus protecting the institution against governmental incursions into its religious beliefs and practices.

A private institution's constitutional protection under the establishment and free exercise clauses is by no means absolute. Its limits are illustrated by *Bob Jones University v. United States,* 461 U.S. 574 (1983) (see Section 12.2.1). Because the university maintained racially restrictive policies on dating and marriage, the Internal Revenue Service had denied it tax-exempt status under federal tax laws. The university argued that its racial practices were religiously based and that the denial abridged its right to free exercise of religion. The U.S. Supreme Court, rejecting this argument, emphasized that the federal government has a "compelling" interest in "eradicating racial discrimination in education" and that that interest "substantially outweighs whatever burden denial of tax benefits places on [the university's] exercise of . . . religious beliefs."

Although the institution did not prevail in *Bob Jones,* the "compelling interest" test that the Court used to evaluate free exercise claims does provide substantial protection for religiously affiliated institutions. A federal statute, the Religious Freedom Restoration Act of 1993 (103 Pub. L. No. 141, 107 Stat. 1488 (1993)), also will provide strong protection for such institutions. This Act reaffirms the compelling interest test as the appropriate standard in religious freedom cases and legislatively overrules a post–*Bob Jones* case (*Employment Division v. Smith,* 494 U.S. 872 (1990)), which severely limited protections available under the free exercise clause. (The Religious Freedom Restoration Act—if the U.S. Supreme Court upholds its constitutionality—will also reaffirm and provide strong protections for *individuals* who assert free exercise claims against *public* institutions, as in the cases in the earlier part of this subsection.)

Although the establishment clause itself imposes no neutrality obligation on private institutions, this clause does have another kind of importance for private institutions that are church related. When government—federal, state, or local—undertakes to provide financial or other support for private postsecondary education, the question arises whether this support, insofar as it benefits church-related education, constitutes government support for religion. If it does, such support would violate the establishment clause because government would have departed from its position of neutrality.

Two 1971 cases decided by the Supreme Court provide the basis for the modern law on government support for church-related schools. *Lemon v. Kurtzman,* 403 U.S. 602 (1971), invalidated two state programs providing aid for church-related elementary and secondary schools. *Tilton v. Richardson,* 403 U.S. 672 (1971), held constitutional a federal aid program providing construction grants to higher education institutions, including those that are church-related. In deciding the cases, the Court developed a three-pronged test for determining when a government support program passes muster under the establishment clause:

First, the statute must have a secular legislative purpose; second, its principal
or primary effect must be one that neither advances nor inhibits religion . . . ;
finally, the statute must not foster "an excessive government entanglement
with religion" (*Walz v. Tax Commission*, 397 U.S. 664, 674 (1970)) [403 U.S.
at 612–13].

The first prong (purpose) has proved easy to meet and has not been of major
significance in subsequent cases. But the other two prongs (effect and entanglement) have been both very important and very difficult to apply in particular
cases. The Court's major explanation of "effect" came in *Hunt v. McNair*, 413
U.S. 734 (1973):

Aid normally may be thought to have a primary effect of advancing religion
when it flows to an institution in which religion is so pervasive that a substantial portion of its functions are subsumed in the religious mission or when it
funds a specifically religious activity in an otherwise substantially secular
setting [413 U.S. at 753].

Its major explanation of "entanglement" appeared in the *Lemon* case:

In order to determine whether the government entanglement with religion is
excessive, we must examine (1) the character and purposes of the institutions
which are benefitted, (2) the nature of the aid that the state provides, and (3)
the resulting relationship between the government and the religious authority
[403 U.S. at 615].

Four Supreme Court cases have applied this complex three-pronged test
to church-related postsecondary institutions. In each case, the aid program
passed the test. In *Tilton*, the Court approved the federal construction grant program, and the grants to the particular colleges involved in that case, by a narrow 5–to–4 vote. In *Hunt v. McNair*, the Court, by a 6–to–3 vote, sustained a
state program that assisted colleges, including church-related colleges, by issuing revenue bonds for their construction projects. In *Roemer v. Board of Public
Works*, 426 U.S. 736 (1976), the Court, by a 5–to–4 vote, upheld Maryland's program of general support grants to private, including church-related, colleges.
And in the fourth case, *Witters v. Washington Department of Services for the
Blind*, 474 U.S. 481 (1986), the Court rejected an Establishment Clause challenge to a state vocational rehabilitation program for the blind that provided
assistance directly to a student enrolled in a religious ministry program at a private Christian college. Distinguishing between institution-based aid and student-
based aid, the unanimous Court concluded that the aid plan did not violate the
second prong of the *Lemon* test, since any state payments that were ultimately
channeled to the educational institution were based solely on the "genuinely
independent and private choices of the aid recipients." Taken together, these

U.S. Supreme Court cases suggest that a wide range of postsecondary support programs can be devised compatibly with the establishment clause and that a wide range of church-related institutions can be eligible to receive government support. The *Roemer* case is perhaps the most revealing. There, the Court refused to find that the grants given a group of church-related schools constituted support for religion—even though the funds were granted annually and could be put to a wide range of uses, and even though the schools had church representatives on their governing boards, employed Roman Catholic chaplains, held Roman Catholic religious exercises, required students to take religion or theology classes taught primarily by Roman Catholic clerics, made some hiring decisions for theology departments partly on the basis of religious considerations, and began some classes with prayers. A very important subsequent case, not involving postsecondary education but further developing the concepts used in these cases, is *Bowen v. Kendrick,* 487 U.S. 589 (1988).

When issues concerning governmental support for religion arise, as in the cases above, the federal Constitution is not the only source of law that may apply. In some states, the state constitution will also play an important role. In *Witters* (above), for example, the U.S. Supreme Court remanded the case to the Supreme Court of Washington (whose decision the U.S. Supreme court had reversed), observing that the state court was free to consider the "far stricter" church-state provision of the state constitution. On remand, the state court concluded that the state constitutional provision—prohibiting use of public moneys to pay for any religious instruction—precluded the grant of state funds to the student enrolled in the religious ministry program (*Witters v. State Commission for the Blind,* 771 P.2d 1119 (Wash. 1989)). First, the court held that providing vocational rehabilitation funds to the student would violate the state constitution because the funds would pay for "a religious course of study at a religious school, with a religious career as [the student's] goal" (771 P.2d at 1119).

Distinguishing the establishment clause of the U.S. Constitution from the state constitution's provision, the court noted that the latter provision "prohibits not only the *appropriation* of public money for religious instruction but also the *application of* public funds to religious instruction" (771 P.2d at 1121). Then, the court held that the student's federal constitutional right to free exercise of religion was not infringed by denial of the funds, because he is "not being asked to violate any tenet of his religious beliefs nor is he being denied benefits 'because of conduct mandated by religious belief'" (771 P.2d at 1123). Third, the court held that denial of the funds did not violate the student's equal protection rights under the Fourteenth Amendment, because the state has a "compelling interest in maintaining the strict separation of church and state set forth" in its constitution, and the student's "individual interest in receiving a religious education must . . . give way to the state's greater need to uphold its constitution" (771 P.2d at 1123).

Though the federal cases have been quite hospitable to the inclusion of church-related institutions in government support programs for postsecondary education, administrators of church-related institutions should still be most sensitive to establishment clause issues. As *Witters* indicates, state constitutions may contain clauses that restrict government support for church-related institutions more vigorously than the federal establishment clause does. The statutes creating funding programs may also contain provisions that restrict the program's application to religious institutions or activities. Moreover, even the federal establishment clause cases have historically been decided by close votes, with great disagreement among the justices. That trend continues, and a number of the justices have accelerated it by raising doubts concerning *Lemon*. The law has not yet settled. Thus, administrators should exercise great care in using government funds and should keep in mind that, at some point, religious influences within the institution can still jeopardize government funding.

SEC. 1.7. ORGANIZING THE POSTSECONDARY INSTITUTION'S LEGAL AFFAIRS

1.7.1. Organizational Arrangements

There are numerous organizational arrangements by which postsecondary institutions can obtain legal counsel. Debate has been growing in recent years concerning which arrangements are most effective and cost-efficient. The issues, which are especially visible in private institutions, range from escalating legal costs, to the appropriate balance between in-house and outside counsel, to new roles and fee schedules for outside counsel, to the use of legal consultants for staff training and other special projects.

The arrangements for public postsecondary institutions often differ from those for private institutions. The latter have a relatively free hand in deciding whom to employ or retain as counsel and how to utilize their services, and will frequently have in-house counsel and campus-based services. Public institutions, on the other hand, may be served by the state attorney general's office or, for some community colleges, by a county or city attorney's office. Other public institutions that are part of a statewide system may be served by system attorneys appointed by the system's governing authority. In either case, working relationships may vary with the state and the campus, and legal counsel may be located at an off-campus site and may serve other campuses as well. In general, administrators in such situations should seek to have services centralized in one or a small number of assistant attorneys general or other government counsel who devote a considerable portion of their time to the particular campus and become thoroughly familiar with its operations.

1.7.2. Treatment Law and Preventive Law

With each of the organizational arrangements above, serious consideration must be given to the particular functions that counsel will perform and to the relationships that will be fostered between counsel and administrators. Broadly stated, counsel's role is to identify and define actual or potential legal problems and provide options for resolving or preventing them. There are two basic, and different, ways to fulfill this role: through treatment law or through preventive law. To analogize to another profession, treatment law is aimed at curing legal diseases, whereas preventive law seeks to maintain legal health. Under either approach, counsel will be guided not only by legal considerations and institutional goals and policies but also by ethical requirements of the legal profession, which shape the responsibilities of individual practitioners to their clients and the public.

Treatment law is the more traditional of the two practice approaches. It focuses on actual challenges to institutional practices and on affirmative legal steps by the institution to protect its interests when they are threatened. When suit is filed against the institution, or litigation is threatened; when a government agency cites the institution for noncompliance with its regulations; when the institution needs formal permission of a government agency to undertake a proposed course of action; when the institution wishes to sue some other party—then treatment law operates. The goal is to resolve the specific legal problem at hand. Treatment law today is indispensable to the functioning of a postsecondary institution, and virtually all institutions have such legal service.

Preventive law, in contrast, focuses on initiatives that the institution can take before actual legal disputes arise. Preventive law involves administrator and counsel in a continual process of setting the legal parameters within which the institution will operate to avoid litigation or other legal disputes. Counsel identifies the legal consequences of proposed actions; pinpoints the range of alternatives for avoiding problems and the legal risks of each alternative; sensitizes administrators to legal issues and the importance of recognizing them early; and determines the impact of new or proposed laws and regulations, and new court decisions, on institutional operations.

Prior to the 1980s, preventive law was not a general practice of postsecondary institutions. But this approach became increasingly valuable as the presence of law on the campus increased, and acceptance of preventive law within postsecondary education grew substantially. Today, preventive law is as indispensable as treatment law and provides the more constructive posture from which to conduct institutional legal affairs.

Institutions using or considering the use of preventive law face some difficult questions: To what extent will administrators and counsel give priority to the practice of preventive law? Which institutional administrators will have direct access to counsel? Will counsel advise only administrators, or will he or she also be available to recognized faculty or student organizations or committees, or perhaps to other members of the university community on certain matters? What working arrangements will ensure that administrators are alert to incipient legal problems and that counsel is involved in institutional decision making at an early stage? What degree of autonomy will counsel have to influence institutional decision making, and what authority will counsel have to halt legally unwise institutional action?

The following steps are suggested for administrators and counsel seeking to implement a preventive law system:

1. Review the institution's current organizational arrangement for obtaining legal counsel. Determine whether changes that might facilitate preventive lawyering—for example, from part-time to full-time counsel or from outside firm to house counsel—are appropriate and feasible.

2. Develop a teamwork relationship between administrator and counsel; both should be substantially involved in legal affairs, cooperating with one another on a regular basis, for preventive law to work best. Since the dividing line between the administrators' and the lawyers' functions is not always self-evident, roles should be developed through mutual interchange between the two sets of professionals. While considerable flexibility is possible, institutions should be careful to maintain a distinction between the two roles. The purpose of preventive law is not to make the administrator into a lawyer or the lawyer into an administrator. It is the lawyer's job to resolve doubts about the interpretation of statutes, regulations, and court decisions; to stay informed of legal developments and predict the directions in which law is evolving; and to suggest legal options and advise on their relative effectiveness in achieving the institution's goals. In contrast, it is the administrator's job (and that of the board of trustees) to stay informed of developments in the theory and practice of administration; to devise policy options within the constraints imposed by law and determine their relative effectiveness in achieving institutional goals; and ultimately, at the appropriate level of the institutional hierarchy, to make the policy decisions that give life to the institution.

3. To assist teamwork relationships, arrange for training for administrators that focuses on the legal implications of their administrative responsibilities. Management workshops for new deans and department chairs, or periodic workshops for middle managers, or counseling sessions for the staff of a particular office would be examples of such training. The institution's legal staff may conduct training sessions, or they may be provided on or off site by third parties. In conjunction with such training, the institution should ensure the availability of relevant and up-to-date legal information for administrators, through distribution of one or more of the newsletters and periodicals available from outside sources, or through legal counsel memos crafted to the particular circumstances of the institution.

4. Have the lawyer-administrator team perform legal audits periodically. A legal audit is a legal "checkup" to determine the legal "health" of the institution. A complete audit would include a survey of every office and function in the institution. For each office and function, the lawyer-administrator team would develop the information and analysis necessary to determine whether that office or function is in compliance with the full range of legal constraints to which it is subject.

5. To supplement legal audits, develop an early-warning system that will apprise counsel and administrators of potential legal problems in their incipiency. The early-warning system should be based on a list of situations that are likely to create significant legal risk for the institution. Such a list might include the following situations: an administrator is revising a standard form contract used by the institution or creating a new standard form contract to cover a type of transaction for which the institution has not previously used such a contract; administrators are reviewing the institution's code of student conduct, student bill of rights, or similar documents; a school or department is seeking to terminate a faculty member's tenure; a committee is drafting or modifying an affirmative action plan; administrators are preparing policies to implement a new set of federal administrative regulations; or administrators are proposing a new security system for the campus or temporary security measures for a particular emergency. Under an early-warning system, all such circumstances, or others that the institution may specify, would trigger a consultative process between administrator and counsel aimed at resolving legal problems before they erupt into disputes.

6. Using the data obtained through legal audits, an early-warning system, and other devices, engage in a continuing course of legal planning. If audits and other means provide detection and diagnosis, legal planning provides measures for legal health maintenance. Legal planning establishes the process and the individual steps by which the institution determines the degree of legal risk exposure it is willing to assume in particular situations, and avoids or resolves legal risks it is unwilling to assume. Successful legal planning depends on a careful sorting out and interrelating of legal and policy issues. Teamwork between administrator and lawyer is therefore a critical ingredient in legal planning. Sensitivity to the authority structure of the institution is also a critical ingredient, so that legal planning decisions are made at the prescribed levels of authority.

7. For the inevitable percentage of potential legal problems that do develop into actual disputes, establish internal grievance mechanisms. These mechanisms may utilize various techniques for dispute resolution, from informal consultation, to mediation or arbitration, to hearings before panels drawn from the academic community. Whatever techniques are adopted should be generally available to students, faculty, and staff members who have complaints concerning actions taken against them by other members of the academic commu-

nity. Some summary procedure should be devised for dismissing complaints that are frivolous or that contest general academic policy rather than a particular action that has harmed the complainant. Not every dispute, of course, is amenable to internal solution, since many disputes involve outside parties (such as business firms, government agencies, or professional associations). But for disputes among members of the campus community, grievance mechanisms provide an on-campus forum that can be attuned to the particular characteristics of academic institutions. Grievance mechanisms can encourage collegial resolution of disputes, thus forestalling the complainant's resort to courts or other external bodies.

SELECTED ANNOTATED BIBLIOGRAPHY

General

Bickel, Robert, & Brechner, Jane. *The College Administrator and the Courts* (College Administration Publications, 1977, plus periodic supp.). A basic casebook written for administrators that briefs and discusses leading court cases. Topics include the legal system, sources of law, the role of counsel, distinctions between public and private colleges, and the state action concept. Updated quarterly by Barbara A. Lee and Peter H. Ruger.

Sec. 1.1 (How Far Does the Law Reach and How Loud Does It Speak?)

Edwards, Harry T. *Higher Education and the Unholy Crusade Against Governmental Regulation* (Institute for Educational Management, Harvard University, 1980). Reviews and evaluates the federal regulatory presence on the campus. Author concludes that much of the criticism directed by postsecondary administrators at federal regulation of higher education is either unwarranted or premature.

Folger, Joseph, & Shubert, J. Janelle. "Resolving Student-Initiated Grievances in Higher Education: Dispute Resolution Procedures in a Non-Adversarial Setting," 3 *NIDR Reports* (National Institute for Dispute Resolution, 1986). A short monograph exploring the various methods employed at twenty different institutions to resolve conflicts. Includes a flow chart entitled "Model of Possible Options for Pursuing Resolutions to Student-Initiated Grievances" and a set of criteria for evaluating the effectiveness of particular grievance procedures.

Gouldner, Helen. "The Social Impact of Campus Litigation," 51 *J. Higher Educ.* 328 (1980). Explores the detrimental effects on the postsecondary community of "the tidal wave of litigation . . . awash in the country"; identifies "increased secrecy on campus," "fragile friendships among colleagues," a "crisis in confidence" in decision making, and "domination by legal norms" as major effects to be dealt with.

Helms, Lelia B. "Litigation Patterns: Higher Education and the Courts in 1988," 57 *West's Educ. Law Rptr.* 1 (1990). Reviews and classifies litigation involving higher education during a one-year period. Uses the geographical area, the court, the parties, and the issue as classifying factors. Includes tables summarizing litigation patterns. Article provides "baseline data for later comparison" and a methodology for collecting later data. See also the Helms entry for Section 1.2.

Hobbs, Walter C. "The Courts," in Philip G. Altbach, Robert O. Berdahl, & Patricia J. Gumport (eds.), *Higher Education in American Society* (3d ed., Prometheus Books, 1994). Reviews the concept of judicial deference to academic expertise and analyzes the impact of courts on postsecondary institutions. Includes illustrative cases. Author concludes that, despite complaints to the contrary from academics, the tradition of judicial deference to academic judgments is still alive and well.

J. Coll. & Univ. Law. "The Law of Higher Education and the Courts: l9XX in Review." A series of annual articles reviewing cases decided in the prior year in federal and state courts. Each article discusses trends in education law while summarizing the important cases regarding First Amendment problems, tort liability, search and seizure on campus, due process, institutional contracts, sovereign and individual immunities, funding, employment discrimination, and other topics.

Kaplin, William A. *The Importance of Process in Campus Administrative Decision-Making,* IHELG Monograph 91–10 (Institute for Higher Education Law and Governance, University of Houston, 1992). Distinguishes between the *substance* and the *process* of internal decision making by campus administrators; develops a "process taxonomy" with six generic classifications (rule making, adjudication, mediation, implementation, investigation, and crisis management); examines the "process values" that demonstrate the importance of campus processes; and sets out criteria for identifying "good" processes.

Olivas, Michael A. *The Law and Higher Education: Cases and Materials on Colleges in Court,* 2d ed. (Carolina Academic Press, 1997). A casebook presenting both foundational and contemporary case law on major themes in higher education law and governance. Includes supportive commentary by the author, news accounts, and excerpts from and cites to writings of others.

Pavela, Gary (ed.). *Synfax Weekly Report* and *Synfax Bulletin* (Synfax, Inc.). Interrelated newsletter-style publications delivered by FAX technology to maintain optimum currency. Each publication digests and critiques important legal and policy developments as reflected in court opinions, news media accounts, and other sources.

Weeks, Kent M., & Davis, Derek (eds.). *Legal Deskbook for Administrators of Independent Colleges and Universities* (2d ed., Center for Constitutional Studies, Baylor University/National Association of College and University Attorneys, 1993). A resource containing legal analysis, practical advice, and bibliographical sources on issues of particular import to administrators and counsel at private institutions.

West's Education Law Reporter (West Publishing Co.). A biweekly publication covering education-related case law on both elementary/secondary and postsecondary education. Includes complete texts of opinions, brief summaries written for the layperson, articles and case comments, and a cumulative table of cases and index of legal principles elucidated in the cases.

Sec. 1.2 (Evolution of the Law Relating to Postsecondary Education)

Beach, John A. "The Management and Governance of Academic Institutions," 12 *J. Coll. & Univ. Law* 301 (1985). Reviews the history and development of institutional governance, broadly defined. Discusses the corporate character of postsecondary institutions, the contradictions of "managing" an academic organization, academic freedom, and the interplay among the institution's various constituencies.

Bok, Derek. "Universities: Their Temptations and Tensions," 18 *J. Coll. & Univ. Law* 1 (1991). Author addresses the need for universities to maintain independence with regard to research and public service. Discusses three sources of temptation: politicization, diversion of faculty time and interest from teaching and research to consulting, and the indiscriminate focus on commercial gain when one is seeking funding.

Bureau of National Affairs. *Computer Data Security: A Legal and Practical Guide to Liability, Loss Prevention, and Criminal and Civil Remedies* (Bureau of National Affairs, 1990). Discusses federal and state laws related to fraud, electronic trespass, and other relevant theories. Offers suggestions for storing and protecting confidential data on computer. The book is written for professionals without technical expertise in computer use.

Clark, Burton R. *The Academic Life: Small Worlds, Different Worlds* (Carnegie Foundation for the Advancement of Teaching, 1987). Traces the evolution of postsecondary institutions, the development of academic disciplines, the nature of academic work, the culture of academe, and academic governance. The book emphasizes the rewards and challenges of the faculty role, addressing the significance of the "postmodern" academic role.

El-Khawas, Elaine. *Campus Trends* (American Council on Education). Published annually, this report analyzes survey data from a cross-section of colleges and universities. Includes data on enrollments, student and faculty characteristics, financial issues, and other significant information.

Fass, Richard A., Morrill, Richard L., & Mount, C. Eric, Jr. "In Loco Parentis Revisited?" 18 *Change* 34 (Jan./Feb. 1986). Provides two perspectives (one by Fass, the second by Morrill and Mount) on whether *in loco parentis* should be reestablished, in what manner, and what alternatives to that doctrine are appropriate for postsecondary institutions.

Fishbein, Estelle A. "New Strings on the Ivory Tower: The Growth of Accountability in Colleges and Universities," 12 *J. Coll. & Univ. Law* 381 (1985). Examines the impact of external forces on the management of colleges and universities. Focusing primarily on the effect of federal regulation (including that by federal courts), the author discusses the significance of internal accountability in responding to external regulation.

Helms, Lelia B. "Patterns of Litigation in Postsecondary Education: A Case Law Study," 14 *J. Coll. & Univ. Law* 99 (1987). Analyzes reported cases in one state (Iowa) from 1850 to 1985. Categorizes cases in a variety of ways and develops findings that provide "perspective on patterns of litigation and possible trends."

Kaplin, William A. "Law on the Campus, 1960–1985: Years of Growth and Challenge," 12 *J. Coll. & Univ. Law* 269 (1985). Discusses the legal implications of social and political changes for colleges and universities. Issues addressed in historical context include the concepts of "public" and "private," the distinctions between secular and religious institutions, and preventive legal planning.

Kerr, Clark. *The Great Transformation in Higher Education, 1960–1980* (State University of New York Press, 1991). A collection of essays written over three decades by an eminent participant in and observer of American higher education's era of greatest expansion, development, and change. The essays are collected under four broad rubrics: The American System in Perspective; The Unfolding of the Great Transformation: 1960–1980; Governance and Leadership Under Pressure; and Academic Innovation and Reform: Much Innovation, Little Reform.

Kerr, Clark. *Troubled Times for American Higher Education: The 1990s and Beyond* (State University of New York Press, 1994). Also a collection of essays, this book addresses contemporary issues that face colleges and universities. Part I examines "possible contours of the future and . . . choices to be made by higher education"; Part II concerns the relationship between higher education and the American economy; Part III examines specific issues, such as quality in undergraduate education, teaching about ethics, the "racial crisis" in American higher education, and elitism in higher education.

Lautsch, John C. "Computers and the University Attorney: An Overview of Computer Law on Campus," 5 *J. Coll. & Univ. Law* 217 (1978–79). Explores the developing relationship between computers and the law and the impact of this relationship on the campus. Includes analysis of the role of contract law as it affects computers; the impact of computers on labor questions; the relationship of patent, copyright, and trade-secret laws to computers; and other areas.

Metzger, Walter, et al. *Dimensions of Academic Freedom* (University of Illinois Press, 1969). A series of papers presenting historical, legal, and administrative perspectives on academic freedom. Considers how the concept has evolved in light of changes in the character of faculties and student bodies and in the university's internal and external commitments.

Pavela, Gary (ed.). *Synthesis: Law and Policy in Higher Education* (College Administration Publications). A five-times-yearly periodical primarily for administrators. Each issue focuses on a single topic or perspective of contemporary concern. Includes practical analysis, commentary from and interviews with experts, case studies, samples of documents, and bibliographies and case citations.

Reidhaar, Donald L. "The Assault on the Citadel: Reflections on a Quarter Century of Change in the Relationship Between the Student and the University," 12 *J. Coll. & Univ. Law* 343 (1985). Reviews changes in the legal relationships between students and institutions, with particular emphasis on student protest and equal opportunity challenges.

Stallworth, Stanley B. "Higher Education in America: Where Are Blacks Thirty-Five Years After *Brown?*" 1991 *Wis. Multi-Cultural Law J.* 36 (1991). Reviews the history of historically black colleges, discusses the effect of *Brown v. Board of Education,* analyzes the effect of federal attempts to desegregate public systems of higher education, and reviews the attitudes of alumni of black colleges toward the quality of their educational experience.

Stark, Joan S., et al. *The Many Faces of Education Consumerism* (Lexington Books, 1977). A collection of essays on the history and status of the educational consumerism movement. Discusses the roles of the federal government, state government, accrediting agencies, and the courts in protecting the consumers of education; the place of institutional self-regulation; and suggestions for the future. Provides a broad perspective on the impact of consumerism on postsecondary education.

Tatel, David, & Guthrie, R. Claire. "The Legal Ins and Outs of University-Industry Collaboration," 64 *Educ. Record* 19 (Spring 1983). Examines the complex legal and business issues that arise when universities and businesses seek to join forces to develop new technologies. Reviews various legal arrangements already effectuated, such as the Harvard University–Monsanto Company joint venture; outlines issues, such as conflict of interest, confidentiality, and patent rights, that arise in such arrangements; and discusses the federal government's role in encouraging university-industry relationships.

Terrell, Melvin C. (ed.). *Diversity, Disunity, and Campus Community* (National Association of Student Personnel Administrators, 1992). Describes problems related to an increasingly diverse student body and recommends ways in which the campus climate can be improved. Discusses cultural diversity in residence halls, relationships with campus law enforcement staff, student and faculty perspectives on diversity and racism, and strategies for reducing or preventing hate crimes.

Weiler, William C. "Post-Baccalaureate Educational Choices of Minority Students," 16 *Rev. Higher Educ.* 439 (1993). Analyzes data from the U.S. Department of Education's "High School and Beyond" database to ascertain why minority students are less likely than whites to earn graduate degrees. The author provides suggestions for the development of programs to encourage undergraduates to seek postbaccalaureate education.

Wright, Thomas W. "Faculty and the Law Explosion: Assessing the Impact—A Twenty-Five Year Perspective (1960–85) for College and University Lawyers," 12 *J. Coll. & Univ. Law* 363 (1985). Assesses developments in the law with regard to college faculty. Issues addressed include the impact of the law on teaching (for example, the Buckley Amendment and student challenges to grading decisions), research (federal regulations, academic misconduct), and faculty-administration relationships (for example, in collective bargaining).

Sec. 1.3 (Sources of Postsecondary Education Law)

Bakken, Gordon M. "Campus Common Law," 5 *J. Law & Educ.* 201 (1976). A theoretical overview of custom and usage as a source of postsecondary education law. Emphasizes the impact of custom and usage on faculty rights and responsibilities.

Edwards, Harry T., & Nordin, Virginia D. *An Introduction to the American Legal System: A Supplement to Higher Education and the Law* (Institute for Educational

Management, Harvard University, 1980). Provides "a brief description of the American legal system for scholars, students, and administrators in the field of higher education who have had little or no legal training." Chapters include summary overviews of "The United States Courts," "The Process of Judicial Review," "Reading and Understanding Judicial Opinions, State Court Systems," "Legislative and Statutory Sources of Law," and "Administrative Rules and Regulations as Sources of Law."

Farnsworth, E. Allan. *An Introduction to the Legal System of the United States* (2d ed., Oceana, 1983). An introductory text emphasizing the fundamentals of the American legal system. Written for the layperson.

Gifis, Steven. *Law Dictionary* (3d ed., Barron's Educational Series, 1991). A paperback study aid for students or laypersons who seek a basic understanding of unfamiliar legal words and phrases. Also includes a table of abbreviations used in legal citations, a map and chart of the federal judicial system, and the texts of the U.S. Constitution and the ABA *Model Rules of Professional Conduct*.

Sec. 1.4 (Litigation in the Courts)

Kane, Mary Kay. *Civil Procedure in a Nutshell* (3d ed., West, 1991). A book-length summary of the entire law of civil procedure, written in clear language; well organized and outlined. Explains the basics of the law and uses case examples for illustration. Includes a discussion of the structure of the court system and a step-by-step guide through a civil case from filing of the complaint to final disposition.

Lieberman, Jethro K. (principal ed.). *The Role of Courts in American Society: The Final Report of the Council on the Role of the Courts* (Council on the Role of the Courts, 1984). A short report discussing sociological, political, and legal issues involving the American legal system. Considers problems with the system, such as overburdened court dockets and the expense of litigation, as well as possible solutions, such as mediation and arbitration.

O'Connell, John B. *Remedies in a Nutshell* (2d ed., West, 1985). A clearly written summary of the entire law of remedies. Explains the basics of the law without the use of case examples. Topics include contempt of court, basic contract remedies, injunctions, and methods of assessing damages.

Reynolds, William L. *Judicial Process in a Nutshell* (2d ed., West 1991). Summarizes the operation of the American court system. Written clearly, the book uses case examples to illustrate such matters as the role of the Constitution, judicial precedent, and general court structure. Topics include the nature of common law, the use of precedent, the use of statutes, and the methods of constitutional interpretation.

Sec. 1.5 (The Public-Private Dichotomy)

Faccenda, Philip, & Ross, Kathleen. "Constitutional and Statutory Regulations of Private Colleges and Universities," 9 *Valparaiso U.L. Rev.* 539 (1975). An overview of the ways in which private institutions are subjected to federal constitutional and regulatory requirements; draws distinctions between public and private institutions. Written primarily for administrators, with footnotes designed for counsel.

Howard, A. E. Dick. *State Aid to Private Higher Education* (Michie, 1977). A comprehensive treatment of state aid programs in each of the fifty states, as well as a general national overview. Provides legal analysis of state and federal constitutional law, historical developments, and descriptive information on aid programs; emphasizes church-state issues, such as those discussed in Section 1.6 of this chapter.

Thigpen, Richard. "The Application of Fourteenth Amendment Norms to Private Colleges and Universities," 11 *J. Law & Educ.* 171 (1982). Reviews the development of various theories of state action, particularly the public function and government contacts theories, and their applications to private postsecondary institutions. Also examines theories other than traditional state action for subjecting private institutions to requirements comparable to those that the Constitution places on public institutions. Author concludes: "It seems desirable to have a public policy of protecting basic norms of fair and equal treatment in nonpublic institutions of higher learning."

Sec. 1.6 (Religion and the Public-Private Dichotomy)

Moots, Philip R., & Gaffney, Edward M. *Church and Campus: Legal Issues in Religiously Affiliated Higher Education* (University of Notre Dame Press, 1979). Directed primarily to administrators and other leaders of religiously affiliated colleges and universities. Chapters deal with the legal relationship between colleges and affiliated religious bodies, conditions under which liability might be imposed on an affiliated religious group, the effect that the relationship between a college and a religious group may have on the college's eligibility for governmental financial assistance, the "exercise of religious preference in employment policies," questions of academic freedom, the influence of religion on student admissions and discipline, the use of federally funded buildings by religiously affiliated colleges, and the determination of property relationships when a college and a religious body alter their affiliation. Ends with a set of conclusions and recommendations and three appendices discussing the relationships between three religious denominations and their affiliated colleges.

Note, "The First Amendment and Public Funding of Religiously Controlled or Affiliated Higher Education," 17 *J. Coll. & Univ. Law* 381 (1991). Distinguishes between "institution-directed" aid and "student-directed" aid, and reviews the federal establishment clause law applicable to each. Covers the leading U.S. Supreme Court cases with a special emphasis on the *Witters* case and its aftermath in the Washington Supreme Court. Also analyzes the viability, under the free exercise clause, of various state restrictions on the funding of religiously affiliated higher education.

See Howard entry for Section 1.5.

Sec. 1.7 (Organizing the Postsecondary Institution's Legal Affairs)

Bickel, Robert. "A Revisitation of the Role of College and University Legal Counsel," 85 *West's Educ. Law Rptr.* 989 (1993), updating the author's earlier article published at 3 *J. Law & Educ.* 73 (1974). Explores the various roles of an institution's legal counsel. Roles include representing the university in formal legal proceedings, giving administrators advice in order to prevent legal problems, and preventing unnecessary extensions of technical legal factors into institutional administration. Includes commentary on the viewpoints of others since the author's original publication in 1974 and concludes that the earlier observations are still valid.

Block, Dennis J., & Epstein, Michael A. *The Corporate Counsellor's Deskbook* (4th ed., Prentice-Hall Law & Business, 1992). A sourcebook in loose-leaf binder format. Provides practical information and analysis, checklists, and sample documents on selecting outside counsel, controlling costs of services, managing litigation and other work assignments, and protecting the attorney-client privilege. Designed for counsel of nonprofit institutions, including colleges and universities. Periodic supplements.

Brown, Louis M., & Dauer, Edward A. *Planning by Lawyers: Materials on a Nonadversarial Legal Process* (Foundation Press, 1978). A comprehensive set of materials presenting various perspectives on legal planning. Includes chapters on "Thinking About Planning" and "Techniques and Devices," with a particularly helpful section on "Legal Audit and Periodic Checkup."

Daane, Roderick K. "The Role of University Counsel," 12 *J. Coll. & Univ. Law* 399 (1985). Addresses the ways in which social changes and differences among institutions have affected the role of attorneys that serve colleges and universities. Examines "the way law is now practiced on campuses," focusing especially on counsel's roles as "Advisor-Counsellor," "Educator-Mediator," "Manager-Administrator," "Draftsman," "Litigator," and "Spokesman."

McCarthy, Jane (ed.). *Resolving Conflict in Higher Education*, New Directions for Higher Education, no. 32 (Jossey-Bass, 1980). Describes and discusses mechanisms (such as mediation) that can be used by postsecondary institutions to resolve internal disputes without the necessity of lawsuits. Includes both legal and policy perspectives on alternative dispute-resolution techniques.

National Association of College and University Attorneys. *The Formbook* (2d ed., NACUA, 1994). Includes nearly one hundred legal forms and checklists covering a wide range of institutional functions and transactions. A practical resource for counsel and administrators at both public and private institutions.

Symposium, "Focus on Ethics and the University Attorney," 19 *J. Coll. & Univ. Law* 305 (1993). A collection of three articles examining the role and the ethical duties of the university attorney, especially with respect to other members of the campus community: Robert F. Drinan, "Lawyer-Client Confidentiality in the Campus Setting"; Stephen S. Dunham, "Case Studies on Wrongdoing on Campus: Ethics and the Lawyer's Role"; and Robert M. O'Neil, "The Lawyer and the Client in the Campus Setting: Who Is the Client, What Does the Client Expect and How May the Attorney Respond?"

Weeks, Kent M. (ed.). *A Legal Inventory for Independent Colleges and Universities* (Center for Constitutional Studies, Mercer University (now at Baylor University), 1981). A short monograph presenting a checklist of questions to use in conducting a legal audit of a private institution.

CHAPTER TWO

The College and Trustees, Administrators, and Staff

SEC. 2.1. THE QUESTION OF AUTHORITY

Trustees, officers, and administrators of postsecondary institutions—public or private—can take only those actions and make only those decisions that they have authority to take or make. Acting or deciding without authority to do so can have legal consequences, both for the responsible individual and for the institution. It is thus critical, from a legal standpoint, for administrators to understand and adhere to the scope and limits of their authority and that of other institutional functionaries with whom they deal. Such sensitivity to authority questions will also normally be good administrative practice, since it can contribute order and structure to institutional governance and make the governance system more understandable, accessible, and accountable to those who deal with it.

Authority generally originates from some fundamental legal source that establishes the institution as a legal entity. For public institutions, the source is usually the constitution or statutes of the state; for private institutions it is usually articles of incorporation, sometimes in combination with some form of state license. This source, though fundamental, is only the starting point for legal analysis of authority questions. To be fully understood and utilized, an institution's fundamental authority must be construed and implemented in light of all the sources of law described in Section 1.3. For public institutions, state administrative law (administrative procedure acts or similar statutes, as well as court decisions) and agency law (court decisions) provide the backdrop against which authority is construed and implemented; for private institutions state corporation or trust law (statutes and court decisions) and agency law (court decisions) are the bases. Authority is particularized and dispersed (delegated) to institutional officers, employees, and organizations by institutional rules and regulations and the institution's employment contracts and, for public institutions, by administrative regulations of the state education boards or agencies. Gaps and ambiguities in authority may be filled in by resort to custom and usage at the institution. And authority may be limited by individual rights guarantees of federal and state constitutions (see especially Section 2.2.3 and Chapters Seven through Nine) and by federal and state statutes and administrative regulations or adjudications (see especially Sections 11.6, 12.1, and 12.4).

There are several generic types of authority. As explained in *Brown v. Wichita State University* (Section 2.3.2), authority may be either express, implied, or apparent. Express authority is that which is found within the plain meaning of a written grant of authority. Implied authority is that which is necessary or appropriate for exercising express authority and can therefore be inferred from the express authority. Apparent authority is not actual authority at all; the term is used to describe the situation where someone acting for the institution induces a belief in other persons that authority exists when in fact it does not. Administrators should avoid this appearance of authority and should not rely on apparent authority as a basis for acting, because the institution may be held liable, under the doctrine of "estoppel," for resultant harm to persons who rely to their detriment on an appearance of authority (see Section 2.2.1). When an institutional officer or employee does mistakenly act without authority, the action can sometimes be corrected through "ratification" by the board of trustees or another officer or employee who does have authority to undertake the act in question (see Section 2.2.1).

One other type of authority is occasionally referred to in the postsecondary context: inherent authority. In *Morris v. Nowotny*, 323 S.W.2d 301 (Tex. 1959), for instance, the court remarked that the statutes establishing the University of Texas "imply the power, and, if they do not so imply, then the power is inherent in university officials to maintain proper order and decorum on the premises of the university." In *Esteban v. Central Missouri State College*, 415 F.2d 1077 (8th Cir. 1969), the court held that the college had "inherent authority to maintain order and to discipline students." And in *Waliga v. Board of Trustees of Kent State University*, 488 N.E.2d 850 (Ohio 1986), it found inherent authority in the university's trustees to revoke an academic degree that had been obtained by fraud. (For the facts and reasoning of this case, see Section 6.1.2.) The inherent authority concept is often loosely used in judicial opinions and has no clear definition. Sometimes, courts appear to apply the phrase to what is really a very broad construction of the institution's implied powers. In *Goldberg v. Regents of the University of California*, 57 Cal. Rptr. 463 (Cal. Ct. App. 1967), the court held that broad disciplinary authority over students was implicit in the state constitution's grant of power to the university, but then it called that authority "inherent." At other times, the inherent authority concept is more clearly distinguished from implied authority; inherent authority then is said to exist not because of any written words but because it would not be sensible, as measured by the norms of postsecondary education, for an institution to be without authority over the particular matter at issue. In all, inherent authority is an elusive concept of uncertain stature and questionable value, and it is a slender reed to rely on to justify actions and decisions. If administrators need broader authority, they should, with counsel's help, seek to expand their express authority or to justify a broader construction of their implied authority.

The law is not clear on how broadly or narrowly authority should be construed in the postsecondary context. To some extent, the answer will vary from state to state and, within a state, may depend on whether the institution is established by the state constitution, by state statutes, or by articles of incorporation. Although authority issues have been addressed in judicial opinions, such as those discussed in Section 2.2, analysis is sometimes cursory, and authority problems are sometimes overlooked. There is debate among courts and commentators about whether postsecondary institutions should be subject to traditional legal principles for construing authority or whether such principles should be applied in a more flexible, less demanding way that takes into account the unique characteristics of postsecondary education. Given the uncertainty, administrators should rely when possible on express rather than implied or inherent authority and should seek clarity in statements of express authority, in order to avoid leaving authority questions to the vagaries of judicial interpretation. If institutional needs require greater flexibility and generality in statements of authority, administrators should consult legal counsel to determine how much breadth and flexibility the courts of the state would permit in construing the various types of authority.

Miscalculations of the institution's authority, or the authority of particular officers or employees, can have various adverse legal consequences. For public institutions, unauthorized acts may be invalidated in courts or administrative agencies under the ultra vires doctrine of administrative law (a doctrine applied to acts that are beyond the delegated authority of a public body or official). For private institutions, a similar result occasionally can be reached under corporation law.

When the unauthorized act is a failure to follow institutional regulations and the institution is public, courts will sometimes hold that the act violated procedural due process. In *Escobar v. State University of New York/College at Old Westbury*, 427 F. Supp. 850 (E.D.N.Y. 1977), a student sought to enjoin the college from suspending him or taking any further disciplinary action against him. The student had been disciplined by the judicial review committee, acting under the college's "Code of Community Conduct." After the college president learned of the disciplinary action, he rejected it and imposed more severe penalties on the student. The president purported to act under the "Rules of Public Order" adopted by the board of trustees of the State University of New York rather than under the college code. The court found that the president had violated the rules, and it enjoined enforcement of his decision:

> Even if we assume the president had power to belatedly invoke the Rules, it is clear that he did not properly exercise that power, since he did not follow the requirements of the Rules themselves. The charges he made against the plaintiff were included in the same document which set forth the plaintiff's suspension and the terms for his possible readmission. Contrary to the Rules, the president did not convene the hearing committee, did not give notice of any hearing, and received no report from the hearing committee. There is no authority in either the Rules or the Code for substituting the hearing before the Code's judicial review committee for the one required to be held before the Rule's hearing committee. . . .
>
> Of course, not every deviation from a university's regulations constitutes a deprivation of due process. . . . But where, as here, an offending student has been formally charged under the college's disciplinary code, has been subjected to a hearing, has been officially sentenced, and has commenced compliance with that sentence, it is a denial of due process of law for the chief administrative officer to step in, conduct his own in camera review of the student's record, and impose a different punishment without complying with any of the procedures which have been formally established for the college. Here the president simply brushed aside the college's formal regulations and procedures and, without specific authority, imposed a punishment of greater severity than determined by the hearing panel, a result directly contrary to the Code's appeal provisions [427 F. Supp. at 858].

For both public and private institutions, an unauthorized act violating institutional regulations may also be invalidated as a breach of an express or implied contract with students or the faculty. *Lyons v. Salve Regina College,* 422 F. Supp. 1354 (D.R.I. 1976), *reversed,* 565 F.2d 200 (1st Cir. 1977), involved a student who had received an F grade in a required nursing course because she had been absent from several classes and clinical sessions. After the student appealed the grade under the college's published "Grade Appeal Process," the grade appeal committee voted that the student receive an Incomplete rather than an F. Characterizing the committee's action as a recommendation rather than a final decision, the associate dean overruled the committee, and the student was dismissed from the nursing program.

The parties agreed that the "Grade Appeal Process" was part of the terms of a contract between them. Though the grade appeal committee's determination was termed a "recommendation" in the college's publications, the lower court found that, as the parties understood the process, the recommendation was to be binding on the associate dean. The associate dean's overruling of the committee was therefore unauthorized and constituted a breach of contract. The lower court ordered the college to change the student's grade to an Incomplete and reinstate her in the nursing program. The appellate court reversed but did not disavow the contract theory of authority. Instead, it found that the committee's determination was not intended to be binding on the associate dean and that the dean therefore had not exceeded his authority in overruling the committee.

Authority questions are also central to a determination of various questions concerning liability for harm to third parties. The institution's tort liability may depend on whether the officer or employee committing the tort was acting within the scope of his authority (see Section 2.3.1). The institution's contract liability may depend on whether the officer or employee entering the contract was authorized to do so (Section 2.3.2). And, under the estoppel doctrine, both the institution and the individual may be liable where the institution or individual had apparent authority to act (Section 2.2.1).

Because of these various legal ramifications, a postsecondary institution should carefully organize and document its authority and the delegation of this authority among institutional officers, employees, and organizations. Counsel should be involved in this process. Organizational statements or charts should be generally available to the campus community, so that persons with questions or grievances can know where to turn for assistance. Delegations should be reviewed periodically, to determine whether they accurately reflect actual practice within the institution and maintain an appropriate balance of specificity and flexibility. Where a gap in authority or an unnecessary overlap or ambiguity is found, it should be corrected. Where questions concerning the permissible scope of authority are uncovered, they should be resolved.

Similarly, administrators should understand the scope of their own authority and that of the officers, employees, and organizations with whom they deal. They should understand where their authority comes from and which higher-level administrators may review or modify their acts and decisions. They should attempt to resolve unnecessary gaps or ambiguities in their authority. They should consider what part of their authority may and should be subdelegated to lower-level administrators or faculty and what checks or limitations should be placed on those delegations. And they should attempt to ensure that their authority is adequately understood by the members of the campus community with whom they deal.

SEC. 2.2. SOURCES AND SCOPE OF AUTHORITY

2.2.1. Officers and Administrators

The authority of the highest-ranking officers and administrators of postsecondary institutions may occasionally be set out in statutes or state board regulations (for public institutions) or in corporate charters (for private institutions). But more often, even the highest-ranking officers and employees, and almost always the lower-ranking ones, derive their authority not directly from statute, state board regulation, or charter but rather from subdelegation by the institution's board of trustees. The lower the administrator in the administrative hierarchy, the greater the likelihood of subsubdelegation—that is, subdelegation of authority from the board of trustees to an officer or administrator who in turn subdelegates part of this authority to some other administrator or employee.

Silverman v. University of Colorado, 555 P.2d 1155 (Colo. 1976), illustrates the subdelegation of authority. A terminated assistant professor claimed that her termination constituted a breach of contract. In December 1972, the associate dean of the professor's school wrote the professor that she would be reappointed for 1973–74 if certain federal funding was renewed and if the professor's peers recommended reappointment. The professor claimed that, although both conditions were fulfilled, the school did not renew her contract, thus violating the terms of the December 1972 letter. The trial court held for the university, reasoning that the associate dean's letter could not create a contract because, by statute, only the board of regents had authority to appoint faculty members. The intermediate appellate court reversed, reasoning that the associate dean could have created a contract because he could have been acting under authority subdelegated to him by the board. The Supreme Court of Colorado then reversed the intermediate court and reinstated the trial court's decision, holding that hiring authority is not delegable unless "expressly authorized by the legislature."

In *People v. Ware*, 368 N.Y.S.2d 797 (N.Y. App. Div. 1975), however, an appellate court upheld a delegation of power from a systemwide board of trustees to the president of an individual institution and thence to campus police officers employed by that institution. The trial court had dismissed a prosecution against an illegal trespasser at the State University of New York (SUNY) at Buffalo because the officer making the arrest did not have authority to do so. According to this court, the New York Education Law (§355(2)(m)) designated the SUNY board of trustees to appoint peace officers, whereas the arresting officer had been appointed by the president of the university. In reversing, the appellate court reasoned that the board had authority under the Education Law to promulgate rules and regulations, and the rules and regulations promulgated by the board provided for the delegation of power to SUNY's executive and administrative officers. By resolution passed under these rules and regulations, the board had authorized administrative officers of each state institution to appoint peace officers for their campuses. Since the SUNY president had properly appointed the arresting officer pursuant to this resolution, the officer had authority to make the arrest.

Even when an institutional officer or administrator acts beyond the scope of his delegated power, so that the act is unauthorized, the board of trustees may subsequently "ratify" the act if that act was within the scope of the board's own authority. "Ratification" converts the initially unauthorized act into an authorized act. In *Silverman v. University of Colorado* (above), for instance, the intermediate appellate court held that, even if the associate dean did not have authority to reappoint the professor, the professor was entitled to prove that the offer of reappointment had been ratified by the board of regents (541 P.2d 93, 96 (1975)). Similarly, in *Tuskegee Institute v. May Refrigeration Co.*, 344 So. 2d 156 (Ala. 1977), two employees of a special program operated by Tuskegee had ordered an air conditioning unit from the May Company. May delivered and installed the unit but was not paid the agreed-upon price. An intermediate appellate court reversed a damages award for May on the theory that the Tuskegee employees who ordered the unit had no authority to do so. The highest state court then reversed the intermediate court. It reasoned that, even though the employees had no actual or apparent authority, Tuskegee had kept and used the unit that the employees ordered and therefore could have ratified their unauthorized acts.

Even when an officer or administrator acts without authority and a higher officer or administrator or the board of trustees has not ratified the act, a court will occasionally estop the institution from denying the validity of the act. Under this doctrine of estoppel, courts may—in order to prevent injustice to persons who had justifiably relied on an unauthorized act—treat the unauthorized act as if it had been authorized. In the *Silverman* case, the plaintiff professor argued that various officials of the school had "advised her that her position was secure for the coming academic year" and that she had "reasonably relied on these representations to her detriment in that she did not seek other employment." The intermediate appellate court ruled that, if the plaintiff's allegations regarding the assurances, the reasonableness of her reliance, and the detriment were true, then "the doctrine of estoppel may be invoked if necessary to prevent manifest injustice." The Colorado Supreme Court reversed, recognizing the estoppel doctrine but holding that the facts did not justify its application in this case. The court reasoned that, since the professor had received adequate notice of nonrenewal, there was no "manifest injustice" necessitating estoppel and that, since the faculty handbook clearly stated that the board of regents makes all faculty appointments, the professor's "reliance on statements made by university officials was misplaced."

Another illustration of estoppel is provided by *Blank v. Board of Higher Education of the City of New York*, 273 N.Y.S.2d 796 (N.Y. Sup. Ct. 1966). The plaintiff student sought to compel the defendant board to award him a Bachelor of Arts degree. The question about the student's degree developed after he was advised that he could take advantage of a Professional Option Plan allowing him to complete a certain minimum amount of coursework without attending any classes. This arrangement enabled him to begin law school in Syracuse before he had finished all his course work at Brooklyn College. The student had been advised by faculty members, the head of the department of psychology, and a member of the counseling and guidance staff, and the arrangement had been approved by the professors of the psychology courses involved, each of whom gave him the necessary assignments. At the time of his expected graduation, however, the student was denied his degree because he had not completed the courses "in attendance."

In defending its refusal to grant the degree, the college argued that only the dean of the faculty had the authority to determine a student's eligibility for the Professional Option Plan and that the dean had not exercised such authority regarding the plaintiff. The college further argued that the dean had devised regulations concerning the Professional Option Plan and that these regulations contained residence requirements which the student had not met. While the court did not dispute these facts, it emphasized, as a contrary consideration, that the plaintiff had "acted in obvious reliance upon the counsel and advice of members of the staff of the college administration to whom he was referred and who were authorized to give him such counsel and advice." Moreover:

> The authority of an agent is not only that conferred upon him by his commission, but also as to third persons that which he is held out as possessing. The principal is often bound by the act of his agent in excess or abuse of his authority, but this is only true between the principal and third persons who, believing and having a right to believe that the agent was acting within and not exceeding his authority, would sustain loss if the act was not considered that of the principal (*Walsh v. Hartford Fire Insurance Co.*, 73 N.Y. 5, 10).
>
> The dean of faculty may not escape the binding effect of the acts of his agents performed within the scope of their apparent authority, and the consequences that must equitably follow therefrom. Having given permission to take the subject courses in the manner prescribed, through his agents . . . , he cannot, in the circumstances, later assert that the courses should have been taken in another manner [273 N.Y.S.2d at 802–03].

Thus, "all of the elements of an estoppel exist" and the "doctrine should be invoked" against the college. The court ordered the college to award the plaintiff the A.B. degree.

In cases involving apparent authority, plaintiffs must convince a court that reliance on that apparent authority was reasonable. In *Sipfle v. Board of Governors of the University of North Carolina*, 318 S.E.2d 256 (N.C. Ct. App. 1984), the plaintiff had signed up for a trip to China organized by a university faculty member and had paid him $52,000 for the cost of the trip. When the travel agency arranging the tour went bankrupt and did not provide the trip or return the plaintiff's money, she sued the university, claiming that the faculty member was its agent and thus the university was responsible for refunding her money. Although the faculty member had used university stationery to advertise the trip, the university escaped liability for his actions because the court ruled that the plaintiff's belief that the university was the sponsor was unreasonable.

Another institution also escaped contract liability on the theory that the defendant could not properly rely on the representations of a college employee. In *Student House, Inc. v. Board of Regents of Regency Universities*, 254 N.E.2d 496 (Ill. 1969), a corporation that owned and operated a private student housing facility at Northern Illinois University sued the university for building additional residence halls. The plaintiffs stated that several years earlier, the university's director of housing had told them that the university would not build additional residence halls; and in reliance on that representation, the plaintiffs formed the corporation and built a private residence hall. The court found that the board of regents had the authority to decide to build residence halls and that the board had not delegated such authority to the housing director. The plaintiffs had relied on the representations of the director without discussing the matter with the president or any board member, said the court; and such reliance on the statements of "lower echelon members of the University staff" (254 N.E.2d at 499) was not reasonable.

2.2.2. The College's Staff

Authority questions occasionally concern college staff—most notably, whether a particular staff member is an agent of the institution or has actual or apparent authority to bind the institution (Section 2.1). But other questions, primarily those related to the staff member's employment, are arising with greater frequency as staff join the various groups that are making increasing demands on colleges.

The legal disputes between a college and its nonfaculty staff do not differ significantly, in most respects, from those between a college and its faculty. With the important exceptions of academic freedom and tenure, which would typically not provide a nonacademic staff member (and one without a faculty appointment) the protections enjoyed by faculty, most of the legal doctrines that apply to faculty also apply to staff.

The legal relationship between a college and its staff is defined by an increasingly complex web of principles and authorities. The core of the relationship is contract law, but that core is encircled by expanding layers of labor relations law, employment discrimination law, and, in public institutions, constitutional law and public employment statutes and regulations. Federal regulations also affect the employment relationship (see Section 12.1). This section will review briefly some of the major principles protecting a college's staff from unlawful practices; for a more comprehensive discussion of these principles, see Chapter 3 of *The Law of Higher Education,* 3d edition (1995).

Contract law is an important source of protections for staff members, whether they are employed by a public or private institution. The written contract may range from a brief notice of appointment on a standard form, to a lengthy collective bargaining agreement negotiated under state or federal labor laws. Or it may not be called a contract at all but a handbook or institutional policy manual. For example, the question of whether an employee handbook is a binding contract has arisen with regard to a staff handbook (see, for example, *Wall v. Tulane University,* 499 So. 2d 375 (La. Ct. App. 1986), and *Gilbert v. Tulane University,* 909 F.2d 124 (5th Cir. 1990)). Contracts are governed by common law, which may vary considerably by state. Employee handbooks and oral promises have been ruled to create binding contracts in some states, while other state courts have rejected this theory. Wrongful-discharge claims may be brought under either contract or tort theories; again, the type of action that may be brought is determined by state law.

Staff at many public and private institutions are represented by unions for the purpose of collective bargaining. Issues of bargaining unit composition, organization and recognition of the bargaining agent, and appropriate subjects of bargaining arise under either state or federal law (depending on whether the college is public or private), although they may be resolved differently for staff than for faculty. For example, in some public colleges and universities, staff (but not faculty) are covered by a state's civil service provisions. These provisions are derived from state statutes and regulations, and thus differ by state and between state systems of higher education. Issues typically involve the classification or reclassification of positions (see *Sindlinger v. State Board of Regents,* 503 N.W.2d 387 (Iowa 1993)), or the amount of due process protection that a college must afford a staff member who is disciplined, discharged, or laid off (see, for example, *Bockes v. Fields,* 999 F.2d 788 (4th Cir. 1993) and *Page v. DeLaune,* 837 F.2d 233 (5th Cir. 1988)).

College staff at public institutions may also be able to assert constitutional claims when they are discharged or disciplined. In two landmark cases, *Board of Regents v. Roth,* 408 U.S. 564 (1972), and *Perry v. Sindermann,* 408 U.S. 593 (1972), the U.S. Supreme Court established that public employees have a right to a fair hearing whenever a personnel decision deprives them of a "property interest" or a "liberty interest" under the Fourteenth Amendment's due process clause. The "property" and "liberty" terminology is derived from the wording of the Fourteenth Amendment itself, which provides that states shall not "deprive any person of life, liberty, or property, without due process of law." Whether or not a staff member has a property interest in continued employment depends on the terms of the employment contract and also may be governed by state law or regulations such as civil service regulations. (The identification of property and liberty interests is also important to many procedural due process questions concerning students; see Sections 4.2.1, 4.2.7.2, 5.2.1, and 7.3.2.)

In identifying property and liberty interests, one must make the critical distinction between staff members who are under continuing contracts and those whose contracts have expired. It is clear, as *Roth* notes, that "public . . . college professors and staff members dismissed during the terms of their contracts . . . have interests in continued employment that are safeguarded by due process." Moreover, if a personnel decision infringes a property or liberty interest, as in dismissal, questions then arise concerning the particular procedures that the institution must follow. These Supreme Court precedents thus provide due process protections against arbitrary or capricious discipline or discharge for staff of public colleges whose employment security is protected by contract. Staff whose contracts have expired, however, or staff who are at-will (who do not have a term contract and are not protected by state law or regulation), are not entitled to due process protections under a property interest theory.

Whether or not they enjoy contractual or state law protections for job security, public college staff are protected against discipline or discharge for speech that is protected by the First Amendment (see, for example, *Wilson v. University of Texas Health Center*, 973 F.2d 1263 (5th Cir. 1992)). A line of U.S. Supreme Court cases has narrowed that protection, however, to speech that is of "public concern" and does not interfere with the employment relationship or the efficient operation of the college. The requirements that the college must meet in discharging an employee who alleges a free speech violation are described in *Pickering v. Board of Education*, 391 U.S. 563 (1968) and *Connick v. Myers*, 461 U.S. 138 (1983), both discussed in Section 6.4.2. In *Waters v. Churchill*, 114 S. Ct. 1878 (1994), the Supreme Court relied upon its *Connick* analysis, ruling that an employer can discipline or discharge the employee for expressive activity if it conducts a reasonable investigation and has a reasonable belief that its version of the facts is correct. For discharges or serious discipline involving either property or liberty interests or First Amendment claims, constitutional due process protections must be provided before the decision becomes final. The crux of these protections is notice and opportunity for a hearing; the college must notify the staff member of the reasons for the decision and provide a fair opportunity for him or her to challenge these reasons in a hearing before an impartial body.

State and federal nondiscrimination laws also protect college staff. The federal government has no less than nine major employment discrimination statutes and one major executive order applicable to postsecondary education, each with its own comprehensive set of administrative regulations or guidelines. All states also have fair employment practices statutes, some of which may exclude educational institutions (such as Md. Ann. Code art. 49B, sec. 18), and others of which may apply to educational institutions and overlap federal statutes.

Because of their national scope and comprehensive coverage of problems and remedies, and because they provide greater protection than the laws of many states, the federal antidiscrimination statutes have assumed greater importance than the state statutes. The federal statutes, moreover, supplemented by those of the states, have outstripped the importance of the federal Constitution as a remedy for employment discrimination. The statutes cover almost all major categories of discrimination and tend to impose more affirmative and stringent requirements on employers than does the Constitution.

Race discrimination in employment is prohibited by Title VII of the Civil Rights Act of 1964 as amended, by 42 U.S.C. sec. 1981, and by Executive Order 11246 as amended. Sex discrimination is prohibited by Title VII, by Title IX of the Education Amendments of 1972, by the Equal Pay Act, and by Executive Order 11246. Age discrimination is outlawed by the Age Discrimination in Employment Act. Discrimination against employees with disabilities is prohibited by both the Americans with Disabilities Act and the Rehabilitation Act of 1973. Discrimination on the basis of religion is outlawed by Title VII and Executive Order 11246. Discrimination on the basis of national origin is prohibited by Title VII and by Executive Order 11246. Discrimination against aliens is prohibited specifically by the Immigration Reform and Control Act and indirectly under Title VII. Discrimination against veterans is covered in part by 38 U.S.C. sec. 4212.

State nondiscrimination laws add more categories of protection, such as marital status or, in a few states, sexual orientation. Although federal law has typically been used to challenge employment decisions by college faculty and staff, some state nondiscrimination statutes provide greater protection or the opportunity for higher damage awards; colleges often find themselves defending discrimination claims brought under both state and federal law.

Although enforcement of the nondiscrimination laws originally focused on alleged bias in making employment decisions, recent years have witnessed an explosion of litigation claiming harassment by an employer or coworker(s) on the basis of some protected characteristic such as race, gender, or sexual orientation. Sexual harassment claims, in particular, have increased and involve staff as well as faculty or students (see, for example, *Townsend v. Indiana University,* 995 F.2d 691 (7th Cir. 1993) and *Giordano v. William Paterson College,* 804 F. Supp. 637 (D.N.J. 1992)). The U.S. Supreme Court has addressed sexual harassment twice under Title VII of the Civil Rights Act of 1964. In both *Meritor Savings Bank v. Vinson,* 477 U.S. 57 (1986) and *Harris v. Forklift Systems,* 114 S. Ct. 367 (1993), the Court has recognized sexual harassment as a form of sex discrimination, ruled that employers may be found liable for harassment of their employees by supervisors, coworkers, or nonemployees, and determined that the creation of a "hostile environment" as a result of unwanted sexual behavior may be challenged under Title VII.

Affirmative action (discussed in the context of student admissions in Section 4.1.5), is also a concern in the employment context. Affirmative action became a major issue because the federal government's initiatives regarding discrimination have a dual aim. The goal is not only to "bar like discrimination in the future" but also to "eliminate the discriminatory effects of the past" (*Albemarle Paper Co. v. Moody*, 422 U.S. 405 (1975)). Addressing this latter objective under Title VII, courts may "order such affirmative action as may be appropriate" (*Franks v. Bowman Transportation Co.*, 424 U.S. 747 (1976), quoting *Albemarle*). Affirmative action can be appropriate under *Franks* even though it may adversely affect other employees, since "a sharing of the burden of the past discrimination is presumptively necessary." Under statutes other than Title VII, and under Executive Orders 11246 and 11375, courts or administrative agencies may similarly require employers, including public and private postsecondary institutions, to engage in affirmative action to eliminate the present effects of past discrimination.

Race- or gender-conscious employment decisions must meet the standards elaborated by the U.S. Supreme Court in a line of cases beginning with *Weber v. Kaiser Aluminum Co.*, 443 U.S. 193 (1979), a case brought under Title VII in which a white steelworker challenged a voluntary affirmative action plan that gave preferences for access to a training program to less-senior black workers. The Court created a test against which subsequent affirmative action plans must be measured to determine their lawfulness: whether the plan is designed to correct a "manifest imbalance" in the workforce, whether it "unnecessarily trammels" the rights of nonminority employees, whether it is an absolute bar to the advancement of nonminority employees, and whether it is temporary. Subsequent rulings by the U.S. Supreme Court have upheld affirmative action plans that meet the *Weber* test, and the race- and gender-conscious employment decisions made under the authority of these plans, in hiring and promotion situations (see, for example, *Johnson v. Transportation Agency, Santa Clara County*, 480 U.S. 616 (1987) (promotion)), but not for layoffs (see, for example, *Wygant v. Jackson Board of Education*, 476 U.S. 267 (1986)). Other affirmative action cases involving public contracting, rather than employment, suggest that the U.S. Supreme Court may be moving away from its earlier support for voluntary affirmative action; a sharply divided Court has invalidated two public contracting laws that required affirmative action (*City of Richmond v. J.A. Croson Co.*, 488 U.S. 469 (1989), and *Adarand Constructors v. Pena*, 115 S. Ct. 2097 (1995)).

A federal appellate opinion involving racial preferences in a layoff of a high school teacher has important implications for affirmative action in employment. In *Taxman v. Board of Education of the Township of Piscataway*, 91 F.3d 1547 (3d Cir. 1996), an *en banc* ruling (8–4), the court found that the school board's use of race to choose between two equally qualified teachers in a layoff decision violated Title VII and the New Jersey Law Against Discrimination. The school board had not claimed that its use of race to make the decision was motivated by the need to remedy past or present discrimination; but rather, the school board had selected the white teacher for layoff in order to increase the diversity of its teaching staff.

The *en banc* court looked to Supreme Court precedent, most notably *Weber*, in order to determine whether the use of race in this situation was permissible under Title VII. The majority interpreted *Weber* to require the defendant to prove that (1) its action "mirrored the purpose of the statute" (that race-conscious decisions increasing diversity was a goal of Title VII when enacted); and (2) its decision did not "unnecessarily trammel" the interests of nonminority employees. The court found that Title VII's sole purpose was remedial and that fostering diversity had not been a motivation for the statute's enactment. Therefore, the only permissible motive for a race-conscious employment decision would be to remedy the school district's own prior discrimination. Since there was no evidence of such prior discrimination (in fact, the district's workforce was racially and ethnically diverse), the school district's action violated Title VII.

Furthermore, said the court, the decision caused a tenured teacher to lose her job, which meant that the interests of a nonminority employee (the plaintiff) were "unnecessarily trammeled." The court distinguished the *Johnson* case, in which the plaintiff was merely eligible for a promotion and did not lose his job, as did Ms. Taxman.

At present, *Taxman* is binding only in New Jersey, Pennsylvania, Delaware, and the Virgin Islands. Although the opinion focuses on layoffs, its reasoning appears to apply to any employment decision. Given the court's broad language rejecting ethnic or racial diversity as a goal of Title VII, the opinion would apparently restrict the affirmative action efforts of colleges and universities that have no record of discrimination but that wish to increase the diversity of their workforce. The broad sweep of the majority opinion's language suggests that the court has effectively equated Title VII and the equal protection clause of the Constitution by stating that the only permissible purpose for race-conscious decisions under Title VII is remediation of the employer's own past or present discrimination. This is a far narrower interpretation of Title VII than that of the Supreme Court in *Weber* or *Johnson v. Transportation Agency,* and the interpretation relies on the Supreme Court's reasoning in equal protection clause cases such as *Wygant v. Jackson.*

Although the layoff decision in *Taxman* involved a race discrimination claim, layoff decisions may also involve contract claims, age or sex discrimination claims, and sometimes constitutional challenges to the institution's determination that financial exigency exists. The legal issues involved in staff layoffs are somewhat less complex than those involving tenured faculty, but careful planning and attention to potential legal claims are critical. For a review of potential legal issues in staff layoffs, see Martin Michaelson and Lawrence White, *Staff Layoffs and Terminations—Managing the Risks,* 1996.

Given the myriad protections for staff and the increasing propensity for individuals who disagree with a negative employment decision to attempt to have that decision overturned by a court, evaluation and documentation of administrative and staff performance are increasingly significant. For assistance, see P. Seldin, *Evaluating and Developing Administrative Performance* (Jossey-Bass, 1988).

2.2.3. Campus Organizations

Authority in postsecondary institutions may be delegated not only to individual officers or administrators but also to various campus organizations that are accorded some role in governance. Common examples include academic senates, faculty assemblies, department faculties, and student or university judicial systems. (See Section 7.1.3 for a discussion of judicial systems.)

Searle v. Regents of the University of California, 100 Cal. Rptr. 194 (Cal. Ct. App. 1972) is a leading case. By a standing order of the regents, the academic senate was given authority to "authorize and supervise all courses and curricula." Pursuant to this authority, the senate approved a course in which 50 percent of the lectures would be taught by a nonfaculty member (Eldridge Cleaver). Subsequent to the senate's approval of the course, the regents adopted two pertinent resolutions. One resolution provided that a person without an appropriate faculty appointment could not lecture more than once during a university quarter in a course offering university credit; the other provided that the course to be taught by Cleaver could not be offered for credit if it could not be restructured.

The course was taught as originally planned. When the regents resolved that the course not be given academic credit, sixteen students who had taken the course and six faculty members sued to compel the regents to grant the credit and to rescind the two resolutions. The plaintiffs argued that the standing order granting the academic senate authority over courses and curricula deprived the regents of power to act. The court, however, found that the regents had specifically retained the power to appoint faculty members and concluded that this case involved an appointment to the faculty rather than just the supervisory power over courses provided by the standing order: "To designate a lecturer for a university course is to name the person to conduct the course, at least to the extent of the lectures to be given by him. When the designation is of one to conduct a full half of the course, it appears to be a matter of appointment to the faculty, which is clearly reserved to the regents." Moreover, the court indicated that the authority of the academic senate was subject to further diminishment by the regents. The court therefore determined that the regents, and not the senate, had authority over the structuring of the course in question.

Another case illustrating delegation of authority to a campus organization—this time a student rather than a faculty group—is *Student Association of the University of Wisconsin-Milwaukee v. Baum*, 246 N.W.2d 622 (Wis. 1976). The

Wisconsin legislature had passed a statute that accorded specific organizational and governance rights to students in the University of Wisconsin system:

> The students of each institution or campus subject to the responsibilities and powers of the board [of regents], the president, the chancellor, and the faculty shall be active participants in the immediate governance of and policy development for such institutions. As such, students shall have primary responsibility for the formulation and review of policies concerning student life, services, and interests. Students, in consultation with the chancellor and subject to the final confirmation of the board, shall have the responsibility for the disposition of those student fees which constitute substantial support for campus student activities. The students of each institution or campus shall have the right to organize themselves in a manner they determine and to select their representatives to participate in institutional governance [Wis. Stat. §36.09(5)].

The chancellor of the Milwaukee campus asserted that, despite the statute's passage, he retained the right to make student appointments to the Physical Environment Committee and the Segregated Fee Advisory Committee. The Student Association—the campuswide student government—argued that the chancellor no longer had this authority because the statute had delegated it to the association. Applying traditional techniques of statutory interpretation, the court agreed with the students. Concerning the student appointments to the Physical Environment Committee, the court held:

> When §36.09(5), Stats., became effective in July 1974, the chancellor lost his authority to make these appointments. The statute gave this authority to the students as of that time. It is well settled that if a rule or directive of an administrative body or officer is in conflict with a newly enacted statute, the statute must take precedence. The students had the right to select their representatives on the Physical Environment Committee [246 N.W.2d at 626].

Using a similar analysis, the court reached the same result with respect to the Segregated Fee Advisory Committee.

2.2.4. Captive and Affiliated Organizations

The activities of higher education institutions are no longer conducted under the umbrella of a single corporate entity. In addition to the degree-granting entity itself, there may be numerous spin-off or related organizations such as alumni and booster clubs, hospitals and clinics, organizations to support research or market products, television or radio stations, museums, and foundations of various kinds. Although often created by action of the institution itself, these organizations may have a corporate existence of their own and may be at least partially independent of the institution. In other situations, the related organization may have originated and developed completely apart from the institution but later enters an affiliation agreement with the institution, maintaining its separate corporate existence and autonomy but cooperating with the institution in some area of mutual interest. The creation and dissolution of these captive and affiliated organizations, and their authority in relation to that of the institution itself, have been the subject of recent debate as well as litigation. The potential liabilities of these organizations, and the potential liabilities the institution might sustain as a result of its relationship with such an organization, have also raised concerns (see, for example, the *Brown* case in Section 2.3.2 (contract liability), and *Jaar v. University of Miami,* 474 So. 2d 239 (Fla. Dist. Ct. App. 1985) (tort liability)).

The problem may arise in different contexts. In one scenario, an institution may wish to sever part or all of a particular function or department, creating a separately incorporated entity. The separate entity then may operate apart from certain legal requirements that would attach if it were still subsumed within the institution's corporate structure. The question then may become whether the institution has sufficiently relinquished its control over the separate entity so that it may operate independently of the institution and free of restrictions that would apply to the institution itself. In *Colorado Association of Public Employees v. Board of Regents of the University of Colorado,* 804 P.2d 138 (Colo. 1990), for example, the court explored the status of a university hospital. The state had promulgated legislation that purported to reorganize the hospital into a private, nonprofit corporation. The legislation provided that the board of regents of the University of Colorado would still control the hospital through regulations and that, "[s]hould the corporation dissolve, the assets of the corporation less amounts owed to creditors will revert to the Regents." The hospital was also required to secure the approval of the state legislature if it wished to transfer the corporation to anyone other than the regents, or if it were to exceed a sixty-million-dollar debt level within two years of its creation.

Under this reorganization scheme, over two thousand state civil servants employed at the hospital had a choice of either continuing as regular members of the hospital staff, in which case they would lose their civil service status, or being assigned by the university to the hospital for a period of two years, at which point they would have to relinquish their employment. The employees filed a complaint alleging that this action would violate the Colorado constitution. The complaint included alternative theories of unconstitutionality. If the legislation were construed to create an entity having the status of a *private* corporation, the plaintiffs claimed that it would violate Articles V and XI of the state constitution, which prohibit private corporations from receiving public funds or assets. If the legislation were construed to create an entity having the status of a *public* corporation, the plaintiffs claimed that it would violate Article XII, Section 13 (the State Civil Service Amendment) and Article XI, Section 3, which forbids state indebtedness except in limited circumstances.

The Supreme Court of Colorado, with two dissents, held that the legislation reorganized the hospital into a public corporation subject to all laws that governed the University of Colorado itself. The court determined that the state maintained control of the hospital by granting the regents power to appoint and remove the hospital directors and to control certain aspects of the hospital's budgeting, spending, and indebtedness. Thus, despite language in the legislation that expressly precluded the hospital from being considered an agency of state government, "it is evident that the Regents have not sufficiently divested themselves of power over the hospital to enable the new corporation to operate independently as a private corporation. Thus, we find that the reorganized hospital is still a public entity."

Since the hospital remained a state entity, and since the legislation would require over two thousand of the hospital's employees to relinquish their civil service status, the court held that the legislation violated the State Civil Service Amendment (Article XII, Section 13 of the state constitution), "which protects state personnel from legislative measures designed to circumvent the constitutional amendment." The court also held that the financing provisions of the reorganizing legislation, allowing the hospital to become indebted, violated Article XI, which prohibits the state from incurring debts.

A different type of structural issue arose in *Gulf Regional Education Television Affiliates v. University of Houston,* 746 S.W.2d 803 (Tex. 1988). The university, because it disapproved of the way in which certain finances were handled by Gulf Regional Education Television (GRETA), had summarily stopped issuing checks to GRETA and had basically dismantled its operations, which the university claimed to be under its control. GRETA hired its own attorney and sued the university. The university challenged GRETA's authority to bring suit, claiming that, as an auxiliary enterprise of the university, it was an arm of the state, and that the attorney general of Texas was the only person authorized to bring suit on the state's behalf. The court had to decide whether GRETA was an agency of the state, which could be represented only by the attorney general, or an independent organization that was merely affiliated with the university and could sue on its own behalf. Relying largely on a letter from the university to GRETA outlining the relationship between the two, the court sided with the university:

> The letter states that auxiliary enterprises are considered part of the University "family" and speaks of the necessity of following University policy on some matters to facilitate the meshing of their operations into the overall institution. Also, auxiliary enterprise employees are employees of the University. Even the language allowing auxiliary enterprises a *major* role in the selection of personnel suggests that the University reserves the option to participate. Finally, and most importantly, while auxiliary enterprises can enter directly into contracts, the University recognizes that, particularly in the case of major contracts, the

contracting parties ultimately hold the University legally responsible
[746 S.W.2d at 808].

Thus, as in the *University of Colorado* case, the institution's retention of considerable control over the affiliated organization demonstrated that the organization was part of the institution rather than an independent entity. GRETA was thus "subject to governance by the Board of Regents and . . . a suit brought by or on its behalf must be authorized by the Board of Regents."

The creation or reorganization of separate entities may also give rise to taxation issues. Resolution of these issues may also depend on the legal status of the organization in relation to the degree-granting entity and the degree of control the latter asserts over the former (as in cases like the *Colorado* case). In addition, the resolution of taxation problems may depend on the functions that the organization performs and their relation to the functions of the institution itself. In *Yale Club of Chicago v. Department of Revenue*, 574 N.E.2d 31 (Ill. 1991), for example, the court considered whether an alumni association that recruited for Yale University qualified for a purchaser's exemption from the state sales tax. The Yale Club of Chicago (YCC) is a nonprofit corporation that dedicates its efforts to promoting Yale University. One of its central purposes is to use its members to interview potential Yale students in the Chicago area. Although the club follows admissions guidelines prepared by Yale, it is not controlled in any way by the university and does not receive any funding from the university. The club sponsors social events for its members: Yale alumni, parents of alumni, and current Yale students.

The appellate court held that the YCC did not qualify for an educational or a charitable tax exemption under Illinois law. Regarding the educational exemption, the club had argued that "because Yale University is a school to which the exemption would apply, and the YCC is performing the same functions that Yale could, the exemption should apply to those activities performed [to further] Yale's educational objectives." In rejecting this argument, the court, under the statute and case law, reasoned that the club could claim exemption based on its relationship with Yale only if the club's activities were "reasonably necessary" to Yale's pursuit of its educational mission. The court ruled that they were not. Thus, the *Yale Club* case demonstrates that an affiliated organization performing beneficial functions for the institution does not necessarily qualify for a tax exemption, even though the institution itself could receive an exemption on the basis of the same activities.

Creation of or affiliation with another entity may also raise questions about the application of state regulatory statutes. Various state statutes apply to state agencies or public bodies, for instance, but not to private entities. If a public institution creates or affiliates with another entity, the question would be

whether the entity is sufficiently controlled by or related to the public institution that the former would be considered an agency or body subject to these
state laws.

In *Weston v. Carolina Research and Development Foundation,* 401 S.E.2d 161
(S.C. 1991), for example, the issue was whether South Carolina's Freedom of
Information Act (S.C. Code Ann. §§30–4–10 to 30–4–110) applied to the Carolina
Research and Development Foundation, a nonprofit corporation operating
"exclusively for the benefit of the University of South Carolina" (401 S.E.2d at
162), thus allowing the plaintiff media organizations to inspect the foundation's
records. The Act applies to all "public bodies," defined in part as "any organization, corporation, or agency supported in whole or in part by public funds or
expending public funds" (S.C. Code Ann. §30–4–20(a)). The court determined
that the foundation had received public funds on at least four separate occasions. The foundation had accepted almost 40 percent of the consideration
the University of South Carolina received for selling one of the university's
buildings; it had accepted over sixteen million dollars in federal grant money
on behalf of the university and managed the expenditure of these funds for construction of an engineering center for the university; it had accepted grants of
money from the city of Columbia and from Richland County, and a conveyance
of real estate from the city, as part of the process of developing a real estate project for the university; and it had retained 15 to 25 percent of the total payments
from private third parties under research and development contracts that the
university had entered and channeled through the foundation. The court held
that any one of these transactions qualified the foundation as a public body
under the language of the Act. The foundation was thus required to permit the
plaintiffs to inspect its records.

Similarly, in *State v. Nicholls College Foundation,* 564 So. 2d 682 (La. 1990),
the inspector general of the state of Louisiana sought to view the records of the
foundation pursuant to the state Public Records Act (La. Rev. Stat. Ann. §§44:1
et seq.). The foundation, a nonprofit corporation organized to promote the welfare of Nicholls College, had received funds from the Nicholls State University
Alumni Federation, another nonprofit organization promoting the college's interests. The federation received its funding through a mandatory fee charged to all
Nicholls students registered for more than seven credit hours; it then transferred
10 percent of these funds to the foundation. Under the Public Records Act, the
foundation's records would be "public records" subject to public inspection if
either (a) the Foundation were a "public body" or (b) the records concerned
"the receipt or payment" of public funds. Using the second rationale, the
Louisiana Supreme Court determined that the federation's close affiliation with
Nicholls College (including its occupying a building on campus at only nominal rent, its use of state employees in its operations, and its inclusion in the col-

lege's yearly budget) made the federation a public body and that the student fees provided to the federation were public funds. The foundation's records of its receipt and use of these funds were thus public records subject to the Act (as, presumably, were the federation's records). The state's inspector general thus had a right to view the records. (For further clarifications in later proceedings, see *State v. Nicholls College Foundation*, 592 So. 2d 419 (La. 1991) and 593 So. 2d 651 (La. 1992); see also Section 11.6.2.)

A quite different set of problems arises when an organization that is not already part of the institution's structure attempts to connect itself to the institution in some way. The general question then is whether an institution has any obligation to allow particular outside entities to become affiliated with it, and whether and how an institution may restrict the rights of such an organization to claim or publicly assert an affiliation with the school. In *Ad Hoc Committee of Baruch Black and Hispanic Alumni Association v. Bernard M. Baruch College*, 835 F.2d 980 (2d Cir. 1987), the plaintiff committee alleged that the college had improperly refused to recognize its proposed alumni association dedicated to the needs of minority students. This refusal, the committee argued, was a violation of the First Amendment and the equal protection clause of the Fourteenth Amendment. The college countered that an officially recognized alumni organization, which included minority alumni, already existed and that the creation of another alumni association could overburden alumni with fund solicitations and thus dilute the current association's power to raise funds.

After a district court dismissed the committee's complaint, the U.S. Court of Appeals reversed and remanded, holding:

> [I]t is possible that plaintiffs could demonstrate that the College's selective denial of official recognition to their alumni association was improperly motivated by discrimination based on political viewpoint or race. . . . In this case, the College has not yet offered any justification for its denial of recognition to the Black and Hispanic Alumni Association, and thus it is impossible to determine at this stage whether this action was motivated by a desire to "discourage one viewpoint and advance another" in violation of the First Amendment [835 F.2d at 982].

On remand, the district court held that universities generally have no responsibilities to their graduates, other than to supply transcripts. In particular:

> The First Amendment does not require colleges to fund or recognize alumni groups. Moreover, a college does not unlawfully impede the associational rights of its alumni when it declines to recognize an alumni group. . . . However, if a college does involve itself in establishing an alumni relationship structure, it must act non-discriminatorily [726 F. Supp. at 523].

The court then held that the committee could show no discrimination or other improper motive by the college in not recognizing the proposed alumni association, and that the college was thus not required to acknowledge and support the new association.[1]

In light of these case illustrations, it is clear that an institution must carefully structure and document its relationships with each organization it creates or with which it affiliates. In so doing, it should focus on the purposes it seeks to fulfill, the degree of control it needs to attain or retain, and the consequences of particular structural relationships on the respective rights of the parties to act autonomously of one another. In addition, the institution should consider how the structural arrangements would affect the applicability of particular regulatory and tax laws to the institution's activities, as well as ascertain whether the institution may be liable for actions of the other entity (see generally Section 2.3) and, if so, how the institution would control that risk (see generally Section 2.5).

SEC. 2.3. INSTITUTIONAL LIABILITY FOR ACTS OF OTHERS

2.3.1. Institutional Tort Liability

A tort is broadly defined as a civil wrong, other than a breach of contract, for which the courts will allow a damage remedy. While there is a broad range of actions that may expose an institution to tort liability, and any act fitting this definition may be considered a tort, there are certain classic torts for which the essential elements of the plaintiff's prima facie case and the defendant's acceptable defenses are already established. The two classic torts that most frequently arise in the setting of postsecondary education are negligence and defamation, both of which are discussed in this section; but other tort theories, such as common law fraud, are also appearing in lawsuits against colleges and universities. Various techniques are available to postsecondary institutions for managing the risks of tort liability, as discussed in Section 2.5.

A postsecondary institution is not subject to liability for every tortious act of its trustees, administrators, or other agents. But the institution will generally be liable, lacking immunity or some other recognized defense, for tortious acts committed within the scope of the actor's employment or otherwise authorized by the institution or subject to its control. In the *Lombard* case discussed in Section 2.3.1.1, for instance, the institution was liable for the acts of its janitors committed in the course of their building maintenance duties. And in *Butler v.*

---

[1]Eventually, the parties resolved their dispute. By agreement, the Black and Hispanic Alumni Association is allowed to use the college's name and some office space, and the committee expressed willingness to discuss a possible relationship with the Baruch Alumni Association ("College Settles Lawsuit Filed by Minority Alumni," *Chron. Higher Educ.*, May 2, 1990, A2).

Louisiana State Board of Education, 331 So. 2d 192 (La. 1976), after finding that a professor had been negligent in allowing a biology experiment to be conducted without appropriate safeguards, the court asserted that the professor's "negligence must be attributed to the defendant university and to the state board of education."

Unless they are employees of the institution, torts caused by students generally will not result in liability for the institution. Medical students, moreover, will not always be considered agents of the institution. In *Gehling v. St. George's University School of Medicine,* 705 F. Supp. 761 (E.D.N.Y. 1989), *affirmed without opin.,* 891 F.2d 277 (2d Cir. 1989), for example, students who treated a colleague after he collapsed in a road race did not expose the medical school to malpractice liability, because they had not acted as agents of the school.

Even if an individual is not an employee of the institution, however, the college may be found liable under the concept of "gratuitous employee." In *Foster v. Board of Trustees of Butler County Community College,* 771 F. Supp. 1122 (D. Kan. 1991), a basketball coach had asked a student to pick up a potential recruit at the airport and drive him to a nearby motel. On his return from the airport, the student ran a red light and hit a truck, resulting in his death and the injuries of the recruit and the truck driver. Both injured parties sued the college.

A jury awarded the injured recruit $2.26 million against the college and the estate of the driver. On appeal, the college argued that it was not responsible for the actions of the student driver. The court, noting that the student's car was uninsured and unregistered and that the student had no valid driver's license, ruled that "the Butler Community College defendants could have discovered [the driver's] unfitness for the task had any investigation been conducted" (771 F. Supp. at 1128). The college had policies requiring students driving on the college's behalf to be licensed; the college's failure to follow its policies and its failure to ascertain whether the student was qualified to undertake the responsibility it assigned him resulted in the court's determination that, for purposes of *respondeat superior* liability, the student was a "gratuitous employee" of the college. (Under the doctrine of *respondeat superior,* an employer is legally responsible for an employee's torts.)

In some circumstances, a postsecondary institution may also be liable for the acts of its student organizations. In *Wallace v. Weiss,* 372 N.Y.S.2d 416 (N.Y. Sup. Ct. 1975), a libel action based on material printed in a student publication, the University of Rochester moved for judgment in its favor on the ground that it was not responsible for the acts of a student organization. The court denied the motion because "the question of the university's responsibility should not be determined until all the facts are presented at the trial." According to this court:

> [A university] may be in a position to take precautions against the publication of libelous matter in its student publications. . . .

> The university, by furnishing and providing to the organization money, space, and in lending its name, may well be responsible for the acts of the organization at least insofar as the university has the power to exercise control. By assisting the organization in its activities, it cannot avoid responsibility by refusing to exercise control or by delegating that control to another student organization [372 N.Y.S.2d at 422].

A 1981 New York State Court of Claims case, *Mazart v. State,* 441 N.Y.S.2d 600 (N.Y. Ct. Cl. 1981) (see Section 8.2.5), contains a valuable analysis of an institution's liability for the tortious acts of its student organizations. The case concerned a libelous letter to the editor, published by the student newspaper at SUNY-Binghamton. The court's opinion addressed the liability theories proposed in *Wallace v. Weiss.* The court noted two possible theories for holding post-secondary institutions liable: (1) that the student organization was acting as an agent of the institution, and the institution, as principal, is vicariously liable for its agents' torts (the *respondeat superior* doctrine); and (2) that the institution had a legal duty to supervise the student organization, even if it was not acting as the institution's agent, because the institution supported or provided the environment for the organization's operation. In a lengthy analysis, the court refused to apply either theory against the institution, holding that (1) the institution did not exercise sufficient control over the newspaper to establish an agency relationship; and (2) given the relative maturity of college students and the rudimentary need and generally understood procedure for verifying information, the institution had no legal duty to supervise the newspaper's editorial process.

The second theory articulated in *Mazart,* the institution's purported "duty to control," became an issue in a case that, although it did not involve a tort claim, addressed issues similar to those addressed in tort actions against colleges. An attempt to hold a university responsible for acts of individual students and a faculty member was rejected by the Supreme Court of Vermont. In *Doria v. University of Vermont,* 589 A.2d 317 (Vt. 1991), an unsuccessful political candidate sued the University of Vermont under several sections of the state constitution, arguing that the university had a duty to supervise and control its students and faculty members in order to preserve his constitutional right to a fair election. The students had worked as telephone pollers for a faculty member and two newspapers; and, the plaintiff alleged, the questions and the ensuing poll results had given other candidates an unfair advantage.

The court rejected the plaintiff's "duty to control" theory, stating that "requiring defendant to strictly regulate and control the activity involved here, or any other student and faculty activity that might have an impact on the electoral process, would be basically inconsistent with the academic environment" (589 A.2d at 321). The result in *Doria* is deferential to the activities of faculty members and their students, particularly in matters related to curriculum or faculty research.

Even if the individual causing the injury is acting in a volunteer capacity rather than within the scope of employment, a college may be liable for injury caused by that person. In *Smith v. University of Texas*, 664 S.W.2d 180 (Tex. Ct. App. 1984), the court refused to award summary judgment to the university on its theory that the tortfeasor (the individual whose actions resulted in injury) was acting as a volunteer referee at a sporting event. Questions about the university's duty to supervise the event, the fact that these "volunteers" were also employees of the university, and unresolved questions of fact dictated that the matter go to trial.

An additional source of potential liability for colleges and universities is found in their status as landowners or landlords. The institution may be held liable for the acts of strangers on the campus under certain circumstances. In *Peterson v. San Francisco Community College District*, 685 P.2d 1193 (Cal. 1984), a student was assaulted in a campus parking lot by an unidentified man who had been hiding behind bushes and trees next to the parking lot. The court found that the college had breached its duty to invitees (individuals lawfully on the campus, whether they were students, staff, or members of the general public) because of the foreseeability of this incident, given the history of violent crime in the area in which the assault occurred. (For a discussion of campus security issues, see Section 5.2.)

Public institutions can sometimes escape tort liability by asserting sovereign or governmental immunity. Sovereign immunity is a common law doctrine that protects the state as an entity, and its agencies, from litigation concerning common law or certain statutory claims. (Immunity of a state and its agencies from suit in federal courts is also guaranteed by the Eleventh Amendment to the U.S. Constitution and is discussed in Section 2.3.3.)

The availability of this defense varies greatly from state to state. While the sovereign immunity doctrine was generally recognized in early American common law, the doctrine has been abrogated or modified in many states by judicial decisions, state legislation, or a combination of the two. When a public institution raises a defense of sovereign immunity, the court must first determine whether the institution is an arm of the state. Because the doctrine does not protect the state's political subdivisions, entities that are separate and distinct from the state are not protected by sovereign immunity. If the court finds that the institution is a state entity, then the court must determine whether the state has taken some action that would divest the institution of sovereign immunity, at least for purposes of the lawsuit. Some states, for example, have passed tort claims acts, which define the types of lawsuits that may be brought against the state and the procedures that must be followed. Other exceptions have been created by decisions of state supreme courts, such as in *Morash v. Commonwealth*, 363 Mass. 612 (1973), in which the Massachusetts Supreme Court ruled that the state could be sued for intentional torts or for a limited category of negligence claims.

In *Brown v. Wichita State University,* 540 P.2d 66 (Kan. 1975), *vacated in part,* 547 P.2d 1015 (Kan. 1976), the university faced both tort and contract claims for damages arising from the crash of an airplane carrying the university's football team. In Kansas, the university's home state, the common law doctrine of immunity had been partly abrogated by judicial decision in 1969, the court holding that the state and its agencies could be liable for negligence in the conduct of "proprietary" (as opposed to "governmental") activities. But in 1970, the Kansas legislature had passed a statute reinstituting the immunity abrogated by the court. The university in *Brown* relied on this statute to assert immunity to the tort claim. The court, after reconsidering the issue, vacated its prior judgment to the contrary and rejected plaintiffs' arguments that the statute was unconstitutional, thus allowing the university's immunity defense.

A public institution does not necessarily lose its immunity defense even if it subsumes—and then must answer for the actions of—an entity that, when independent, did not enjoy such immunity. In *Kroll v. Board of Trustees of the University of Illinois,* 934 F.2d 904 (7th Cir. 1991), a former employee of an athletic association sued the trustees for wrongful discharge. Although the athletic association had been a nonprofit corporation independent of the university, the state legislature had merged the association into the university through special legislation. The court ruled that the board had not waived its immunity when it absorbed the association, nor had the legislature so provided. Therefore, the university's immunity extended to acts of the former association, and the case was dismissed.

Sovereign immunity may be unavailable as a defense if the institution does not assert this defense in its response to a lawsuit. In *University of Kentucky Board of Trustees v. Hayse,* 782 S.W.2d 609 (Ky. 1989), the Kentucky Supreme Court rejected the university's claim of sovereign immunity in litigation over a tenure denial because it had not been asserted at the beginning of the proceedings. Sovereign immunity is also unavailable in situations where the state entity is not performing a governmental function, but one that a private entity could perform. For example, in *Brown v. Florida State Board of Regents,* 513 So. 2d 184 (Fla. Dist. Ct. App. 1987), a student at the University of Florida drowned in a lake owned and maintained by the university. In response to the university's defense of sovereign immunity in the ensuing wrongful death claim, the appellate court ruled that since the type of activity was not a governmental one, the university could not assert the immunity defense; once the university decided to operate a lake, it then assumed the common law duty of care to those who used it.

Although private institutions can make no claim to sovereign immunity, nonprofit schools may sometimes be able to assert a limited "charitable" immunity defense to certain tort actions. The availability of this defense also varies considerably from state to state. Overall, the charitable immunity defense appears to be more limited and less recognized than sovereign immunity. In a leading precedent, *President and Directors of Georgetown College v. Hughes,* 130 F.2d 810 (D.C. Cir. 1942), the court struck a common note by heavily criticizing charitable immunity and refusing to apply it to a tort suit brought by a special nurse injured on the premises of the college's hospital. And in *Mullins v. Pine Manor College,* 449 N.E.2d 331 (Mass. 1983) (discussed in Section 5.2.2), the Supreme Court of Massachusetts, noting that the state legislature had abrogated charitable immunity for torts committed in the course of activity that was primarily commercial (Mass. Gen. Laws ch. 231, §85K), rejected the college's charitable immunity defense. The court also refused the college president's request to apply a good-faith standard, rather than a negligence standard, to his actions. (A good-faith standard would absolve the president of liability even if he were found negligent, as long as he had acted in good faith.)

2.3.1.1. Negligence. Higher education institutions are facing a growing array of negligence lawsuits, often related to students or others injured on campus or at off-campus functions. Although most college students have reached the age of majority and, theoretically, are responsible for their own behavior, injured students and their parents are increasingly asserting that the institution has a duty of supervision or a duty based on its "special relationship" with the student that goes beyond the institution's ordinary duty to invitees, tenants, or trespassers. When the postsecondary institution is not immune from negligence suits under either sovereign or charitable immunity, liability depends, first, on whether the institution's actions fit the legal definition of the tort with which it is charged; and, second, on whether the institution's actions are covered by one of the recognized defenses that protect against liability for the tort with which it is charged. For the tort of negligence, the legal definition will be met if the institution owed a duty to the injured party but failed to exercise due care to avoid the injury. Whether or not a duty exists is a matter of state common law. In *Lombard v. Fireman's Fund Insurance Co.,* 302 So. 2d 394 (La. Ct. App. 1974), the duty was found to depend on the plaintiff's status while on the institution's property. The plaintiff was a student going to a class held on the second floor of a Southern University building. When the student reached the second floor, she noticed that it was slippery but continued to walk the fifteen feet to her classroom. The student slipped and fell, injuring her back. The slipperiness was caused by an excess amount of oil that janitors had placed on the floors. In holding the university liable, the court determined that the plaintiff was an "invitee" on the university's property, as opposed to a trespasser, and applied the general tort law principle "that the owner of property owes to invitees . . . the duty of exercising reasonable care to keep the premises in a safe condition, or of warning invitees of hidden or concealed perils of which he knows or should have known in the exercise of reasonable care."

In addition to the general duty owed to invitees on its campus, there may be a "special relationship" between the institution and its students that gives rise to a duty beyond that owed to invitees or to the general public. For example, when the institution sponsors an activity such as intercollegiate sports, a court may find that the institution owes a duty to student athletes on the basis of a special relationship. In *Kleinknecht v. Gettysburg College*, 989 F.2d 1360 (3d Cir. 1993) (discussed in Section 10.6), a federal appellate court applying Pennsylvania law held that a special relationship existed between the college and a student who collapsed as a result of cardiac arrest and died during lacrosse practice, and that because of this special relationship, the college had a duty to provide treatment to the student in the event of such a medical emergency. On the other hand, if the student is pursuing private social activities that the institution has not undertaken to supervise or control, a court may find that no duty exists. In *University of Denver v. Whitlock*, 744 P.2d 54 (Colo. 1987), for example, the Supreme Court of Colorado reversed a $5.26 million judgment against the University of Denver for a student rendered a quadriplegic in a trampoline accident.

The accident in *Whitlock* occurred in the front yard of a fraternity house on the university campus. The university had leased the land to the fraternity. Whitlock asserted that the university had a duty, based on a "special relationship," to make sure that the fraternity's trampoline was used only under supervised conditions. The special relationship, Whitlock asserted, arose either from his status as a student or the university's status as landowner and lessor to the fraternity. But the court held that the university's power to regulate student conduct on campus did not give rise to a duty to regulate student conduct or to monitor the conduct of every student on campus. Nothing the university had done justified Whitlock's reliance on the university for aid or protection, the court noted. Citing earlier cases in which no duty to supervise social activity was found (*Bradshaw v. Rawlings* and *Baldwin v. Zoradi*, discussed below), the court concluded that the university did not have a special relationship based merely on the fact that Whitlock was a student. Inspection of the lease between the university and the fraternity disclosed no right to direct or control the activities of the fraternity members, and the fire inspections and drills conducted by the university did not create a special relationship.

In determining whether a duty exists, the court may consider whether the harm that befell the individual was foreseeable. For example, in *Kleinknecht v. Gettysburg College*, discussed above, the court noted that the specific event need not be foreseeable, but that the risk of harm must be both foreseeable and unreasonable. In analyzing the standard of care required, the court noted that the potential for life-threatening injuries occurring during practice or an athletic event was clearly foreseeable, and thus the college's failure to provide facilities for emergency medical attention was unreasonable. In another case, *Nero v. Kansas State University*, 861 P.2d 768 (Kan. 1993) (discussed in Section 5.2.2), the Kansas Supreme Court ruled that the rape of a student by a fellow student in a residence hall was reasonably foreseeable because the alleged rapist had been found guilty of an earlier sexual assault on campus.

If the injury is unforeseeable, however, the court will refuse to create a duty. For example, the Supreme Court of Vermont refused to hold Norwich University liable for injuries to two railroad engineers shot by university students, because the injuries were not foreseeable and the students were legally adults (*Smith v. Day*, 538 A.2d 157 (Vt. 1987)). Lack of foreseeability also undergirded a ruling by New York's highest court that the State University of New York at Buffalo had no legal duty to screen applicants who were ex-convicts for violent tendencies before admitting them. In *Eiseman v. State*, 518 N.Y.S.2d 608, 511 N.E.2d 1128 (N.Y. 1987), the court overturned rulings by two lower courts that the university and the state's prison system were jointly liable for an ex-convict's rape and murder of a fellow student:

> [I]mposing liability on the College for failing to screen out or detect potential danger signals in [the ex-convict] would hold the College to a higher duty than society's experts in making such predictions—the correction and parole officers, who in the present case have been found to have acted without negligence [518 N.Y.S.2d at 616].

On the other hand, when the institution attempts to prohibit, or to control, inherently dangerous activities in which its students participate, a court may find that it has a duty to those students. In *Furek v. University of Delaware*, 594 A.2d 506 (Del. 1991), the Supreme Court of Delaware ruled that the university's pervasive regulation of hazing during fraternity rush created a duty to protect students from injuries suffered as a result of that hazing. Furek, who had pledged the local chapter of Sigma Phi Epsilon, was seriously burned and permanently scarred when a fraternity member poured a lye-based liquid oven cleaner over his back and neck as part of a hazing ritual. After he withdrew from the university and lost his football scholarship, he sued the university and was awarded $30,000 by a jury, 93 percent of which was to be paid by the university and the remainder by the student who poured the liquid on Furek.

The university asserted on appeal that it had no duty to Furek. While agreeing that "the university's duty is a limited one," the court was "not persuaded that none exists" (594 A.2d at 517). Rejecting the rationales of *Bradshaw* (discussed below) and its progeny, the court used a public policy argument to find that the University did have a duty:

> It seems . . . reasonable to conclude that university supervision of potentially dangerous student activities is not fundamentally at odds with the nature of the parties' relationship, particularly if such supervision advances the health and safety of at least some students [594 A.2d at 518].

Although it refused to find a special duty based on the dangerous activities of fraternities and their members, the court held that:

> Certain established principles of tort law provide a sufficient basis for the imposition of a duty on the [u]niversity to use reasonable care to protect resident students against the dangerous acts of third parties. . . . [W]here there is direct university involvement in, and knowledge of, certain dangerous practices of its students, the university cannot abandon its residual duty of control [594 A.2d at 519–20].

The court determined that the university's own policy against hazing, and its repeated warnings to students against the hazards of hazing, "constituted an assumed duty" (594 A.2d at 520). Relying on Section 314A of the *Restatement (Second) of Torts,* the court determined that the "pervasive" regulation of hazing by the university amounted to an undertaking by the university to protect students from the dangers related to hazing, and created a duty to do so.

Once a legal duty is found to exist, the boundaries of that duty must be delineated. That is, a court must determine what standard of care the defendant will be held to under the circumstances. This issue was considered in *Mortiboys v. St. Michael's College,* 478 F.2d 196 (2d Cir. 1973). A student sued the institution for injuries sustained while he was skating on an outdoor ice rink maintained by the college for student pleasure skating. The student had fallen when his skate hit a one-inch-high lump of ice. The court refused to hold the college liable and articulated the standard of care owed by the college as "reasonable care under all the circumstances." For the college to be held liable, the dangerous condition would either have to be "known . . . or [to] have existed for such a time that it was [the college's] duty to know it." The court concluded that it was "a matter of speculation what caused the lump to be formed and whether it had been there for any substantial length of time." Expensive maintenance equipment, which would be used for indoor intercollegiate hockey rinks, "cannot reasonably be required of a college providing an outdoor rink for the kind of use contemplated and to which this rink was actually being put at the time of the accident."

But if the institution undertakes to provide a service, particularly to individuals who depend on the institution for their safety, the court may determine that a higher standard of care exists than that owed to a mere invitee. In *Nova University v. Wagner,* 491 So. 2d 1116 (Fla. 1986), the Supreme Court of Florida ruled that the university, which operated a residential rehabilitation center for children with behavioral problems, could be liable for actions of those children. Two residents at the center had escaped and, while at large, had killed one younger child and severely injured a second. The resident supervisors were university employees, and the court ruled that in operating the facility, they had failed to meet the standard of reasonable care to avoid harm to the general public.

Even if a duty and the requisite standard of care have been established, the postsecondary institution still will not be found negligent unless the plaintiff is able to prove that the institution's breach of duty was the proximate cause of the injury. In *Mintz v. State*, 362 N.Y.S.2d 619 (N.Y. App. Div. 1975), the State University at New Paltz was found not liable for the deaths of two students who drowned on a canoe trip sponsored by an outing club. The court held that "it was the terrible, severe, and unforeseen weather conditions on the lake, and not any negligence on the part of the university, which were the proximate cause of the deaths herein."

Even when the plaintiff establishes all the elements for a prima facie case of negligence, as discussed above, the postsecondary institution may avoid liability by asserting and proving the defense of "contributory negligence" or "assumption of risk" of injury by the plaintiff.

While failing to find the plaintiff contributorily negligent, the court in the *Lombard* case discussed earlier acknowledged the acceptability of such a defense. "The invitee in a slip and fall case is under a duty to see dangers which are obvious and can be detected and avoided by the degree of care exercised by a reasonably prudent person"; under the facts presented, however, "it was not unreasonable for plaintiff to traverse the slippery floor [for only a few feet] after she discovered its slippery condition."

Liability also will not be imposed where the plaintiff is found to have assumed the risk of the injury that occurred. This "assumption-of-risk" doctrine was applied in *Rubtchinsky v. State University of New York at Albany*, 260 N.Y.S.2d 256 (N.Y. Ct. Cl. 1965), where a student was injured in a pushball game between freshmen and sophomores conducted by the student association as part of an orientation program. The court found that the student voluntarily assumed the risks of the game, since the student, who was offered various orientation activities, chose to play pushball.

2.3.1.2. Alcohol consumption and negligence. Contemporary problems concerning the consumption of alcohol by college students provide a particularly useful illustration of negligence law's operation on campus. For postsecondary administrators and legal counsel, student drinking is a persistent and troubling issue. Vandalism of campus property is one consequence of alcohol-related student activity. Of more serious concern, however, are the injuries and deaths that result from accidents caused by student drinking, and the potential tort liability of postsecondary institutions for such occurrences. Surveys have found that alcohol is a factor in most incidents leading to injury or death of students or campus visitors. For example, a survey of claims by an insurer of a national fraternity between 1987 and 1991 showed that 86 percent of all fatalities, 86 percent of injuries resulting in paralysis, 72 percent of the serious injuries reported, 88 percent of psychological injuries, and 97 percent of reported cases of sexual abuse involved alcohol use (Harris & Harris 1992 Fraternity Claims Analysis). Although many institutions have attempted to curb drinking, especially by underage students, their success has been limited (C. Shea, "Party Schools Find the Image Is Difficult to Shed as Efforts to Curb Alcohol Abuse Have Limited Success," *Chron. Higher Educ.,* Apr. 7, 1993, A31–32).

Two cases from Pennsylvania and California consider the responsibility of postsecondary institutions to control student drinking on campus and at college-sponsored activities off campus. The cases also add generally to an understanding of negligence liability by analyzing the relationship between the institution and its students, and the ensuing legal duty of care arising from this relationship. Both of these cases have been relied on in subsequent cases where students claimed that the institution had a duty to protect them from the consequences of their own actions.

In *Bradshaw v. Rawlings,* 612 F.2d 135 (3d Cir. 1979), a sophomore at Delaware Valley College in Doylestown, Pennsylvania, was seriously injured in an automobile accident following the annual sophomore class picnic, which had been held off campus. The injured student was a passenger in a car driven by another student, who had become intoxicated at the picnic. Flyers announcing the picnic were mimeographed by the college duplicating facility. They featured drawings of beer mugs and were prominently displayed across the campus. The sophomore class's faculty adviser, who did not attend the picnic, cosigned the check that was used to purchase beer. The injured student brought his action against the college, as well as the beer distributor and the municipality, alleging that the college owed him a duty of care to protect him from harm resulting from the beer drinking at the picnic. The jury in the trial court awarded the student, who was rendered quadriplegic, damages in the amount of $1,108,067 against all defendants, and each appealed on separate grounds.

The college argued on appeal that the plaintiff had failed to establish that the college owed him a legal duty of care. The appellate court agreed with this argument. Its opinion began with a discussion of the custodial character of postsecondary institutions. Changes that have taken place on college campuses in recent decades lessen the duty of protection that institutions once owed to their students:

> There was a time when college administrators and faculties assumed a role
> *in loco parentis.* . . . A special relationship was created between college and
> student that imposed a duty on the college to exercise control over students'
> conduct and, reciprocally, gave the students certain rights of protection by the
> college. . . . A dramatic reapportionment of responsibilities and social interests
> [has taken] place. . . . College administrators no longer control the broad arena
> of general morals. At one time by exercising their rights and duties *in loco paren-*
> *tis,* colleges were able to impose strict regulations. But today students vigorously
> claim the right to define and regulate their own lives [612 F.2d at 139].

The concept of legal duty is neither rigid nor static. A court can create a new duty if, after evaluating the interests of the parties, it decides that a plaintiff should be entitled to legal protection against a defendant's conduct. According to the *Bradshaw* court, "The plaintiff in this case possessed an important interest in remaining free from bodily injury, and thus the law protects his right to recover compensation from those who negligently cause his injury. The college, on the other hand, has an interest in the nature of its relationship with its adult students, as well as an interest in avoiding responsibilities that it is incapable of performing."

The student had the burden of proving the existence of a legal duty by identifying specific interests that arose from his relationship with the college. Concentrating on the college's regulation prohibiting the possession or consumption of alcoholic beverages on campus or at off-campus, college-sponsored functions, he argued that this regulation created a custodial relationship between the college and its students. A basic principle of law holds that one who voluntarily takes custody of another is under a duty to protect that person. The plaintiff reasoned that he was entitled to the protection voluntarily assumed by the college when it promulgated the regulation. The court dismissed this argument on the ground that the college regulation merely tracks state law, which prohibits persons under the age of twenty-one from drinking intoxicants.[2] By promulgating the regulation, then, the college did not voluntarily assume a custodial relationship but only reaffirmed the necessity of student compliance with Pennsylvania law.

Besides creating new legal duties, courts may rely on existing case or statutory law that recognizes a legal duty arising from the particular relationship at issue. Some states impose a legal duty on a provider of intoxicants to an intoxicated person, making the provider responsible to third parties for the negligent acts of the intoxicated person (known as "social host" liability theories). The plaintiff in *Bradshaw* argued that this duty, already existing in some states, also existed in Pennsylvania. By analogy, the college would then have a duty to protect third persons from the negligent acts of intoxicated student drivers, because it had furnished, or condoned the furnishing of, the alcoholic beverages. Pennsylvania does establish by statute a duty of care to third persons if the provider has a liquor license, but the Pennsylvania Supreme Court had held that a private host who supplies intoxicants to a visibly intoxicated guest may not be held civilly liable for injuries to third persons caused by the intoxicated guest's negligence. The *Bradshaw* court predicted that, since the Pennsylvania courts had refused to impose a legal duty on the private host, "it

---

[2]In actuality, the regulation went beyond the statute because it applied to every student regardless of age—a point that could have favored the plaintiff had the court been sensitive to it. Lawyers will thus want to exercise caution in relying on the court's analysis of this particular issue.

would be even less willing to find a relationship between a college and its student under the circumstances of this case." (The Pennsylvania Supreme Court has since ruled that individuals who knowingly serve intoxicants to minors are negligent per se and liable for any ensuing damages (*Congino v. Portersville*, 470 A.2d 515 (Pa. 1983).)

Consequently, unable to find a legal duty based on a special relationship existing as a matter of law, and unwilling to obligate the college by creating a new duty, the appellate court reversed the trial court's judgment of liability.

The *Bradshaw* case was quoted with approval in a California case, *Baldwin v. Zoradi*, 176 Cal. Rptr. 809 (Cal. Ct. App. 1981). In *Baldwin*, the drinking occurred on campus in a dormitory room, and the plaintiff student was injured by an intoxicated student driver involved in a drag-racing contest. The plaintiff alleged that her dormitory room agreement, which prohibited alcoholic beverages in the residence halls, created a special relationship between her and the dormitory advisers and that the advisers therefore owed her a duty to enforce the provisions of the agreement. Although California courts are particularly willing to find a duty of protection where the defendant stands in a special relationship to both the victim and the person causing the harm, as was argued here, the *Baldwin* court determined that practicality prevented the imposition of a legal duty on the college to control student drinking. The prevalence of alcohol consumption on the modern college campus would make compliance with such a duty almost impossible, and the use of alcohol by college students is not so harshly judged by contemporary standards as to require special efforts to eradicate it.

Bradshaw and *Baldwin* have influenced many courts in subsequent litigation regarding whether the institution owed its students a duty to protect them from drinking, either their own or that of fellow students. In *Beach v. University of Utah*, 726 P.2d 413 (Utah 1986), an underage student who consumed alcohol on a university-sponsored field trip, in full view of the faculty adviser, fell off a cliff, sustaining serious injuries. The court refused to find a duty, based on special relationship, on the university's part, despite the fact that the university had promulgated regulations against drinking and the fact that the faculty adviser had failed to enforce those regulations.

Similarly, in *Crow v. State of California*, 271 Cal. Rptr. 349 (Cal. Ct. App. 1990), a California appellate court rejected a student's claim that the university owed him a duty to protect him from assault by an intoxicated fellow student. The assailant, of legal drinking age, had become intoxicated at a party held in a university residence hall. On a previous occasion, he had also assaulted a residence hall adviser. Despite the plaintiff's assertion that the fellow student was "inherently dangerous" and that the prior assault made this one foreseeable, the court found no duty to supervise either the beer party or the assailant.

And in *Van Mastrigt v. Delta Tau Delta*, 573 A.2d 1128 (Pa. Super. Ct. 1990), another university escaped liability when a student, incarcerated for murder, claimed that the alcohol and drugs he consumed at a campus fraternity party induced him to commit the crime and that both the university and the fraternity were liable for his actions. The appellate court dismissed the claim, finding no duty and thus no breach.

With regard to liability for injuries related to alcohol consumption by students, college administrators, in all probability, may safely rely on *Bradshaw* and *Baldwin* insofar as they reject the notion of a general custodial relationship between the postsecondary institution and its students. Colleges with drinking regulations that do not merely track state law, however, could still be held liable, despite *Bradshaw,* if the regulations can be interpreted as a voluntary assumption of a specific custodial duty regarding alcoholic beverages (such as was found with regard to the University of Delaware's hazing regulations in *Furek,* discussed above). Although many college communities are responding to alcohol abuse by establishing task forces for responsible student drinking and by operating alcohol education clinics, there is also a trend toward initiating or strengthening institutional regulations on alcohol use. Since courts could construe such regulations to constitute voluntary assumption of custodial duty, institutions should have counsel review all drinking regulations.

Moreover, student alcohol abuse is increasingly recognized as a serious campus problem, and special efforts are being made to eradicate it. Despite the apparent vitality of the *Baldwin* doctrine, the intractability of the problem and increasingly vigorous institutional efforts to control underage drinking and its associated violence may encourage students to continue to attempt to hold colleges responsible for injuries resulting from student alcohol abuse on campus or at college-sponsored activities off campus.

Additional sources of liability may arise in states where case or statutory law establishes civil liability for private hosts who furnish intoxicating beverages (see *Kelly v. Gwinnell,* 476 A.2d 1219 (N.J. 1984), and *Bauer v. Dann,* 428 N.W.2d 658 (Iowa 1988)) or for retail establishments that sell alcohol to minors. Sponsors of parties at which intoxicants are served, particularly to minors, could be found negligent under the social host doctrine. A court in such a jurisdiction could rely on this law to impose a legal duty on the institution when alcohol is served at college-sponsored activities. Many states also have Dram Shop Acts, which strictly regulate licensed establishments engaged in the sale of intoxicants and impose civil liability for dispensing intoxicants to an intoxicated patron. A college or university that holds a liquor license, or contracts with a concessionaire who holds one, may wish to enlist the aid of legal counsel to assess its legal obligations as a license holder.

2.3.1.3. Defamation. The second typical tort asserted against a postsecondary institution—defamation—is committed by the oral or written publication of matter that tends to injure a person's reputation. The matter must have been published to some third person and must have been capable of defamatory meaning and understood as referring to the plaintiff in a defamatory sense. (See Sections 8.2.4 and 8.2.5 for a further discussion of defamation.) Defamation claims are also asserted against officials of the institution, such as deans or department chairs. These claims are discussed in Section 2.4.1.

One of the most important defenses against a defamation action is the conditional or qualified privilege of fair comment and criticism. An application of this privilege occurred in *Olsson v. Indiana University Board of Trustees,* 571 N.E.2d 585 (Ind. Ct. App. 1991). A prospective teacher, who had graduated from the university and had performed her student teaching under the supervision of one of its faculty, sued the university, claiming that a letter of reference written by a faculty member was libelous. The faculty member had described both the plaintiff's strengths and weaknesses with apparent candor.

The court ruled that the faculty member and the university were protected by a qualified privilege that may be asserted "if a need exists for full and unrestricted communication regarding matters on which the parties have a common interest or duty" (571 N.E.2d at 587). Such a privilege would cover any communication "if made in good faith on any subject matter in which the party making the communication has an interest or in reference to which he has a duty, either public or private, whether legal or moral, or social, if made to a person having a corresponding interest or duty" (571 N.E.2d at 587). Noting that the university had a responsibility to prepare teachers, the court ruled that this letter of recommendation was an appropriate occasion for the use of the qualified privilege.

Another conditional privilege that is important for administrators in state institutions is the privilege afforded to executive and administrative officers of government. In *Shearer v. Lambert,* 547 P.2d 98 (Or. 1976), an assistant professor at Oregon State University brought a libel action against the head of her department. While admitting that the statement was defamatory, the defendant argued that the privilege of government officers should be extended to lesser executive or administrative officers, such as the head of a department. The court agreed, reasoning that, since "the privilege is designed to free public officials from intimidation in the discharge of their duties, we are unable to explain why this policy would not apply equally to inferior as well as to high-ranking officers." This qualified privilege is available, however, only where the defendant "publishes the defamatory matter in the performance of his official duties."

A constitutional "opinion" privilege based on the First Amendment is also sometimes assertable as a defense in a defamation action. Under this privilege, defamation may be considered protected speech under the First Amendment if the speech meets certain requirements. In *Gertz v. Robert Welch,* 418 U.S. 323, 339–40 (1974), the U.S. Supreme Court stated that "there is no such thing as a false idea." *Gertz* has been interpreted to mean that an allegedly defamatory statement of opinion is actionable only if it implies that "undisclosed defamatory facts" have formed the basis for the opinion (*Restatement (Second) of Torts* §566 at 170). An example of the application of this doctrine is found in *Belliveau v. Rerick*, 504 A.2d 1360 (R.I. 1986), in which a professor denied tenure by Providence College sued his department chair for defamation, arguing that the chair had undercounted his "publications" and thus given false information. The court characterized the chair's statement as opinion and said that the chair and the plaintiff had a difference of opinion about what "counted" as a publication. Since the chair and the plaintiff had referred to the same list of "publications," there were no undisclosed facts, and the court applied the constitutional privilege. Furthermore, noted the court, even if the chair's statements could be characterized as fact, rather than opinion, he was protected by a qualified privilege of commenting on the qualifications of tenure candidates, as required by his position.

If a defamation lawsuit is brought against a prominent administrator, trustee, or faculty member who would be considered a "public figure," the standard of proof changes to one of "actual malice," and the privilege to defame is thus broader than for defamation of private figures. In *Avins v. White*, 627 F.2d 637 (3d Cir. 1980), for example, the question was whether the dean of the Delaware Law School was a public figure. After examining his role "as creator, chief architect, and the first dean" of the school, and his active involvement in the school's efforts to achieve accreditation, the court answered the question affirmatively.

If a person is a public figure, another person will not be held liable for defaming him unless that other person's comment "was made with knowledge of its falsity or in reckless disregard of whether it was false or true" (*Garrison v. Louisiana*, 379 U.S. 64, 74 (1964)). Thus, to the extent that members of the academic community are placeable in the public-figure category, the institution's potential liability for defamation is reduced. Under factors such as those considered by the court in *Avins v. White*, however, it is unlikely on any given campus at any particular time that a substantial proportion of the community would be considered public figures.

2.3.1.4. Other sources of tort liability. One area of potential liability that combines several theories of liability revolves around the issue of acquired immune deficiency syndrome (AIDS, or HIV). Although the potential consequences of contracting AIDS are very serious, since the disease itself is usually fatal, the limited avenues of transmission of the disease mean that the liability of most institutions is limited. However, those with medical or dental schools face potential liability for infection of patients, staff, and the general public.

Students and staff who have AIDS or who are HIV-positive are protected by the Rehabilitation Act and the Americans with Disabilities Act (see Sections 12.1.6 and 12.4.4) against discrimination on the basis of that status. Potential tort issues involving individuals who are HIV-positive could include invasion of privacy for breaches of confidentiality, negligent treatment by student health service personnel, assault and/or battery, fraud, and intentional or negligent infliction of emotional distress.

When an HIV-positive employee or student is involved in clinical programs, such as medicine or dentistry, in which that employee or student comes in contact with members of the general public in university-sponsored clinics, potential negligence liability exists if that employee or student infects a patient. Concern over this liability persuaded Washington University to deny further enrollment in the dental program to an HIV-positive dental student. The student sued the university under Section 504 of the Rehabilitation Act. (For discussion of this and related cases, see Section 12.4.4.)

Another potential source of tort liability, albeit a generally unsuccessful one for plaintiffs, is the doctrine of "educational malpractice." The claim (which may also be based on contract law, as discussed in Sections 2.3.2 and 3.2) arises from the duty assumed by a professional not to harm the individuals relying on the professional's expertise. An individual who performs "one of the professions, or a trade, calling or business, . . . [is] required to exercise that degree of skill (a special form of competence) and knowledge usually had by members of such profession or such trade in good standing" (S. Speiser, *The American Law of Torts* (Clark Boardman Callaghan, 1985), 319).

Although they often sympathize with students who claim that they have not learned what they should have learned, or that their professors were negligent in teaching or supervising them, courts have been reluctant to create a cause of action for educational malpractice. In *Ross v. Creighton University,* 740 F. Supp. 1319 (N.D. Ill. 1990), discussed in Section 10.2, a trial judge dismissed the claim by a former athlete that the university had failed to educate him. Asserting that the university's curriculum was too difficult for him, the former basketball player argued that Creighton had a duty to educate him and not simply allow him to attend while maintaining his athletic eligibility. The judge disagreed, ruling that the student was ultimately responsible for his academic success. The appellate court affirmed (957 F.2d 410 (7th Cir. 1992)).

A similar result was reached in *Moore v. Vanderloo,* 386 N.W.2d 108 (Iowa 1986), although the plaintiff in this case was a patient injured by a chiropractor trained at Palmer College of Chiropractic. The patient sued the college, claiming that the injuries were a cause of the chiropractor's inadequate training. After reviewing cases from other jurisdictions, the Iowa Supreme Court decided against permitting a cause of action for educational malpractice.

The court gave four reasons for its decision:

1. There is no satisfactory standard of care by which to measure an educator's conduct.

2. The cause of the student's failure to learn is inherently uncertain, as is the nature of damages.

3. Permitting such claims would flood the courts with litigation and would thus place a substantial burden on educational institutions.

4. The courts are not equipped to oversee the day-to-day operation of educational institutions.

The Supreme Court of Kansas reached a similar conclusion in *Finstand v. Washburn University of Topeka*, 845 P.2d 685 (Kan. 1993). Several students in the university's court-reporting program sued the university for consumer fraud (since, they alleged, it had falsely claimed that its program was accredited) and for malpractice (since, they alleged, the performance of students in the program on the state's certification test was worse than that of other students). Although the court found that the students' latter allegation was true, there was no evidence that the students' failure rate was caused by poor instruction. Citing *Ross* and a case in which New York's highest court rejected a malpractice claim against a school system (*Donohue v. Copiague Unified Free School District*, 391 N.E.2d 1352 (N.Y. 1979)), the Kansas Supreme Court refused to recognize such a claim for essentially the same reasons cited in *Moore*.

2.3.2. Institutional Contract Liability

The institution may be characterized as a "principal" and its trustees, administrators, and other employees as "agents" for purposes of discussing the potential liability of each on contracts transacted by an agent for, or on behalf of, the institution. The fact that an agent acts with the principal in mind does not necessarily excuse the agent from personal liability (see Section 2.4.2), nor does it automatically make the principal liable. The key to the institution's liability is authorization; that is, the institution may be held liable if it authorized the agent's action before it occurred or if it subsequently ratified the action. However, even when an agent's acts were properly authorized, an institution may be able to escape liability by raising a legally recognized defense such as sovereign immunity. As mentioned in Section 2.3.1, this defense is available in some states to public institutions but not to private institutions.

The existence and scope of sovereign immunity from contract liability vary from state to state. In *Charles E. Brohawn & Bros., Inc. v. Board of Trustees of Chesapeake College*, 304 A.2d 819 (Md. 1973), the court recognized a very broad immunity defense. The plaintiffs had sued the trustees to compel them to pay the agreed-upon price for work and materials provided under the contract, including the construction of buildings for the college. In considering the college's defense, the court reasoned:

> The doctrine of sovereign immunity exists under the common law of Maryland. By this doctrine, a litigant is precluded from asserting an otherwise meritorious cause of action against this sovereign state or one of its agencies which has inherited its sovereign attributes, unless [sovereign immunity has been] expressly waived by statute or by a necessary inference from such a legislative enactment. . . . The doctrine of sovereign immunity or, as it is often alternatively referred to, governmental immunity was before this court in *University of Maryland v. Maas,* 173 Md. 554, 197 A. 123 (1938), where our predecessors reversed a judgment recovered against the university for breach of contract in connection with the construction of a dormitory at College Park. That opinion, after extensively reviewing the prior decisions of this court, succinctly summed up [our predecessors'] holdings: "So it is established that neither in contract nor tort can a suit be maintained against a governmental agency, first, where specific legislative authority has not been given, second, even though such authority is given, if there are no funds available for the satisfaction of the judgment, or no power reposed in the agency for the raising of funds necessary to satisfy a recovery against it" (173 Md. at 559, 197 A. at 125) [304 A.2d at 820; notes and citations omitted].

Finding that the cloak of the sovereign's immunity was inherited by the community college and had not been waived, the court rejected the plaintiff's contract claim.

Regarding contract liability, there is little distinction to be made among trustees, administrators, employees, and other agents of the institution. Whether the actor is a member of the board of trustees or its equivalent—the president, the athletic director, the dean of arts and sciences, or some other functionary—the critical question is whether the action was authorized by the institution.

The issue of authorization can become very complex, as illustrated by *Brown v. Wichita State University,* 540 P.2d 66 (Kan. 1975). As mentioned in Section 2.3.1, the *Brown* case arose after the crash of a plane carrying the Wichita State football team. The survivors and personal representatives of the deceased passengers sued Wichita State University (WSU) and the Physical Education Corporation (PEC) at the school for breaching their Aviation Service Agreement by failing to provide passenger liability insurance for the football team and other passengers. The plaintiffs claimed that they were third-party beneficiaries of the service agreement entered into by WSU, the PEC, and the aviation company. The service agreement was signed by the athletic director of WSU and by an agent of the aviation company. The university asserted that it did not have the authority to enter the agreement without the board of regents' approval, which it did not have; that it did not grant the athletic director the authority to enter the agreement on its behalf; that the athletic director only had authority to act as the agent of the PEC; that WSU could not ratify the agreement because it lacked authority to enter it initially; and that, as a state agency, it could not be estopped from denying the validity of the agreement.

The court held that the PEC was the agent of the university and that the athletic director, "as an officer of the corporate agent [PEC], had the implied power and authority to bind the principal—Wichita State University." The court further held that failure to obtain the board of regents' approval did not invalidate the contract:

> The legislature has delegated to the board of regents the authority to control, operate, manage, and supervise the universities and colleges of this state. "For such control, operation, management, or supervision, the board of regents may make contracts and adopt orders, policies, or rules and regulations and do or perform such other acts as are authorized by law or are appropriate for such purposes" (K.S.A. 1974 Supp. 76–712). . . . However, no policy, rule, or regulation of the board of regents has been cited or furnished to this court regarding contract matters, and none can be found in the Kansas Administrative Regulations. . . . Absent any such rules or regulations, Wichita State cannot use the statute to deny the validity of the Aviation Service Agreement following execution and partial performance. Common honesty forbids repudiation now [540 P.2d at 76–77].

The fact that the agreement had been partly performed was particularly persuasive to the court:

> Today, the use of separate corporate entities in collegiate athletics appears to be common, perhaps widespread, but indeed shadowy as to involvement and responsibility. Whether such arrangements should continue is not a question for this court. But when the involvement is such as presented in the instant case, then it begs logic to hold [that] no agency relations exist and that the principles thereof do not apply. Performance under the contract had begun and payments [were] made; this constituted tacit, effective approval of the Aviation Agreement Contract [540 P.2d at 77].

An institution sued on a contract can raise defenses arising from the contract itself or from some circumstance unique to the institution. Defenses that arise from the contract include the other party's fraud, the other party's breach of the contract, and the absence of one of the requisite elements (offer, acceptance, consideration) in the formation of a contract. Defenses unique to the institution may include a counterclaim against the other party, the other party's previous collection of damages from the agent, or, for public institutions, the sovereign immunity defense discussed earlier. Even if one of these defenses—for instance, that the agent or institution lacked authority or that a contract element was absent—is successfully asserted, a private institution may be held liable for any benefit it received as a result of the other party's performance. But public institutions may sometimes not even be required to pay for benefits received under such circumstances.

Institutions also face potential contract liability from policy documents or student catalogues (see Section 3.2) and from student athletes who argue that the college made contractually binding representations during the recruitment process (see, for example, *Ross v. Creighton University,* discussed in Section 10.2).

The variety of contract and agency law principles that may bear on contract liability makes the area a complex one, calling for frequent involvement of legal counsel. The postsecondary institution's main concern in managing liability should be the delineation of the contracting authority of each of its agents. By carefully defining such authority, and by repudiating any unauthorized contracts of which they become aware, postsecondary administrators can protect the institution from unwanted liability. While protection may also be found in other defenses to contract actions, such as sovereign immunity, advance planning of authority is the surest way to limit contract liability and the fairest to the parties with whom the institution's agents may deal.

2.3.3. Institutional Liabilities for Violations of Federal Constitutional Rights

The tort and contract liabilities of postsecondary institutions (discussed in Sections 2.3.1 and 2.3.2) are based in state law and, for the most part, are relatively well settled. The institution's potential constitutional rights liability, in contrast, is primarily a matter of federal law, which has undergone a complex evolutionary development. The key statute governing the enforcement of constitutional rights, commonly known as "Section 1983," reads:

Every person who, under color of any statute, ordinance, regulation, custom, or usage, of any state or territory or the District of Columbia, subjects, or causes to be subjected, any citizen of the United States or other person within the jurisdiction thereof to the deprivation of any rights, privileges, or immunities secured by the Constitution and laws, shall be liable to the party injured in an action at law, suit in equity, or other proper proceeding for redress [42 U.S.C. §1983].

Section 1983's coverage is limited in two major ways. First, it imposes liability only for actions carried out "under color of" state law, custom, or usage. Under this language, the statute applies only to actions attributable to the state, in much the same way that, under the state action doctrine (see Section 1.5.2), the U.S. Constitution applies only to actions attributable to the state. While public institutions clearly meet this statutory test, private postsecondary institutions cannot be subjected to Section 1983 liability unless the action complained of was so connected with the state that it can be said to have been done under color of state law, custom, or usage.

Second, Section 1983 imposes liability only on a "person"—a term not defined in the statute. Thus, Section 1983's application to postsecondary education also depends on whether the particular institution or system being sued is considered to be a person, as the courts construe that term. Although private institutions would usually meet this test because they are corporations, which are considered to be legal persons under state law, most private institutions would be excluded from Section 1983 anyway under the color-of-law test. Thus, the crucial coverage issue under Section 1983 is one that primarily concerns administrators of public institutions: whether a public postsecondary institution is a person for purposes of Section 1983 and thus subject to civil rights liability under that statute.

A related issue, which also helps shape a public institution's liability for violations of constitutional rights, is whether the institution is immune from suit in federal courts under Article III and the Eleventh Amendment of the U.S. Constitution. If the suit is against the state itself, or if the suit is against a state official acting in his or her "official capacity" and seeks money damages that would come from the state treasury, the immunity from federal court suit will apply unless the state has consented to suit, expressly or by clear implication, thus waiving its immunity. As discussed below, the courts have used Eleventh Amendment immunity law as a backdrop against which to fashion a definition of "person" under Section 1983.

In a series of cases beginning in 1978, the U.S. Supreme Court dramatically expanded the potential liability of government entities under Section 1983. As a result of these cases, it is now clear that any political subdivision of a state may be sued under this statute; that such governmental defendants may not assert a qualified immunity from liability based on the reasonableness or good faith of their actions; that they may be liable not only for violations of an individual's federal constitutional rights but also for violations of other rights secured by federal law (*State of Maine v. Thiboutot*, 448 U.S. 1 (1980)); and that they may not require claimants to resort to state administrative forums before seeking redress in court.

The first, and key, case in this series is the U.S. Supreme Court's decision in *Monell v. Department of Social Services of the City of New York*, 436 U.S. 658 (1978). Overruling prior precedents that had held the contrary, the Court decided that local government units, such as school boards and municipal corporations, are "persons" under Section 1983 and thus subject to liability for violating civil rights protected by that statute. Since the definition of "person" is central to Section 1983's applicability, the question is whether the Court's definition in *Monell* is broad enough to encompass postsecondary institutions: Are all or some public postsecondary institutions sufficiently like local government units that they will be considered "persons" subject to Section 1983 liability?

The answer depends not only on a close analysis of *Monell* but also on an analysis of the particular institution's organization and structure under state law. Locally based institutions, such as community colleges established as an arm of a county or a community college district, are the most likely candidates for "person" status. At the other end of the spectrum, institutions established as state agencies under the direct control of the state are apparently the least likely candidates. This distinction between local agencies and state agencies is appropriate because the Eleventh Amendment immunizes states, but not local governments, from certain suits in federal courts. Consequently, the *Monell* Court limited its "person" definition "to local government units which are not considered part of the state for Eleventh Amendment purposes." And in a subsequent case, *Quern v. Jordan*, 440 U.S. 332 (1979), the Court emphasized this limitation in *Monell* and asserted that neither the language nor the history of Section 1983 evidences any congressional intention to abrogate the states' Eleventh Amendment immunity.

The clear implication, reading *Monell* and *Quern* together, is that local governments—such as school boards, cities, and counties—are persons suable under Section 1983 and are not immune from suit under the Eleventh Amendment, whereas state governments and state agencies controlled by the state are not persons under Section 1983 and are immune under the Eleventh Amendment. The issue in any particular case, then, as phrased by the Court in another case decided the same day as *Quern,* is whether the entity in question "is to be regarded as a political subdivision" of the state (and thus not immune) or as "an arm of the state subject to its control" (and thus immune) (*Lake County Estates v. Tahoe Regional Planning Agency,* 440 U.S. 391, 401–02 (1979)).

This case law added clarity to what once had been the confusing and uncertain status of postsecondary institutions under Section 1983 and the Eleventh Amendment. But courts continued to have difficulty determining whether to place particular institutions on the immune or nonimmune side of the liability line. A 1982 U.S. Court of Appeals case, *United Carolina Bank v. Board of Regents of Stephen F. Austin State University,* 665 F.2d 553 (5th Cir. 1982), provides an instructive illustration of the problem. The plaintiff in this case was a professor who had been dismissed from his position. He brought a Section 1983 suit against the board of regents, the president of the university, and four university administrators, alleging violations of his First Amendment free speech and Fourteenth Amendment due process rights. When the professor died during the course of the action, the bank, as administrator of his estate, became the plaintiff. The threshold question was whether the Eleventh Amendment barred the federal court from taking jurisdiction over the Section 1983 claims against the university, as opposed to the claims against the four administrators sued in their individual capacities (see Section 2.4.3). To answer this question, the court had to "decide whether the Board of Regents of SFA is to be treated as an arm of the State, partaking of the State's eleventh amendment immunity, or is instead to be treated as a municipal corporation or other political subdivision to which the eleventh amendment does not extend."

The district court determined that the Eleventh Amendment did not bar suit against SFA. The appellate court disagreed and dismissed the claim, characterizing the university as an arm of the state not subject to Section 1983 suits in federal courts:

> Our analysis will first examine the status of the Board of Regents of SFA under Texas law. . . . Texas law provides: "'state agency' means a university system or an institution of higher education as defined in section 61.003 Texas Education Code, other than a public junior college." . . . By contrast, Texas statutory definitions of "political subdivision" typically exclude universities in the category of SFA. . . .
>
> [W]e next examine the state's degree of control over SFA, and SFA's fiscal autonomy. SFA was created by the legislature in 1921, and in 1969 was placed under the control of its own Board of Regents. Texas' statutes authorizing the operation of SFA and providing for its governance are codified at Tex. Educ. Code Ann. §95.01 *et seq.* and §101.01 *et seq.* These statutes provide that members of the Board of Regents are to be appointed by the Governor with the advice and consent of the Senate. Tex. Educ. Code Ann. §101.11. Texas also subjects SFA to some control by the Coordinating Board, Texas College and University System, which exercises broad managerial powers over all of the public institutions of higher learning in Texas. . . .
>
> SFA's Board has the power of eminent domain, but "the taking of the land is for the use of the state." Tex. Educ. Code Ann. §95.30. The University's real property is state property, Tex. Rev. Civ. Stat. Ann. art. 601b §1.02; . . . and the funds used to purchase it were appropriated by the legislature from the general revenues of the state. . . . State law is the source of the University's authority to purchase, sell, or lease real and personal property. *See* Tex. Rev. Civ. Stat. Ann. art. 601b. The University's operating expenses come largely through legislative appropriation. 1981 Tex. Sess. Law Serv. ch. 875 at 3695. Even those public funds which do not originate with the state are reappropriated to the University, *id.* ch. 875 at 3720, and become subject to rigid control by the state when received. *Id.* ch. 875 at 3719–21. . . .
>
> In addition to the functions cited above, because SFA is a state agency it is subject to state regulation in every other substantial aspect of its existence. . . . Also Texas courts have held repeatedly that suits against Universities within SFA's classification are suits against the state for sovereign immunity purposes. . . . In short, under Texas law SFA is more an arm of the state than a political subdivision [665 F.2d at 557–58].

The court carefully noted that its conclusion concerning Stephen F. Austin University would not necessarily apply to state universities in other states, or to all other postsecondary institutions in Texas: "Each situation must be addressed individually because the states have adopted different schemes, both intra and interstate, in constituting their institutions of higher learning." As an example, the court noted the distinction between Texas institutions such as SFA, on the one hand, and Texas junior colleges, on the other. Relying on Texas statutes, the court reaffirmed its earlier decisions in *Hander v. San Jacinto Junior College*, 519 F.2d 273 (5th Cir. 1975), and *Goss v. San Jacinto Junior College*, 588 F.2d 96 (5th Cir. 1979), that Texas junior colleges are not arms of the state because they can levy taxes for their support and because their trustees are elected rather than appointed by the governor. Thus they are suable under Section 1983.

Eleventh Amendment and Section 1983 case law since *United Carolina Bank* has developed along similar lines, with courts frequently equating the Eleventh Amendment immunity analysis with the "person" analysis under Section 1983 (see, for example, *Thompson v. City of Los Angeles*, 885 F.2d 1439 (9th Cir. 1989), upholding dismissal of a claim against the board of regents of the University of California). In the process, the law has become clearer and more refined. In *Kashani v. Purdue University*, 813 F.2d 843 (7th Cir. 1987), for example, the court reaffirmed the proposition that the Eleventh Amendment shields most state universities from damages liability in Section 1983 actions. The plaintiff, an Iranian graduate student, asserted that his termination from a doctoral program during the Iranian hostage crisis was based on his national origin. In dismissing his claim for monetary relief, the court suggested that, although the states have structured their educational systems in many ways and courts review each case on its facts, "it would be an unusual state university that would not receive immunity" (813 F.2d at 845). The court also reaffirmed, however, that under the doctrine of *Ex parte Young*, 209 U.S. 123 (1908), the Eleventh Amendment does not bar claims against university officers in their official capacities for the injunctive relief of reinstatement. In determining whether the defendant, Purdue University, was entitled to Eleventh Amendment immunity, the court placed primary importance on the "extent of the entity's financial autonomy from the state," the relevant considerations being "the extent of state funding, the state's oversight and control of the university's fiscal affairs, the university's ability independently to raise funds, whether the state taxes the university, and whether a judgment against the university would result in the state increasing its appropriations to the university." Applying these considerations, the court concluded that Purdue was entitled to immunity because it "is dependent upon and functionally integrated with the state treasury."

Other courts, particularly in the Third and Sixth Circuits, have applied a more expansive set of nine factors to resolve Eleventh Amendment immunity questions. These factors, known variously as the "*Urbano* factors" or "*Blake* factors" to credit the cases from which they derived, have gained increasing popularity in recent higher education cases. In the case that first articulated these factors, *Urbano v. Board of Managers of New Jersey State Prison*, 415 F.2d 247 (3d Cir. 1969), the court explained:

(1) [L]ocal law and decisions defining the status and nature of the agency involved in its relation to the sovereign are factors to be considered, but only one of a number that are of significance. Among the other factors, no one of which is conclusive, perhaps that most important is (2) whether, in the event plaintiff prevails, the payment of the judgment will have to be made out of the state treasury; significant here also is (3) whether the agency has the funds or the power to satisfy the judgment. Other relevant factors are (4) whether the agency is performing a governmental or proprietary function; (5) whether it has been separately incorporated; (6) the degree of autonomy over its operations; (7) whether it has the power to sue and be sued and to enter into contracts; (8) whether its property is immune from state taxation; and (9) whether the sovereign has immunized itself from responsibility for the agency's operations [415 F.2d at 5051; numbering added].

This nine-factor test was applied to higher education in *Hall v. Medical College of Ohio at Toledo*, 742 F.2d 299 (6th Cir. 1984), a case in which a student who had been dismissed from medical school alleged racial discrimination in violation of Section 1983. The district court, looking generally to the extent of the school's functional autonomy and fiscal independence, had held that the school was an "arm of the state" entitled to Eleventh Amendment immunity. Although the appellate court affirmed the district court, it emphasized that the nine-part *Urbano/Blake* test "is the better approach for examining the 'peculiar circumstances' of the different colleges and universities."

Similarly, the court in *Skehan v. State System of Higher Education*, 815 F.2d 244 (3d Cir. 1987), used the *Urbano/Blake* test to determine that the defendant State System "is, effectively, a state agency and therefore entitled to the protection of the eleventh amendment." In contrast, however, the court in *Kovats v. Rutgers, The State University*, 822 F.2d 1303 (3d Cir. 1987), determined that Rutgers is not an arm of the state of New Jersey and thus is not entitled to Eleventh Amendment immunity. The case involved Section 1983 claims of faculty members who had been dismissed. Focusing on *Urbano/Blake* factors 2 and 3, the court considered whether a judgment against Rutgers would be paid by Rutgers or the state and determined that Rutgers in its discretion could pay the judgment either with segregated nonstate funds or with nonstate funds that were commingled with state funds. Rutgers argued that, if it paid the judgment, the state would have to increase its appropriations to the university, thus affecting the state treasury. The court held that such an appropriations increase following a judgment would be in the legislature's discretion, and that "[i]f the state structures an entity in such a way that the other relevant criteria indicate it to be an arm of the state, then immunity may be retained even where damage awards are funded by the state at the state's discretion." Then, considering the other *Urbano/Blake* factors, the court determined that, although Rutgers "is now, at least in part, a state-created entity which serves a state purpose with a large degree of state financing, it remains under state law an independent entity able to direct its own actions and responsible on its own for judgments resulting from those actions."

Since the Eleventh Amendment provides states with immunity only from federal court suits, it does not apply to Section 1983 suits in state courts. The definition of "person" under Section 1983 is thus the sole focus of the analysis. In *Will v. Michigan Department of State Police*, 491 U.S. 58 (1989), the U.S. Supreme Court ruled that neither the state nor state officials sued in their official capacities are "persons" for the purposes of Section 1983 suits in state courts. But in *Howlett v. Rose*, 496 U.S. 356 (1990), the Court reaffirmed that Section 1983 suits may be brought in state courts against other government entities that are considered "persons" under Section 1983. In such cases, *state* law protections of sovereign immunity and other state procedural limitations on suits against the sovereign (see *Felder v. Casey*, 487 U.S. 131 (1988)) will not generally be available to the government defendants.

Fuchilla v. Layman, 537 A.2d 652 (N.J. 1988), provides an example of a higher education case brought in state court under Section 1983. The case also illustrates how courts may continue to rely on Eleventh Amendment analysis in such suits, even though the amendment's immunity applies only in federal courts. A former employee of the University of Medicine and Dentistry of New Jersey sued the university, alleging sexual harassment. The Supreme Court of New Jersey reasoned that if "a governmental entity enjoys immunity as the state or its alter ego under the eleventh amendment, it cannot be liable as a 'person' under Section 1983." The court then looked at Eleventh Amendment law— specifically, the nine-factor *Urbano/Blake* test—to determine whether UMDNJ is a "person" under Section 1983. The court concluded that the "factors tip in favor of finding [that] the UMDNJ is not the alter ego of the State for eleventh amendment purposes and, therefore, is liable as a person under Section 1983."

Even if the institution is characterized as a Section 1983 "person" with no Eleventh Amendment immunity, it may still be able in particular cases to avoid liability. According to *Monell:*

> Local governing bodies . . . can be sued directly under [Section] 1983 . . . [where] the action that is alleged to be unconstitutional implements or executes a policy statement, ordinance, regulation, or decision officially adopted and promulgated by the body's officers. Moreover, although the touchstone of the Section 1983 action against a government body is an allegation that official policy is responsible for a deprivation of rights protected by the Constitution, local governments, like every other Section 1983 "person," by the very terms of the statute, may be sued for constitutional deprivations visited pursuant to governmental "custom" even though such a custom has not received formal approval through the body's official decision-making channels. . . .

On the other hand, the language of Section 1983 . . . compels the conclusion that Congress did not intend municipalities to be held liable unless action pursuant to official municipal policy of some nature caused a constitutional tort. In particular, we conclude that a municipality cannot be held liable solely because it employs a tortfeasor—or, in other words, a municipality cannot be held liable under Section 1983 on a *respondeat superior* theory [436 U.S. at 690–91].

Thus, along with its expansion of the "persons" suable under Section 1983, *Monell* also clarifies and limits the types of government actions for which newly suable entities can be held liable.

The liability of political subdivisions under the *Monell* decision is not limited by the "qualified immunity" that officers and employees would have if sued personally (see Section 2.4.3). This type of immunity claim was rejected by the U.S. Supreme Court in *Owen v. City of Independence*, 445 U.S. 622 (1980):

[N]either history nor policy supports a construction of Section 1983 that would justify the qualified immunity. . . . We hold, therefore, that the municipality may not assert the good faith of its officers or agents as a defense to liability under Section 1983.

. . . [O]wing to the qualified immunity enjoyed by most government officials, see *Scheuer v. Rhodes*, 416 U.S. 232 (1974), many victims of municipal malfeasance would be left remediless if the city were also allowed to assert a good-faith defense.

. . . We believe that today's decision, together with prior precedents in this area, properly allocates [the costs of official misconduct] among the three principals in the scenario of the Section 1983 cause of action: the victim of the constitutional deprivation; the officer whose conduct caused the injury; and the public, as represented by the municipal entity. The innocent individual who is harmed by an abuse of governmental authority is assured that he will be compensated for his injury. The offending official . . . may go about his business secure in the knowledge that a qualified immunity will protect him from personal liability for damages that are more appropriately chargeable to the populace as a whole. And the public will be forced to bear only the costs of injury inflicted by the "execution of a government's policy or custom, whether made by its lawmakers or by those whose edicts or acts may fairly be said to represent official policy" [445 U.S. at 638, 651, 657; quoting *Monell v. New York City Dept. of Social Services*, 436 U.S. at 694].

Although *Monell* and *Owen* made clear that political subdivisions could be held liable under Section 1983 for compensatory monetary damages, the cases did not determine whether political subdivisions could also be liable for punitive damages. In an earlier case, *Carey v. Piphus*, 435 U.S. 247 (1978), the Supreme Court had held that punitive damages could be assessed in an appropriate case against a government employee "with the specific purpose of deterring or punishing violations of constitutional rights." But in *City of Newport v. Fact Concerts, Inc.*, 453 U.S. 247 (1981), the Court refused to extend this ruling to political subdivisions. The Court found that the goal of deterrence would not be served by awards of punitive damages against political subdivisions, since it was far from clear that policy-making officials would be deterred from wrongdoing by the knowledge that awards could be assessed against their governments.

In another case, *Memphis Community School District v. Stachura*, 477 U.S. 299 (1986), the Court also determined that compensatory damages awards in Section 1983 cases may not be based on the "value" or "importance" of the constitutional right that has been violated. Citing *Carey v. Piphus*, the Court underscored that actual injuries are the only permissible bases for an award of compensatory damages caused by the denial of a constitutional right.

Various procedural issues of importance to colleges and universities have also arisen in the wake of *Monell*. For instance, in *Patsy v. Board of Regents of the State of Florida*, 457 U.S. 496 (1982), a suit by a staff employee of Florida International University alleging race and sex discrimination, the U.S. Supreme Court had to decide whether a Section 1983 plaintiff must "exhaust" available state administrative remedies before a court may consider her claim (see Section 1.4.2). Invoking such an exhaustion requirement would be yet another way for governmental defendants to ameliorate the impact of decisions expanding Section 1983 liability. For many years preceding *Patsy*, however, the Court had refused to impose an exhaustion requirement on Section 1983 suits. The Court in *Patsy* declined the Florida board of regents' invitation to overrule this line of decisions. And in *Burnett v. Grattan*, 468 U.S. 42 (1984), the Court rejected yet another procedural device for limiting the impact of Section 1983. The defendant, a state university, argued that the federal court should "borrow" and apply a six-month state statute of limitations to the case—the same time period as applied to the filing of discrimination complaints with the state human rights commission—and that the plaintiffs' complaint should be dismissed because it was not filed within six months of the harm (employment discrimination) that the plaintiffs alleged. The Court concluded that, in order to accomplish the goals of Section 1983, it was necessary to apply a longer, three-year, time period for bringing this particular suit—the same period generally allowed for civil actions under the law of the state whose statutes of limitations were being borrowed.

Given these substantial and complex legal developments, at least some public postsecondary institutions are now subject to Section 1983 liability, both in federal courts and state courts, for violations of federal constitutional rights. Those that are subject may be exposed to extensive judicial remedies, which they are unlikely to escape by using procedural technicalities. Moreover, institutions and systems that can escape Section 1983 liability because they are not "persons" or are otherwise protected by the Eleventh Amendment will likely find that they are subject in other ways to liability for violations of constitutional rights. They will be suable under other federal civil rights laws establishing statutory rights that parallel those protected by the Constitution. They may also be suable under similar state civil rights laws or under state statutes similar to Section 1983 that authorize access to state courts for the vindication of federal or state constitutional rights. Moreover, trustees and administrators of public institutions are sometimes suable in their individual capacities under Section 1983 even where the institution could not be sued (see Section 2.4.3).

In such a legal environment, administrators should foster full and fair enjoyment of federal civil rights on their campuses. Even when a particular institution's Section 1983 status is unclear, administrators should seek to comply with the spirit of Section 1983, which compels that where officials "may harbor doubt about the lawfulness of their intended actions . . . [they should] err on the side of protecting citizens' . . . rights" (*Owen*, 445 U.S. at 652).

SEC. 2.4. PERSONAL LIABILITY OF TRUSTEES, ADMINISTRATORS, AND STAFF

2.4.1. Personal Tort Liability

A trustee, administrator, or other agent of a postsecondary institution who commits a tort may be liable even if the tort was committed while he or she was conducting the institution's affairs. The individual must actually have committed the tortious act, directed it, or otherwise participated in its commission, however, before personal liability will attach. The individual will not be personally liable for torts of other institutional agents merely because he or she represents the institution for whom the other agents were acting. The elements of a tort and the defenses against a tort claim (see Section 2.3.1) in suits against the individual personally are generally the same as those in suits against the institution. An individual sued in his or her personal capacity, however, is usually not shielded by the sovereign immunity and charitable immunity defenses that sometimes protect the institution.

If a trustee, administrator, or other institutional agent commits a tort while acting on behalf of the institution and within the scope of the authority delegated to him or her, both the individual and the institution may be liable for the harm caused by the tort. But the institution's potential liability does not relieve the individual of any measure of liability; the injured party could choose to collect a judgment solely from the individual, and the individual would have no claim against the institution for any part of the judgment he or she was required to pay. However, where individual and institution are both potentially liable, the individual may receive practical relief from liability if the injured party squeezes the entire judgment from the institution or the institution chooses to pay the entire amount.

If a trustee, administrator, or other institutional agent commits a tort while acting outside the scope of delegated authority, he or she may be personally liable but the institution would not be liable (Section 2.3.1). Thus, the injured party could obtain a judgment only against the individual, and only the individual would be responsible for satisfying the judgment. The institution, however, may affirm the individual's unauthorized action ("affirmance" is similar to the "ratification" discussed in connection with contract liability in Section 2.3.2), in which case the individual will be deemed to have acted within his or her authority, and both institution and individual will be potentially liable.

Officers and employees of public institutions can sometimes escape tort liability by proving the defense of "official immunity." For this defense to apply, the individual's act must have been within the scope of his or her authority and must have been a discretionary act involving policy judgment, as opposed to a "ministerial duty" (the person performing such a duty has little or no discretion with regard to the choices to be made). Because it involves this element of discretion and policy judgment, official immunity is more likely to apply to a particular individual the higher in the authority hierarchy he is.

For example, in *Staheli v. Smith*, 548 So. 2d 1299 (Miss. 1989), the Supreme Court of Mississippi was asked to determine whether the dean of the School of Engineering at the University of Mississippi was a public official for purposes of governmental immunity against a defamation lawsuit. A faculty member sued the dean, stating that a letter from the dean recommending against tenure for the plaintiff was libelous. The court found that the dean was, indeed, a public figure and thus protected by qualified government immunity. Since the faculty handbook authorized administrators to make "appropriate" comments, and since making a subjective evaluation of a faculty member's performance is a discretionary, rather than a ministerial, duty, the court found that the dean had acted within the scope of his authority and had not lost the privilege by exceeding his authority.

On the other hand, the Supreme Court of Virginia in *James v. Jane*, 267 S.E.2d 108 (Va. 1980), rejected a defense of sovereign immunity asserted by physicians who were full-time faculty members at the state university medical center and members of the hospital staff. The defendants had argued that, as state employees, they were immune from a suit charging them with negligence in their treatment of certain patients at the university's hospital. The trial court accepted the physicians' defense. Although agreeing that under Virginia law certain state employees and agents could share the state's own sovereign immunity, the Virginia Supreme Court reversed the trial court and refused to extend this immunity to these particular employees. The court reasoned that the state's interest in the competent management of the state university medical center was no different from its interest in the competent management of a private medical center, nor did the state exercise more control over the university's medical center than it did over nonpublic medical centers. Thus, the defendant physicians were not entitled to sovereign immunity.

The "sovereign" or "state employee" immunity thus created by the Virginia court is potentially broader than the "official immunity" recognized in some other jurisdictions. In states recognizing "official immunity," the likelihood of successfully invoking the defense is, as mentioned, proportional to the officer's or employee's level in the authority hierarchy. This official immunity doctrine seeks to protect the discretionary and policy-making functions of higher-level decision makers, a goal that the *James v. Jane* opinion also recognized. The sovereign immunity defense articulated in *James,* however, encompasses an additional consideration: the degree of state control over the employee's job functions. In weighing this additional factor, the Virginia sovereign immunity doctrine also seeks to protect state employees who are so closely directed by the state that they should not bear individual responsibility for negligent acts committed within the scope of this controlled employment. Sovereign immunity Virginia-style may thus extend to lower-echelon employees not reached by official immunity. Although *James* held that this theory does not apply to physicians treating patients in a state university medical center, the theory could perhaps be applied to other postsecondary employees—such as middle- or low-level administrative personnel (*Messina v. Burden,* 321 S.E.2d 657 (Va. 1984), concerning the superintendent of buildings at a community college), or support staff.

Although *James* is binding law only in Virginia, it illustrates nuances in the doctrine of personal tort immunity that may also exist, or may now develop, in other states. When contrasted with the cases relying on the official immunity doctrine, *James* also illustrates the state-by-state variations that can exist in this area of the law.

In *Tarasoff v. Regents of the University of California,* 551 P.2d 334 (Cal. 1976), the parents of a girl murdered by a psychiatric patient at the university hospital sued the university regents, four psychotherapists employed by the hospital, and the campus police. The patient had confided his intention to kill the daughter to a staff psychotherapist. Though the patient was briefly detained by the campus police at the psychotherapist's request, no further action was taken to protect the daughter. The parents alleged that the defendants should be held liable for a tortious failure to confine a dangerous patient and a tortious failure to warn them or their daughter of a dangerous patient. The psychotherapists and campus police claimed official immunity under a California statute freeing "public employee(s)" from liability for acts or omissions resulting from "the exercise of discretion vested in [them]" (Cal. Govt. Code §820.2). The court accepted the official immunity defense in relation to the failure to confine, because that failure involved a "basic policy decision" sufficient to constitute discretion under the statute. But regarding the failure to warn, the court refused to accept the psychotherapists' official immunity claim, because the decision whether to warn was not a basic policy decision. The campus police needed no official immunity from their failure to warn, because, the court held, they had no legal duty to warn in light of the facts in the complaint.

A federal appellate court found several members of the athletic staff protected by a qualified immunity against liability for negligence in the death of a student. In *Sorey v. Kellett,* 849 F.2d 960 (5th Cir. 1988), a football player at the University of Southern Mississippi collapsed during practice and died shortly thereafter. The court applied Mississippi's qualified immunity for public officials performing discretionary, rather than ministerial, acts to the trainer, the team physician, and the football coach, finding that the first two were performing a discretionary act in administering medical treatment to the student. The coach was entitled to qualified immunity because of his general authority over the football program. Noting that "a public official charged only with general authority over a program or institution naturally is exercising discretionary functions" [849 F.2d at 964], the court denied recovery to the plaintiff.

Defamation claims against faculty and administrators have proliferated over the past few years, but few have been successful. For example, a female associate professor denied promotion sued her department chair, claiming that a memo he wrote to her and distributed to higher-level administrators was defamatory. The court rejected the claim on several grounds. First, the plaintiff had requested the promotion and thus "opened herself" to evaluation. Second, the memo had a limited audience and thus did not meet the "publication" requirement for defamation (see Section 2.3.1.2). And third, the memo expressed the chair's opinion, and thus was constitutionally protected (*Gernander v. Winona State University,* 428 N.W.2d 473 (Minn. Ct. App. 1988)).

But a recent ruling by the U.S. Supreme Court in *Milkovich v. Lorain Journal Co.,* 497 U.S. 1 (1990), suggests that this third reason may not be legally sound when applied to a "public figure" (see Section 2.3.1.2). The plaintiff claimed that an article in which he was portrayed as a perjurer was defamatory. The defendant, a newspaper, asserted an "opinion privilege" as its entire defense to the defamation claim. In an opinion by Chief Justice Rehnquist, the Supreme Court denied that an "opinion privilege" existed, although it said that "statements on matters of public concern must be provable as false before liability attaches," at least in situations where "a media defendant is involved" (497 U.S. at 19). Although future nonmedia defendants may attempt to limit *Milkovich* to its narrow facts, the opinion's wholesale rejection of the "opinion privilege" appears to apply to all defendants, not just the media.

The official immunity and state employee immunity defenses are not available to officers and employees of private institutions. But it appears that at least the trustees of private nonprofit institutions will be leniently treated by some courts out of deference to the trustees' special discretionary functions. As a result, the personal liability of such trustees may be limited in a way somewhat akin to the official immunity limitation available to officers and employees of public institutions.

Administrators acting within the scope of their authority may be protected by a common law qualified privilege for communications between persons sharing a common duty or interest, such as communications between individuals within a business or an academic organization. "The conditional nature of this privilege, or its 'qualification,' depends on whether or not the communication was made on a proper occasion, in good faith and without excessive publication" (F. Bazluke, *Defamation Issues in Higher Education* (National Association of College and University Attorneys, 1990), 8). In *Kraft v. William Alanson White Psychiatric Foundation,* 498 A.2d 1145 (D.C. 1985), the court applied an "absolute privilege" to communications among faculty members about the plaintiff's inadequate academic performance in a postgraduate certificate program. The court stated:

> A person who seeks an academic credential and who is on notice that satisfactory performance is a prerequisite to his receipt of that credential consents
> to frank evaluation by those charged with the responsibility to supervise him
> [498 A.2d at 1149].

In addition, certain university administrators or trustees may be viewed as "public figures" by a court; in such instances the plaintiff would have to demonstrate that the defendants acted with "actual malice" in publishing the defamatory information. The constitutional standard that a public figure must meet was established by the U.S. Supreme Court in *New York Times v. Sullivan,* 376 U.S. 254 (1964), in which the court defined actual malice to include knowledge of the falsity of the statement or reckless disregard for its truth or falsity. Athletic coaches, university trustees and administrators, and even prominent faculty have been determined to be public figures; thus, public comment on their activities or decisions must meet a high standard in order to be actionable.

Defendants in certain defamation cases may be protected by the concept of "invited libel" and thus found not to have been responsible for the "publication" element of a defamation claim. In *Sophianopoulous v. McCormick,* 385 S.E.2d 682 (Ga. Ct. App. 1989), a state appellate court rejected a faculty member's defamation claim against his department chair. The professor had complained to the American Association of University Professors (AAUP) that his chair had mistreated him. When the AAUP contacted the chair to inquire about the professor's performance, the chair sent the AAUP copies of memoranda critical of the professor's performance. The judges ruled that, by involving the

AAUP in the dispute with his chair, the plaintiff consented to having the offending information published to the AAUP.

Institutions should consider whether or not they wish to protect their personnel from the financial consequences of personal tort liability. Insurance coverage and indemnification agreements, discussed in Section 2.5.2, may be utilized for this purpose.

2.4.2. Personal Contract Liability

A trustee, administrator, or other agent who signs a contract on behalf of an institution may be personally liable for its performance if the institution breaches the contract. The extent of personal liability depends on whether the agent's participation on behalf of the institution was authorized—either by a grant of express authority or by an implied authority, an apparent authority, or a subsequent ratification by the institution. (See the discussion of authority in Section 2.3.2.) If the individual's participation was properly authorized, and if that individual signed the contract only in the capacity of an institutional agent, he or she will not be personally liable for performance of the contract. If, however, the participation was not properly authorized, or if the individual signed in an individual capacity rather than as an institutional agent, he or she may be personally liable.

In some cases, the other contracting party may be able to sue both the institution and the agent or to choose between them. This option is presented when the contracting party did not know at the time of contracting that the individual participated in an agency capacity, but later learned that was the case. The option is also presented when the contracting party knew that the individual was acting as an institutional agent, but the individual also gave a personal promise that the contract would be performed. In such situations, if the contracting party obtains a judgment against both the institution and the agent, the judgment may be satisfied against either or against both, but the contracting party may receive no more than the total amount of the judgment. Where the contracting party receives payment from only one of the two liable parties, the paying party may have a claim against the nonpayor for part of the judgment amount.

An agent who is a party to the contract in a personal capacity, and thus potentially liable on it, can assert the same defenses that are available to any contracting party. These defenses may arise from the contract (for instance, the absence of some formality necessary to complete the contract, or fraud, or inadequate performance by the other party), or they may be personal to the agent (for instance, a particular counterclaim against the other party).

Quasi-contractual theories, such as detrimental reliance, may be used to assert personal liability against trustees or administrators. In *Student House, Inc. v. Board of Regents of Regency Universities*, 254 N.E.2d 496 (Ill. 1969), a private housing developer sought to enjoin the trustees of Northern Illinois University from building additional student housing. The developer claimed that several administrators, such as the director of student housing and the director of research, had promised that the university would not build housing if private housing met the university's needs. The Illinois Supreme Court ruled that, as a matter of law, the developer's reliance on these oral representations of lower-level administrators was unreasonable, and refused to apply the plaintiff's agency law and estoppel theories.

2.4.3. Personal Liability for Violations of Federal Constitutional Rights

The liability of trustees, administrators, and other employees of postsecondary institutions for constitutional rights violations is determined under the same body of law that determines the liability of the institutions themselves, and presents many of the same legal issues (see Section 2.3.3). As with institutional liability, an individual's action must usually be done "under color of" state law, or must be characterizable as "state action," before liability will attach. But, as with tort and contract liability, the liability of individual trustees, administrators, and other employees is not coterminous with that of the institution itself. Defenses that may be available to the institution (such as the constitutional immunity defense) may not be available to individuals sued in their individual (or personal) capacities; conversely, defenses that may be available to individuals (such as the qualified immunity discussed later in this section) may not be available to the institution.

The federal statute referred to as Section 1983, quoted in Section 2.3.3, is again the key statute. Individual state and local government officials and employees sued in their personal capacities are clearly "persons" under Section 1983 and thus subject to its provisions whenever they are acting under color of state law (*Hafer v. Melo,* 112 S. Ct. 358 (1991)). But courts have long recognized a qualified immunity for certain public officials and employees from liability for monetary damages under Section 1983. In 1974 and again in 1975, the U.S. Supreme Court attempted to explain the scope of this immunity as it applies to school officials.

In *Scheuer v. Rhodes,* 416 U.S. 232 (1974), the Court considered a suit for damages brought on behalf of three students killed in the May 1970 disturbances at Kent State University. The Court rejected the contention that the president of Kent State and other state officials had an absolute "official immunity" protecting them from personal liability. The Court instead accorded the president and officials a "qualified immunity" under Section 1983: "In varying scope, a qualified immunity is available to officers of the executive branch of government, the variation being dependent upon the scope of discretion and responsibilities of the office and all the circumstances as they reasonably appeared at the time of the action on which liability is sought to be based." Because the availability of this immunity depended on facts not yet in the record, the Supreme Court remanded the case to the trial court for further proceedings.[3]

In *Wood v. Strickland,* 420 U.S. 308 (1975), the Supreme Court extended, and added enigma to, its discussion of Section 1983 immunity in the institutional context. After the school board in this case had expelled some students from high school for violating a school disciplinary regulation, several of them sued the members of the school board for damages and injunctive and declaratory relief. In a controversial decision with strong dissents, the Court held that school board members, as public school officials, are entitled to a qualified immunity from such suits:

> We think there must be a degree of immunity if the work of the schools is to go forward; and, however worded, the immunity must be such that public school officials understand that action taken in the good-faith fulfillment of their responsibilities and within the bounds of reason under all the circumstances will not be punished and that they need not exercise their discretion with undue timidity. . . .
>
> The official must himself be acting sincerely and with a belief that he is doing right, but an act violating a student's constitutional rights can be no more justified by *ignorance or disregard of settled, indisputable law* on the part of one entrusted with supervision of students' daily lives than by the presence of actual malice. To be entitled to a special exemption from the categorical remedial language of Section 1983 in a case in which his action violated a student's constitutional rights, a school board member, who has voluntarily undertaken the task of supervising the operation of the school and the activities of the students, must be held to a standard of conduct based not only on permissible intentions but also on *knowledge of the basic, unquestioned constitutional rights of his charges.* Such a standard neither imposes an unfair burden upon a person assuming a responsible public office requiring a high degree of intelligence and judgment for the proper fulfillment of its duties, nor an unwarranted burden in light of the value which civil rights have in our legal system. Any lesser standard would deny much of the promise of Section 1983. Therefore, in the specific context of school discipline, we hold that a school board member is not immune from liability for damages under Section 1983 (1) if he knew or reasonably should have known that the action he took within his sphere of official responsi-

---

[3]On remand, the case proceeded to trial against all defendants. No defendant was held immune from suit. The president of Kent State was eventually dismissed as a defendant, however, because the facts indicated that he had not personally violated any of the plaintiffs' rights (see *Krause v. Rhodes,* 570 F.2d 563 (6th Cir. 1977)). Eventually, the case was settled and an award of $600,000 plus attorney's fees made to the plaintiffs (see *Krause v. Rhodes,* 640 F.2d 214 (6th Cir. 1981)).

bility would violate the constitutional rights of the student affected, or (2) if he took the action with the malicious intention to cause a deprivation of constitutional rights or other injury to the student [420 U.S. at 321–22; emphasis and numbering added].

The Court's reliance on the *Scheuer* case at several points in its *Wood* opinion indicates that the *Wood* liability standard applies to public officials in postsecondary education as well. Clearly, this qualified immunity would be available to trustees and executive heads of public postsecondary institutions. The immunity of lower-level administrators and faculty members is less clear; for, as the Court noted in *Scheuer* and reaffirmed in *Wood,* the immunity's existence and application would depend in each case on the "scope of discretion and responsibilities of the office."

In 1982, the Court modified its *Wood* analysis in ruling on a suit brought against two senior aides in the Nixon administration. The immunity test developed in *Wood* had two parts. One part was subjective; it focused on the defendant's "permissible intentions," asking whether he had acted "with the malicious intention to cause a deprivation of constitutional rights or other injury" to the plaintiff (420 U.S. at 322). The other part was objective; it focused on the defendant's "knowledge of . . . basic, unquestioned constitutional rights," asking whether he "knew or reasonably should have known that the action he took . . . would violate the constitutional rights" of the plaintiff (420 U.S. at 322). The 1982 case, *Harlow v. Fitzgerald,* 457 U.S. 800, deleted the subjective part of the test because it had inhibited courts from dismissing insubstantial lawsuits prior to trial:

> We conclude today that bare allegations of malice should not suffice to subject government officials either to the costs of trial or to the burdens of broad-reaching discovery. We therefore hold that government officials performing discretionary functions generally are shielded from liability for civil damages insofar as their conduct does not violate clearly established statutory or constitutional rights of which a reasonable person would have known (see *Procunier v. Navarette,* 434 U.S. 555, 565 (1978); *Wood v. Strickland,* 420 U.S. at 321).
>
> Reliance on the objective reasonableness of an official's conduct, as measured by reference to clearly established law, should avoid excessive disruption of government and permit the resolution of many insubstantial claims on summary judgment. On summary judgment, the judge appropriately may determine not only the currently applicable law but whether that law was clearly established at the time an action occurred. If the law at that time was not clearly established, an official could not reasonably be expected to anticipate subsequent legal developments, nor could he fairly be said to "know" that the law forbade conduct not previously identified as unlawful. Until this threshold immunity question is resolved, discovery should not be allowed. If the law was clearly established, the immunity defense ordinarily should fail, since a reasonably competent public

official should know the law governing his conduct. Nevertheless, if the official pleading the defense claims extraordinary circumstances and can prove that he neither knew nor should have known of the relevant legal standard, the defense should be sustained. But again, the defense would turn primarily on objective factors [457 U.S. at 817–18].

In litigation, qualified immunity is an affirmative defense to be pleaded by the individual seeking to assert the immunity claim (*Gomez v. Toledo,* 446 U.S. 635 (1980)). Once the defendant has asserted the claim, the court must determine (1) whether the plaintiff's complaint alleges the violation of a right protected by Section 1983; and (2), if so, whether this right "was clearly established at the time of [the defendant's] actions" (*Siegert v. Gilley,* 111 S. Ct. 1789, 1793–94 (1991)). If the court answers both of these inquiries affirmatively, it will reject the immunity claim unless the defendant can prove that, because of "extraordinary circumstances," he "neither knew nor should have known" the clearly established law applicable to the case (*Harlow,* above). The burden of proof here is clearly on the defendant, and it would be a rare case in which the defendant would sustain this burden.

Other complexities are illustrated by *Mangaroo v. Nelson,* 864 F.2d 1202 (5th Cir. 1989). The plaintiff had been demoted from a deanship to a tenured faculty position. She sued both Nelson, the acting president who demoted her, and Pierre, Nelson's successor, alleging that their actions violated her procedural due process rights. She sued the former in his *individual* (or personal) capacity, seeking monetary damages, and the latter in his *official* capacity, seeking injunctive relief. The court held that Nelson was entitled to claim the qualified immunity, since the plaintiff sought money damages from him in his individual capacity for the harm he had caused. In contrast, the court held that Pierre was not entitled to qualified immunity, because the plaintiff sued him only in his official capacity, seeking an injunctive order compelling him, as president, to take action to remedy the violation of her due process rights.

As a result of this line of cases, personnel of public colleges and universities are charged with responsibility for knowing "clearly established law" (*Harlow,* above). Unless "extraordinary circumstances" prevent an individual from gaining such knowledge, the disregard of clearly established law is considered unreasonable and thus unprotected by the cloak of immunity. It will often be debatable whether particular principles of law are sufficiently "clear" to fall within the Court's characterization. Moreover, the applicability of even the clearest principles may depend on the particular facts of each case. Since it is therefore extremely difficult to predict what unlawful actions would fall within the qualified immunity, administrative efforts will be far better spent taking preventive measures to ensure that Section 1983 violations do not occur, rather than making weak predictions about whether immunity would exist if violations did occur.

Officers and administrators found personally liable under Section 1983 are subject to both court injunctions and money damage awards in favor of the prevailing plaintiff(s). Unlike governmental defendants (see *City of Newport v. Fact Concerts, Inc.,* Section 2.3.3 of this volume), individual defendants may be held liable for punitive as well as compensatory damages. To collect compensatory damages, a plaintiff must prove "actual injury," tangible or intangible; courts usually will not presume that damage occurred from a violation of civil rights and will award compensatory damages only to the extent of proven injury (*Carey v. Piphus,* 435 U.S. 247 (1978)). To collect punitive damages, a plaintiff must show that the defendant's actions either manifested "reckless or callous disregard for the plaintiff's rights" or constituted "intentional violations of federal law" (*Smith v. Wade,* 461 U.S. 30, 51 (1983)).

Besides having a potentially broad scope of liability and a limited, unpredictable immunity from damages under Section 1983, institutional personnel are also generally unprotected by the Eleventh Amendment immunity that sometimes protects their institutions from federal court suits (see Section 2.3.3). In the *Scheuer* case (discussed earlier in this section), for example, the Court held that the president of Kent State had no such immunity:

> The Eleventh Amendment provides no shield for a state official confronted by a claim that he had deprived another of a federal right under the color of state law. . . . When a state officer acts under a state law in a manner violative of the federal Constitution, he "comes into conflict with the superior authority of that Constitution, and he is in that case stripped of his official or representative character and is subjected *in his person* to the consequences of his individual conduct" [416 U.S. at 237; quoting *Ex parte Young,* 209 U.S. 123, 159 (1908)].

If a state university president has no immunity under the Constitution, it follows that lower-level administrators and faculty members (and probably trustees) would also usually have no such immunity. The *Scheuer* case notes one important circumstance, however, under which such persons would enjoy the constitutional immunity: when they are sued only as titular parties in a suit that is actually seeking money damages from the state treasury. In this type of suit, the individual is sued for damages in his or her official (or representational)—rather than personal (or individual)—capacity (see *Papasan v. Allain,* 478 U.S. 265, 276–79 (1986)). In such circumstances, the suit will be considered to be against the state itself and thus barred by the Eleventh Amendment.

The state of the law under Section 1983 and the Eleventh Amendment, taken together, gives administrators of public postsecondary institutions no cause to feel confident that either they or other institutional officers or employees are insulated from personal civil rights liability. To minimize the liability risk in this critical area of law and social responsibility, administrators should make legal counsel available to institutional personnel for consultation, encourage review by counsel of institutional policies that may affect civil rights, and provide personnel with information on or training in basic civil rights law and other legal principles. To absolve personnel of the financial drain of any liability that does occur, administrators may wish to consider the purchase of special insurance coverage or the development of indemnity plans. As discussed in Section 2.5.2, however, public policy in some states may limit the use of these techniques in the civil rights area.

SEC. 2.5. INSTITUTIONAL MANAGEMENT OF LIABILITY RISK

The risk of financial liability for injury to another party remains a major concern for postsecondary institutions as well as their governing board members and personnel. This section examines some methods for controlling such risk exposure and thus minimizing the detrimental effect of liability on the institution and its personnel. Risk management may be advisable not only because it helps stabilize the institution's financial condition over time but also because it can improve the morale and performance of institutional personnel by alleviating their concerns about potential personal liability. In addition, risk management can implement the institution's humanistic concern for minimizing and compensating any potential injuries that its operations may cause to innocent third parties. The major methods of risk management may be called risk avoidance, risk control, risk transfer, and risk retention. See generally J. Adams and J. Hall, "Legal Liabilities in Higher Education: Their Scope and Management" (Part II), 3 *J. Coll. & Univ. Law* 335, 360–69 (1976).

2.5.1. Risk Avoidance and Risk Control

The most certain method for managing a known exposure to liability is risk avoidance—the elimination of the behavior, condition, or program that is the source of the risk. This method is often not realistic, however, since it could require institutions to forgo activities important to their educational missions. It might also require greater knowledge of the details of myriad campus activities than administrators typically can acquire and greater certainty about the legal principles of liability (see Sections 2.3 and 2.4) than the law typically affords.

Risk control is less drastic than risk avoidance. The goal is to reduce, rather than eliminate entirely, the frequency or severity of potential exposures to liability—mainly by improving the physical environment or modifying hazardous behavior or activities in ways that reduce the recognized risks. Although this method may have less impact on an institution's educational mission than risk avoidance, it may similarly require considerable detailed knowledge of campus facilities and functions and of legal liability principles.

2.5.2. Risk Transfer

By purchasing commercial insurance, entering "hold-harmless" or "indemnification" agreements, or employing releases and waivers, institutions can transfer their own liability risks to others or transfer to themselves the liability risks of their officers and employees or of third parties.

2.5.2.1. Insurance. A commercial insurance policy shifts potential future financial losses (up to a maximum amount) to the insurance company in exchange for payment of a specified premium. The institution can insure against liability for its own acts, as well as liability transferred to it by a hold-harmless agreement with its personnel. With the advice of insurance experts, the institution can determine the kinds and amounts of liability protection it needs and provide for the necessary premium expenditures in its budgeting process.

There are two basic types of insurance policies important to higher education institutions. The first and primary type is general liability insurance; it provides broad coverage of bodily injury and property damage claims such as would arise in the case of a negligently caused injury to a student or staff member. The second type is directors and officers insurance ("D & O" coverage, or sometimes "errors and omissions" coverage). It covers property and nonbodily injury claims such as employment claims, defamation, and violations of due process.

General liability insurance policies usually exclude from their coverage both intentionally or maliciously caused damage and damage caused by acts that violate penal laws. In *Brooklyn Law School v. Aetna Casualty and Surety Co.*, 849 F.2d 788 (2d Cir. 1988), for example, the school had incurred numerous costs in defending itself against a lawsuit in which a former professor alleged that the school, its trustees, and faculty members had intentionally conspired to violate his constitutional rights. The school sued its insurer—which insured the school under an umbrella policy—to recover its costs in defending against the professor's suit. The appellate court held that, under New York law, the insurer was not required to defend the insured against such a suit, which alleged intentional harm, when the policy terms expressly excluded from coverage injuries caused by the insured's intentional acts.

Liability arising from the violation of an individual's constitutional or civil rights is also commonly excluded from general liability insurance coverage—an exclusion that can pose considerable problems for administrators and institutions, whose exposure to such liability has escalated greatly since the 1960s. In specific cases, questions about this exclusion may become entwined with questions concerning intent or malice. In *Andover Newton Theological School, Inc. v. Continental Casualty Company,* 930 F.2d 89 (1st Cir. 1991), the defendant insurance company had refused to pay on the school's claim after a court had found that the school violated the Age Discrimination in Employment Act (ADEA) when it dismissed a tenured, sixty-two-year-old professor. The jury in the professor's case found that the school had impermissibly considered the professor's age in deciding to dismiss him, but the evidence did not clearly establish that the school's administrators had acted deliberately. Under the ADEA, behavior by the school that showed "reckless disregard" for the law was enough to sustain the verdict against it. When the school sought to have its insurance carrier pay the judgment, the insurer objected on grounds that it is against Massachusetts public policy (and that of most other states) to insure against intentional or deliberate conduct of the insured. The district court agreed and held the school's loss to be uninsurable.

On appeal, the appellate court reasoned that the school's suit against the insurer revolved around the following question:

> Does a finding of willfulness under the Age Discrimination in Employment Act (ADEA), if based on a finding of "reckless disregard as to whether [defendant's] conduct is prohibited by federal law," constitute "deliberate or intentional . . . wrongdoing" such as to preclude indemnification by an insurer under the public policy of Massachusetts as codified at Mass. Gen. L. ch. 175, section 47 Sixth (b)? [930 F.2d at 91].

The appellate court certified this question to the Massachusetts Supreme Judicial Court, which answered in the negative. The federal appellate court then reversed the federal district court's decision and remanded the case to that court for further proceedings. The appellate court reasoned that, since the jury verdict did not necessitate a conclusion that the school had acted intentionally or deliberately, the losses incurred by the school were insurable and payment would not contravene public policy.

Exclusions from coverage, as in the examples above, may exist either because state law requires the exclusion or because the insurer has made its own business decision to exclude certain actions from its standard coverages. When the exclusion is of the latter type, institutions may nevertheless be able to cover such risks by combining a standard policy with one or more specialty endorsements or companion policies, such as a directors' and officers' policy. If this arrangement still does not provide all the coverage the institution desires, and if the institution can afford the substantial expense, it may request a "manuscript" policy tailored to its specific needs.

2.5.2.2. Hold-harmless and indemnification agreements. A second method of risk transfer is a hold-harmless or indemnification agreement. In a broad sense, the term "indemnification" refers to any compensation for loss or damage. Insurance is thus one method of indemnifying someone. But in the narrower sense used here, indemnification refers to an arrangement whereby one party (for example, the institution) agrees to hold another party (for example, an individual officer or employee) harmless from financial liability for certain acts or omissions of that party which cause damage to another. Institutions typically require that the individual to be indemnified have acted in good faith and within his or her institutional authority.

Although, with respect to its own personnel, the institution would typically be the "indemnitor"—that is, the party with ultimate financial liability—the institution can sometimes also be an "indemnitee," the party protected from liability loss. The institution could negotiate for hold-harmless protection for itself, for instance, in contracts it enters with outside contractors or lessees. In an illustrative case, *Bridston v. Dover Corp. and University of North Dakota v. Young Men's Christian Association*, 352 N.W.2d 194 (N.D. 1984), the university had leased a campus auditorium to a dance group. One of the group's members was injured during practice, allegedly because of the negligence of a university employee, and sued the university for damages. The university invoked an indemnity clause in the lease agreement and successfully avoided liability by arguing that the clause required the lessee to hold the university harmless even for negligent acts of the university's own employees.

Like insurance policies, indemnification agreements often do not cover liability resulting from intentional or malicious action or from action violating the state's penal laws. Just as public policy may limit the types of acts or omissions that may be insured against, it may also limit those for which indemnification may be received.

Both public and private institutions may enter indemnification agreements. A public institution, however, may need specific authorizing legislation, while private institutions usually can rely on the general laws of their states for sufficient authority. Some states also provide for indemnification of all state employees for injuries caused by their acts or omissions on behalf of the state.

2.5.2.3. Releases and waivers. A third method of risk transfer is the release or waiver agreement. This type of arrangement releases one of two related parties from liability to the other for injuries arising from the relationship. In postsecondary education, this mechanism is most likely to be used in situations such as intercollegiate athletics, provision of medical services, student field trips, and tours of construction sites, where the participant or recipient is required to execute a release or waiver as a precondition to participation or receipt. See generally *The Law of Higher Education*, 3d ed., Section 2.5.4. Administrators should refer all questions concerning the use and validity of releases to legal counsel.

2.5.3. Risk Retention

The most practical option for the institution in some circumstances may be to retain the risk of financial liability. Risk retention may be appropriate, for instance, in situations where commercial insurance is unavailable or too costly, the expected losses are so small that they can be considered normal operating expenses, or the probability of loss is so remote that it does not justify any insurance expense. Both insurance policy deductibles and methods of self-insurance are examples of risk retention. The deductible amounts in an insurance policy allocate the first dollar coverage of liability, up to the amount of the deductible, to the institution. The institution becomes a self-insurer by maintaining a separate bank account to pay appropriate claims. The institution's risk managers must determine the amount to be available in the account and the frequency and amount of regular payments to the account. This approach is distinguished from simple noninsurance by the planning and actuarial calculations that it involves.

SELECTED ANNOTATED BIBLIOGRAPHY

Sec. 2.1 (The Question of Authority)

Bess, James L. *Collegiality and Bureaucracy in the Modern University* (Teachers College Press, 1988). Examines governance in the contemporary university. Discusses the relationship between authority structures, power, and collegiality; and between organizational characteristics and faculty perceptions of administrators. A framework for analysis of university governance is provided.

Hornby, D. Brock. "Delegating Authority to the Community of Scholars," 1975 *Duke L.J.* 279 (1975). Provides excellent legal and policy analysis regarding delegations of authority in public systems of postsecondary education. Considers constitutional and statutory delegations to statewide governing boards and individual boards of trustees, and subdelegations of that authority to officials, employees, and other bodies in individual institutions. Contains many useful citations to legal and policy materials.

Sec. 2.2 (Sources and Scope of Authority)

American Association for Higher Education. "Special Issue: Divestment," 38 *AAHE Bulletin* no. 9 (May 1986). Examines issues that arise when an institution decides to divest itself of the stock it holds in corporations doing business in countries whose human rights policies are contrary to democratic principles. Various divestment options are described, and suggestions are made for dealing with the campus community when the institution is considering divestment.

Bakaly, Charles G., Jr., & Grossman, Joel M. *Modern Law of Employment Contracts: Formation, Operation and Remedies for Breach* (Prentice-Hall Law & Business, 1983 and periodic supp.). Analyzes judicial precedents, state and federal employment laws, and recent developments in the employment-at-will doctrine. Also included is information about drug testing, medical screening and HIV, alternative dispute resolution, the drafting of employment policies and manuals, and tort theories that are often appended to contract claims.

Christie, George C. "Legal Aspects of Changing University Investment Strategies," 58 *N.C. L. Rev.* 189 (1980). Examines legal aspects of the effort, currently undertaken by most postsecondary institutions, to increase the rate of return from existing endowments. Although it focuses on North Carolina law, the article is also valuable for institutions in other states because of its discussions of the Uniform Management of Institutional Funds Act, Treasury regulations issued under the Internal Revenue Code, and various other sources of federal guidance.

Gross, Allen J. *Employee Dismissal Law: Forms and Procedures* (2d ed., Wiley, 1992). Discusses suits alleging wrongful dismissal. Follows the litigation path from the time a decision to litigate is made through interrogatories, depositions, the trial, and its closing arguments. Useful for attorneys representing either party, the book focuses on the litigation process rather than the substance of the legal claims. Model forms and policies are included, as are suggestions for presenting wrongful-discharge cases before a jury.

Ingram, Richard T., & Associates. *Governing Public Colleges and Universities: A Handbook for Trustees, Chief Executives, and Other Campus Leaders* (Jossey-Bass, 1993). A resource book for college trustees. Divided into three parts: "Understanding the Environment of Public Higher Education," "Fulfilling Board Functions," and "Developing the Public Board." Each part is subdivided into chapters and topics, many of which address legal considerations. Appendices contain resources, including sample statements of board members' responsibilities and desirable qualifications for trustees; a survey of public governing boards' characteristics, policies, and practices; and self-study criteria for public multicampus and system boards. Also included is an extensive annotated list of recommended readings.

Larson, Lex K. *Employment Screening* (Matthew Bender, 1988, and annual updates). Discusses employment testing and reference checking, drug and alcohol screening, HIV testing, polygraph and honesty testing, genetic testing, and background checks. Additional chapters address judicial precedent on negligent hiring claims and examine state, federal, and constitutional laws relevant to employee screening. Appendices include model policies, forms, and other practice aids.

Larson, Lex K., & Borowsky, Philip. *Unjust Dismissal* (Matthew Bender, 1985). Provides a comprehensive review and analysis of a variety of claims under the umbrella of "unjust dismissal," including whistleblowing, free speech, workplace privacy, lie detector tests, and personnel manuals. Also discusses the covenant of good faith and fair dealing and other tort claims related to dismissal. Each step of the litigation process is described, and litigation-prevention recommendations for employers are included.

Leonard, Arthur S. "A New Common Law of Employment Termination," 66 *N.C. L. Rev.* 631 (1988). Discusses the assortment of contract and tort theories that state courts have recognized as limiting the employment-at-will doctrine.

Seldin, Peter. *Evaluating and Developing Administrative Performance* (Jossey-Bass, 1988). Presents a comprehensive system for assessing administrative performance and helping administrators improve their performance. Chapters discuss the demand for accountability and its effect on evaluation, the use of evaluative information in personnel decisions, characteristics of a successful evaluation system, the process of creating an evaluation system, and legal pitfalls of evaluation.

Sec. 2.3 (Institutional Liability for Acts of Others)

Aiken, Ray, Adams, John F., & Hall, John W. *Legal Liabilities in Higher Education: Their Scope and Management* (Association of American Colleges, 1976), printed simultaneously in 3 *J. Coll. & Univ. Law* 127 (1976). Provides an in-depth examination of legal and policy issues of institutional liability and the problems of protecting institutions and their personnel against liability by insurance and risk management.

Bazluke, Francine T. *Defamation Issues in Higher Education* (National Association of College and University Attorneys, 1990). A layperson's guide to defamation law. Author reviews the legal framework for a defamation claim and the possible defenses, and then discusses specific employment issues and student disciplinary actions that may give rise to defamation claims. Also discussed is the institution's potential liability for defamatory student publications. Guidelines are provided to minimize the institution's exposure to defamation claims.

Bickel, Robert D., & Lake, Peter F. "Reconceptualizing the University's Duty to Provide a Safe Learning Environment: A Criticism of the Doctrine of *In Loco Parentis* and the Restatement (Second) of Torts," 20 *J. Coll. & Univ. Law* 261 (1994). Criticizes the majority rule regarding institutional liability from *Rabel* (discussed in Section 4.17.2) and *Bradshaw* and argues that courts have improperly interpreted the *Restatement (Second) of Torts* and its "special relationship" requirement. The authors assert that colleges have a duty to protect, warn, and control their students, and that they should be found liable if they fail to act reasonably to protect students from foreseeable harm.

Bookman, Mark. *Contracting Collegiate Auxiliary Services* (Education and Nonprofit Consulting, 1989). Discusses legal and policy issues related to contracting for auxiliary services on campus. An overview chapter reviews legal terminology, the advantages and disadvantages of contracting, and the ways in which contracting decisions are made. Another chapter explains what should be negotiated when the contract is developed and how contracted services should be managed. Sample documents are included.

Burling, Philip. *Crime on Campus: Analyzing and Managing the Increasing Risk of Institutional Liability* (National Association of College and University Attorneys, 1990). Reviews the legal analyses that courts undertake in responding to claims that liability for injuries suffered on campus should be shifted from the victim to the institution. Includes a review of literature about reducing crime on campus and managing the risk of liability to victims whom the institution may have a duty to protect.

Evans, Richard B. Note, " 'A Stranger in a Strange Land': Responsibility and Liability for Students Enrolled in Foreign-Study Programs," 18 *J. Coll. & Univ. Law* 299 (1991). Examines the doctrine of "special relationship" that has been applied to the student-institution relationship and discusses its significance to claims of students injured while participating in a study-abroad program. Suggestions for limiting institutional liability are provided.

Gaffney, Edward M., & Sorensen, Philip M. *Ascending Liability in Religious and Other Non Profit Organizations* (Center for Constitutional Studies, Mercer University (now at Baylor University), 1984). Provides an overview of liability case law related to nonprofit and religiously affiliated organizations, discusses constitutional issues, and provides suggestions for structuring the operations of such organizations to limit liability.

Gehring, Donald D., & Geraci, Christy P. *Alcohol on Campus: A Compendium of the Law and a Guide to Campus Policy* (College Administration Publications, 1989). Examines legal and policy issues related to alcohol on college campuses. Included are chapters reviewing research on student consumption of alcohol, including differences by students' race and gender; sources of legal liability for colleges if intoxicated students injure themselves or others; and procedural and substantive considerations in developing alcohol policies and risk management procedures. A state-by-state analysis of laws relevant to alcohol consumption, sale, and social host liability is included. The book is updated annually.

Miyamoto, Tia. "Liability of Colleges and Universities for Injuries During Extracurricular Activities," 15 *J. Coll. & Univ. Law* 149 (1988). Examines four theories under which students have attempted to hold institutions liable for injuries incurred while participating in extracurricular activities: (1) *in loco parentis,* (2) the duty to supervise students, (3) the duty to control the acts of third persons who have injured the student, and (4) the duty to protect students as invitees. Cases in which one or more of these theories were used are analyzed. Author concludes that the fourth theory is the one under which the student is most likely to prevail.

Moots, Philip R. *Ascending Liability: Planning Memorandum* (Center for Constitutional Studies, Mercer University (now at Baylor University), 1987). Discusses planning issues such as risk management, contract drafting, and restructuring of certain activities of the organization. Also discusses the role of the governing board and the institution's role vis-à-vis related organizations.

National Association of College and University Attorneys. *Am I Liable? Faculty, Staff, and Institutional Liability in the College and University Setting* (NACUA, 1989). A collection of articles on selected liability issues. Included are analyses of general tort liability theories, liability for the acts of criminal intruders, student groups and alcohol-related liability, academic advising and defamation, and workers' compensation. Also discusses liability releases. A final chapter addresses risk management and insurance issues. Written by university counsel, these articles provide clear, useful information to counsel, administrators, and faculty.

Richmond, Douglas. "Institutional Liability for Student Activities and Organizations," 19 *J. Law & Educ.* 309 (1990). Provides an overview of a variety of tort theories, and judicial precedents related to these theories, in which the institution's liability for the allegedly wrongful acts of student organizations was at issue.

Stevens, George E. "Evaluation of Faculty Competence as a 'Privileged Occasion,'" 4 *J. Coll. & Univ. Law* 281 (1979). Discusses the law of defamation as it applies to institutional evaluations of professional competence.

Strohm, Leslie Chambers (ed.). *AIDS on Campus: A Legal Compendium* (National Association of College and University Attorneys, 1991). A collection of materials related to a range of legal, medical, and policy issues concerning AIDS. Included are Centers for Disease Control recommendations, guidelines, and updates regarding precautions to take if employees, patients, or students have AIDS; journal articles; occupational safety and health guidelines; institutional policy statements; and an extensive list of resources.

Sec. 2.4 (Personal Liability of Trustees, Administrators, and Staff)

Crandall, Deborah. *The Personal Liability of Community College Officials,* Topical Paper no. 61 (ERIC Clearinghouse for Junior Colleges, 1977). A guide for administrators that "illustrates the kinds of actions taking place in the courts and provides useful background information on personal liability." Though written for community college administrators, can be useful for other postsecondary administrators as well.

Hopkins, Bruce R., & Anderson, Barbara S. *The Counselor and the Law* (3d ed., American Association for Counseling and Development, 1990). Discusses confidentiality, privilege, and civil and criminal liability for counselors in educational, institutional, and community settings.

See Moots and NACUA entries for Section 2.3.

Sec. 2.5 (Institutional Management of Liability Risk)

Burling, Philip, & United Educators Risk Retention Group. "Managing Athletic Liability: An Assessment Guide," 72 *West's Educ. Law Rptr.* 503 (1993). A practical guide for developing and implementing risk management programs for athletics. Covers institutional duties to supervise; to provide safe facilities, adequate equipment, safe transportation, and medical treatment; and to protect spectators. Includes basic requirements and suggestions for risk management programs, "risk management action steps" for effectuating the institution's various duties, suggestions for selection and training of athletic staff, and a list of case citations.

Hollander, Patricia. *Computers in Education: Legal Liabilities and Ethical Issues Concerning Their Use and Misuse* (College Administration Publications, 1986). A monograph cataloguing negligence, contract, criminal, and other problems in one of the newest areas of potential liability. Provides practical guidance for identifying potential liabilities and avoiding or resolving the problems.

Stone, Byron, & North, Carol. *Risk Management and Insurance for Nonprofit Managers* (Society for Nonprofit Organizations, 1988). Provides practical guidance to nonprofit entities in devising risk management programs, including selection and maintenance of insurance coverage.

See Aiken and NACUA entries for Section 2.3.

CHAPTER THREE

The Legal Status of Students

SEC. 3.1. OVERVIEW

3.1.1. The Evolutionary Process

The legal status of students in postsecondary institutions changed dramatically in the 1960s, changed further in the 1970s and 1980s, and is still evolving. For most purposes, students are no longer second-class citizens under the law. They are recognized under the federal Constitution as "persons" with their own enforceable constitutional rights. They are recognized as adults, with the rights and responsibilities of adults, under many state laws. And they are accorded their own legal rights under various federal statutes. The background of this evolution is traced in Section 1.2; the legal status that emerges from these developments, and its impact on postsecondary administration, is explored throughout this chapter and Chapters Four through Ten.

Perhaps the key case in forging the new student status was *Dixon v. Alabama State Board of Education* (1961), discussed in Section 7.3.2. The court in this case rejected the notion that education in state schools is a "privilege" to be dispensed on whatever conditions the state in its sole discretion deems advisable; it also implicitly rejected the *in loco parentis* concept, under which the law had bestowed on schools all the powers over students that parents had over minor children. The *Dixon* approach became a part of U.S. Supreme Court jurisprudence in cases such as *Tinker v. Des Moines School District* (see Section 8.1), *Healy v. James* (Sections 8.1 and 9.1.1), and *Goss v. Lopez* (Section 7.3.2). The

137

impact of these public institution cases spilled over onto private institutions, as courts increasingly viewed students as contracting parties having rights under express and implied contractual relationships with the institution. Congress gave students at both public and private schools new rights under various civil rights acts and, in the Buckley Amendment (Section 3.3.1), gave postsecondary students certain rights that were expressly independent of and in lieu of parental rights. State statutes lowering the age of majority also enhanced the independence of students from their parents and brought the bulk of postsecondary students, even undergraduates, into the category of adults.

The latest stage in the evolution of the legal status of students is the stage of institutional self-regulation. Increasingly, higher education associations and commentators have urged, and assisted, individual institutions to redefine and extend their own internal regulations as an alternative or supplement to government regulation. (See generally E. El-Khawas, "Solving Problems Through Self-Regulation," 59 *Educ. Record* 323 (1978); C. Saunders, "How to Keep the Government from Playing the Featured Role," 59 *Educ. Record* 61 (1978).) But self-regulation has not displaced the continuing flow of federal regulation regarding student rights and responsibilities (see Sections 5.3.3 and 12.3.3).

3.1.2. The Age of Majority

The age of majority is established by state law in all states. There may be a general statute prescribing an age of majority for all or most business and personal dealings in the state, or there may be specific statutes or regulations establishing varying ages of majority for specific purposes. Until the 1970s, twenty-one was typically the age of majority in most states. But since the 1971 ratification of the Twenty-Sixth Amendment, lowering the voting age to eighteen, most states have lowered the age of majority to eighteen or nineteen for many other purposes as well. The Michigan statute (Mich. Comp. Laws Ann. §722.52) illustrates the comprehensive approach adopted by some states:

> Notwithstanding any other provision of law to the contrary, a person who is eighteen years of age but less than twenty-one years of age when this Act takes effect, and a person who attains eighteen years of age thereafter, is deemed to be an adult of legal age for all purposes whatsoever and shall have the same duties, liabilities, responsibilities, rights, and legal capacity as persons heretofore acquired at twenty-one years of age.

Other states have adopted more limited or more piecemeal legislation, sometimes using different minimum ages for different purposes. Given the lack of uniformity, administrators and counsel should carefully check state law in their own states.

The age-of-majority laws can affect many postsecondary regulations and policies. For example, students at age eighteen may be permitted to enter binding contracts without the need for a cosigner, give consent to medical treatment, declare financial independence, or establish a legal residence apart from the parents. But although students' legal capacity enables institutions to deal with them as adults at age eighteen, it does not necessarily require that institutions do so. Particularly in private institutions, administrators may still be able as a policy matter to require a cosigner on contracts with students, for instance, or to consider the resources of parents in awarding financial aid, even though the parents have no legal obligation to support the student. An institution's legal capacity to adopt such policy positions depends on the interpretation of the applicable age-of-majority law and the possible existence of special state law provisions for postsecondary institutions. A state loan program, for instance, may have special definitions of dependency or residency, which may not conform to general age-of-majority laws. Administrators will thus confront two questions: What do the age-of-majority laws require that I do in particular areas? And should I, where I am under no legal obligation, establish age requirements higher than the legal age in particular areas, or should I instead pattern institutional policies on the general legal standard?

SEC. 3.2. THE CONTRACTUAL RIGHTS OF STUDENTS

Both public and private institutions often have express contractual relationships with students. The most common examples are probably the housing contract or lease, the food service contract, and the loan agreement. When problems arise in these areas, the written contract, including institutional regulations incorporated by reference in the contract, is usually the first source of legal guidance.

The contractual relationship between student and institution, however, extends beyond the terms of express contracts. There also exists the more amorphous contractual relationship recognized in *Carr v. St. John's University, New York*, 187 N.E.2d 18 (N.Y. 1962), the modern root of the contract theory of student status. In reviewing the institution's dismissal of students for having participated in a civil marriage ceremony, the court based its reasoning on the principle that "when a student is duly admitted by a private university, secular or religious, there is an implied contract between the student and the university that, if he complies with the terms prescribed by the university, he will obtain the degree which he sought." Construing a harsh and vague regulation in the university's favor, the court upheld the dismissal because the students had failed to comply with the university's prescribed terms.

Although *Carr* dealt only with a private institution, a subsequent New York case, *Healy v. Larsson,* 323 N.Y.S.2d 625, *affirmed,* 318 N.E.2d 608 (N.Y. 1974) (discussed later in this section), indicated that "there is no reason why . . . the *Carr* principle should not apply to a public university or community college."

Other courts have increasingly utilized the contract theory for both public and private institutions, as well as for both academic and disciplinary disputes. The theory, however, does not necessarily apply identically to all such situations. A public institution may have more defenses against a contract action. *Eden v. Board of Trustees of State University,* 374 N.Y.S.2d 686 (N.Y. App. Div. 1975), for instance, recognizes both an ultra vires defense and the state's power to terminate a contract when necessary in the public interest. ("Ultra vires" means "beyond authority," and the defense is essentially, "You can't enforce this contract against us because we didn't have authority to make it in the first place.") And courts may accord both public and private institutions more flexibility in drafting and interpreting contract terms involving academics than they do contract terms involving discipline. In holding that Georgia State University had not breached its contract with a student by withholding a master's degree, for example, the court in *Mahavongsanan v. Hall,* 529 F.2d 448 (5th Cir. 1976), recognized the "wide latitude and discretion afforded by the courts to educational institutions in framing their academic requirements."

In general, courts have applied the contract theory to postsecondary institutions in a deferential manner. Courts have accorded institutions considerable latitude to select and interpret their own contract terms and to change the terms to which students are subjected as they progress through the institution. In *Mahavongsanan,* for instance, the court rejected the plaintiff student's contract claim in part because an institution "clearly is entitled to modify [its regulations] so as to properly exercise its educational responsibility." Nor have institutions been subjected to the rigors of contract law as it applies in the commercial world. The plaintiff student in *Slaughter v. Brigham Young University* (Sections 7.2.2 and 7.3.4) had been awarded $88,283 in damages in the trial court in a suit alleging erroneous dismissal from school. The appellate court reversed:

> The trial court's rigid application of commercial contract doctrine advanced by plaintiff was in error, and the submission on that theory alone was error. . . .
>
> It is apparent that some elements of the law of contracts are used and should be used in the analysis of the relationship between plaintiff and the university to provide some framework into which to put the problem of expulsion for disciplinary reasons. This does not mean that "contract law" must be rigidly applied in all its aspects, nor is it so applied even when the contract analogy is extensively adopted. . . . The student-university relationship is unique, and it should not be and cannot be stuffed into one doctrinal category [514 F.2d at 676].

Despite the generally deferential judicial attitude, the contract theory creates a two-way street; it has become a source of meaningful rights for students as well as for institutions. In *Healy v. Larsson,* for instance, the plaintiff student had transferred to the Schenectady County Community College and had taken all the courses his guidance counselors specified, but he was denied a degree. The court held that he was contractually entitled to the degree because he had "satisfactorily completed a course of study at . . . [the] community college as prescribed to him by authorized representatives of the college." Similarly, in the *Steinberg* and *Eden* cases, discussed in Section 4.1.3, students won victories in admissions cases. Other examples include *Paynter v. New York University,* 319 N.Y.S.2d 893 (N.Y. App. Div. 1971), and *Zumbrun v. University of Southern California,* 101 Cal. Rptr. 499 (Cal. Ct. App. 1972), both suits seeking tuition refunds after classes had been canceled for part of a semester during antiwar protests. Although in *Paynter* the court held in favor of the university and in *Zumbrun* it remanded the case to the trial court for further proceedings, both opinions recognized that the courses to be taken by a student and the services to be rendered in the courses are part of the student-institution contract. Moreover, the opinions indicate that the institution may make only "minor" changes in the schedule of classes and in the course of study that a student has undertaken for a particular semester; more substantial deviations could constitute a breach of contract.

But in *Doherty v. Southern College of Optometry,* 862 F.2d 570 (6th Cir. 1988), the court rejected a student's claim that deviations from the stated curriculum breached his contractual rights. The college's handbook had specifically reserved the right to change degree requirements, and the college had uniformly applied curricular changes to current students in the past. Therefore, the court ruled that the changes were neither arbitrary nor capricious, and dismissed the student's contract claim.

An express disclaimer in a state university's catalogue defeated a student's contract claim in *Eiland v. Wolf,* 764 S.W.2d 827 (Tex. Ct. App. 1989). Although the catalogue stated that the student would be entitled to a diploma if he successfully completed required courses and met other requirements, the express disclaimer that the catalogue was not an enforceable contract and was subject to change without notice convinced the court to dismiss the student's challenge to his academic dismissal.

A reservation-of-rights clause was also present, but less important, in *Beukas v. Fairleigh Dickinson University,* 605 A.2d 776 (N.J. Super. Ct. Law Div. 1991), *affirmed,* 605 A.2d 708 (N.J. Super. Ct. App. Div. 1992). The court ruled that no express contract existed between the dental students and the university and that, under principles of "quasi-contract," the university could close the dental school as long as it acted in good faith (see Section 4.1.3).

The contract theory is still developing. Debate continues on issues such as the means for identifying the terms and conditions of the student-institution contract, the extent to which the school catalogue constitutes part of the contract, and the extent to which the institution retains implied or inherent authority (see Section 2.1) not expressed in any written regulation or policy. For example, in *Prusack v. State,* 498 N.Y.S.2d 455 (N.Y. App. Div. 1986), the court rejected the student's claim that a letter of admission from the university that had quoted a particular tuition rate was an enforceable contract, since other university publications expressly stated that tuition was subject to change. In *Eiland v. Wolf,* 764 S.W.2d 827 (Tex. Ct. App. 1989), reservation-of-rights language in a catalogue for the University of Texas Medical School at Galveston absolved the institution of contractual liability. The catalogue stated, "The provisions of this catalogue are subject to change without notice and do not constitute an irrevocable contract between any student . . . and the University." Furthermore, the catalogue gave the faculty the right to determine whether a student's performance was satisfactory, and stated that "the Faculty of the School of Medicine has the authority to drop any student from the rolls . . . if circumstances of a legal, moral, health, social, or academic nature justify such a request" (764 S.W.2d at 838). The court said, "Given the express disclaimers in the document alleged to be a contract here, it is clear that no enforceable 'contract' existed" (764 S.W.2d at 838).

Also still debatable is the extent to which courts will rely on certain contract law concepts, such as "unconscionable" contracts and "contracts of adhesion." An unconscionable contract is one that is so harsh and unfair to one of the parties that a reasonable person would not freely and knowingly agree to it. Unconscionable contracts are not enforceable in the courts. In *Albert Merrill School v. Godoy,* 357 N.Y.S.2d 378 (Civ. Ct., N.Y. City, 1974), for example, the school sought to recover money due on a contract to provide data-processing training. Finding that the student did not speak English well and that the bargaining power of the parties was uneven, the court held the contract unconscionable and refused to enforce it. A contract of adhesion is one offered by one party (usually the party in the stronger bargaining position) to the other party on a "take-it-or-leave-it" basis, with no opportunity to negotiate the terms. Although courts will often construe adhesion contracts in favor of the weaker party where there is ambiguity, such contracts are enforceable unless a court holds that they are unconscionable. In *K. D. v. Educational Testing Service,* 386 N.Y.S.2d 747 (N.Y. Sup. Ct. 1976), the court viewed the plaintiff's agreement with ETS to take the Law School Admissions Test (LSAT) as a contract of adhesion, explaining:

> Where the court finds that an agreement is a contract of adhesion, effort will frequently be made to protect the weaker party from the agreement's harsher terms

by a variety of pretexts, while still keeping the elementary rules of the law of contracts intact (Kessler, "Contracts of Adhesion—Some Thoughts About Freedom of Contract," 43 *Columbia L. Rev.* 629, 633 (1943)). The court may, for example, find the obnoxious clause "ambiguous," even where no ambiguity exists, and then construe it against its author; or it may find the clause to be against public policy and declare it unenforceable [386 N.Y.S.2d at 752].

Nevertheless, the court held the agreement valid because it was not "so unfair and unreasonable" that it should be disregarded by use of the available "pretexts."

Since these contract principles depend on the weak position of one of the parties, and on overall determinations of "fairness," courts are unlikely to apply them against institutions that deal openly with their students—for instance, by following a good-practice code, operating grievance mechanisms for student complaints (see Sections 7.1.1 through 7.1.3), and affording students significant opportunity to participate in institutional governance.

Other contractual issues may arise as a result of the action of institutional or state-level actors. For example, in *Arriaga v. Members of Board of Regents*, 825 F. Supp. 1 (D. Mass. 1992), students challenged the constitutionality of retroactive tuition increases ordered by the state board of regents after the state legislature, responding to a fiscal crisis, passed a law increasing tuition for nonresident students. Claiming that the institution's statements about the amount of tuition for nonresident students was a contract, the students argued that the regents' action impaired their contractual rights in violation of the U.S. Constitution's contracts clause, Article I, Section 10.

The regents filed a motion to dismiss the lawsuit, arguing that they had the unilateral power to impose tuition increases, and thus it was not the legislature's action that was dispositive of the constitutional claim. The court was required to determine whether it was the action of the legislature or the regents that resulted in the tuition increase, for the contracts clause would apply only to the acts of the legislature unless it had delegated its power to the executive branch (here, the regents). The court concluded that, although the regents determined that tuition increases were necessary before the legislature formally passed the law, their action was in anticipation of the law and thus was controlled by the provisions of the contracts clause.

As further developments unfold, postsecondary administrators should be sensitive to the language used in all institutional rules and policies affecting students. Language suggestive of a commitment (or promise) to students should be used only when the institution is prepared to live up to the commitment. Limitations on the institution's commitments should be clearly noted where possible. Administrators should consider the adoption of an official policy, perhaps even a "code of good practice," on fair dealing with students.

SEC. 3.3. STUDENT FILES AND RECORDS

3.3.1. The Buckley Amendment

The Family Educational Rights and Privacy Act of 1974 (20 U.S.C. §1232g), popularly known as the Buckley Amendment or FERPA, has created a substantial role for the federal government with respect to student records. The Act and its implementing regulations, 34 C.F.R. Part 99, apply to all public and private educational agencies or institutions that receive federal funds from the U.S. Department of Education or whose students receive such funds (under the Guaranteed Student Loan program, for example) and pay them to the agency or institution (34 C.F.R. §99.1). While FERPA does not invalidate common law or state statutory law applicable to student records (see this volume, Section 3.3.2), the regulations are so extensive that they are the predominant legal consideration in dealing with student records.

FERPA and its regulations establish requirements pertaining to (1) students' right of access to their education records (34 C.F.R. §§99.10–99.12); (2) students' right to challenge the content of their records (34 C.F.R. §§99.20–99.22); (3) disclosure of "personally identifiable" information from these records to personnel of the institution or to outsiders (34 C.F.R. §§99.30–99.37); (4) the institution's obligation to notify students of their rights under the Act and regulations (34 C.F.R. §§99.6–99.7); and (5) recourse for students and the federal government when an institution may have violated the Act or regulations (34 C.F.R. §§99.60–99.67). Recourse includes a formal system for receipt, investigation, and adjudication of complaints by the Family Policy Compliance Office of the Department of Education and by a review board (34 C.F.R. §99.60). All students enrolled or formerly enrolled in postsecondary institutions have rights under the Act and regulations regardless of whether they are eighteen and regardless of whether they are dependent on their parents (34 C.F.R. §99.5). (If students are dependents for federal income tax purposes, however, they cannot prevent their parents from seeing their education records (§99.3 (1)(a)(8)).)

The records that are protected under FERPA are all "those records that are (1) [d]irectly related to a student; and (2) [m]aintained by an educational agency or institution or by a party acting for the agency or institution" (20 U.S.C. §1232g(a)(4)(A), 34 C.F.R. §99.3). This section of the regulations contains five exceptions to this definition, which exclude from coverage certain personal and private records of institutional personnel, certain campus law enforcement records, certain student employment records, certain records regarding health care, and "records . . . [such as alumni records] that only contain information about an individual after he or she is no longer a student at [the] . . . institution." There is also a partial exception for "directory information," which is exempt from the regulations' nondisclosure requirements under certain conditions (34 C.F.R. §99.37).

The key to success in dealing with FERPA is a thorough understanding of the implementing regulations. Administrators should keep copies of the regulations at their fingertips and should not rely on secondary sources to resolve particular problems. Counsel should review the institution's record-keeping policies and practices, and every substantial change in them, to ensure compliance with the regulations. Administrators and counsel should work together to maintain appropriate legal forms to use in implementing the regulations, such as forms for a student's waiver of his or her rights under the Act or regulations, forms for securing a student's consent to release personally identifiable information from his or her records (34 C.F.R. §99.30), and forms for notifying parties to whom information is disclosed of the limits on the use of that information (34 C.F.R. §99.34). Questions concerning the interpretation or application of the regulations may be directed to the Family Policy Compliance Office at the U.S. Department of Education.

Since FERPA has been in effect, questions about who has access, and to what types of records, have proliferated. For example, a student rejected for admission to a graduate program in chemistry at the University of Texas attempted to use FERPA to gain access to the letters of recommendation written in his behalf. The U.S. Court of Appeals for the Fifth Circuit affirmed the judgment of a federal trial court that the student, although he had audited some courses at the University, did not meet FERPA's definition of "student" (*Tarka v. Franklin*, 891 F.2d 102 (5th Cir. 1989). A few years later, students admitted to Harvard University who wished to examine the comments that admissions staff had made about them on "summary sheets" filed a complaint with the Department of Education when Harvard denied their request. Harvard had told the students that the summary sheets were kept in a file separate from the student's academic record, that they included direct quotes from the confidential letters of recommendation, and that they had no further significance once a student was admitted. Therefore, Harvard believed that these documents were not accessible under FERPA.

In an advisory letter, reprinted in 22 *Coll. Law Dig.* 299 (July 16, 1992), the Department of Education ruled that the students had a right to examine the summary sheets. Applying FERPA's definition of an "education record" (documents containing information related to a student that are maintained by an educational agency—20 U.S.C. §1232g(a)(4)(A)), the Department of Education determined that the summary sheets met that definition. However, the department ruled that the university could redact from the documents any excerpts specifically derived from confidential letters of recommendation if the student had waived his or her right of access to these letters.

Questions also have been raised about the status of campus law enforcement records under FERPA. Originally, the Department of Education had interpreted the law to mean that any record released by the campus law enforcement unit to other campus officials became part of the student's "education record" and could not be shared, even with other law enforcement agencies, without the student's permission. A federal trial judge ruled, however, that the department's interpretation of FERPA regarding arrest records violated certain constitutional provisions. In *Student Law Press Center v. Alexander,* 778 F. Supp. 1227 (D.D.C. 1991), student journalists challenged a FERPA provision authorizing the withdrawal of federal funds from a college or university that discloses to the public personally identifiable information contained in campus police reports. The plaintiffs sought a preliminary injunction against the enforcement of that provision, claiming that the restriction violated their First Amendment right to receive information and their implied Fifth Amendment right to equal protection. The court ruled that the plaintiffs had demonstrated the likelihood of success on their claim. It therefore granted the preliminary injunction, noting that there was no legitimate privacy interest in arrest records and thus no constitutional basis for upholding that provision of FERPA.

Similar cases have also been brought under state open-records laws (see Section 11.6.2), with similar results. In *Bauer v. Kincaid,* 759 F. Supp. 575 (W.D. Mo. 1991), the editor of the student newspaper at Southwest Missouri State University, suing under the state's sunshine law, charged that the university's refusal to provide access to campus law enforcement records was unlawful. A federal trial court ruled that FERPA did not protect these records from disclosure and that, alternatively, if it did protect law enforcement records from disclosure, FERPA violated the Constitution's equal protection clause by creating a classification (student vs. nonstudent) that had no rational basis. But another federal trial court rejected the request of a nonstudent to gain access to campus law enforcement records in *Norwood v. Slammons,* 788 F. Supp. 1020 (W.D. Ark. 1991), ruling that the general public had no First Amendment right to a college's disciplinary or law enforcement records.

Following this flurry of judicial activity, Congress passed the Higher Education Amendments of 1992 (Pub. L. No. 102–325, codified at 20 U.S.C. §1232 g(a)(4)(B)(ii)), which amended FERPA to exclude from the definition of "education records" records that are maintained by a law enforcement unit of an educational agency or institution for the purpose of law enforcement. This change enables institutions to disclose information about campus crime contained in law enforcement unit records to parents, the media, other students, and other law enforcement agencies. The Department of Education has issued final revised regulations to implement the amendments to FERPA at 34 C.F.R. §99.8 (69 Fed. Reg. 3464 (Jan. 17, 1995)).

The Education Department has also revised the FERPA regulations to clarify the definition of a disciplinary record and to specify the conditions for its release. Disciplinary records are considered "education records" and thus subject to FERPA's limitations on disclosure. However, the revised regulations permit the institution to disclose to the alleged victim of a violent crime the results of a disciplinary proceeding involving the student accused of the crime (34 C.F.R. §99.3). Student press groups have sought access to disciplinary records, in some cases successfully, under state open-records laws (see the discussion of *The Red and the Black* case, Section 11.6.1).

Although federal courts have consistently refused to find a private right of action under FERPA, several have ruled that students may challenge alleged violations of their FERPA rights under Section 1983 of the Civil Rights Act (see Section 2.3.3) (*Tarka v. Franklin,* 891 F.2d 102 (Fifth Cir. 1989); (*Fay v. South Colonie Central School District,* 802 F.2d 21 (2d Cir. 1986)). And a federal district court permitted students to base a constitutional claim on the deprivation of their rights under FERPA. In *Krebs v. Rutgers, The State University of New Jersey,* 797 F. Supp. 1246 (D.N.J. 1992), students filed claims under Section 1983 and the federal Privacy Act (discussed in Section 3.3.3), challenging Rutgers' use of their Social Security numbers as identification numbers on class rosters, identification cards, meal tickets, and other university documents. Although the judge granted summary judgment for Rutgers on the Privacy Act claim (noting that the university was not subject to that law because it is not a state agency), he issued a preliminary injunction requiring the university to halt the practice of some faculty members who took attendance by circulating rosters containing students' names and their Social Security numbers. The university and the students settled the case, with Rutgers agreeing to remove the numbers from meal cards, to stop mailing letters to students with the numbers on the outside of the envelope, to permit students to obtain substitute identification numbers, and to hold public hearings on student privacy twice a year for the next two years.

The judge acknowledged that the students had no private right of action under FERPA. However, he stated that limiting the students to the administrative complaint procedure was unsatisfactory because he did not believe that the Education Department would withhold federal funds from the university for the relatively minor violation of disclosing Social Security numbers. Therefore, he ruled, the students had rights under federal law that were being violated. Since Section 1983 permitted individuals to claim violations of their federally guaranteed rights, he ruled that the students could make out a Section 1983 claim based on the underlying federal law (FERPA).

3.3.2. State Law

In a majority of states, courts now recognize a common law tort of invasion of privacy, which, in some circumstances, protects individuals against the public disclosure of damaging private information about them and against intrusions into their private affairs. A few states have similarly protected privacy with a statute or constitutional provision. Although this body of law has seldom been applied to educational record-keeping practices, the basic legal principles appear applicable to record-keeping abuses by postsecondary institutions. This body of right-to-privacy law could protect students against abusive collection and retention practices where clearly intrusive methods are used to collect information concerning private affairs. In *White v. Davis,* 533 P.2d 222 (Cal. 1975) (see Section 11.4), for example, the court held that undercover police surveillance of university classes and meetings violated the right to privacy because "no professor or student can be confident that whatever he may express in class will not find its way into a police file." Similarly, right-to-privacy law could protect students against abusive dissemination practices that result in unwarranted public disclosure of damaging personal information.

In addition to this developing right-to-privacy law, many states also have statutes or administrative regulations dealing specifically with record keeping. These include subject-access laws, open-record or public-record laws, and confidentiality laws. Such laws usually apply only to state agencies, and a state's postsecondary institutions may or may not be considered state agencies subject to record-keeping laws (see Section 11.6.2). Occasionally, a state statute deals specifically with postsecondary education records. A Massachusetts statute, for instance, makes it an "unfair educational practice" for any "educational institution," including public and private postsecondary institutions, to request information or make or keep records concerning certain arrests or misdemeanor convictions of students or applicants (Mass. Gen. Laws Ann. ch. 151C, §2(f)).

Since state laws on privacy and records vary greatly from state to state, administrators should check with counsel to determine the law in their particular state. Since state record requirements may occasionally conflict with FERPA regulations, counsel must determine whether any such conflict exists. Regarding right-to-privacy concepts, an institution in compliance with FERPA regulations is not likely to be violating any state right to privacy. The two exceptions concern information collection practices and the particular types of records kept, which are not treated in the FERPA regulations (except that FERPA (§99.32) requires that a "record of disclosures" of information be kept). In these situations, developing state laws may carve out requirements, as in the *White* case and the Massachusetts statute above, independent of and supplementary to FERPA.

3.3.3. The Federal Privacy Act

The Privacy Act of 1974 (88 Stat. 1896, partly codified in 5 U.S.C. §552a) applies directly to federal government agencies and, with two exceptions discussed below, does not restrict postsecondary education institutions. The Act accords all persons—including students, faculty members, and staff members—certain rights enforceable against the federal government regarding information about them in federal agency files, whether collected from a postsecondary institution or from any other source. The Act grants the right to inspect, copy, and correct such information and limits its dissemination by the agency. Regulations implementing the Privacy Act are found at 34 C.F.R. Part 5b.

Section 7 of the Act prohibits federal, state, and local government agencies from requiring persons to disclose their Social Security numbers. This provision applies to public but not to private postsecondary institutions (see the *Krebs* case in Section 3.3.1, which also discusses when an institution is considered a state agency for purposes of this provision) and thus prevents public institutions from requiring either students or employees to disclose their Social Security numbers. The two exceptions to this nondisclosure requirement permit an institution to require disclosure (1) where it is required by some other federal statute and (2) where the institution maintains "a system of records in existence and operating before January 1, 1975, if such disclosure was required under statute or regulation adopted prior to such date to verify the identity of an individual" (88 Stat. 1896 at 1903).

The second provision of the Act potentially relevant to some postsecondary institutions is Section 3(m) (5 U.S.C. §552a(m)), which applies the Act's requirements to government contractors who operate record-keeping systems on behalf of a federal agency pursuant to the contract.

SELECTED ANNOTATED BIBLIOGRAPHY

Sec. 3.2 (The Contractual Rights of Students)

Cherry, Robert L., Jr. "The College Catalog as a Contract," 21 *J. Law & Educ.* 1 (1992). A review of litigation regarding the contractual status of college catalogues. Discusses disclaimers, reservation-of-rights clauses, and other significant drafting issues.

Dodd, Victoria J. "The Non-Contractual Nature of the Student-University Relationship," 33 *U. Kan. Law Rev.* 701 (1985). Reviews breach-of-contract claims by students, and concludes that courts have manipulated traditional contract law principles in order to defer to institutional autonomy. Analyzes the elements of the student-institution "contract" and argues that courts should impose duties on institutions in addition to their "contract" obligations.

Jennings, Eileen K. "Breach of Contract Suits Against Postsecondary Institutions: Can They Succeed?" 7 *J. Coll. & Univ. Law* 191 (1980–81). A detailed study of suits brought by students alleging breach of contract. Cases are divided into the categories of "Tuition and Fees," "Scholarships," "Student Discipline," "Miscellaneous," and "The Academic Relationship." In the last category, cases are subdivided into "Program Termination," "Quality of Academic Program," "Refusal to Grant Degree," "Change of Requirements During Student's Tenure," and "Academic Dismissal Procedures."

LaTourette, Audrey Wolfson, & King, Robert D. "Judicial Intervention in the Student-University Relationship: Due Process and Contract Theories," 65 *U. Detroit L. Rev.* 199 (1988). Reviews constitutional and contract law disputes between students and colleges. Authors conclude that heightened judicial scrutiny of institutional due process has strengthened students' procedural rights, but that courts remain deferential to substantive academic judgments. Includes a comprehensive analysis of due process in academic and disciplinary decisions, as well as an overview of the application of contract law to student-institution relationships.

Nordin, Virginia D. "The Contract to Educate: Toward a More Workable Theory of the Student-University Relationship," 8 *J. Coll. & Univ. Law* 141 (1981–82). A historical and theoretical overview of the development and current interpretation of the "contract to educate." Includes discussion of the academic abstention doctrine, the application of implied contract and quasi-contract theories to education, the reasonable expectations of the parties, and the legal significance of the college bulletin.

Olswang, Steven G., Cole, Elsa Kircher, & Wilson, James B. "Program Elimination, Financial Emergency, and Student Rights," 9 *J. Coll. & Univ. Law* 163 (1982–83). Analyzes one particular aspect of the contract relationship between institution and student: the obligations the institution may have to the student when the institution has slated an academic program for elimination. A useful supplement to the Jennings and the Nordin entries above.

Sec. 3.3 (Student Files and Records)

American Association of Collegiate Registrars and Admissions Officers, Task Force on Buckley Amendment. *A Guide to Postsecondary Institutions for Implementation of the Family Educational Rights and Privacy Act of 1974 as Amended* (AACRAO, 1976). Explains the Act and its regulations, as well as the procedures and strategies for compliance, and provides sample forms for use in complying and a copy of the Act and its regulations.

Schatken, Steven N. "Student Records at Institutions of Postsecondary Education: Selected Issues Under the Family Educational Rights and Privacy Act of 1974," 4 *J. Coll. & Univ. Law* 147 (1977). Identifies the major Buckley issues, explains why they are issues, suggests resolutions, and gives practical advice for administrators and counsel dealing with student records.

See Van Tol entry for Section 4.1.

CHAPTER FOUR

Admissions and Financial Aid

SEC. 4.1. ADMISSIONS

4.1.1. Basic Legal Requirements

Postsecondary institutions have traditionally been accorded wide discretion in formulating admissions standards. The law's deference to administrators' autonomy stems from the notion that tampering with admissions criteria is tampering with the expertise of educators. In recent years, however, some doorways have been opened in the wall of deference, as dissatisfied applicants have successfully pressed the courts for relief, and legislatures and administrative agencies have sought to regulate certain aspects of the admissions process.

Administrators are subject to three general constraints in formulating admissions policies: (1) the selection process must not be arbitrary or capricious; (2) the institution may be bound, under a contract theory, to adhere to its published admissions standards and to honor its admissions decisions; and (3) the institution may not have admissions policies that unjustifiably discriminate on the basis of race, sex, age, disability, or citizenship.

Although administrators are also constrained in the admissions process by the "Buckley" regulations on school records (Section 3.3.1), the regulations have only limited applicability to admissions records. The regulations do not apply to the records of persons who are not or have not been students at the institution; thus, admissions records are not covered until the applicant has been accepted and is in attendance at the institution (34 C.F.R. §§99.1(d), 99.3 ("student")). The institution may also maintain the confidentiality of letters of recommendation if the student has waived the right of access; such a waiver may be sought during the application process (34 C.F.R. §99.12). Moreover, when a student from one component unit of an institution applies for admission to another unit of the same institution, the student is treated as an applicant rather than a student with respect to the second unit's admissions records; those records are therefore not subject to Buckley until the student is in attendance in the second unit (34 C.F.R. §99.5).

Falsification of information on an application may be grounds for discipline or expulsion. In *North v. West Virginia Board of Regents*, 332 S.E.2d 141 (W. Va. 1985), a medical student provided false information on his application concerning his grade point average, courses taken, degrees, birth date, and marital status. The court upheld the expulsion on two theories: that the student had breached the university's disciplinary code (even though he was not a student at the time) and that the student had committed fraud.

Students may also make constitutional claims, based on the due process and equal protection provisions of the Fourteenth Amendment. For example, in *Martin v. Helstad*, 578 F. Supp. 1473 (W.D. Wis. 1983), a law school revoked its acceptance of an applicant when the school learned he had neglected to include on his application that he had been convicted of a felony and incarcerated. The court held that, although the applicant was entitled to minimal procedural due process to respond to the school's charge that he had falsified information on his application, the school had provided him sufficient due process in allowing him to explain his nondisclosure.

In *Phelps v. Washburn University of Topeka*, 634 F. Supp. 556 (D. Kan. 1986), rejected applicants attempted to state due process claims, asserting that the university denied them admission because they were active in racial justice issues and because of similar activities of their father. The court found no racial discrimination and also ruled that the plaintiffs had no property interest in being admitted to the university, thus defeating their procedural due process claims.

4.1.2. Arbitrariness

The "arbitrariness" standard of review is the one most protective of the institution's prerogatives. The cases reflect a judicial hands-off attitude toward any admissions decision arguably based on academic qualifications. Under the arbitrariness standard, the court will overturn an institution's decision only if there is no reasonable explanation for its actions. *Lesser v. Board of Education of New York*, 239 N.Y.S.2d 776 (N.Y. App. Div. 1963), provides a classic example. Lesser sued Brooklyn College after being rejected because his grade average was below the cutoff. He argued that the college acted arbitrarily and unreasonably in not considering that he had been enrolled in a demanding high school honors program. The court declined to overturn the judgment of the college:

> Courts may not interfere with the administrative discretion exercised by agencies which are vested with the administration and control of educational institutions, unless the circumstances disclosed by the record leave no scope for the use of that discretion in the matter under scrutiny. . . .
>
> More particularly, a court should refrain from interjecting its views within those delicate areas of school administration which relate to the eligibility of applicants and the determination of marking standards, unless a clear abuse of statutory authority or gross error has been shown [239 N.Y.S.2d at 779].

The court in *Arizona Board of Regents v. Wilson,* 539 P.2d 943 (Ariz. Ct. App. 1975), expressed similar sentiment. In that case, a woman was refused admission to the graduate school of art at the University of Arizona because the faculty did not consider her art work to be of sufficiently high quality. She challenged the admissions process on the basis that it was a rolling admissions system with no written guidelines. The court entered judgment in favor of the university:

> This case represents a prime example of when a court should not interfere in the academic program of a university. It was incumbent upon appellee to show that her rejection was in bad faith, or arbitrary, capricious, or unreasonable. The court may not substitute its own opinions as to the merits of appellee's work for that of the members of the faculty committee who were selected to make a determination as to the quality of her work [539 P.2d at 946].

Another court, in considering whether a public university's refusal to admit a student to veterinary school involved constitutional protections, rejected arbitrariness claims based on the due process and equal protection clauses. In *Grove v. Ohio State University,* 424 F. Supp. 377 (S.D. Ohio 1976), the plaintiff, denied admission to veterinary school three times, argued that the use of a score from a personal interview introduced subjective factors into the admissions decision process that were arbitrary and capricious, thus depriving him of due process. Second, he claimed that the admission of students less well qualified than he deprived him of equal protection. And third, he claimed that a professor had told him he would be admitted if he took additional courses.

Citing *Board of Regents v. Roth,* 408 U.S. 564 (1972), a landmark case involving a public employee's right to constitutional due process, the court determined that the plaintiff had a liberty interest in pursuing veterinary medicine. The court then examined the admissions procedure and concluded that, despite its subjective element, it provided sufficient due process protections. The court deferred to the academic judgment of the admissions committee with regard to the weight that should be given to the interview score. The court also found no property interest, since the plaintiff had no legitimate entitlement to a space in a class of 130 when over 900 individuals had applied.

The court rejected the plaintiff's second and third claims as well. The plaintiff had not raised discrimination claims but had asserted that the admission of students with lower grades was a denial of equal protection. The court stated, "This Court is reluctant to find that failure to adhere exactly to an admissions formula constitutes a denial of equal protection" (424 F. Supp. at 387), citing *Bakke* (see Section 4.1.5). Nor did the professor's statement that the plaintiff would be reconsidered for admission if he took additional courses constitute a promise to admit him once he completed the courses.

The review standards in these cases establish a formidable barrier for disappointed applicants to cross. But occasionally someone succeeds. *State ex rel. Bartlett v. Pantzer,* 489 P.2d 375 (Mont. 1971), arose after the admissions committee of the University of Montana Law School had advised an applicant that he would be accepted if he completed a course in financial accounting. He took such a course and received a D. The law school refused to admit him, claiming that a D was an "acceptable" but not a "satisfactory" grade. The student argued that it was unreasonable for the law school to inject a requirement of receiving a "satisfactory grade" after he had completed the course. The court agreed:

> Thus, we look to the matter of judgment or "discretion" in the legal sense. To cause a young man, who is otherwise qualified and whose entry into law school would not interfere with the educational process in any discernible fashion, to lose a year and an opportunity for education on the technical, unpublished distinction between the words "satisfactory" and "acceptable" as applied to a credit-earning grade from a recognized institution is, in our view, an abuse of discretion [489 P.2d at 379].

All these cases involve public institutions, and whether their principles would apply to private institutions is unclear. The "arbitrary and capricious" standard apparently arises from concepts of due process and administrative law that are applicable only to public institutions. Courts may be even less receptive to arbitrariness arguments lodged against private schools, although common law may provide some relief even here. In *In re Press,* 45 U.S.L.W. 2238 (N.Y. Sup. Ct., Oct. 27, 1976), for instance, the court held that an arbitrariness claim was a valid basis on which New York University, a private institution, could be sued. And in *Levine v. George Washington University* and *Paulsen v. Golden Gate University* (Section 4.1.6), common law principles protected students at private institutions against arbitrary interpretation of institutional policy.

The cases discussed in this section demonstrate that, if the individuals and groups who make admissions decisions adhere carefully to their published (or unwritten) criteria, give individual consideration to every applicant, and provide reasonable explanations for the criteria they use, judicial review will be deferential.

4.1.3. The Contract Theory

The plaintiffs in *Eden v. Board of Trustees of the State University,* 374 N.Y.S.2d 686 (N.Y. App. Div. 1975), had been accepted for admission to a new school of podiatry being established at the State University of New York at Stony Brook. Shortly before the scheduled opening, the state suspended its plans for the school, citing fiscal pressures in state government. The students argued that they had a contract with SUNY entitling them to instruction in the podiatry school. The court agreed that SUNY's "acceptance of the petitioners' applications satisfies the classic requirements of a contract." Though the state could legally abrogate its contracts when necessary in the public interest to alleviate a fiscal crisis, and though "the judicial branch . . . must exercise restraint in questioning executive prerogative," the court nevertheless ordered the state to enroll the students for the ensuing academic year. The court found that a large federal grant as well as tuition money would be lost if the school did not open, that the school's personnel were already under contract and would have to be paid anyway, and that postponement of the opening therefore would not save money. Since the fiscal crisis would not be alleviated, the state's decision was deemed "arbitrary and capricious" and a breach of contract.

The *Eden* case establishes that a prospective student has a contract with the school once the school accepts his or her admission application. A subsequent case takes the contract analysis one step further, applying it to applicants not yet accepted. In *Steinberg v. University of Health Sciences/Chicago Medical School,* 354 N.E.2d 586 (Ill. App. Ct. 1976), the court held that a rejected applicant could sue for breach of contract on the theory that the medical school had deviated from the admissions criteria in its catalogue. The applicant alleged that the school had used unstated criteria, such as the existence of alumni in the applicant's family and the ability to pledge large sums of money to the school. Although conceding that it had no authority to interfere with the substance of a private school's admissions requirements, the court asserted that the school had a contractual duty to its applicants to judge their qualifications only by its published standards unless it had specifically reserved the right to reject any applicant.

The court reasoned that the school's catalogue was an invitation to make an offer; the plaintiff's application in response to that invitation was an offer; and the medical school's retention of the application fee was the acceptance of the offer.

We believe that he [Steinberg] and the school entered into an enforceable contract; that the school's obligation under the contract was stated in the school's bulletin in a definitive manner; and that by accepting his application fee—a valuable consideration—the school bound itself to fulfill its promises. Steinberg accepted the school's promises in good faith, and he was entitled to have his application judged according to the school's stated criteria [354 N.E.2d at 591].

The court thus ordered a trial on the applicant's allegations that the school had breached a contract. The Illinois Supreme Court affirmed the order and also held that the applicant had a cause of action for fraud (371 N.E.2d 634 (Ill. 1977)).

Thus, the contract theory clearly applies to both public and private schools, although, as *Eden* suggests, public institutions may have defenses not available to private schools. While the contract theory does not require administrators to adopt or to forgo any particular admissions standard, it does require that administrators honor their acceptance decisions once made and honor their published policies in deciding whom to accept and to reject. Administrators should thus carefully review their published admissions policies and any new policies to be published. The institution may wish to omit standards and criteria from its policies in order to avoid being pinned down under the contract theory. Conversely, the institution may decide that full disclosure is the best policy. In either case, administrators should make sure that published admissions policies state only what the institution is willing to abide by. If the institution needs to reserve the right to depart from or supplement its published policies, such reservation should be clearly inserted, with counsel's assistance, into all such policies.

Even if a catalogue is not viewed as a contract, a court may hold an institution to a good-faith standard. In *Beukas v. Fairleigh Dickinson University*, 605 A.2d 776 (N.J. Super. Ct. Law Div. 1991), *affirmed*, 605 A.2d 708 (N.J. Super. Ct. App. Div. 1992), former dental students sued the university for closing its dental school when the state withdrew its subsidy. The university pointed to language in the catalogue reserving the right to eliminate programs and schools, arguing that the language was binding on the students. But instead of applying a contract theory, the trial court preferred to analyze the issue using quasi-contract theory, and applied an arbitrariness standard:

[T]his court rejects classic contract doctrine to resolve this dispute. . . . [T]he "true" university-student "contract" is one of mutual obligations implied, not in fact, but by law; it is a quasi-contract which is "created by law, for reasons of justice without regard to expressions of assent by either words or acts" [citing *West Caldwell v. Caldwell*, 26 N.J. 9 (1958)]. . . . This theory is the most efficient and legally-consistent theory to resolve a university-student conflict resulting from an administrative decision to terminate an academic or professional program. The inquiry should be: did the university act in good faith and, if so, did it deal fairly with its students? [605 A.2d at 783, 784].

The court explained its reasoning for using a good-faith standard rather than contract law:

This approach will give courts broader authority for examining university decisionmaking in the administrative area than would a modified standard of judicial deference and will produce a more legally cohesive body of law than will application of classic contract doctrine with its many judicially created exceptions, varying as they must from jurisdiction to jurisdiction [605 A.2d at 784–85].

The state's appellate court upheld the result and the reasoning but stated that if the catalogue was a contract (a question that this court did not attempt to answer), the reservation-of-rights language would have permitted the university to close the dental school.

The existence of a contractual relationship between student and institution is significant if the student wishes to assert constitutional claims based on a property interest. In *Unger v. National Residents Matching Program*, 928 F.2d 1392 (3d Cir. 1991), the plaintiff, admitted to Temple University's residency program in dermatology, challenged the university's decision to terminate the program five months before she was to enroll. Unger claimed constitutional violations of both liberty and property interests. The court rejected the liberty interest claim, stating that Unger was inconvenienced by Temple's actions but was not precluded from seeking other training.

To Unger's claim that Temple's decision deprived her of a property interest, based on her contract with the university, the court replied that the claim failed for two reasons. First, Unger had no legitimate expectation that she would continue her graduate medical training; second, she had no entitlement to the training provided by the program. The court did find that Temple's offer of admission was a contract, but it was not the type of contract that created a property interest enforceable under federal civil rights law (see Section 2.3.3).

Common law developments in employment contract interpretation (see Section 2.2.2) have implications for student admissions as well. Oral promises, the effect of disclaimers, and other issues related to whether a contract exists and how it should be interpreted may affect student challenges to admission decisions. For an examination of some of these issues, see E. Bunting, "The Admissions Process: New Legal Questions Creep Up the Ivory Tower," 60 *West's Educ. Law Rptr.* 691 (1990).

4.1.4. The Principle of Nondiscrimination

Postsecondary institutions are prohibited in varying degrees and by varying legal authorities from discriminating in their admissions process on the basis of race, sex, disability, age, residence, and alien status. The first four are discussed in this section. The other two types—discrimination against nonresidents (residents of other states) and discrimination against aliens (citizens of other countries who are residing in the United States)—are discussed in Sections 4.2.5 and 4.2.6 because the leading cases concern financial aid rather than admissions. The legal principles in these sections also apply generally to admissions. Under these principles, generally speaking, admissions preferences for state residents (see, for example, Cal. Educ. Code §22522) may be permissible (see *Rosenstock v. Board of Governors of the University of North Carolina,* 423 F. Supp. 1321, 1326–27 (M.D.N.C. 1976)), but among state residents a preference for those who are United States citizens or a bar to those who are nationals of particular foreign countries is probably impermissible (see *Tayyari v. New Mexico State University,* 495 F. Supp. 1365 (D.N.M. 1980)). For an analysis of residency requirements, see M. Olivas, "*Plyler v. Doe, Toll v. Moreno* and Postsecondary Admissions: Undocumented Adults and Enduring Disability," 15 *J. Law & Educ.* 19 (1986).

4.1.4.1. Race. It is clear under the Fourteenth Amendment's equal protection clause that, in the absence of a "compelling state interest" (see Section 4.1.5), no public institution may discriminate in admissions on the basis of race. The leading case is *Brown v. Board of Education,* 347 U.S. 483 (1954), which, although it concerned elementary and secondary schools, clearly applies to postsecondary education as well. The Supreme Court affirmed its relevance to higher education in *Florida ex rel. Hawkins v. Board of Control,* 350 U.S. 413 (1956). Cases involving postsecondary education have generally considered racial segregation within a state postsecondary system rather than within a single institution, and suits have been brought under Title VI of the Civil Rights Act of 1964 as well as the Constitution. These cases are discussed in Section 12.4.2.

Although most of the racial segregation cases focus on a broad array of issues, a recent decision by the U.S. Supreme Court addressed admissions issues, among others. In *United States v. Fordice,* 112 S. Ct. 2727 (1992), private plaintiffs and the U.S. Department of Justice asserted that the Mississippi public higher education system was segregated, in violation of both the U.S. Constitution and Title VI of the Civil Rights Act of 1964. Although a federal trial judge had found the state system to be in compliance with both Title VI and the Constitution, a federal appellate court and the U.S. Supreme Court disagreed. (This case is discussed at length in Section 12.4.2.)

Justice White, writing for a unanimous Court, found that the state's higher education system retained vestiges of its prior de jure segregation. With regard to admissions, Justice White cited the state's practice (initiated in 1963, just prior to Title VI's taking effect) of requiring all applicants for admission to the three flagship universities (which were predominantly white) to have a minimum composite score of 15 on the American College Testing (ACT) Program. Testimony had demonstrated that the average ACT score for white students was

18, and the average ACT score for black students was 7. Justice White wrote, "Without doubt, these requirements restrict the range of choices of entering students as to which institution they may attend in a way that perpetuates segregation" (112 S. Ct. at 2739).

These admissions standards were particularly revealing of continued segregation, according to Justice White, when one considered that institutions given the same mission within the state (regional universities) had different admissions standards, depending on the race of the predominant student group. For example, predominantly white regional universities had ACT requirements of 18 or 15, compared to minimum requirements of 13 at the black universities. Because the differential admissions standards were "remnants of the dual system with a continuing discriminatory effect" (112 S. Ct. at 2739), the state was required to articulate an educational reason for those disparities, and it had not done so.

Furthermore, the institutions looked only at ACT scores and did not consider high school grades as a mitigating factor for applicants who could not meet the minimum ACT score. The gap between the grades of black and white applicants was narrower than the gap between their ACT scores, "suggesting that an admissions formula which included grades would increase the number of black students eligible for automatic admission to all of Mississippi's public universities" (112 S. Ct. at 2740). Although the state had argued that grade inflation and the lack of comparability among high schools' course offerings and grading practices made grades an unreliable indicator, the Court dismissed that argument:

> In our view, such justification is inadequate because the ACT was originally adopted for discriminatory purposes, the current requirement is traceable to that decision and seemingly continues to have segregative effects, and the State has so far failed to show that the "ACT-only" admission standard is not susceptible to elimination without eroding sound educational policy [112 S. Ct. at 2740].

The use of high school grades as well as scores on standardized tests is common in higher education admissions decisions, and the state's attempt to rely solely on ACT scores was an important element of the Court's finding of continued segregation.

Although most challenges to allegedly discriminatory admissions requirements have come from black students, Asian and Latino students have filed challenges as well. In *United States v. League of United Latin American Citizens*, 793 F.2d 636 (5th Cir. 1986), black and Latino college students raised Title VI and constitutional challenges to the state's requirement that college students pass a reading and mathematics skills test before enrolling in more than six hours of professional education courses at Texas public institutions. Passing rates on these tests were substantially lower for minority students than for white, non-Latino students.

Although the trial court had enjoined the practice, the appellate court vacated the injunction, noting that the state had validated the tests and that they were appropriate:

The State's duty . . . to eliminate the vestiges of past discrimination would
indeed be violated were it to thrust upon minority students, both as role models
and as pedagogues, teachers whose basic knowledge and skills were inferior
to those required of majority race teachers [793 F.2d at 643].

In response to the students' equal protection claim, the court found that the state had demonstrated a compelling interest in teacher competency and that the test was a valid predictor of success in the courses. Because the students could retake the test until they passed it, their admission was only delayed, not denied. In response to the students' liberty interest claim, the court found a valid liberty interest in pursuing a chosen profession but also found that the state could require a reasonable examination for entry into that profession.

Latino students and civil rights groups also challenged the state's funding for public colleges and universities located near the Mexican border, arguing that they were more poorly funded because of their high proportion of Latino students. A jury, applying the state constitution's requirement of equal access to education, found that the state higher education system did not provide equal access to citizens in southern Texas, although it also found that state officials had not discriminated against these persons (K. Mangan, "Texas Jury Faults State on Equal Access to Top Universities," *Chron. Higher Educ.*, Nov. 27, 1991, A25). A state court judge later ordered the state to eliminate the funding inequities among state institutions (K. Mangan, "9 State Colleges in South Texas to Get Massive Budget Increase," *Chron. Higher Educ.*, June 23, 1993, A23). But in *Richards v. League of United Latin American Citizens,* 868 S.W.2d 306 (Tex. 1993), the Texas Supreme Court ruled later that year that allegedly inequitable resource allocation to predominantly Hispanic public colleges did not violate students' equal protection rights.

Asian students have challenged the admissions practices of several institutions, alleging that they either have "quotas" limiting the number of Asians who may be admitted or that the institutions exclude Asians from minority admissions programs. Complaints filed with the Education Department's Office for Civil Rights, which enforces Title VI (see this volume, Section 12.4.2), have resulted in changes in admissions practices at both public and private colleges and universities. For a discussion of this issue, see Note, "Assuring Equal Access of Asian Americans to Highly Selective Universities," 90 *Yale L.J.* 659 (1989).

In addition to the Constitution's equal protection clause and the desegregation criteria developed under Title VI, there are two other major legal bases for attacking racial discrimination in higher education. The first is the civil rights statute called "Section 1981" (42 U.S.C. §1981). A post–Civil War statute guaranteeing the freedom to contract, Section 1981 has particular significance because (like Title VI) it applies to private as well as public institutions. In the leading case of *Runyon v. McCrary*, 427 U.S. 160 (1976), the U.S. Supreme Court used Section 1981 to prohibit two private, white elementary schools from discriminating against blacks in their admissions policies. Since the Court has applied Section 1981 to discrimination against white persons as well as blacks (*McDonald v. Santa Fe Trail Transportation Co.*, 427 U.S. 273 (1976)), this statute would also apparently prohibit predominantly minority private institutions from discriminating in admissions against white students.

The other legal source is federal income tax law. In Revenue Ruling 71–447, 1971–2 C.B. 230 (*Cumulative Bulletin*, an annual multivolume compilation of various tax documents published by the IRS), the Internal Revenue Service revised its former policy and ruled that schools practicing racial discrimination were violating public policy and should be denied tax-exempt status. Other IRS rulings enlarged on this basic rule. Revenue Procedure 72–54, 1972–2 C.B. 834, requires schools to publicize their nondiscrimination policies. Revenue Procedure 75–50, 1975–2 C.B. 587, requires that a school carry the burden of "show[ing] affirmatively . . . that it has adopted a racially nondiscriminatory policy as to students" and also establishes record-keeping and other guidelines through which a school can demonstrate its compliance. And Revenue Ruling 75–231, 1975–1 C.B. 158, furnishes a series of hypothetical cases to illustrate when a church-affiliated school would be considered to be discriminating and in danger of losing tax-exempt status. The U.S. Supreme Court upheld the basic policy of Revenue Ruling 71–447 in *Bob Jones University v. United States*, 461 U.S. 574 (1983), which is discussed in Section 12.2.1.

The combined impact of these various legal sources—the equal protection clause, Title VI, Section 1981, and IRS tax rulings—is clear: neither public nor private postsecondary institutions may maintain admissions policies (with a possible exception for affirmative action policies, as discussed in Section 4.1.5) that discriminate against students on the basis of race, nor may states maintain plans or practices that perpetuate racial segregation in a statewide system of postsecondary education.

4.1.4.2. Sex. Title IX of the Education Amendments of 1972 (20 U.S.C. §1681 *et seq.*) (see Section 12.4.3) is the primary legal source governing sex discrimination in admissions policies. While Title IX and its implementing regulations, 34 C.F.R. Part 106, apply nondiscrimination principles to both public and private institutions receiving federal funds, there are special exemptions concerning admissions. For the purposes of applying these admissions exemptions, each "administratively separate unit" of an institution is considered a separate institution (34 C.F.R. §106.15(b)). An "administratively separate unit" is "a school, department, or college . . . admission to which is independent of admission to any other component of such institution" (34 C.F.R. §106.2(o)). Private undergraduate institutions are not prohibited from discriminating in admissions on the basis of sex (20 U.S.C. §1681(a)(1), 34 C.F.R. §106.15(d)). Nor are public undergraduate institutions that have always been single-sex institutions (20 U.S.C. §1681(a)(5), 34 C.F.R. §106.15(e); but compare the *Hogan* case, discussed later in this section). In addition, religious institutions, including all or any of their administratively separate units, may be exempted from nondiscrimination. The remaining institutions, which are prohibited from discriminating in admissions, are (1) graduate schools; (2) professional schools, unless they are part of an undergraduate institution exempted from Title IX's admissions requirements (see 34 C.F.R. §106.2(m)); (3) vocational schools, unless they are part of an undergraduate institution exempted from Title IX's admissions requirements (see 34 C.F.R. §106.2(n)); and (4) public undergraduate institutions that are not, or have not always been, single-sex schools.[1]

Institutions subject to Title IX admissions requirements are prohibited from treating persons differently on the basis of sex in any phase of admissions and recruitment (34 C.F.R. §§106.21–106.23). Specifically, Section 106.21(b) of the regulations provides that a covered institution, in its admissions process, shall not

  (i) Give preference to one person over another on the basis of sex, by ranking applicants separately on such basis, or otherwise;

 (ii) Apply numerical limitations upon the number or proportion of persons of either sex who may be admitted; or

(iii) Otherwise treat one individual differently from another on the basis of sex.

Section 106.21(c) prohibits covered institutions from treating the sexes differently in regard to "actual or potential parental, family, or marital status"; from discriminating against applicants because of pregnancy or conditions relating to childbirth; and from making preadmission inquiries concerning marital status. Sections 106.22 and 106.23(b) prohibit institutions from favoring single-sex or predominantly single-sex schools in their admissions or recruitment practices, if such practices have "the effect of discriminating on the basis of sex."

---

[1]The admissions exemption for private undergraduate institutions in the regulations may be broader than that authorized by the Title IX statute. For an argument that "administratively separate" professional and vocational components of private undergraduate institutions should not be exempt and that private undergraduate schools which are primarily professional and vocational in character should not be exempt, see W. Kaplin & M. McGillicuddy, "Scope of Exemption for Private Undergraduate Institutions from Admissions Requirements of Title IX," memorandum printed in 121 *Congressional Record* 1091 (94th Cong., 1st Sess., 1975).

Institutions that are exempt from Title IX admissions requirements are not necessarily free to discriminate at will on the basis of sex. Some will be caught in the net of other statutes or of constitutional equal protection principles. A state statute such as the Massachusetts statute prohibiting sex discrimination in vocational training institutions may catch other exempted undergraduate programs (Mass. Gen. Laws Ann. ch. 151C, §2A(a)). More important, the Fourteenth Amendment's equal protection clause places restrictions on public undergraduate schools, even if they are single-sex schools exempt from Title IX.

After a period of uncertainty concerning the extent to which equal protection principles would restrict a public institution's admissions policies, the U.S. Supreme Court considered the question in *Mississippi University for Women v. Hogan,* 458 U.S. 718 (1982). In this case, the plaintiff challenged an admissions policy that excluded males from a professional nursing school. Ignoring the dissenting justices' protestations that Mississippi provided baccalaureate nursing programs at other state coeducational institutions, the majority of five struck down the institution's policy as unconstitutional sex discrimination. In the process, the Court developed an important synthesis of constitutional principles applicable to sex discrimination claims. These principles would apply not only to admissions but also to all other aspects of a public institution's operations:

> Because the challenged policy expressly discriminates among applicants on the basis of gender, it is subject to scrutiny under the equal protection clause of the Fourteenth Amendment (*Reed v. Reed,* 404 U.S. 71, 75 (1971)). That this statute discriminates against males rather than against females does not exempt it from scrutiny or reduce the standard of review (*Caban v. Mohammed,* 441 U.S. 380, 394 (1979); *Orr v. Orr,* 440 U.S. 268, 279 (1979)). Our decisions also establish that the party seeking to uphold a statute that classifies individuals on the basis of their gender must carry the burden of showing an "exceedingly persuasive justification" for the classification (*Kirchberg v. Feenstra,* 450 U.S. 455, 561 (1981); *Personnel Administrator of Massachusetts v. Feeney,* 442 U.S. 256, 273 (1979)). The burden is met only by showing at least that the classification serves "important governmental objectives and that the discriminatory means employed" are "substantially related to the achievement of those objectives" (*Wangler v. Druggists Mutual Insurance Co.,* 446 U.S. 142, 150 (1980)).
>
> Although the test for determining the validity of a gender-based classification is straightforward, it must be applied free of fixed notions concerning the roles and abilities of males and females. Care must be taken in ascertaining whether the statutory objective itself reflects archaic and stereotypic notions. Thus, if the statutory objective is to exclude or "protect" members of one gender because they are presumed to suffer from an inherent handicap or to be innately inferior, the objective itself is illegitimate (see *Frontiero v. Richardson,* 411 U.S. 677, 684–85 (1973) (plurality opinion)).
>
> If the state's objective is legitimate and important, we next determine whether the requisite direct, substantial relationship between objective and

means is present. The purpose of requiring that close relationship is to assure that the validity of a classification is determined through reasoned analysis rather than through the mechanical application of traditional, often inaccurate, assumptions about the proper roles of men and women [458 U.S. at 723–24].

Applying the principles regarding the legitimacy and importance of the state's objective, the Court noted that the state's justification for prohibiting men from enrolling in the nursing program was to compensate for discrimination against women. On the contrary, the Court pointed out, women had never been denied entry to the nursing profession, and limiting admission to women actually perpetuated the stereotype that nursing is "women's work." The state had made no showing that women needed preferential treatment in being admitted to nursing programs, and the Court did not believe that that was the state's purpose in discriminating against men.

Even if the state had a valid compensatory objective, its policy would still be unconstitutional, according to the Court, because it also violated other equal protection principles:

> The state has made no showing that the gender-based classification is substantially and directly related to its proposed compensatory objective. To the contrary, MUW's policy of permitting men to attend classes as auditors fatally undermines its claim that women, at least those in the school of nursing, are adversely affected by the presence of men.
>
> MUW permits men who audit to participate fully in classes. Additionally, both men and women take part in continuing education courses offered by the school of nursing, in which regular nursing students also can enroll. . . . The uncontroverted record reveals that admitting men to nursing classes does not affect teaching style, . . . and that men in coeducational nursing schools do not dominate the classroom. . . . In sum, the record in this case is flatly inconsistent with the claim that excluding men from the school of nursing is necessary to reach any of MUW's educational goals [458 U.S. at 730–31].

The Court's opinion on its face invalidated single-sex admissions policies only at MUW's school of nursing and, by extension, other public postsecondary nursing schools. The majority noted, "We decline to address the question of whether MUW's admissions policy, as applied to males seeking admission to schools other than the school of nursing, violates the Fourteenth Amendment," and "We are not faced with the question of whether states can provide 'separate but equal' undergraduate institutions for males and females." But the majority's reasoning cannot so easily be confined, as two of the three dissenting opinions pointed out. It is likely that this reasoning would also invalidate single-sex policies in programs other than nursing and in entire institutions. The most arguable exception to this broad reading would be a single-sex policy that redresses the effects of past discrimination on a professional program in which one sex is substantially underrepresented. But even such a compensatory policy would be a form of explicit sexual quota, which could be questioned by analogy to the racial affirmative action cases (this volume, Section 4.1.5).

Whatever the remaining ambiguity about the scope of the *Hogan* decision, it will not be resolved by further litigation at the Mississippi University for Women. After the Supreme Court decision, MUW's board of trustees—perhaps anticipating a broad application of the Court's reasoning—voted to admit men to all divisions of the university.

The *Hogan* opinion provided important guidance in a challenge to the lawfulness of male-only public military colleges. In *United States v. Commonwealth of Virginia*, 766 F. Supp. 1407, *vacated*, 976 F.2d 890 (4th Cir. 1992), the U.S. Department of Justice challenged the admissions policies of the Virginia Military Institute (VMI), which admitted only men. The government claimed that those policies violated the equal protection clause (it did not include a Title IX claim, since military academies and historically single-sex institutions are exempt from Title IX). Equal protection challenges to sex discrimination require the state to demonstrate "an exceedingly persuasive justification" for the classification (*Hogan*, 458 U.S. at 739). In this case, the state argued that enhancing diversity by offering a distinctive, single-sex military education to men was an important state interest. The district court found that the single-sex policy was justified because of the benefits of a single-sex education, and that requiring VMI to admit women would "fundamentally alter" the "distinctive ends" of the educational system (766 F. Supp. at 1411).

The appellate court vacated the district court's opinion, stating that Virginia had not articulated an important objective sufficient to overcome the burden on equal protection. While the appellate court agreed with the trial court's finding that the admission of women would materially affect several key elements of VMI's program—physical training, lack of privacy, and the adversative approach to character development—it was homogeneity of gender, not maleness, that justified the program (976 F.2d at 897). The appellate court also accepted the trial court's findings that single-sex education has important benefits. But these findings did not support the trial court's conclusion that VMI's male-only policy passed constitutional muster. Although VMI's single-gender education and "citizen-soldier" philosophy were permissible, the state's exclusion of women from such a program was not, and no other public postsecondary education institution in Virginia was devoted to educating only one gender.

The court did not order VMI to admit women but remanded the case to the district court to give Virginia the option to (1) admit women to VMI, (2) establish parallel institutions or programs for women, or (3) terminate state support for VMI. On appeal, the U.S. Supreme Court refused to hear the case (508 U.S. 946 (1993)). Following that action, the trustees of VMI voted to underwrite a parallel program at a neighboring private women's college, Mary Baldwin College. The program differed in many respects, however, from the VMI approach to military education; it lacked many of the military aspects of the VMI program (the wearing of uniforms, the "adversative method" of leadership development), and Mary Baldwin did not offer the range of degrees that is offered by VMI.

The U.S. Department of Justice challenged the plan, saying that it was based on gender stereotypes, and asked the court to order VMI to admit women and to integrate them into its full program. A trial judge approved the parallel program at Mary Baldwin College, and a divided panel of the U.S. Court of Appeals for the Fourth Circuit affirmed, finding that providing single-gender education was a legitimate objective of the state, and that the leadership program at Mary Baldwin College was "sufficiently comparable" to the VMI program to satisfy the demands of the equal protection clause (44 F.3d 1229 (4th Cir. 1995)). The dissenting judge argued that the state's justification for excluding women from VMI was not "exceedingly persuasive" and that the women's leadership program at Mary Baldwin College did not provide substantially equal tangible and intangible educational benefits; he thus concluded that maintaining VMI as a single-sex public institution violated the equal protection clause. A petition for rehearing *en banc* was denied.

The United States again asked the Supreme Court to review the appellate court's ruling, and this time the Court agreed. In a 7-to-1 decision (Justice Thomas did not participate), the Court ruled that VMI's exclusion of women violated the equal protection clause (116 S. Ct. 2264 (1996)). Since strict scrutiny is reserved for classifications based on race or national origin (see Section 4.1.4.1), the Court used intermediate scrutiny, which Justice Ginsburg, the author of the majority opinion, termed "skeptical scrutiny," to analyze the state of Virginia's claim that single-sex education provides important educational benefits. Reviewing the state's history of providing higher education for women, the Court concluded that women had first been excluded from public higher education and then admitted to once all-male public universities, but that no public, single-sex institution had been established for women, and thus the state had not provided equal benefits for women. With regard to the state's argument that VMI's adversative training method provided important educational benefits that could not be made available to women and thus their admission would "destroy" VMI's unique approach to education, the Court noted that both parties had agreed that some women could meet all of the physical standards imposed upon VMI cadets; moreover, the experience with women cadets in the military academies suggested that the state's fear that the presence of women would force change upon VMI was based on overbroad generalizations about women as a group, rather than on an analysis of how individual women could perform.

The Court then turned to the issue of the remedy for VMI's constitutional violation. Characterizing the women's leadership program at Mary Baldwin College as "unequal in tangible and intangible facilities" and offering no opportunity for the type of military training for which VMI is famous, the Court stressed the differences between the two programs and institutions in terms of the quality of the faculty, the range of degrees offered, athletic and sports facilities, endowments, and the status of the degree earned by students. Criticizing the Fourth Circuit for applying an overly deferential standard of review that the Court characterized as one "of its own invention," the Court reversed its decision and held that the separate program did not cure the constitutional violation.

Chief Justice Rehnquist voted with the majority but wrote a separate concurring opinion because he disagreed with Justice Ginsburg's analysis of the remedy. The "parallel program" at Mary Baldwin College was "distinctly inferior" to VMI, said Justice Rehnquist, but the state could cure the constitutional violation by providing a public institution for women that offered the "same quality of education and [was] of the same overall calibre" as VMI. Justice Rehnquist's opinion thus differs sharply from that of Justice Ginsburg, who characterized the exclusion of women as the constitutional violation, while Justice Rehnquist characterized the violation as the maintenance of an all-male institution without providing a comparable institution for women.

Justice Scalia, the sole dissenter, attacked the Court's interpretation of equal protection jurisprudence, saying that the Court had used a higher standard than the intermediate scrutiny that is typically used to analyze categories based on gender. Furthermore, stated Justice Scalia, since the Constitution does not specifically forbid distinctions based upon gender, the political process, not the courts, should be used to change state behavior. Finding that the maintenance of single-sex education is an important educational objective, Justice Scalia would have upheld the continued exclusion of women from VMI.

The only other all-male public college in the United States, The Citadel, was ordered by a panel of the U.S. Court of Appeals for the Fourth Circuit in 1993 to admit a female applicant whom that college had admitted on the mistaken belief that she was male (*Faulkner v. Jones,* 1993 U.S. App. LEXIS 29885 (4th Cir. 1993); see also "Military College Is Ordered to Admit Woman," *New York Times,* Nov. 18, 1993, B16). The court ordered that she be admitted as a day student and remanded to the district court the issue of whether she can become a full member of the college's corps of cadets. On remand, the trial judge ordered that she become a member of the corps of cadets. The college appealed this ruling, and an appeals court panel ordered her status as a cadet to be delayed until the court could hear the college's arguments. The court later ruled that Ms. Faulkner be admitted to the Citadel. Although Ms. Faulkner dropped out after a few days, several women were admitted to the Citadel in the fall of 1996.

Important as *Hogan* and *U.S. v. Virginia* may be to the law regarding sex discrimination in admissions, it is only part of the bigger picture, which already includes Title IX. Thus, to view the law in its current state, one must look both to the equal protection clause (for public institutions) and to Title IX. *Hogan* and its progeny have at least limited, and apparently undermined, the Title IX exemption for public undergraduate institutions that have always had single-sex admissions policies (20 U.S.C. §1681(a)(5), 34 C.F.R. §106.15(e)). Thus, given the outcome of the disputes over public single-sex military colleges, the only programs and institutions that are still legally free to have single-sex admissions policies are (1) private undergraduate institutions and their constituent programs and (2) religious institutions, including their graduate, professional, and vocational programs, if they have obtained a waiver of Title IX admission requirements on religious grounds (20 U.S.C. §1681(a)(3); 34 C.F.R. §106.12).

Another potential area for sex discrimination in admissions is in the use of standardized tests for making admission decisions. Some of the standardized tests used to make admission decisions—the Scholastic Aptitude Test, for example—have been challenged because of the systematic gender differences in scores. When these test scores are used to make decisions about awarding scholarships, they may be especially vulnerable to legal challenge. In *Sharif v. New York State Education Department* (discussed in Section 4.2.3), a federal district court ruled that this practice violated Title IX and the Fourteenth Amendment's equal protection clause. The American Civil Liberties Union has filed a sex discrimination complaint with the Office for Civil Rights, alleging that the use of scores on the Scholastic Aptitude Test to determine the winners of National Merit Scholarships disproportionately favors boys (M. Winerip, "Merit Scholarship Program Faces Sex Bias Complaint," *New York Times*, Feb. 16, 1994, A18). For analysis of the potential discriminatory effects of standardized testing, see K. Connor and E. Vargyas, "The Legal Implications of Gender Bias in Standardized Testing," *Berkeley Women's Law J.* 13 (1992).

In addition to Title IX, other laws include prohibitions on sex discrimination in admissions. For example, one section of the Public Health Service Act's provisions on nurse education (42 U.S.C. §298(b)(2)) prohibits the secretary of health and human services from making grants, loan guarantees, or interest subsidy payments to schools of nursing unless the schools provide "assurances satisfactory to the Secretary that the school will not discriminate on the basis of sex in the admission of individuals to its training programs."

4.1.4.3. Disability. The country's conscience has awakened to the problem of discrimination against people with disabilities. Accommodating students with disabilities is a particularly significant issue for colleges and universities because of the sheer numbers of these students. According to a study by the American Council on Education, in 1992 nearly one in eleven freshmen reported that they had a disability, compared with one in thirty-eight in 1978 (*College Freshmen with Disabilities: a Statistical Profile* (American Council on Education, 1992)). And disability discrimination complaints by students are increasing in proportion to their growth in numbers. In 1992, for example, the Education Department found that forty-six colleges had violated the rights of either students or employees with disabilities (S. Jaschik, "46 Colleges Found to Have Violated Rights of Disabled, U.S. Documents Show," *Chron. Higher Educ.*, Apr. 21, 1993, A18).

Two pieces of landmark federal legislation—Section 504 of the Rehabilitation Act of 1973 (29 U.S.C. §794) and the Americans with Disabilities Act (ADA) (42 U.S.C. §12101 *et seq.*)—prohibit discrimination against individuals with disabilities. Before those laws were passed, these individuals had been the subject of a few scattered federal provisions (such as 20 U.S.C. §1684, which prohibits discrimination against blind persons by institutions receiving federal funds) and a few constitutional equal protection cases (such as *PARC v. Pennsylvania*, 334 F. Supp. 1257 (E.D. Pa. 1971), which challenged discrimination against disabled students by public elementary and secondary schools). But none of these developments have had nearly the impact on postsecondary admissions that Section 504 and the ADA have.

As applied to postsecondary education, Section 504 generally prohibits discrimination on the basis of disability in federally funded programs and activities (see this volume, Section 12.4.4). Section 104.42 of the implementing regulations, 34 C.F.R. Part 104, prohibits discrimination on the basis of disability in admissions and recruitment. This section contains several specific provisions similar to those prohibiting sex discrimination in admissions under Title IX (see this volume, Section 4.1.4.2). These provisions prohibit (1) the imposition of limitations on "the number or proportion of individuals with disabilities who may be admitted" (§104.42(b)(1)); (2) the use of any admissions criterion or test "that has a disproportionate, adverse effect" on individuals with disabilities, unless the criterion or test, as used, is shown to predict success validly and no alternative, nondiscriminatory criterion or test is available (§104.42(b)(2)); and (3) any preadmission inquiry about whether the applicant has a disability, unless the recipient needs the information in order to correct the effects of past discrimination or to overcome past conditions that resulted in limited participation by people with disabilities (§§104.42(b)(4) and 104.42(c)).

These prohibitions apply to discrimination directed against "qualified" individuals with disabilities. A disabled person is qualified, with respect to postsecondary and vocational services, if he or she "meets the academic and technical standards requisite to admission or participation in the recipient's education program or activity" (§104.3(k)(3)). Thus, while the regulations do not prohibit an institution from denying admission to a person with a disability who does not meet the institution's "academic and technical" admissions standards, they do prohibit an institution from denying admission on the basis of the disability as such. (After a student is admitted, however, the institution can make confidential inquiry concerning the disability (34 C.F.R. §104.42(b)(4)); in this way the institution can obtain advance information about disabilities that may require accommodation.)

In addition to these prohibitions, the institution has an affirmative duty to ascertain that its admissions tests are structured to accommodate applicants with disabilities that impair sensory, manual, or speaking skills, unless the test is intended to measure these skills. Such adapted tests must be offered as often and in as timely a way as other admissions tests and must be "administered in facilities that, on the whole, are accessible" to people with disabilities (§104.42(b)(3)).

In *Southeastern Community College v. Davis,* 442 U.S. 397 (1979), the U.S. Supreme Court issued its first interpretation of Section 504. The case concerned a nursing school applicant who had been denied admission because she is deaf. The Supreme Court ruled that an "otherwise qualified handicapped individual" is one who is qualified *in spite of* (rather than except for) his disability. Since an applicant's disability is therefore relevant to his or her qualification for a specific program, Section 504 does not preclude a college or university from imposing "reasonable physical qualifications" on applicants for admission, where such qualifications are necessary for participation in the school's program. The Department of Education's regulations implementing Section 504 provide that a disabled applicant is "qualified" if he or she meets "the academic and technical standards" for admission; the Supreme Court has made it clear, however, that "technical standards" may sometimes encompass reasonable physical requirements. Under *Davis,* an applicant's failure to meet such requirements can be a legitimate ground for rejection.

The Court's 9-to-0 ruling was a disappointment to many advocates on behalf of people with disabilities. They feared the decision's effects on their entry into academic and professional pursuits and, more generally, on an institution's willingness to accommodate the needs of people with disabilities. The impact of *Davis* may be substantially limited, however, by the rather narrow and specific factual context in which the case arose. The plaintiff, who was severely hearing-impaired, sought admission to a nursing program. The college denied her admission, believing that she would not be able to perform nursing duties in a safe manner and could not participate fully in the clinical portion of the program.

The U.S. District Court had decided the case in favor of the college, concluding that the plaintiff's disability "prevents her from safely performing in both her training program and her proposed profession" and that she therefore was not "otherwise qualified" under Section 504 (424 F. Supp. 1341 (E.D.N.C. 1976)). The U.S. Court of Appeals had reversed, concluding that the district court had erred in taking the plaintiff's handicap into account in determining whether she was "otherwise qualified" (574 F.2d 1158 (4th Cir. 1978)). Determining that the district court had the better of the argument, the Supreme Court reversed the appellate court:

Section 504 by its terms does not compel educational institutions to disregard the disabilities of handicapped individuals or to make substantial modifications in their programs to allow disabled persons to participate. Instead, it requires only that an "otherwise qualified handicapped individual" not be excluded from participation in a federally funded program "solely by reason of his handicap," indicating only that mere possession of a handicap is not a permissible ground for assuming an inability to function in a particular context.

The court [of appeals], however, believed that the "otherwise qualified" persons protected by Section 504 include those who would be able to meet the requirements of a particular program in every respect except as to limitations imposed by their handicap. Taken literally, this holding would prevent an institution from taking into account any limitation resulting from the handicap, however disabling. It assumes, in effect, that a person need not meet legitimate physical requirements in order to be "otherwise qualified." We think the understanding of the district court is closer to the plain meaning of the statutory language. An otherwise qualified person is one who is able to meet all of a program's requirements in spite of his handicap [442 U.S. at 405–07].

The Court cited the regulations interpreting Section 504, noting that the individual must be able to meet both academic and "technical" standards in order to be deemed a "qualified" individual with a disability (34 C.F.R. §104.3(k)(3)). Furthermore, the Court noted, the regulations emphasize that legitimate physical qualifications could be essential to participation in particular programs.

The plaintiff had argued that Section 504 requires affirmative action and that the court should order the college to modify the program by giving her individualized instruction, exempting her from required courses, and adapting the program in other ways to enable her to participate. The Court rejected this argument:

[I]t . . . is reasonably clear that Section 84.44(a) [of the regulations, now 34 C.F.R. §104.44(a)] does not encompass the kind of curricular changes that would be necessary to accommodate respondent in the nursing program. In light of respondent's inability to function in clinical courses without close supervision, Southeastern with prudence could allow her to take only academic classes. Whatever benefits respondent might realize from such a course of study, she would not receive even a rough equivalent of the training a nursing program normally gives. Such a fundamental alteration in the nature of a program is far more than the "modification" the regulation requires.

Moreover, an interpretation of the regulations that required the extensive modifications necessary to include respondent in the nursing program would raise grave doubts about their validity. If these regulations were to require substantial adjustments in existing programs beyond those necessary to eliminate discrimination against otherwise qualified individuals, they would do more than clarify the meaning of Section 504. Instead, they would constitute an unauthorized extension of the obligations imposed by that statute.

The language and structure of the Rehabilitation Act of 1973 reflect a recognition by Congress of the distinction between the evenhanded treatment of qualified handicapped persons and affirmative efforts to overcome the disabilities caused by handicaps. . . . Congress understood [that] accommodation of the needs of handicapped individuals may require affirmative action and knew how to provide for it in those instances where it wished to do so. . . .

Here neither the language, purpose, nor history of Section 504 reveals an intent to impose an affirmative action obligation on all recipients of federal funds. Accordingly, we hold that, even if HEW has attempted to create such an obligation itself, it lacks the authority to do so [442 U.S. at 409–12].

The Court carefully limited its holding to the circumstances of this case, noting that technological advances might one day enable certain persons with disabilities to qualify for certain programs that they were not presently qualified for.

It is important to emphasize that *Davis* involved admission to a professional, clinical training program. The demands of such a program, designed to train students in the practice of a profession, raise far different considerations from those involved in admission to an undergraduate or a graduate academic program, or even a nonclinically oriented professional school. While the Court approved the imposition of "reasonable physical qualifications," it did so only for requirements that the institution can justify as necessary to the applicant's successful participation in the particular program involved. In *Davis*, the college had shown that an applicant's ability to understand speech without reliance on lipreading was necessary to ensure patient safety and to enable the student to realize the full benefit of its nursing program. For programs without clinical components, or without professional training goals, it would be much more difficult for the institution to justify such physical requirements. Even for other professional programs, the justification might be much more difficult than in *Davis*. In a law school program, for example, the safety factor would be lacking. Moreover, in most law schools, clinical training is offered as an elective rather than a required course. By enrolling only in the nonclinical courses, a deaf student would be able to complete the required program with the help of an interpreter.

Furthermore, the Court did not say that affirmative action is never required to accommodate the needs of disabled applicants. Although the Court asserted that Section 504 does not require institutions "to lower or to effect substantial modifications of standards" or to make "fundamental alteration[s] in the nature of a program," the Court did suggest that less substantial and burdensome program adjustments may sometimes be required. The Court also discussed, and did not question, the regulation requiring institutions to provide certain "auxiliary aids," such as interpreters for students with hearing impairments, to qualified students with disabilities (see Sections 5.3.1 and 12.4.4). This issue was addressed in *United States v. Board of Trustees for the University of Alabama*,

908 F.2d 740 (11th Cir. 1990), in which the court ordered the university to provide additional transportation for students with disabilities. Moreover, the Court
said nothing that in any way precludes institutions from voluntarily making
major program modifications for applicants who are disabled.

Several appellate court cases have applied the teachings of *Davis* to other admissions problems. The courts in these cases have refined the *Davis* analysis,
especially in clarifying the burdens of proof in a discrimination suit under Section 504. In *Pushkin v. Regents of the University of Colorado*, 658 F.2d 1372 (10th
Cir. 1981), the court affirmed the district court's decision that the plaintiff, a
medical doctor suffering from multiple sclerosis, had been wrongfully denied
admission to the university's psychiatric residency program. Agreeing that *Davis*
permitted consideration of handicaps in determining whether an applicant is
"otherwise qualified" for admission, the court outlined what the plaintiff had
to prove in order to establish his case of discrimination:

1. The plaintiff must establish a prima facie case by showing that he was
   an otherwise qualified handicapped person *apart from* his handicap,
   and was rejected under circumstances which gave rise to the inference
   that his rejection was based solely on his handicap.

2. Once plaintiff establishes his prima facie case, defendants have the burden of going forward and proving that plaintiff was not an otherwise
   qualified handicapped person—that is, one who is able to meet all of
   the program's requirements *in spite of* his handicap—or that his rejection
   from the program was for reasons other than his handicap.

3. The plaintiff then has the burden of going forward with rebuttal evidence
   showing that the defendants' reasons for rejecting the plaintiff are based
   on misconceptions or unfounded factual conclusions, and that reasons
   articulated for the rejection other than the handicap encompass unjustified consideration of the handicap itself [658 F.2d at 1387].

In another post-*Davis* case, *Doe v. New York University*, 666 F.2d 761 (2d Cir.
1981), the court held that the university had not violated Section 504 when it
denied readmission to a woman with a long history of "borderline personality"
disorders. This court also set out the elements of the case a plaintiff must make
to comply with the *Davis* reading of Section 504:

Accordingly, we hold that in a suit under Section 504 the plaintiff may make
out a prima facie case by showing that he is a handicapped person under the
Act and that, although he is qualified apart from his handicap, he was denied
admission or employment because of his handicap. The burden then shifts
to the institution or employer to rebut the inference that the handicap was
improperly taken into account by going forward with evidence that the handicap
is relevant to qualifications for the position sought (cf. *Dothard v. Rawlinson*,

433 U.S. 321 . . . (1977)). The plaintiff must then bear the ultimate burden of showing by a preponderance of the evidence that in spite of the handicap he is qualified and, where the defendant claims and comes forward with some evidence that the plaintiff's handicap renders him less qualified than other successful applicants, that he is at least as well qualified as other applicants who were accepted [666 F.2d at 776–77].

The *Doe* summary of burdens of proof is articulated differently from the *Pushkin* summary, and the *Doe* court disavowed any reliance on *Pushkin*. In contrast to the *Pushkin* court, the *Doe* court determined that a defendant institution in a Section 504 case "does not have the burden, once it shows that the handicap is relevant to reasonable qualifications for readmission (or admission), of proving that . . . [the plaintiff is not an otherwise qualified handicapped person]" (666 F.2d at 777 n.7).

The *Doe* case is also noteworthy because, in deciding whether the plaintiff was "otherwise qualified," the court considered the fact that she had a recurring illness, even though it was not present at the time of the readmission decision. This was an appropriate factor to consider because the illness could reappear and affect her performance after readmission:

> The crucial question to be resolved in determining whether Doe is "otherwise qualified" under the Act is the substantiality of the risk that her mental disturbances will recur, resulting in behavior harmful to herself and others. The district court adopted as its test that she must be deemed qualified if it appeared "more likely than not" that she could complete her medical training and serve as a physician without recurrence of her self-destructive and antisocial conduct. We disagree with this standard. In our view she would not be qualified for readmission if there is a significant risk of such recurrence. It would be unreasonable to infer that Congress intended to force institutions to accept or readmit persons who pose a significant risk of harm to themselves or others, even if the chances of harm were less than 50 percent. Indeed, even if she presents any appreciable risk of such harm, this factor could properly be taken into account in deciding whether, among qualified applicants, it rendered her less qualified than others for the limited number of places available. In view of the seriousness of the harm inflicted in prior episodes, NYU is not required to give preference to her over other qualified applicants who do not pose any such appreciable risk at all [666 F.2d at 777].

Doe is thus the first major case to deal directly with the special problem of disabling conditions that are recurring or degenerative. The question posed by such a case is this: To what extent must the university assume the risk that an applicant capable of meeting program requirements at the time of admission may be incapable of fulfilling these requirements at a later date because of changes in his or her disabling conditions? *Doe* makes clear that universities may weigh such risks in making admission or readmission decisions and may consider an applicant unqualified if there is "significant risk" of recurrence (or degeneration) that would incapacitate the applicant from fulfilling program requirements. This risk factor thus becomes a relevant consideration for both parties in carrying their respective burdens of proof in Section 504 litigation. In appropriate cases, where there is medical evidence for doing so, universities may respond to the plaintiff's prima facie case by substantiating the risk of recurrence or degeneration that would render the applicant unqualified. The plaintiff would then have to demonstrate that his condition is sufficiently stable or, if it is not, that any change during his enrollment as a student would not render him unable to complete program requirements.

Another case interpreting Section 504 in light of *Davis* is *Kling v. County of Los Angeles,* 633 F.2d 876 (9th Cir. 1980), 769 F.2d 532 (9th Cir. 1985), *reversed without opin.,* 474 U.S. 936 (1985). The appellate court granted a preliminary injunction admitting the plaintiff, who suffered from Crohn's disease, into the defendant's school of nursing pending the completion of litigation. The school did not argue that the plaintiff failed to meet its admissions requirements but rather that, because of her disability, she would miss too many classes. In rejecting the school's argument, the court relied on the opinion of the plaintiff's physician that she would be able to complete the program and that hospitalization, if necessary, could be planned to minimize interruptions in her schooling. The appellate court remanded the case to the district court, directing it to grant a preliminary injunction.

The district court, however, determined that the plaintiff had been properly denied admission to the college, and denied damages. In its second opinion, the appellate court said that the plaintiff was otherwise qualified and that damages were appropriate. It again remanded the case for calculation of damages.

The U.S. Supreme Court granted review and reversed the appellate court on the same day, ordering it to reconsider its ruling in light of *Anderson v. Bessemer City,* 470 U.S. 564 (1985), a case that addresses the standard for determining whether a district court's fact-finding is clearly erroneous. Three justices filed dissents to the reversal. Justice Stevens pointed out that the college's doctor had never evaluated the plaintiff on an individual basis but had made generalized assumptions about the nature of her disability, which Section 504 prohibits.

In *Doherty v. Southern College of Optometry,* 862 F.2d 570 (6th Cir. 1988), a federal appellate court considered the relationship between Section 504's "otherwise qualified" requirement and the institution's duty to provide a "reasonable accommodation" for a student with a disability. The plaintiff—a student with retinitis pigmentosa (RP), which restricted his field of vision, and a neurological condition that affected his motor skills—asserted that the college should exempt him from recently introduced proficiency requirements related to the operation of optometric instruments. The student could not meet these requirements and claimed that they were a pretext for discrimination on the basis of disability, since he was "otherwise qualified" and therefore had the right to be accommodated.

In ruling for the school, the district court considered the "reasonable accommodation" inquiry to be separate from the "otherwise qualified" requirement; thus, in its view, the institution was obligated to accommodate only a student with a disability who has already been determined to be "otherwise qualified." The appeals court disagreed, indicating that the "inquiry into reasonable accommodation is one aspect of the 'otherwise qualified' analysis" (862 F.2d at 577). To explain the relationship, the court quoted from *Brennan v. Stewart*, 834 F.2d 1248, 1261–62 (5th Cir. 1988):

> [I]t is clear that the phrase "otherwise qualified" has a paradoxical quality; on the one hand, it refers to a person who has the abilities or characteristics sought by the [institution]: but on the other, it cannot refer only to those already capable of meeting all the requirements—or else no reasonable requirement could ever violate Section 504, no matter how easy it would be to accommodate handicapped individuals who cannot fulfill it. This means that we can no longer take literally the assertion of *Davis* that "an otherwise qualified person is one who is able to meet all of a program's requirements in spite of his handicap." The question . . . is the rather mushy one of whether some "reasonable accommodation" is available to satisfy the legitimate interests of both the [institution] and the handicapped person [862 F.2d at 575].

The appellate court's interpretation did not change the result in the case; since the proficiency requirements were reasonably necessary to the practice of optometry, waiver of these requirements would not have been a "reasonable accommodation." But the court's emphasis on the proper relationship between the "otherwise qualified" and "reasonable accommodation" inquiries does serve to clarify and strengthen the institution's obligation to accommodate the particular needs of students with disabilities.

In another case concerning the qualifications of a student with a disability, the court determined that the plaintiff was not qualified for admission. In *Wood v. President and Trustees of Spring Hill College*, 978 F.2d 1214 (11th Cir. 1992), the plaintiff, who had schizophrenia, attended college for one week, and alleged constructive dismissal from the college on the basis of her disability. Resting her claim on Section 504, the plaintiff said that the college's insistence that she take remedial courses was based on her disability. The college disagreed, arguing that its admission decision had been erroneous and that its request that she defer her admission for one semester while taking remedial courses was reasonable. A jury found for the college, and the plaintiff appealed.

Because the plaintiff was seeking compensatory damages, she was required to demonstrate intentional discrimination, said the appellate court, which she had not done. And although the judge should have instructed the jury to consider whether the college had acted "solely on the basis of handicap" (as articulated in 29 U.S.C. §794(a)), the lack of objection at trial to this omission prevented its assertion on appeal. Furthermore, the plaintiff had presented no evidence that she had requested an accommodation, so there was no need for the jury to determine whether the college should have provided the plaintiff with a reasonable accommodation.

The Rehabilitation Act and the ADA also prohibit retaliation against students with disabilities who request accommodations or who file complaints alleging discrimination. In *Rothman v. Emory University*, 828 F. Supp. 537 (N.D. Ill. 1993), a former law student who had epilepsy charged that the university had failed to give him appropriate accommodations (including additional time to take examinations) and, when he complained, had retaliated by writing a letter to the Illinois Board of Law Examiners asserting that he was hostile and attributing his behavior to "chronic epilepsy." In considering the university's motion for summary judgment, the court ruled that, if proven, such actions could support a claim of discrimination and retaliation against a person with disabilities.

Students alleging discrimination on the basis of disability may file a complaint with the Education Department's Office for Civil Rights (OCR), or they may file a private lawsuit and receive compensatory damages (*Tanberg v. Weld County Sheriff*, 787 F. Supp. 970 (D. Colo. 1992)). Section 504 does not, however, provide a private right of action against the secretary of education, who enforces Section 504 (*Salvador v. Bennett*, 800 F.2d 97 (7th Cir. 1986)).

The provisions of the ADA are similar in many respects to those of Section 504, upon which, in large part, it was based. In addition to employment (see Section 2.2.2), Title II of the ADA prohibits discrimination in access to services or programs of a public entity (such as a public college or university), and Title III prohibits discrimination in access to places of public accommodation (such as private colleges and universities).

The ADA specifies ten areas in which colleges and universities may not discriminate against a qualified individual with a disability: eligibility criteria; modifications of policies, practices, and procedures; auxiliary aids and services; examinations and courses; removal of barriers in existing facilities; alternatives to barriers in existing facilities; personal devices and services; assistive technology; seating in assembly areas; and transportation services (28 C.F.R. §36.301–310). The law also addresses accessibility issues for new construction or renovation of existing facilities (28 C.F.R. §36.401–406). The law is discussed more fully in Section 12.4.4.

The law's language regarding "eligibility criteria" means that in their admissions or placement tests or other admission-related activities, colleges and universities must accommodate the needs of applicants or students with disabilities. For example, one court held that, under Section 504, the defendant medical school must provide a dyslexic student with alternate exams unless it could demonstrate that its rejection of all other testing methods was based on rational reasons (*Wynne v. Tufts University School of Medicine*, 932 F.2d 19 (1st Cir. 1991)).

Students with learning disabilities are protected by both Section 504 and the ADA, and legal challenges by such students are on the rise. For example, in *Fruth v. New York University*, 2 A.D. Cases 1197 (S.D.N.Y. 1993), a student with learning disabilities challenged the university's decision to rescind his acceptance because he had failed to attend a required summer orientation session for students with learning disabilities. Relying heavily on *Doe v. New York University* (discussed above), the court ruled that, since the student's grades were lower than the university's required grade point average, the university's insistence that the student attend the summer program was reasonable and not in violation of the ADA. It is likely that courts will continue to rely on precedent developed under Section 504 until a body of ADA law has developed.

In sum, postsecondary administrators should still proceed very sensitively in making admission decisions concerning disabled persons. *Davis* can be expected to have the greatest impact on professional and paraprofessional health care programs; beyond that, the circumstances in which physical requirements for admission may be used are unclear. Furthermore, while *Davis* relieves colleges and universities of any obligation to make substantial modifications in their program requirements, a refusal to make lesser modifications may in some instances constitute discrimination. Furthermore, interpretation of Section 504's requirements has evolved since *Davis*, as evidenced by the *Doherty* case; and in some cases the ADA provides additional protections for students. Administrators and counsel should watch for further litigation involving different factual settings, as well as for possible new policy interpretations by the Department of Education.

4.1.4.4. Age. In *Massachusetts Board of Retirement v. Murgia*, 427 U.S. 307 (1976), the U.S. Supreme Court held that age discrimination is not subject to the high standard of justification that the equal protection clause of the Constitution requires, for instance, for race discrimination. Rather, age classifications are permissible if they "rationally further" some legitimate governmental objective. The Court confirmed the use of the "rational basis" standard for age discrimination cases in *City of Dallas v. Stanglin*, 490 U.S. 19 (1989), saying that this standard is "the most relaxed and tolerant form of judicial scrutiny under the Equal Protection Clause" (490 U.S. at 26).

In *Miller v. Sonoma County Junior College District*, No. C–74–0222 (N.D. Cal. 1974) (unpublished opinion decided before *Murgia*), two sixteen-year-old students won the right to attend a California junior college. The court held that the college's minimum-age requirement of eighteen was an arbitrary and irrational basis for exclusion because it was not related to the state's interest in providing education to qualified students.

In *Purdie v. University of Utah,* 584 P.2d 831 (Utah 1978), a case that can usefully be compared with *Miller,* the court considered the constitutional claim of a fifty-one-year-old woman who had been denied admission to the university's department of educational psychology. Whereas the Miller plaintiffs were allegedly too young for admission, Purdie was allegedly too old. But in both cases, the courts used the equal protection clause to limit the institution's discretion to base admission decisions on age. In *Purdie,* the plaintiff alleged, and the university did not deny, that she exceeded the normal admissions requirements and was rejected solely because of her age. The trial court held that her complaint did not state a viable legal claim and dismissed the suit. On appeal, the Utah Supreme Court reversed, holding that rejection of a qualified fifty-one-year-old would violate equal protection unless the university could show that its action bore a "rational relationship to legitimate state purposes." Since the abbreviated trial record contained no evidence of the department's admissions standards or its policy regarding age, the court remanded the case to the trial court for further proceedings.

Both public and private institutions that receive federal funds are subject to the federal Age Discrimination Act of 1975 (42 U.S.C. §6101 *et seq*). Section 6101 of the Act, with certain exceptions listed in Sections 6103(b) and 6103(c), originally prohibited "unreasonable discrimination on the basis of age in programs or activities receiving federal financial assistance." In 1978, Congress deleted the word "unreasonable" from the Act (see this volume, Section 12.4.5), thus lowering the statute's tolerance for discrimination and presumably making its standards more stringent than the Constitution's "rationality" standard used in *Purdie.* As amended and interpreted in the implementing regulations (45 C.F.R. Part 90), the Age Discrimination Act clearly applies to the admissions policies of postsecondary institutions.

The age discrimination regulations, however, do not prohibit all age distinctions. Section 90.14 of the regulations permits age distinctions that are necessary to the "normal operation" of, or to the achievement of a "statutory objective" of, a program or activity receiving federal financial assistance (see this volume, Section 12.4.5). Moreover, Section 90.15 of the regulations permits recipients to take an action based on a factor other than age—"even though that action may have a disproportionate effect on persons of different ages"—if the factor has a "direct and substantial relationship" to the program's operation or goals. The practical impact of these provisions on admissions policies is illustrated by two examples in the explanatory commentary accompanying the regulations:

1. A medical school receiving federal financial assistance generally does not admit anyone over 35 years of age, even though this results in turning away highly qualified applicants over 35. The school claims it has an objective, the teaching of qualified medical students who, upon graduation, will practice as long as possible. The school believes that this objective requires it to select younger applicants over older ones. The use of such an age distinction is *not necessary* to normal operation of the recipient's program because it does not meet the requirement of Section 90.14(b). Age of the applicant may be a reasonable measure of a nonage characteristic (longevity of practice). This characteristic may be impractical to measure directly on an individual basis. Nevertheless, achieving a high average of longevity of practice cannot be considered a program objective for a medical school within the meaning of the Act. The "normal operation" exception is not intended to permit a recipient to use broad notions of efficiency or cost-benefit analysis to justify exclusion from a program on the basis of age. The basic objectives of the medical school involve training competent and qualified medical school graduates. These objectives are not impaired if the average length of time its graduates practice medicine is lowered by a fraction of a year (or even more) by the admission of qualified applicants over 35 years of age.

2. A federally assisted training program uses a physical fitness test as a factor for selecting participants to train for a certain job. The job involves frequent heavy lifting and other demands for physical strength and stamina. Even though older persons might fail the test more frequently than younger persons, the physical fitness test measures a characteristic that is *directly and substantially related* to the job for which persons are being trained and is, therefore, permissible under the Act [44 Fed. Reg. 33773–74 (June 12, 1979)].

State law also occasionally prohibits age discrimination against students. In its Fair Educational Practices statute, for example, Massachusetts prohibits age discrimination in admissions to graduate programs and vocational training institutions (Mass. Gen. Laws Ann. ch. 151C, §§2(d), 2A(a)).

Taken together, the Constitution, the federal law and regulations, and occasional state laws now appear to create a substantial legal barrier to the use of either maximum- or minimum-age policies in admissions. The federal Age Discrimination Act, applicable to both public and private institutions regardless of whether they receive federal funds, is the most important of these developments; administrators should watch for further implementation of this statute.

4.1.5. Affirmative Action Programs

Designed to increase the number of minority persons admitted to educational programs, affirmative action policies pose delicate social and legal questions. Educators have agonized over the extent to which the social goal of greater minority representation justifies the admission of less or differently qualified applicants into educational programs, particularly in the professions, while courts have grappled with the complaints of qualified but rejected nonminority applicants who claim to be victims of "reverse discrimination" because minority applicants were admitted in preference to them. Though two cases have reached the U.S. Supreme Court, *DeFunis* and *Bakke* (both discussed later), neither case established comprehensive requirements regarding affirmative action. But the varied opinions of the justices in the *Bakke* decision, 438 U.S. 265 (1978), contain valuable insight and guidance concerning the legal and social issues of affirmative action. Read together with two lower court cases (discussed later) that followed it, *Bakke* forms a baseline against which all affirmative action programs have been measured. A recent federal appellate court opinion, *Hopwood v. Texas*, 78 F.3d 932 (5th Cir. 1996), *cert. denied*, 116 S. Ct. 2581 (1996), calls into question the continuing vitality of the *Bakke* line of cases, however, and the Supreme Court's refusal to review this case raises many questions about how to devise admissions programs that may lawfully take affirmative action considerations into account.

The legal issues can be cast in both constitutional and statutory terms and apply to both public and private institutions. The constitutional issues, pertaining only to public institutions, arise under the Fourteenth Amendment's equal protection clause. The statutory issues arise under Title VI of the Civil Rights Act of 1964 and Title IX of the Education Amendments of 1972, which prohibit race and sex discrimination by public and private institutions receiving federal funds (see Sections 4.1.4.1 and 4.1.4.2) and under 42 U.S.C. §1981, which has been construed to prohibit race discrimination in admissions by private schools, whether or not they receive federal money (see Section 4.1.4.1). In the *Bakke* case, a majority of the justices agreed that Title VI uses constitutional standards for determining the validity of affirmative action programs (see 438 U.S. at 284–87, 328–41, 414–18). Standards comparable to the Constitution's would presumably also be used for any affirmative action question arising under 42 U.S.C. §1981 or under Title IX. Thus, *Bakke* establishes the foundation for a core of uniform legal parameters for affirmative action, applicable to public and private institutions alike.

Both the Title VI and the Title IX regulations address the subject of affirmative action. These regulations preceded *Bakke* and are brief and somewhat ambiguous. After *Bakke*, HEW issued a "policy interpretation" of Title VI, indicating that the department had reviewed its regulations in light of *Bakke* and "concluded that no changes in the regulation are required or desirable" (44 Fed. Reg. 58509, at 58510 (Oct. 10, 1979)). In this policy interpretation, however, HEW did set forth guidelines for applying its affirmative action regulation consistent with *Bakke*.

When an institution has discriminated in the past, the Title VI and Title IX regulations require it to implement affirmative action programs to overcome the effects of that discrimination (34 C.F.R. §§100.3(b)(6)(i) and 100.5(i); 34 C.F.R.

§106.3(a)). When the institution has not discriminated, the regulations nevertheless permit affirmative action to overcome the effects of societal discrimination (34 C.F.R. §§100.3(b)(6)(ii) and 100.5(i); 34 C.F.R. §106.3(b)). The HEW policy interpretation contains guidelines for such voluntary uses of affirmative action to increase minority student enrollments.

The first case to confront the constitutionality of affirmative action admissions programs in postsecondary education was *DeFunis v. Odegaard,* 507 P.2d 1169 (Wash. 1973), *dismissed as moot,* 416 U.S. 312 (1973), *on remand,* 529 P.2d 438 (Wash. 1974). After DeFunis, a white male, was denied admission to the University of Washington law school, he filed suit alleging that less qualified minority applicants had been accepted and that, but for the affirmative action program, he would have been admitted. He claimed that the university discriminated against him on the basis of his race, in violation of the equal protection clause.

The law school admissions committee had calculated each applicant's predicted first-year average (PFYA) through a formula that considered the applicant's Law School Admissions Test (LSAT) scores and junior-senior undergraduate average. The committee had attached less importance to a minority applicant's PFYA and had considered minority applications separately from other applications. Although the committee accepted minority applicants whose PFYAs were lower than those of other applicants, in no case did it accept any person whose record indicated that he or she would not be able to complete the program successfully. The committee established no quotas; rather, its goal was the inclusion of a reasonable representation of minority groups. DeFunis's PFYA was higher than those of all but one of the minority applicants admitted in the year he was rejected.

The state trial court ordered that DeFunis be admitted, and he entered the law school. The Washington State Supreme Court reversed the lower court and upheld the law school's affirmative action program as a constitutionally acceptable admissions tool justified by several "compelling" state interests. Among them were the "interest in promoting integration in public education," the "educational interest . . . in producing a racially balanced student body at the law school," and the interest in alleviating "the shortage of minority attorneys—and, consequently, minority prosecutors, judges, and public officials."

When DeFunis sought review in the U.S. Supreme Court, he was permitted to remain in school pending the Court's final disposition of the case. Subsequently, in a per curiam opinion with four justices dissenting, the Court declared the case moot because, by then, DeFunis was in his final quarter of law school and the university had asserted that his registration would remain effective regardless of the case's final outcome. The Court vacated the Washington State Supreme Court's judgment and remanded the case to that court for appropriate disposition. Though the per curiam opinion does not discuss the merits of the case, Justice Douglas's dissent presents a thought-provoking analysis of affirmative action in admissions:

> The equal protection clause did not enact a requirement that law schools employ as the sole criterion for admissions a formula based upon the LSAT and undergraduate grades, nor does it prohibit law schools from evaluating an applicant's prior achievements in light of the barriers that he had to overcome. A black applicant who pulled himself out of the ghetto into a junior college may thereby demonstrate a level of motivation, perseverance, and ability that would lead a fair-minded admissions committee to conclude that he shows more promise for law study than the son of a rich alumnus who achieved better grades at Harvard. That applicant would be offered admission not because he is black but because as an individual he has shown he has the potential, while the Harvard man may have taken less advantage of the vastly superior opportunities offered him. Because of the weight of the prior handicaps, that black applicant may not realize his full potential in the first year of law school, or even in the full three years, but in the long pull of a legal career his achievements may far outstrip those of his classmates whose earlier records appeared superior by conventional criteria. There is currently no test available to the admissions committee that can predict such possibilities with assurance, but the committee may nevertheless seek to gauge it as best it can and weigh this factor in its decisions. Such a policy would not be limited to blacks, or Chicanos, or Filipinos, or American Indians, although undoubtedly groups such as these may in practice be the principal beneficiaries of it. But a poor Appalachian white, or a second-generation Chinese in San Francisco, or some other American whose lineage is so diverse as to defy ethnic labels, may demonstrate similar potential and thus be accorded favorable consideration by the committee.
>
> The difference between such a policy and the one presented by this case is that the committee would be making decisions on the basis of individual attributes, rather than according a preference solely on the basis of race. To be sure, the racial preference here was not absolute—the committee did not admit all applicants from the four favored groups. But it did accord all such applicants a preference by applying, to an extent not precisely ascertainable from the record, different standards by which to judge their applications, with the result that the committee admitted minority applicants who, in the school's own judgment, were less promising than other applicants who were rejected. Furthermore, it is apparent that because the admissions committee compared minority applicants only with one another, it was necessary to reserve some proportion of the class for them, even if at the outset a precise number of places were not set aside. That proportion, apparently 15 to 20 percent, was chosen because the school determined it to be "reasonable," although no explanation is provided as to how that number rather than some other was found appropriate. Without becoming

embroiled in a semantic debate over whether this practice constitutes a "quota," it is clear that given the limitation on the total number of applicants who could be accepted, this policy did reduce the total number of places for which DeFunis could compete—solely on account of his race [416 U.S. at 331–33].

Justice Douglas did not conclude that the university's policy was therefore unconstitutional but, rather, that it would be unconstitutional unless, after a new trial, the court found that it took account of "cultural standards of a diverse rather than a homogeneous society" in a "racially neutral" way.

Five years after it had avoided the issue in *DeFunis*, the Supreme Court considered the legality of affirmative action in *Regents of the University of California v. Bakke*, 438 U.S. 265 (1978). The plaintiff, a white male twice rejected from the medical school of the University of California at Davis, had challenged the affirmative action program that the school used to select a portion of its entering class each year that he was rejected. The particular facts concerning this program's operation were critical to its legality and were subject to dispute in the court proceedings. They are best taken from Justice Powell's opinion in the U.S. Supreme Court, in a passage with which a majority of the justices agreed:

The faculty devised a special admissions program to increase the representation of "disadvantaged" students in each medical school class. The special program consisted of a separate admissions system operating in coordination with the regular admissions process. . . .

The special admissions program operated with a separate committee, a majority of whom were members of minority groups. On the 1973 application form, candidates were asked to indicate whether they wished to be considered as "economically and/or educationally disadvantaged" applicants; on the 1974 form, the question was whether they wished to be considered as members of a "minority group" which the medical school apparently viewed as "blacks," "Chicanos," "Asians," and "American Indians." If these questions were answered affirmatively, the application was forwarded to the special admissions committee. No formal definition of "disadvantaged" was ever produced, but the chairman of the special committee screened each application to see whether it reflected economic or educational deprivation. Having passed this initial hurdle, the applications then were rated by the special committee in a fashion similar to that used by the general admissions committee, except that special candidates did not have to meet the 2.5 grade point average cutoff applied to regular applicants. About one fifth of the total number of special applicants were invited for interviews in 1973 and 1974. Following each interview, the special committee assigned each special applicant a benchmark score. The special committee then presented its top choices to the general admissions committee. The latter did not rate or compare the special candidates against the general applicants but could reject recommended special candidates for failure to meet course requirements or other specific deficiencies. The special committee continued to recommend special applicants until a number prescribed by faculty vote were admitted. While the overall class size was still fifty, the prescribed number was eight; in 1973 and 1974, when the class size had doubled to 100, the prescribed number of special admissions also doubled, to sixteen.

From the year of the increase in class size—1971—through 1974, the special program resulted in the admission of twenty-one black students, thirty Mexican-Americans, and twelve Asians, for a total of sixty-three minority students. Over the same period, the regular admissions program produced one black, six Mexican-Americans, and thirty-seven Asians, for a total of forty-four minority students. Although disadvantaged whites applied to the special program in large numbers, none received an offer of admission through that process. Indeed, in 1974 at least, the special committee explicitly considered only "disadvantaged" special applicants who were members of one of the designated minority groups [438 U.S. at 272–76].

The university sought to justify its program by citing the great need for doctors to work in underserved minority communities, the need to compensate for the effects of societal discrimination against minorities, the need to reduce the historical deficit of minorities in the medical profession, and the need to diversity the student body. In analyzing these justifications, the California Supreme Court had applied a "compelling state interest" test, such as that used in *DeFunis,* along with a "less objectionable alternative test" (*Bakke v. Regents of the University of California,* 553 P.2d 1152 (Cal. 1976)). Although it assumed that the university's interests were compelling, this court held the affirmative action program unconstitutional because the university had not demonstrated that the program was the least burdensome alternative available for achieving its goals. The court suggested these alternatives:

> The university is entitled to consider, as it does with respect to applicants in the special program, that low grades and test scores may not accurately reflect the abilities of some disadvantaged students, and it may reasonably conclude that although their academic scores are lower, their potential for success in the school and the profession is equal to or greater than that of an applicant with higher grades who has not been similarly handicapped.
>
> In addition, the university may properly, as it in fact does, consider other factors in evaluating an applicant, such as the personal interview, recommendations, character, and matters relating to the needs of the profession and society, such as an applicant's professional goals. . . .
>
> In addition to flexible admission standards, the university might increase minority enrollment by instituting aggressive programs to identify, recruit, and provide remedial schooling for disadvantaged students of all races who are interested in pursuing a medical career and have an evident talent for doing so.

Another ameliorative measure which may be considered is to increase the number of places available in the medical schools, either by allowing additional students to enroll in existing schools or by expanding the schools. . . .

None of the foregoing measures can be related to race, but they will provide for consideration and assistance to individual applicants who have suffered previous disabilities, regardless of their surname or color [553 P.2d at 1166–67].

Thus concluding that the university's program did not satisfy applicable constitutional tests, the California court held that the program operated to exclude Bakke on account of his race and ordered that Bakke be admitted to medical school. It further held that the Constitution prohibited the university from giving any consideration to race in its admissions process and enjoined the university from doing so.

The U.S. Supreme Court affirmed this decision in part and reversed it in part (438 U.S. 265 (1978)). The justices wrote six opinions (totaling 157 pages), none of which commanded a majority of the Court. Three of these opinions deserve particular consideration: (1) Justice Powell's opinion—in some parts of which various of the other justices joined; (2) Justice Brennan's opinion—in which Justices White, Marshall, and Blackmun joined (referred to below as the "Brennan group"); and (3) Justice Stevens's opinion—in which Justices Stewart, Rehnquist, and Chief Justice Burger joined (referred to below as the "Stevens group").

A bare majority of the justices, four (the "Stevens group") relying on Title VI and one (Justice Powell) relying on the equal protection clause of the Fourteenth Amendment, agreed that the University of California at Davis program unlawfully discriminated against Bakke, thus affirming the first part of the California court's judgment (ordering Bakke's admission). A different majority of five justices—Justice Powell and the "Brennan group"—agreed that "the state has a substantial interest that legitimately may be served by a properly devised admissions program involving the competitive consideration of race and ethnic origin" (438 U.S. at 320), thus reversing the second part of the California court's judgment (prohibiting the consideration of race in admissions). The various opinions debated the issues of what equal protection tests should apply, how Title VI should be interpreted in this context, what the appropriate justifications for affirmative action programs are, and to what extent such programs can be race conscious. No majority agreed on any of these issues, however, except that Title VI embodies constitutional principles of equal protection.

Since the Supreme Court's decision in *Bakke*, two state court decisions have applied the teachings of the *Bakke* opinions to uphold affirmative action programs of state professional schools in Washington and California. The first of these two cases was *McDonald v. Hogness*, 598 P.2d 707 (Wash. 1979). The particular facts, like the facts in *Bakke*, were singularly important to the outcome. McDonald, a white male, sought admission to the University of Washington's medical school. After being rejected, he challenged the school's admissions policy as racially discriminatory against whites.

According to its published admissions policy then in effect, the medical school considered candidates "comparatively on the basis of academic performance, medical aptitude, motivation, maturity, and demonstrated humanitarian qualities." Unlike the admissions policy at issue in *Bakke*, the University of Washington's policy did not provide for any separate treatment or consideration of minority applicants. Nor did the policy explicitly recognize race as an admission criterion. It did, however, provide that "extenuating background circumstances are considered as they relate to [the five listed] selection factors." Similarly, the guidelines given members of the school's interviewing committee listed "special considerations, including extenuating circumstances" as one of the criteria for rating applicants. According to the Washington Supreme Court's analysis of the school's admissions practices, the race of applicants could be and was considered under this criterion.

In its opinion, the Washington court further described the school's admissions policy and its application to McDonald:

> Medical school personnel believe grade point average (GPA) is the best measure of academic performance, while the Medical College Admissions Test (MCAT) score is the best measure of medical aptitude. Noncognitive criteria—motivation, maturity, and demonstrated humanitarian qualities—are assessed from the applicant's file and the interview. . . .

The "first screen" score calculated upon receipt of an application is based on GPA and MCAT. It is the "bright-line" test for referral to the admissions committee and is considered later by admissions committee application readers and interview-conference committee members. Of the 1,703 applicants, 816 were referred to the reading committee. Interviews were granted to 546 applicants considered potentially competitive by reading committee analyses. . . .

> After the twenty- to thirty-minute interview, the candidate is excused and each member [of the interview-conference committee] independently places the applicant in one of four categories: (1) Unacceptable (specific deficiencies); (2) Possible (with comparative deficiencies academically and/or with regard to noncognitive features); (3) Acceptable (no deficiencies that are not balanced by other abilities, would be an average medical student); and (4) Outstanding (no apparent deficiencies, high probability of making an excellent physician and scholar). Following each interview-conference, committee staff calculate an average of the individual committee members' ratings based on a scale of 4 for "outstanding" downward through 1 for "unacceptable." The average is entered on the interview-conference summary.

The Skeletal Consideration List (SCL) serves as a rough agenda for EXCOM selection meetings. Placement is determined by one's total score—first screen score plus interview-conference score—grouped again in categories 4, 3, 2, and 1. Placement in category 2 or 1 nearly always leads to application denial. McDonald averaged 2.17 on the interview and was placed in category 2. His SCL position was at the number 237 level. When corrected for "ties" of 546 candidates interviewed for 175 slots, more than 300 placed higher than McDonald. However, every black, Chicano, and American Indian placing higher than McDonald on the SCL had a lower "first screen" score than he did. On April 30, 1976, EXCOM voted that all candidates not otherwise acted upon, which included McDonald, be considered noncompetitive for the [1976 entering] class and his application was denied [598 P.2d at 709–10].

Noting at the outset that McDonald would not have been admitted even if the race of applicants had not been considered, the court held that this fact alone justified denying relief. But because of the public importance of the case and the likelihood of its recurrence, the court proceeded to address the merits of McDonald's discrimination claim. It based its analysis on the equal protection clause and noted, as a majority of the justices in *Bakke* had held, that an admissions program which was consistent with the Fourteenth Amendment would also be consistent with Title VI of the Civil Rights Act of 1964.

In holding that the medical school's admissions program was constitutional, the court relied heavily on Justice Powell's opinion in *Bakke*. That opinion, according to the Washington court, discouraged the separate consideration of minority applicants but permitted race to be considered as a factor in an admissions policy when its consideration "(1) is designed to promote a compelling state interest and (2) does not insulate an applicant from competition with remaining applicants." Like Justice Powell, the Washington court acknowledged that the attainment of a diverse student body is a compelling interest because it is central to the university's academic freedom:

The University of Washington argues that the denial of McDonald's application was an exercise of its constitutionally protected freedom to decide who shall be admitted to study. It quotes Mr. Justice Frankfurter's concurring opinion in *Sweezy v. New Hampshire*, 354 U.S. 234, 263 . . . (1957), also quoted by Mr. Justice Powell in *Bakke*, 438 U.S. at 312 . . .

It is the business of a university to provide that atmosphere which is most conducive to speculation, experiment, and creation. It is an atmosphere in which there prevail "the four essential freedoms" of a university— to determine for itself on academic grounds who may teach, what may be taught, how it shall be taught, and who may be admitted to study.

Like Mr. Justice Powell, we believe that the atmosphere of "speculation, experimentation, and creation" is promoted by a diverse student body. We agree that, in seeking diversity, the U.W. medical school must be viewed "as seeking to achieve a goal that is of paramount importance in the fulfillment of its mission" (438 U.S. at 313 . . .). But though a university must have wide discretion in making admission judgments, "constitutional limitations protecting individual rights may not be disregarded" (438 U.S. at 314 . . .) [598 P.2d at 712–13 n.7].

The Washington court then compared the medical school's admissions program with another program—the Harvard plan—that had been cited approvingly in *Bakke,* finding the two plans similar because they used race as one of several factors to be considered. For further support, the Washington court also relied on the opinion of Justice Brennan's group of four justices in *Bakke* and its own earlier opinion in *DeFunis:*

> In the second *Bakke* opinion which supports the UW medical school on this issue, Justices Brennan, White, Marshall, and Blackmun pronounce the [University of California at] Davis program constitutionally valid. In their opinion, the state need only show [that the racial criterion] (1) serves an important, articulated purpose, (2) does not stigmatize any discrete group, and (3) is reasonably used in light of the program's objectives (438 U.S. at 361 . . .). The Brennan group believes Davis's goal of admitting students disadvantaged by effects of past discrimination is sufficiently important. They reasonably read Mr. Justice Powell's opinion as agreeing [that] this can constitute a compelling purpose (438 U.S. at 366 n.42 . . .).

In the instant case, the trial court determined the school had decided that, in order to serve the educational needs of the school and the medical needs of the region, the school should seek greater representation of minorities "where there has been serious underrepresentation in the school and in the medical profession." Thus, the program furthers a compelling purpose of eliminating racial imbalance within public medical education.

> Furthermore, the program here meets the additional elements of the Brennan group's test. The racial classification does not stigmatize any discrete group and is reasonably used in light of its objectives [598 P.2d at 713–14].

The court in *McDonald* thus accepted the authority of both the Powell opinion and the Brennan group's opinion in *Bakke,* holding that the University of Washington plan met the tests established by each of these opinions. In so doing, the court also accepted two separate interests—attainment of a diverse student body and elimination of racial imbalance by admitting minority students disadvantaged by past societal discrimination—as compelling interests that can justify the use of affirmative action plans.

The second affirmative action case, to be read in tandem with *McDonald,* is *DeRonde v. Regents of the University of California,* 625 P.2d 220 (Cal. 1981). The plaintiff was an unsuccessful applicant for admission to King Hall, the University of California at Davis law school. Following his rejection, the plaintiff was accepted at and graduated from a different law school and was admitted to the state bar. The California court chose not to dismiss the case as moot, however, citing the need for "appellate resolution of important issues of substantial and continuing public interest."

The court first examined the operation of the law school's admissions policy:

The record discloses that, in selecting candidates for admission to King Hall in 1975, the university relied principally on a formula which combined an applicant's previous academic grade point average (GPA) with his or her score on the standardized Law School Admissions Test (LSAT). This formula yielded a predicted first-year average (PFYA) which, it was hoped, measured, at least roughly, the applicant's potential for law study.

Believing, however, that the foregoing formula tended to ignore other significant and relevant selection factors, the university considered several additional background elements to supplement or mitigate a lower PFYA. These factors included (1) growth, maturity, and commitment to law study (as shown by prior employment, extracurricular and community activities, advanced degrees or studies, and personal statements and recommendations); (2) factors which, while no longer present, had affected previous academic grades (such as temporary physical handicaps or disruptive changes in school or environment); (3) wide discrepancies between grades and test scores where there was indicated evidence of substantial ability and motivation; (4) rigor of undergraduate studies; (5) economic disadvantage; and (6) "ethnic minority status" contributing to diversity.

It is the consideration by the university of the final factor, "ethnic minority status," which is the principal target of DeRonde's attack. Trial testimony established that "ethnic minority status" was defined by the university as including Asians, blacks, Chicanos, Native Americans, and Filipinos. This grouping generally corresponds to the ethnic categories defined by the federal Equal Employment Opportunity Commission in its public reports. The record reflects that the university's reasons for considering minority status were primarily twofold: First, an appreciable minority representation in the student body will contribute a valuable cultural diversity for both faculty and students; and, second, a minority representation in the legal pool from which future professional and community leaders, public and private, are drawn will strengthen and preserve minority participation in the democratic process at all levels. In short, it was believed that the individual and group learning experience is enriched with broadly beneficial consequences both to the profession and to the public at large. We carefully emphasize that, although minority status was included as one of several pertinent selection factors, the university did not employ any quota system or reserve a fixed number of positions for any minority applicants in its entering class.

Just as a relatively low PFYA might be increased by utilization of any of the foregoing factors, alternatively, a relatively high PFYA could be reduced by considering (1) the applicant's prior schools attended, (2) the difficulty of his or her prior course of study, (3) variations in an applicant's multiple LSAT scores, (4) the absence of any factors indicating maturity or motivation, and (5) the applicant's advanced age.

As a consequence of this formulation, in 1975 the 406 students to whom the university offered admission included 135 minority applicants, and more than 1,800 applicants, including DeRonde, were rejected. DeRonde's 3.47 GPA and 575 LSAT score produced a 2.70 PFYA. The PFYAs of successful applicants ranged from 2.24 to 3.43. Sixty-nine minority applicants were accepted with PFYAs lower than DeRonde's. On the other hand, the more than 800 unsuccessful applicants who had higher PFYAs than DeRonde included 35 minority applicants [625 P.2d at 222–23].

Noting that the *McDonald* court had employed similar analysis, the *DeRonde* court focused on the equal protection clause and began its analysis by referring to Justice Powell's *Bakke* opinion. The court then compared the Davis program to the Harvard plan discussed by Justice Powell and similarly found it acceptable:

> In our view the admissions procedures used by the university to select its 1975 entering class at King Hall does not vary in any significant way from the Harvard program. Minority racial or ethnic origin was one of several competing factors used by the university to reach its ultimate decision whether or not to admit a particular applicant. Each application, as contemplated by the program, was individually examined and evaluated in the light of the various positive and negative admission factors. As Justice Powell pointedly observed, the primary and obvious defect in the quota system in *Bakke* was that it *precluded* individualized consideration of every applicant without regard to race (438 U.S. at 31718 and n.52 . . .). That fatal flaw does not appear in the admissions procedure before us. This is not a quota case. Thus, we conclude that the race-attentive admissions procedure used by the university in 1975 would have passed federal constitutional muster under the standards prescribed by Justice Powell in *Bakke* [625 P.2d at 225].

The *DeRonde* court then turned, as had the *McDonald* court, to Justice Brennan's opinion:

> The Brennan opinion, representing the views of four justices, would have upheld the Davis quota system invalidated by the majority in *Bakke*. It may fairly be concluded that a race-conscious law school admissions program that did not involve a quota, *a fortiori*, would be sustained by those holding the Brennan view [625 P.2d at 225].

The court noted that the Brennan group had also explicitly approved the Harvard plan but had focused on different interests than those relied on by Powell:

> Justice Brennan "agree[d] with Mr. Justice Powell that a plan like the 'Harvard' plan . . . is constitutional under our approach, at least so long as the use of race

to achieve an integrated student body is necessitated by the lingering effects of past discrimination" (438 U.S. at 326, n.1 . . . ; see also 438 U.S. at 378–79 . . . (expressing the view that the Harvard plan is "no more or less constitutionally acceptable" than the Davis quota system ruled invalid by the majority)). Justice Brennan expands the foregoing requirement of a past discriminatory effect and would hold that even a racial quota system such as involved in *Bakke* was constitutional if its purpose "is to remove the disparate racial impact [the university's] actions might otherwise have and if there is reason to believe that the disparate impact is itself the product of past discrimination, whether its own or that of society at large" [625 P.2d at 225; quoting 438 U.S. at 369].

Since the *DeRonde* trial had preceded the U.S. Supreme Court's *Bakke* opinions, the question of whether the university's admissions program was "necessitated by the lingering effects of past discrimination" was neither framed nor litigated by the parties. The court nevertheless studied the record and found evidence that a race-conscious admissions program was needed to prevent a disproportionate underrepresentation of minorities at King Hall. The primary evidence was the testimony of a former dean of the law school, who "stressed that if admission selection was based solely upon numbers (i.e., GPA and LSAT scores), 'the greatest bulk of the minority applicants' would be excluded." The court then looked to the Brennan opinion to develop a nexus between past societal discrimination and present underrepresentation of minorities:

Finally, the existence of a nexus between past discrimination and present disproportionate academic and professional underrepresentation was fully acknowledged in the Brennan opinion itself, wherein it was readily assumed that societal discrimination against minorities has impaired their access to equal educational opportunity. As the opinion states, "Davis clearly could conclude that the serious and persistent underrepresentation of minorities in medicine . . . *is the result of handicaps under which minority applicants labor as a consequence of a background of deliberate, purposeful discrimination against minorities in education and in society generally,* as well as in the medical profession (438 U.S. at 370–71 . . .). . . . Judicial decrees recognizing discrimination in public education in California testify to the fact of widespread discrimination suffered by California-born minority applicants. . . . The conclusion is inescapable that applicants to medical school must be few indeed who endured the effects of *de jure* segregation, the resistance to *Brown I* [*Brown v. Board of Education,* 347 U.S. 483 (1954)], or the equally debilitating pervasive private discrimination fostered by our long history of official discrimination, and yet come to the starting line with an education equal to whites" (438 U.S. at 372 . . . , italics added, footnotes omitted) [625 P.2d at 226].

Combining its reliance on the Brennan opinion with its reliance on the Powell opinion, the court concluded:

Accordingly, we conclude that, whether based on the Powell reasoning of assuring an academically beneficial diversity among the student body, or on the Brennan rationale of mitigating the effects of historical discrimination, it is abundantly clear that the university's 1975 admissions program would, on its face, meet federal constitutional standards as declared by a majority of the justices of the high Court [625 P.2d at 226].

Having upheld the facial validity of the Davis law school's admissions policy, the court next considered DeRonde's argument that the policy had been unconstitutionally applied to his particular circumstances. In rejecting this argument, the court again relied heavily on the Powell opinion in *Bakke:*

We readily acknowledge, of course, that a facially valid procedure may in its actual application produce a constitutionally discriminatory result. Indeed, Justice Powell in *Bakke* fully and fairly both raised the possibility and anticipated the answer, noting:

> It has been suggested that an admissions program which considers race only as one factor is simply a subtle and more sophisticated—but no less effective—means of according racial preference than the Davis program. A facial intent to discriminate, however, is evident in petitioner's preference program and not denied in this case. *No such facial infirmity exists in an admissions program where race or ethnic background is simply one element—to be weighed fairly against other elements—in the selection process.* . . . And a court would not assume that a university, professing to employ a facially nondiscriminatory admissions policy, would operate it as a cover for the functional equivalent of a quota system. In short, *good faith would be presumed in the absence of a showing to the contrary* in the manner permitted by our cases (438 U.S. at 318–19. . . , italics added; but see 438 U.S. at 378–79 . . . (opn. of Brennan, J.)).

Again, we emphasize Justice Powell's analysis on the point because the Brennan group presumably would permit even a deliberate and systematic exclusion of white applicants if supported by the requisite showing of past discrimination.

Justice Powell further observed that "So long as the university proceeds on an individualized, case-by-case basis, there is no warrant for judicial interference in the academic process. If an applicant can establish that the institution does not adhere to a policy of individual comparisons, or can show that a systematic exclusion of certain groups results, the presumption of legality might be overcome, creating the necessity of proving legitimate educational purpose" (438 U.S. at 319, n.53 . . .).

The record before us is barren of any evidence showing that the university was deliberately using the challenged admissions procedure either as a "cover" for a quota system or as a means of systematic exclusion of, or discrimination against, white male applicants such as DeRonde. The trial court made no such finding. Without proof of such an intent, the university's procedures must be upheld against a claim of unlawful racial discrimination even if accompanied by some evidence of a disproportionate impact (see *Bakke,* 438 U.S. at 289, n.27 (opn. of Powell, J.); *Arlington Heights v. Metropolitan Housing Corp.* (1977), 429 U.S. 252, 264–66 . . .).

Moreover, the evidence fails to support a finding of such disproportionate impact. The record does reflect that, between 1971 and 1977, the percentage of minorities in the entering classes at King Hall has been substantial, fluctuating from a low of 22.78 percent in 1971 to a high of 41.6 percent in 1976. From this arithmetic, DeRonde argues that "for six straight years, from 1971 to 1976, the percentage of minority students entering classes at Davis law school averaged 33 percent of those classes. This was at a time when more *highly qualified* male Caucasians were applying for admission than in the history of the school. . . . How can there be said to exist no 'disproportionate' impact when *extremely well-qualified* male Caucasian applicants outnumber *poorly qualified* minority applicants by over three to one and are admitted to the school in a lesser percentage?" (Italics added.)

As the italicized portion of the argument reveals, the principal difficulty with DeRonde's statistical analysis is that it is based upon the faulty premise that it is only a high PFYA or GPA which truly "qualifies" an applicant for admission to law school. Yet as Justice Powell carefully explained in *Bakke,* racial or ethnic origin, as well as other "nonobjective" factors, such as personal talents, work experience, or leadership potential, properly may be considered in weighing each applicant's qualifications (438 U.S. at 317–20 . . . ; for a probing analysis of the concept of "merit" within the academic context, see Fallon, "To Each According to His Ability, from None According to His Race: The Concept of Merit in the Law of Anti-discrimination," 60 *Boston University L. Rev.* 815, 871–76 (1980)).

DeRonde's statistics may indicate that the university has placed considerable weight upon racial or ethnic factors in determining the composition of its entering law classes. Yet nothing in *Bakke* prohibits such a practice, so long as individualized personal consideration is given to the varied qualifications of each applicant. Furthermore, the fact remains that male Caucasian applicants to King Hall continue to gain admission in respectable numbers. For example, according to DeRonde's own figures, in 1975, the year of DeRonde's application, 157 white males were offered admission as opposed to 133 minority applicants. We do not know the number of white females who were admitted. These statistics alone, however, would appear to contradict any assertion that the university has adopted or implemented a systematic plan or scheme to exclude male Caucasians [625 P.2d at 226–28].

Taken together, *McDonald* and *DeRonde* add considerably to the law on affirmative action. The courts adopted the same analytical approach to determining the validity of particular admissions policies. In developing this analysis, both courts affirmed the authority of the Powell opinion and the Brennan group's opinion in *Bakke,* illustrating how these two opinions may be read together to provide a guide to the validity of affirmative action admissions plans. By accepting both opinions, the *McDonald* and *DeRonde* courts also accepted two separate justifications for implementing affirmative action: the "diverse student body" justification espoused by Powell and the "alleviation of past discrimination" justification espoused by the Brennan group.

More recently, the affirmative action debate has looked more closely at the "diverse student body" rationale, analyzing whether Title VI and the U.S. Constitution permit the use of affirmative action programs to promote "diversity." Despite the salience of the diversity argument to many educators, it has been difficult to persuade courts that this goal justifies race-conscious admissions programs. A federal district court applied the teachings of *Bakke* and its progeny to evaluate the claim of a white male applicant to CUNY Law School at Queens College that his rejection violated Titles VI and IX and the equal protection clause. The plaintiff had applied to, and been rejected by, the law school eight times. In *Davis v. Halperin*, 768 F. Supp. 968 (E.D.N.Y. 1991), the plaintiff challenged the school's use of "diversity" as one of the criteria on which admissions decisions were made. Although the court rejected the plaintiff's sex discrimination claim, it applied strict scrutiny to his race discrimination claim, saying that the provisions of Title VI have been interpreted to proscribe discrimination that also violates the equal protection clause. The court found that the plaintiff had made out a prima facie case of race discrimination because the law school had admitted minority applicants with lower LSAT scores and lower undergraduate grades than the plaintiff's. In response to the law school's motion for summary judgment, the judge ruled that, although the law school had rebutted the plaintiff's prima facie case of race discrimination by demonstrating that it had followed an affirmative action plan, the court could not determine whether the plan's purpose was to remedy past discrimination by the law school itself (which was permissible) or to remedy past societal discrimination (which was impermissible). The court remarked: "*Bakke* makes it clear that in the absence of prior discrimination by the university the consideration of race as one factor among many by a university admissions process is constitutional only so far as it seeks to procure for the university the educational benefits which flow from having a diverse student body (768 F. Supp. at 981)." The judge ordered the matter to be tried to a jury.

As interpreted and applied in *McDonald, DeRonde,* and *Davis,* the *Bakke* case has brought some clarity to the law of affirmative action in admissions. A recent case, however, has challenged the continuing vitality of Justice Powell's opinion in *Bakke,* as well as the authority of colleges to use "diversity" as a lawful rationale for considering race, gender, or other such characteristics as a "plus" factor in admissions. In *Hopwood v. Texas,* 78 F.3d 932 (5th Cir. 1996), four individuals who were denied admission to the University of Texas Law School sued the state and the Law School under the equal protection clause of the U.S. Constitution's Fourteenth Amendment, Sections 1981 and 1983 of the federal civil rights statutes (see Section 4.1.4.1), and Title VI of the Civil Rights Act of 1964 (see Section 12.4.2), claiming that they were denied admission on the basis of their race. The law school's affirmative action admissions program gave preferences to black and Mexican American applicants only and used a separate committee to evaluate their applications. "Cutoff scores" used to allocate applicants to various categories in the admissions process were lower for blacks and Mexican Americans than for other applicants, resulting in the admission of students in the "minority" category whose college grades and LSAT scores were lower than those of some white applicants who had been rejected.

The trial and appellate courts used the strict scrutiny standard of review (see Section 4.1.4.1), under which the defendant must establish (1) that it has a compelling interest that justifies the "discrimination," and (2) that its use of racial classifications is narrowly tailored to achieve its compelling interest. The law school had presented five justifications for its affirmative action admissions program, each of which, it argued, met the compelling state interest test: (1) to achieve the law school's mission of providing a first-class legal education to members of the two largest minority groups in Texas; (2) to achieve a diverse student body; (3) to remedy the present effects of past discrimination in the Texas public school system; (4) to comply with the 1983 consent decree with the Office of Civil Rights, U.S. Department of Education, regarding recruitment of black and Mexican American students; and (5) to comply with the standards of the American Bar Association and Association of American Law Schools regarding diversity.

Although the federal district court ruled that the portions of the law school's admissions program that gave "minority" applicants a separate review process violated the Fourteenth Amendment, that court had found, using the strict scrutiny standard, that two of the law school's justifications for the program (numbers 2 and 3) passed constitutional muster. Thus, the trial court had held that the affirmative action plan furthered the compelling interest of attaining diversity in the student body and that it served to remedy prior discrimination by the state of Texas in its entire public school system (including elementary and secondary schools). A three-judge panel of the appellate court rejected these justifications, finding that each failed one part of the strict scrutiny test.

The appellate panel first addressed the law school's argument that its admissions program was justified because it increased the diversity of the student body. It examined the opinion of Justice Powell in *Regents of the University of California v. Bakke,* 438 U.S. 265 (1978) and his response to the university's argument that a race-conscious admissions program was necessary to ensure a diverse student body for the medical school and that attaining a diverse student body was a compelling governmental interest. Although Justice Powell had stated that setting aside places in the medical school for which only minorities were eligible did not meet the strict scrutiny standard, he did state that attaining a diverse student body was a "constitutionally permissible goal for an institution of higher education" (438 U.S. at 311). The Fifth Circuit panel rejected Justice Powell's argument, however, stating that "achieving a diverse student body is not a compelling interest under the Fourteenth Amendment" (78 F.3d at 944) and noted that Justice Powell's opinion had never gained the support of a majority of the Supreme Court—in *Bakke* or in any subsequent case. Furthermore, "no case since *Bakke* has accepted diversity as a compelling state interest under a strict scrutiny analysis" (78 F.3d at 944). Under recent Supreme Court precedent, said the court, racial classifications are only permissible for remedial purposes.

The court then addressed the district court's finding that the law school's admission program had a remedial purpose. Although the court recognized that the state of Texas had discriminated on the basis of race and ethnicity in its public education system, the law school's admission program was not designed to remedy that prior unlawful conduct because the program gave preferences to minorities from outside Texas and to some who had attended private school. Furthermore, said the court, in order for the admissions program to comply with constitutional requirements, the law school would have had to present evidence of a history of its own prior unlawful segregation. "A broad program that sweeps in all minorities with a remedy that is in no way related to past harms cannot survive constitutional scrutiny" (78 F.3d at 951). Once prior discrimination had been established, the law school would then have to trace present effects from the prior discrimination, to establish the size of those effects, and to develop a limited plan to remedy the harm. The "present effects" cited by both the law school and the district court—a bad reputation in the minority community and a perceived hostile environment in the law school for minority students—were insufficient, said the court, citing the Fourth Circuit's opinion in *Podberesky v. Kirwan* (see Section 4.2.4).

One appellate judge, although concurring in the result of the plaintiffs' constitutional claim, disagreed with the majority's statement that diversity could never be a compelling state interest. The lack of Supreme Court precedent on what constitutes a compelling interest and on whether diversity could provide such an interest in a public graduate school program, convinced this judge that the proper approach was to assume, without deciding, that diversity was a compelling state interest, and to consider whether the law school admissions program was narrowly tailored to achieve diversity. The judge's concern was that "diversity," as defined by the law school, covered only two groups: blacks and Mexican Americans. Limiting the program to these two groups, said the judge, "more closely resembles a set aside or quota system for those two disadvantaged minorities than it does an academic admissions program narrowly tailored to achieve true diversity" (78 F.3d at 966).

When the panel's opinion was announced, two other Fifth Circuit judges sought to have the case heard by the full seventeen-judge appellate bench (called an *en banc* review), despite the fact that neither party sought such review. A majority of the circuit judges voted not to hear the case *en banc* (84 F.3d 720 (5th Cir. 1996)). Two judges dissented vigorously from the denial of *en banc* review. Stating that the panel opinion "goes out of its way to break ground that the Supreme Court itself has been careful to avoid" (84 F.3d at 721), the dissenters accused the majority of "purport[ing] to overrule" the *Bakke* decision, calling the outcome "radical" and insisting that "every active judge on this court" should review the case because it would "literally change the face of public educational institutions throughout Texas, the other states of this circuit, and this nation."

The dissenters were particularly outraged at the panel's dismissal of Justice Powell's decision in *Bakke,* stating that the panel had strung together "pieces and shards of recent Supreme Court opinions" dealing with a variety of affirmative action issues in noneducational settings and had created "a gossamer chain which it proffers as a justification for overruling *Bakke*" (84 F.3d at 722). Characterizing the panel decision as "overreaching," a second judge reminded the court of the legacy of de jure segregation against black applicants, most notably in the *Sweatt v. Painter* litigation in which the U.S. Supreme Court found the admissions policies of the University of Texas Law School to violate the equal protection clause because they excluded blacks (399 U.S. 629 (1950)).

The U.S. Supreme Court rejected the law school's request that it review the Fifth Circuit's opinion (116 S. Ct. 2581 (1996)), a decision that leaves the legal status of racial or other minority preferences in public college admissions decisions in limbo. The decision of the Fifth Circuit is binding on public institutions in the states that make up the Fifth Circuit—Louisiana, Mississippi, and Texas— but is not binding on public institutions in other states until and unless federal courts in other circuits, or the state courts themselves, make similar rulings. Given the Fourth Circuit's rejection of race-based financial aid at public institutions in *Podberesky* (Section 4.2.4), it is possible that that circuit would adopt the reasoning of *Hopwood,* should a relevant case reach that court.

Until other courts speak, it is inappropriate to declare nonremedial affirmative action in admissions "dead." Even though another federal circuit did recently rule that using race to choose between equally qualified teachers when making a layoff decision violated Title VII (see Section 2.2.2), that court limited its ruling to employment, stating specifically that *Bakke* did not apply in the employment setting.

Hopwood does, however, raise questions for public colleges outside the Fifth Circuit and also for private colleges whose affirmative action programs could face challenges under Title VI (see Section 12.4.2), given *Bakke's* assertion that Title VI must be interpreted under equal protection clause principles. In response, colleges should review their affirmative action programs (in both admissions and financial aid) in light of the ongoing public dialogue about affirmative action, and in light of both of the prongs of the strict scrutiny test. Special attention should be given to any mechanisms that use separate committees, criteria, or cutoff scores for minority applicants; these mechanisms are clearly subject to legal challenge, as happened in *Hopwood.* If need be, colleges should also clarify exactly why and how they use racial preferences, how they identify present effects of past discrimination, how they define diversity (and why they define it this way), and the value that diversity adds to the academic environment. (For an excellent discussion of the pitfalls of limiting affirmative action programs to selected minority groups, see Gabriel J. Chin, "*Bakke* to the Wall: The Crisis of Diversity," 4 *William & Mary Bill of Rights Journal* 881 (1996)). Moreover, in light of *Hopwood,* colleges should give renewed attention to the possible use of "uniform" or "differential systems" of affirmative action as alternatives to "preferential" systems. These alternatives (discussed below) are much less vulnerable than preferential systems to the types of legal challenges made in *Hopwood.*

The legal and social issues of affirmative action are sensitive, and administrators should involve legal counsel fully when considering any adoption or change of an affirmative action admissions policy. The following five guidelines can assist institutions in any such consideration:

1. As a threshold matter, the institution should consider whether it or the educational system of which it is a part has ever discriminated against minorities or women in its admissions policies. If any illegal discrimination has occurred, the law will require that the institution use affirmative action to the extent necessary to overcome the present effects of the past discrimination. (See the discussion in the *Bakke* opinions, 438 U.S. at 284, 328, and 414.) The limits that the *Bakke* decision places on the use of racial preferences do not apply to situations where "an institution has been found, by a court, legislature, or administrative agency, to have discriminated on the basis of race, color, or national origin. Race-conscious procedures that are impermissible in voluntary affirmative action programs may be required [in order] to correct specific acts of past discrimination committed by an institution or other entity to which the institution is directly related" (U.S. Dept. HEW, Policy Interpretation of Title VI, 44 Fed. Reg. 58509 at 58510 (Oct. 10, 1979)).

For example, in *Geier v. Alexander,* 801 F.2d 799 (6th Cir. 1986), a federal appellate court upheld a consent decree that required race-conscious recruitment and admissions practices at the formerly *de jure* segregated Tennessee system of public higher education. (For a discussion of this case and its history, see Section 12.4.2.) The Department of Justice had attacked the consent decree, asserting that it denied equal protection to nonminority students because it was not victim-specific. The court applied strict scrutiny to the challenged practices, finding that the elimination of persistent racial segregation in public higher education was a "compelling state interest," that the five-year life of the consent decree was reasonable, that its goals regarding the admission of minority students were "modest," and that the plan was "narrowly tailored" to achieve the purpose of remedying prior discrimination.

2. In considering whether to employ an affirmative action program, the institution should carefully determine its purposes and objectives and make its decisions in the context of these purposes and objectives. The institution may choose one or a combination of three basic approaches to affirmative action: the uniform system, the differential system, and the preferential system. While all three systems can be implemented lawfully, the potential for legal challenge increases as the institution proceeds down the list. The potential for substantially increasing minority enrollments also increases, however, so that an institution which is deterred by the possibility of legal action may also be forsaking part of the means to achieve its educational and societal goals.

3. A uniform system of affirmative action consists of changing the institution's general admissions standards or procedures so that they are more sensitively attuned to the qualifications and potential contributions of disadvantaged and minority individuals. These changes are then applied uniformly to all applicants. For example, all applicants might be given credit for work experience, demonstrated commitment to working in a particular geographical area, or overcoming handicaps or disadvantages. Such a system would thus allow all candidates—regardless of race, ethnicity, or sex—to demonstrate particular qualities that may not be reflected in grades or test scores. It would not preclude the use of numerical cutoffs where administrators believe that applicants with grades or test scores above or below a certain number should be automatically accepted or rejected. In *DeFunis*, Justice Douglas discussed aspects of such a system (416 U.S. at 331–32), as did the California Supreme Court in *Bakke* (553 P.2d at 1165–66).

4. A differential system of affirmative action is based on the concept that equal treatment of differently situated individuals may itself create inequality; different standards for such individuals become appropriate when use of uniform standards would in effect discriminate against them. If, for instance, the institution determined, using appropriate psychometric procedures, that a standardized admissions test that it used was culturally biased as applied to its disadvantaged or minority applicants, it might use a different standard for assessing their performance on the test or employ some other criterion in lieu of the test.

In *Bakke*, Justice Powell referred to a differential system by noting, "Racial classifications in admissions conceivably could serve a . . . purpose . . . which petitioner does not articulate: fair appraisal of each individual's academic promise in light of some bias in grading or testing procedures. To the extent that race and ethnic background were considered only to the extent of curing established inaccuracies in predicting academic performance, it might be argued that there is no 'preference' at all" (438 U.S. at 306 n.43). Justice Douglas's *DeFunis* opinion also referred extensively to differential standards and procedures:

> Professional persons, particularly lawyers, are not selected for life in a computerized society. The Indian who walks to the beat of Chief Seattle of the Muckleshoot tribe in Washington has a different culture than examiners at law schools. . . .
>
> The admissions committee acted properly in my view in setting minority applications apart for separate processing. These minorities have cultural backgrounds that are vastly different from the dominant Caucasian. Many Eskimos, American Indians, Filipinos, Chicanos, Asian Indians, Burmese, and Africans come from such disparate backgrounds that a test sensitively tuned for most applicants would be wide of the mark for many minorities. . . .
>
> I think a separate classification of these applicants is warranted, lest race be a subtle force in eliminating minority members because of cultural differences. . . .
>
> The reason for the separate treatment of minorities as a class is to make more certain that racial factors do not militate *against an applicant or on his behalf.* . . .
>
> The key to the problem is consideration of such applications *in a racially neutral way* [416 U.S. at 334–36, 340].

To remain true to the theory of a differential system, an institution can modify standards or procedures only to the extent necessary to counteract the discriminatory effect of applying uniform standards; and the substituted standards or procedures must be designed to select only candidates whose qualifications and potential contributions are comparable to those of candidates selected under the general standards.

5. A preferential system of affirmative action is explicitly "race conscious" and allows some form of preference for minority applicants. The admissions programs at issue in the cases discussed above can be viewed, for the most part, as preferential systems. It is the preference available only to minorities that creates the reverse discrimination claim. Depending on the institution's objectives, some form of racial preference may indeed be necessary. In *Bakke,* the Brennan group of justices agreed that:

> There are no practical means by which . . . [the university] could achieve its ends in the foreseeable future without the use of race-conscious measures. With respect to any factor (such as poverty or family educational background) that may be used as a substitute for race as an indicator of past discrimination, whites greatly outnumber racial minorities simply because whites make up a far larger percentage of the total population and therefore far outnumber minorities

in absolute terms at every socioeconomic level. . . . Moreover, while race is posi-
tively correlated with differences in . . . [grades and standardized test] scores,
economic disadvantage is not. Thus, it appears that economically disadvantaged
whites do not score less well than economically advantaged whites while economically advantaged blacks score less well than do disadvantaged whites.
These statistics graphically illustrate that the university's purpose to integrate
its classes by compensating for past discrimination could not be achieved by a
general preference for the economically disadvantaged or the children of parents
of limited education unless such groups were to make up the entire class
[438 U.S. at 376–77].

Preferential systems may fulfill objectives broader than those of differential
systems. As *McDonald* and *DeRonde* demonstrate, the leading examples are the
objectives of diversifying the student body and alleviating the effects of past institutional discrimination. In a preferential system, the institution must exercise
special care in determining its objectives and relating its system to them. Administrators should rely demonstrably on the institution's educational expertise and
involve policy makers at the highest levels of authority over the institution. As
emphasized by the court in an important pre-*Bakke* case, *Hupart v. Board of
Higher Education of the City of New York,* 420 F. Supp. 1087 (S.D.N.Y. 1976):

Every distinction made on a racial basis . . . must be justified. . . . It cannot be
accomplished thoughtlessly or covertly, then justified after the fact. The defendants cannot sustain their burden of justification by coming to court with an
array of hypothetical and *post facto* justifications for discrimination that has
occurred either without their approval or without their conscious and formal
choice to discriminate as a matter of official policy. It is not for the court to
supply a rational or compelling basis (or something in between) to sustain the
questioned state action. That task must be done by appropriate state officials
before they take any action [420 F. Supp. at 1106].

The permissible types and scope of preference are also subject to continuing
debate. Under *Bakke,* a preferential system that employs explicit racial or ethnic quotas is, by a 5–to–4 vote, reverse discrimination and thus prohibited. But
other forms of preference may be permissible. Until the U.S. Supreme Court
speaks again, the best guideline is Justice Powell's opinion in *Bakke.* The Brennan group of justices approved of explicit, specific preferences; a fifth vote was
needed to form a majority; and of the remaining justices, only Powell acknowledged support for any form of preferential admissions system. Justice Powell's
opinion thus sets a boundary that administrators should stay within to reasonably ensure legality.

Although the Supreme Court has not addressed affirmative action preferences
in college admissions since *Bakke,* it has considered such preferences in the

employment context and in the allocation of public funding. For example, the Supreme Court, in *Johnson v. Transportation Agency,* 480 U.S. 616 (1987), cited with approval Justice Powell's opinion in *Bakke* in a case upholding affirmative action plans that allowed employers to consider "ethnicity or sex" as "a factor" in making hiring decisions. This case is discussed in Section 2.2.2. And the Court, in analyzing another voluntary affirmative action plan under the equal protection clause, determined that the "strict scrutiny" test would be applied. This case, *City of Richmond v. J. A. Croson Co.,* combined with another Supreme Court ruling in *Adarand Constructors v. Pena,* 115 S. Ct. 2097 (1995), suggests that attempts of public entities to remedy "societal discrimination" when there is no evidence that the organization itself has engaged in discrimination will run afoul of the equal protection clause. Although the Court's rulings in the employment and public contracting contexts must be interpreted with great care when applied to college admissions, these cases are clearly relevant for the determination of how affirmative action programs may lawfully be developed and implemented, and both *Croson* and *Adarand* were relied upon in *Hopwood* to invalidate the university's affirmative action program.

For Justice Powell, and thus currently for administrators, the key to a lawful preference system is "a policy of individual comparisons" that "assures a measure of competition among all applicants" and does not result in any "systematic exclusion of certain groups" on grounds of race or ethnicity from competition for a portion of the places in a class (see 438 U.S. at 319 n.53). In such a system, "race or ethnic background may be deemed a 'plus' in a particular applicant's file" as long as it is only "one element—to be weighed fairly against other elements—in the selection process. . . . A court would not assume that a university, professing to employ [such] a racially nondiscriminatory admissions policy, would operate it as a cover for the functional equivalent of a quota system" (438 U.S. at 317–18). (As discussed above, Powell's model of a constitutional preference policy is the Harvard plan, a copy of which is set out in an appendix to his opinion.)

But affirmative action programs that reserve a certain number of slots for minority applicants or that evaluate minority applicants only against each other and not against the entire group of applicants, will likely run afoul of the Constitution and/or Title VI. In 1992, the U.S. Department of Education and the University of California at Berkeley entered an agreement whereby the law school at Berkeley agreed to halt its practice of separating applicants by race into separate pools for admissions purposes. The law school had admission goals for each minority or ethnic group, and had separate waiting lists by ethnic or minority group as well. Berkeley, and other law schools as well, now require admissions committee members to read and evaluate a random group of applicants rather than having particular individuals evaluate and make admissions decisions only for minority applicants.

Institutions should also take care that they do not exclude certain underrepresented groups from their affirmative action programs. The Office for Civil Rights ruled that a decision by the state of Connecticut to exclude Asians and Native Americans from programs to recruit and retain minority students violated Title VI. The ruling was based on an examination of representation of students from these groups at each institution, rather than the statewide figures that had been used to justify the exclusion. Asian groups had argued that their exclusion was based on stereotypes (S. Jaschik, "Affirmative-Action Ruling on Connecticut Called a 'Big Step' for Asian Americans," *Chron. Higher Educ.*, May 19, 1993, A19).

By following the five guidelines presented in this section and by tailoring its affirmative action program to recent concerns articulated by the Office for Civil Rights, an institution—with the active involvement of legal counsel—may still be able to maximize the elbow room it has to make policy choices about affirmative action. By carefully considering and justifying its choices under these guidelines, the institution may be able to present a compelling defense to an attack on its affirmative action system. The future of these systems is in question, however, and until the Supreme Court speaks again on this issue, the debate, and the uncertainty, will continue.

4.1.6. Readmission

The readmission of previously excluded students can pose additional legal problems for postsecondary institutions. Although the legal principles in Section 4.1 apply generally to readmissions, the contract theory (Section 3.2) may assume added prominence, because the student-institution contract may include provisions concerning exclusion and readmission. The principles in Sections 6.1, 7.2, and 7.3 may also apply generally to readmissions where the student challenges the validity of the original exclusion.

Institutions should have an explicit policy on readmission, even if that policy is simply, "Excluded students will never be considered for readmission." An explicit readmission policy can give students advance notice of their rights, or lack of rights, concerning readmission and, where readmission is permitted, can provide standards and procedures to promote fair and evenhanded decision making. If the institution has an explicit admissions policy, administrators should take pains to follow it, especially since its violation could be considered a breach of contract. Similarly, if administrators make an agreement with a student concerning readmission, they should firmly adhere to it. *Levine v. George Washington University*, C.A. (Civil Action) 8230–76 (D.C. Super. Ct. 1976), for instance, concerned a medical student who had done poorly in his first year but was allowed to repeat the year, with the stipulation that he would be excluded for a "repeated performance of marginal quality." On the second try, he passed all his courses but ranked low in each. The school excluded him. The court used contract principles to overturn the exclusion, finding that the school's subjective and arbitrary interpretation of "marginal quality," without prior notice to the student, breached the agreement between student and school. In contrast, the court in *Giles v. Howard University*, 428 F. Supp. 603 (D.D.C. 1977), held that the university's refusal to readmit a former medical student was not a breach of contract, because the refusal was consistent with the "reasonable expectations" of the parties.

The California case of *Paulsen v. Golden Gate University* illustrates the flexibility that courts may accord institutions in devising and applying readmission standards; at the same time, the case illustrates the legal and practical difficulties an institution may encounter if it has no written readmission policy or does not administer its policy evenhandedly. The plaintiff in *Paulsen* had been excluded from law school at the end of his third year and petitioned the school to be allowed to attend for another year to make up his deficiencies. The school ultimately permitted him to continue on the condition that he could not receive a degree, but only a "certificate of attendance," no matter how high his grades were. After attending for a fourth year and removing his deficiencies, the student sued for a degree. The trial court ordered the institution to award the degree, and the intermediate appellate court affirmed (156 Cal. Rptr. 190 (Cal. Ct. App. 1979)). This court found that the school "apparently maintained an unwritten policy" of permitting deficient students to continue for an extra year but that no other students who had done so had been subjected to the "no-degree" condition. On this basis, the intermediate appellate court held for the student because the no-degree condition was "arbitrary, a manifest abuse of discretion, and an unreasonable discrimination between students."

On further appeal in *Paulsen*, the California Supreme Court reversed the intermediate appellate court (159 Cal. Rptr. 858 (Cal. 1979)). Although the school had allowed other students to return for an additional year without imposing the "no-degree" condition, the Court noted, none of the other students had "flunked out," as Paulsen had.

> The imposition of reasonable conditions on the readmission of academically disqualified students was apparently a regular practice of Golden Gate. Although the no-degree condition may have been novel at the time, this fact in itself does not demonstrate its impermissibility. The only unacceptable conditions are those imposed for reasons extraneous to a student's qualifications for a degree (*Shuffer v. Board of Trustees*, 67 Cal. App. 3d 208, 220, 136 Cal. Rptr. 527). Here, there was an obvious relationship between Paulsen's special fourth-year program, even if unique, and his remarkably unsatisfactory academic record [159 Cal. Rptr. at 862].

Even though the institution ultimately prevailed, a written and consistently adhered-to readmission policy might have saved it from the uncertainties of having others guess about the bases for its decisions.

Another case, decided in 1980, illustrates the importance of carefully considering the procedures to be used in making readmission decisions. In *Evans v. West Virginia Board of Regents,* 271 S.E.2d 778 (W. Va. 1980), a student in good standing at a state school of osteopathic medicine had been granted a one-year leave of absence because of illness. When he sought reinstatement two months after termination of the leave, he was informed that because of his lateness he would have to reapply for admission. He did so but was rejected without explanation. The West Virginia Supreme Court of Appeals found that the student was "not in the same class as an original applicant to a professional school." Nor was he in the same position as a student who had been excluded for academic reasons, since "nothing appears of record even remotely suggesting his unfitness or inability to complete the remainder of his education." Rather, since he had voluntarily withdrawn after successfully completing two and a half years of his medical education, the student had a "reasonable expectation that he would be permitted to complete his education." He thus had "a sufficient property interest in the continuation and completion of his medical education to warrant the imposition of minimal due process protections." The court prescribed that the following procedures be accorded the student if the school again sought to deny him readmission: "(1) a formal written notice of the reasons should he not be permitted to continue his medical education; (2) a sufficient opportunity to prepare a defense to the charges; (3) an opportunity to have retained counsel at any hearings on the charges; (4) a right to confront his accusers and present evidence on his own behalf; (5) an unbiased hearing tribunal; and (6) an adequate record of the proceedings" (271 S.E.2d at 781).

The appellate court in *Evans* did not indicate the full terms of the school's policies regarding leave of absence and readmission or the extent to which these policies were put in writing. Perhaps, as in *Paulsen,* other schools in the defendant's position may avoid legal hot water by having a clear statement of their policies, including any procedural protections that apply and the consequences of allowing a leave of absence to expire.

Although private institutions would not be subject to the Fourteenth Amendment due process reasoning in *Evans,* they should nevertheless note the court's assertion that readmission decisions encompass different considerations and consequences than original admission decisions. Even private institutions may therefore choose to clothe readmission decisions with greater procedural safeguards than they apply to admission decisions. Moreover, private institutions, like public institutions, should clearly state their readmission policies in writing and coordinate them with their policies on exclusion and leaves of absence.

Once such policies are stated in writing, or if the institution has a relatively consistent practice of readmitting former students, contract claims may ensue if the institution does not follow its policies. For discussion of an unsuccessful contract claim by a student seeking readmission to medical school, see *North v. State of Iowa,* 400 N.W.2d 566 (Iowa, 1987).

Students may also allege that denials of readmission are grounded in disability or race discrimination. In *Anderson v. University of Wisconsin,* 841 F.2d 737 (7th Cir. 1988), a black former law student sued the university when it refused to readmit him for a third time because of his low grade point average. To the student's race discrimination claim, the court replied that the law school had consistently readmitted black students with lower grades than those of whites it had readmitted; thus, no systemic race discrimination could be shown against black students. With regard to the plaintiff's claim that the law school had refused to readmit him, in part, because of his alcoholism, the court determined that Section 504 requires a plaintiff to demonstrate that he is "otherwise qualified" before relief can be granted. Given the plaintiff's inability to maintain the minimum grade point average required for retention, the court determined that the plaintiff was not "otherwise qualified," and ruled that "[l]aw schools may consider academic prospects and sobriety when deciding whether an applicant is entitled to a scarce opportunity for education" (841 F.2d at 742).

SEC. 4.2. FINANCIAL AID

4.2.1. General Principles

The legal principles affecting financial aid have a wide variety of sources. Some principles apply generally to all financial aid, whether awarded as scholarships, assistantships, loans, fellowships, preferential tuition rates, or in some other form. Other principles depend on the particular source of funds being used and thus may vary with the aid program or the type of award. Sections 4.2.2 through 4.2.7 discuss the principles, and specific legal requirements resulting from them, that present the most difficult problems for financial aid administrators. This section discusses more general principles affecting financial aid.

The principles of contract law may apply to financial aid awards, since an award once made may create a contract between the institution and the aid recipient. Typically, the institution's obligation is to provide a particular type of aid at certain times and in certain amounts. The student recipient's obligation depends on the type of aid. With loans, the typical obligation is to repay the principal and a prescribed rate of interest at certain times and in certain amounts. With other aid, the obligation may be only to spend the funds for specified academic expenses or to achieve a specified level of academic performance in order to maintain aid eligibility. Sometimes, however, the student recipient may have more extensive obligations—for instance, to perform instructional or laboratory duties, play on a varsity athletic team, or provide particular services after graduation. The defendant student in *State of New York v. Coury,* 359 N.Y.S.2d 486 (N.Y. Sup. Ct. 1974), for instance, had accepted a scholarship and agreed, as a condition of the award, to perform internship duties in a welfare agency for one year after graduation. When the student did not perform the duties, the state sought a refund of the scholarship money. The court held for the state because the student had "agreed to accept the terms of the contract" and had not performed as the contract required.

The law regarding gifts, grants, wills, and trusts may also apply to financial aid awards. These legal principles would generally require aid administrators to adhere to any conditions that the donor, grantor, testator, or settlor placed on use of the funds. But the conditions must be explicit at the time of the gift. For example, in *Hawes v. Emory University,* 374 S.E. 2d 328 (Ga. Ct. App. 1988), a scholarship donor demanded that the university return the gift, asserting that the funds had not been dispersed as agreed upon. The court found the contribution to be a valid gift without any indication that its use was restricted in the way the donor later alleged.

Funds provided by government agencies or private foundations must be used in accordance with conditions in the program regulations, grant instrument, or other legal document formalizing the transaction. Section 4.2.2 illustrates such conditions in the context of federal aid programs.

Similarly, funds made available to the institution under wills or trusts must be used in accordance with conditions in the will or trust instrument, unless those conditions are themselves illegal. Conditions that discriminate by race, sex, or religion have posed the greatest problems in this respect. If a public agency or entity has compelled or affirmatively supported the imposition of such conditions, they will usually be considered to violate the federal Constitution's equal protection clause (see *In re Wilson,* 465 N.Y.S.2d 900 (N.Y. 1983)). But if such conditions appear in a privately established and administered trust, they will usually be considered constitutional because no state action is present. In *Shapiro v. Columbia Union National Bank and Trust Co.* (see Section 1.4.2), for instance, the Supreme Court of Missouri refused to find state action to support a claim of sex discrimination lodged against a university's involvement in a private trust established to provide scholarships exclusively for male students. Even in the absence of state action, however, a discriminatory condition in a private trust may still be declared invalid if it violates one of the federal nondiscrimination requirements applicable to federal fund recipients (see Sections 4.2.3 and 4.2.4).

Conditions in testamentary or inter vivos trusts can sometimes be modified by a court under the *cy pres* doctrine. In *Howard Savings Institution v. Peep,* 170 A.2d 39 (N.J. 1961), Amherst College was unable to accept a trust establishing a scholarship loan fund, because one of its provisions violated the college's charter. The provision, stipulating that recipients of the funds had to be "Protestant" and "Gentile," was deleted by the court. Similarly, in *Wilbur v. University of Vermont,* 270 A.2d 889 (Vt. 1970), the court deleted a provision in a financial aid trust that had placed numerical restrictions on the size of the student body at the university's college of arts and sciences. In each case, the court found that the dominant purpose of the person establishing the trust could still be achieved with the restriction removed. As the court in the *Peep* case explained:

> The doctrine of *cy pres* is a judicial mechanism for the preservation of a charitable trust when accomplishment of the particular purpose of the trust becomes impossible, impracticable, or illegal. In such a situation, if the settlor manifested an intent to devote the trust to a charitable purpose more general than the frustrated purpose, a court, instead of allowing the trust to fail, will apply the trust funds to a charitable purpose as nearly as possible to the particular purpose of the settlor [170 A.2d at 42].

Given the numerous legal and public relations issues involved in institutional fundraising and gift acceptance, administrators should develop a clear policy on the acceptance of gifts. For assistance with the development of such a policy, see F. S. Smith, *Looking the Gift Horse in the Mouth* (National Association of College and University Attorneys, 1993).

A third relevant body of legal principles is that of constitutional due process. These principles apply generally to public institutions; they also apply to private institutions when those institutions make awards from public funds (see Section 1.5.2). Since termination of aid may affect both "property" and "liberty" interests (see Section 2.2.2) of the student recipients, courts may sometimes require that termination be accompanied by some form of procedural safeguard. *Corr v. Mattheis*, 407 F. Supp. 847 (D.R.I. 1976), for instance, involved students who had had their federal aid terminated in midyear, under a federal "student unrest" statute, after they had participated in a campus protest against the Vietnam War. The court found that the students had been denied a property interest in continued receipt of funds awarded to them, as well as a liberty interest in being free from stigmas foreclosing further educational or employment opportunities. Termination thus had to be preceded by notice and a meaningful opportunity to contest the decision. In other cases, if the harm or stigma to students is less, the required procedural safeguards may be less stringent. Moreover, if aid is terminated for academic rather than disciplinary reasons, procedural safeguards may be almost nonexistent, as courts follow the distinction between academic deficiency problems and misconduct problems drawn in Section 7.3.3.

In *Conrad v. University of Washington*, 834 P.2d 17 (Wash. 1992), the Washington Supreme Court ruled that student athletes do not have a constitutionally protected property interest in the renewal of their athletic scholarships. The court reversed a lower court's finding that the students, who had been dropped from the football team after several instances of misconduct, had a property interest in renewal of their scholarships. The financial aid agreements that the students had signed were for one academic year only and did not contain promises of renewal. The supreme court interpreted the financial aid agreements as contracts that afforded the students the right to *consideration* for scholarship renewal and—citing *Board of Regents v. Roth* (see Section 2.2.2)—refused to find a "common understanding" that athletic scholarships were given for a four-year period. Furthermore, the court said, the fact that both the university and the NCAA provided minimal due process guarantees did not create a property interest (see Section 10.1.2).

Federal and state laws regulating lending and extensions of credit provide a fourth body of applicable legal constraints. At the federal level, for example, the Truth-in-Lending Act (15 U.S.C. §1601 *et seq.*) establishes various disclosure requirements for loans and credit sales. Such provisions are of concern not only to institutions with typical loan programs but also to institutions with credit plans allowing students or parents to defer payment of tuition for extended periods of time. The federal Truth-in-Lending Act, however, exempts National Direct Student Loans (now Perkins Loans), and Guaranteed Student Loans (now Federal Family Education Loans) (see Section 4.2.2) from its coverage (15 U.S.C. §1603(6)).

As tuition increases have outpaced the rate of inflation and tax law changes have depressed the incentives for savings, state policy makers have looked for other ways to help parents finance their children's college education. One strategy that has received substantial attention in recent years is the creation of prepaid tuition plans by individual colleges and also by some states. For example, a few institutions adopted a program whereby parents of a baby could pay a specified amount to the institution at the time the child was born; later, if the child was admitted, no tuition would be due. If the child was not admitted or did not wish to attend, the payment would be returned with little or no interest. Several states have adopted such plans as well. For example, in 1987 Michigan adopted a prepaid tuition plan that promised to pay four years of tuition at a state institution (or the equivalent amount if the child attended college elsewhere) for a one-time payment by the parents. The funds were put into a trust fund, which invested the money. The assumption underlying the plan was that the investment would produce the anticipated returns and that tuition increases would be stable. That assumption later proved to be incorrect. (For a description of state prepaid tuition plans, see A. Gunn, "Economic and Tax Aspects of Prepaid-Tuition Plans, 17 *J. Coll. & Univ. Law* 243 (1990).) Michigan suspended its program in 1991 ("Michigan Halts Sale of Prepaid-Tuition Contracts While It Re-Examines the Pioneering Program," *Chron. Higher Educ.*, Oct. 2, 1991, A29). Ohio did the same in the spring of 1994 (J. Carmona, "Ohio Agency Suspends Marketing of Prepaid-Tuition Program," *Chron. Higher Educ.*, Apr. 27, 1994, A24).

Because of the potential problems with prepaid tuition plans, other states have adopted savings plans rather than prepayment plans. In many states, parents are encouraged to buy general-obligation bonds issued by the state for the construction and renovation of campus buildings, with the interest tax free. In other states, parents who buy U.S. Savings Bonds pay no state income tax on interest from the bonds if the funds are used to pay college tuition. (Interest on the bonds is also free of federal tax.) Critics of the savings plans say that they will not produce enough income to meet tuition costs; but others believe that plans that encourage saving for college costs will reduce pressure on federal student loan funds and will benefit students who need financial assistance the most.

Given the multitude of tax, contract, and other legal complications of prepaid tuition plans, institutions should consult with counsel knowledgeable in these areas of the law before implementing such plans.

The gap between the cost of inflation and tuition increases, combined with growing pressure to reduce expenditures for federal student assistance, may lead to changes in student financial assistance policies, both by colleges and by the federal and state governments. Some colleges, when making admission decisions, are considering the prospective student's ability to pay; others are targeting students from affluent communities for heavy recruitment. (See S. Lubman, "A 'Student of Value' Means a Student Who Can Pay the Rising Cost of College," *Wall Street Journal,* Jan. 5, 1994, B1.) Although these are policy rather than legal issues for the moment, they may have legal consequences.

4.2.2. Federal Programs

The federal government provides or guarantees many millions of dollars per year in student aid for postsecondary education through a multitude of programs.[2] To protect its investment and ensure the fulfillment of national priorities and goals, the federal government imposes many requirements on the way institutions manage and spend funds under federal programs. Some are general requirements applicable to student aid and all other federal assistance programs. Others are specific programmatic requirements applicable to one student aid program or to a related group of such programs. These requirements constitute the most prominent—and, critics would add, most prolific and burdensome—source of specific restrictions on an institution's administration of financial aid.

The most prominent general requirements are the nondiscrimination requirements discussed in Section 4.2.3, which apply to all financial aid, whether or not it is provided under federal programs. In addition, the federal Buckley Amendment (FERPA) (discussed in Section 3.3.1) imposes various requirements on the institution's record-keeping practices for all the financial aid that it disburses.

---

[2]The number, complexity, and volatility of federal student assistance programs pose legal issues far too lengthy and specialized for treatment in this volume. The discussion in this section relies heavily on D. Rigney & B. Butler, *Federal Student Financial Aid Programs: A Legal and Policy Overview* (National Association of College and University Attorneys, 1993). The annotated bibliography provides additional sources for individuals wishing more detailed information about these programs.

The FERPA regulations, however, do partially exempt financial aid records from nondisclosure requirements. They provide that an institution may disclose personally identifiable information from a student's records, without the student's consent, to the extent "necessary for such purposes as" determining the student's eligibility for financial aid, determining the amount of aid and the conditions that will be imposed regarding it, or enforcing the terms or conditions of the aid (34 C.F.R. §99.31(a)(4)).

Also important are the Student Assistance General Provisions, 34 C.F.R. Part 668, which impose numerous requirements on institutions participating in programs under the Higher Education Act (see below). In determining a student's eligibility for federal assistance, for instance, an institution must ascertain whether the student is in default on any federally subsidized or guaranteed loan or owes a refund on a federal grant, and must obtain the student's "financial aid transcript(s)" from other institutions to assist in this task (34 C.F.R. §668.19).

Most of the federal student aid programs were created by the Higher Education Act of 1965 (20 U.S.C. §§1070–1099), which has been reauthorized and amended regularly since that year. The most recent changes are contained in the Higher Education Amendments of 1992 (106 Stat. 448, 479–652). Financial aid programs for students in health-related studies are in the Public Health Service Act (42 U.S.C. §294 *et seq.* and §297 *et seq.*), and programs for veterans and military personnel are in various acts (see Section 12.3.2). The names and requirements of most of the federal student assistance programs have changed in recent years, and Congress has imposed new accountability requirements on colleges and universities participating in these programs.

The specific programmatic restrictions on federal student aid depend on the particular program. There are various types of programs, with different structures, by which the government makes funds available:

1. Programs in which the federal government provides funds to institutions to establish revolving loan funds—as in the Perkins Loan program (20 U.S.C. §§1087aa–1087hh, 34 C.F.R. Part 674) and the Health Professions Student Loan program (42 U.S.C. §294m *et seq.*, 42 C.F.R. Part 57, subpart C).

2. Programs in which the government grants funds to institutions, which in turn grant them to students—as in the Supplemental Educational Opportunity Grant (SEOG) program (20 U.S.C. §§1070b–1070b-3, 34 C.F.R. Part 676) and the Federal Work-Study (FWS) program (42 U.S.C. §§2751–2756(a), 34 C.F.R. Part 675).

3. Programs in which students receive funds from the federal government—as in the GI Bill program (38 U.S.C. §§3451–4393, 38 C.F.R. 21.1020) and the Pell Grant program (20 U.S.C. §§1070a–1070a-6, 34 C.F.R. Part 690).

4. Programs in which students receive funds from the federal government through the states—as in the State Student Incentive Grant (SSIG) program (20 U.S.C. §1070c *et seq.*, 34 C.F.R. Part 692).

5. Programs in which students receive funds from third-party lenders— as in the Federal Family Educational Loan program (20 U.S.C. §§1071–1087–2, 34 C.F.R. Part 682).

The Federal Family Educational Loan program includes three types of loans: Stafford Loans, Supplemental Loans for Students (SLS), and Parent Loans for Undergraduate Students (PLUS). Each of these programs has its own regulations placing various requirements on the institution. The new Federal Direct Student Loan Program (FDSLP) allows institutions, authorized by the Department of Education, to lend money directly to students through loan capital provided by the federal government (20 U.S.C. §1087a *et seq.*, 34 C.F.R. Part 685). Since the Direct Loan Program eliminates third-party lenders, the Department of Education hopes eventually to replace the FFEL program with this program in order to streamline the student loan system.

A further complication was interjected into the student aid arena in 1982, when Congress amended the Military Selective Service Act to require that students subject to the draft registration law must register as a condition of receiving federal student financial aid (Defense Department Authorization Act of 1983, 50 U.S.C. §462(f)). In order to receive aid, students required to register with Selective Service must file statements with the institutions they attend, certifying that they have complied with the Selective Service law and regulations. The validity of this requirement was upheld by the U.S. Supreme Court in *Selective Service System v. Minnesota Public Interest Research Group*, 468 U.S. 841 (1984). Regulations implementing the certification requirement are published in 34 C.F.R. Part 668 (the Student Assistance General Provisions), §§668.31–668.36.

A section of the Higher Education Act of 1965 requires institutions that participate in any federal financial aid program to make certain information "readily available, through appropriate publications and mailings," to prospective or enrolled students upon request and to the secretary of education on an annual basis (20 U.S.C. §1092(a)). This information must accurately describe (1) the financial aid programs available to students and the methods by which such aid is distributed; (2) the forms, applications, and other requirements that students must complete to be eligible for such assistance; (3) the responsibilities of students receiving such assistance; and (4) the personnel who can assist students with questions regarding financial assistance (20 U.S.C. §1092(a)(1)(A-D, H)). The institution also must provide other information, such as the cost of attendance (tuition, fees, books and supplies, room and board, and related items); its refund policy; the services available to students with disabilities; the institution's standards for "satisfactory progress" toward completion of the degree;

and the terms and conditions under which students receiving guaranteed student loans or direct loans may receive deferral of repayment or partial cancellation under the Peace Corps Act or the Domestic Volunteer Service Act, or for comparable full-time community service (20 U.S.C. §1092(a)(1)(E–G, I–L). Regulations implementing these requirements are found at 34 C.F.R. §§668.41–668.45 (the Student Assistance General Provisions). In 1990, the Student Right-to-Know and Campus Security Act (Pub. L. No. 101–542, 104 Stat. 2381, 20 U.S.C. §1001 *et seq.* (also discussed in Section 10.1.4 of this volume)) added more consumer information requirements to the Higher Education Act, particularly with regard to graduation rates of the student body and of athletes, and crime statistics. Regulations interpreting these new disclosure requirements will also be published in 34 C.F.R. Part 668.

The Immigration Reform and Control Act of 1986 (IRCA) amended Section 484 of the Higher Education Act of 1965 (20 U.S.C. §1091) by conditioning the receipt of Title IV funds upon compliance with a number of verification measures affecting both educational institutions and alien students. In order to participate in grants, loans, or work assistance under Title IV programs, all students must declare in writing that they are U.S. citizens or in an immigrant status that does not preclude their eligibility (§121(a)(3) of IRCA). The IRCA also requires alien students to provide the institution with documentation that clearly establishes their immigration status, and further requires the institution to verify the status of such students with the Immigration and Naturalization Service (INS). Institutions are prohibited from denying, delaying, reducing, or terminating Title IV funds without providing students with a reasonable opportunity to establish eligibility. If, after complying with these requirements, an institution determines that a student is ineligible, it is required to deny or terminate Title IV aid and provide the student with an opportunity for a hearing concerning his or her eligibility (34 C.F.R. §668.1 36(c)).

Another provision of the Higher Education Act requires an institution participating in the federal student aid program to certify "that it has in operation a drug abuse prevention program that is determined by the institution to be accessible to any officer, employee, or student at the institution" (20 U.S.C. §1094-(a)(10)). Similar provisions in other laws that place obligations on institutions receiving federal funds are discussed in Section 12.3.3.

Much of the controversy surrounding the federal student aid programs has concerned the sizable default rates on student loans, particularly at institutions that enroll large proportions of low-income students. Several reports issued by the General Accounting Office have been sharply critical of the practices of colleges, loan guaranty agencies, and the Department of Education in implementing the federally guaranteed student loan programs. As a result, substantial changes have been made in the laws and regulations related to eligibility, repayment, and collection practices. Collection requirements of federal student loan programs are discussed in Section 4.2.7.3. For an extensive analysis of many troubling issues facing federal student aid policy makers, see R. P. Guerre, Note, "Financial Aid in Higher Education: What's Wrong, Who's Being Hurt, What's Being Done," 17 *J. Coll. & Univ. Law* 483 (1991).

Institutions that participate in federal student aid programs must have their program records audited annually by an independent auditor. Regulations regarding the conduct of the audit and reporting requirements appear at 34 C.F.R. §668.24.

Finally, the program integrity provisions of the Higher Education Act Amendments of 1992 (Pub. L. No. 102–325) will enable the federal government, with the help of state entities, to keep a watchful eye over institutions participating in federal financial aid programs. These provisions allow State Postsecondary Review Entities (SPREs) to perform an extensive review of institutions identified by the Department of Education, through statutory criteria, as troublesome. One trigger for this extensive review is an institution's high default rate on federal student loans (20 U.S.C. §1099a *et seq.*).

Federal courts have refused to authorize a private right of action under the Higher Education Act for students to enforce the financial assistance laws and regulations (see, for example, *L'ggrke v. Benkula,* 966 F.2d 1346 (10th Cir. 1992)). But a few courts have permitted students to use state common law fraud or statutory consumer protection theories against the Education Department, colleges, or lenders when the college either ceased operations or provided a poor-quality education (see, for example, *Tipton v. Alexander,* 768 F. Supp. 540 (S.D. W. Va. 1991)). (See Section 12.3.4 for a discussion of private rights of action under federal funding laws.) One court has permitted students to file a RICO (Racketeer Influenced Corrupt Organization) claim against a trade school, alleging mail fraud. In *Gonzalez v. North American College of Louisiana,* 700 F. Supp. 362 (S.D. Tex. 1988), the students charged that the school induced them to enroll and to obtain federal student loans, which they were required to repay. The school was unaccredited; and, after it had obtained the federal funds in the students' name, it closed and did not refund the loan proceeds.

Federal student aid programs bring substantial benefits to students and the colleges they attend. Their administrative and legal requirements, however, are complex and change constantly. It is imperative that administrators and counsel become conversant with these requirements and monitor legislative and judicial developments closely.

4.2.3. Nondiscrimination

The legal principles of nondiscrimination apply to the financial aid process in much the same way they apply to the admissions process (see Sections 4.1.4 and 4.1.5). The same constitutional principles of equal protection apply to financial aid. The relevant statutes and regulations on nondiscrimination—Title VI,

Title IX, Section 504, the Americans with Disabilities Act, and the Age Discrimination Act—all apply to financial aid, although Title IX's and Section 504's coverage and specific requirements for financial aid are different from those for admissions. And affirmative action poses difficulties for financial aid programs similar to those it poses for admissions programs.

Of the federal statutes, Title IX has the most substantial impact on the financial aid programs and policies of postsecondary institutions. The regulations (34 C.F.R. §106.37), with four important exceptions, prohibit the use of sex-restricted scholarships and virtually every other sex-based distinction in the financial aid program. Section 106.37(a)(1) prohibits the institution from providing "different amount[s] or types" of aid, "limit[ing] eligibility" for "any particular type or source" of aid, "apply[ing] different criteria," or otherwise discriminating "on the basis of sex" in awarding financial aid. Section 106.37 (a)(2) prohibits the institution from giving any assistance, "through solicitation, listing, approval, provision of facilities, or other services," to any "foundation, trust, agency, organization, or person" that discriminates on the basis of sex in providing financial aid to the institution's students. Section 106.37 (a)(3) also prohibits aid eligibility rules that treat the sexes differently "with regard to marital or parental status."

The four exceptions to this broad nondiscrimination policy permit sex-restricted financial aid under certain circumstances. Section 106.37(b) permits an institution to "administer or assist in the administration of" sex-restricted financial assistance that is "established pursuant to domestic or foreign wills, trusts, bequests, or similar legal instruments or by acts of a foreign government." Institutions must administer such awards, however, in such a way that their "overall effect" is "nondiscriminatory" according to standards set out in Section 106.37(b)(2). Section 106.31(c) creates the same kind of exception for sex-restricted foreign-study scholarships awarded to the institution's students or graduates. Such awards must be established through the same legal channels specified for the first exception, and the institution must make available "reasonable opportunities for similar [foreign] studies for members of the other sex." The third exception, for athletic scholarships, is discussed in Section 10.2. A fourth exception was added by an amendment to Title IX included in the Education Amendments of 1976. Section 412(a)(4) of the amendments (20 U.S.C. §1681(a)(9)) permits institutions to award financial assistance to winners of pageants based on "personal appearance, poise, and talent," even though the pageant is restricted to members of one sex.

Section 504 of the Rehabilitation Act of 1973 (see Section 12.4.4), as implemented by the Department of Education's regulations, restricts postsecondary institutions' financial aid processes as they relate to disabled persons. Section 104.46(a) of the regulations (34 C.F.R. Part 104) prohibits the institution from providing "less assistance" to qualified disabled students, from placing a "limit

[on] eligibility for assistance," and from otherwise discriminating or assisting any other entity to discriminate on the basis of disability in providing financial aid. The major exception to this nondiscrimination requirement is that the institution may still administer financial assistance provided under a particular discriminatory will or trust, as long as "the overall effect of the award of scholarships, fellowships, and other forms of financial assistance is not discriminatory on the basis of handicap" (34 C.F.R. §104.46(a)(2)).

The Americans with Disabilities Act also prohibits discrimination on the basis of disability in allocating financial aid. Title II, which covers state and local government agencies, applies to public colleges and universities that meet the definition of a state or local government agency. The regulations prohibit institutions from providing a benefit (here, financial aid) "that is not as effective in affording equal opportunity . . . to reach the same level of achievement as that provided to others" (34 C.F.R. §35.130(b)(1)(iii)). Both public and private colleges and universities are covered by Title III as "places of public accommodation" (34 C.F.R. §36.104), and are prohibited from limiting the access of individuals with disabilities to the benefits enjoyed by other individuals (34 C.F.R. §36.202(b)).

Regulations interpreting the Age Discrimination Act of 1975 (42 U.S.C. §6101 *et seq.*) (see Section 12.4.5 of this volume) include the general regulations applicable to all government agencies dispensing federal aid as well as regulations governing the federal financial assistance programs for education. These regulations are found at 34 C.F.R. Part 110 and were published at 58 Fed. Reg. 40194 (July 27, 1993).

The regulations set forth a general prohibition against age discrimination in "any program or activity receiving Federal financial assistance" (34 C.F.R. §110.10(a)) but permit funding recipients to use age as a criterion if the recipient "reasonably takes into account age as a factor necessary to the normal operation or the achievement of any statutory objective of a program or activity" (34 C.F.R. §110.12) or if the action is based on "reasonable factors other than age," even though the action may have a disproportionate effect on a particular age group (34 C.F.R. §110.13). With respect to the administration of federal financial aid, the regulations would generally prohibit age criteria for the receipt of student financial assistance.

The affirmative action/reverse discrimination dilemma first hit the financial aid area in *Flanagan v. President and Directors of Georgetown College,* 417 F. Supp. 377 (D.D.C. 1976). The law school at Georgetown had allocated 60 percent of its financial aid for the first-year class to minority students, who constituted 11 percent of the class. The remaining 40 percent of the aid was reserved for nonminorities, the other 89 percent of the class. Within each category, funds were allocated on the basis of need; but, because of Georgetown's allocation policy, the plaintiff, a white law student, received less financial aid than some minority students, even though his financial need was greater. The school's threshold argument was that this program did not discriminate by race because disadvantaged white students were also included within the definition of minority. The court quickly rejected this argument:

> Certain ethnic and racial groups are automatically accorded "minority" status, while whites or Caucasians must make a particular showing in order to qualify. . . . Access to the "favored" category is made more difficult for one racial group than another. This in itself is discrimination as prohibited by Title VI as well as the Constitution [417 F. Supp. at 382].

The school then defended its policy as part of an affirmative action program to increase minority enrollment. The student argued that the policy discriminated against nonminorities in violation of Title VI of the Civil Rights Act (see this volume, Section 12.4.2). The court sided with the student:

> Where an administrative procedure is permeated with social and cultural factors (as in a law school's admission process), separate treatment for "minorities" may be justified in order to insure that all persons are judged in a racially neutral fashion.
>
> But in the instant case, we are concerned with the question of financial need, which, in the final analysis, cuts across racial, cultural, and social lines. There is no justification for saying that a "minority" student with a demonstrated financial need of $2,000 requires more scholarship aid than a "nonminority" student with a demonstrated financial need of $3,000. To take such a position, which the defendants have, is reverse discrimination on the basis of race, which cannot be justified by a claim of affirmative action [417 F. Supp. at 384].

Although *Flanagan* broadly concludes that allotment of financial aid on an explicit racial basis is impermissible, the subsequent decision in *Bakke* (see Section 4.1.5) and its progeny appear to provide some room for racial considerations in financial aid programs. Exactly how much room remains, however, is presently uncertain, given the *Podberesky* litigation (discussed in Section 4.2.4).

Criteria used to make scholarship awards may have discriminatory effects even if they appear facially neutral. For example, research demonstrates that women students tend to score approximately sixty points lower on the Scholastic Aptitude Test than male students do, although women's high school and college grades tend to be higher than men's. In *Sharif by Salahuddin v. New York State Education Department*, 709 F. Supp. 345 (S.D.N.Y. 1989), a class of female high school students filed an equal protection claim, seeking to halt New York's practice of awarding Regents and Empire State Scholarships exclusively on the basis of SAT scores. The plaintiffs alleged that the practice discriminated against female students. The judge issued a preliminary injunction, ruling that the state should not use SAT scores as the sole criterion for awarding scholarships.

4.2.4. Minority Scholarships

Many U.S. colleges and universities reserve a portion of their financial aid funds for scholarships given only to members of certain racial or ethnic groups. A 1993 study conducted by the General Accounting Office, an independent federal agency, found that 5 percent of the financial aid awards for undergraduates, and 4 percent of the financial aid funds, were given to minority students through exclusive scholarships. Although the percentages are relatively low, the study found that two-thirds of undergraduate institutions, one-third of graduate schools, and three-fourths of professional schools awarded at least one minority scholarship during the 1991–92 academic year (S. Jaschik, "Government Finds Few Scholarships Reserved for Ethnic or Racial Minorities," *Chron. Higher Educ.*, Jan. 26, 1994, A36).

The legal status of race-exclusive minority scholarships was challenged in several federal court actions. One case is particularly instructive, showing the complexity of the interplay between forbidden racial discrimination and the recognition that prior discrimination, whether by an institution or by society, has resulted in unequal educational opportunities for some individuals. In *Podberesky v. Kirwan*, 764 F. Supp. 364 (D. Md. 1991), a Hispanic student brought Title VI and equal protection challenges against the University of Maryland–College Park's Banneker Scholarship program, which was restricted to black students. Defending the program against strict scrutiny analysis, the university argued that the program served the compelling state interest of remedying prior *de jure* discrimination (see Section 12.4.2), given the fact that the state was still under order by the Office for Civil Rights to remedy its formerly segregated system of public higher education. The university also argued that its goal of diversity was served by the Banneker Scholarship program.

The district court ruled that the university had provided "overwhelming" evidence of present effects of prior discrimination and found the program lawful without considering the university's diversity argument. The federal appeals court, however, reversed the district court in *Podberesky v. Kirwan*, 956 F.2d 52 (4th Cir. 1992). Although the appellate court agreed that the university had provided sufficient evidence of prior discrimination, it found the Office for Civil Rights' observations about the present effects of discrimination unconvincing because they had been made too long ago (between 1969 and 1985); and it ordered the district court to make new findings regarding the present effects of prior discrimination. The appellate court also noted that race-exclusive programs violate the *Bakke* precedent if their purpose is to increase diversity and not to remedy prior discrimination.

On remand, the university focused solely on the "present effects of prior discrimination" argument, and presented voluminous evidence, including surveys of black high school students and their parents, information on the racial climate at the university, research on the economic status of black citizens in

Maryland and the effect of unequal educational opportunity, and other studies. In *Podberesky v. Kirwan*, 838 F. Supp. 1075 (D. Md. 1993), the trial court found that the university had demonstrated a "strong basis in evidence" for four present effects of past discrimination: the university's poor reputation in the black community, underrepresentation of blacks in the student body, the low retention and graduation rates of black students at the university, and a racially hostile campus climate. Furthermore, the court found that the Banneker program was narrowly tailored to remedy the present effects of past discrimination because it demonstrated the university's commitment to black students, it increased the number of peer mentors and role models available to black students, it increased the enrollment of high-achieving black students, and it improved the recipients' academic performance and persistence. Less restrictive alternatives would not produce these results.

With regard to the university's evidence of the present effects of past discrimination, the court made this comment:

> It is worthy of note that the University is (to put it mildly) in a somewhat unusual situation. It is not often that a litigant is required to engage in extended self-criticism in order to justify its pursuit of a goal that it deems worthy [838 F. Supp. at 1082 n.47].

The plaintiff again appealed the district court's ruling to the U.S. Court of Appeals for the Fourth Circuit, and again he was successful (*Podberesky v. Kirwan*, 38 F.3d 147 (4th Cir. 1994)). Despite the university's voluminous evidence of present effects of prior racial discrimination, the appellate court found that there was insufficient proof of such present effects to establish a compelling interest for the race-exclusive scholarships; furthermore, said the court, the program was not narrowly tailored and thus failed both prongs of the strict scrutiny test.

The appellate court was sharply critical of all the findings made by the district court on the "present effects of prior discrimination." With respect to the lower court's findings that the university has a poor reputation in the minority community and that there is a hostile racial environment on campus, the court ruled that these present conditions were not closely related to the university's prior discrimination but were more directly a result of present societal discrimination which cannot form the basis for a race-conscious remedy. Regarding the findings of low retention and graduation rates of minority students, the appellate court held that this condition was not directly linked to the university's prior discrimination but was a result of economic and other, unrelated factors. Similarly, regarding the underrepresentation of black students at the university, the court held that this condition could not be traced directly to the university's prior discrimination; other factors, such as student preference for predominantly minority public colleges in Maryland, the decision to apply only to out-of-state colleges, or the decision not to attend college at all could explain all or part of the underrepresentation.

The court then criticized the university for arguing that its program was narrowly tailored to increase the number of black Maryland residents at the university because the Banneker program was open to out-of-state students. The court also rejected the trial court's finding that the program provided role models and mentors to other black students, noting that the Supreme Court had "rejected the role-model theory as a basis for implementing a race-conscious remedy" (38 F.3d 147 at 159). Added the court, "the program more resembles outright racial balancing than a tailored remedial program" (38 F.3d at 160).

Although the university had originally used two rationales—remediation of its own prior discrimination and enhancement of student diversity—for its race-exclusive scholarship program, the trial court had addressed only the remediation rationale on remand. In *Podberesky I,* the appellate court had rejected diversity as a rationale for race-exclusive programs; thus, the university did not argue that rationale in *Podberesky II,* and neither the trial nor the appellate court discussed it in the second round of litigation.

The university appealed the ruling of the Fourth Circuit to the U.S. Supreme Court, but its petition was denied. Given that denial, the ruling in *Podberesky* applies directly only to those states in the Fourth Circuit (Maryland, North Carolina, South Carolina, Virginia, and West Virginia). Because of its reliance on Supreme Court jurisprudence in *Croson* (see Section 2.2.2), and given the subsequent opinion of the U.S. Court of Appeals in the *Hopwood* case (see Section 4.1.5), *Podberesky* signals that race- or gender-based scholarship programs at public colleges and universities may be in jeopardy, at least for institutions that have no history of *de jure* segregation or cannot present strong evidence of present effects of their own past discrimination; remedying societal discrimination, at least in the Fourth Circuit, is not a compelling interest sufficient to survive strict scrutiny.

Although *Podberesky*'s impact is geographically limited, it provides an opportunity for college administrators and faculty to review and reconsider their affirmative action programs. At this point, public institutions outside the Fourth Circuit, and private institutions (which face potential challenges under Title VI (see Section 12.4.2)), do not need to change their policies to comply with a court decree that is not binding on them. However, institutions may wish to examine their minority scholarship programs to ascertain whether they are responsive to the issues raised in *Podberesky.* Are minority students underrepresented at the college in relation to their representation in the state (for public institutions) or the college's applicant pool (for private institutions)? Is the program based on a "remedy-for-discrimination" or a diversity rationale? If the former, is there strong evidence of present effects of past discrimination? If the latter, are "disadvantaged" nonminority students also eligible for the financial assistance under the program? How broad is the college's definition of "minority," and how does the college justify this particular definition?

In December 1991, as the *Podberesky* litigation was proceeding, the U.S. secretary of education in the Bush administration, Lamar Alexander, issued a proposed Title VI policy guidance that would have required race neutrality in scholarships awarded by colleges and universities unless a court, administrative agency, or local legislative body had found present effects of past discrimination (*Nondiscrimination in Federally Assisted Programs: Title VI of the Civil Rights Act of 1964; Proposed Policy Guidance,* 56 Fed. Reg. 64548). The proposed policy guidance would have permitted colleges to use privately funded, race-exclusive scholarship funds for scholarships awarded to minority students on a race-neutral basis but would have prohibited colleges from using race as a criterion for awarding scholarships.

Shortly after the proposed policy guidance was issued, several members of Congress asked the General Accounting Office to ascertain how many students received race-exclusive scholarships and how much funding these scholarships represented. Secretary Alexander agreed to postpone the effective date of the policy guidance until the GAO report was completed. By the time the study was completed, President Clinton had replaced President Bush; and the new education secretary, Richard Riley, issued a statement on February 17, 1994, which said that college scholarships could be awarded on the basis of race to remedy past discrimination *and* to promote diversity on college campuses. The proposed guidelines permit colleges to determine on their own—without the need for court, administrative, or legislative findings—that present effects of prior discrimination exist. The policy guidelines are published at 59 Fed. Reg. 8756–8764 (Feb. 23, 1994).

Affirmative action doctrine is in flux, and college faculty and administrators are understandably perplexed about how they may lawfully maintain or increase the proportion of members of underrepresented groups in their student body. Given the recent judicial activity with regard to scholarships (*Podberesky*) and admission (*Hopwood*), re-examination of the purposes and effects of affirmative action in both these areas is well advised.

Much has been written about the legality, social need for, and effect of minority scholarships. For an account of the *Podberesky* litigation by one of the university's attorneys, see A. H. Baida, "Not All Minority Scholarships Are Created Equal: Why Some May Be More Constitutional Than Others," 18 *J. Coll. & Univ. Law* 333 (1992). For a criticism of the Bush Administration's policy on minority scholarships, see M. A. Olivas, "Federal Law and Scholarship Policy: An Essay on the Office for Civil Rights, Title VI, and Racial Restrictions," 18 *J. Coll. & Univ. Law* 21 (1991). For an analysis that concludes that minority scholarships are not permissible to address societal discrimination but may be used to redress prior institutional discrimination, see J. A. Ward, "Comment: Race-

Exclusive Scholarships: Do They Violate the Constitution and Title VI of the Civil Rights Act of 1964?" 18 *J. Coll. & Univ. Law* 73 (1991). See also, J.W.D. Stokes & M. B. Pachman, "Are Race-Based Scholarships Illegal?" 69 *West's Educ. Law Rptr.* 663 (1991).

4.2.5. Discrimination Against Nonresidents

State institutions have often imposed significantly higher tuition fees on out-of-state students, and courts have generally permitted such discrimination in favor of the state's own residents. The U.S. Supreme Court, in the context of a related issue, said, "We fully recognize that a state has a legitimate interest in protecting and preserving the quality of its colleges and universities and the right of its own bona fide residents to attend such institutions on a preferential tuition basis" (*Vlandis v. Kline,* 412 U.S. 441, 452–53 (1973)). Not all preferential tuition systems, however, are beyond constitutional challenge.

In a variety of cases, students have questioned the constitutionality of the particular criteria used by states to determine who is a resident for purposes of the lower tuition rate. In *Starns v. Malkerson,* 326 F. Supp. 234 (D. Minn. 1970), students challenged a regulation that stipulated, "No student is eligible for resident classification in the university, in any college thereof, unless he has been a bona fide domiciliary of the state for at least a year immediately prior thereto " The students argued, as have the plaintiffs in similar cases, that discrimination against nonresidents affects "fundamental" rights to travel interstate and to obtain an education and that such discrimination is impermissible under the equal protection clause unless necessary to the accomplishment of some "compelling state interest." The court dismissed the students' arguments, concluding that "the one-year waiting period does not deter any appreciable number of persons from moving into the state. There is no basis in the record to conclude, therefore, that the one-year waiting period has an unconstitutional 'chilling effect' on the assertion of the constitutional right to travel." The U.S. Supreme Court affirmed the decision without opinion (401 U.S. 985 (1971)).

Other cases are consistent with *Starns* in upholding durational residency requirements of up to one year for public institutions. Courts have agreed that equal protection law requires a high standard of justification when discrimination infringes fundamental rights. But, as in *Starns,* courts have not agreed that the fundamental right to travel is infringed by durational residency requirements. Since they have also rejected the notion that access to education is a fundamental right (see *San Antonio Independent School District v. Rodriguez,* 411 U.S. 1 (1973)), courts have not applied the "compelling interest" test to durational residency requirements of a year or less. In *Sturgis v. Washington,* 414 U.S. 1057 (1973), *affirming* 368 F. Supp. 38 (W.D. Wash. 1973), the Supreme Court again recognized these precedents by affirming, without opinion, the lower court's approval of Washington's one-year durational residency statute.

However, in *Vlandis v. Kline* (cited earlier in this section), the Supreme Court held another kind of residency requirement to be unconstitutional. A Connecticut statute provided that a student's residency at the time of application for admission would remain her residency for the entire time she was a student. The Supreme Court noted that, under such a statute, a person who had been a lifelong state resident, except for a brief period in another state just prior to admission, could not reestablish Connecticut residency as long as she remained a student. But a lifelong out-of-state resident who moved to Connecticut before applying could receive in-state tuition benefits even if she had lived in the state for only one day. Because such unreasonable results could flow from Connecticut's "permanent irrebuttable presumption" of residency, the Court held that the statute violated due process. At the same time, the Court reaffirmed the state's broad discretion to use more flexible and individualized criteria for determining residency, such as "year-round residence, voter registration, place of filing tax returns, property ownership, driver's license, car registration, marital status, vacation employment," and so on. In subsequent cases, the Court has explained that *Vlandis* applies only to "those situations in which a state 'purports to be concerned with [domicile but] at the same time den[ies] to one seeking to meet its test of [domicile] the opportunity to show factors clearly bearing on that issue'" (*Elkins v. Moreno*, 435 U.S. 647 (1978), quoting *Weinberger v. Salfi*, 422 U.S. 749, 771 (1975)).

Lower courts have considered other types of residency criteria, sometimes (like the Supreme Court in *Vlandis*) finding them invalid. In *Kelm v. Carlson*, 473 F.2d 1267 (6th Cir. 1973), for instance, a U.S. Court of Appeals invalidated a University of Toledo requirement that a law student show proof of employment in Ohio before being granted resident status. And in *Samuel v. University of Pittsburgh*, 375 F. Supp. 1119 (W.D. Pa. 1974), *affirmed*, 538 F. 2d 991 (3d Cir. 1976), a class action brought by female married students, a federal district court invalidated a residency determination rule that made a wife's residency status dependent on her husband's residency. While the state defended the rule by arguing the factual validity of the common law presumption that a woman has the domicile of her husband, the court held that the rule discriminated on the basis of sex and thus violated equal protection principles.

Other courts (like the Supreme Court in *Starns* and in *Sturgis*) have upheld particular residency criteria against constitutional as well as state administrative law objections. In the most recent case, *Peck v. University Residence Committee of Kansas State University*, 807 P.2d 652 (Kan. 1991), the student plaintiff had applied to the defendant Residence Committee for approval to pay the lower tuition charge for Kansas resident students. The committee denied his request despite the fact that he "(1) registered to vote and voted in Kansas; (2) registered an automobile in Kansas and paid personal property tax in Kansas; (3) insured his automobile in Kansas; (4) acquired a Kansas driver's license; (5)

had a checking and savings account in Kansas; and (6) registered with the selective service in Kansas" (807 P.2d at 656). The state district court overruled the committee's decision, stating that its "action in denying Peck resident status is not supported by substantial evidence." Reversing the district court, the Supreme Court of Kansas held that, although the student had established physical residence in Kansas, he had not established the requisite intent to remain permanently in Kansas after graduation. Reviewing the committee's application of eight primary and nine secondary factors set out in state regulations for use in determining intent, the court concluded that most of the student's evidence related to secondary factors, which, standing alone, were "not probative for an intent determination because many are capable of being fulfilled within a few days of arriving in Kansas." The court also rejected the student's arguments that the residency regulations were inconsistent with the authorizing state statute (Kan. Stat. Ann. §76729(c)(4)) and that the regulations violated equal protection and procedural due process. The court therefore reinstated the findings and decision of the Residence Committee.

In addition to establishing acceptable criteria, institutions must ensure that the procedures they follow in making residency determinations will not be vulnerable to challenges. For instance, they will be expected to follow any procedures established by state statutes or administrative regulations. Their procedures also must not violate the notice requirements of the federal due process clause. In *Lister v. Hoover*, 706 F.2d 796 (7th Cir. 1983), however, the court held that the due process clause did not obligate the University of Wisconsin to provide students denied resident status with a written statement of reasons for the denial; see also *Michaelson v. Cox*, 476 F. Supp. 1315 (S.D. Iowa, 1979).

4.2.6. Discrimination Against Aliens

In *Nyquist v. Jean-Marie Mauclet*, 432 U.S. 1 (1977), the U.S. Supreme Court set forth constitutional principles applicable to discrimination against resident aliens in student financial aid programs. The case involved a New York state statute that barred resident aliens from eligibility for regents' college scholarships, tuition assistance awards, and state-guaranteed student loans. Resident aliens denied financial aid argued that the New York law unconstitutionally discriminated against them in violation of the equal protection clause of the Fourteenth Amendment. The Supreme Court agreed.

The Court's opinion makes clear that alienage, somewhat like race, is a "suspect classification." Discrimination against resident aliens in awarding financial aid can thus be justified only if the discrimination is necessary in order to achieve some compelling governmental interest. The *Nyquist* opinion indicates that offering an incentive for aliens to become naturalized, or enhancing the educational level of the electorate, is not a state governmental interest sufficient to justify discrimination against resident aliens with regard to financial aid.

Since the case was brought against the state rather than against individual postsecondary institutions, *Nyquist's* most direct effect is to prohibit states from discriminating against resident aliens in state financial aid programs. It does not matter whether the state programs are for students in public institutions, in private institutions, or both, since in any case the state has created the discrimination. In addition, the case clearly would prohibit public institutions from discriminating against resident aliens in operating their own separate financial aid programs. Private institutions are affected by these constitutional principles only to the extent that they are participating in government-sponsored financial aid programs or are otherwise engaging in "state action" (see Section 1.5.2) in their aid programs.

It does not necessarily follow from *Nyquist* that all aliens must be considered eligible for financial aid. *Nyquist* concerned legal resident aliens and determined that such aliens as a class do not differ sufficiently from United States citizens to permit different treatment. Courts might not reach the same conclusion about temporary nonresident aliens. In *Ahmed v. University of Toledo*, 664 F. Supp. 282 (N.D. Ohio 1986), for example, the court considered a challenge to the University of Toledo's requirement that all international students purchase health insurance. Students not able to show proof of coverage were deregistered, and their financial aid was discontinued. The trial court ruled that the affected international students were not a suspect class for equal protection purposes, because only nonresident aliens were required to purchase the insurance; resident aliens were not. Since the situation was thus unlike *Nyquist*, where the challenged policy had affected resident rather than nonresident aliens, the court used the more relaxed "rational relationship" standard of review for equal protection claims rather than the strict scrutiny standard and held that the university's policy was rational and therefore constitutional. The U.S. Court of Appeals dismissed the students' appeal as moot (822 F.2d 26 (6th Cir. 1987)). In an earlier case, however, the court in *Tayyari v. New Mexico State University*, 495 F. Supp. 1365 (D.N.M. 1980), did invalidate a university policy denying reenrollment (during the Iranian hostage crisis) to Iranian students who were nonimmigrant aliens in this country on student visas. The court considered the students to be a suspect class and determined that the university's reasons for treating them differently could not pass strict scrutiny.

Despite the *Tayyari* reasoning, administrators whose institutions are subject to the *Nyquist* principles can probably comply by making sure that they do not require students to be U.S. citizens or to show evidence of intent to become citizens in order to be eligible for financial aid administered by the institution. (The U.S. Department of Education has a similar eligibility standard for the federal Stafford Loan program (34 C.F.R. §668.7).) Institutions thus may deem temporary nonresident aliens ineligible, at least if they have no demonstrable present intention to become permanent residents. The distinction between resident and temporary nonresident aliens may be justifiable on grounds that institutions (and states) need not spend their financial aid resources on individuals who have no intention to remain in and contribute to the state or the United States. Whether institutions may also make undocumented resident aliens ineligible for financial assistance is a separate question not controlled by *Nyquist* and is discussed below.

Moreover, since *Nyquist* does not affect state residency requirements, aliens who are not state residents may still be deemed ineligible when the principles discussed in Section 4.2.5 permit it—not because they are aliens but because they are nonresidents of the state. Although state residency for aliens may be determined in part by their particular status under federal immigration law (see especially 8 U.S.C. §1101(a)(15)), it is well to be cautious in relying on federal law. In *Elkins v. Moreno*, 435 U.S. 647 (1978), the University of Maryland had denied "in-state" status, for purposes of tuition and fees, to aliens holding G–4 nonimmigrant visas (for employees of international treaty organizations and their immediate families) under federal law. The university argued that their federal status precluded such aliens from demonstrating an intent to become permanent Maryland residents. The U.S. Supreme Court rejected this argument, holding that G–4 aliens (unlike some other categories of nonimmigrant aliens) are not incapable under federal law of becoming permanent residents and thus are not precluded from forming an intent to reside permanently in Maryland. The Court then certified to the Maryland Court of Appeals the question whether G–4 aliens or their dependents are incapable of establishing Maryland residency under the state's common law.

In "act 2" of this litigation drama, *Toll v. Moreno*, 397 A.2d 1009 (Md. 1979), *judgment vacated*, 441 U.S. 458 (1979), the Maryland court answered no to the Supreme Court's question. In the interim, however, the university had adopted a new in-state policy, which no longer used state residency as the paramount factor in determining in-state status for tuition and fees. Because the changed policy raised new constitutional issues, the Supreme Court ended act 2 by vacating the Maryland court's judgment and remanding the case to the federal district court where the *Elkins* case had begun.

After the district court invalidated Maryland's new policy and the U.S. Court of Appeals affirmed, the case returned to the U.S. Supreme Court (*Toll v. Moreno*, 458 U.S. 1 (1982)) for act 3. The Court held that the university's new policy, insofar as it barred G–4 aliens and their dependents from acquiring in-state status, violated the supremacy clause (Art. VI, para. 2) of the United States Constitution. The supremacy clause recognizes the primacy of federal regulatory authority over subjects within the scope of federal constitutional power and prevents state law from interfering with federal law regarding such subjects. Since the federal government's broad constitutional authority over immigration has long been recognized, federal law on immigration is supreme, and states may not interfere with it. Applying these principles in *Toll*, the Court reasoned:

[Our cases] stand for the broad principle that "state regulation not congression-ally sanctioned that discriminates against aliens lawfully admitted to the country is impermissible if it imposes additional burdens not contemplated by Con-gress." *De Canas v. Bica,* 424 U.S. 351, 358 n.6 (1976). . . .

The Immigration and Nationality Act of 1952, 66 Stat. 163, as amended, 8 U.S.C. §1101 et seq., . . . recognizes two basic classes of aliens, immigrant and nonimmigrant. With respect to the nonimmigrant class, the Act establishes vari-ous categories, the G–4 category among them. For many of these nonimmigrant categories, Congress has precluded the covered alien from establishing domicile in the United States. . . . But significantly, Congress has allowed G–4 aliens— employees of various international organizations, and their immediate families— to enter the country on terms permitting the establishment of domicile in the United States. . . . In light of Congress' explicit decision not to bar G–4 aliens from acquiring domicile, the State's decision to deny "in-state" status to G–4 aliens, *solely* on account of the G–4 alien's federal immigration status, surely amounts to an ancillary "burden not contemplated by Congress" in admitting these aliens to the United States [458 U.S. at 12–14; citations and footnotes omitted].

As a result of the *Elkins/Toll* litigation, it is now clear that postsecondary institutions may not use G–4 aliens' immigration status as a basis for denying them in-state status for tuition and fees purposes. It does not follow, however, that institutions are similarly limited with respect to other categories of nonim-migrant aliens. Most nonimmigrant categories, other than G–4, are made up of aliens who enter the United States temporarily for a specific purpose and must maintain domicile in a foreign country (see, for example, 8 U.S.C. §1101(a)-(15)(B) (temporary visitors for pleasure or business); §1101(a)(15)(C) (aliens in transit); §1101(a)(15)(F) (temporary foreign students); §1101(a)(15)(H) (tem-porary workers); see generally, Section 12.1.4). Such restrictions, not applica-ble to G–4s, preclude these other classes of nonimmigrant aliens from forming an intent to establish permanent residency (or domicile), which is required under the residency laws of most states. Thus, federal and state law would apparently still allow public institutions to deny in-state status to nonimmigrant aliens other than G–4s or to other narrow categories that are not required to maintain domicile in their home countries.

It also remains important, after *Elkins/Toll,* to distinguish between nonim-migrant (nonresident) and immigrant (resident) aliens. Because immigrant aliens, like G–4 aliens, are permitted under federal law to establish United States and state residency, denial of in-state status because of their alienage would apparently violate the federal supremacy principles relied on in *Toll* (act 3). Such discrimination against immigrant aliens is also prohibited by the equal protec-tion clause of the Fourteenth Amendment, as established in *Nyquist v. Jean-Marie Mauclet,* discussed earlier in this section.

Since the *Elkins/Toll* litigation, yet another critical distinction has emerged: the distinction between legal (immigrant or nonimmigrant) aliens and illegal (undocumented) aliens. In some circumstances, the equal protection clause will also protect undocumented aliens from state discrimination in the delivery of educational services. In *Plyler v. Doe,* 457 U.S. 202 (1982), for instance, the U.S. Supreme Court used equal protection principles to invalidate a Texas statute that "den[ied] to undocumented school age children the free public education that [the state] provides to children who are citizens of the United States or legally admitted aliens." Reasoning that the Texas law was "directed against children [who] can have little control" over their undocumented status, and that the law "den[ied] these children a basic education," thereby saddling them with the "enduring disability" of illiteracy, the Court held that the state's interests in protecting its education system and resources could not justify this discriminatory burden on the affected children. *Plyler* dealt with elementary education; the key question, then, is whether the case's reasoning and the equal protection principles that support it would apply to higher education as well—in particular to state policies that deny to undocumented aliens financial aid or instate tuition status that is available to U.S. citizens and documented aliens.

This question has attracted a great deal of attention in California, where courts have wrestled with it in a complex chain of litigation. In 1983, the California legislature passed a statute providing that "[a]n alien, including an unmarried minor alien, may establish his or her residence, unless precluded by the Immigration and Nationality Act (8 U.S.C. §1101 *et seq.*) from establishing domicile in the United States" (Cal. Educ. Code §68062(h)). It was not clear how this statute would apply to undocumented aliens who had been living in California and sought to establish residency for in-state tuition purposes. At the request of the chancellor of the California State University, the attorney general of California issued an interpretation of the statute, indicating that an illegal alien's incapacity to establish residence in the United States under federal immigration law precluded that same alien from establishing residency in California for in-state tuition purposes (67 *Opinions of the Attorney General* 241 (Cal.) (1984), Opinion No. 84–101). Subsequently, the University of California and the California State University and College System formulated identical policies charging all undocumented aliens out-of-state tuition.

In *Leticia A. v. Regents of the University of California,* No. 588–982–5 (Cal. Super. Ct., Alameda County, Apr. 3, 1985), *judgment vacated,* June 10, 1985, *judgment amended and reinstated,* June 19, 1985, four undocumented alien students challenged the constitutionality of these policies on equal protection grounds. The plaintiffs had been brought into this country during their minority and had graduated from California high schools. Relying on the Supreme Court's reasoning in *Plyler,* and on the equal protection clause of the *state* constitution, the *Leticia A.* court determined that "higher education is an 'important' interest in California" and that the defendants' policies can survive equal protection scrutiny only if "there is a 'substantial' state interest served by the [blanket] classification" of undocumented aliens as nonresidents. The court then compared the rationales supporting this classification and those supporting the federal immigration laws:

> The policies underlying the immigration laws and regulations are vastly different from those relating to residency for student fee purposes. The two systems are totally unrelated for purposes of administration, enforcement and legal analysis. The use of unrelated policies, statutes, regulations or case law from one system to govern portions of the other is irrational. The incorporation of policies governing adjustment of status for undocumented aliens into regulations and administration of a system for determining residence for student fee purposes is neither logical nor rational [*Leticia A.* at 9–10].

The court therefore declared the defendants' policies unconstitutional (without rendering any judgment on the validity of Section 68062(h), on which the policies were based) and ordered the defendants to determine the state residence status of undocumented students and applicants for purposes of in-state tuition in the same way as it would make that determination for U.S. citizens.

Neither defendant appealed the *Leticia A.* decision. In 1990, however, a former employee of the University of California sued that institution to require it to reinstate its pre-*Leticia* policy. The employee, Bradford, had been terminated by the University of California for his "unwillingness to comply with the ruling of the [*Leticia A.*] court." The trial court granted summary judgment in favor of the employee. On appeal, in *Regents of the University of California v. Superior Court,* 276 Cal. Rptr. 197 (Cal. Ct. App. 1990) (known as the *Bradford* case), the court reviewed the purpose and constitutionality of the defendant's pre-*Leticia A.* residency policy, as well as of Section 68062(h) itself. The court held that, as originally argued by the defendants in the *Leticia A.* litigation, Section 68062(h) "precludes undocumented alien students from qualifying as residents of California for tuition purposes." Then the court examined whether such an interpretation denied undocumented alien students the equal protection of the laws. Reasoning that undocumented aliens are commonly and legitimately denied basic rights and privileges under both state and federal law, that the university also denies the lower tuition rate to residents of other states and to aliens holding student visas, and that the state had "manifest and important" interests in extending this denial to undocumented aliens, the appellate court upheld the trial court's ruling.

Unlike the *Leticia A.* court, the appellate court in the *Bradford* case did not rely on the Supreme Court's *Plyler* decision but distinguished it on the basis of the "significant difference between an elementary education and a university education." Thus, the *Bradford* court's decision is in direct conflict with *Leticia A.* and serves to uphold the constitutionality of Section 68062(h) as well as the University of California's pre-*Leticia A.* policy. Since *Bradford,* litigation has continued in the California superior courts to work out the implementation of that decision and its application to the California State University and College System, which was not a defendant in *Bradford.*

4.2.7. Collection of Student Debts

When a postsecondary institution extends financial aid to its students in the form of loans, it has the additional problem of making sure that students repay their loans according to the schedule and conditions in the loan agreement. Enforcing payment of loans can involve the institution in a legal quagmire, several aspects of which are discussed in this section.

4.2.7.1. Federal bankruptcy law. Student borrowers have often sought to extinguish their loan obligations to their institutions by filing for bankruptcy under the federal Bankruptcy Code contained in Title XI of the *United States Code.* The Bankruptcy Code supersedes all state law inconsistent with its provisions or with its purpose of allowing the honest bankrupt a "fresh start," free from the burden of indebtedness. A debtor may institute bankruptcy proceedings by petitioning the appropriate federal court for discharge of all his provable debts. Following receipt of the bankruptcy petition, the court issues an order fixing times for the filing and hearing of objections to the petition before a bankruptcy judge. Notice of this order is given to all potential creditors, usually by mail.

Debtors may petition for bankruptcy under either Chapter 7 or Chapter 13 of the Bankruptcy Code. Under a Chapter 7 "straight" bankruptcy, debts are routinely and completely discharged unless the creditors can show reasons why no discharge should be ordered (11 U.S.C. §727) or unless a creditor can demonstrate why its particular claim should be "excepted" from the discharge order as a "nondischargeable debt" (11 U.S.C. §523). Chapter 13, on the other hand, provides for the adjustment of debts for debtors with regular income. After filing a Chapter 13 petition, the debtor must submit a plan providing for full or partial repayment of debts (11 U.S.C. §§1321–1323), and the bankruptcy court must hold a hearing and decide whether to confirm the plan (11 U.S.C. §§1324–1325, 1327). Prior to the hearing, the bankruptcy court must notify all creditors whom the debtor has included in the plan; these creditors may then object to the plan's confirmation (11 U.S.C. §1324). If the plan is confirmed and the debtor makes the payments according to the plan's terms, the bankruptcy court will issue a discharge of those debts included in the plan (11 U.S.C. §1328(a)).

In 1976, responding to an escalation in defaults on student loans and in the number of students seeking discharge of their loans in bankruptcy, Congress amended the Higher Education Act to prohibit the discharge, under certain circumstances, of loans guaranteed or insured under the federal Guaranteed Student Loan program (20 U.S.C. §1087–3). Subsequently, Congress replaced this provision with a broader provision, included in the Bankruptcy Reform Act of 1978. In 1979, Congress amended this new provision in order to clarify its language and correct some inequities that it had inadvertently created. As amended, the new student bankruptcy provision took effect, along with the rest of the revised Bankruptcy Code, on October 1, 1979. Further amendments were made in 1990 to extend the statutory period from five to seven years. The provision is contained in 11 U.S.C. §523(a)(8):

Section 523. Exceptions to discharge:
(a) A discharge under Section 727, 1141, 1228(a), 1228(b), or 1328(b) of this title does not discharge an individual debtor from any debt—
 . . . (8) for an educational benefit overpayment or loan made, insured, or guaranteed by a governmental unit, or made under any program funded in whole or in part by a governmental unit or nonprofit institution of higher education, or for an obligation to repay funds received as an educational benefit, scholarship or stipend, unless—
(A) such loan, benefit, scholarship or stipend overpayment first became due more than seven years (exclusive of any applicable suspension of the repayment period) before the date of the filing of the petition; or
(B) excepting such debt from discharge under this paragraph will impose an undue hardship on the debtor and the debtor's dependents.

The 1990 amendments also made student loans nondischargeable under Chapter 13 (11 U.S.C. §1328(a)).

Section 523(a)(8) covers loans made under any Department of Education student loan program as well as student loans made, insured, guaranteed, or funded by other "governmental units," such as state and local governments, and by nonprofit higher education institutions. Loans made by profit-making postsecondary institutions or privately owned banks (and not guaranteed or insured under a government program) are not covered by the provision and thus continue to be dischargeable. Moreover, Section 523(a)(8) applies to bankruptcies under both Chapter 7 and Chapter 13.

In re Shore, 707 F.2d 1337 (11th Cir. 1983), illustrates the broad scope of the "governmental unit" language of Section 523(a)(8). A student at Columbus College, part of the University of Georgia System, had borrowed money from the Greentree-Sevier Trust, a trust to benefit Columbus College and its students. The student sought to discharge the loan in bankruptcy, arguing that the loan was made by a trust fund rather than a governmental unit and therefore did not fall within the reach of Section 523. The court disagreed:

Columbus College is the beneficiary of the Greentree-Sevier Trust. Columbus College made the educational loan to Shore using funds from this trust. Appellant agreed "to pay to Columbus College" the sum of the amount signed for in the space provided on the Loan Agreement. An educational loan "made by" a governmental unit within the meaning of Section 523(a)(8) is one in which a governmental unit is the lender and the holder of the loan obligation. The particular fund on which the governmental unit draws to fund the loan does not alter the definition [707 F.2d at 1339].

The student loan bankruptcy provision defuses what previously had been a major issue in Chapter 7 student bankruptcies: the issue of "provability." In *State v. Wilkes,* 41 N.Y.2d 655 (N.Y. 1977), for example (decided when the old code was in effect), a college had initiated collection procedures against a student who claimed that his prior bankruptcy had discharged his student loans (a point not made clear in the bankruptcy proceeding). The New York Court of Appeals rejected the student's claim. It held that contingencies such as a repayment plan extending over ten years, provision for termination of the debt if the student died or became disabled, and provision for reduction of the debt if the student taught in certain schools made the "ultimate amount of liability impossible to ascertain or even approximate." The debt was therefore not "provable," and because not provable it was nondischargeable.

Section 523(a)(8) obviates the need for an institution to claim lack of provability in order to prevent the discharge of student loans that have been due for less than seven years. During that period, the student loan is ordinarily nondischargeable, regardless of provability. Thus, the institution no longer has the burden of filing a proof of claim and asserting lack of provability as a bar to discharge unless the debt has been due for seven years or more. Instead, Section 523(a)(8) "is intended to be self-executing and the lender or institution is not required to file a complaint to determine the nondischargeability of any student loan" (S. Rep. No. 95–989, 95th Cong., 2d Sess., reprinted in 1978 *U.S. Code Cong. & Admin. News,* 5865).

Even if a student loan is nondischargeable under Chapter 7, the filing of a bankruptcy petition may nevertheless affect the institution's efforts to collect the debt. Under the Bankruptcy Code, creditors are automatically prohibited during the pendency of the bankruptcy proceedings from continuing with collection efforts (11 U.S.C. §362). The bankruptcy judge may modify or cancel this prohibition during the proceedings, however, if the institution can show cause why such action should be taken (11 U.S.C. §362(d)(1)).

There has been considerable litigation on the scope of the "undue hardship" exception to nondischargeability in Section 523(a)(8)(B). In general, bankruptcy courts have interpreted this exception narrowly, looking to the particular facts of each case. Primary importance has been attached to whether the student debtor's economic straits were foreseeable and within his control. Although several courts have established tests for undue hardship, the test created in *Brunner v. New York State Higher Education Services Corp.*, 831 F.2d 395 (2d Cir. 1987), has been adopted by several federal appellate courts. The three-part test requires the court to determine

1. that the debtor cannot maintain, based on current income and expenses, a "minimal" standard of living for [himself or] herself and [his or] her dependents if forced to repay the loans; and

2. that additional circumstances exist indicating that this state of affairs is likely to persist for a significant portion of the repayment period of the student loans; and

3. that the debtor has made good faith efforts to repay the loans [831 F.2d at 396].

In *In re Perkins,* 11 Bankr. Rptr. (*Bankruptcy Reporter)* 160 (D. Vt. 1980), the court held that the undue hardship exception "is not intended to shelter the debtor from self-imposed hardship resulting from a reluctance to live within his means." *In re Price,* 1 Bankr. Rptr. 768 (D. Haw. 1980), held that the bankrupt's sending three children to private schools constituted a failure to live within means; and *In re Brock,* 4 Bankr. Rptr. 491 (S.D.N.Y. 1980), held that "the necessity of careful budgeting is not evidence of undue hardship." Even unemployment or underemployment will not suffice for a hardship discharge when future prospects are bright (see, for example, *In re Hemmen,* 7 Bankr. Rptr. 63 (N.D. Ala. 1980); *In re Tobin,* 18 Bankr. Rptr. 560 (W.D. Wis. 1982)). In *Matter of Robinson, 999* F.2d 1132 (7th Cir. 1993), the court ruled that, because the debtor's hardship was temporary, he had not met the test for undue hardship. On the other hand, courts will consider such factors as insufficient income to maintain a minimum standard of living, excessive unavoidable debts and expenses, and the failure of education to increase the debtor's earning power. In *In re Diaz,* 5 Bankr. Rptr. 253 (W.D.N.Y. 1980), for instance, the bankruptcy judge discharged the student loans of a debtor with personal and family medical problems and poor employment prospects; and in *In re Birden,* 17 Bankr. Rptr. 891 (E.D. Pa. 1982), the bankruptcy judge, in deciding to discharge the student loans, considered the presence of large, nondischargeable obligations for taxes and child support payments. A debtor's longstanding and serious mental and emotional problems convinced a judge that her situation met the "undue hardship" test in *Kline v. United States,* 155 Bankr. Rptr. 762 (W.D. Mo. 1993).

Cosigners and nonstudents (such as parents) who take out federally guaranteed student loans also appear to be covered by the nondischargeability provisions of the bankruptcy law. In *Webb v. Student Loan Funding Corp.,*

151 Bankr. Rptr. 804 (N.D. Ohio 1992), the parent, the obligor on a federal PLUS loan (Parent Loans for Undergraduate Students) taken out for her daughter's college education, argued that she had not received a direct benefit from the loan (her daughter, not she, had received the education). The court disagreed, stating that the parent did receive at least an indirect benefit, and that this reason was insufficient to exempt PLUS loans from the clear intent of the bankruptcy law's statutory language. Similarly, in *In re Hammarstrom*, 95 Bankr. Rptr. 160 (N.D. Cal. 1989), the court held that the exception to dischargeability in Section 523(a)(8) unambiguously applied to the debtor, whether or not the debtor received a direct benefit from the loan. And in *In re Pelkowski*, 990 F.2d 737 (3d Cir. 1993), the court overturned a lower court ruling that the loan was not an "educational" loan if the debtor was a cosigner or guarantor of the loan for the student borrower. After analyzing the legislative history of the amendments to the Bankruptcy Code related to federal student loans, the court concluded that Congress had acted for the purpose of reducing debtor abuse of the federal student loan program; extending the nondischargeability provisions to nonstudent debtors would further the intent of Congress in this regard.

Students may be precluded from further borrowing under the federal student loan program if they have had earlier loans discharged in bankruptcy. In *Elter v. Great Lakes Higher Education Corp.*, 95 Bankr. Rptr. 618 (E.D. Wis. 1989), a bankruptcy court allowed a state guaranty agency to deny a new educational loan to such students.

For suggestions regarding appropriate institutional actions in collecting student loans from debtors in bankruptcy (written prior to the amendments to Chapter 13), see R. W. Rieder, "Student Loans and Bankruptcies: What Can a University-Creditor Do?" 56 *West's Educ. Law Rptr.* 691 (1989).

4.2.7.2. Withholding certified transcripts. Like its predecessor, the revised (1978) Bankruptcy Code generally forbids creditors from resorting to the courts or other legal process to collect debts discharged in bankruptcy (11 U.S.C. §524(a)(2)). Under the old Bankruptcy Act, however, there was considerable debate on whether informal means of collection, such as withholding certified grade transcripts from a student bankrupt, were permissible. In *Girardier v. Webster College*, 563 F.2d 1267 (8th Cir. 1977), decided under the old Act, the court held that the Act did not prohibit private institutions from withholding certified transcripts. Besides reducing the scope of this problem by limiting the dischargeability of student loans, the 1978 Bankruptcy Act appears to have legislatively overruled the result in the *Girardier* case.

The provision of the old Act that was applied in *Girardier* prohibited formal attempts, by "action" or "process," to collect discharged debts. In the 1978 Act, this provision was amended to read (with further amendments in 1984):

> A discharge in a case under this title . . . operates as an injunction against the commencement or continuation of an action, the employment of process, or an act, to collect, recover or offset any such debt as a personal liability of the debtor, whether or not discharge of such debt is waived [11 U.S.C. §524(a)(2)].

The language, especially the phrase "or an act," serves to extend the provision's coverage to informal, nonjudicial means of collection, thus "insur[ing] that once a debt is discharged, the debtor will not be pressured in any way to repay it" (S. Rep. No. 95989, 95th Cong., 2d Sess., reprinted in 1978 *U.S. Code Cong. Admin. News* 5866).

The 1978 Act also added the words "any act" to a related provision, Section 362(a)(6), which prohibits creditors from attempting to collect debts during the pendency of a bankruptcy proceeding. Bankruptcy courts have construed this new language to apply to attempts to withhold certified transcripts (see *In re Lanford,* 10 Bankr. Rptr. 132 (D. Minn. 1981)). This legislative change, together with the change in Section 524(a)(2), apparently prevents postsecondary institutions from withholding transcripts both during the pendency of a bankruptcy proceeding and after the discharge of debts, under either Chapter 7 or Chapter 13.

The charge typically made when a college refuses to provide a transcript for a student who has filed a bankruptcy petition is that the college has violated the "automatic stay" provisions of the Bankruptcy Code (11 U.S.C. §362) (*In re Parham,* 56 Bankr. Rptr. 531 (E.D. Va. 1986); *Parraway v. Andrews University,* 50 Bankr. Rptr. 316 (W.D. Mich. 1986)). Even though the debt is nondischargeable, the college may not withhold the transcript during the automatic stay period (*California State University, Fresno v. Gustafson,* 934 F.2d 216 (9th Cir. 1990); *In re Weiner Merchant, Debtor,* 958 F.2d 738 (6th Cir. 1992)).

The situation is different if, as in the majority of situations, the student has not filed a bankruptcy petition. Nothing in the Bankruptcy Code would prohibit postsecondary institutions from withholding transcripts from such student debtors. Moreover, the code does not prevent institutions from withholding transcripts if the bankruptcy court has refused to discharge the student loan debts. In *Johnson v. Edinboro State College,* 728 F.2d 163 (3d Cir. 1984), for example, the bankruptcy court had declared a former student to be bankrupt but did not discharge his student loans because he had failed to prove that a hardship existed. Nevertheless, the bankruptcy court had held that the college was obligated to issue the student a transcript because of the Bankruptcy Code's policy to guarantee debtors "fresh starts." When the college appealed, the Court of Appeals overruled the bankruptcy court, holding that when a bankrupt's student loans are nondischargeable under Section 523(a)(8), the policy of that section overrides the code's general fresh-start policy. The college therefore remained free to withhold transcripts from the student.

Similarly, nothing in the federal Family Educational Rights and Privacy Act (FERPA) concerning student records (see Section 3.3.1) prohibits institutions from withholding certified transcripts from student debtors. If an institution enters grades in a student's records, FERPA would give the student a right to see and copy the grade records. But FERPA would not give the student any right to a *certified* transcript of grades, nor would it obligate the institution to issue a certified transcript or other record of grades to third parties (see *Girardier v. Webster College,* 421 F. Supp. 45, 48 (D. Mo. 1976), *vacated on other grounds,* 563 F. 2d 1267 (8th Cir. 1977)).

The most likely legal difficulty would arise under the federal Constitution's due process clause, whose requirements limit only public institutions (see Section 1.5.2). The basic question is whether withholding a certified transcript deprives the student of a "liberty" or "property" interest protected by the due process clause (see generally Section 2.2.2). If so, the student would have the right to be notified of the withholding and the reason for it, and to be afforded some kind of hearing on the sufficiency of the grounds for withholding. Courts have not yet defined liberty or property interests in this context. But under precedents in other areas, if the institution has regulations or policies entitling students to certified transcripts, these regulations or policies could create a property interest that would be infringed if the institution withholds a transcript without notice or hearing. And withholding certified transcripts from a student applying to professional or graduate school, or for professional employment, may so foreclose the student's freedom to pursue educational or employment opportunities as to be a deprivation of liberty. Thus, despite the lack of cases on point, administrators at public institutions should consult counsel before implementing a policy of withholding transcripts for failure to pay loans, or for any other reason.

4.2.7.3. Debt collection requirements in federal student loan programs. The Perkins Loan (formerly NDSL) program's statute and regulations contain several provisions affecting the institution's debt collection practices. The statute provides (in 20 U.S.C. §1087cc(4)), that where a note or written agreement evidencing such a loan has been in default for at least six months despite the institution's due diligence in attempting to collect the debt, the institution, under certain circumstances, may assign its rights under the note or agreement to the United States. If the debt is thereafter collected by the United States, the amount, less 30 percent, is returned to the institution as an additional capital contribution. The Perkins Loan regulations (34 C.F.R. §674.41 *et seq.*) provide that each institution maintaining a Perkins Loan fund must accept responsibility for, and use due diligence in effecting, collection of all amounts due and payable to the fund. Due diligence includes the following elements: (1) providing borrowers with information about changes in the program that affect their rights and responsibilities (34 C.F.R. §674.41(a)); (2) conducting exit interviews with borrowers when they leave the institution and providing them with copies of repayment schedules that indicate the total amount of the loans and the dates and amounts of installments as they come due (34 C.F.R. §674.42(a)); (3) keeping a written record of interviews and retaining signed copies of borrowers' repayment schedules (34 C.F.R. §674.42(a)(3)); and (4) staying in contact with borrowers both before and during the repayment period, in order to facilitate billing and keep the borrowers informed of changes in the program that may affect rights and obligations (34 C.F.R. §674.42(b)). The institution must also use specified "billing procedures" (set forth at 34 C.F.R. §674.43), including statements of notice and account and demands for payment on accounts that are more than fifteen days overdue. If an institution is unable to locate a borrower, it must conduct an address search (34 C.F.R. §674). If the billing procedures are unsuccessful, the institution must either obtain the services of a collection agency or utilize its own resources to compel repayment (34 C.F.R. §675(a)).

The Federal Family Education Loan (FFEL, formerly GSL) program includes fewer provisions related to debt collection, since postsecondary institutions are not usually the lenders under the program. The regulations require (at 34 C.F.R. §682.610(a)), that participating institutions establish and maintain such administrative and fiscal procedures and records as may be necessary to protect the United States from unreasonable risk of loss due to defaults. Another approach to debt collection, with more specifics than FFEL but fewer than Perkins, is illustrated by the Health Professions Student Loan program (42 C.F.R. Part 57, subpart C). Participating institutions must exercise "due diligence" in collecting loan payments (42 C.F.R. §57.210(b)) and must maintain complete repayment records for each student borrower, including the "date, nature, and result of each contact with the borrower or proper endorser in the collection of an overdue loan" (42 C.F.R. §57.215(c)). The regulations also establish a quantitative performance standard, requiring institutions to maintain a "defaulted principal amount outstanding" rate of not more than 5 percent (42 C.F.R. §57.216(a)).

In order to step up collection activities under the Health Education Assistance Loan (HEAL) program (42 U.S.C. §294 et seq., 42 C.F.R. Part 60), the Public Health Service of the Department of Health and Human Services issued regulations authorizing institutions to withhold transcripts of HEAL defaulters. The regulations also require schools to note student loan defaults on *academic* transcripts. (For a discussion of the lawfulness of withholding student transcripts, see Section 4.2.7.2.)

Prior to 1991, the statute of limitations for defaulted student loans was six years. However, the Higher Education Technical Amendments of 1991 (Pub. L. No. 102–26, 105 Stat. 123, codified as amended at 20 U.S.C. §1091(a)) deleted the six-year statute of limitations temporarily. The Higher Education

Amendments of 1992 made the deletion permanent. Following passage of the amendments, the question before the courts was whether student loans in default for more than six years prior to the amendments' enactment were now subject to collection. The courts have ruled that they are (see, for example, *United States v. Glockson*, 998 F.2d 896 (11th Cir. 1993); see also *United States v. Mastrovito*, 830 F. Supp. 1281 (D. Ariz. 1993), *affirmed without opinion*, 46 F. 3d 1147 (9th Cir. 1994)).

In 1986, the Department of Education, in order to stimulate repayment of Title IV obligations, amended the regulations governing the Perkins Loan program to revise the definition of "default" status. Under the former default provisions, a borrower in default could remain eligible to receive federal loans if he or she submitted to the institution a written statement of intent to repay. The new provision (codified at 34 C.F.R. §668.7) directs that borrowers who default on their student loans forfeit eligibility for continued Title IV assistance.

A law passed by Congress in October 1990, the Student Loan Default Prevention Initiative Act of 1990 (Pub. L. No. 101–508, 104 Stat. 1388, codified at various sections of 20 U.S.C.), is aimed at reducing the number of defaulted loans by rendering institutions with high default rates ineligible to participate in certain student loan programs. Section 1085 provides that any institution whose "cohort default rate" exceeds a certain threshold percentage for three consecutive years loses its eligibility for participation in the FFEL program for the fiscal year in which the determination is made and for the two succeeding years. The regulations specifying how default rates are calculated appear at 34 C.F.R. §668.15. The process for calculating the cohort default rate was described in *Canterbury Career School, Inc. v. Riley*, 833 Supp. 1097 (D.N.J. 1993). In this case, the threshold beyond which termination would occur was 30 percent. The court also discussed the due process protections (particularly the opportunity for a hearing) available to schools threatened with termination of their eligibility to participate in federal student aid programs.

In another case, a chain of cosmetology schools challenged the secretary of education's decision to terminate the schools' eligibility to participate in the FFEL program. The plaintiffs charged that a "paper" appeal process, rather than a full-blown adversary hearing on the record, violated their rights of due process on both procedural and substantive grounds. The schools also charged that the secretary had miscalculated the default rate. In *Pro Schools, Inc. v. Riley*, 824 F. Supp. 1314 (E.D. Wis. 1993), the trial court disagreed, noting that the secretary was permitted to use default data from years prior to the enactment of the Student Loan Default Prevention Initiative Act, and that the use of these data did not make the Act itself retroactive because the issue was the schools' present eligibility, not their past eligibility (citing *Association of Accredited Cosmetology Schools v. Alexander*, 979 F.2d 859 (D.C. Cir. 1992)). Although the court accepted the plaintiffs' argument that continued eligibility for participation in the federal programs was both a property and a liberty interest (citing *Continental Training Services, Inc. v. Cavazos*, 893 F.2d 877 (7th Cir. 1990)), it viewed the written appeal process as sufficient to protect the schools' due process rights.

Institutions have several weapons in their fight to collect Perkins Loans from defaulting student borrowers. The Student Loan Default Prevention Initiative Act permits colleges to use collection agencies to recover defaulted loans and also permits judges to award attorney's fees to institutions that must litigate to recover the unpaid loans. In *Trustees of Tufts College v. Ramsdell*, 554 N.E.2d 34 (Mass. 1990), the court noted these provisions but limited the attorney's fees to the state law standard, rather than the more generous ceiling that the university argued was permitted by federal regulations. The regulations interpreting the Act are found at 34 C.F.R. §§675 and 676.

For those loans that have been assigned to the federal government for collection, federal agency heads may seek a tax offset against the debtor's tax refunds by request to the Internal Revenue Service (as provided in 26 U.S.C. §6402(d)). According to *Thomas v. Bennett*, 856 F.2d 1165 (8th Cir. 1988), the six-year statute of limitations on actions for money damages brought by the United States (28 U.S.C. §2415(a)) does not bar the tax offset, because the statute of limitations does not negate the debt but only bars a court suit as a means of collection; the debt is still collectible by other means. By regulation, however, the Internal Revenue Service has provided that it will not use the offset procedure for any debt that has been delinquent for more than ten years at the time offset is requested (26 C.F.R. §301.6402–6(c)(1)). This regulation was upheld in *Grider v. Cavazos*, 911 F.2d 1158 (5th Cir. 1990). The appellate court refused to permit the secretary of education to intercept the tax refunds of two individuals who had defaulted on their loans fifteen and eleven years earlier. Although the secretary had argued that the loans became delinquent when the banks assigned the loans to the secretary for collection, the court sided with the debtors' argument that the loans went into default when the required payments to the bank (the lender) were not made. The court commented:

> [We] take no pleasure in giving aid and comfort to those former students who shirk their loan repayment obligations by hiding behind statutes of limitation. We can only ask in rhetorical wonderment why the Secretary continues quixotically to pursue judicial construction of the Regulation instead of simply asking his counterpart in the Department of the Treasury to close the loophole in the Regulation with a proverbial stroke of his pen [911 F.2d at 1164].

Students challenging their obligation to repay federal student loans are finding some creative solutions in situations where the college involved either has closed or did not provide the promised educational services. In some cases, students have argued that the lending banks or the state agency guarantors of their federal student loans must be subject to state law regarding secured transactions. For example, in *Tipton v. Alexander,* 768 F. Supp. 540 (S.D. W. Va. 1991), former students of a defunct business college sued the secretary of education, the banks, and the state guaranty agency, asserting that the school had fraudulently misrepresented the training it would provide the students. The students claimed that the defendants could not enforce the repayment obligation because the students had rights under state consumer protection laws. Although the defendants argued that the Higher Education Act of 1965 preempted state law defenses to collection attempts under the federal student loan program, the trial court disagreed, stating that the defendants were subject to the students' state law defenses regarding secured transactions. The law in West Virginia provides that, in making a consumer loan, the lender is subject to the borrower's defenses against the seller if the lender participated in or was connected with the sales transaction. The students argued that the lender (the bank) and the school worked together to induce the students to take out the federally guaranteed loans. Because of their concern that students might successfully avoid their student loan obligations under state law, some banks may become hesitant to participate in the federal student loan programs; and their reluctance to participate could, in turn, limit the access of some students to these loans. See S. Jaschik, "U.S. Court Ruling on Bank Liability Worries Aid Experts," *Chron. Higher Educ.,* Aug. 7, 1991, A17 (discussing *Tipton*).

Students arguing under other state law theories, however, have been less successful. In *Bogart v. Nebraska Student Loan Program,* 858 S.W.2d 78 (Ark. 1993), the Supreme Court of Arkansas rejected a group of students' claim that the guaranty agency and the banks who actually loaned the money to the students were agents of the stenographic school, against which the students had obtained a judgment for fraud, which they were then unable to collect. The court ruled that the Higher Education Act preempted the students' claims under agency law. A similar result occurred in *Veal v. First American Savings Bank,* 914 F.2d 909 (7th Cir. 1990). And in *Jackson v. Culinary School of Washington,* 811 F. Supp. 714 (D.D.C. 1993), the court rejected the claims of students seeking to have their loan obligations declared null and void because of the secretary of education's negligent supervision of the school's default rate and the quality of its curriculum. The court said that the student loan program

> is not a warranty or guarantee of the quality of the educational program. As a matter of policy, the plaintiffs would require the current defendants [the banks and the Department of Education] to police the curriculum and activities of all schools throughout the nation, and the practicalities of this would effectively bring about the end of the student loan program as we have known it in this country over the last several years [811 F. Supp. at 719].

The former students appealed, and the U.S. Court of Appeals for the District of Columbia Circuit, ruling on procedural grounds, remanded the case to the trial court for dismissal (*Jackson v. Culinary School of Washington, Ltd.*, 27 F.3d 573 (D.C. Cir. 1994)). The students appealed to the U.S. Supreme Court; that court vacated the D.C. Circuit's opinion and remanded it for the appellate court's consideration of the standard for reviewing a trial court's granting of declaratory relief (115 S. Ct. 2573 (1995)). On remand (59 F.3d 254 (D.C. Cir. 1995)), the appellate court determined that the students had no legally enforceable right against the secretary of education (upholding the trial court's ruling on the merits of the plaintiffs' federal claim); but remanded the issue of whether state law claims could be resolved by declaratory relief for further and more extensive consideration by the trial court.

Collection of student loans is a critical issue for colleges and universities, for legal reasons and because of the implications of student default rates for continued eligibility. College and university officials should use experienced counsel and student aid professionals to develop and enforce student financial aid policies that fully comply with state and federal requirements.

SELECTED ANNOTATED BIBLIOGRAPHY

Sec. 4.1 (Admissions)

Crockett, Richard B., & Shelley Sanders Kehl. *Accommodating Students with Learning and Emotional Disabilities: A Legal Compendium.* (National Association of College and University Attorneys, 1996). Reprints articles from law and social science journals, as well as conference outlines, on the requirements of Section 504 and the ADA; the accommodation of learning disabilities and emotional disabilities; and on the characteristics of certain learning disabilities. Also includes material on how the laws are enforced, institutional policies and handbooks on accommodating disabled students, and several guides for faculty concerning assisting disabled students.

Hurley, Brigid. Note, "Accommodating Learning Disabled Students in Higher Education: Schools' Legal Obligations Under Section 504 of the Rehabilitation Act," 32 *Boston College L. Rev.* 1051 (1991). Reviews statutory and regulatory provisions of Section 504 of the Rehabilitation Act of 1973, as well as judicial interpretations of Section 504 for higher education. Examines the reasonable accommodation requirement, the feasibility of the "undue financial burden" defense on behalf of the college, and the practice of "flagging" disabled students in institutional records.

Johnson, Alex M., Jr. "Bid Whist, Tonk and *United States v. Fordice:* Why Integrationism Fails African-Americans Again," 81 *Cal. L. Rev.* 1401 (1993). Criticizes the Supreme Court's *Fordice* opinion regarding the present effects of former *de jure* segregation in public colleges and universities, particularly the potential effect of the opinion on traditionally black colleges.

McCormack, Wayne (ed.). *The Bakke Decision—Implications for Higher Education Admissions* (American Council on Education, 1978). A report of the American Council on Education/Association of American Law Schools committee convened to study *Bakke*. Reviews the various opinions in *Bakke* and discusses their implications for admissions and financial aid. The report also "analyzes the various objectives to be served by race and ethnic group-conscious admission programs and examines several models of admission procedures and criteria that might be used to serve these objectives."

Orleans, Jeffrey H. "Memorandum: First Thoughts on *Southeastern Community College v. Davis*," 6 *J. Coll. & Univ. Law* 263 (1979–80). Analyzes the U.S. Supreme Court's *Davis* opinion and explores its impact on the postsecondary institution's obligations to students with disabilities. Also explores the potential impact of *Davis* on issues such as "academic treatment, adjustments, and assistance" and "preadmission inquiries."

Sindler, Allan P. *Bakke, DeFunis, and Minority Admissions: The Quest for Equal Opportunity* (Longman, 1978). A thought-provoking analysis of the various issues raised by affirmative admissions policies. Traces the issues and their implications through the U.S. Supreme Court's pronouncement in *Bakke*.

"Symposium: *Regents of the University of California v. Bakke*," 67 *Cal. L. Rev.* 1 (1979). Contains articles, comments, and a book review on issues relating to *Bakke*. Lead articles, all by noted legal scholars, are Derrick A. Bell, Jr., "*Bakke*, Minority Admissions, and the Usual Price of Racial Remedies"; Vincent Blasi, "*Bakke* as Precedent: Does Mr. Justice Powell Have a Theory?"; Robert G. Dixon, Jr., "*Bakke*: A Constitutional Analysis", R. Kent Greenawalt, "The Unresolved Problems of Reverse Discrimination"; Louis Henkin, "What of a Right to Practice a Profession?"; Robert M. O'Neil, "*Bakke* in Balance: Some Preliminary Thoughts"; and Richard A. Posner, "The *Bakke* Case and the Future of Affirmative Action."

Van Tol, Joan E. (ed.). *College and University Student Records: A Legal Compendium* (National Association of College and University Attorneys, 1989). A collection of articles, sample policies and forms, and state and federal statutes concerning student records. Included are discussions of fraudulent academic credentials, degree revocation, maintenance of computerized academic records, and requests for information from student records.

Sec. 4.2 (Financial Aid)

Butler, Blaine B., & Rigney, David P. *Managing Federal Student Aid Programs* (National Association of College and University Attorneys, 1993). An overview of the federal student aid programs. Discusses institutional eligibility for participation in these programs, federal oversight of institutional participation, and the audit process. A primer for attorneys unfamiliar with federal student aid programs and their complexity.

Dorian, James C., & Ward, Diane M. *Student Loan Programs: Management and Collection* (National Association of College and University Business Officers, 1991). A guidebook to the management of federal student loan programs. In addition to chapters on each of the major federal loan programs, the book includes chapters on administrative and fiscal standards, loan collection, contracting for services, litigation and bankruptcy, audits and program reviews, the regulatory process, and consumer credit protection. Appendices provide forms, sample letters, federal regulations, a glossary of terms, and a list of references and resources.

Lines, Patricia M. "Tuition Discrimination: Valid and Invalid Uses of Tuition Differentials," 9 *J. Coll. & Univ. Law* 241 (1982–83). Addresses the constitutional validity of tuition differentials between state residents, on one hand, and nonresidents, aliens, or new residents, on the other. Reviews issues arising under equal protection clauses of federal and state constitutions, the federal privileges and immunities clause, the "irrebuttable presumption" doctrine of federal due process, and the federal supremacy clause.

Olivas, Michael A. "*Plyler v. Doe, Toll v. Moreno,* and Postsecondary Admissions: Undocumented Adults and 'Enduring Disability,'" 15 *J. Coll. & Univ. Law* 19 (1986). Examines the impact of two important U.S. Supreme Court cases on the rights of undocumented aliens to attend and receive resident status at public higher education institutions. Proposes that the Court's treatment of undocumented alien elementary school students in Texas (in *Plyler v. Doe)* may be extended to other jurisdictions as well as to the higher education arena. Includes a table, with accompanying explanatory text, of the regulatory or policy-making entities that formulate higher education residency requirements in each of the states.

Olivas, Michael A. "Administering Intentions: Law, Theory, and Practice of Postsecondary Residency Requirements," 59 *J. Higher Educ.* 263 (1988). Traces the legal basis for resident and nonresident tuition charges through examination of the statutes, regulations, and administrative practices governing the fifty state systems and the District of Columbia. Explores seven types of alternative models for making residency determinations and sets out suggestions for reform. Includes four helpful tables organizing and summarizing data.

Sagner, Dianne. "Consumer Credit and Higher Education," 6 *J. Coll. & Univ. Law* 3 (1979). Discusses the truth-in-lending provisions of the Consumer Credit Protection Act of 1968 (15 U.S.C. §160 *et seq.*) and the university's obligations in disclosing the terms of student loans and credit sales.

Tanaka, Paul. *The Permissibility of Withholding Transcripts Under the Bankruptcy Law* (National Association of College and University Attorneys, 1986). Discusses provisions of the bankruptcy law relevant to an institution's right to withhold a transcript.

CHAPTER FIVE

The Campus Community

Institutions of higher education typically undertake to create and maintain a campus community that provides a nurturing academic and social environment for students. Institutions with residential campuses also have residential communities. To maintain these communities, institutions must provide a range of services for students extending far beyond courses and instructors. This chapter surveys various types of services and the legal issues to which each has given rise.

SEC. 5.1. STUDENT HOUSING

5.1.1. Housing Regulations

Postsecondary institutions with residential campuses usually have policies specifying which students may, and which students must, live in campus housing. Such regulations sometimes apply only to certain groups of students, using classifications based on the student's age, sex, class, or marital status. Institutions also typically have policies regulating living conditions in campus housing. Students in public institutions have sought to use the federal Constitution to challenge such housing policies.

In *Prostrollo v. University of South Dakota*, 507 F.2d 775 (8th Cir. 1974), students claimed that the university's regulation requiring all single freshmen and sophomores to live in university housing was unconstitutional because it denied them equal protection under the Fourteenth Amendment and infringed their constitutional rights of privacy and freedom of association. The university admitted that one purpose of the regulation was to maintain a certain level of dormitory occupancy to secure revenue to repay dormitory construction costs. But the university also offered testimony that the regulation was instituted to ensure that younger students would educationally benefit from the experience in self-government, community living, and group discipline and the opportunities for relationships with staff members that dormitory life provides. In addition, university officials contended that the dormitories provided easy access to study facilities and to films and discussion groups.

After evaluating these justifications, the lower court determined that the primary purpose of the housing regulation was financial and that the regulation's differentiation of freshmen and sophomores from upper-division students had no rational relationship to the purpose of ensuring housing income. The lower court therefore held the regulation unconstitutional under the equal protection clause. The appellate court reversed the lower court's decision. It reasoned that, even if the regulation's primary purpose was financial, there was no denial of equal protection because there was another rational basis for differentiating freshmen and sophomores from upper-division students: the university officials' belief that the regulation contributed to the younger students' adjustment to college life. The appellate court also rejected the students' right-to-privacy and freedom-of-association challenges. The court gave deference to school authorities' traditionally broad powers in formulating educational policy.

A similar housing regulation that used an age classification to prohibit certain students from living off campus was at issue in *Cooper v. Nix,* 496 F.2d 1285 (5th Cir. 1974). The regulation required all unmarried, full-time undergraduate students, regardless of age and whether or not emancipated, to live on campus. The regulation contained an exemption for certain older students, which in practice the school enforced by simply exempting all undergraduates twenty-three years old and over. Neither the lower court nor the appeals court found any justification in the record for a distinction between twenty-one-year-old students and twenty-three-year-old students. Though the lower court had enjoined the school from requiring students twenty-one and older to live on campus, the appeals court narrowed the remedy to require only that the school not automatically exempt all twenty-three-year-olds. Thus, the school could continue to enforce the regulation if it exempted students over twenty-three only on a case-by-case basis.

A regulation that allowed male students but not female students to live off campus was challenged in *Texas Woman's University v. Chayklintaste,* 521 S.W.2d 949 (Tex. Civ. App. 1975), and found unconstitutional. Though the university convinced the court that it did not have the space or the money to provide on-campus male housing, the court held that mere financial reasons could not justify the discrimination. The court concluded that the university was unconstitutionally discriminating against its male students by not providing them with any housing facilities and also was unconstitutionally discriminating against its female students by not permitting them to live off campus.

The university subsequently made housing available to males and changed its regulations to require both male and female undergraduates under twenty-three to live on campus. Although the regulation was now like the one found unconstitutional in *Cooper,* above, the Texas Supreme Court upheld its constitutionality in a later appeal of *Texas Woman's University v. Chayklintaste,* 530 S.W.2d 927 (Tex. 1975). In this case the university justified the age classification with reasons similar to those used in *Prostrollo,* above, which upheld the freshman and sophomore classification. The university argued that on-campus dormitory life added to the intellectual and emotional development of its students and supported this argument with evidence from two professional educational journals and the testimony of a vice president of student affairs, a professor of education, and an instructor of social work.

In *Bynes v. Toll,* 512 F.2d 252 (2d Cir. 1975), another university housing regulation was challenged—in this case a regulation that permitted married students to live on campus but barred their children from living on campus. The court found that there was no denial of equal protection, since the university had several very sound safety reasons for not allowing children to reside in the dormitories. The court also found that the regulation did not interfere with the marital privacy of the students or their natural right to bring up their children.

Housing regulations limiting dormitory visitors have also been constitutionally challenged. In *Futrell v. Ahrens,* 540 P.2d 214 (N.M. 1975), students claimed that a regulation prohibiting visits by members of the opposite sex in dormitory bedrooms violated their rights of privacy and free association. The regulation did not apply to the lounges or lobbies of the dorms. The court held for the institution, reasoning that even if the regulation affected rights of privacy and association, it was a reasonable time-and-place restriction on exercise of those rights, since it served legitimate educational interests and conformed with accepted standards of conduct.

Taken together, these cases indicate that the Constitution affords public universities broad leeway in regulating on-campus student housing. An institution may require some students to live on campus; may regulate living conditions to fulfill legitimate health, safety, or educational goals; and may apply its housing policies differently to different student groups. If students are treated differently, however, the Constitution requires that the basis for classifying them be reasonable. The cases above suggest that classification based solely on financial considerations may not meet that test. Administrators should thus be prepared to offer sound nonfinancial justifications for classifications in their residence rules—such as the promotion of educational goals, the protection of the health and safety of students, or the protection of other students' privacy interests. Differing treatment of students based on sex may require a relatively stronger showing of justification, and differing treatment based on race would require a justification so compelling that perhaps none exists.

Besides these limits on administrators' authority over student housing, the Constitution also limits public administrators' authority to enter student rooms (see Section 5.1.2) and to regulate solicitation, canvassing, and voter registration in student residences (see Sections 11.3 and 11.5.4).

For private as well as public institutions, federal civil rights regulations limit administrators' authority to treat students differently on grounds of race, sex, age, or disability. The Title VI regulations (see Section 12.4.2) apparently prohibit any and all different treatment of students by race (34 C.F.R. §§100.3(b)(1)(b)(5) and 100.4(d)). The Title IX regulations (see Section 12.4.3) require that the institution provide amounts of housing for female and male students proportionate to the number of housing applicants of each sex, that such housing be comparable in quality and in cost to the student, and that the institution not have different housing policies for each sex (34 C.F.R. §§106.32 and 106.33). Furthermore, a provision of Title IX (20 U.S.C. §1686) states:

> Notwithstanding anything to the contrary contained in this chapter, nothing contained herein shall be construed to prohibit any educational institution receiving funds under this Act from maintaining separate living facilities for the different sexes.

The Section 504 regulations on discrimination against people with disabilities (see Section 12.4.4) require institutions to provide "comparable, convenient, and accessible" housing for students with disabilities at the same cost as for nondisabled students (34 C.F.R. §104.45). The regulations also provide that colleges provide a variety of housing and that students with disabilities be given a choice among several types of housing (34 C.F.R. §104.45(a)).

In *Fleming v. New York University*, 865 F.2d 478 (2d Cir. 1989), a graduate student who used a wheelchair claimed that the university overcharged him for his room, in violation of Section 504 of the Rehabilitation Act. The trial court dismissed his claim, and the appellate court affirmed. The student had requested single occupancy of a double room as an undergraduate; the university charged him twice the rate that a student sharing a double room paid. After intervention by the U.S. Office for Civil Rights, the university modified its room charge to 75 percent of the rate for two students in a room.

When the student decided to enroll in graduate school at the university, he asked to remain in the undergraduate residence hall. The university agreed and charged him the 75 percent fee. However, because of low occupancy in the graduate residence halls, graduate students occupying double rooms there were charged a single-room rate. When the student refused to pay his room bills, the university withheld his master's degree. The court ruled that the student's claim for his undergraduate years was time-barred. The claim for disability discrimination based on the room charges during his graduate program was denied because the student had never applied for graduate housing; he had requested undergraduate housing. There was no discriminatory denial of cheaper graduate housing, the court said, because the student never requested it.

The Age Discrimination Act regulations (see Section 12.4.5) apparently apply to discrimination by age in campus housing. As implemented in the general regulations, the ADA apparently limits administrators' authority to use explicit age distinctions (such as those used in *Cooper v. Nix* and *Texas Woman's University v. Chayklintaste)* in formulating housing policies. Policies that distinguish among students according to their class (such as those used in *Prostrollo v. University of South Dakota)* may also be prohibited by the ADA, since they may have the effect of distinguishing by age. Such age distinctions will be prohibited (under §90.12 of the general regulations) unless they fit within one of the narrow exceptions specified in the regulations (in §§90.13, 90.14, and 90.15) or constitute affirmative action (under §90.49). The best bet for fitting within an exception may be the regulation that permits age distinctions "necessary to the normal operation . . . of a program or activity" (§90.14). But administrators should note that the four-part test set out in the regulation carefully circumscribes this exception. For policies based on the class of students, administrators may also be helped by the regulation that permits the use of a nonage factor with an age-discriminatory effect "if the factor bears a direct and substantial relationship to the normal operation of the program or activity" (§90.15).

Moreover, the Fair Housing Act prohibits discrimination in housing on the basis of "familial status" (42 U.S.C. §3604 (1989)). An advisory letter from the U.S. Department of Housing and Urban Development discussing the application of the law to accommodations for students and their children in college or university residence halls is reproduced at 20 *Coll. Law Dig.* 326–29 (July 19, 1990). This statute may create rights for married students greater than they are afforded under the Constitution in cases such as *Bynes v. Toll* (above).

Another group protesting discrimination in housing policies is same-sex couples. These couples have claimed that because they are not allowed to marry, they are unfairly excluded from a benefit extended to married students. Furthermore, since many colleges and universities prohibit discrimination on the basis of sexual orientation, gay couples have argued that denying them housing violates the institution's nondiscrimination regulations. Several universities, including the University of Pennsylvania and Stanford University, have provided university housing to unmarried couples, including those of the same sex.

5.1.2. Searches and Seizures

The Fourth Amendment secures an individual's expectation of privacy against government encroachment by providing that "the right of the people to be secure in their persons, houses, papers, and effects, against unreasonable searches and seizures, shall not be violated, and no warrants shall issue, but upon probable cause, supported by oath or affirmation, and particularly describing the place to be searched, and the persons or things to be seized." Searches or seizures conducted pursuant to a warrant meeting the requirements of this provision are deemed reasonable. Warrantless searches may also be found reasonable if they are conducted with the consent of the individual involved, if they are incidental to a lawful arrest, or if they come within a few narrow judicial exceptions, such as an emergency situation.

The applicability of these Fourth Amendment mandates to postsecondary institutions has not always been clear. In the past, when administrators' efforts to provide a "proper" educational atmosphere resulted in noncompliance with the Fourth Amendment, the deviations were defended by administrators and often upheld by courts under a variety of theories. While the previously common justification of *in loco parentis* is no longer appropriate (see Section 3.1.1), several remaining theories retain vitality. The leading case of *Piazzola v. Watkins,* 442 F.2d 284 (5th Cir. 1971), provides a good overview of these theories and their validity.

In *Piazzola,* the dean of men at a state university, at the request of the police, pledged the cooperation of university officials in searching the rooms of two students suspected of concealing marijuana there. At the time of the search, the university had the following regulation in effect: "The college reserves the right to enter rooms for inspection purposes. If the administration deems it necessary, the room may be searched and the occupant required to open his personal baggage and any other personal material which is sealed." The students' rooms were searched without their consent and without a warrant by police officers and university officials. When police found marijuana in each room, the students were arrested, tried, convicted, and sentenced to five years in prison. The U.S. Court of Appeals for the Fifth Circuit reversed the convictions, holding that "a student who occupies a college dormitory room enjoys the protection of the Fourth Amendment" and that the warrantless searches were unreasonable and therefore unconstitutional under that amendment.

Piazzola and similar cases establish that administrators of public institutions cannot avoid the Fourth Amendment simply by asserting that a student has no reasonable expectation of privacy in institution-sponsored housing. (Compare *State v. Dalton,* 716 P.2d 940 (Wash. Ct. App. 1986).) Similarly, administrators can no longer be confident of avoiding the Fourth Amendment by asserting the *in loco parentis* concept or by arguing that the institution's landlord status, standing alone, authorizes it to search to protect its property interests. Nor does the landlord status, by itself, permit the institution to consent to a search by police, since it has been held that a landlord has no authority to consent to a police search of a tenant's premises (see, for example, *Chapman v. United States,* 365 U.S. 610 (1961)).

However, two limited bases remain on which administrators of public institutions or their delegates can enter a student's premises uninvited and without the authority of a warrant.[1] Under the first approach, the institution can obtain the student's general consent to entry by including an authorization to enter in a written housing agreement or in housing regulations incorporated in the housing agreement. *Piazzola* explains the limits on this approach. Citing the regulation quoted above, the court explained:

> The university retains broad supervisory powers which permit it to adopt . . . [this regulation], provided that regulation is reasonably construed and is limited in its application to further the university's function as an educational institution. The regulation cannot be construed or applied so as to give consent to a search for evidence for the primary purpose of a criminal prosecution. Otherwise, the regulation itself would constitute an unconstitutional attempt to require a student to waive his protection from unreasonable searches and seizures as a condition to his occupancy of a college dormitory room [442 F.2d at 289].

Thus, housing agreements or regulations must be narrowly construed to permit only such entry and search as is expressly provided, and in any case to permit only entries undertaken in pursuit of an educational purpose rather than a criminal enforcement function. *State v. Hunter,* 831 P.2d 1033 (Utah App. 1992), illustrates the type of search that may come within the *Piazzola* guidelines. The director of housing at Utah State University had instigated and conducted a room-to-room inspection to investigate reports of vandalism on the second floor of a dormitory. Upon challenge by a student in whose room the director discovered stolen university property in plain view, the court upheld the search because the housing regulations expressly authorized the room-to-room inspection and because the inspection served the university's interest in protecting university property and maintaining a sound educational environment.

---

[1]In *New Jersey v. T.L.O.,* 469 U.S. 325 (1985), the U.S. Supreme Court created a judicial exception to the warrant requirement for certain searches of public school students. However, the Court's opinion directly applies only to public elementary and secondary schools. Moreover, the opinion applies (1) only to searches of the person or property (such as a purse) carried on the person, as opposed to searches of dormitory rooms, lockers, desks, or other such locations (469 U.S. at 337 n.5), and (2) only to "searches carried out by school authorities acting alone and on their own authority," as opposed to "searches conducted by school officials in conjunction with or at the behest of law enforcement agencies" (469 U.S. at 341 n.7).

Under the second approach to securing entry to a student's premises, the public institution can sometimes conduct searches (often called "administrative searches") whose purpose is to protect health and safety—for instance, to enforce health regulations or fire and safety codes. Although such searches, if conducted without a student's consent, usually require a warrant, it may be obtained under less stringent standards than those for obtaining a criminal search warrant. The leading case is *Camara v. Municipal Court,* 387 U.S. 523 (1967), where the U.S. Supreme Court held that a person cannot be prosecuted for refusing to permit city officials to conduct a warrantless code-enforcement inspection of his residence. The Court held that such a search required a warrant, which could be obtained "if reasonable legislative or administrative standards for conducting an area inspection are satisfied"; such standards need "not necessarily depend upon specific knowledge of the condition of the particular dwelling."

In emergency situations where there is insufficient time to obtain a warrant, health and safety searches may be conducted without one. The U.S. Supreme Court emphasized in the *Camara* case (387 U.S. at 539) that "nothing we say today is intended to foreclose prompt inspections, even without a warrant, that the law has traditionally upheld in emergency situations." In other cases, courts have recognized firefighters' authority to enter "a burning structure to put out the blaze" and remain there to investigate its cause (*Michigan v. Tyler,* 436 U.S. 499 (1978)), and police officers' authority to "enter a dwelling without a warrant to render emergency aid and assistance to a person whom they reasonably believe to be in distress and in need of that assistance" (*Root v. Gauper,* 438 F.2d 361 (8th Cir. 1971)).

Before entering a room pursuant to the housing agreement or an administrative (health and safety) search, administrators should usually seek to notify and obtain the specific consent of the affected students when it is feasible to do so. Such a policy not only evidences courtesy and respect for privacy but would also augment the validity of the entry in circumstances where there may be some doubt about the scope of the administrator's authority under the housing agreement or the judicial precedents on administrative searches.

In addition to these two limited approaches (housing agreements and administrative searches) to securing entry, other even narrower exceptions to Fourth Amendment warrant requirements may be available to security officers of public institutions who have arrest powers. Such exceptions involve the intricacies of Fourth Amendment law on arrests and searches. The case of *State of Washington v. Chrisman,* 102 S. Ct. 812 (1982), is illustrative. A campus security guard at Washington State University had arrested a student, Overdahl, for illegally possessing alcoholic beverages. The officer accompanied Overdahl to his dormitory room when Overdahl offered to retrieve his identification. Overdahl's roommate, Chrisman, was in the room. While waiting at the doorway for Overdahl to find his identification, the officer observed marijuana seeds and a pipe lying on a desk in the room. The officer then entered, confirmed the identity of the seeds, and seized them. Chrisman was later convicted of possession of marijuana and LSD, which security officers also found in the room.

By a 6–to–3 vote, the U.S. Supreme Court applied the "plain view" exception to the Fourth Amendment and upheld the conviction. The plain view doctrine allows a law enforcement officer to seize property that is clearly incriminating evidence or contraband when that property is in "plain view" in a place where the officer has a right to be. The Court determined that, since an arresting officer has a right to maintain custody of a subject under arrest, this officer lawfully could have entered the room with Overdahl and remained at Overdahl's side for the entire time Overdahl was in the room. Thus, the officer not only had the right to be where he could observe the drugs; he also had the right to be where he could seize the drugs. According to the Court, "It is of no legal significance whether the officer was in the room, on the threshold, or in the hallway, since he had a right to be in any of these places as an incident of a valid arrest. . . . This is a classic instance of incriminating evidence found in plain view when a police officer, for unrelated but entirely legitimate reasons, obtains lawful access to an individual's area of privacy."

Chrisman thus recognizes that a security officer may enter a student's room "as an incident of a valid arrest" of either that student or his roommate. The case also indicates that an important exception to search warrant requirements— the plain view doctrine—retains its full vitality in the college dormitory setting. The Court accorded no greater or lesser constitutional protection from search and seizure to student dormitory residents than to the population at large. Clearly, under *Chrisman* students do enjoy Fourth Amendment protections on campus; but, just as clearly, the Fourth Amendment does not accord dormitory students special status or subject campus security officials to additional restrictions that are not applicable to the nonacademic world.

The Supreme Court placed an important restriction on the plain view doctrine in *Arizona v. Hicks*, 480 U.S. 321 (1987). A police officer, who had entered an apartment lawfully for Fourth Amendment purposes, noticed some stereo equipment that he believed might be stolen. He moved the equipment slightly to locate the serial numbers and later ascertained that the equipment was, in fact, stolen. The Court ruled that the search and seizure were unlawful because the police officer did not have probable cause to believe the equipment was stolen—only a reasonable suspicion, which is insufficient for Fourth Amendment purposes.

Administrators at private institutions are generally not subject to Fourth Amendment restraints, since their actions are usually not state action (Section 1.5.2). But if local, state, or federal law enforcement officials are in any way involved in a search at a private institution, such involvement may be sufficient to make the search state action and therefore subject to the Fourth Amendment. In *People v. Boettner,* 362 N.Y.S.2d 365 (N.Y. Sup. Ct. 1974), *affirmed,* 376 N.Y.S.2d 59 (N.Y. App. Div. 1975), for instance, the question was whether a dormitory room search by officials at the Rochester Institute of Technology, a private institution, was state action. The court answered in the negative only after establishing that the police had not expressly or implicitly requested the search; that the police were not aware of the search; and that there was no evidence of any implied participation of the police by virtue of a continuing cooperative relationship between university officials and the police. A Virginia appellate court reached a similar conclusion in *Duarte v. Commonwealth,* 407 S.E.2d 41 (Va. Ct. App. 1991), because the dean of students at a private college had told college staff to search the plaintiff's room, and police were not involved in the search. And in a leading case involving a security officer of a private business firm, another court judged the validity of the search by determining whether the officer had "acted at the behest or suggestion, with the aid, advice, or encouragement, or under the direction or influence of" government law enforcement officials (*United States v. Clegg,* 509 F.2d 605 (5th Cir. 1975)). Thus, a private institution's authority to conduct searches unshackled by the Fourth Amendment depends on the absence of direct or indirect involvement of such officials in such searches. In addition, if security officers at a private institution have been given public arrest or search powers, they and their institution will be subject to Fourth Amendment strictures in exercising these state-delegated powers (see *People v. Zelinski,* 594 P.2d 1000 (Cal. 1979), discussed in Section 5.2.1).

SEC. 5.2. CAMPUS SECURITY

Crime is an unfortunate fact of life on many college campuses. Consequently, campus security and the role of security officers have become high-visibility issues. Although contemporary jurisprudence rejects the concept that colleges are responsible for the safety of students (see Section 2.3.1), institutions of higher education have, in some cases, been found liable for injury to students when the injury was foreseeable or when there was a history of criminal activity on campus.

5.2.1. Security Officers

The powers and responsibilities of campus security officers should be carefully delineated. Administrators must determine whether such officers should be permitted to carry weapons and under what conditions. They must determine the security officers' authority to investigate crime on campus or to investigate violations of student codes of conduct. Record-keeping practices also must be devised.[2] The relationship that security officers will have with local and state police must be cooperatively worked out with local and state police forces. Because campus security officers may play dual roles, partly enforcing public criminal laws and partly enforcing the institution's codes of conduct, administrators should carefully delineate the officers' relative responsibilities in each role.

Administrators must also determine whether their campus security guards have, or should have, arrest powers under state or local law. For public institutions, state law may grant full arrest powers to certain campus security guards. In *People v. Wesley,* 365 N.Y.S.2d 593 (City Ct., Buffalo, 1975), for instance, the court determined that security officers at a particular state campus were "peace officers" under the terms of Section 355(2)(m) of the New York Education Law. For public institutions not subject to such statutes, and for private institutions, deputization under city or county law or the use of "citizen's arrest" powers may be options (see *Hall v. Virginia,* 389 S.E.2d 921 (Va. Ct. App. 1990)).

Although security guards may have authority to make arrests off campus as well as on campus, their off-campus authority may be more limited. In *State v. Lyon,* 584 P.2d 844 (Utah 1978), for instance, the Supreme Court of Utah vacated the conviction of a motorcyclist (Lyon) who had been arrested by a college security officer four blocks from the campus. The state argued that, under Utah law, the officer had "all of the powers possessed by a policeman" and was "required" to make the arrest to protect the interests of the college. The court rejected this argument, noting that the officer's "suspicion" that Lyon had committed vandalism or theft did not justify the off-campus arrest. Rather, the court stated, for the arrest to be valid, a "present danger" to the college, its students, or its employees must have been evident. (See D. Berman, "Law and Order on Campus: An Analysis of the Role and Problems of the Security Police," 49 *J. Urban Law* 49 (1971–72).)

Conversely, in *Commonwealth of Pennsylvania v. Mitchell,* 554 A.2d 542 (Pa. Super. Ct. 1989), a state court defined the territorial jurisdiction within which campus police in that state may exercise their authority. The defendants, suspected of attempted theft, had been arrested by University of Pennsylvania campus police on the sidewalk of a commercial district on the university's property. The defendants argued that Pennsylvania law did not authorize the campus police to arrest them on commercial property owned and held by the university for investment purposes. Under the applicable statute (71 Pa. Stat. §646),

---

[2]For a general discussion of the legal restrictions on record keeping, see Section 3.3. The Federal Educational Rights and Privacy Act, discussed in Section 3.3.1, has a specific provision on law enforcement records (20 U.S.C. §1232(a)(4)(B) (ii)). Regulations implementing this provision are in 34 C.F.R. §§99.3 (definitions of "disciplinary action or proceeding" and "education records") and 99.8 (definition of "law enforcement unit" and "law enforcement records").

security and campus police may exercise their powers and perform their duties only on the "premises" and "grounds and buildings" of state colleges and universities. Relying on the statute's legislative history and purpose, the court concluded that these statutory terms include not only academic and residential areas but also commercial property used for investment purposes. It reasoned that to limit "premises" to academic and residential areas would ignore the layout and everyday operations of colleges and universities, because business establishments owned by institutions are typically frequented by students. Thus, the court upheld the validity of the arrest.

State laws vary considerably regarding the off-campus authority of campus police officers, and the particular facts of each incident may also have an effect on the court's determination.

Police work is also subject to a variety of constitutional restraints concerning such matters as investigations, arrests, and searches and seizures of persons or private property. Security officers for public institutions are subject to all these restraints. In private institutions, security officers who are operating in conjunction with local or state police forces (see Section 5.1.2) or who have arrest powers (see *Zelinski* case below) may also be subject to constitutional restraints under the state action doctrine (Section 1.5.2). In devising the responsibilities of such officers, therefore, administrators should be sensitive to the constitutional requirements regarding police work.

In *People v. Zelinski,* 594 P.2d 1000 (Cal. 1979), the California Supreme Court issued a major opinion concerning the applicability of constitutional restraints to private security personnel. Although it concerned security guards at a department store rather than a college campus, and applied the state constitution rather than the United States Constitution, the case nevertheless speaks meaningfully to the question of when a private college's security officers would be subject to state or federal constitutional restraints on their activities. In reversing the conviction of a person who had been arrested and searched by private store detectives, the *Zelinski* court reasoned:

> Here the store security forces did not act in a purely private capacity but rather were fulfilling a public function in bringing violators of the law to public justice. For reasons hereinafter expressed, we conclude that under such circumstances— that is, *when private security personnel conduct an illegal search or seizure while engaged in a statutorily authorized citizen's arrest and detention of a person in aid of law enforcement authorities*—the constitutional proscriptions of Article I, Section 13 [whose words parallel the Fourth Amendment to the U.S. Constitution] are applicable. . . .
>
> Persons so acting should be subject to the constitutional proscriptions that secure an individual's right to privacy, for their actions are taken pursuant to statutory authority to promote a state interest in bringing offenders to public accounting. Unrestrained, such action would subvert state authority in defiance

of its established limits. It would destroy the protection those carefully defined limits were intended to afford to everyone, the guilty and innocent alike. It would afford de facto authorizations for searches and seizures incident to arrests or detentions made by private individuals that even peace officers are not authorized to make. Accordingly, we hold that in any case *where private security personnel assert the power of the state to make an arrest or to detain another person for transfer to custody of the state,* the state involvement is sufficient for the court to enforce the proper exercise of that power (cf. *People v. Haydel* (524 P.2d 866 (Cal. 1974)) by excluding the fruits of illegal abuse thereof [594 P.2d at 1006; emphasis added].

Administrators should also be sensitive to the tort law principles applicable to security work (see generally Sections 2.3.1, 2.4.1, and 2.5). Like athletic activities (Section 10.6), campus security actions are likely to expose the institution to a substantial risk of tort liability. Using physical force or weapons, detaining or arresting persons, entering or searching private property can all occasion tort liability if they are undertaken without justification or accomplished carelessly. *Jones v. Wittenberg University,* 534 F.2d 1203 (6th Cir. 1976), for example, dealt with a university security guard who had fired a warning shot at a fleeing student. The shot pierced the student's chest and killed him. The guard and the university were held liable for the student's death, even though the guard did not intend to hit the student and may have had justification for firing a shot to frighten a fleeing suspect. The appellate court reasoned that the shooting could nevertheless constitute negligence "if it was done so carelessly as to result in foreseeable injury."

Institutions may also incur liability for malicious prosecution if an arrest or search is made in bad faith. In *Wright v. Schreffler,* 618 A.2d 412 (Pa. Super. Ct. 1992), a former college student's conviction for possession and delivery of marijuana was reversed because the court found that the defendant had been entrapped by campus police at Pennsylvania State University. The former student then sued the arresting officer for malicious prosecution, stating that the officer had no probable cause to arrest him, since the arrest was a result of the entrapment. The court agreed, and denied the officer's motion for dismissal.

Campus police may also be held liable under tort law for their treatment of individuals suspected of criminal activity. In *Hickey v. Zezulka,* 443 N.W.2d 180 (Mich. Ct. App. 1989), a university public-safety officer had placed a Michigan State University student in a holding cell at the university's department of public safety. The officer had stopped the student for erratic driving, and a breathalyzer test had shown that the student had blood alcohol levels of between 0.15 and 0.16 percent. While in the holding cell, the student hanged himself by a noose made from his belt and socks that he connected to a bracket on a heating unit attached to the ceiling of the cell.

The student's estate brought separate negligence actions against the officer and the university, and both were found liable after trial. Although an intermediate appellate court upheld the trial verdict against both the university and the officer, the state's supreme court, in *Hickey v. Zezulka,* 487 N.W.2d 106 (Mich. 1992), reversed the finding of liability against the university, applying Michigan's sovereign immunity law. The court upheld the negligence verdict against the officer, however, noting that the officer had violated university policies about removing harmful objects from persons before placing them in holding cells and about checking on them periodically. The court characterized the officer's actions as "ministerial" rather than discretionary, which, under Michigan law, eliminated her governmental immunity defense.

In light of *Hickey,* universities with local holding cells should make sure that campus police regulations are clear about the proper procedures to be used, particularly in handling individuals who are impaired by alcohol and drugs, and should ensure that the procedures are followed to reduce both the potential for harm to individuals and liability to the institution or its employees.

5.2.2. Protection Against Violent Crime on Campus

The extent of the institution's obligation to protect students from crime on campus—particularly, violent crimes committed by outsiders from the surrounding community—has become a sensitive issue for higher education. The number of such crimes reported, especially sexual attacks on women, has increased steadily over the years. As a result, postsecondary institutions now face substantial tactical and legal problems concerning the planning and operation of their campus security systems, as well as a federal law requiring them to report campus crime statistics.

In an early case, *P.D. v. Catholic University,* Civ. No. 75–2198 (D.D.C. 1976), a jury found the defendant liable for injuries incurred by a student who was raped in the locker room of the campus gym. While the case supports the general proposition that institutions have some legal duty to protect their students against outside criminal assailants, the court did not issue any opinion explaining the source or extent of this duty. Since then, however, a number of other courts have provided answers to these questions.

The court's response may depend, in part, on where the attack took place and whether the assailant was a student or an intruder. When students have encountered violence in residence halls from intruders, the courts have found a duty to protect the students similar to that of a landlord. For example, in *Mullins v. Pine Manor College,* 449 N.E.2d 331 (Mass. 1983), the court approved several legal theories for establishing institutional liability in residence hall security cases. The student in *Mullins* had been abducted from her dormitory room and raped on the campus of Pine Manor College, a women's college located in a suburban area. Although the college was located in a low-crime area and there was relatively little crime on campus, the court nevertheless held the college liable.

Developing its first theory, the court determined that residential colleges have a general legal duty to exercise due care in providing campus security:

> We think it can be said with confidence that colleges of ordinary prudence customarily exercise care to protect the well-being of their resident students, including seeking to protect them against the criminal acts of third parties. An expert witness hired by the defendant testified that he had visited eighteen area colleges, and, not surprisingly, all took steps to provide an adequate level of security on their campus. He testified also that standards had been established for determining what precautions should be taken. Thus, the college community itself has recognized its obligation to protect resident students from the criminal acts of third parties. This recognition indicates that the imposition of a duty of care is firmly embedded in a community consensus.
>
> This consensus stems from the nature of the situation. The concentration of young people, especially young women, on a college campus, creates favorable opportunities for criminal behavior. The threat of criminal acts of third parties to resident students is self-evident, and the college is the party which is in the position to take those steps which are necessary to ensure the safety of its students. No student has the ability to design and implement a security system, hire and supervise security guards, provide security at the entrance of dormitories, install proper locks, and establish a system of announcement for authorized visitors. Resident students typically live in a particular room for a mere nine months and, as a consequence, lack the incentive and capacity to take corrective measures. College regulations may also bar the installation of additional locks or chains. Some students may not have been exposed previously to living in a residence hall or in a metropolitan area and may not be fully conscious of the dangers that are present. Thus, the college must take the responsibility on itself if anything is to be done at all [449 N.E.2d at 335].

Developing its second theory, the court determined "that a duty voluntarily assumed must be performed with due care." Quoting from Section 323 of the *Restatement (Second) of Torts,* a scholarly work of the American Law Institute, the court held that when a college has taken responsibility for security, it is "subject to liability . . . for physical harm resulting from [the] failure to exercise reasonable care to perform [the] undertaking." An institution may be held liable under this theory, however, only if the plaintiff can establish that its "failure to exercise due care increased the risk of harm, or . . . the harm is suffered because of the student's reliance on the undertaking."

Analyzing the facts of the case under these two broad theories, the appellate court affirmed the trial court's judgment in favor of the student. The facts relevant to establishing the college's liability included the ease of scaling or opening the gates that led to the dormitories, the small number of security guards on night shift, the lack of a system for supervising the guards' performance of their duties, and the lack of dead bolts or chains for dormitory room doors.

Courts have ruled in two cases that universities provided inadequate residence hall security and that lax security was the proximate cause of a rape in one case and a death in a second. In *Miller v. State*, 478 N.Y.S.2d 829 (N.Y. App. Div. 1984), a student was abducted from the laundry room of a residence hall and taken through two unlocked doors to another residence hall where she was raped. The court noted that the university was on notice that nonresidents frequented the residence hall, and it criticized the university for failing to take "the rather minimal security measure of keeping the dormitory doors locked when it had notice of the likelihood of criminal intrusions" (478 N.Y.S.2d at 833). "Notice" consisted of knowledge by university agents that nonresidents had been loitering in the lounge of the residence hall, and the occurrence of numerous robberies, burglaries, criminal trespass, and a rape. The court applied traditional landlord-tenant law and increased the trial court's damage award of $25,000 to $400,000.

In the second case, *Nieswand v. Cornell University*, 692 F. Supp. 1464 (N.D.N.Y. 1988), a federal trial court refused to grant summary judgment for Cornell University when it denied that its residence hall security was inadequate and thus the proximate cause of a student's death. A rejected suitor (not a student) had entered the residence hall without detection and shot the student and her roommate. The roommate's parents filed both tort and contract claims (see Sections 2.3.1 and 2.3.2) against the university. The court, citing *Miller*, ruled that whether or not the attack was foreseeable was a question of material fact, which would have to be determined by a jury. Furthermore, the representations made by Cornell in written documents, such as residence hall security policies and brochures, regarding the locking of doors and the presence of security personnel could have constituted an implied contract to provide appropriate security. Whether a contract existed and, if so, whether it was breached was again a matter for the jury.

In another case involving Cornell, the university was found not liable for an assault in a residence hall by an intruder. The intruder had scaled a two-story exterior metal grate and then kicked open the victim's door, which had been locked and deadbolted. In *Vangeli v. Schneider*, 598 N.Y.S.2d 837 (N.Y. App. Div. 1993), the court ruled that Cornell had met its duty to provide "minimal security" as a landlord.

Although colleges and universities have a duty to provide security for students living in residence halls, courts have distinguished between their duty as a landlord and the more general duty to provide security on campus. For example, in *Nola M. v. University of Southern California*, 20 Cal. Rptr. 2d 97 (Cal. Ct. App. 1993), the court refused to find the university liable for a sexual assault on campus. Although there was a history of violent crimes on the campus, the court did not believe that additional security measures would have prevented the injury to the plaintiff. The university's duty as a landowner does not extend, said the court, to ensuring absolute safety against random acts of violence. This result is the majority rule, since most cases involving colleges and universities charged with liability when a student is injured by the violent act of a stranger have resulted in findings of no liability for the college.

Campus security issues also arise when the assailant is a fellow student. Again, in most instances the college is absolved of liability unless the violent act was clearly foreseeable. Although courts have continued to reject the claim that colleges must ensure the safety of their students, a few courts have applied the common law duty imposed on landlords to protect their invitees against foreseeable harm. For example, in *Nero v. Kansas State University*, 861 P.2d 768 (Kan. 1993), the Supreme Court of Kansas ruled that the university might be found negligent for permitting a student who had earlier been found guilty of a sexual assault on campus to live in a coeducational residence hall, where he sexually assaulted the plaintiff, a fellow student. The court reversed a summary judgment for the university, declaring that a jury would have to determine whether the attack was foreseeable and, if so, whether the university had breached a duty to the plaintiff. The court said:

> We hold [that] the university-student relationship does not in and of itself impose a duty upon universities to protect students from the actions of fellow students or third parties. The *in loco parentis* doctrine is outmoded and inconsistent with the reality of contemporary college life.
>
> There are, however, other theories under which a university might be held liable. . . . [A] university has a duty of reasonable care to protect a student against certain dangers, including criminal actions against a student by another student or a third party if the criminal act is reasonably foreseeable and within the university's control [861 P.2d at 778, 780].

In most cases where the assailants were students, however, the courts have found for the college. In *Rabel v. Illinois Wesleyan University*, 514 N.E.2d 552 (Ill. App. Ct. 1987), the court ruled that the university had no duty to protect a student against a "prank" by fellow students that involved her abduction from a residence hall, despite the fact that the assailant had violated the college's policy against underage drinking. A similar result was reached in *Tanja H. v. Regents of the University of California*, 278 Cal. Rptr. 918 (Cal. Ct. App. 1991); the court stated that the university had no duty to supervise student parties in residence halls or to prevent underage consumption of alcohol. Even in *Eiseman v. State*, 518 N.Y.S.2d 608 (N.Y. 1987), the highest court of New York State refused to find that the university had a legal duty to screen applicants who were ex-convicts for violent tendencies before admitting them. (For analysis of this case, see D. M. Kobasic, E. R. Smith, & L. S. Barmore Zucker, "*Eiseman v. State of New York*: The Duty of a College to Protect Its Students from Harm by Other Students Admitted Under Special Programs," 14 *J. Coll. & Univ. Law* 591 (1988).)

Although colleges typically prevail in situations where plaintiffs allege that security was lax and thus directly linked to their injuries, liability may attach if an agent of the college has knowledge of the particular threat of harm to the victim and does not act with appropriate care. In *Jesik v. Maricopa County Community College District,* 611 P.2d 547 (Ariz. 1980), a student, during registration at the college, reported to a security guard employed by the college that, following an argument, another individual had threatened to kill him. The security guard took no steps to protect the student. About an hour after the report, the assailant returned to campus carrying a briefcase. The student pointed out the assailant to the same security guard, and the guard assured him that he would be protected. The guard then questioned the assailant, turned to walk away, and the assailant shot and killed the student.

The plaintiff, the father of the murdered student, sued the president and the individual members of the governing board of the Community College District, the executive dean and dean of students at Phoenix College, the security guard (Hilton), and the Community College District. The trial court summarily dismissed the case against all defendants except the security guard. The plaintiff appealed this dismissal to the Arizona Supreme Court, which first considered the potential liability of the officials and administrators. The plaintiff argued that "[the individual] defendants controlled an inadequate and incompetent security force [and thus should be] liable for any breach of duty by that security force." To establish the "duty" that had been breached, the plaintiff relied on a series of Arizona statutes that required the Community College District's governing board, where necessary, to appoint security officers (Ariz. Rev. Stat. Ann. §15–679(A)(3) and (9)); "to adopt rules and regulations for the maintenance of public order" (§13–1093); and to prevent "trespass upon the property of educational institutions [or] interference with its lawful use" (§13–1982). The court rejected this argument, finding that the statutes in question did not establish any specific standard of care but "only set forth a general duty to provide security to members of the public on school property."

Having discovered no specific legal duty chargeable to the individual defendants (excluding the security officer, whose potential liability the trial court had not rejected), the Arizona court next considered the liability of the Community College District itself. The court found this principle controlling in Arizona:

> A public school district in Arizona is liable for negligence when it fails to exercise ordinary care under the circumstances. [Arizona cases have] established that students are invitees and that schools have a duty to make the premises reasonably safe for their use. If a dangerous condition exists, the invitee must show that the employees of the school knew of or created the condition at issue [611 P.2d at 550].

The court then determined that the *respondeat superior* doctrine applies to governmental defendants under Arizona law, so that the Community College

District could be held liable for the negligence of its employees. Therefore, if the plaintiff could show at trial that the district's security guard had breached the duty set out above, while acting within the scope of employment, the district would be liable (along with the employee) for the death of the plaintiff's son.

The *Jesik* court also discussed an Arizona statute (Ariz. Rev. Stat. Ann. §15442(A)(16)) that imposes a standard of care on public school districts and community college districts (see 611 P.2d at 550 (original opinion) and 551 (supplemental opinion)). The court did not base its decision on this statute, since the statute was not yet in effect at the time the crime was committed. But the court's discussions provide a useful illustration of how state statutes may affect liability questions about campus security. In a later case, *Peterson v. San Francisco Community College District*, 205 Cal. Rptr. 842 (Cal. 1984), the court did rely on a statutory provision to impose liability on the defendant. The plaintiff was a student who had been assaulted while leaving the campus parking lot. Her assailant had concealed himself behind "unreasonably thick and untrimmed foliage and trees." Several other assaults had occurred at the same location and in the same manner. Community college officials had known of these assaults but did not publicize them. The court held that the plaintiff could recover damages under Section 835 of the California Tort Claims Act (Cal. Govt. Code §810 *et seq.*), which provides that "a public entity is liable for injury caused by a dangerous condition of its property" if the dangerous condition was caused by a public employee acting in the scope of his employment or if the entity "had actual or constructive notice of the dangerous condition" and failed to correct it. The court concluded that the failure to trim the foliage or to warn students of the earlier assaults constituted the creation of such a dangerous condition.

The cases in this section illustrate a variety of campus security problems and a variety of legal theories for analyzing them. Each court's choice of theories depended on the common and statutory law of the particular jurisdiction and the specific factual setting of the case. The theories used in *Nero,* where the security problem occurred in campus housing and the institution's role was comparable to a landlord's, differ from the theories used in *Jesik,* where the security problems occurred elsewhere and the student was considered the institution's "invitee." Similarly, the first theory used in *Mullins,* establishing a standard of care specifically for postsecondary institutions, differs from theories in the other cases, which borrow and apply standards of care for landlords or landowners generally. Despite the differences, however, a common denominator can be extracted from these cases that can serve as a guideline for postsecondary administrators: When an institution has foreseen or ought to have foreseen that criminal activity will likely occur on campus, it must take reasonable, appropriate steps to safeguard its students and other persons whom it has expressly or implicitly invited onto its premises. In determining whether this duty has been met in a specific case, courts will consider the foreseeability of violent criminal activity on the particular campus and the reasonableness and appropriateness of the institution's response to that particular threat.

5.2.3. Federal and State Statutes on Campus Security

Following what appears to be an increase in violent crime on campus, the legislatures of several states and the U.S. Congress passed laws requiring colleges and universities to provide information on the numbers and types of crimes on and near campus. The federal legislation, known as the "Crime Awareness and Campus Security Act" (Title II of Pub. L. No. 101–542 (1990)), amends the Higher Education Act of 1965 (this volume, Section 4.2.2) at 20 U.S.C. §1092. The Campus Security Act, in turn, was amended by the Higher Education Amendments of 1992 (Pub. L. No. 102–325) and imposes requirements on colleges and universities for preventing, reporting, and investigating sex offenses that occur on campus.

The Campus Security Act, as amended by the Higher Education Amendments of 1992, requires colleges to report, on an annual basis,

> statistics concerning the occurrence on campus, during the most recent calendar year, and during the 2 preceding calendar years for which data are available, of the following criminal offenses reported to campus security authorities or local police agencies—
>
> > (i) murder;
> >
> > (ii) sex offenses, forcible or nonforcible;
> >
> > (iii) robbery;
> >
> > (iv) aggravated assault;
> >
> > (v) burglary; and
> >
> > (vi) motor vehicle theft.

The law requires that colleges report the number of arrests for liquor law violations, drug abuse violations, and weapons possessions as well. The law also requires colleges to develop and distribute to students, prospective students and their parents, and the secretary of education,

> (1) a statement of policy regarding—
>
> > (i) such institution's campus sexual assault programs, which shall be aimed at prevention of sex offenses; and
> >
> > (ii) the procedures followed once a sex offense has occurred.

The law also requires colleges to include in their policy (1) educational programs to promote the awareness of rape and acquaintance rape, (2) sanctions that will follow a disciplinary board's determination that a sexual offense has occurred, (3) procedures students should follow if a sex offense occurs, and (4) procedures for on-campus disciplinary action in cases of alleged sexual assault.

The Campus Security Act also requires colleges to provide information on their policies regarding the reporting of other criminal actions and regarding campus security and campus law enforcement. They must also provide a description of the type and frequency of programs designed to inform students and employees about campus security.

In one of its most controversial provisions, the law defines "campus" as

(i) any building or property owned or controlled by the institution of higher education within the same reasonably contiguous geographic area and used by the institution in direct support of, or related to its educational purposes; or

(ii) any building or property owned or controlled by student organizations recognized by the institution.

The second part of the definition would, arguably, make fraternity and sorority houses part of the "campus," even if they are not owned by the college and are not on land owned by the college.

The secretary of education has implemented the Campus Security Act by amending 34 C.F.R. §668 to add a new §668.48, which sets out the procedures an institution must follow in reporting campus crimes and its obligations in instances of campus sexual assault, summarized above. These regulations require that crimes reported to counselors be included in the college's year-end report, but they do not require counselors to report crimes to the campus community at the time that they learn of them if the student victim requests that no report be made. The regulations require other college officials, however, to make timely reports to the campus community about crimes that could pose a threat to other students.

Several states have also promulgated laws requiring colleges and universities either to report campus crime statistics or to open their law enforcement logs to the public. For example, a Massachusetts law (Mass. Ann. Laws ch. 41, §98F (1993)) has the following requirement:

Each police department and each college or university to which officers have been appointed pursuant to the provisions of [state law] shall make, keep and maintain a daily log, written in a form that can be easily understood [, of] . . . all responses to valid complaints received [and] crimes reported. . . . All entries in said daily logs shall, unless otherwise provided by law, be public records available without charge to the public.

Pennsylvania law requires colleges to provide students and employees, as well as prospective students, with information about crime statistics and security measures on campus. It also requires colleges to report to the Pennsylvania

State Police all crime statistics for a three-year period (24 Pa. Cons. Stat. Ann. §2502 (1992)).

These federal and state requirements to give "timely warning" may be interpreted as creating a legal duty for colleges to warn students, staff, and others about persons on campus who have been accused of criminal behavior. If the college does not provide such a warning, its failure to do so could result in successful negligence claims against it in the event that a student or staff member is injured by someone who one or more administrators know has engaged in allegedly criminal behavior in the past. (For analysis of institutional liability and potential defenses, see Section 2.3.1.)

SEC. 5.3. SUPPORT SERVICES

Institutions provide numerous support services to students. Health services, counseling services, auxiliary aids for students with disabilities, child-care services, birth control services, and legal services are prominent examples that are discussed in this section. Other examples include housing services and campus security (both discussed above), placement services, resident life programming, parking, food services, and various other student convenience services. An institution may provide some of these services directly through its own staff members; other services may be performed by outside third parties under a contract with the institution or by student groups subsidized by the institution. Funding may come from the institution's regular budget, from mandatory student fees, from revenues generated by charging for the service, or from grants or other governmental assistance. In all of these contexts, the provision of support services may give rise to a variety of legal issues and liability concerns, some of which are illustrated below.

5.3.1. Auxiliary Aids for Disabled Students

When students need support services in order to remove practical impediments to their full participation in the institution's educational program, provocative questions arise concerning the extent of the institution's obligation to provide such services. Courts have considered these questions in two contexts: auxiliary aids for disabled students—in particular, interpreter services for hearing-impaired students; and child-care facilities for students with young children (discussed in section 5.3.2).

University of Texas v. Camenisch, 451 U.S. 390 (1981), was an early, and highly publicized, case on interpreter services. A deaf graduate student at the University of Texas alleged that the university had violated Section 504 of the Rehabilitation Act of 1973 by refusing to provide him with sign-language interpreter services, which he claimed were necessary to the completion of his master's degree. The university had denied the plaintiff's request for such services on the grounds that he did not meet the university's established criteria for financial assistance to graduate students and should therefore pay for his own interpreter. The district court had issued a preliminary injunction ordering the university to provide the interpreter services, irrespective of the student's ability to pay for them. The U.S. Court of Appeals affirmed the district court (616 F.2d 127 (5th Cir. 1980)). The U.S. Supreme Court, however, held that the issue concerning the propriety of the preliminary injunction had become moot because the plaintiff had graduated. Thus, the *Camenisch* case did not furnish answers to questions concerning institutional responsibilities to provide interpreter services and other auxiliary aids to disabled students. A regulation promulgated under Section 504 (34 C.F.R. §104.44(d)) does obligate institutions to provide such services, and this obligation apparently is not negated by the student's ability to pay. But the courts have not ruled definitively on whether this regulation, so interpreted, is consistent with the Section 504 statute. That is the issue raised but not answered in *Camenisch.*

A related issue concerns the obligations of federally funded state vocational rehabilitation (VR) agencies to provide auxiliary services for eligible college students. The plaintiff in *Camenisch* argued that the Section 504 regulation (now §104.44(d)) does not place undue financial burdens on the universities because "a variety of outside funding sources," including the VR agencies, "are available to aid universities" in fulfilling their obligation. This line of argument suggests two further questions: whether the state VR agencies are legally obligated to provide auxiliary services to disabled college students and, if so, whether their obligation diminishes the obligation of universities to pay the costs (see J. Orleans and M. A. Smith, "Who Should Provide Interpreters Under Section 504 of the Rehabilitation Act?" 9 *J. Coll. & Univ. Law* 177 (1982–83)).

Two cases decided since *Camenisch* provide answers to these questions. In *Schornstein v. New Jersey Division of Vocational Rehabilitation Services,* 519 F. Supp. 773 (D.N.J. 1981), *affirmed,* 688 F.2d 824 (3d Cir. 1982), the court held that Title I of the Rehabilitation Act of 1973 (29 U.S.C. §100 *et seq.*) requires state VR agencies to provide eligible college students with interpreter services they require to meet their vocational goals. In *Jones v. Illinois Department of Rehabilitation Services,* 504 F. Supp. 1244 (N.D. Ill. 1981), *affirmed,* 689 F.2d 724 (7th Cir. 1982), the court agreed that state VR agencies have this legal obligation. But it also held that colleges have a similar obligation under Section 104.44(d) and asked whose responsibility is primary. The court concluded that the state VR agencies have primary financial responsibility, thus diminishing universities' responsibility in situations where the student is eligible for state VR services. There is a catch, however, in the application of these cases to the *Camenisch* problem. As the district court in *Schornstein* noted, state VR agencies may consider the financial need of disabled individuals in determining the extent to which the agency will pay the costs of rehabilitation services (see 34 C.F.R.

§361.47). Thus, if a VR agency employs a financial-need test and finds that a particular disabled student does not meet it, the primary obligation would again fall on the university, and the issue raised in *Camenisch* would again predominate.

5.3.2. Child-Care Services

Child care, the second context in which a court has addressed a claim for support services needed to overcome some practical impediment to education, was the focus of *De La Cruz v. Tormey*, 582 F.2d 45 (9th Cir. 1978). Several low-income women brought suit in a federal district court, challenging the lack of child-care facilities on the campuses of the San Mateo Community College District. The plaintiffs alleged that the impact of the district's decision not to provide child-care facilities fell overwhelmingly on women, effectively barring them from the benefits of higher education and thus denying them equal educational opportunity. The women claimed that the policy constituted sex discrimination in violation of the equal protection clause and Title IX of the Education Amendments of 1972. The district court dismissed the case for failure to state any claim on which relief could be granted, and the plaintiffs appealed.

The appellate court, reversing the district court, ruled that the complaint could not be summarily dismissed on the pleadings and remanded the case for a trial on the plaintiffs' allegations. Although the district's policy did not rest on an explicit gender classification, the appellate court acknowledged that a facially neutral policy could still violate equal protection if it affected women disproportionately and was adopted or enforced with discriminatory intent. And while Title IX would similarly require proof of disproportionate impact, "a standard less stringent than intentional discrimination" may be appropriate when a court is considering a claim under that statute. (For more recent developments regarding discriminatory intent, see Section 12.4.7.2.)

Regarding disproportionate impact, the court explained:

> There can be little doubt that a discriminatory effect, as that term is properly understood and has been used by the Supreme Court, has been adequately alleged. The concrete human consequences flowing from the lack of sufficient child care facilities, very practical impediments to beneficial participation in the District's educational programs, are asserted to fall overwhelmingly upon women students and would-be students. . . .
>
> [T]he essence of the plaintiffs' grievance is that the absence of child care facilities renders the *included* benefits less valuable and less available to women; in other words, that the effect of the District's child care policy is to render the entire "package" of its programs of lesser worth to women than to men. . . . Were the object of their challenge simply a refusal to initiate or support a program or course of particular interest and value to women—women's studies, for instance—the case might be a much easier one [582 F.2d at 53, 56–57].

After remand, the parties in *De La Cruz* agreed to an out-of-court settlement that provided for the establishment of child-care centers on the defendant's campuses. A trial was never held. It is therefore still not known whether the novel claim raised in *De La Cruz*, or similar claims regarding other support services or other forms of discrimination, will be recognized by the courts.

5.3.3. Birth Control Services

Other types of legal issues may arise when members of the campus community object on grounds of conscience to the institution's provision of a particular service. Health services involving birth control—abortion, sterilization, and distribution of contraceptive devices—are a primary example. The problem may be compounded when the contested service is funded by a student activities fee or other mandatory fee. Students who oppose abortion on grounds of conscience, for instance, may also object to the mandatory fees and the use of their own money to fund such services. The sparse law on this point suggests that such challenges will not often succeed. In *Erzinger v. Regents of the University of California*, 187 Cal. Rptr. 164 (Cal. Ct. App. 1982), for instance, students objected to the defendants' use of mandatory fees to provide abortion and pregnancy counseling as a part of campus student health services. The court rejected the students' claim that such use infringed their free exercise of religion.

Similarly, in the recent case of *Goehring v. Brophy*, 94 F. 3d 1294 (9th Cir. 1996), the U.S. Court of Appeals for the Ninth Circuit relied in part on *Erzinger* to uphold a University of California at Davis mandatory student registration fee used to subsidize a university health insurance program that covered the cost of abortion services. The university requires that all its graduate and professional students have health insurance. Students may acquire this insurance through the Graduate Student Health Insurance Program that provides a subsidy of $18.50 per insured student, per quarter, to reduce the cost of the premiums; funds generated by the mandatory student fees cover the cost of the subsidy. Students may opt out of this program by proving that they have health insurance from another provider.

The plaintiffs claimed that the university's insurance program violated their free exercise of religion because their sincerely held religious beliefs prevented them from subsidizing, or in any way financially contributing to, abortion services. In analyzing this claim, the appellate court looked to the Religious Freedom Restoration Act, 42 U.S.C. §2000bb (see this volume, Sec. 1.6). Applying section (a) of the Act, the court held that the plaintiffs had failed to "establish that the university's subsidized health insurance program imposes a substantial burden on a central tenet of their religion." Several factors were critical to the court's conclusion:

The plaintiffs are not required to purchase the University's subsidized health insurance—undergraduate students are not required to have health insurance and graduate students may purchase insurance from any provider. Moreover, the student health insurance subsidy is not a substantial sum of money and the subsidy, taken from registration fees, is distributed only for those students who elect to purchase University insurance. Furthermore, the plaintiffs are not required to accept, participate in, or advocate in any manner for the provision of abortion services. Abortions are not provided on the University campus. Students who request abortion services are referred to outside providers [94 F. 3d at 1300].

The court also concluded—under section (b) of the Act—that "even if the plaintiffs were able to satisfy the substantial burden requirement, the university's health insurance system nonetheless survives constitutional attack because it . . . is the least restrictive means of furthering a compelling government interest." Three "compelling" university interests supported the health insurance program: providing students with affordable health insurance that many would be unable to obtain if it was not available through the university; helping prevent the spread of communicable disease among students who must eat, sleep, and study in close quarters; and protecting students from the distractions of undiagnosed illnesses and unpaid medical bills that could interfere with their studies. Moreover, according to the court, the use of mandatory student fees to subsidize the insurance program was the "least restrictive means" of furthering these university interests. Relying on cases that rejected free exercise challenges to the federal government's collection and expenditure of tax dollars, the court reasoned that:

[T]he fiscal vitality of the University's fee system would be undermined if the plaintiffs in the present case were exempted from paying a portion of their student registration fee on free exercise grounds. Mandatory uniform participation by every student is essential to the insurance system's survival. . . . There are few, if any, University funded activities to which one student or another would not object [94 F.3d at 1301].

Other questions concerning abortion services arose during Congress's consideration of the Civil Rights Restoration Act of 1987 (see Section 12.4.7.4). The basic issue was whether an institution's decision to exclude abortion services from its campus health care or its student health insurance coverage could be considered sex discrimination under the Title IX regulations (see 34 CFR §§106.39 and 106.40). Congress responded by including two "abortion neutrality" provisions in the 1987 Act: Section 3(a), which adds a new Section 909 (20 U.S.C. §1688) to Title IX, and Section 8 (20 U.S.C. §1688 note). Under these provisions, neither Title IX nor the Civil Rights Restoration Act may be construed (1) to require an institution to provide abortion services, (2) to prohibit an institution from providing abortion services, or (3) to permit an institution to penalize a person for seeking or receiving abortion services related to legal abortion.

Also affecting abortion services were the 1988 amendments to the regulations for Title X of the Public Health Service Act (42 U.S.C. §§300 to 300a–6), which provides federal funds for family planning clinics. These amendments (codified at 42 C.F.R. §§59.2, 59.5, and 59.7–59.10) prohibited fund recipients (some of whom are campus health clinics or university-affiliated hospitals) from providing counseling or referrals regarding abortion. The U.S. Supreme Court upheld these regulations against a challenge that they violated the free speech rights of physicians and the privacy rights of pregnant women (*Rust v. Sullivan*, 500 U.S. 173 (1991)). However, after President Clinton assumed office, he issued a memorandum directing the secretary of HHS to suspend the so-called Gag Rule (58 Fed. Reg. 7455 (1993)). The secretary issued an interim rule (58 Fed. Reg. 7462 (1993)) temporarily reinstating the pre-1988 rules and also published proposed new regulations (58 Fed. Reg. 7464 (1993)). (The comment period for the proposed rules ended in 1993, but no final rules had yet been published as this book went to press.)

5.3.4. Student Legal Services

In yet another context—student legal services—the case of *Student Government Assn. v. Board of Trustees of the University of Massachusetts*, 868 F.2d 473 (1st Cir. 1989), illustrates complex questions concerning the First Amendment. The court held that the First Amendment did not bar the university from terminating its existing campus legal services office (LSO), which represented students in criminal matters and in suits against the university. In order for students' access to legal services to be protected under the First Amendment, the legal services office must be considered a "public forum" (see Section 8.1.2) that provides a "channel of communication" between students and other persons (868 F.2d at 476). Here, the students sought to communicate with two groups through the LSO: persons with whom they have disagreements, and the attorneys staffing the LSO. Since the court system, rather than the LSO itself, was the actual channel of communication with the first group, the only channel of communication the LSO provided was with the LSO attorneys in their official capacities. The court did not extend First Amendment public forum protection to this channel because the university was not *regulating* communication in the marketplace of ideas, but only determining whether to *subsidize* communication. Having only extended a subsidy to the LSO, the university could terminate this subsidy unless the plaintiffs could prove that the university was doing so for a reason that itself violated the First Amendment—for instance, to penalize students who had brought suits against the university, or to suppress the assertion (in legal proceedings) of ideas the university considered dangerous or offensive. The court determined that the termination was "nonselective," applying to all litigation rather than only to litigation that reflected a "particular viewpoint," and thus did not serve to penalize individual students or suppress particular ideas. The termination therefore did not violate the free speech clause of the First Amendment. (See Comment, "*Student Government Association v. Board of Trustees of the University of Massachusetts*: Forum and Subsidy Analysis Applied to University Funding Decisions," 17 *J. Coll. Univ. Law* 65 (1990).)

SEC. 5.4. AUXILIARY ENTERPRISES AND ACTIVITIES

5.4.1. The Growth of Campus Auxiliary Operations

With increasing frequency and vigor, postsecondary institutions have expanded the scope of "auxiliary" operations that involve the institution in the sale of goods, services, or leasehold (rental) interests in real estate.[3] Such activities, engaged in by the institution itself or by a subsidiary or affiliated organization (see Section 2.2.4), may be an important means for serving students, and thus sales of goods or services may be restricted to students. In other situations, sales may be made to faculty and staff as well as students; sales may also be made incidentally to the general public, or the general public or particular noncampus customers may be the primary sales target.

Examples include the sale of personal computers and software to students; child-care services provided for a fee at campus child-care centers; barbering and hairstyling services; travel services; computing services; graphics, printing, and copying services; credit card services; the sale of sundries, snack food, greeting cards, musical recordings, or trade paperbacks by campus bookstores or convenience stores; the sale of hearing aids at campus speech and hearing clinics; the sale of books by university presses; the sale of prescription drugs at university medical centers; summer sports camps on the campus; training programs for business and industry; entertainment and athletic events open to the public for an admission charge; hotel or dining facilities open to university guests or the public; rental of dormitory rooms to travelers or outside groups; rental of campus auditoriums, conference facilities, and athletic facilities; leasing of campus space to private businesses that operate on campus; conference management services; entrepreneurial uses of radio or television stations and related telecommunication facilities; and the sale of advertising space on athletic scoreboards or in university publications.

---

[3]The phrases "auxiliary enterprises," "auxiliary operations," and "auxiliary activities," as used throughout this section, refer to a broad range of functions that are claimed to be "auxiliary" to the education and research that are the central mission of a higher education institution.

In addition, institutions may sell "rights" to other sellers, who then can market particular products or services on campus—for example, a sale of exclusive rights to a soft-drink company to market its soft drinks on campus. Similarly, institutions may sell other "rights" for a profit, such as broadcast rights for intercollegiate athletic contests or rights to use the institution's trademarks.

Institutions may engage in such activities for a variety of reasons. The goal may be to provide clinical-training opportunities for students (for example, speech and hearing clinics or hotel administration schools); to make campus life more convenient and self-contained, thus enhancing the quality of life (banks, fast-food restaurants, travel services, barber shops and hairstyling salons, convenience stores); to increase institutional visibility and good will with professional and corporate organizations or the general public (training programs, conference management services, rental of campus facilities); or to make productive use of underutilized space, especially in the summer (summer sports camps, rental of dormitory rooms and conference facilities). Increasingly, however, in addition to or in lieu of these goals, institutions may operate auxiliary enterprises in response to budgetary pressures or initiatives that necessitate the generation of new revenues or prompt particular institutional units to be self-supporting.

When auxiliary operations are for educational purposes and involve goods, services, or facilities not generally available from local businesses, few controversies arise. Those that do usually involve tort and contract liability issues fitting within the scope of Sections 2.3 and 2.4 or issues concerning government licenses and inspections (for example, for a campus food service). But when auxiliary operations arguably extend beyond educational purposes or put the institution in a competitive position, numerous new issues may arise. Critics may charge that the institution's activities are drawing customers away from local businesses; that the competition is unfair because of the institution's tax-exempt status, funding sources, and other advantages; that the institution's activities are inconsistent with its academic mission and are diverting institutional resources from academic to commercial concerns; or that the institution's activities expose it to substantial new risks that could result in monetary loss or loss of prestige from commercial contract and bill collection disputes and tort liability claims. Problems may arise in the areas of public relations, government relations (especially with state legislatures), budgets and resources, and insurance and other risk management practices (see Section 2.5), in addition to the legal issues discussed next.

5.4.2. The Contract Law Basis for Auxiliary Operations

When a higher education institution operates auxiliary enterprises or engages in other auxiliary activities, it thrusts itself into the world of business and thus exposes itself to a substantial dose of commercial law. Since most commercial arrangements are embodied in contracts that define the core rights and responsibilities of the contracting parties, contract law is the foundation on which the institution's business relationships are built. This section discusses the basics of contract law as they apply to relationships between the institution and the business world.

A contract is a promise, or a performance or forbearance, given in exchange for some type of compensation. The three basic elements of a contract are the offer, the acceptance, and the compensation—legally referred to as "consideration." A contract may involve goods, services, real estate, or any combination thereof. A contract may be either written or oral. Virtually all states have a "statute of frauds," however, providing that certain types of contracts (for example, contracts for the sale of real property) must be in writing in order to be enforceable. A written contract may be either a standard form contract or an instrument specifically designed to meet individual circumstances. While contracts typically are viewed as an exchange (for example, money for goods), they also can take the form of cooperative arrangements such as affiliation agreements or joint venture agreements.

The types of clauses contained in a contract depend on the purposes of the contract, the interests of the parties, and the scope and complexity of the transaction. Most commercial contracts include clauses specifying the scope and duration of the contract; price, payment, or profit-sharing arrangements; delivery, installation, or implementation requirements; and definitions of contract terms. Most commercial contracts also include general clauses containing representations of authority to contract and to perform; warranties of products or performance; limitations on liability (indemnification or hold-harmless clauses); provisions for termination, renewal, or amendment; definitions of breach or default; remedies for breach; dispute-resolution techniques (for example, arbitration); and a "choice of law," that is, a selection of a body of state law that will govern the transaction. Some contracts also may include special clauses containing representations that a party has complied with applicable law; has clear title to certain property; holds necessary licenses, bonds, or insurance coverages; or has certain copyright or patent rights. Overall, the parties can include any provisions they agree on that are not prohibited by state or federal law. They are, by a process of "private ordering," creating the private law that will govern their relationship.

Prior to 1954, state common law (see this volume, Section 1.3.1.4) governed all contracts. From 1954 to 1967, every state except Louisiana adopted some form of the Uniform Commercial Code (U.C.C.). The U.C.C. now governs contracts for the sale of goods, except for certain issues (for example, defenses) that the U.C.C. does not address. These issues are still governed by the common law (see

U.C.C. §1–103), as are domestic contracts that do not involve the sale of goods. For international transactions between parties in the United States and parties in certain other countries, the United Nations Convention on Contracts for the International Sale of Goods (15 U.S.C.A. Appendix (West Supp. 1993)) will govern the contract if the contract does not otherwise specify the applicable law.

For the most part, the U.C.C. is consistent with the common law of contract. Departures from the common law are contained primarily in Article 2, dealing with the sale of goods, and in Article 9, dealing with the assignment of contract rights. (See generally J. D. Calamari and J. M. Perillo, *The Law of Contracts* (3d ed., West, 1987).) When the U.C.C. does depart from the common law, the effect is that the rules applicable to the sale of goods will differ from those for the sale of labor, services, or land. Thus, it is important to know whether a particular contract is for the sale of goods, and thus subject to the U.C.C., or for the sale of services, labor, or land, and subject to the common law.

The starting point for making this distinction is the U.C.C.'s definition of "goods"—that is, "all things (including specifically manufactured goods) which are movable at the time of identification to the contract for sale" (U.C.C. §2–105). This definition will sometimes be difficult to apply. In *Advent Systems Ltd. v. Unysis Corp.*, 925 F.2d 670 (3d Cir. 1991), for instance, a computer software producer sued a computer manufacturer for breach of contract. The plaintiff argued that the U.C.C. should not control the case because "the 'software' referred to in the agreement as a 'product' was not a 'good' but intellectual property outside the ambit of the [U.C.C.]." The court rejected the argument: "[A] computer program may be copyrightable as intellectual property [but this] does not alter the fact that once in the form of a floppy disc or other medium, the program is tangible, movable and available in the marketplace. The fact that some programs may be tailored for specific purposes need not alter their status as 'goods' because the code definition includes 'specifically manufactured goods.'"

5.4.3. State Noncompetition Statutes

Consistent with recent trends, several states now have statutes that prohibit institutions from engaging in certain types of competitive commercial transactions; and the number of such statutes is increasing. Virtually all these statutes focus on public institutions and do not cover private institutions. Some statutes apply generally to state agencies and boards but include special provisions for state institutions of higher education; other statutes apply specifically and only to state higher education institutions. Some statutes apply broadly to sales of goods and services as well as to the commercial use of facilities, while others are limited to sales of goods. Yet others are even narrower, applying only to the sale of a particular type of goods or service—for example, hearing aids (Idaho Code §54–2902(d)); uses of television or telecommunications facilities

(Del. Code Ann. tit. 14, §129(e)); or uses of other revenue-producing buildings and facilities (Iowa Code §262.44). Some statutes set out specific prohibitions and rules; others delegate rule-making authority to the state board or the institutions. University medical centers and health care services often are exempted from these statutes.

An excellent example of the broader type of statute is a 1987 Arizona law on state competition with private enterprise (Ariz. Rev. Stat. Ann. §41–2751 *et seq.*). The Arizona statute includes a specific section (41–2753) regulating state community colleges and universities. Subsection A(3) of this section covers sales to "students, faculty, staff, or invited guests." It prohibits community colleges and universities from providing such persons with "goods, services or facilities that are practically available from private enterprise *except as authorized by the state governing board*" (emphasis added), thus delegating responsibility and discretion regarding such matters to the board of regents and the board of directors for community colleges.

Subsection (A)(1) of this section covers sales to "persons other than students, faculty, staff, and invited guests." It prohibits community colleges and universities from selling such persons "goods, services or facilities that are practically available from private enterprise." However, three important exceptions to this prohibition make it inapplicable: (1) when the "provision of the goods, service or facility offers a valuable educational or research experience for students as part of their education or fulfills the public service mission" of the institution; (2) when the institution is "sponsoring or providing facilities for recreational, cultural and athletic events or . . . facilities providing food services and sales"; and (3) when the institution is "specifically authorized by statute" to provide a particular type of goods, service, or facility.

Other subsections contain special provisions regarding competitive bidding (§41–2753(A)(2)) and special provisions regarding the institution's sale of "products and by-products which are an integral part of research or instruction" (§41–2753(B)). The entire section is implemented through rules adopted by the state governing board (§41–2753(C)) and is enforced through a complaint process administered by the governing board and through judicial review (§41–2753(D)).

Colorado has a statute similar to Arizona's, passed in 1988 (Colo. Rev. Stat. §24–113–101 *et seq.*). Other states have different types of laws. The state of Washington law requires state higher education institutions, "in consultation with local business organizations and representatives of the small business community," to develop policies and mechanisms regarding the sale of goods and services that could be obtained from a commercial source (Wash. Rev. Code §28B.63.010 *et seq.*). The Illinois University Retail Sales Act restricts sales by any "retail store carrying any line of general merchandise" that is operated by a state higher education institution or by a contractor or lessee located on the property of such an institution (S.H.A. 110 ILCS 115/1 (1994)). The Illinois statute also restricts credit sales by retail stores operated by state higher education institutions. And the Iowa statute (Iowa Code. ch. 23A) applies broadly to state agencies "engage[d] in the manufacturing, processing, sale, offering for sale, rental, leasing, delivery, dispensing, distributing, or advertising of goods or services to the public which are also offered by private enterprise," but it provides substantial exemptions for public higher education institutions (§§23 A.2(2) and 23 A.2(10)(K)).

Since most of these statutes are relatively new, and since not all of them permit enforcement by private lawsuits (see *Board of Governors of the University of North Carolina v. Helpingstine*, 714 F. Supp. 167, 175 (M.D.N.C. 1989)), there are few court opinions interpreting and applying the statutory provisions. A leading example thus far is *American Asbestos Training Center, Ltd. v. Eastern Iowa Community College*, 463 N.W.2d 56 (Iowa 1990), in which a private training center sought to enjoin a public community college from offering asbestos removal courses in competition with the center. The center relied on Chapter 23A of the Iowa Code (discussed earlier), arguing that the college's training programs were "services" that could not be offered in competition with private enterprise. The court disagreed. Construing the term "services," as applied to a community college, it held that "[t]eaching and training are distinct from, rather than included within, the meaning of 'services,'" and that the statute therefore was inapplicable to a community college's training programs. Alternatively, the court concluded that, even if training programs were considered "services," the statute still would not apply. The statute does not restrict services that are authorized specifically by some other statute, and other sections of the Iowa Code specifically do authorize community colleges to offer vocational and technical training.

In light of these statutory developments, student affairs professionals involved in auxiliary operations at public institutions will need to understand the scope of any noncompetition statute in effect in their state and to ensure that their institution's programs comply with any applicable statutory provisions. In addition, whether or not their state has a noncompetition statute, public institutions should monitor state legislative activities regarding noncompetition issues and participate in the legislative process for any bill that is proposed. Some of the existing statutes are not well drafted, and it will behoove institutions faced with new proposals to avoid the weaknesses in some existing statutes. The state of Washington statute, discussed earlier, appears to embody the best approach and best drafting thus far available. And perhaps most important, both public and private institutions with substantial auxiliary enterprises—whether or not they are subject to a noncompetition statute—should maintain a system of self-study and self-regulation, including consultation with local business representatives, to help ensure that the institution's auxiliary operations serve the institutional mission and strike an appropriate balance between the institutional's interests and those of private enterprise.

5.4.4. Administering Auxiliary Enterprises

Decisions on establishing and operating auxiliary enterprises pose considerable challenges for public and private institutions alike, and involve considerations and judgments different from those that predominate in decision making on academic matters. Student affairs professionals should ensure that, through self-regulation and other means, questions about auxiliary enterprises receive high-level and continuing attention. Specifically, institutions should establish procedures and guidelines for reviewing and approving proposals for auxiliary enterprises, as well as processes for monitoring their operations; centralize decision making on major policy issues, to promote consistency in institutional objectives and to mobilize all institutional expertise; identify and resolve threshold questions about the institution's state statutory authority to operate and to fund particular enterprises (see *LHE* 3d, sections 9.3.2 and 9.3.3); and consult with representatives of local businesses as part of the review and approval process, in order to alleviate concerns of unfair competition.

Structural arrangements will also be important. An auxiliary enterprise may be operated by the institution itself, either through the central administration or by a school or an academic department. Alternatively, an enterprise may be operated by an outside entity with whom the institution negotiates a lease of land or facilities, a joint venture or partnership agreement, or other arrangement; or an institution may establish a subsidiary corporation or other affiliate, either profit or nonprofit (see Section 2.2.4), to operate an auxiliary enterprise. The various choices may have different consequences for institutional control, availability of business expertise, legal liability, and tax liability.

To attend to the mix of considerations, institutions will need to engage in substantial legal and business planning. Student affairs professionals will need to work together with legal counsel, business officers, and risk managers. Lines of communication to the local business community will need to be opened and cooperative relationships cultivated. And involvement and oversight by the highest-ranking *academic* officers will need to be maintained, to ensure that auxiliary ventures are not inconsistent with and do not detract from the institution's academic mission. Probably the single most important factor for administrators to emphasize—if they seek to minimize legal authority problems and tax liabilities and to maximize good will with the campus community, the local business community, and local and state legislatures—is a correlative relationship between the objectives of the auxiliary enterprise and the academic mission of the institution.

SELECTED ANNOTATED BIBLIOGRAPHY

Sec. 5.1 (Student Housing)

Delgado, Richard. "College Searches and Seizures: Students, Privacy and the Fourth Amendment," 26 *Hastings L.J.* 57 (1975). Discusses the legal issues involved in dormitory searches and analyzes the validity of the various legal theories used to justify such searches.

Gehring, Donald D. (ed.). *Administering College and University Housing: A Legal Perspective* (rev. ed., College Administration Publications, 1992). An overview of legal issues that can arise in the administration of campus housing. Written in layperson's language and directed to all staff involved with campus housing. Contains chapters by Gehring, Pavela, and others, covering the application of constitutional law, statutory and regulatory law, contract law, and tort law to the residence hall setting, and provides suggestions for legal planning. Includes an appendix with a "Checklist of Housing Legal Issues" for use in legal audits of housing programs.

Note, "Admissibility of Evidence Seized by Private University Officials in Violation of Fourth Amendment Standards, " 56 *Cornell L. Rev.* 507 (1971). Discusses the applicability of Fourth Amendment standards to actions by private universities, as well as the degree of involvement by school and police authorities that may render private university actions subject to the state action doctrine.

Sec. 5.2 (Campus Security)

Hauserman, Nancy, & Lansing, Paul. "Rape on Campus: Postsecondary Institutions as Third Party Defendants," 8 *J. Coll & Univ. Law* 182 (1981–82). Traces the evolution of tort actions by rape and assault victims against third-party institutional defendants. Reviews the procedural issues that may be raised by such suits, the availability and scope of sovereign and charitable immunity defenses, the elements a plaintiff must prove in order to establish the case, and the potential availability of Title IX as an additional ground for litigation.

Oshagan, Georgi-Ann. "Obscuring the Issue: The Inappropriate Application of *in loco parentis* to the Campus Crime Victim Duty Question," 39 *Wayne L. Rev.* 1335 (1993). Reviews the propensity for crime victims and/or their parents to attempt to hold the university liable for the acts of third parties or the negligence of the students themselves.

Raddatz, Anita. *Crime on Campus: Institutional Tort Liability for the Criminal Acts of Third Parties* (National Association of College and University Attorneys, 1988). A pamphlet for college administrators that reviews the basic elements of negligence liability and discusses their implications for campus security. Includes a statement from the American Council on Education regarding campus security and a selected list of references on institutional liability for crimes on campus.

Smith, Michael Clay. *Coping with Crime on Campus* (American Council on Education/Macmillan, 1988). Reviews the increase in campus crime since the late 1960s, the effect of alcohol and drugs on campus crime, sexual assaults, and security issues.

Smith, Michael Clay. *Crime and Campus Police: A Handbook for Campus Police Officers and Administrators* (College Administration Publications, 1989). Discusses risk management, the proper procedure for searches and seizures and arrests on campus, campus judicial procedures, frequent problems encountered by campus police and administrators, white-collar crime on campus, and alcohol issues.

Sec. 5.3 (Support Services)

See Hurley entry for Section 4.1.

Sec. 5.4 (Auxiliary Enterprises and Activities)

Calamari, John D., and Perillo, Joseph M. *The Law of Contracts* (3d ed., West, 1987). A comprehensive discussion of the principles of the law of contracts. Individual chapters are devoted to such subjects as offer and acceptance, consideration, promissory estoppel, breach, and damages.

Weltzenbach, Lanora (ed.). *Contracting for Services* (National Association of College and University Business Officers, 1982). An overview of the various phases of the contracting process as it relates to services. Provides practical assistance in managing each phase. Includes case studies; analysis of particular contract clauses; sample contracts for nine service areas (cleaning and custodial, food, bookstore, vending, security, professional, consultant, construction, and equipment maintenance); and technical discussions applying contracting principles to four specific types of services (food, professional design, risk management consultant, and billing and collection).

See Bookman entry for Section 2.3.

CHAPTER SIX

Academic Policies
and Concerns

SEC. 6.1. GRADES, CREDITS, AND DEGREES

When an institution applies its academic standards to students, it is subject to fewer legal restrictions than is the case when it applies disciplinary standards (see Chapter Seven). Courts are more deferential to academia when evaluation of academic work is the issue, believing that such evaluation resides in the expertise of the faculty rather than the court.

6.1.1. Awarding of Grades and Degrees

When a student alleges that a grade has been awarded improperly or a degree has been denied unfairly, the courts must determine whether the defendant's action reflected the application of academic judgment or an arbitrary or unfair application of institutional policy. In one leading case, *Connelly v. University of Vermont*, 244 F. Supp. 156 (D. Vt. 1965), a medical student challenged his dismissal from medical school. He had failed the pediatrics-obstetrics course and was excluded, under a College of Medicine rule, for having failed 25 percent or more of his major third-year courses. The court described its role, and the institution's legal obligation, in such cases as follows:

> Where a medical student has been dismissed for a failure to attain a proper standard of scholarship, two questions may be involved; the first is, was the student in fact delinquent in his studies or unfit for the practice of medicine? The second

question is, were the school authorities motivated by malice or bad faith in dismissing the student, or did they act arbitrarily or capriciously? In general, the first question is not a matter for judicial review. However, a student dismissal motivated by bad faith, arbitrariness, or capriciousness may be actionable. . . .

This rule has been stated in a variety of ways by a number of courts. It has been said that courts do not interfere with the management of a school's internal affairs unless "there has been a manifest abuse of discretion or where [the school officials'] action has been arbitrary or unlawful" (*State ex rel. Sherman v. Hyman*, 180 Tenn. 99, 171 S.W.2d 822, *certiorari denied*, 319 U.S. 748 . . . (1942)), or unless the school authorities have acted "arbitrarily or capriciously" (*Frank v. Marquette University*, 209 Wis. 372, 245 N.W. 125 (1932)), or unless they have abused their discretion (*Coffelt v. Nicholson*, 224 Ark. 176, 272 S.W.2d 309 (1954); *People ex rel. Bluett v. Board of Trustees of University of Illinois*, 10 Ill. App. 2d 207, 134 N.E.2d 635, 58 A.L.R.2d 899 (1956)), or acted in "bad faith" (*Barnard v. Inhabitants of Shelburne* . . . [102 N.E. 1095 (Mass. 1913)] and see . . . 109 N.E. 818 (same case)).

The effect of these decisions is to give the school authorities absolute discretion in determining whether a student has been delinquent in his studies, and to place the burden on the student of showing that his dismissal was motivated by arbitrariness, capriciousness, or bad faith. The reason for this rule is that, in matters of scholarship, the school authorities are uniquely qualified by training and experience to judge the qualifications of a student, and efficiency of instruction depends in no small degree upon the school's faculty's freedom from interference from other noneducational tribunals. It is only when the school authorities abuse this discretion that a court may interfere with their decision to dismiss a student [244 F. Supp. at 159–60].

The plaintiff had alleged that his instructor decided before completion of the course to fail him regardless of the quality of his work. The court held that these allegations met its requirements for suits. They therefore stated a cause of action, which if proven at trial would justify the entry of judgment against the college.

In 1975, a federal appeals court issued an important reaffirmation of the principles underlying the *Connelly* case. *Gaspar v. Bruton*, 513 F.2d 843 (10th Cir. 1975), concerned a practical nurse student who had been dismissed for deficient performance in clinical training. In rejecting the student's suit against the school, the court held that:

Courts have historically refrained from interfering with the authority vested in school officials to drop a student from the rolls for failure to attain or maintain prescribed scholastic rating (whether judged by objective and/or subjective standards), absent a clear showing that the officials have acted arbitrarily or have abused the discretionary authority vested in them. . . .

The courts are not equipped to review academic records based upon academic standards within the particular knowledge, experience, and expertise of academicians. Thus, when presented with a challenge that the school authorities suspended or dismissed a student for failure re academic standards, the court may grant relief, as a practical matter, only in those cases where the student presents positive evidence of ill will or bad motive [513 F.2d at 850–51].

The U.S. Supreme Court has twice addressed the subject of the standard of review of academic judgments. It first considered this subject briefly in *Board of Curators of the University of Missouri v. Horowitz*, 435 U.S. 78 (1978) (discussed in Section 7.3.3). A dismissed medical student claimed that the school applied stricter standards to her because of her sex, religion, and physical appearance. Referring particularly to *Gaspar v. Bruton*, the Court rejected the claim in language inhospitable to substantive judicial review of academic decisions:

> A number of lower courts have implied in dictum that academic dismissals from state institutions can be enjoined if "shown to be clearly arbitrary or capricious." . . . Even assuming that the courts can review under such a standard an academic decision of a public educational institution, we agree with the district court that no showing of arbitrariness or capriciousness has been made in this case. Courts are particularly ill equipped to evaluate academic performance. The factors discussed . . . with respect to procedural due process [see Section 7.3.3] speak *a fortiori* here and warn against any such judicial intrusion into academic decision making [435 U.S. at 91–92].

In a case in which the Court relied heavily on *Horowitz*, a student filed a substantive due process challenge to his academic dismissal from medical school. The student, whose entire record of academic performance in medical school was mediocre, asserted that the school's refusal to allow him to retake the National Board of Medical Examiners examination violated his constitutional rights because other students had been allowed to retake the exam. In *Regents of the University of Michigan v. Ewing*, 474 U.S. 214 (1985), the Court assumed without deciding the issue that Ewing had a property interest in continued enrollment in medical school. The Court noted that it was not the school's procedures that were under review—the question was "whether the record compels the conclusion that the University acted arbitrarily in dropping Ewing from the Inteflex program without permitting a reexamination" (474 U.S. at 225). The court then stated:

> Ewing's claim, therefore, must be that the University misjudged his fitness to remain a student in the Inteflex program. The record unmistakably demonstrates, however, that the faculty's decision was made conscientiously and with careful deliberation, based on an evaluation of the entirety of Ewing's academic career [474 U.S. at 225].

Citing *Horowitz,* the Court emphasized:

When judges are asked to review the substance of a genuinely academic decision, such as this one, they should show great respect for the faculty's professional judgment. Plainly, they may not override it unless it is such a substantial departure from accepted academic norms as to demonstrate that the person or committee responsible did not actually exercise professional judgment [474 U.S. at 225].

Citing *Keyishian* (discussed in Section 6.4.1), the Court reminded the parties that concerns about institutional academic freedom also limited the nature of judicial review of substantive academic judgments.

Although the result in *Ewing* represents the standard to be used by lower courts, the Court's willingness to assume the existence of a property or liberty interest is questionable in light of a subsequent Supreme Court ruling. In *Siegert v. Gilley,* 111 S. Ct. 1789 (1991), the Court ruled that when defendants who are state officials or state agencies raise a defense of qualified immunity (see Section 2.3.3), federal courts must determine whether a property or liberty interest was "clearly established" at the time the defendant acted. Applying *Siegert,* the Supreme Court of Hawaii in *Soong v. University of Hawaii,* 825 P.2d 1060 (Haw. 1992), ruled that a student had no clearly established substantive constitutional right to continued enrollment in an academic program.

Courts may resolve legal questions concerning the award of grades, credits, or degrees not only by applying standards of arbitrariness or bad faith but also by applying the terms of the student-institution contract (Section 3.2). A 1979 Kentucky case, *Lexington Theological Seminary v. Vance,* 596 S.W.2d 11 (Ky. Ct. App. 1979), illustrates the deference that may be accorded postsecondary institutions—especially church-related institutions—in identifying and construing the contract. The case also illustrates the problems that may arise when institutions attempt to withhold academic recognition from students because of their homosexuality.

The Lexington Theological Seminary, a seminary that trains ministers for the Disciples of Christ and other denominations, had denied Vance, a student who had successfully completed all his academic requirements, a Master of Divinity degree because of his admitted homosexuality. The student had enrolled in the seminary in 1972. In September 1975, he advised the dean of the school and the president of the seminary of his homosexuality. In January 1976, the student was informed that his degree candidacy would be deferred until he completed one additional course. In May 1976, after he had successfully completed the course, the faculty voted to grant the Master of Divinity degree. The seminary's executive committee, however, voted not to approve the faculty recommendation, and the board of trustees subsequently ratified the committee's decision. The student brought suit, seeking conferral of the degree.

The trial court dealt with the suit as a contract case and held that the seminary had breached its contract with the plaintiff student. The Kentucky Court of Appeals, although it overruled the trial court, also agreed to apply contract principles to the case. "The terms and conditions for graduation from a private college or university are those offered by the publications of the college at the time of enrollment and, as such, have some of the characteristics of a contract."

The appellate court relied on various phrases from the seminary's catalogue—such as "Christian ministry," "gospel transmitted through the Bible," "servants of the Gospel," "fundamental character," and "display traits of character and personality which indicate probable effectiveness in the Christian ministry"—which it determined to be contract terms. It held that these terms created "reasonably clear standards" and interpreted them to permit the seminary to bar a homosexual student from receiving a degree. The court found that the seminary, being a religious institution preparing ministers to preach the gospel, had "a most compelling interest" in allowing only "persons possessing character of the highest Christian ideals" to graduate and that it had exercised sound discretion in denying the degree.

The court's reasoning sparked a strong dissenting opinion, which examined not only the language in the seminary catalogue but also the conduct of the seminary's dean, president, and faculty. The dissenting judge said, "Since neither the dean, the president, nor the faculty understood the catalogue to clearly exclude homosexuals, their view certainly cloud[ed] any contrary meaning." The dissent also argued that the language used in the catalogue was not sufficiently clear. "In the future, the board should consider revising the catalogue to be more explicit on what is meant by 'fundamental character.' The board might also make it clear that applications for degree candidacy will not only be 'evaluated by the faculty' but will also be reviewed by the board."

The *Lexington Theological Seminary* case illustrates that courts may resolve questions of academic credits or degrees by viewing the school catalogue as a contract that is binding on both student and institution. The majority opinion also illustrates the flexibility that courts may accord postsecondary institutions in drafting and interpreting this contract, and the special deference that may be accorded church-related institutions in enforcing terms dealing with morality. The dissent in this case, however, deserves as much attention as the majority opinion. It cautions administrators against construing ambiguous catalogue or policy language in a way that is inconsistent with their prior actions (see Section 1.3.2.3) and illustrates the potential for ambiguity that resides in general terms such as "fundamental character." Postsecondary administrators should heed these warnings. Other courts may not be as deferential to the institution as the Kentucky Court of Appeals was, especially in cases that involve life-style or off-campus behavior rather than the quality of academic work as such. Even if administrators could confidently expect broad deference from the courts, the dissent's cautions are still valuable as suggestions for how institutions can do better, of their own accord rather than through judicial compulsion, in ordering their own internal affairs.

An example of a court's refusal to defer to a college's interpretation of its catalogue and policy documents is *Russell v. Salve Regina College,* 890 F.2d 484 (1st Cir. 1989). Sharon Russell had been asked to withdraw from the nursing program at the college because the administrators believed her obesity was unsatisfactory for a nursing student. Although Russell's academic performance in all but one course was satisfactory or better, the instructor in one clinical course gave her a failing grade, which the jury found was related to her weight, not to her performance. Although the nursing program's rules specified that failing a clinical course would result in expulsion, the college promised Russell that she could remain in the program if she would sign a contract promising to lose weight on a regular basis. She did so, and attended Weight Watchers during that year, but did not lose weight. At the end of her junior year, Russell was asked to withdraw from Salve Regina, and she transferred to another nursing program, where she was required to repeat her junior year because of a two-year residency requirement. She completed her nursing degree, but in five years rather than four.

Although the trial judge dismissed her tort claims of intentional infliction of emotional distress and invasion of privacy (stemming from administrators' conduct regarding her obesity), the contract claim had been submitted to the jury, which had found for Russell and had awarded her approximately $144,000. On appeal, the court discussed the terms of the contract:

> From the various catalogs, manuals, handbooks, etc., that form the contract between student and institution, the district court, in its jury charge, boiled the agreement between the parties down to one in which Russell on the one hand was required to abide by disciplinary rules, pay tuition, and maintain good academic standing, and the College on the other hand was required to provide her with an education until graduation. The court informed the jury that the agreement was modified by the "contract" the parties signed during Russell's junior year. The jury was told that, if Russell "substantially performed" her side of the bargain, the College's actions constituted a breach [890 F.2d at 488].

The college had objected to the trial court's use of commercial contract principles of substantial performance rather than using a more deferential approach, such as was used in *Slaughter v. Brigham Young University* (Sections 7.2.2 and 7.3.4). But the appellate court disagreed, noting that the college's actions were based not on academic judgments but on a belief that the student's weight was inappropriate, despite the fact that the college knew of the student's obesity when it admitted her to both the college and the nursing program:

Under the circumstances, the "unique" position of the College as educator becomes less compelling. As a result, the reasons against applying the substantial performance standard to this aspect of the student-college relationship also become less compelling. Thus, Salve Regina's contention that a court cannot use the substantial performance standard to compel an institution to graduate a student merely because the student has completed 124 out of 128 credits, while correct, is inapposite. The court may step in where, as here, full performance by the student has been hindered by some form of impermissible action [890 F.2d at 489].

Unlike the student in the *Lexington Theological Seminary* case, Russell was not asking the court to award her a degree; she was asking for contract damages, which included one year of forgone income (while she attended the other college for the extra year). The appellate court found that this portion of the award—$25,000—was appropriate.[1]

Although infrequent, challenges to grades or examination results have been brought by students. For example, in *Olsson v. Board of Higher Education of the City of New York*, 402 N.E.2d 1150 (N.Y. 1980), a student had not passed a comprehensive examination and therefore had not been awarded the M.A. degree for which he had been working. He claimed that his professor had misled him about the required passing grade on the examination. The professor had meant to say that a student must score three out of a possible five points on four of the five questions; instead, the professor said that a student must pass three of five questions. The student invoked the estoppel doctrine—the doctrine that justifiable reliance on a statement or promise estops the other from contradicting it if the reliance led directly to a detriment or injustice to the promisee. He argued that (1) he had justifiably relied on the professor's statement in budgeting both his study and test time, (2) he had achieved the grade the professor had stated was necessary, and (3) injustice would result if the university was not estopped from denying the degree.

The trial court and the intermediate appellate court both accepted the student's argument. The state's highest appellate court, however, did not. Deferring to the academic judgment of the institution, and emphasizing that the institution had offered the student an opportunity to retake the exam, the court refused to grant a "degree by estoppel":

In reversing the determinations below, we are mindful that this case involves more than a simple balancing of equities among various competing commercial

---

[1]The U.S. Supreme Court subsequently reversed and remanded the appellate court's decision (499 U.S. 225 (1991)); on remand, the appellate court reinstated its prior judgment and opinion (938 F.2d 315 (1st Cir. 1991)).

interests. While it is true that in the ordinary case, a principal must answer for the misstatements of his agent when the latter is clothed with a mantle of apparent authority (see, for example, *Phillips v. West Rockaway Land Co.*, 226 N.Y. 507, 124 N.E. 87), such hornbook rules cannot be applied mechanically where the "principal" is an educational institution and the result would be to override a determination concerning a student's academic qualifications. Because such determinations rest in most cases upon the subjective professional judgment of trained educators, the courts have quite properly exercised the utmost restraint in applying traditional legal rules to disputes within the academic community (see, for example, *Board of Curators, University of Missouri v. Horowitz*, 435 U.S. 78 . . .).

This judicial reluctance to intervene in controversies involving academic standards is founded upon sound considerations of public policy. When an educational institution issues a diploma to one of its students, it is, in effect, certifying to society that the student possesses all of the knowledge and skills that are required by his chosen discipline. In order for society to be able to have complete confidence in the credentials dispensed by academic institutions, however, it is essential that the decisions surrounding the issuance of these credentials be left to the sound judgment of the professional educators who monitor the progress of their students on a regular basis. Indeed, the value of these credentials from the point of view of society would be seriously undermined if the courts were to abandon their longstanding practice of restraint in this area and instead began to utilize traditional equitable estoppel principles as a basis for requiring institutions to confer diplomas upon those who have been deemed to be unqualified.

Certainly [in this case John Jay College] was not obliged to confer a diploma upon Olsson before he demonstrated his competence in accordance with the institution's academic standards. The mere circumstance that Olsson may have been misled by Professor Kim's unfortunate remark cannot serve to enhance the student's position in this regard. Despite Olsson's speculative contention that he might have passed the examination had he not been misinformed about the grading criteria, the fact remains that neither the courts nor the college authorities have any way of knowing whether the outcome of the testing would have been different if Olsson had not "relied" upon Professor Kim's misstatement. Indeed, the fact that 23 of the 35 students enrolled in Professor Kim's review course managed to pass the examination despite the faculty member's "slip-of-the-tongue" serves to demonstrate that there was no necessary connection between Olsson's exposure to the "three out of five" comment and his failure to achieve a passing score. Under these circumstances, requiring the college to award Olsson a diploma on equitable estoppel grounds would be a disservice to society, since the credential would not represent the college's considered judgment that Olsson possessed the requisite qualifications [402 N.E.2d at 1152–53].

Although the court refused to apply the estoppel doctrine to the particular facts of this case, it indicated that in other, more extreme, circumstances estoppel could apply to problems concerning grading and other academic judgments.

The court compared Olsson's situation to that of the plaintiff in *Blank v. Board of Higher Education of the City of New York*, 273 N.Y.S.2d 796 (see this volume, Section 2.2.1), in which the student had completed all academic requirements for his bachelor's degree but had not spent his final term "in residence." The student demonstrated reliance on the incorrect advice of several advisers and faculty members and had only failed to satisfy a technical requirement rather than an academic one. The court explained:

> The outstanding feature which differentiates *Blank* from the instant case is the unavoidable fact that in *Blank* the student unquestionably had fulfilled the academic requirements for the credential he sought. Unlike the student here, the student in *Blank* had demonstrated his competence in the subject matter to the satisfaction of his professors. Thus, there could be no public policy objection to [the court's] decision to award a "diploma by estoppel.". . . Moreover, although the distinction is not dispositive, it cannot be overlooked that the student in *Blank* had relied upon a continuous series of deliberate and considered assurances from several faculty members, while Olsson, the student in this case, premised his estoppel claim upon a single inadvertent "slip-of-the-tongue" made by one professor during the course of a single presentation [402 N.E.2d at 1154].[2]

The *Olsson* case thus provides both an extensive justification of "academic deference"—that is, judicial deference to an educational institution's academic judgments—and an extensive analysis of the circumstances in which courts, rather than deferring, should invoke estoppel principles to protect students challenging academic decisions. Synthesizing its analysis, the court concluded:

> It must be stressed that the judicial awarding of an academic diploma is an extreme remedy which should be reserved for the most egregious of circumstances. In light of the serious policy considerations which militate against judicial intervention in academic disputes, the courts should shun the "diploma by estoppel" doctrine whenever there is some question as to whether the student seeking relief has actually demonstrated his competence in accordance with the standards devised by the appropriate school authorities. Additionally, the courts should be particularly cautious in applying the doctrine in cases such

---

[2]Another case in which the court ordered the award of a degree is *Kantor v. Schmidt*, 423 N.Y.S.2d 208 (N.Y. App. Div. 1979), a mandamus proceeding under New York law. The State University of New York at Stony Brook had withheld the degree because the student had not made sufficient progress, within established time limits, toward completion of the degree. A New York trial court ordered the defendant to award a B.A. degree to the student because the university had not complied with the state commissioner of education's regulations on student progress and informing students of progress. The appellate court affirmed but, on reargument, vacated its decision and dismissed the appeal as moot (432 N.Y.S.2d 156 (1980)).

as this, where a less drastic remedy, such as retesting, may be employed without seriously disrupting the student's academic or professional career [402 N.E.2d at 1154].

A challenge to grades in two law school courses provided the New York courts with an opportunity to address another issue similar to that in *Olsson*— the standard of review to be used when students challenge particular grades. In *Susan M v. New York Law School,* 544 N.Y.S.2d 829 (N.Y. App. Div. 1989), *reversed,* 556 N.E.2d 1104 (N.Y. 1990), a law student dismissed for inadequate academic performance sought judicial review of her grades in her constitutional law and corporations courses. The student claimed that she had received poor grades because of errors made by the professors in both courses. In the constitutional law course, she alleged, the professor gave incorrect instructions on whether the exam was open-book; in the corporations course, the professor evaluated a correct answer as incorrect. The law school asserted that these allegations were beyond judicial review because they were a matter of professional discretion.

Although Susan M's claims were dismissed by the trial court, the intermediate appellate court disagreed with the law school's characterization of both grade disputes as beyond judicial review. It agreed that the dispute over the constitutional law examination was "precisely the type of professional, educational judgment the courts will not review" (544 N.Y.S.2d at 830); but the student's claim regarding her answer in the corporations exam, for which she received no credit, was a different matter. The court said:

> At least when a student's very right to remain in school depends on it, we think the school owes the student some manner of safeguard against the possibility of arbitrary or capricious error in grading, and that, in the absence of any such safeguards, concrete allegations of flagrant misapprehension on the part of the grader entitle the student to a measure of relief [544 N.Y.S.2d at 831–32].

The court then described the type of review it believed appropriate, an approach that, had it been upheld on appeal, would have subjected the professor's reasoning process in grading the examination to judicial scrutiny:

> At issue is not what grade petitioner should have received but whether the grade received was arbitrary and capricious; not whether petitioner deserved a C+ instead of a D in Corporations but whether she deserved a zero on this particular essay; not the quality of petitioner's answer but the rationality of the professor's grading [544 N.Y.S.2d at 832].

The court remanded this issue to the law school "for further consideration of petitioner's grade in Corporations." It asked the school to provide "reasonable assurances that the zero given her on the essay in question was a rational exercise of discretion by the grader" (544 N.Y.S.2d at 832). The law school appealed, and the state's highest court unanimously reversed the appellate division's holding, reinstating the outcome in the trial court.

The court strongly endorsed the academic deference argument made by the law school, stating in the opinion's first paragraph:

> Because [the plaintiff's] allegations are directed at the pedagogical evaluation of her test grades, a determination best left to educators rather than the courts, we conclude that her petition does not state a judicially cognizable claim [556 N.E.2d at 1105].

After reviewing the outcomes in earlier challenges to the academic determinations of colleges and universities, the state's highest court stated:

> As a general rule, judicial review of grading disputes would inappropriately involve the courts in the very core of academic and educational decision making. Moreover, to so involve the courts in assessing the propriety of particular grades would promote litigation by countless unsuccessful students and thus undermine the credibility of the academic determinations of educational institutions. We conclude, therefore, that, in the absence of demonstrated bad faith, arbitrariness, capriciousness, irrationality or a constitutional or statutory violation, a student's challenge to a particular grade or other academic determination relating to a genuine substantive evaluation of the student's academic capabilities, is beyond the scope of judicial review [556 N.E.2d at 1107].

Concluding that the plaintiff's claims concerned substantive evaluation of her academic performance, the court refused to review them.

Although students apparently may not obtain academic credentials through litigation, they occasionally obtain them fraudulently, either by claiming degrees from "diploma mills" or by altering transcripts to make it appear that they completed a degree. For analysis of this issue, see J. Van Tol, "Detecting, Deterring and Punishing the Use of Fraudulent Academic Credentials: A Play in Two Acts," 29 *Santa Clara L. Rev.* 1 (1990).

6.1.2. Degree Revocation

Generally, both public and private colleges and universities have authority to revoke improperly awarded degrees when good cause for doing so, such as the discovery of fraud or misrepresentation, is shown. Public institutions must afford the degree recipient notice and an opportunity for a hearing before making a decision on whether to revoke a degree, following due process guidelines (see Section 7.3.2). Private institutions, although generally not subject to constitutional requirements, are subject to contract law, and generally must use procedures that will protect the degree recipient from potentially arbitrary or capricious conduct by the institution (see Section 7.3.4).

Degree revocations by both public and private institutions have been challenged in lawsuits. In *Waliga v. Board of Trustees of Kent State University*, 488 N.E.2d 850 (Ohio 1986), the Ohio Supreme Court upheld the university's right to rescind a degree. Two individuals had been awarded baccalaureate degrees, one in 1966 and one in 1967, from Kent State University. University officials discovered, over ten years later, discrepancies such as credits granted for courses the students never took, and grades on official records that were different from those reported by course professors. The university rescinded the degrees on the grounds that the students had not completed the appropriate number of credits for graduation.

The students sought a declaratory judgment on the university's power to rescind a degree. The Ohio Supreme Court found such power under two theories. First, the court interpreted Ohio law as permitting any action necessary for operating the state university unless such action was expressly prohibited by statute. As long as a fair hearing had been held, the university had the power to rescind a degree procured by fraud. Second, the court addressed the significance of the public's confidence in the integrity of degrees awarded by colleges and universities:

> Academic degrees are a university's certification to the world at large of the recipient's educational achievement and the fulfillment of the institution's standards. To hold that a university may never withdraw a degree, effectively requires the university to continue making a false certification to the public at large of the accomplishment of persons who in fact lack the very qualifications that are certified [488 N.E.2d at 852].

Just as a university has the power to refuse to confer a degree if a student does not complete the requirements for graduation, it also has the power, the court ruled, to rescind a degree awarded to a student who did not complete those requirements.

Given an institution's power to rescind a degree, what procedural protections must the institution give the student? If the institution is public, the Fourteenth Amendment's due process clause may require certain protections, particularly if the court finds a property interest in the student's possession of the degree. In *Crook v. Baker*, 813 F.2d 88 (6th Cir. 1987), a federal appeals court addressed this issue.

After awarding Crook an M.A. in geology, the University of Michigan determined that the data he had used in his master's thesis were fabricated, and notified him that a hearing would be held to determine whether the degree should be revoked. Crook filed a complaint in federal court, asserting that the university lacked the power to rescind a degree and, if such power were present, that the procedures used by the university violated his due process rights because they did not permit him to cross-examine witnesses.

The court first considered whether the university had the power to rescind the degree. Summarizing the opinion in *Waliga* at some length, the court determined that "there is nothing in Michigan constitutional, statutory or case law that indicates that the Regents do not have the power to rescind the grant of a degree" (813 F.2d at 92), and noted that the state constitution gave the university significant independence in educational matters.

Turning to the student's procedural claims, the court applied the teachings of *Goss v. Lopez* (Section 7.3.2) to evaluate the sufficiency of the procedural protections afforded Crook. Although the trial court had ruled that the hearing violated Crook's right to due process, the appellate court found that the university had given Crook sufficient notice of the charges against him and that the hearing—at which he was permitted to have counsel present, to present witnesses in his behalf, and to respond to the charges against him—complied with the requirements of *Goss*. Although the hearing was "informal," in that hearing panel members asked questions and neither the university nor Crook was permitted to ask questions of the witnesses, the court held that Crook had no procedural due process right to have his attorney examine and cross-examine witnesses and that the university's procedures for questioning witnesses were sufficient for due process purposes.

Crook had also claimed violation of his substantive due process rights, alleging no rational basis for the rescission of his degree. Citing *Ewing* (see Section 6.1.1), the court found that the hearing committee had exercised professional judgment and that the committee's determination that Crook's data were fabricated was neither arbitrary nor capricious.

Waliga and *Crook* establish the power of a public institution to rescind a degree, and *Crook* discusses the type of procedural protection required to meet constitutional due process standards. When private institutions are involved, however, constitutional requirements typically do not apply. Unless the institution can meet the "state action" test (see Section 1.5.2), constitutional protections are not available to the student (see *Imperiale v. Hahnemann University*, 966 F.2d 125 (3d Cir. 1992)).

In another case, which was brought by a student whose doctoral degree was revoked on the grounds that his dissertation was plagiarized, a California appellate court analyzed the university's actions under a deferential standard of review—whether or not the university abused its discretion. In *Abalkhail v. Claremont University Center*, 2d Civ. No. B014012 (Cal. Ct. App. 1986), the court detailed the procedures used to determine whether the degree should be revoked. The university had received a report that portions of the dissertation might have been plagiarized, and it appointed a committee of investigation to determine whether plagiarism had occurred and degree revocation was warranted.

After the committee concluded that plagiarism might have occurred, the graduate school dean informed Abalkhail that a hearing would be held and described the procedures that would be followed. Abalkhail did not receive a copy of the letter that instigated the investigation until the day of the hearing, but he was given the opportunity to respond to the charges against him and was asked if there were additional procedures necessary to give him a fair hearing. The hearing committee met again with Abalkhail to inform him of additional evidence against him and to permit him to respond to that evidence by a particular time. After the time for response had elapsed, the committee found that much of Abalkhail's dissertation was plagiarized and recommended that his degree be rescinded. The university did so, and Abalkhail filed a complaint, alleging deprivation of due process and fairness protections.

Applying the California common law doctrine of fair procedures required of nonprofit groups, the court ruled that Abalkhail was entitled to "the minimum requisites of procedural fairness" (2d Civ. No. B014012 at 15). These "minimum requisites" included notice of the charges and the probable consequences of a finding that the charges would be upheld, a fair opportunity to present his position, and a fair hearing. These had been provided to the plaintiff, according to the court. (For analysis of *Waliga, Crook,* and *Abalkhail,* see B. Reams, Jr., "Revocation of Academic Degrees by Colleges and Universities," 14 *J. Coll. & Univ. Law* 283 (1987).)

Although institutions of higher education appear to have the authority to revoke degrees, the revocation must be an act of the same entity that has the authority to award the degree. In *Hand v. Matchell,* 957 F.2d 791 (10th Cir. 1992), a federal appellate court affirmed a federal trial court's award of summary judgment to a former student who challenged his degree revocation. The board of regents of New Mexico State University had not acted on the degree revocation but had delegated that decision to the graduate dean and, when the student appealed the dean's decision, to the executive vice president. Although the university had developed a procedure that involved both faculty and external experts in the determination that the plaintiff's dissertation had been plagiarized, the court, interpreting New Mexico law, said that the board could not delegate its authority to revoke a degree to a subordinate individual or body.

SEC. 6.2. SEXUAL HARASSMENT BY FACULTY

Although students typically have not prevailed in challenges to grades or the denial of degrees on academic grounds, they may be somewhat more successful when they allege that sexual harassment influenced the grading decision or the faculty member's conduct toward them. Sexual harassment of students is a violation of Title IX of the Education Amendments of 1972 (discussed in Section

12.4.3) in that it may interfere with a student's ability to benefit from an educational program by subjecting the student to behavioral or grading criteria not applied to other students. If the student works for the college or university and is harassed by a coworker or supervisor, the harassment may also be a violation of Title VII or the state's fair employment law (see, for example, *Karibian v. Columbia University*, 14 F.3d 773 (2d Cir. 1994), where the university was held strictly liable for the sexual harassment of a student employee by her supervisor).

The existence and extent of sexual harassment against students is well documented (see, for example, B. W. Dziech and L. Weiner, *The Lecherous Professor: Sexual Harassment on Campus* (Beacon Press, 1984)). Colleges and universities that have promulgated policies prohibiting harassment of students have forbidden such behaviors as sexist behavior (using sexual images or sexual language when sex is irrelevant to the subject matter, or sexual joking that embarrasses or humiliates students of one sex). Also forbidden are romantic relationships between professors and students and unwanted demands for sexual favors with overt or implied threats or promises of academic rewards or punishments.

Although Title IX has been in effect for over two decades, only in recent years have students succeeded in litigation charging faculty and their institutions with liability for sexual harassment, and most of these cases have turned on procedural issues. In an early case, *Alexander v. Yale University*, 631 F.2d 178 (2d Cir. 1980), five female students alleged that Yale's practices and procedures for dealing with sexual harassment of students violated Title IX of the Education Amendments of 1972. One of the plaintiffs alleged that a faculty member had "offered to give her a grade of 'A' in the course in exchange for her compliance with his sexual demands" and that, when she refused, he gave her a C, which "was not the result of a fair evaluation of her academic work but the result of her failure to accede to [the professor's] sexual demands." The remaining plaintiffs made other allegations concerning acts of harassment and the inadequacies of campus procedures to deal with them.

The district court entered judgment for Yale, and the U.S. Court of Appeals affirmed. With the exception of the lowered-grade claim of one plaintiff, all the various claims and plaintiffs were dismissed for technical reasons: the plaintiffs had graduated and their claims were therefore "moot"; Yale had already adopted procedures for dealing with sexual harassment and thus, in effect, had already granted the primary remedy requested in the suit; other claims of harm were too "speculative" or "uncertain." The lowered-grade claim was dismissed because the plaintiff, at trial, did not prove the allegations.

Although it rejected all claims, the *Alexander* court by no means shut the door on Title IX actions alleging that the integrity of grading or other academic processes has been compromised by faculty's sexual harassment of students. Both trial and appellate courts made clear that the grade claim was a "justifiable claim for relief under Title IX." A denial or threatened denial of earned academic awards would be a deprivation of an educational benefit protected by Title IX; and when imposed for sexual reasons, that deprivation becomes sex discrimination prohibited by Title IX. As the district court held, and the appellate court quoted with apparent approval, "Academic advancement conditioned upon submission to sexual demands constitutes sex discrimination in education" (459 F. Supp. 1, 4 (D. Conn. 1977), 631 F.2d at 182).

A federal appellate court clarified several significant issues relating to sexual harassment in *Lipsett v. University of Puerto Rico*, 864 F.2d 881 (1st Cir. 1988). Lipsett, a female surgical resident at the university hospital, was dismissed from her residency after complaining on several occasions about sexual harassment from both her fellow residents and some of the faculty members supervising her. The harassment involved statements by her fellow students and faculty supervisors that women should not be surgeons, sexual advances and unwelcome touching by some residents, name-calling, and the posting of centerfolds from *Playboy* magazine in the residents' dining area. Her supervisors ignored her complaints and dismissed her from the program for insubordination and violation of rules, behavior that Lipsett either denied or asserted was general practice among the residents.

Lipsett filed claims under Title IX against the residents and under Section 1983 (on equal protection grounds) against the faculty and program staff. In reviewing the district court's grant of summary judgment to the university and its administrators, the appellate court evaluated whether, using Lipsett's version of the facts, she could have prevailed on her discrimination claims. Because Lipsett was both a student and an employee of the university, the court used Title VII precedent to interpret Title IX's application to the plaintiff's claims that the sexual harassment had created a hostile environment. The court found that Lipsett had established a prima facie case of hostile work environment and quid pro quo sexual harassment by the residents,[3] that the complaints about her work performance were "infused with discriminatory bias," that most of her supervisors knew of the harassment, and that the failure of the supervising faculty to investigate her complaints could constitute gross negligence. These findings suggested that the supervising faculty could be held individually liable under Section 1983 (Section 2.3.3).

With regard to the standard for determining liability for quid pro quo harassment, the court held that an educational institution is "absolutely liable" whether or not it knew, should have known, or approved of a supervisor's actions (864

---

[3]"Hostile work environment" sexual harassment is sexually oriented conduct by peers, nonemployees, or supervisors that creates an abusive or hostile work environment on the basis of the individual's gender. Quid pro quo sexual harassment is an exchange of sexual favors in return for a supervisor's promise either to grant employment benefits or to refrain from taking adverse action against an employee.

F.2d at 901). With regard to hostile environment harassment, the court adopted an agency theory of liability, stating:

> [I]n a Title IX case, an educational institution is liable upon a finding of hostile environment sexual harassment perpetrated by its supervisors upon employees *if* an official representing that institution knew, or in the exercise of reasonable care, should have known, of the harassment's occurrence, *unless* that official can show that he or she took appropriate steps to halt it [864 F.2d at 901].

While the analysis in *Lipsett* is useful in those unusual cases where the student is both an employee and a student, it may have limited application in cases in which the student is not an employee.

Two federal courts addressed the issue of whether Title IX permitted claims of hostile environment sexual harassment, with different outcomes. In *Moire v. Temple University School of Medicine*, 613 F. Supp. 1360 (E.D. Pa. 1985), *affirmed without opin.*, 800 F.2d 1136 (3d Cir. 1986), the court rejected for lack of evidence a female medical student's claim that her supervisor's sexually oriented comments had created a hostile environment. The court did, however, express its willingness to apply Title VII theories of hostile environment harassment to claims brought under Title IX:

> [H]arassment from an abusive environment occurs where multiple incidents of offensive conduct lead to an environment violative of a victim's civil rights. Here there is no allegation of *quid pro quo* harassment. . . . The issue is whether plaintiff because of her sex was in a harassing or abusive environment [613 F. Supp. at 1366–67].

Conversely, a federal district court refused to find that Title IX permitted hostile environment claims. In *Bougher v. University of Pittsburgh*, 713 F. Supp. 139 (W.D. Pa. 1989), *affirmed*, 882 F.2d 74 (3d Cir. 1989), the court rejected the plaintiff's argument that Title VII theories should be applied to Title IX:

> [T]o suggest, as plaintiff must, that unwelcome sexual advances, from *whatever* source, official or unofficial constitute Title IX violations is a leap into the unknown which, whatever its wisdom, is the duty of Congress or an administrative agency to take. Title IX simply does not permit a "hostile environment" claim as described for the workplace [713 F. Supp. at 145].

Because the appellate court found that the plaintiff's claim was barred by the state statute of limitations, it did not determine whether Title IX includes hostile environment claims. It made this comment, however: "[W]e decline to adopt [the district court's] reasoning *in toto* and we find it unnecessary to reach the question, important though it may be, whether evidence of a hostile environment is sufficient to sustain a claim of sexual discrimination in education in violation of Title IX" (882 F.2d at 77).

Another federal district court stated unequivocally that Title IX contemplated hostile environment claims. In *Patricia H. v. Berkeley Unified School District*, 830 F. Supp. 1288 (N.D. Cal. 1993), the court decided that the continuing presence of a teacher who had allegedly molested a high school student created a hostile environment, and that the student's claim was actionable under Title IX.

Students have used theories in addition to Title IX to seek remedies for alleged sexual harassment. In *George v. University of Idaho*, 822 P.2d 549 (Idaho Ct. App. 1991), a law student, who had ended a consensual relationship with a law professor, filed a breach-of-contract claim against the university, asserting that the professor's efforts to resume the relationship, and his retaliation in the form of actions disparaging her character within the law school and the legal community, constituted breach of an implied contract. The court denied summary judgment for the university, noting the existence of several questions of fact concerning the nature and scope of the university's responsibility to the student. First of all, the court noted, the university had an implied contract with the student—as evidenced by the university's sexual harassment policy and by its statement in the faculty handbook that it would "fulfill its responsibilities in pursuit of the academic goals and objectives of all members of the community." Furthermore, when the student brought the professor's actions to the attention of the school, a written agreement had been executed, in which the professor promised to stop harassing the plaintiff if she would drop claims against him and the law school. The court found that the university had an obligation under that agreement independent of its implied contract with the plaintiff, an obligation that extended beyond her graduation, to take reasonable measures to enforce the agreement.

An unpublished case brought under Minnesota's nondiscrimination law illustrates the nature of contemporary judicial review of student sexual harassment claims. In *Smith v. Hennepin County Technical Center*, 1988 U.S. Dist. LEXIS 4876 (D. Minn. 1988), two students charged the instructor in a dental laboratory with offensive touching and with retaliation when they complained of his conduct. The court, using Title VII law by analogy, adopted a five-step prima facie test for establishing a prima facie case of sexual harassment in an educational setting:

[The plaintiff must show that]

1. she was a member of a protected class;

2. she was subject to unwelcome harassment;

3. the harassment was based on sex;

4. the harassment had the purpose or effect of unreasonably interfering with her education or created an intimidating, hostile, or offensive learning environment; and

> 5. the educational institution knew or should have known of the harass-
> ment and failed to take proper remedial action [1988 U.S. Dist. LEXIS
> 4876 at 39].

Because the instructor was an employee of the institution, the court ruled
that the institution was directly liable for torts committed by its employee if the
employer could have prevented the tort through the exercise of reasonable care.

Although it appears that the federal courts are willing to hold colleges and
universities liable for sexual harassment by their employees, plaintiffs have not
been successful in their attempts to hold the harasser individually liable under
Title IX. For example, in *Nelson v. Temple University and Lee Dowling*, 920 F.
Supp. 633 (E.D. Pa. 1996), a student who alleged harassment by a college administrator sought to hold him individually liable under Title IX. The court
examined the language of Title IX and concluded that, in the absence of language suggesting that Title IX was intended to cover individuals, the phrase
"recipients of federal assistance" should apply only to institutions. However, administrators or faculty at public institutions who are accused of harassing students may be sued under Section 1983 of the federal civil rights statutes (this
volume, Section 2.4.3; see, for example, *Doe v. Petaluma City School District*, 54
F.3d 1447 (9th Cir. 1995)).

The U.S. Supreme Court's decision in *Franklin v. Gwinnett County* (discussed
in Section 12.4.3), ruling that plaintiffs demonstrating intentional discrimination under Title IX may be awarded money damages, has raised the stakes for
both plaintiffs and institutions in these cases. Students, for instance, may argue
that they left college as a result of harassment and therefore suffered the loss of
career opportunities as well as emotional distress. Courts have made it very
clear in the employment context that prompt and effective remedial action must
be taken when the organization is on notice that sexual harassment may have
occurred. That standard is now being applied to the responses of colleges and
universities, since students—increasingly aware of their rights and the availability of remedies—are losing their reluctance to complain about sexual harassment by faculty.

To protect themselves from liability, and to provide a means for working
through these difficult issues internally, institutions of higher education have
developed policies that both define prohibited sexually harassing conduct and
provide a grievance system for students who believe they have been sexually
harassed by a faculty member or an administrator. One particularly difficult
decision institutions may face in drafting such policies is whether to prohibit all
sexual relationships between students and faculty, consensual or not. Proponents of the total ban argue that the unequal power relationships between
student and faculty member mean that no relationship is truly consensual.
Opponents of total bans, on the other hand, argue that students are beyond the

legal age of consent, and that institutions infringe on constitutional rights of free association or risk invasion-of-privacy claims if they attempt to regulate the personal lives of faculty and students. For discussions of this difficult issue, see M. Chamallas, "Consent, Equality and the Legal Control of Sexual Conduct," 61 *Southern Cal. L. Rev.* 777 (1988); P. DeChiara, "The Need for Universities to Have Rules on Consensual Sexual Relationships Between Faculty Members and Students," 21 *Columbia J. of Law & Social Problems* 137 (1988); and E. Keller, "Consensual Amorous Relationships Between Faculty and Students: The Constitutional Right to Privacy," 15 *J. Coll. & Univ. Law* 21 (1988).

Institutions must also determine what complaint procedures they will use to enforce their harassment policies. If there are existing procedures for disciplining faculty, the institution could use them. The AAUP has released a statement on "Sexual Harassment: Suggested Policy and Procedures for Handling Complaints" (in *AAUP Policy Documents and Reports* (AAUP, 1995), 171–173), which includes due process protections for the accused and a faculty committee as fact finder. If the institution's procedure permits the faculty member to have an attorney present, the institution should determine whether it will provide counsel for the student, particularly if the faculty member sues the student as a result of the harassment complaint. Of course, the institution is exposed to potential litigation by both the accused faculty member and the student (see K. S. Mangan, "Thorny Legal Issues Face Colleges Hit by Sexual-Harassment Cases," *Chron. Higher Educ.*, Aug. 4, 1993, A13).

Although it now appears established that institutions will face liability under Title IX for harassment by staff or faculty, the issue of institutional liability for peer sexual harassment remains to be resolved. While students are not agents of the institution (unless, perhaps, they are also employees), some commentators have argued that Title IX creates a duty upon colleges and universities to provide equal access to academic programs, and that sexual harassment, whether by students or faculty, denies women students that equal access. Although recent U.S. Supreme Court rulings in free speech cases (see Section 8.3) have complicated the efforts of public institutions to outlaw harassing or threatening speech, Title IX may provide victims an avenue for relief in cases of harassing conduct or unprotected speech of which the institution was aware.

Several issues come into play when a student attempts to hold an institution liable under Title IX for sexual harassment by a fellow student (or other non-employee). First, the courts have been required to determine whether, in a case of peer harassment, students may base their Title IX claim on the "hostile educational environment" theory. A few federal courts have applied the standards developed under Title VII for hostile work environment to student claims that sexual harassment by peers created a hostile learning environment (*Bosley v. Kearney R-1 School District*, 904 F. Supp. 1006, 1022 (W.D. Mo. 1995); *Burrow v. Postville Community School District*, 929 F. Supp. 1193 (N.D. Iowa 1996)). But a plaintiff's ability to state such a claim does not guarantee success, for several courts have ruled that a plaintiff seeking to hold an educational organization liable for peer harassment must show that the institution's response (or lack of response) to the harassment constituted intentional discrimination on the basis of gender. For example, a federal appellate court has ruled that Title IX does not impose liability on a school district for peer hostile environment harassment unless the district itself discriminated by responding to harassment against girls differently than harassment against boys (*Rowinsky v. Bryan Independent School District*, 80 F.3d 1006 (5th Cir. 1996)). This result has been criticized by the federal Office for Civil Rights as rejecting "the authority of other Federal courts and OCR's longstanding construction of Title IX." In draft Guidance that describes the analytical approach OCR uses when investigating complaints of alleged peer harassment, the agency states that "Title IX does not make a school responsible for the actions of the harassing student, but rather for its own discrimination in failing to act and permitting the harassment to continue once a school official knows that it is happening" (*OCR Policy Guidance Regarding Peer Sexual Harassment* (August 1996, p. 15)). Since Title IX doctrine for peer harassment is still developing, it is not clear whether the federal appellate courts will defer to the OCR Guidelines. Administrators should monitor with care the legal developments in this volatile area of the law.

For analysis of the complex legal issues involved in peer harassment and institutional liability, see J. Faber, "Expanding Title IX of the Education Amendments of 1972 to Prohibit Student to Student Sexual Harassment," 2 *UCLA Women's Law J.* 85 (1992). For a report on peer sexual harassment, see *Peer Harassment: Hassles for Women on Campus* (Center for Women Policy Studies, 1992).

SEC. 6.3. STUDENTS WITH DISABILITIES

As noted in Section 4.1.4.3, the Rehabilitation Act and the Americans with Disabilities Act of 1990 require colleges and universities to provide reasonable accommodations for students with disabilities. Although the laws do not require institutions to change their academic criteria for disabled students, they may need to change the format of tests; to provide additional time, or readers or aides to help students take examinations; or to change minor aspects of course requirements.

The question of how much change is required arose in *Wynne v. Tufts University School of Medicine*, 976 F.2d 791 (1st Cir. 1992). A medical student dismissed on academic grounds asserted that the medical school had refused to accommodate his learning disability by requiring him to take a multiple-choice test rather than an alternative type of test that would have minimized the impact of his learning disability. Initially, the trial court granted summary judgment for

Tufts, but the appellate court reversed on the grounds that the record was insufficient to enable the court to determine whether Tufts had attempted to accommodate Wynne and whether Tufts had evaluated the impact of the requested accommodation on its academic program (932 F.2d 19 (1st Cir. 1991, *en banc*)).

On remand, the university provided extensive evidence to the trial court that it had permitted Wynne to repeat his first year of medical school, had paid for the neuropsychological testing of Wynne that had identified his learning disabilities, and had provided him with tutors, note takers, and other assistance. It had permitted him to take make-up examinations for courses he failed, and had determined that there was not an appropriate alternative method of testing his knowledge in the biochemistry course.

On the strength of the school's evidence of serious consideration of alternatives to the multiple-choice test, the district court again awarded summary judgment for Tufts, and the appellate court affirmed. In deferring to the school's judgment on the need for a certain testing format, the court said:

> [T]he point is not whether a medical school is "right" or "wrong" in making program-related decisions. Such absolutes rarely apply in the context of subjective decision-making, particularly in a scholastic setting. The point is that Tufts, after undertaking a diligent assessment of the available options, felt itself obliged to make "a professional, academic judgment that [a] reasonable accommodation [was] simply not available" [976 F.2d at 795].

Given the multiple forms of assistance that Tufts had provided Wynne, and the school's ability to demonstrate that it had evaluated alternate test forms and determined that none would be an appropriate substitute for the multiple-choice format, the court was satisfied that the school had satisfied the requirements of the Rehabilitation Act.

In *Halasz v. University of New England,* 816 F. Supp. 37 (D. Me. 1993), a federal trial court relied on *Wynne* to review the challenge of a student, dismissed from the University of New England on academic grounds, that the school had failed to provide him with necessary accommodations and had discriminated against him on the basis of his disability. The school had a special program for students with learning disabilities who lacked the academic credentials necessary for regular admission to the university. The program provided a variety of support services for these students and gave them an opportunity for regular admission to the university after they completed the special one-year program. Despite the special services, such as tutoring, taped texts, untimed testing, and readers for some of his classes, the plaintiff was unable to attain an academic record sufficient for regular admission to the university. His performance in the courses and tests that he took during his year in the special program indicated, the university alleged, that he was not an "otherwise qualified" student with a disability and thus was not protected by the Rehabilitation Act. The university was able to demonstrate the academic rationale for its program requirements and to show that the plaintiff had been given the same amount and quality of assistance that had been given to other students who later were offered admission to the university's regular academic program.

The decisions in *Wynne* and *Halasz* stress the significance of an institution's consideration of potential accommodations for students with disabilities. Given the tendency of courts to defer to academic judgments, but to hold colleges and universities to strict procedural standards, those institutions that can demonstrate, as could Tufts, that they gave careful consideration to the student's request, and reached a decision on *academic* grounds that the accommodation was either unnecessary or unsuitable, should be able to prevail against challenges under either the Rehabilitation Act or the ADA.

SEC. 6.4. STUDENT ACADEMIC FREEDOM

6.4.1. General Concepts and Principles

The concept of academic freedom eludes precise definition. It draws meaning from both the world of education and the world of law. Moreover, academic freedom refers not only to the prerogatives of faculty members and students but also to the prerogatives of institutions ("institutional academic freedom" or "institutional autonomy"). As the court stated in *Piarowski v. Illinois Community College,* 759 F.2d 625 (7th Cir. 1985), "though many decisions describe 'academic freedom' as an aspect of the freedom of speech that is protected against governmental abridgment by the First Amendment, . . . the term is equivocal. It is used to denote both the freedom of the academy to pursue its ends without interference from the government . . . and the freedom of the individual teacher (or in some versions—indeed in most cases—the student) to pursue his ends without interference from the academy; and these two freedoms are in conflict." And in *Regents of the University of Michigan v. Ewing,* 474 U.S. 214, 226 n.12 (1985), the U.S. Supreme Court itself confirmed that "[a]cademic freedom thrives not only on the independent and uninhibited exchange of ideas among teachers and students . . . but also, and somewhat inconsistently, on autonomous decision making by the academy itself."

Educators usually use the term "academic freedom" in reference to the custom and practice, and the ideal, by which *faculty members* may best flourish in their work as teachers and researchers (see, for example, the AAUP's 1940 "Statement of Principles on Academic Freedom and Tenure," in *AAUP Policy Documents and Reports* (AAUP, 1990), 3–10). Lawyers and judges often use "academic freedom" as a catch-all term to describe the legal rights and responsibilities of *faculty members,* and courts hearing such cases attempt to reconcile basic constitutional principles with prevailing views of academic freedom's social and intellectual role in American life. Thus, the scope of student academic freedom can be understood only in relation to faculty academic freedom, especially in cases of conflict. The following discussion emphasizes the case law on faculty academic freedom and the impact that claims of faculty academic freedom may have on students and their claims to academic freedom.

In the realm of law and courts (the primary focus of this section), it is important to distinguish between academic freedom claims based on constitutional law and those based on contract law. Though courts usually discuss academic freedom in cases concerning the constitutional rights of faculty members, the legal boundaries of academic freedom are initially defined by contract law. Faculty members possess whatever academic freedom is guaranteed them under their faculty contracts. The AAUP's 1940 "Statement of Principles on Academic Freedom and Tenure," its 1970 "Interpretive Comments," and its 1982 "Recommended Institutional Regulations on Academic Freedom and Tenure" (all included in *AAUP Policy Documents and Reports* (AAUP, 1990), 3–10, 21–30) are often considered the preeminent policy statements on academic freedom, and it is crucial for administrators to determine whether either document has been— or should be—incorporated into the faculty contract. For any document that has been incorporated, courts will interpret and enforce its terms by reference to contract law principles. Even when these documents have not been incorporated into the contract, they may be an important source of academic "custom and usage" that courts will consider in interpreting unclear contract terms (see Section 1.3.2.3).

In public institutions, administrators are limited by both contract law and constitutional concepts of academic freedom, and perhaps also by state statutes or administrative regulations on academic freedom. But in private institutions (see Sections 1.5.1 and 1.5.3), the faculty contract and the student contract (see Section 3.1) may provide the only legal restrictions on the administrator's authority to limit academic freedom. In religiously affiliated institutions, concern for the institution's special mission may add additional complexities to contract law's application to academic freedom problems. In addition, concerns regarding the establishment and free exercise of religion may limit the capacity of the courts to entertain lawsuits against religiously affiliated institutions by faculty members or students alleging breach of contract.

Constitutional principles of academic freedom have developed in two stages, each occupying a distinct time period and including distinct types of cases. The earlier cases of the 1950s and 1960s focused on faculty and institutional freedom from external (political) intrusion. These cases pitted the faculty and the institution against the state. Since the early 1970s, academic freedom cases have focused primarily on faculty freedom from institutional intrusion. In these later cases, faculty academic freedom has collided with institutional academic freedom.

In the 1950s and 1960s cases, the U.S. Supreme Court gave academic freedom constitutional status under the First Amendment freedoms of speech and association, and to a lesser extent under the Fifth Amendment protection against self-incrimination and the Fourteenth Amendment guarantee of procedural due process. The opinions in these cases include a number of ringing declarations on the importance of academic freedom. In *Sweezy v. New Hampshire*, 354 U.S. 234 (1957), for example, both the plurality opinion and Justice Frankfurter's concurring opinion lauded academic freedom in the course of reversing a contempt judgment against a professor who had refused to answer questions concerning a lecture delivered at the state university. In *Shelton v. Tucker*, 364 U.S. 479 (1960), where it invalidated a state statute that compelled public school and college teachers to reveal all organizational affiliations or contributions for the previous five years, the Court remarked:

> The vigilant protection of constitutional freedoms is nowhere more vital than in the community of American schools. "By limiting the power of the states to interfere with freedom of speech and freedom of inquiry and freedom of association, the Fourteenth Amendment protects all persons, no matter what their calling. But, in view of the nature of the teacher's relation to the effective exercise of the rights which are safeguarded by the Bill of Rights and by the Fourteenth Amendment, inhibition of freedom of thought, and of action upon thought, in the case of teachers brings the safeguards of those amendments vividly into operation. Such unwarranted inhibition upon the free spirit of teachers . . . has an unmistakable tendency to chill that free play of the spirit which all teachers ought especially to cultivate and practice; it makes for caution and timidity in their associations by potential teachers" (*Wieman v. Updegraff*, 344 U.S. 183, 195 . . . (concurring opinion)) [1364 U.S. at 487].

And in *Keyishian v. Board of Regents*, 385 U.S. 589 (1967), in the course of invalidating a New York State law used to punish "seditious" words and acts of faculty members, the Court added:

> Our nation is deeply committed to safeguarding academic freedom, which is of transcendent value to all of us and not merely to the teachers concerned. That freedom is therefore a special concern of the First Amendment, which does not tolerate laws that cast a pall of orthodoxy over the classroom. . . . The classroom is peculiarly the "marketplace of ideas." The nation's future depends upon leaders trained through wide exposure to that robust exchange of ideas which discovers truth "out of a multitude of tongues, [rather] than through any kind of authoritative selection" (*United States v. Associated Press*, 52 F. Supp. 362, 372) [385 U.S. at 603].

One year after *Keyishian*, the U.S. Supreme Court stepped gingerly into a new type of academic freedom controversy that became the primary focus for the second stage of academic freedom's development in the courts. *Pickering v. Board of Education,* 391 U.S. 563 (1968), concerned a public high school teacher who had been dismissed for writing the local newspaper a letter in which he criticized the board of education's financial plans for the high schools. Pickering brought suit alleging that the dismissal violated his First Amendment freedom of speech. The school board argued that the dismissal was justified because the letter "damaged the professional reputations of . . . [the school board] members and of the school administrators, would be disruptive of faculty discipline, and would tend to foment 'controversy, conflict, and dissension' among teachers, administrators, the board of education, and the residents of the district."

The Court balanced the teacher's free speech interests against the state's interest in maintaining an efficient educational system, using the following considerations in the balance: (1) Was there a close working relationship between the teacher and those he criticized? (2) Is the substance of the letter a matter of legitimate public concern? (3) Did the letter have a detrimental impact on the administration of the educational system? (4) Was the teacher's performance of his daily duties impeded? (5) Was the teacher writing in his professional capacity or as a private citizen? The Court found that Pickering had no working relationship with the board, that the letter dealt with a matter of public concern, that Pickering's letter was greeted with public apathy and therefore had no detrimental effect on the schools, that Pickering's performance as a teacher was not hindered by the letter, and that he wrote as a citizen, not as a teacher. The Court concluded that under all these facts, the school administration's interest in limiting teachers' opportunities to contribute to public debate was not significantly greater than its interest in limiting a similar contribution by any member of the general public and that "in a case such as this, absent proof of false statements knowingly or recklessly made by him, a teacher's exercise of his right to speak on issues of public importance may not furnish the basis for his dismissal from public employment."

The *Pickering* balancing test was further explicated in *Connick v. Myers,* 461 U.S. 138 (1983). The issue was whether *Pickering* protects public employees who communicate views to office staff about office personnel matters. The plaintiff, Myers, was an assistant district attorney who had been scheduled for transfer to another division of the office. In opposing the transfer, she circulated a questionnaire on office operations to other assistant district attorneys. Later on the same day, she was discharged. In a 5-to-4 decision, applying the *Pickering* factors, the Court majority determined that the questions posed by Myers (with one exception) "do not fall under the rubric of matters of 'public concern'"; that Myers spoke "not as a citizen upon matters of public concern, but instead as an employee upon matters only of personal interest"; and that circulation of the questionnaire interfered with "close working relationships" within the office. The balance of factors therefore indicated that the discharge did not violate the plaintiff's freedom of speech.

Connick emphasizes the need to distinguish between communications on matters of public concern and communications on matters of private or personal concern—a distinction that does not depend on whether the communication is itself made in public or in private. The dispute between the majority and dissenters in *Connick* reveals how slippery this distinction can be. Although *Connick* may appear to limit the protections originally provided by *Pickering*, the Court emphasized that its opinion was limited to the case's specific facts and that courts must remain attentive to the "enormous variety of fact situations" that other cases may present.

In recent years, lower courts have had occasion to apply U.S. Supreme Court precedents to a variety of academic freedom disputes pitting faculty members against students and against their institutions. The source of law most frequently invoked in these cases is the First Amendment's free speech clause, as interpreted in the *Pickering/Connick* line of cases. Some cases have also relied on *Keyishian* and its forerunners, either in lieu of or as a supplement to the *Pickering/Connick* line. As could be expected, courts have reached varying conclusions that depend on the specific facts of the case, the particular court's disposition on liberal construction of First Amendment protections, and its sensitivities to the nuances of academic freedom.

Even more recently, the U.S. Supreme Court has made a major academic freedom pronouncement focused specifically on students. In *Rosenberger v. Rector and Visitors of University of Virginia*, 115 S. Ct. 2510 (1995) (discussed in Section 9.1.4), in protecting students' rights, the Court declared that dangers to free speech are:

> especially real in the University setting, where the State acts against a . . . tradition of thought . . . that is at the center of our intellectual and philosophic tradition. . . . In ancient Athens, and, as Europe entered into a new period of intellectual awakening, in places like Bologna, Oxford, and Paris, universities began as voluntary and spontaneous assemblages or concourses for students to speak and to write and to learn. . . . The quality and creative power of student intellectual life to this day remains a vital measure of a school's influence and attainment. For the University, by regulation, to cast disapproval on particular viewpoints of its students risks the suppression of free speech and creative inquiry in one of the vital centers for the nation's intellectual life, its college and university campuses [115 S. Ct. at 2520].

This pronouncement has the potential to influence the course of protection for student academic freedom; future developments should be watched carefully.

6.4.2. Academic Freedom in the Classroom

Academic freedom disputes concerning course content, teaching methods, grading, or classroom behavior usually get to court because a faculty member (rather than a student) files suit. The suit is usually against the institution or its academic officers who have sought to regulate the faculty member's teaching activities. But students nonetheless have an important stake in these disputes, and indeed students may have lodged the complaints which precipitated them. The faculty member's actions may have hindered the students' freedom to learn; if the faculty member prevails in the dispute, student academic freedom may therefore diminish (see, for example, the *Bishop* case below). Or the faculty member may have used methods or materials that intrude upon other student interests—for example, the use of fair grading practices or freedom from sexual harassment; if the faculty member prevails, these student interests would receive less protection (see, for example, the *Lovelace* and *Cohen* cases below). Or, conversely, the faculty member may have been acting to guard the students' freedom to learn or to promote other student interests; if the faculty member prevails in this situation, the students win too. Since students are thus understandably concerned about these disputes between faculty and institution, and about the scope of faculty academic freedom, student affairs professionals will need to be familiar with the pertinent law and policy considerations.

Courts are generally reticent to intervene on behalf of faculty members in disputes concerning the classroom, viewing these matters as best left to the competence of the officers and administrators who have primary responsibility over academic affairs. Two classical cases from the early 1970s illustrate this judicial attitude.

Hetrick v. Martin, 480 F.2d 705 (6th Cir. 1973), concerned a state university's refusal to renew a nontenured faculty member's contract. Her troubles with the school administration apparently began when unnamed students and the parents of one student complained about certain of her in-class activities. To illustrate the "irony" and "connotative qualities" of the English language, for example, the faculty member once told her freshman students, "I am an unwed mother." At that time, she was a divorced mother of two, but she did not reveal that fact to her class. On occasion, she also apparently discussed the war in Vietnam and the military draft with one of her freshman classes.

The faculty member sued the university, alleging an infringement of her First Amendment rights. The court ruled that the university had not based the nonrenewal on any statements the faculty member had made but rather on her "pedagogical attitude." The faculty member believed that her students should be free to organize assignments in accordance with their own interests, while the university expected her to "go by the book." Thus, viewing the case as a dispute over teaching methods, the court refused to equate the teaching methods of professors with constitutionally protected speech:

> We do not accept plaintiff's assertion that the school administration abridged her First Amendment rights when it refused to rehire her because it considered her teaching philosophy to be incompatible with the pedagogical aims of the university. Whatever may be the ultimate scope of the amorphous "academic

freedom" guaranteed to our nation's teachers and students . . . , it does not encompass the right of a nontenured teacher to have her teaching style insulated from review by her superiors . . . just because her methods and philosophy are considered acceptable somewhere in the teaching profession [480 F.2d at 709].

Clark v. Holmes, 474 F.2d 928 (7th Cir. 1972), also involved a teacher's methods and behavior. Clark was a nontenured, temporary substitute teacher at Northern Illinois University, a state institution. He had been told that he could be rehired if he was willing to remedy certain deficiencies—namely, that he "counseled an excessive number of students instead of referring them to NIU's professional counselors; he overemphasized sex in his health survey course; he counseled students with his office door closed; and he belittled other staff members in discussions with students." After discussions with his superiors, in which he defended his conduct, Clark was rehired; but in the middle of the year he was told that he would not teach in the spring semester because of these same problems.

Clark brought suit, claiming that, under *Pickering*, the university had violated his First Amendment rights by not rehiring him because of his speech activities. The court, disagreeing, refused to apply *Pickering* to this situation: (1) Clark's disputes with his colleagues about course content were not matters of public concern, as were the matters raised in Pickering's letter; and (2) Clark's disputes involved him as a teacher, not as a private citizen, whereas Pickering's situation was just the opposite. The court then held that the institution's interest as employer overcame any free speech interest the teacher may have had:

> But we do not conceive academic freedom to be a license for uncontrolled expression at variance with established curricular contents and internally destructive of the proper functioning of the institution. First Amendment rights must be applied in light of the special characteristics of the environment in the particular case (*Tinker v. Des Moines Indep. Community School Dist.*, 393 U.S. 503, 506 . . . (1969); *Healy v. James*, 408 U.S. 169 (1972)). The plaintiff here irresponsibly made captious remarks to a captive audience, one, moreover, that was composed of students who were dependent upon him for grades and recommendations. . . .
>
> Furthermore, *Pickering* suggests that certain legitimate interests of the state may limit a teacher's right to say what he pleases: for example, (1) the need to maintain discipline or harmony among coworkers; (2) the need for confidentiality; (3) the need to curtail conduct which impedes the teacher's proper and competent performance of his daily duties; and (4) the need to encourage a close and personal relationship between the employer and his superiors, where that relationship calls for loyalty and confidence [474 F.2d at 931].

Most of the more recent cases are consistent with *Hetrick* and *Clark*. In *Lovelace v. Southeastern Massachusetts University*, 793 F.2d 419 (1st Cir. 1986), for instance, the court rejected the free speech claim of a faculty member whose contract was not renewed after he rejected administration requests to lower the academic standards he applied to his students. Citing *Hetrick* and *Clark*, the court concluded that universities must themselves have the freedom to set their own standards on "matters such as course content, homework load, and grading policy" and that "the first amendment does not require that each nontenured professor be made a sovereign unto himself."

Similarly, in *Wirsing v. Board of Regents of the University of Colorado*, 739 F. Supp. 551 (D. Colo. 1990), *affirmed without opin.*, 945 F.2d 412 (10th Cir. 1991), a tenured professor of education taught her students "that teaching and learning cannot be evaluated by any standardized test." Consistent with these beliefs, the professor refused to administer the university's standardized course evaluation forms for her classes. The dean denied her a pay increase because of her refusal. The professor sought a court injunction ordering the regents to award her the pay increase and to desist from requiring her to use the form. She argued that the forms were "contrary to her theory of education. Hence, by being forced to give her students the standardized form, the university is interfering arbitrarily with her classroom method, compelling her speech, and violating her right to academic freedom." The court rejected her argument:

> Here, the record is clear that Dr. Wirsing was not denied her merit salary increase because of her teaching methods, presentation of opinions contrary to those of the university, or otherwise presenting controversial ideas to her students. Rather, she was denied her merit increase for her refusal to comply with the University's teacher evaluation requirements. . . . [A]lthough Dr. Wirsing may have a constitutionally protected right under the First Amendment to disagree with the University's policies, she has no right to evidence her disagreement by failing to perform the duty imposed upon her as a condition of employment [739 F. Supp. at 553].

Since the professor remained free to "use the form as an example of what not to do . . . [and to] criticize openly both the [standardized] form and the University's evaluation form policy," the university's requirement was "unrelated to course content [and] in no way interferes with . . . academic freedom." Moreover, according to the court, adoption of a method of teacher evaluation "is part of the University's own right to academic freedom."

Similarly, in *Martin v. Parrish*, 805 F.2d 583 (5th Cir. 1986), the court upheld the dismissal of an economics instructor at Midland College in Texas, ruling that the instructor's use of vulgar and profane language in a college classroom did not fall within the scope of First Amendment protection. Applying *Connick v. Myers*, the court held that the instructor's language did not constitute speech on "matters of public concern." In the process, the court noted the professor's claim that, apart from *Connick*, he had "a first amendment right to 'academic freedom' that permits use of the language in question," but refused to address this claim because "such language was not germane to the subject matter in his class and had no educational function" (805 F.2d at 584 n.2). The court also approved an alternative for upholding the dismissal. Applying elementary/secondary education precedents (see *Bethel School District v. Fraser,* 478 U.S. 675 (1986)), it held that the instructor's use of the language was unprotected because "it was a deliberate, superfluous attack on a 'captive audience' with no academic purpose or justification." In a separate opinion, a concurring judge accepted the court's reasoning based on *Connick* but rejected its alternative analysis, on the grounds that the precedents the court had invoked should not apply to higher education. The concurring judge also agreed with the court in refusing to address the professor's argument based on an independent "first amendment right to 'academic freedom'": "While some of [his] comments arguably bear on economics and could be viewed as relevant to Martin's role as a teacher in motivating the interest of his students, his remarks *as a whole* are unrelated to economics and devoid of any educational function."

A leading 1990s case, *Bishop v. Aronov,* 926 F.2d 1066 (11th Cir. 1991), strikes a similar note while treading into new areas that involve religion as well as speech. An exercise physiology professor, as the court explained, "occasionally referred to his religious beliefs during instructional time. . . . Some of his references concerned his understanding of the creative force behind human physiology. Other statements involved brief explanations of a philosophical approach to problems and advice to students on coping with academic stresses." He also organized an optional after-class meeting, held shortly before the final examination, to discuss "Evidences of God in Human Physiology." But "[h]e never engaged in prayer, read passages from the Bible, handed out religious tracts, or arranged for guest speakers to lecture on a religious topic during instructional time." Some students nevertheless complained about the in-class comments and the optional meeting. The university responded by sending the professor a memo requiring that he discontinue "(1) the interjection of religious beliefs and/or preferences during instructional time periods and (2) the optional classes where a 'Christian Perspective' of an academic topic is delivered." The professor challenged the university's action as violating both his freedom of speech and his freedom of religion (see Section 1.6) under the First Amendment. The district court emphasized that "the university has created a forum for students and their professors to engage in a free interchange of ideas" and granted summary judgment for the professor (732 F. Supp. 1562 (N.D. Ala. 1990)). The U.S. Court of Appeals disagreed and upheld the university's actions.

With respect to the professor's free speech claims, the appellate court, like the majority in *Martin* (above), applied recent elementary/secondary education precedents that display considerable deference to educators (see *Hazelwood School District v. Kuhlmeier,* 484 U.S. 260 (1988)). Using *Kuhlmeier* especially, and without satisfactorily justifying its extension either to higher education in general or to faculty members (since *Kuhlmeier* concerned the free speech of *students),* the court asserted that administrators "do not offend the First Amendment by exercising editorial control over style and content of student [or professor] speech in school-sponsored expressive activities so long as their actions are reasonably related to legitimate pedagogical concerns." Addressing the academic freedom implication of its position, the court concluded:

> Though we are mindful of the invaluable role academic freedom plays in our
> public schools, particularly at the post-secondary level, we do not find support
> to conclude that academic freedom is an independent First Amendment right.
> And, in any event, we cannot supplant our discretion for that of the University.
> Federal judges should not be ersatz deans or educators. In this regard, we trust
> that the University will serve its own interests as well as those of its professors
> in pursuit of academic freedom [926 F.2d at 1075].

In upholding the university's authority in matters of course content as superior to that of the professor, the court accepted the validity and applicability of two particular institutional concerns underlying the university's decision to limit the professor's instructional activities. First was the university's "concern . . . that its courses be taught without personal religious bias unnecessarily infecting the teacher or the students." Second was the concern that optional classes not be conducted under circumstances that give "the impression of official sanction, which might [unduly pressure] students into attending and, at least for purposes of examination, into adopting the beliefs expressed" by the professor. Relying on these two concerns, against the backdrop of its general deference to the institution in curricular matters, the court concluded:

> In short, Dr. Bishop and the University disagree about a matter of content in the
> course he teaches. The University must have the final say in such a dispute.
> Though Dr. Bishop's sincerity cannot be doubted, his educational judgment can
> be questioned and redirected by the University when he is acting under its aus-
> pices as a course instructor, but not when he acts as an independent educator
> or researcher. The University's conclusions about course content must be
> allowed to hold sway over an individual professor's judgments. By its memo
> to Dr. Bishop, the University seeks to prevent him from presenting his religious
> viewpoint during instructional time, even to the extent that it represents his
> professional opinion about his subject matter. We have simply concluded that
> the University as an employer and educator can direct Dr. Bishop to refrain from
> expression of religious viewpoints in the classroom and like settings [926 F.2d
> at 1076–77].

Though the appellate court's opinion may seem overly deferential to the institution's prerogatives as employer, and insufficiently sensitive to the particular role of faculty academic freedom in higher education (see R. O'Neil, "*Bishop v. Aronov:* A Comment," 18 *J. Coll. & Univ. Law* 381 (1992)), at least the court was careful to demarcate limits on its holding. These limits are very important. Regarding the professor's classroom activities, the court clearly stated that the university's authority applies only "to the classroom speech of the professor, . . . wherever he purports to conduct a class for the university." "[T]he university has not suggested that [the professor] cannot hold his particular views; express them, on his own time, far and wide and to whomever will listen; or write and publish, no doubt authoritatively, on them; nor could it so prohibit him." The court also conceded that "[o]f course, if a student asks about [the professor's] religious views, he may fairly answer the question." Moreover, regarding the optional meetings, the court noted that "[t]he University has not suggested that [the professor] cannot organize such meetings, make notice of them on campus, or request University space to conduct them; nor could it so prohibit him." As long as the professor "makes it plain to his students that such meetings are not mandatory, not considered part of the coursework, and not related to grading, the university cannot prevent him from conducting such meetings."

The court rejected the professor's free exercise of religion claim in a single paragraph, noting that the professor "has made no true suggestion, much less demonstration, that any proscribed conduct of his impedes the practice of religion. . . . [T]he university's restrictions of him are not directed at his efforts to practice religion, per se, but rather are directed at his practice of teaching." The court likewise gave scant attention to the potential establishment clause ramifications of the case: "we do not reach the establishment clause questions raised by [the professor's] conduct. The university can restrict speech that falls short of an establishment violation, and we have already disposed of the university's restrictions of [the professor] under the free speech clause."[4]

Although the cases discussed earlier strongly support institutional authority over professors' instructional activities, it does not follow that institutions invariably prevail. The courts in *Wirsing, Martin,* and *Bishop,* in limiting their holdings, all suggest situations in which faculty members could prevail. In the following four cases, faculty members—and thus faculty academic freedom—actually did prevail over institutional authority.

In a 1996 case, *Cohen v. San Bernardino Valley College,* 92 F.3d 968 (9th Cir. 1996), reversing 883 F. Supp. 1407 (C.D. Cal. 1995), the appellate court used the constitutional "void for vagueness" doctrine to invalidate a college's attempt to discipline a teacher for classroom speech. The case provides the most pointed

[4]For an example of a classroom case in which the court did find an establishment clause violation, see *Lynch v. Indiana State University Board of Trustees,* 378 N.E.2d 900 (Ind. 1978).

discussion to date of the tension between faculty academic freedom and students' claims to be free from sexual harassment in the classroom.

The plaintiff, Cohen, was a tenured professor at San Bernardino Valley College. A student in his remedial English class was offended by his alleged use of vulgarities and obscenities in class, and his alleged focus on pornography. According to the court:

> One student in the class . . . became offended by Cohen's repeated focus on topics of a sexual nature, his use of profanity and vulgarities, and by his comments which she believed were directed intentionally at her and other female students in a humiliating and harassing manner. During this class Cohen began a class discussion on the issue of pornography and played the "devil's advocate" by asserting controversial viewpoints. Cohen has for many years typically assigned provocative essays such as Jonathan Swift's "A Modest Proposal" and discussed subjects such as obscenity, cannibalism, and consensual sex with children in a "devil's advocate" style. During classroom discussion on pornography in the remedial English class . . . Cohen stated in class that he wrote for Hustler and Playboy magazines and he read some articles out loud in class. Cohen concluded the class discussion by requiring his students to write essays defining pornography. When Cohen assigned the "Define Pornography" paper, [the student] asked for an alternative assignment but Cohen refused to give her one.
>
> [The student] stopped attending Cohen's class and received a failing grade for the semester [F.3d at 970].

The student filed a grievance against Cohen, alleging that his behavior violated the college's new sexual harassment policy, which provided that:

> Sexual harassment is defined as unwelcome sexual advances, requests for sexual favors, and other verbal, written, or physical conduct of a sexual nature.
> It includes, but is not limited to, circumstances in which: . . .
> (2) Such conduct has the purpose or effect of unreasonably interfering with an individual's academic performance or creating an intimidating, hostile, or offensive learning environment . . . [92 F.3d at 971].

After a hearing and appeal, the college found that Cohen had violated part (2) of the policy and ordered him to:

(1) [P]rovide a syllabus concerning his teaching style, purpose, content, and method to his students at the beginning of class and to the department chair . . . ;

(2) [A]ttend a sexual harassment seminar . . . ;

(3) [U]ndergo a formal evaluation procedure . . . ; and

(4) [B]ecome sensitive to the particular needs and backgrounds of his

> students, and to modify his teaching strategy when it becomes apparent
> that his techniques create a climate which impedes the students' ability
> to learn [92 F.3d at 971].

The district court rejected Cohen's claim that application of the sexual harassment policy violated his right to academic freedom:

> [T]he concept of academic freedom . . . is more clearly established in academic
> literature than it is in the courts . . . [and] judicial application is far from clear.
> [Furthermore], [a] review of the case law shows that, despite eloquent rhetoric
> on "academic freedom," the courts have declined to cede all classroom control
> to teachers [883 F. Supp. at 1412, 1414].

That court also rejected Cohen's claim that, under *Connick v. Myers,* 461 U.S. 138 (1983) (see Sec. 6.4.1, this volume), the college had violated his free speech rights as a public employee. The court divided Cohen's speech into two categories—(1) vulgarities and obscenities, and (2) comments related to the curriculum and focusing on pornography and other sexual topics. It concluded that the speech in the first category was not on matters of public concern but that the speech in the second category was on matters of public concern because Cohen did not speak merely to advance some purely private interest.

Thus, under *Connick,* the college could regulate the first type of speech but could regulate the second only if it could justify a restriction in terms of the speaker's job duties and the efficient operation of the college. The court agreed that the college had demonstrated sufficient justification:

> [A]lthough there is evidence in the record that Cohen's teaching style was effec-
> tive for at least some students, [and that] Cohen's colleagues have stated that he
> is a gifted and enthusiastic teacher . . . [whose] teaching style falls within the
> range of acceptable academic practice . . . the learning process for a number of
> students was hampered by the hostile learning environment created by Cohen.
> According to one peer evaluator who observed a class in which Cohen discussed
> . . . the topic of consensual sex with children, Cohen's "specific focus impedes
> academic success for some students" [883 F. Supp. at 1419].

In an important qualification, however, the court cautioned that:

> In applying a "hostile environment" prohibition, there is the danger that the most
> sensitive and the most easily offended students will be given veto power over
> class content and methodology. Good teaching should challenge students and
> at times make them uncomfortable. Colleges and universities . . . must avoid a
> tyranny of mediocrity in which all discourse is made bland enough to suit the
> tastes of all the students. However, colleges and universities must have the

power to require professors to effectively educate all segments of the university population, including those students unused to the rough and tumble of intellectual discussion. If colleges and universities lack this power, each classroom becomes a separate fiefdom in which the educational process is subject to professorial whim. Universities must be able to ensure that the more vulnerable as well as the more sophisticated students receive a suitable education. . . . Within the educational context, the university's mission is to effectively educate students, keeping in mind students' varying backgrounds and sensitivities. Furthermore, the university has the right to preclude disruption of this educational mission through the creation of a hostile learning environment. . . . The College's substantial interest in educating all students, not just the thick-skinned ones, warrants . . . requiring Cohen to put potential students on notice of his teaching methods [883 F. Supp. at 1419–20].

Moreover, "this ruling goes only to the narrow and reasonable discipline which the College seeks to impose. A case in which a professor is terminated or directly censored presents a far different balancing question. Further, the Court must avoid restricting creative and engaging teaching, even if some oversensitive students object to it" (883 F. Supp. at 1422).

On appeal, the United States Court of Appeals for the Ninth Circuit unanimously overruled the district's decision but did so on different grounds than those explored by the district court. The court emphasized that neither it nor the U.S. Supreme Court had yet determined the scope of First Amendment protection to be given to a professor's classroom speech. Rather than engage this analysis, the court focused its opinion and analysis on the vagueness of the college's sexual harassment policy and held that "the Policy's terms [are] unconstitutionally vague as applied to Cohen in this case." The court did not address whether or not the "college could punish speech of this nature if the policy were more precisely construed by authoritative interpretive guidelines or if the college were to adopt a clearer and more precise policy."

In its analysis, the appellate court noted three objections to vague college policies:

First, they trap the innocent by not providing fair warning. Second, they impermissibly delegate basic policy matters to low level officials for resolution on an ad hoc and subjective basis, with the attendant dangers of arbitrary and discriminatory application. Third, a vague policy discourages the exercise of first amendment academic freedoms [92 F.3d at 972].

Guided by these concerns, the court reasoned that:

Cohen's speech did not fall within the core region of sexual harassment as defined by the Policy. Instead, officials of the College, on an entirely ad hoc

basis, applied the Policy's nebulous outer reaches to punish teaching methods
that Cohen had used for many years. Regardless of what the intentions of the
officials of the College may have been, the consequences of their actions can
best be described as a legalistic ambush. Cohen was simply without any notice
that the Policy would be applied in such a way as to punish his longstanding
teaching style—a style which, until the College imposed punishment upon
Cohen under the Policy, had apparently been considered pedagogically sound
and within the bounds of teaching methodology permitted at the College
[92 F.3d at 972].

Since the appellate court's reasoning is different from the district court's, and
since the appellate court does not disagree with or address the issues that were
dispositive for the district court, the latter's analysis remains a useful illustration of how other courts may handle such issues when they arise under policies that are not unconstitutionally vague.

In *Parate v. Isibor,* 868 F.2d 821 (6th Cir. 1989), the court used the First
Amendment to limit the deference traditionally accorded administrative decisions about grading of students. The defendant, dean of the school in which the
plaintiff was a nontenured professor, ordered the plaintiff, over his objections,
to execute a grade-change form raising the final grade of one of his students.
The plaintiff argued that this incident, and several later incidents alleged to be
in retaliation for his lack of cooperation regarding the grade change, violated
his First Amendment academic freedom. Relying on the free speech clause, the
court agreed that "[b]ecause the assignment of a letter grade is symbolic communication intended to send a specific message to the student, the individual
professor's communicative act is entitled to some measure of First Amendment
protection." The court reasoned (without reliance on the *Pickering/Connick*
methodology) that:

[T]he professor's evaluation of her students and assignment of their grades is
central to the professor's teaching method. . . . Although the individual professor
does not escape the reasonable review of university officials in the assignment
of grades, she should remain free to decide, according to her own professional
judgment, what grades to assign and what grades not to assign. . . . Thus, the
individual professor may not be compelled, by university officials, to change a
grade that the professor previously assigned to her student. Because the individual professor's assignment of a letter grade is protected speech, the university
officials' action to compel the professor to alter that grade would severely
burden a protected activity [868 F.2d at 828].

Thus, the defendant's act of ordering the plaintiff to change the grade, contrary to the plaintiff's professional judgment, violated the First Amendment.
The court indicated, however, that had university administrators changed the

student's grade themselves, this action would not have violated the plaintiff's First Amendment rights. The protection that *Parate* accords to faculty grading and teaching methods is therefore quite narrow—more symbolic than real, perhaps, but nonetheless an important step away from the deference normally paid institutions in these matters. (For a more extended critique and criticism of *Parate,* see D. Sacken, "Making No Sense of Academic Freedom: *Parate v. Isibor,*" 56 *West's Educ. Law Rptr.* 1107 (Jan. 4, 1990).)

Another case, *DiBona v. Matthews,* 269 Cal. Rptr. 882 (Cal. Ct. App. 1990), illustrates that the First Amendment can provide a measure of protection for a professor's artistic and literary expression as it relates to the choice of class content and materials. In this case, the California Court of Appeals held that San Diego Community College District administrators violated a teacher's free speech rights when they canceled a play production and a drama class in which the controversial play was to have been performed. The teacher had selected a play entitled *Split Second* for performance by students enrolled in the drama class. The play was about a black police officer who, in the course of an arrest, shot a white suspect after the suspect had subjected him to racial slurs and epithets. The play's theme closely paralleled the facts of a criminal case that was then being tried in San Diego. The court determined that the college administrators had canceled the class because of the content of the play. While the First Amendment free speech clause did not completely prevent the college from considering the play's content in deciding to cancel the drama class, the court held that the college's particular reasons—that the religious community opposed the play and that the subject was controversial and sensitive—were not valid reasons under the First Amendment. Moreover, distinguishing the present case from those involving minors in elementary and secondary schools, the court held that the college could not cancel the drama class solely because of the vulgar language included in the play.

Yet another case, *McConnell v. Howard University,* 818 F.2d 58 (D.C. Cir. 1987), discussed further in Section 1.4.3.3, provides some academic freedom protection in the private institution context and signals another type of step away from the traditional deference that courts give to administrators' decisions regarding classroom behavior. The *McConnell* court raised questions about the university's handling of a conflict between professor and student and ordered the case remanded for a de novo trial. The case was a breach-of-contract action, and the court's reasoning suggests that, at least in circumstances like those being addressed, the contract claim may be a more promising vehicle for faculty members than the constitutional claims in cases such as *Hetrick* and *Clark.*

6.4.3. Academic Freedom in Research and Publication

Academic freedom protections extend to the research and publication activities of both faculty members and students. Just as with classroom issues, however, the faculty member's academic freedom may clash with the interests of some students. Since research and publication activities are apparently the most ardently protected of all faculty activities, faculty freedoms are more likely to prevail in this arena. The case of *Levin v. Harleston,* 770 F. Supp. 895, *affirmed,* 966 F.2d 85 (2d Cir. 1992), is illustrative.

In *Levin,* a philosophy professor at City College of the City University of New York had advocated in certain writings and publications that blacks are less intelligent on average than whites. In addition, he had opposed all use of affirmative action quotas. As a result of these writings, he became controversial on campus. Student groups staged demonstrations; documents affixed to his door were burned; and students distributed pamphlets outside his classroom. On several occasions, groups of students made so much noise outside his classrooms that he could not continue the class. The college's written regulations prohibited student demonstrations that have the effect of disrupting or obstructing teaching and research activities. Despite this regulation and the professor's repeated reports about the disruptions, the university took no action against the student demonstrators. The college did, however, take two affirmative steps to deal with the controversy regarding the professor. First, the college dean (one defendant) created "shadow sections" (alternative sections) for the professor's required introductory philosophy course. Second, the college president (another defendant) appointed an ad hoc faculty committee "to review the question of when speech both in and outside the classroom may go beyond the protection of academic freedom or become conduct unbecoming a member of the faculty."

To implement the shadow sections, the college dean sent letters to the professor's students, informing them of the option to enroll in these sections. The dean stated in the letter, however, that he was "aware of no evidence suggesting that Professor Levin's views on controversial matters have compromised his performance as an able teacher of Philosophy who is fair in his treatment of students." After implementation of the shadow sections, enrollment in the professor's classes decreased by one-half. The college had never before used such sections to allow students to avoid a particular professor because of his views.

To implement the ad hoc committee, the president charged the members "to specifically review information concerning Professor Michael Levin . . . and to include in its report its recommendations concerning what the response of the College should be." The language of the charge tracked certain language in college bylaws and professional contracts concerning the discipline of faculty members and the revocation of tenure. Three of the seven committee members had previously signed a faculty petition condemning the professor. Moreover, although the committee met more than ten times, it never extended the professor an opportunity to address it. The committee's report, as summarized by the district court, stated "that Professor Levin's writings constitute unprofessional and inappropriate conduct that harms the educational process at the college, and that the college has properly intervened to protect his students from his views by creating the shadow sections."

The professor sought declaratory and injunctive relief, claiming that the defendants' failure to enforce the student demonstration regulations, the creation of the shadow sections, and the operation of the ad hoc committee violated his rights under the federal Constitution's free speech and due process clauses. After trial, the district court issued a lengthy opinion agreeing with the professor.

Relying on *Keyishian* (Section 6.4.1), the court noted the chilling and stigmatizing effect of the ad hoc committee's activities, as demonstrated by the fact that the professor declined over twenty invitations to speak or write about his controversial views. The court thus held that the professor had an objective and reasonable basis to fear losing his position, and that the effects on him were "exactly that predicted in *Keyishian*. . . . Professor Levin was forced to 'stay as far away as possible from utterances or acts which might jeopardize his living.'" To determine whether this infringement on the professor's speech was nonetheless legitimate, the court then undertook a *Pickering/Connick* analysis. It held that there was "no question" that the professor's speech was "protected expression," since his writings and statements addressed matters that were "quintessentially 'issues of public importance.'" The only justification advanced by the defendants for the ad hoc committee and shadow sections was the need to protect the professor's students from harm that could accrue "if they thought, because of the expression of his views, that he might expect less of them or grade them unfairly." The court, however, rejected this justification because City College had presented no evidence at trial to support it. Consequently, the trial court granted injunctive relief, compelling the defendants to investigate the alleged violations of the college's student demonstration regulations and prohibiting the defendants from any further use of the shadow sections or the ad hoc committee.

The federal appeals court disagreed with the district court's conclusion regarding the failure to enforce the student demonstration regulations, since the college generally had not enforced these regulations and there was no evidence that "the college treated student demonstrations directed at Professor Levin any differently than other student demonstrations." The defendants' inaction could thus not be considered a violation of any of the professor's constitutional rights.

The appellate court generally agreed, however, with the district court's conclusion regarding the shadow sections and the ad hoc committee. The court noted that the "formation of the alternative sections would not be unlawful if done to further a legitimate educational purpose that outweighed the infringement on Professor Levin's First Amendment rights." But the defendants had presented no evidence to support their contention that the professor's expression of his ideas outside the classroom harmed the educational process within the classroom. In fact, "none of Professor Levin's students had ever complained of unfair treatment on the basis of race." The court concluded that the defendants' "encouragement of the continued erosion in the size of Professor Levin's class if he does not mend his extracurricular ways is the antithesis of freedom of expression." The appellate court also agreed that the operation of the ad hoc committee had a "chilling effect" on the professor's speech and thus violated his First Amendment rights. Affirming that "governmental action which falls short of direct prohibition on speech may violate the First Amendment by chilling the free exercise of speech," the court determined that, when the president "deliberately formed the committee's inquiry into Levin's conduct to mirror the contractual standard for disciplinary action, he conveyed the threat that Levin would be dismissed if he continued voicing his racial theories."

To implement its conclusions, the appellate court vacated the portion of the trial court's injunction ordering the defendants to investigate the alleged violations of the demonstration regulations. It affirmed the portion of the injunction prohibiting the defendants from using the shadow sections. Regarding the ad hoc committee, the appellate court modified the relief ordered by the trial court. Since the ad hoc committee had recommended no disciplinary action and had no further investigations or disciplinary proceedings pending, the injunction was unnecessary. It was sufficient to issue an order that merely declared the unconstitutionality of the defendants' use of the committee, since such declaratory relief would make clear that "disciplinary proceedings, or the threat thereof, predicated solely upon Levin's continued expression of his views outside of the classroom" would violate his free speech rights.

Levin is an important case for several reasons. It painstakingly chronicles a major academic freedom dispute centering on faculty publication activities; it demonstrates a relationship between academic freedom and the phenomenon of "political correctness";[5] and it strongly supports faculty academic freedom in research by using the federal Constitution as a basic source of protection. The courts' opinions do not break new legal ground, however, since they use established principles and precedents applicable to public employees generally and do not emphasize the unique circumstances of academic freedom on the college campus. Nor is the decision, once limited by its special and unique facts, as broadly applicable as may at first appear. The case dealt with traditionally protected speech—writing and outside publication expressing opinions on matters of public concern—and not with classroom lectures, teaching methods, or

---

[5]According to the trial court, "[t]his case raises serious constitutional questions that go to the heart of the current national debate on what has come to be demonimated as 'political correctness' in speech and thought on the campuses of the nation's colleges and universities" (footnote omitted). See generally P. Berman (ed.), *Debating P.C.: The Controversy over Political Correctness on College Campuses* (Dell, 1992).

course materials, or with intramural speech on institutional affairs. Not only is such speech given the highest protection, but the defendants produced no evidence that the professor's writings and views had any adverse impact on his classroom performance or his treatment of students. Nor did the defendants claim that the professor's statements were false. The college had never before created such shadow sections and had advanced no "legitimate educational interest" in using them in this circumstance. Finally, the numerous procedural flaws in the establishment and operation of the ad hoc committee greatly supported, if only circumstantially, the professor's claims that his constitutional rights were being chilled.

SELECTED ANNOTATED BIBLIOGRAPHY

Sec. 6.1 (Grades, Credits, and Degrees)

Kibler, William L., Nuss, Elizabeth M., Peterson, Brent G., & Pavela, Gary. *Academic Integrity and Student Development* (College Administration Publications, 1988). Examines student academic dishonesty from several perspectives: student development, methods for preventing academic dishonesty, and the legal issues related to student dishonesty. A model code of academic integrity and case studies are included in the appendix.

LaMorte, Michael W., & Meadows, Robert B. "Educationally Sound Due Process in Academic Affairs," 8 *J. Law & Educ.* 197 (1979). Analyzes cases up to and including *Board of Curators of the University of Missouri v. Horowitz,* (discussed in Section 7.3.3). Provides extended discussion of educationally and legally sound practices in student evaluation, academic dismissals, and awarding of degrees.

Schweitzer, Thomas A. "'Academic Challenge' Cases: Should Judicial Review Extend to Academic Evaluations of Students?" 41 *American U. L. Rev.* 267 (1992). Compares judicial review of student discipline cases with "academic challenge" cases (in which the student challenges an academic decision made by the institution). Provides a thorough and penetrating analysis of a variety of challenges to academic decisions, including degree revocation.

Zirkel, Perry A., & Hugel, Paul S. "Academic Misguidance in Colleges and Universities," 56 *West's Educ. Law Rptr.* 709 (1989). Discusses the legal and practical implications of erroneous or inadequate academic advice by faculty and administrators. Reviews four legal theories used by students to seek damages when they are harmed, allegedly by "misguidance," and concludes that most outcomes favor the institution, not the student.

See Jennings entry for Section 3.2, especially at 204–15.

Sec. 6.2 Sexual Harassment by Faculty

Schneider, Ronna G. "Sexual Harassment and Higher Education," 65 *Tex. L. Rev.* 525 (1987). Reviews the federal laws prohibiting sexual harassment and their regulations, including both Title VII and Title IX. Author compares the enforcement of Title IX with that of Title VI, and discusses the U.S. Supreme Court's ruling in *Meritor Savings Bank*. Provides a thorough legal analysis of sexual harassment theory.

Sec. 6.4 (Student Academic Freedom)

"The Academy in the Courts: A Symposium on Academic Freedom," 16 *U. Cal. Davis L. Rev.* 831 (1983). A two-part article. (The second part discusses "Discrimination in the Academy.") The first part contains three articles on First Amendment issues: Robert O'Neil, "Scientific Research and the First Amendment: An Academic Privilege"; Katheryn Katz, "The First Amendment's Protection of Expressive Activity in the University Classroom: A Constitutional Myth"; and Martin Malin & Robert Ladenson, "University Faculty Members' Right to Dissent: Toward a Unified Theory of Contractual and Constitutional Protection." Symposium also includes a foreword by John Poulos, which briefly recounts the history of institutional academic autonomy and reviews each article's critique of this concept.

Byrne, J. Peter. "Academic Freedom: A 'Special Concern of the First Amendment,'" 99 *Yale L.J.* 251 (1989). Develops a framework and foundation for the academic freedom that is protected by the First Amendment. Traces the development of academic freedom as construed by both academics and the courts and then espouses a new theory of "academic freedom based on the traditional legal status of academic institutions and on the appropriate role of the judiciary in academic affairs."

DeChiara, Peter. "The Need for Universities to Have Rules on Consensual Sexual Relationships Between Faculty Members and Students," 21 *Columbia J. Law & Social Problems* 137 (1988). Reviews the issue of faculty-student sexual relationships and possible responses by universities. Reports on the author's survey of thirty-eight institutions. Discusses constitutional right-to-privacy implications of regulation. Author asserts that regulation is needed because consensual sexual relationships between faculty and students can create problems of pressured decisions, sexual harassment, and favoritism.

Menand, Louis (ed.). *Academic Freedom and the Future of the Academy* (University of Chicago Press, forthcoming). A collection of lectures by noted scholars from various disciplines, who debate the cutting-edge issues of academic freedom. This collection is the product of a lecture series sponsored by the AAUP.

Olivas, Michael. "Reflections on Professional Academic Freedom: Second Thoughts on the Third 'Essential Freedom,'" 45 *Stanford L. Rev.* 1835 (1993). Presents the author's perspective on faculty academic freedom, with particular emphasis on conflicts that arise in the classroom. Considers and interrelates professional norms, First Amendment case law, and recent scholarly commentary.

O'Neil, Robert. *Is Academic Freedom a Constitutional Right?* Monograph 84–7 (Institute for Higher Education Law and Governance, University of Houston, 1984), reprinted (under title "Academic Freedom and the Constitution") in 11 *J. Coll. & Univ. Law* 275 (1984). An argument on behalf of the continued vitality of constitutionally based claims of academic freedom. Examines the current status of and conceptual difficulties regarding such claims and makes suggestions for faculty members and other academics to consider before submitting such claims to the courts for vindication.

"Symposium on Academic Freedom," 66 *Tex. L. Rev.* no. 7 (1988). Contains eighteen commentaries and responses preceded by a lengthy foreword by Julius Getman and Jacqueline Mintz. Commentaries include, among others, (1) Walter P. Metzger, "Profession and Constitution: Two Definitions of Academic Freedom in America"; (2) Matthew W. Finkin, "Intramural Speech, Academic Freedom, and the First Amendment"; (3) Charles E. Curran, "Academic Freedom and Catholic Universities"; (4) Lonnie D. Kliever, "Academic Freedom and Church-Affiliated Universities"; (5) Phoebe A. Haddon, "Academic Freedom and Governance: A Call for Increased Dialogue and Diversity"; (6) Rebecca S. Eisenberg, "Academic Freedom and Academic Values in Sponsored Research"; (7) David M. Rabban, "Does Academic Freedom Limit Faculty Autonomy?"; and (8) Douglas Laycock and Susan E. Waelbroeck, "Academic Freedom and the Free Exercise of Religion."

Van Alstyne, William W. (special ed.). "Freedom and Tenure in the Academy: The Fiftieth Anniversary of the 1940 Statement of Principles," 53 *Law & Contemporary Problems* no. 3 (1990); also published as a separate book, *Freedom and Tenure in the Academy* (Duke University Press 1993). A symposium containing nine articles: (1) Walter P. Metzger, "The 1940 Statement of Principles on Academic Freedom and Tenure"; (2) William W. Van Alstyne, "Academic Freedom and the First Amendment in the Supreme Court of the United States: An Unhurried Historical Review"; (3) Judith Jarvis Thomson, "Ideology and Faculty Selection"; (4) Robert M. O'Neil, "Artistic Freedom and Academic Freedom"; (5) Rodney A. Smolla, "Academic Freedom, Hate Speech, and the Idea of a University"; (6) David M. Rabban, "A Functional Analysis of 'Individual' and 'Institutional' Academic Freedom Under the First Amendment"; (7) Michael W. McConnell, "Academic Freedom in Religious Colleges and Universities"; (8) Ralph S. Brown and Jordan E. Kurland, "Academic Tenure and Academic Freedom"; and (9) Matthew W. Finkin, "A Higher Order of Liberty in the Workplace: Academic Freedom and Tenure in the Vortex of Employment Practices and Law." Also includes a helpful bibliography of sources: Janet Sinder, "Academic Freedom: A Bibliography," listing 174 journal articles, books, and reports; and three appendices containing the 1915 AAUP "General Report," the 1940 "Statement of Principles," and the 1967 "Joint Statement on Rights and Freedoms of Students."

See Finkin entry for Section 11.5.

CHAPTER SEVEN

The Disciplinary Process

SEC. 7.1. DISCIPLINARY AND GRIEVANCE SYSTEMS

Colleges and universities develop codes of student conduct (discussed in Section 7.1.2) and standards of academic performance (discussed in Section 6.1), and expect students to conform to those codes and standards. In this chapter, we discuss student challenges to institutional attempts to discipline them for violations of these codes and standards. First, Section 7.1 presents the guidelines for disciplinary and grievance systems that afford students appropriate statutory and constitutional protections. Section 7.2 analyzes the courts' responses to student challenges to colleges' disciplinary rules and regulations, emphasizing the different standards that public and private institutions must meet. Section 7.3 reviews the guidelines developed by courts reviewing challenges to the *procedures* used by colleges when they seek to discipline or expel a student for either social or academic misconduct.

7.1.1. Establishment of Systems

Postsecondary institutions have extensive authority to regulate both the academic and the nonacademic activities and behavior of students. This power is summarized in an often-cited judicial statement:

> In the field of discipline, scholastic and behavioral, an institution may establish
> any standards reasonably relevant to the lawful missions, processes, and functions

of the institution. It is not a lawful mission, process, or function of . . . [a public] institution to prohibit the exercise of a right guaranteed by the Constitution or a law of the United States to a member of the academic community in the circumstances. Therefore, such prohibitions are not reasonably relevant to any lawful mission, process, or function of . . . [a public] institution.

Standards so established may apply to student behavior on and off the campus when relevant to any lawful mission, process, or function of the institution. By such standards of student conduct the institution may prohibit any action or omission which impairs, interferes with, or obstructs the missions, processes, and functions of the institution.

Standards so established may require scholastic attainments higher than the average of the population and may require superior ethical and moral behavior. In establishing standards of behavior, the institution is not limited to the standards or the forms of criminal laws ["General Order on Judicial Standards of Procedure and Substance in Review of Student Discipline in Tax-Supported Institutions of Higher Education," 45 F.R.D. 133, 145 (W.D. Mo. 1968)].

It is not enough, however, for an administrator to understand the extent and limits of institutional authority. The administrator must also skillfully implement this authority through various systems for the resolution of disputes concerning students. Such systems should include procedures for processing and resolving disputes, substantive standards or rules to guide the judgment of the persons responsible for dispute resolution, and mechanisms and penalties with which decisions are enforced. The procedures, standards, and enforcement provisions should be written and made available to all students. Dispute-resolution systems, in their totality, should create a two-way street; that is, they should provide for complaints by students against other members of the academic community as well as complaints against students by other members of the academic community.

The choice of structures for resolving disputes depends on policy decisions made by administrators, preferably in consultation with representatives of various interests within the institution. Should a single system cover both academic and nonacademic disputes, or should there be separate systems for separate kinds of disputes? Should there be a separate disciplinary system for students, or should there be a broader system covering other members of the academic community as well? Will the systems use specific and detailed standards of student conduct, or will they operate on the basis of more general rules and policies? To what extent will students participate in establishing the rules governing their conduct? To what extent will students, rather than administrators or faculty members, be expected to assume responsibility for reporting or investigating violations of student conduct codes or honor codes? To what extent will students take part in adjudicating complaints by or against students? What kinds of sanctions can be levied against students found to have been engaged in misconduct?

Can they be fined, made to do volunteer work on campus, expelled from the institution, given a failing grade in a course or denied a degree, or required to make restitution? To what extent will the president, provost, or board of trustees retain final authority to review decisions concerning student misconduct?

Devices for creating dispute-resolution systems may include honor codes or codes of academic ethics; codes of student conduct; bills of rights, or rights and responsibilities, for students or for the entire academic community; the use of various legislative bodies, such as a student or university senate; a formal judiciary system for resolving disputes concerning students; the establishment of grievance mechanisms for students, such as an ombudsman system or a grievance committee; and mediation processes that provide an alternative or supplement to judiciary and grievance mechanisms. On most campuses, security guards or some other campus law enforcement system will also be involved in the resolution of disputes and regulation of student behavior.

Occasionally, specific procedures or mechanisms will be required by law. Constitutional due process, for instance, requires the use of certain procedures before a student is suspended or dismissed from a public institution (see Section 7.3). The Title IX regulations (this volume, Section 12.4.3) and the Family Educational Rights and Privacy Act (FERPA) regulations (this volume, Section 3.3) require both public and private institutions to establish certain procedures for resolving disputes under those particular statutes. Even when specific mechanisms or procedures are not required by law, the procedures or standards adopted by an institution will sometimes be affected by existing law. A public institution's rules regarding student protest, for instance, must comply with First Amendment strictures protecting freedom of speech (Section 8.3). And its rules regarding administrative access to or search of student rooms, and the investigatory techniques of its campus police, must comply with Fourth Amendment strictures regarding search and seizure (Section 5.1.2). Though an understanding of the law is thus crucial to the establishment of disciplinary and grievance systems, the law by no means rigidly controls their form and operation. To a large extent, the kind of system adopted will depend on the institution's notions of good administrative practice.

Fair and accessible dispute-resolution systems, besides being useful administrative tools in their own right, can also insulate institutions from lawsuits. Students who feel that their arguments or grievances will be fairly considered within the institution may forgo resort to the courts. If students ignore internal mechanisms in favor of immediate judicial action, the courts may refer the students to the institution. Under the "exhaustion-of-remedies" doctrine (see Section 1.4.2), courts may require plaintiffs to exhaust available remedies within the institution before bringing the complaint to court. In *Pfaff v. Columbia-Greene Community College*, 472 N.Y.S.2d 480 (N.Y. App. Div. 1984), for example, the New York courts dismissed the complaint of a student who had sued her college, contesting a C grade entered in a course, because the college had an internal appeal process and the student "failed to show that pursuit of the available administrative appeal would have been fruitless."

7.1.2. Codes of Student Conduct

Three major issues are involved in the drafting or revision of codes of student conduct: the type of conduct the code will encompass, the procedures to be used when infractions of the code are alleged, and the sanctions for code violations.

Codes of student conduct typically proscribe both academic and social misconduct, whether or not the misconduct violates civil or criminal laws, and whether or not the misconduct occurs on campus. Academic misconduct may include plagiarism, cheating, forgery, or alteration of institutional records. In their review of sanctions for academic misconduct, and of the degree of procedural protection required for students accused of such misconduct, courts have been relatively deferential (see Section 7.3.3). For a comprehensive discussion of academic dishonesty, including preventive strategies, disciplinary systems, and a model code of academic integrity, see W. Kibler, E. Nuss, B. Peterson, & G. Pavela, *Academic Integrity and Student Development* (College Administration Publications, 1988).

Social misconduct may include disruption of an institutional function (including teaching and research) and abusive or hazing behavior (but limitations on speech may run afoul of free speech protections, as discussed in Section 8.3). It may also encompass conduct that occurs off-campus, particularly if the misconduct also violates criminal law and the institution can demonstrate that the restrictions are directly related to its educational mission or the campus community's welfare (*Krasnow v. Virginia Polytechnic Institute,* 551 F.2d 591 (4th Cir. 1977); *Wallace v. Florida A&M University,* 433 So. 2d 600 (Fla. Dist. Ct. App. 1983)).

Sanctions for code violations may range from a warning to expulsion, with various intermediate penalties such as suspension or public service requirements. Students who are expelled may seek injunctive relief under the theory that they will be irreparably harmed; some courts have ruled that sanctions short of expulsion would not be appropriate for injunctive relief (*Boehm v. University of Pennsylvania School of Veterinary Medicine,* 573 A.2d 575 (Pa. Super. Ct. 1990), but see *Jones v. Board of Governors,* 557 F. Supp. 263 (W.D.N.C.), *affirmed,* 704 F.2d 713 (4th Cir. 1983)). Students at public institutions may assert constitutional claims related to deprivation of a property and/or liberty interest (see Section 2.2.2), while students at private institutions may file actions based on contract law.

If a code of conduct defines the offenses for which a student may be penalized by a public institution, that code must comply with constitutional due process requirements concerning vagueness. The requirement is a minimal one:

the code must be clear enough for students to understand the standards with which their conduct must comply, and it must not be susceptible to arbitrary enforcement. A public institution's code of conduct must also comply with the constitutional doctrine of overbreadth in any area where the code could affect First Amendment rights. Basically, this doctrine requires that the code not be drawn so broadly and vaguely as to include protected First Amendment activity along with behavior subject to legitimate regulation (see Sections 8.1.2 and 8.3). Finally, a public institution's student conduct code must comply with a general requirement of evenhandedness; that is, the code cannot arbitrarily discriminate in the range and types of penalties, or in the procedural safeguards, afforded various classes of offenders. *Paine v. Board of Regents of the University of Texas System*, 355 F. Supp. 199 (W.D. Tex. 1972), *affirmed per curiam*, 474 F.2d 1397 (5th Cir. 1973), concerned such discriminatory practices. The institution had given students convicted of drug offenses a harsher penalty and fewer safeguards than it gave to all other code offenders, including those charged with equally serious offenses. The court held that this differential treatment violated the equal protection and due process clauses.

As noted in Section 7.1.1, codes of conduct can apply to the off-campus actions as well as the on-campus activity of students. But the extension of a code to off-campus activity can pose significant legal and policy questions. In the *Paine* case discussed earlier, the institution automatically suspended students who had been put on probation by the criminal courts for possession of marijuana. The court invalidated the suspensions partly because they were based on an off-campus occurrence (court probation) that did not automatically establish a threat to the institution. And in *Thomas v. Granville Board of Education*, 607 F.2d 1043 (2d Cir. 1979), a high school case with pertinent ramifications for postsecondary education, several students had been suspended for their off-campus activities in publishing a newspaper of sexual satire. The court also invalidated these suspensions, according the students the same First Amendment rights as citizens generally and emphasizing that "our willingness to grant school officials substantial autonomy within their academic domain rests in part on the confinement of that power within the metes and bounds of the school itself." (For a contrary view, in which the court upheld the authority of a public college to discipline its students for off-campus violations of laws dealing with controlled substances, see *Hart v. Ferris State College*, 557 F. Supp. 1379 (W.D. Mich. 1983).)

To avoid problems in this area, administrators should ascertain that an off-campus act has a direct detrimental impact on the institution's educational functions before using that act as a basis for disciplining students. See, for example, the opinion of the attorney general of Maryland upholding the right of the state university to discipline "for off-campus conduct detrimental to the interests of the institution, subject to the fundamental constitutional safeguards that apply to all disciplinary actions by educational officials" (74 *Opinions of the Attorney General* 1 (Md.) (1989), Opinion No. 89–002).

Private institutions not subject to the state action doctrine (see Section 1.5.2) are not constitutionally required to follow these principles regarding student codes. Yet the principles reflect basic notions of fairness, which can be critical components of good administrative practice; thus, administrators of private institutions may wish to use them as policy guides in formulating their codes.

A question that colleges and universities, irrespective of control, may wish to consider is whether the disciplinary code should apply to student organizations as well as to individual students. Should students be required to assume collective responsibility for the actions of an organization, and should the university impose sanctions, such as withdrawal of institutional recognition, on organizations that violate the disciplinary code? For a model student disciplinary code that includes student organizations within its ambit, see E. Stoner & K. Cerminara, "Harnessing the 'Spirit of Insubordination': A Model Student Disciplinary Code," 17 *J. Coll. & Univ. Law* 89 (1990).

7.1.3. Judicial Systems

Judicial systems that adjudicate complaints of student misconduct must be very sensitive to procedural safeguards. The membership of judicial bodies, the procedures they use, the extent to which their proceedings are open to the academic community, the sanctions they may impose, the methods by which they may initiate proceedings against students, and provisions for appealing their decisions should be set out in writing and made generally available within the institution.

Whenever the charge could result in a punishment as serious as suspension, a public institution's judicial system must provide the procedures required by the due process clause (see Section 7.3.2). The focal point of these procedures is the hearing at which the accused student may present evidence and argument concerning the charge. The institution, however, may wish to include preliminary stages in its judicial process for more informal disposition of complaints against students. The system may provide for negotiations between the student and the complaining party, for instance, or for preliminary conferences before designated representatives of the judicial system. Full due process safeguards need not be provided at every such preliminary stage. *Andrews v. Knowlton*, 509 F.2d 898 (2d Cir. 1975), dealt with the procedures required at a stage preceding an honor code hearing. The court held that due process procedures were not required at that time because it was not a "critical stage" that could have a "prejudicial impact" on the final determination of whether the student violated the honor code. Thus, administrators have broad authority to construct informal preliminary proceedings—as long as a student's participation in such stages does not adversely affect his or her ability to defend the case in the final stage.

A question receiving increased attention is whether the judicial system will permit the accused student to have an attorney present. Several models are possible: (1) Neither the college nor the student will have attorneys. (2) Attorneys may be present to advise the student but may not participate by asking questions or making statements. (3) Attorneys may be present and participate fully in questioning and making opening and closing statements. A federal appellate court was asked to rule on whether a judicial system at Northern Illinois University that followed the second model—attorney present but a nonparticipant—violated a student's due process rights. In *Osteen v. Henley,* 13 F.3d 221 (7th Cir. 1993), the court wrote:

> Even if a student has a constitutional right to *consult* counsel . . . we don't think he is entitled to be represented in the sense of having a lawyer who is permitted to examine or cross-examine witnesses, to submit and object to documents, to address the tribunal, and otherwise to perform the traditional function of a trial lawyer. To recognize such a right would force student disciplinary proceedings into the mold of adversary litigation. The university would have to hire its own lawyer to prosecute these cases and no doubt lawyers would also be dragged in—from the law faculty or elsewhere—to serve as judges. The cost and complexity of such proceedings would be increased, to the detriment of discipline as well as of the university's fisc [13 F.3d at 225].

The court then, citing *Mathews v. Eldridge,* 424 U.S. 319 (1976), balanced the cost of permitting lawyers to participate against the risk of harm to students if lawyers were excluded. Concluding that the risk of harm to students was "trivial," the court refused to rule that attorneys were a student's constitutional right.

Occasionally, a campus judicial proceeding may involve an incident that is also the subject of criminal court proceedings. The same student may thus be charged in both forums at the same time. In such circumstances, the postsecondary institution is not legally required to defer to the criminal courts by canceling or postponing its proceedings. As held in *Paine* (Section 7.1.2) and other cases, even if the institution is public, such dual prosecution is not double jeopardy because the two proceedings impose different kinds of punishment to protect different kinds of state interests. The Constitution's double jeopardy clause applies only to successive criminal prosecutions for the same offense. Nor will the existence of two separate proceedings necessarily violate the student's privilege against self-incrimination. In several cases—for instance, *Grossner v. Trustees of Columbia University,* 287 F. Supp. 535 (S.D.N.Y. 1968)—courts have rejected student requests to stay campus proceedings on this ground pending the outcome of criminal trials. One court emphasized, however, that if students in campus proceedings "are forced to incriminate themselves . . . and if that testimony is offered against them in subsequent criminal proceedings, they can then invoke . . . [Supreme Court precedents] in opposition to the offer" (*Furutani v.*

Ewigleben, 297 F. Supp. 1163 (N.D. Cal. 1969)). In another case, the court rejected as speculative a student's claim that his being identified in campus disciplinary proceedings would jeopardize the fairness of his criminal trial (*Nzuve v. Castleton State College*, 335 A.2d 321 (Vt. 1975)).

While neither double jeopardy nor self-incrimination need tie the administrator's hands, administrators may nevertheless choose, for policy reasons, to delay or dismiss particular campus proceedings when the same incident is in the criminal courts. It is possible that the criminal proceedings will adequately protect the institution's interests. Or, as *Furutani* and *Nzuve* suggest, student testimony at a campus proceeding could create evidentiary problems for the criminal court.

If a public institution proceeds with its campus action while the student is subject to charges still pending in criminal court, the institution may have to permit the student to have a lawyer with him during the campus proceedings. In *Gabrilowitz v. Newman*, 582 F.2d 100 (1st Cir. 1978), a student challenged a University of Rhode Island rule that prohibited the presence of legal counsel at campus disciplinary hearings. The student obtained an injunction prohibiting the university from conducting the hearing without permitting the student the advice of counsel. The appellate court, affirming the lower court's injunction order, held that when a criminal case based on the same conduct giving rise to the disciplinary proceeding is pending in the courts, "the denial to [the student] of the right to have a lawyer of his own choice to consult with and advise him during the disciplinary proceeding would deprive [him] of due process of law."

The court emphasized that the student was requesting the assistance of counsel to consult with and advise him during the hearing, not to conduct the hearing on the student's behalf. Such assistance was critical to the student because of the delicacy of the legal situation he faced:

> Were the appellee to testify in the disciplinary proceeding, his statement could be used as evidence in the criminal case, either to impeach or as an admission if he did not choose to testify. Appellee contends that he is, therefore, impaled on the horns of a legal dilemma: if he mounts a full defense at the disciplinary hearing without the assistance of counsel and testifies on his own behalf, he might jeopardize his defense in the criminal case; if he fails to fully defend himself or chooses not to testify at all, he risks loss of the college degree he is within weeks of receiving, and his reputation will be seriously blemished [582 F.2d at 103].

If a public institution delays campus proceedings and then uses a conviction in the criminal proceedings as the basis for its campus action, the institution must take care to protect the student's due process rights. In the *Paine* case, a university rule required the automatic two-year suspension of any student convicted of a narcotics offense. The court held that the students must be given an opportunity to show that, despite their conviction and probation, they posed "no substantial threat of influencing other students to use, possess, or sell drugs or narcotics." Thus, a criminal conviction does not automatically provide the basis for suspension; administrators should still ascertain that the conviction has a detrimental impact on the campus, and the affected student should have the opportunity to make a contrary showing.

For analysis of this issue in the context of acquaintance rape cases, see P. Burling, *Acquaintance Rape on Campus: A Model for Institutional Response* (National Association of College and University Attorneys, 1993). See also *Statement Concerning Campus Disciplinary Procedures and the Criminal Law in Sexual Assault Cases* (National Association of Student Personnel Administrators, Mar. 1993).

SEC. 7.2. DISCIPLINARY RULES AND REGULATIONS

Postsecondary institutions customarily have rules of conduct or behavior that students are expected to follow. It has become increasingly common to commit these rules to writing and embody them in codes of conduct binding on all students (see Section 7.1.2). Although the trend toward written codes is a sound one, legally speaking, because it gives students fairer notice of what is expected from them and often results in a better-conceived and administered system, written rules also provide a specific target to aim at in a lawsuit.

Students have challenged institutional attempts to discipline them by attacking the validity of the rule they allegedly violated or by attacking the nature of the disciplinary proceeding that determined the occurrence of the alleged violation. This section discusses student challenges to the validity of institutional rules and regulations; Section 7.3 discusses challenges to the procedures used by colleges to determine whether, in fact, violations have occurred.

7.2.1. Public Institutions

In public institutions, students frequently contend that the rules of conduct violate some specific guarantee of the Bill of Rights, as made applicable to state institutions by the Fourteenth Amendment (see Section 1.5.2). These situations, the most numerous of which implicate the free speech and press clauses of the First Amendment, are discussed in Section 2.2.2 and various other sections of this book. In other situations, the contention is a more general one—that the rule is so vague that its enforcement violates due process; that is (as noted in Section 7.1.2), the rule is unconstitutionally "vague" or "void for vagueness."

Soglin v. Kauffman, 418 F.2d 163 (7th Cir. 1969), is illustrative. The University of Wisconsin had expelled students for attempting to block access to an off-campus recruiter as a protest against the Vietnam War. The university had charged the students under a rule prohibiting "misconduct" and argued in court that it had inherent power to discipline, which need not be exercised through specific rules. Both the U.S. District Court and the U.S. Court of Appeals held that the misconduct policy was unconstitutionally vague. The appellate court reasoned:

> No one disputes the power of the university to protect itself by means of disciplinary action against disruptive students. Power to punish and the rules defining the exercise of that power are not, however, identical. Power alone does not supply the standards needed to determine its application to types of behavior or specific instances of "misconduct." As Professor Fuller has observed: "The first desideratum of a system for subjecting human conduct to the governance of rules is an obvious one: there must be rules" (L. Fuller, *The Morality of Law,* p. 46 (rev. ed., [Yale University Press,] 1969)). The proposition that government officers, including school administrators, must act in accord with rules in meting out discipline is so fundamental that its validity tends to be assumed by courts engaged in assessing the propriety of specific regulations. . . . The [doctrine] of vagueness . . . , already applied in academic contexts, [presupposes] the existence of rules whose coherence and boundaries may be questioned. . . . These same considerations also dictate that the rules embodying standards of discipline be contained in properly promulgated regulations. University administrators are not immune from these requirements of due process in imposing sanctions. Consequently, in the present case, the disciplinary proceedings must fail to the extent that the defendant officials of the University of Wisconsin did not base those proceedings on the students' disregard of university standards of conduct expressed in reasonably clear and narrow rules.
>
> . . . The use of "misconduct" as a standard in imposing the penalties threatened here must therefore fall for vagueness. The inadequacy of the rule is apparent on its face. It contains no clues which could assist a student, an administrator, or a reviewing judge in determining whether conduct not transgressing statutes is susceptible to punishment by the university as "misconduct."
>
> Pursuant to appropriate rule or regulation, the university has the power to maintain order by suspension or expulsion of disruptive students. Requiring that such sanctions be administered in accord with preexisting rules does not place an unwarranted burden upon university administration. We do not require university codes of conduct to satisfy the same rigorous standards as criminal statutes. We only hold that expulsion and prolonged suspension may not be imposed on students by a university simply on the basis of allegations of "misconduct" without reference to any preexisting rule which supplies an adequate guide [418 F.2d at 167–68].

While similar language about vagueness is often found in other court opinions, the actual result in *Soglin* (the invalidation of the rule) is unusual. Most university rules subjected to judicial tests of vagueness have survived, sometimes because the rule at issue is less egregious than the "misconduct" rule in *Soglin,* sometimes because a court accepts the "inherent power to discipline" argument raised by the *Soglin* defendants and declines to undertake any real vagueness analysis, and sometimes because the student conduct at issue was so contrary to the judges' own standards of decency that they tended to ignore the defects in the rules in light of the obvious "defect" in behavior. *Esteban v. Central Missouri State College,* 415 F.2d 1077 (8th Cir. 1969), the case most often cited in opposition to *Soglin,* reveals all three of these distinctions. In this case, students contested their suspension under a regulation prohibiting "participation in mass gatherings which might be considered as unruly or unlawful." In upholding the suspension, the court emphasized the need for "flexibility and reasonable breadth, rather than meticulous specificity, in college regulations relating to conduct" and recognized the institution's "latitude and discretion in its formulation of rules and regulations." The approach has often been followed in later cases—for instance, in *Jenkins v. Louisiana State Board of Education,* 506 F.2d 992 (5th Cir. 1975), where the court upheld a series of regulations dealing with disorderly assembly and disturbing the peace on campus.

Although the judicial trend suggests that most rules and regulations will be upheld, administrators should not thus assume that they have a free hand in promulgating codes of conduct. *Soglin* signals the institution's vulnerability where it has no written rules at all or where the rule provides no standard to guide conduct. And even the *Esteban* court warned, "We do not hold that any college regulation, however loosely framed, is necessarily valid." To avoid such pitfalls, disciplinary rules should provide standards sufficient to guide both the students in their conduct and the disciplinarians in their decision making. A rule will likely pass judicial scrutiny if the standard "conveys sufficiently definite warning as to the proscribed conduct when measured by common understanding and practices" (*Sword v. Fox,* 446 F.2d 1091 (4th Cir. 1971), upholding a regulation that "demonstrations are forbidden in any areas of the health center, inside any buildings, and congregating in the locations of fire hydrants"). Regulations need not be drafted by a lawyer—in fact, heavy student involvement in drafting may be valuable to ensure an expression of their "common understanding"—but it would usually be wise to have a lawyer play a general advisory role in the process.

Once the rules are promulgated, institutional officials have some latitude in interpreting and applying them, as long as the interpretation is reasonable. In *Board of Education of Rogers, Ark. v. McCluskey,* 458 U.S. 966 (1982), a public school board's interpretation of one of its rules was challenged as unreasonable. The board had held that its rule against students being under the influence of "controlled substances" included alcoholic beverages. The U.S. Supreme Court, quoting *Wood v. Strickland* (see Section 2.4.3, this volume), asserted that "federal courts [are] not authorized to construe school regulations" unless the board's interpretation "is so extreme as to be a violation of due process" (458 U.S. at 969–70).

7.2.2. Private Institutions

Private institutions, not being subject to federal constitutional constraints (see Section 1.5.2), have even more latitude than public institutions do in promulgating disciplinary rules. Courts are likely to recognize a broad right to make and enforce rules that is inherent in the private student-institution relationship or to find such a right implied in some contractual relationship between student and school. Under this broad construction, private institutional rules will not be held to specificity standards such as those in *Soglin* (discussed in Section 7.2.1). Thus, in *Dehaan v. Brandeis University,* 150 F. Supp. 626 (D. Mass. 1957), the court upheld the plaintiff's suspension for misconduct under a policy where the school "reserves the right to sever the connection of any student with the university for appropriate reason"; and in *Carr v. St. John's University, New York,* 231 N.Y.S.2d 410 (N.Y. App. Div. 1962), *affirmed,* 187 N.E.2d 18 (N.Y. 1962), the courts upheld the dismissal of four students for off-campus conduct under a regulation providing that "in conformity with the ideals of Christian education and conduct, the university reserves the right to dismiss a student at any time on whatever grounds the university judges advisable."

Despite the breadth of such cases, the private school administrator, like his or her public counterpart, should not assume a legally free hand in promulgating disciplinary rules. Under one developing theory or another (see Section 1.5.3), courts can now be expected to protect private school students from clearly arbitrary disciplinary actions. When a school has disciplinary rules, courts may overturn administrators' actions taken in derogation of the rules. And when there is no rule or the applicable rule provides no standard of behavior, courts may overturn suspensions for conduct that the student could not reasonably have known was wrong. Thus, in *Slaughter v. Brigham Young University,* 514 F.2d 622 (10th Cir. 1975), though the court upheld the expulsion of a graduate student for dishonesty under the student code of conduct, it first asked "whether the . . . [expulsion] was arbitrary" and indicated that the university's findings would be accorded a presumption of correctness only "if the regulations concerned are reasonable [and] if they are known to the student or should have been." To avoid such situations, private institutions may want to adhere to much the same guidelines for promulgating rules as are suggested above for public institutions, despite the fact that they are not required by law to do so.

7.2.3. Disciplining Students with Psychiatric Illnesses

Students with mental or psychological disabilities are protected against discrimination by the Rehabilitation Act and the Americans with Disabilities Act (see this volume, Sections 4.1.4.3 and 12.4.4). Yet behavior resulting from a student's mental illness may disrupt campus activities, or the student may be dangerous to herself or to other students, faculty, or administrators. Opinion is divided among educators and mental health professionals as to whether students suffering from mental disorders who violate the institution's code of student conduct should be subject to the regular disciplinary procedure or should be given a "medical withdrawal" if their presence on campus becomes disruptive or dangerous.

Several issues arise in connection with mentally ill students who are disruptive or dangerous. If campus counseling personnel have gained information from a student indicating that he or she is potentially dangerous, the teachings of *Tarasoff v. Regents of the University of California* (Section 2.4.1) and its progeny (as well as many state statutes codifying *Tarasoff)* regarding a duty to warn the potential target(s) of the violence would apply. If administrators or faculty know that the student is potentially dangerous and the student subsequently injures someone, negligence claims based on the foreseeability of harm may arise (Section 2.3.1.1). On the other hand, potential violations of the federal Family Educational Rights and Privacy Act (discussed in Section 3.3.1) could also be implicated if institutional officials warned a student's family or others of suicide threats or other serious medical or psychological conditions.

Given the potential for constitutional claims at public institutions and discrimination claims at all institutions, administrators who are considering disciplinary action against a student with a mental or emotional disorder should provide due process protections (see Section 7.3.2). If the student has violated the institution's code of conduct and is competent to participate in the hearing, some experts recommend subjecting the student to the same disciplinary proceedings that a student without a mental or emotional impairment would receive (see, for example, G. Pavela, *The Dismissal of Students with Mental Disorders* (College Administration Publications, 1985)). For an analysis of the issues facing public colleges and universities in these circumstances, and recommended actions, see J. DiScala, S. G. Olswang, & C. S. Niccolls, "College and University Responses to the Emotionally or Mentally Impaired Student," 19 *J. Coll. & Univ. Law* 17 (1992).

SEC. 7.3. PROCEDURES FOR SUSPENSION, DISMISSAL, AND OTHER SANCTIONS

7.3.1. General Principles

As Sections 6.1 and 7.2 indicate, both public and private postsecondary institutions have the clear right to dismiss, suspend, or impose lesser sanctions on students for behavioral misconduct or academic deficiency. But just as that right is limited by the principles set out in those sections, so it is also circumscribed by a body of procedural requirements that institutions must follow in effecting disciplinary or academic sanctions. These procedural requirements tend to be more specific and substantial than the requirements set out earlier, although they vary depending on whether behavior or academics is involved and whether the institution is public or private (see Section 1.5.2).

At the threshold level, whenever an institution has established procedures that apply to the imposition of sanctions, the law will usually require that they be followed. In *Woody v. Burns,* 188 So. 2d 56 (Fla. 1966), for example, the court invalidated an expulsion from a public institution because a faculty committee had "circumvented . . . [the] duly authorized [disciplinary] committee and arrogated unto itself the authority of imposing its own penalty for appellant's misconduct." And in *Tedeschi v. Wagner College,* 49 N.Y.2d 652 (N.Y. 1980), New York's highest court invalidated a suspension from a private institution, holding that "when a university has adopted a rule or guideline establishing the procedure to be followed in relation to suspension or expulsion, that procedure must be substantially observed."

There are three exceptions, however, to this "follow-the-rules" principle. An institution may be excused from following its own procedures if the student knowingly and freely waives his or her right to them, as in *Yench v. Stockmar,* 483 F.2d 820 (10th Cir. 1973), where the student neither requested that the published procedures be followed nor objected when they were not. Second, deviations from established procedures may be excused when they do not disadvantage the student, as in *Winnick v. Manning,* 460 F.2d 545 (2d Cir. 1972), where the student contested the school's use of a panel other than that required by the rules, but the court held that the "deviations were minor ones and did not affect the fundamental fairness of the hearing." And third, if an institution provides more elaborate protections than constitutionally required, failure to provide nonrequired protections may not imply constitutional violations (see Section 7.3.3).

7.3.2. Public Institutions: Disciplinary Sanctions

State institutions may be subject to state administrative procedure acts, state board of higher education rules, or other state statutes or administrative regulations specifying particular procedures for suspensions or expulsions. In *Moresco v. Clark,* 473 N.Y.S.2d 843 (N.Y. App. Div. 1984), the court refused to apply New York State's Administrative Procedure Act to a suspension proceeding at SUNY-Cortland; but in *Mull v. Oregon Institute of Technology,* 538 P.2d 87 (Or. 1975), the court applied that state's administrative procedure statutes to a suspension for misconduct and remanded the case to the college with instructions to enter findings of fact and conclusions of law as required by one of the statutory provisions.

The primary external source of procedural requirements for public institutions, however, is the due process clause of the federal Constitution, which prohibits the government from depriving an individual of life, liberty, or property without certain procedural protections. Since the early 1960s, the concept of procedural due process has been one of the primary legal forces shaping the administration of postsecondary education. For purposes of due process analysis, courts typically assume, without deciding, that a student has a property interest in continued enrollment at a public institution (see, for example, *Marin v. University of Puerto Rico*, 377 F. Supp. 613, 622 (D.P.R. 1974)). One court stopped short of finding a property interest but said that the Fourteenth Amendment "gives rights to a student who faces expulsion for misconduct at a tax-supported college or university" (*Henderson State University v. Spadoni*, 848 S.W.2d 951 (Ark. Ct. App. 1993)). As did the court in *Marin*, the U.S. Supreme Court has assumed a property interest in continued enrollment in a public institution (for example, in *Ewing* and *Horowitz*, discussed in Sections 6.1.1 and 7.3.3 respectively), but has not yet directly ruled on this point.

A landmark 1961 case on suspension procedures, *Dixon v. Alabama State Board of Education*, 294 F.2d 150 (5th Cir. 1961), is still very instructive. Several black students at Alabama State College had been expelled during a period of intense civil rights activity in Montgomery, Alabama. The students, supported by the NAACP, sued the state board, and the court faced the question "whether [the] due process [clause of the Fourteenth Amendment] requires notice and some opportunity for hearing before students at a tax-supported college are expelled for misconduct." On appeal, this question was answered in the affirmative, with the court establishing standards by which to measure the adequacy of a public institution's expulsion procedures:

> The notice should contain a statement of the specific charges and grounds which, if proven, would justify expulsion under the regulations of the board of education. The nature of the hearing should vary depending upon the circumstances of the particular case. The case before us requires something more than an informal interview with an administrative authority of the college. By its nature, a charge of misconduct, as opposed to a failure to meet the scholastic standards of the college, depends upon a collection of the facts concerning the charged misconduct, easily colored by the point of view of the witnesses. In such circumstances, a hearing which gives the board or the administrative authorities of the college an opportunity to hear both sides in considerable detail is best suited to protect the rights of all involved. This is not to imply that a full-dress judicial hearing, with the right to cross-examine witnesses, is required. Such a hearing, with the attending publicity and disturbance of college activities, might be detrimental to the college's educational atmosphere and impractical to carry out. Nevertheless, the rudiments of an adversary proceeding may be preserved without encroaching upon the interests of the college. In the instant case, the student should be given the names of the witnesses against him and an oral or written report on the facts to which each witness testifies. He should also be given the opportunity to present to the board, or at least to an administrative

official of the college, his own defense against the charges and to produce either oral testimony or written affidavits of witnesses in his behalf. If the hearing is not before the board directly, the results and findings of the hearing should be presented in a report open to the student's inspection. If these rudimentary elements of fair play are followed in a case of misconduct of this particular type, we feel that the requirements of due process of law will have been fulfilled [294 F.2d at 158–59].

Since the *Dixon* case, courts at all levels have continued to recognize and extend the due process safeguards available to students charged by college officials with misconduct. Such safeguards must now be provided for all students in publicly supported schools, not only before expulsion, as in *Dixon,* but before suspension and other serious disciplinary action as well. In 1975, the U.S. Supreme Court itself recognized the vitality and clear national applicability of such developments when it held that even a secondary school student faced with a suspension of less than ten days is entitled to "*some* kind of notice and . . . *some* kind of hearing" (*Goss v. Lopez,* 419 U.S. 565, 579 (1975)).

Although the Court in *Goss* was not willing to afford students the right to a full-blown adversary hearing (involving cross-examination, written transcripts, and representation by counsel), it set out minimal requirements for compliance with the due process clause. The Court said:

We do not believe that school authorities must be totally free from notice and hearing requirements. . . . [T]he student [must] be given oral or written notice of the charges against him and, if he denies them, an explanation of the evidence the authorities have and an opportunity to present his side of the story. The [Due Process] Clause requires at least these rudimentary precautions against unfair or mistaken findings of misconduct and arbitrary exclusion from school [419 U.S. at 581].

In cases subsequent to *Goss,* most courts have applied these "minimal" procedural standards and, for the most part, have ruled in favor of the college.

Probably the case that has set forth due process requirements in greatest detail and, consequently, at the highest level of protection, is *Esteban v. Central Missouri State College,* 277 F. Supp. 649 (W.D. Mo. 1967) (see also later litigation in this case, discussed earlier in Section 7.2.1). The plaintiffs had been suspended for two semesters for engaging in protest demonstrations. The lower court held that the students had not been accorded procedural due process and ordered the school to provide the following protections for them: (1) a written statement of the charges, for each student, made available at least ten days before the hearing; (2) a hearing before the person(s) having power to expel or suspend; (3) the opportunity for advance inspection of any affidavits or exhibits the college intends to submit at the hearing; (4) the right to bring counsel to the hearing to advise them (but not to question witnesses); (5) the opportunity to present their own version of the facts, by personal statements as well as affidavits and witnesses; (6) the right to hear evidence against them and question (personally, not through counsel) adverse witnesses; (7) a determination of the facts of each case by the hearing officer, solely on the basis of the evidence presented at the hearing; (8) a written statement of the hearing officer's findings of fact; and (9) the right, at their own expense, to make a record of the hearing.

The judicial imposition of specific due process requirements rankles many administrators. By and large, courts have been sufficiently sensitive to avoid such detail in favor of administrative flexibility (see, for example, *Moresco v. Clark,* 473 N.Y.S.2d 843 (N.Y. App. Div. 1984); *Henson v. Honor Committee of the University of Virginia,* 719 F.2d 69 (4th Cir. 1983), discussed in Section 7.3.2.2). Yet for the internal guidance of an administrator responsible for disciplinary procedures, the *Esteban* requirements provide a useful checklist. The listed items not only suggest the outer limits of what a court might require but also identify those procedures most often considered valuable for ascertaining facts where they are in dispute. Within this framework of concerns, the constitutional focus remains on the notice-and-opportunity-for-hearing concept of *Dixon.*

Although the federal courts have not required the type of protection provided at formal judicial hearings, deprivations of basic procedural rights can result in judicial rejection of an institution's disciplinary decision. In *Weideman v. SUNY College at Cortland,* 592 N.Y.S.2d 99 (N.Y. App. Div. 1992), the court annulled the college's dismissal of a student who had been accused of cheating on an examination and ordered a new hearing. Specifically, the court found these procedural defects:

1. Evidence was introduced at the hearing of which the student was unaware.

2. The student was not provided the five-day written notice required by the student handbook about evidence supporting the charges against him and had no opportunity to defend against that evidence.

3. The hearing panel contacted a college witness after the hearing and obtained additional evidence without notifying the student.

4. The student was given insufficient notice of the date of the hearing and the appeal process.

5. The student was given insufficient notice (one day) of his right to appeal.

6. The student's attorney had advised college officials of these violations, but the letter had been ignored.

7.3.2.1. Notice. Notice should be given of both the conduct with which the student is charged and the rule or policy that allegedly proscribes the conduct. The charges need not be drawn with the specificity of a criminal indictment, but they should be "in sufficient detail to fairly enable . . . [the student] to present a defense" at the hearing (*Jenkins v. Louisiana State Board of Education,* 506 F.2d 992 (5th Cir. 1975)), holding notice in a suspension case to be adequate, particularly in light of information provided by the defendant subsequent to the original notice). Factual allegations not enumerated in the notice may be developed at the hearing if the student could reasonably have expected them to be included.

There is no clear constitutional requirement concerning how much advance notice the student must have of the charges. As little as two days before the hearing has been held adequate (*Jones v. Tennessee State Board of Education,* 279 F. Supp. 190 (M.D. Tenn. 1968), *affirmed,* 407 F.2d 834 (6th Cir. 1969); see also *Nash v. Auburn University,* 812 F.2d 655 (11th Cir. 1987)). *Esteban* required ten days, however, and in most other cases the time has been longer than two days. In general, courts handle this issue case by case, asking whether the amount of time was fair under all the circumstances.

7.3.2.2. Hearing. The minimum requirement is that the hearing provide students with an opportunity to speak in their own defense and explain their side of the story. Since due process apparently does not require an open or a public hearing, the institution has the discretion to close or partially close the hearing or to leave the choice to the accused student. But courts usually will accord students the right to hear the evidence against them and to present oral testimony or, at minimum, written statements from witnesses. Formal rules of evidence need not be followed. Cross-examination, the right to counsel, the right to a transcript, and an appellate procedure have generally not been constitutional essentials, but where institutions have voluntarily provided these procedures, courts have often cited them approvingly as enhancers of the hearing's fairness. In upholding the validity of the University of Virginia's student-operated honor system, for example, the court in *Henson v. Honor Committee of the University of Virginia,* 719 F.2d 69 (4th Cir. 1983), reasoned that:

> The university's honor system provides the accused student with an impressive array of procedural protections. The student, for example, receives what is essentially an indictment, specifying both the charges and the factual allegations supporting them (Virginia Honor Code, Art. III §C(l)). He has a right to a hearing before a committee of his peers. He is entitled, at no personal cost, to have a student lawyer represent his interests at all critical stages in the proceedings. He may also retain a practicing attorney to assist in his defense, although the attorney can assume no active role in the honor trial itself (Art. III §C(1)). The individuals who brought the charges must face the student at the hearing and state the basis of their allegations (Art. III §D(2)). They, in turn, must submit to cross-

examination by the student, or his designated student counsel, and by the members of the hearing committee. The student then has the right to present evidence in opposition to the charges and to offer witnesses for the sole purpose of bolstering his character (Art. III §D(5)(a)). He may, if he chooses, demand that the hearing be conducted in public, where impartial observers can make an independent assessment of the proceeding's fairness (Art. VIII §E). If, after hearing the evidence, four fifths (4/5) of the committee members find the student guilty beyond a reasonable doubt, he has the right to appeal the decision to a five-member board comprised of members of the student government (Art. V). This board is empowered to review the record of the honor trial and to grant new trials when, in its judgment, the correct procedures were not followed or the evidentiary findings of the trial committee were deficient.

In some respects, these procedures concededly fall short of the stringent protections afforded the criminal defendant; that is not, however, a defect of constitutional dimension. . . . The Supreme Court has made it plain that "the judicial model of an evidentiary hearing is neither a required, nor even the most effective, method of decision making in all circumstances" [quoting *Mathews v. Eldridge*, 424 U.S. 319, 348 (1976)]. . . .

It is true that Henson [the student plaintiff] was not permitted to have a practicing attorney conduct his defense, but this is not a right generally available to students facing disciplinary charges (*Gabrilowitz v. Newman*, 582 F.2d 100, 104 (1st Cir. 1978)). Henson was provided with two student lawyers, who consulted extensively with his personally retained attorney at all critical stages of the proceedings. The due process clause would impose no greater obligations on the university than it placed on itself in conducting its disciplinary proceedings [719 F.2d at 73–74].

When the conduct with which the student is charged in the disciplinary proceeding is also the subject of a criminal court proceeding, the due process obligations of the institution will likely increase. Since the student then faces additional risks and strategic problems, some of the procedures usually left to the institution's discretion may become constitutional essentials. In *Gabrilowitz v. Newman*, 582 F.2d 100 (1st Cir. 1978) (discussed in Section 7.1.3), for example, the court required that the institution allow the student to have a professional lawyer present to advise him during the disciplinary hearing.

The person(s) presiding over the disciplinary proceedings and the person(s) with authority to make the final decision must decide the case on the basis of the evidence presented and must, of course, weigh the evidence impartially. Generally, the student must show malice, bias, or conflict of interest on the part of the hearing officer or panel member before a court will make a finding of partiality. In *Blanton v. State University of New York*, 489 F.2d 377 (2d Cir. 1973), the court held that—at least where students had a right of appeal—due process was not violated when a dean who had witnessed the incident at issue also sat on the hearing committee. And in *Jones v. Tennessee State Board of Education*,

279 F. Supp. 190 (M.D. Tenn. 1968), *affirmed*, 407 F.2d 834 (6th Cir. 1969), the court even permitted a member of the hearing committee to give evidence against the accused student, in the absence of proof of malice or personal interest. But other courts may be less hospitable to such practices, and it would be wise to avoid them whenever possible.

The hearing must normally take place before the suspension or expulsion goes into effect. The leading case on this point has been *Stricklin v. Regents of the University of Wisconsin,* 297 F. Supp. 416 (W.D. Wis. 1969), where the court limited the use of interim suspensions, pending a final decision, to situations where "the appropriate university authority has reasonable cause to believe that danger will be present if a student is permitted to remain on campus pending a decision following a full hearing." The court also noted that "an interim suspension may not be imposed without a prior preliminary hearing, unless it can be shown that it is impossible or unreasonably difficult to accord it prior to an interim suspension," in which case "procedural due process requires that . . . [the student] be provided such a preliminary hearing at the earliest practical time." These requirements would protect a student from being "suspended in ex parte proceedings . . . without any opportunity, however brief and however limited, to persuade the suspending authority that there is a case of mistaken identity or that there was extreme provocation or that there is some other compelling justification for withholding or terminating the interim suspension." While case law on these points has been sparse, the U.S. Supreme Court's 1975 ruling in *Goss v. Lopez* affirms that at least part of *Stricklin* applies nationwide:

> As a general rule notice and hearing should precede removal of the student from school. We agree . . . , however, that there are recurring situations in which prior notice and hearing cannot be insisted upon. Students whose presence poses a continuing danger to persons or property or an ongoing threat of disrupting the academic process may be immediately removed from school . . . [and notice and hearing] should follow as soon as practicable [419 U.S. at 583 (1975)].

The extent to which the notice and hearing procedures set forth above apply to disciplinary sanctions less severe than suspension or expulsion is unclear. On the one hand, a pre-*Goss* case, *Yench v. Stockmar,* 483 F.2d 820 (10th Cir. 1973), held the due process clause inapplicable to disciplinary probation cases in which students are not required to interrupt their education. On the other hand, any penalty that deprives the student of substantial educational benefits or seriously affects his or her reputation and employment prospects is, under *Goss,* arguably subject to at least the "rudimentary" protections of due process. In general, an institution should provide increasingly more formal and comprehensive due process procedures as the severity of the potential penalty increases and should gear its procedures to the maximum penalty that can be meted out in each type of proceeding it authorizes.

A federal appellate court considered the question of the specific protections necessary to satisfy the Constitution's due process clause. In *Gorman v. University of Rhode island,* 837 F.2d 7 (1st Cir. 1988), a student suspended for a number of disciplinary infractions charged that the university's disciplinary proceedings were defective in several respects. He asserted that two students on the student-faculty University Board on Student Conduct were biased against him because of earlier encounters; that he had been denied the assistance of counsel at the hearing; that he had been denied a transcript of the hearing; and that the director of student life had served as adviser to the board and also had prepared a record of the hearing, thereby compromising the board's independence.

Finding no evidence that Gorman was denied a fair hearing, the court commented:

> [T]he courts ought not to extol form over substance, and impose on educational institutions all the procedural requirements of a common law criminal trial. The question presented is not whether the hearing was ideal, or whether its procedure could have been better. In all cases the inquiry is whether, under the particular circumstances presented, the hearing was fair, and accorded the individual the essential elements of due process [837 F.2d at 16].

When students are accused of academic misconduct, such as plagiarism or cheating, conduct issues become mixed with academic evaluation issues (compare the *Napolitano* case in Section 7.3.4). Courts typically require some due process protections for students suspended or dismissed for academic misconduct, but not elaborate ones. For example, in *Easley v. University of Michigan Board of Regents,* 853 F.2d 1351 (6th Cir. 1988), the court found no constitutional deprivation in a law school's decision to suspend a student for one year after finding that he had plagiarized a course paper. The school had given the student an opportunity to respond to the charges against him, and the court also determined that the student had no property interest in his law degree because he had not completed the degree requirements.

But in *Jaksa v. Regents of the University of Michigan,* 597 F. Supp. 1245 (E.D. Mich. 1984), *affirmed without opinion,* 787 F.2d 590 (6th Cir. 1986), a trial court noted that a student challenging a one-semester suspension for cheating on a final examination had both a liberty interest and a property interest in continuing his education at the university. Applying the procedural requirements of *Goss v. Lopez,* the court ruled that the student had been given a meaningful opportunity to present his version of the situation to the hearing panel. It rejected the student's claims that due process was violated because he was not allowed to have a representative at the hearing, was not given a transcript, could not confront the student who charged him with cheating, and was not provided with a detailed statement of reasons by the hearing panel.

7.3.3. Public Institutions: Academic Sanctions

As noted earlier, the Fourteenth Amendment's due process clause also applies to students facing suspension or dismissal from publicly supported schools for deficient academic performance. But even though academic dismissals may be even more damaging to students than disciplinary dismissals, due process affords substantially less protection to students in the former situation. Courts grant less protection because they recognize that they are less competent to review academic evaluative judgments than factually based determinations of misconduct and that hearings and the attendant formalities of witnesses and evidence are less meaningful in reviewing grading than in determining misconduct.

Gaspar v. Bruton, 513 F.2d 843 (10th Cir. 1975), was apparently the first case to provide any procedural due process rights to a student facing an academic suspension or dismissal. The plaintiff was a forty-four-year-old high school graduate pursuing practical nurse training in a vocational-technical school. After completing more than two-thirds of the program, she was dismissed for deficient performance in clinical training. She had been on probation for two months owing to such deficiencies and had been informed that she would be dismissed if they were not corrected. When they were not, she was notified of dismissal in a conference with the superintendent and some of her instructors and was subsequently offered a second conference and an opportunity to question other staff and faculty members who had participated in the dismissal decision.

The trial and appellate courts upheld the dismissal, rejecting the student's contention that before dismissal she should have been confronted with and allowed to challenge the evidence supporting the dismissal and permitted to present evidence in her defense. Although the appellate court recognized a "property interest" in continued attendance, it held that school officials had only minimal due process obligations in this context:

> Gaspar was provided much more due process than that which we hold must be accorded in cases involving academic termination or suspension. We hold that school authorities, in order to satisfy due process prior to termination or suspension of a student for deficiencies in meeting minimum academic performance, need only advise that student with respect to such deficiencies in any form. All that is required is that the student be made aware prior to termination of his failure or impending failure to meet those standards [513 F.2d at 850–51].

More significant protection was afforded in *Greenhill v. Bailey*, 519 F.2d 5 (8th Cir. 1975), where another U.S. Court of Appeals invalidated a medical student's dismissal because he had not been accorded procedural due process. The school had dismissed the student for "lack of intellectual ability or insufficient preparation" and had conveyed that information to the liaison committee of the Association of American Medical Colleges, where it was available to all other medical schools. The court ruled that "the action by the school in denigrating Green-hill's intellectual ability, as distinguished from his performance, deprived him of a significant interest in liberty, for it admittedly 'imposed on him a stigma or other disability that foreclose[s] his freedom to take advantage of other . . . opportunities'" (*Board of Regents v. Roth,* 408 U.S. at 573, 92 S. Ct. at 2707). In such circumstances, due process required more than the school had provided:

> At the very least, Greenhill should have been notified in writing of the alleged deficiency in his intellectual ability, since this reason for his dismissal would potentially stigmatize his future as a medical student elsewhere, and should have been accorded an opportunity to appear personally to contest such allegation.
>
> We stop short, however, of requiring full trial-type procedures. . . . But an "informal give-and-take" between the student and the administrative body dismissing him—and foreclosing his opportunity to gain admission at all comparable institutions—would not unduly burden the educational process and would, at least, give the student "the opportunity to characterize his conduct and put it in what he deems proper context" (*Goss v. Lopez,* 419 U.S. at 584, 95 S. Ct. at 741) [519 F.2d at 9].

The next year, the same U.S. Court of Appeals extended its *Greenhill* ruling in another medical school case, *Horowitz v. Board of Curators of the University of Missouri,* 538 F.2d 1317 (8th Cir. 1976). But on appeal, the U.S. Supreme Court clipped this court's wings and put an apparent halt to the development of procedural due process in academic disputes (*Board of Curators of the University of Missouri v. Horowitz,* 435 U.S. 78 (1978)). The university had dismissed the student, who had received excellent grades on written exams, for deficiencies in clinical performance, peer and patient relations, and personal hygiene. After several faculty members repeatedly expressed dissatisfaction with her clinical work, the school's council on evaluation recommended that Horowitz not be allowed to graduate on time and that, "absent radical improvement" in the remainder of the year, she be dropped from the program. She was then allowed to take a special set of oral and practical exams, administered by practicing physicians in the area, as a means of appealing the council's determination. After receiving the results of these exams, the council reaffirmed its recommendation. At the end of the year, after receiving further clinical reports on Horowitz, the council recommended that she be dropped from school. The school's coordinating committee, then the dean, and finally the provost for health sciences affirmed the decision.

Though there was no evidence that the reasons for the dismissal were conveyed to the liaison committee, as in *Greenhill,* the appellate court held that "Horowitz's dismissal from medical school will make it difficult or impossible for her to obtain employment in a medically related field or to enter another medical school." The court concluded that dismissal would so stigmatize the student as to deprive her of liberty under the Fourteenth Amendment and that, under the circumstances, the university could not dismiss the student without providing "a hearing before the decision-making body or bodies, at which she shall have an opportunity to rebut the evidence being relied upon for her dismissal and accorded all other procedural due process rights."

The Supreme Court found it unnecessary to decide whether Horowitz had been deprived of a liberty or property interest. Even assuming she had, Horowitz had no right to a hearing:

> Respondent has been awarded at least as much due process as the Fourteenth Amendment requires. The school fully informed respondent of the faculty's dissatisfaction with her clinical progress and the danger that this posed to timely graduation and continued enrollment. The ultimate decision to dismiss respondent was careful and deliberate. These procedures were sufficient under the due process clause of the Fourteenth Amendment. We agree with the district court that respondent was afforded full procedural due process by the [school]. In fact, the court is of the opinion, and so finds, that the school went beyond [constitutionally required] procedural due process by affording [respondent] the opportunity to be examined by seven independent physicians in order to be absolutely certain that their grading of the [respondent] in her medical skills was correct [435 U.S. at 85].

The Court relied on the distinction between academic and disciplinary cases that lower courts had developed in cases prior to *Horowitz,* finding that distinction to be consistent with its own due process pronouncements, especially in *Goss v. Lopez* (Section 7.3.2):

> The Court of Appeals apparently read *Goss* as requiring some type of formal hearing at which respondent could defend her academic ability and performance. . . . But we have frequently emphasized that "the very nature of due process negates any concept of inflexible procedures universally applicable to every imaginable situation" (*Cafeteria Workers v. McElroy,* 367 U.S. 886, 895 (1961)). The need for flexibility is well illustrated by the significant difference between the failure of a student to meet academic standards and the violation by a student of valid rules of conduct. This difference calls for far less stringent procedural requirements in the case of an academic dismissal. . . .
>
> A school is an academic institution, not a courtroom or administrative hearing room. In *Goss,* this Court felt that suspensions of students for disciplinary reasons have a sufficient resemblance to traditional judicial and administrative fact finding to call for a "hearing" before the relevant school authority. . . .
>
> Academic evaluations of a student, in contrast to disciplinary determinations, bear little resemblance to the judicial and administrative fact-finding proceedings to which we have traditionally attached a full hearing requirement. In *Goss,*

the school's decision to suspend the students rested on factual conclusions that the individual students had participated in demonstrations that had disrupted classes, attacked a police officer, or caused physical damage to school property. The requirement of a hearing, where the student could present his side of the factual issue, could under such circumstances "provide a meaningful hedge against erroneous action." The decision to dismiss respondent, by comparison, rested on the academic judgment of school officials that she did not have the necessary clinical ability to perform adequately as a medical doctor and was making insufficient progress toward that goal. Such a judgment is by its nature more subjective and evaluative than the typical factual questions presented in the average disciplinary decision. Like the decision of an individual professor as to the proper grade for a student in his course, the determination whether to dismiss a student for academic reasons requires an expert evaluation of cumulative information and is not readily adapted to the procedural tools of judicial or administrative decision making [435 U.S. at 85–90].

Horowitz signals the Court's lack of receptivity to procedural requirements for academic dismissals. Clearly, an adversary hearing is not required. Nor are all the procedures used by the university in *Horowitz* required, since the Court suggested that Horowitz received more due process than she was entitled to. But the Court's opinion does not say that no due process is required. Institutions apparently must afford some minimal protections, the exact character of which is not yet clear. Due process probably requires the institution to inform the student of the inadequacies in performance and their consequences on academic standing. Apparently, due process also generally requires that the institution's decision making be "careful and deliberate." For the former requirements, courts are likely to be lenient on how much information or explanation the student must be given and also on how far in advance of formal dismissal the student must be notified. For the latter requirement, courts are likely to be very flexible, not demanding any particular procedure but rather accepting any decision-making process that, overall, supports reasoned judgments concerning academic quality. Even these minimal requirements would be imposed on institutions only when their academic judgments infringe on a student's "liberty" or "property" interest, and it is not yet clear what constitutes such infringements in the post-secondary context.

Since courts attach markedly different due process requirements to academic sanctions than to disciplinary sanctions, it is crucial to be able to place particular cases in one category or the other. The characterization required is not always easy. The *Horowitz* case is a good example. The student's dismissal was not a typical case of inadequate scholarship, such as poor grades on written exams; rather, she was dismissed at least partly for inadequate peer and patient relations and personal hygiene. It is arguable that such a decision involves "fact-finding," as in a disciplinary case, more than an "evaluative," "academic judgment."

Indeed, the Court split on this issue: five judges applied the "academic" label to the case, two judges applied the "disciplinary" label or argued that no labeling was appropriate, and two judges refused to determine either which label to apply or "whether such a distinction is relevant." For an analysis of *Horowitz* and a criticism of its deference to the university's academic judgment, see W. G. Buss, "Easy Cases Make Bad Law: Academic Expulsion and the Uncertain Law of Due Process," 65 *Iowa L. Rev.* 1 (1979).

Another illustration of the categorization difficulty is provided by a pre-*Horowitz* case, *Brookins v. Bonnell,* 362 F. Supp. 379 (E.D. Pa. 1973). A nursing student was dismissed from a community college for (1) failing to submit a state-required physical examination report, (2) failing to inform the college that he had previously attended another nursing school, and (3) failing to attend class regularly. The student disputed these charges and argued that he should have been afforded a hearing before his dismissal. The court indicated that the right to a hearing depended on whether the student had been dismissed "because of disciplinary misconduct" or "solely because of an academic failure." After noting that the situation "does not fit neatly" into either category, the court decided the issue as follows:

> This case is not the traditional disciplinary situation where a student violates the law or a school regulation by actively engaging in prohibited activities. Plaintiff has allegedly failed to act and comply with school regulations for admission and class attendance by passively ignoring these regulations. These alleged failures do not constitute misconduct in the sense that plaintiff is subject to disciplinary procedures. They do constitute misconduct in the sense that plaintiff was required to do something. Plaintiff contends that he did comply with the requirements. Like the traditional disciplinary case, the determination of whether plaintiff did or did not comply with the school regulations is a question of fact. Most importantly, in determining this factual question, reference is not made to a standard of achievement in an esoteric academic field. Scholastic standards are not involved, but rather disputed facts concerning whether plaintiff did or did not comply with certain school regulations. These issues adapt themselves readily to determination by a fair and impartial "due process" hearing [362 F. Supp. at 383].

The distinction made by the court is sound and is generally supported in the various justices' opinions in *Horowitz*.

But two federal appellate courts weighed in on the "academic" side in cases involving mixed issues of misconduct and poor academic performance. In *Mauriello v. University of Medicine and Dentistry of New Jersey*, 781 F.2d 46 (3d Cir. 1986), the court ruled that the dismissal of a medical student who repeatedly failed to produce thesis data was on academic rather than disciplinary grounds. And in *Harris v. Blake*, 798 F.2d 419 (10th Cir. 1986), in reviewing a student's involuntary withdrawal for inadequate grades, the court held that a professor's letter to a student's file, charging the student with incompetent performance (including absence from class) and unethical behavior in a course, concerned academic rather than disciplinary matters.

When dismissal or other serious sanctions depend more on disputed factual issues concerning conduct than on expert evaluation of academic work, the student should be accorded procedural rights akin to those for disciplinary cases (Section 7.3.2), rather than the lesser rights for academic deficiency cases. Of course, even when the academic label is clearly appropriate, administrators may choose to provide more procedural safeguards than the Constitution requires. Indeed, there may be good reason to provide some form of hearing prior to academic dismissal whenever the student has some basis for claiming that the academic judgment was arbitrary, in bad faith, or discriminatory (see Section 6.1.1). The question for the administrator, therefore, is not merely what procedures are constitutionally required but also what procedures would make the best policy for the particular institution.

There have been several reported opinions applying *Horowitz* to other academic dismissal problems in public institutions. Typical of these is *Schuler v. University of Minnesota*, 788 F.2d 510 (8th Cir. 1986). Schuler was dismissed from the doctoral program in psychology after failing a required oral examination on two occasions. Schuler alleged that she had been misinformed about the subject matter of both examinations, and she used the university's internal process to appeal the dismissal. Her appeal was denied, and she filed constitutional claims, alleging that she had not been notified about the subject matter of the examination or the evaluative criteria. She also alleged that the appeal procedure was defective because department faculty members were on the appeal board. The court noted that she had been given adequate notice of the faculty's dissatisfaction with her performance and, citing *Horowitz*, said that a student need not be made aware of the criteria by which she would be judged:

> The full procedural safeguards of the fourteenth amendment are inapplicable where, as here, a student is dismissed from a state educational institution for failure to meet academic standards. . . . Dismissal of a student for academic reasons comports with the requirements of procedural due process if the student had prior notice of faculty dissatisfaction with his or her performance and of the possibility of dismissal, and if the decision to dismiss the student was careful and deliberate [788 F.2d at 514].

The court addressed a second issue—one that clearly illustrates the deferential standard of review that courts have interpreted *Horowitz* to imply. The plaintiff argued that the university did not follow its written procedures in reviewing her appeal, and that this failure to adhere to its own procedures violated her due process rights. On the contrary, said the court,

the University's noncompliance with its own grievance appeal procedures
would not violate Schuler's right to procedural due process, because the hearing she received at the departmental level exceeded the process constitutionally
required to protect her interest in continued enrollment at that institution
[788 F.2d at 515].

In other words, because academic dismissal does not involve more than minimal due process rights, the university's written policies went beyond constitutional requirements, and failure to follow these policies did not trigger
constitutional protections. (See also *Delaney v. Heimstra,* 288 N.W.2d 769 (S.D.
1980); *Gamble v. University of Minnesota,* 639 F.2d 452 (8th Cir. 1981); *Lunde
v. Iowa Board of Regents,* 487 N.W.2d 357 (Iowa Ct. App. 1992); *Bleicher v. University of Cincinnati College of Medicine,* 604 N.E.2d 783 (Ohio Ct. App. 1992).)

More frequently, courts have relied on *Horowitz* for guidance in contexts
other than student academic dismissals from public institutions—namely, in
challenges to academic decisions other than dismissals, to academic dismissals
from private institutions, and to judgments concerning faculty rather than students. In *Olsson v. Board of Higher Education of the City of New York,* 402
N.E.2d 1150 (N.Y. 1980) (see Section 6.1.1), for example, the court cited *Horowitz* in rejecting a public college student's challenge to an examination grade.
In *Maas v. Corp. of Gonzaga University,* 618 P.2d 106 (Wash. Ct. App. 1980), and
Miller v. Hamline University School of Law, 601 F.2d 970 (8th Cir. 1979), the
courts used *Horowitz* to reject student challenges to academic decisions of private institutions. And in *Clark v. Whiting,* 607 F.2d 634 (4th Cir. 1979), another
court relied on *Horowitz* to reject an associate professor's challenge to a denial
of promotion to full professor.

Overall, two trends are emerging from the reported decisions in the wake of
Horowitz. First, extensive appellate litigation challenging academic dismissals
is not occurring, and the cases that have been reported have usually been
decided in favor of the institutions. Apparently *Horowitz,* with its strong support for institutional discretion in devising academic dismissal procedures, has
depressed the market for such litigation. Second, courts have read *Horowitz* as
a case whose message has meaning well beyond the context of constitutional
due process and academic dismissal. Thus, *Horowitz* also supports the broader
concept of "academic deference," or judicial deference to the full range of an
academic institution's academic decisions. Both trends help insulate postsecondary institutions from judicial intrusion into their dealings with students and
other members of the academic community. But just as surely, these trends
emphasize the institution's own responsibilities to deal fairly with students and
others and to provide appropriate internal means of accountability regarding
institutional academic decision making.

7.3.4. Private Institutions

Federal constitutional guarantees of due process do not bind private institutions unless their imposition of sanctions falls under the state action doctrine explained in Section 1.5.2. But the inapplicability of constitutional protections, as Sections 6.1 and 7.2 suggest, does not necessarily mean that the student stands procedurally naked before the authority of the school.

The old view of a private institution's authority is illustrated by *Anthony v. Syracuse University*, 231 N.Y.S. 435 (N.Y. App. Div. 1928), where a student's dismissal was upheld even though "no adequate reason [for it] was assigned by the university authorities." The court held that "no reason for dismissing need be given," though the institution "must . . . have a reason" that falls within its dismissal regulations. "Of course, the university authorities have wide discretion in determining what situation does and what does not fall within . . . [its regulations], and the courts would be slow indeed in disturbing any decision of the university authorities in this respect."

In more recent times, however, many courts have become faster on the draw with private schools. In *Carr v. St. John's University, New York* (see Section 7.2.2), a case limiting the impact of *Anthony* within New York State, the court indicated, although ruling for the university, that a private institution dismissing a student must act "not arbitrarily but in the exercise of an honest discretion based on facts within its knowledge that justify the exercise of discretion." In subsequently applying this standard to a discipline case, another New York court ruled that "the college or university's decision to discipline that student [must] be predicated on procedures which are fair and reasonable and which lend themselves to a reliable determination" (*Kwiatkowski v. Ithaca College*, 368 N.Y.S.2d 973 (N.Y. Sup. Ct. 1975)).

A federal appellate court has taken a similar approach. *Slaughter v. Brigham Young University*, 514 F.2d 622 (10th Cir. 1975), concerned a student who was dismissed for violating the honesty provision of the student code, having made unauthorized use of a professor's name as coauthor of an article. After the lower court had awarded $88,283 in damages to the student, the appellate court set aside the judgment and upheld the dismissal. But in doing so, it tested "whether the action was arbitrary" by investigating both the "adequacy of the procedure" and the substantiality of the evidence supporting the institution's determination. In judging the procedures, the court used *constitutional* due process as a guide, holding that the "proceedings met the requirements of the constitutional procedural due process doctrine as it is presently applied to public universities," and it is therefore unnecessary "to draw any distinction, *if there be any*, between the requirements in this regard for private and for public institutions" (emphasis added).

Another federal appellate court, however, has made it clear that private colleges and universities are not held to the same constitutional standards as are public institutions, even if state law requires them to promulgate disciplinary rules. In *Albert v. Carovano,* 851 F.2d 561 (2d Cir. 1988), students suspended by Hamilton College for occupying the college's administration building brought constitutional claims under a state action theory (see Section 1.5.2). Section 6450 of New York's Education Law required all institutions of higher education to adopt disciplinary rules and to file them with the state, which the college had done. Although the college's rules and disciplinary procedures provided for a judiciary board that would review the charges and evidence and determine the sanctions to be levied, the procedures also reserved to the president the right to dispense with the written procedures. In dealing with the students, who continued to occupy the building even after the college had secured a court order enjoining the occupation, the president suspended them effective the end of the semester, but invited them to state in writing their views on the situation to either the trustees or himself. The students demanded a hearing before the Judiciary Board, which was not granted. The lawsuit ensued.

The *en banc* court provided a lengthy discussion of the state action doctrine. In this case, it noted, the state law required that the disciplinary rules be placed on file, but the state had made no attempt to evaluate the rules or to ensure that the colleges followed them. Given the lack of state action, the plaintiffs' constitutional claims were dismissed. The court remanded for further consideration the students' claim that the college's selective enforcement of its disciplinary regulations violated Section 1981's prohibitions against race discrimination (see Section 4.1.4.1).

As is true of public institutions, judges are more likely to require procedural protections in the misconduct area than in the academic sphere. For example, in *Melvin v. Union College,* 600 N.Y.S.2d 141 (N.Y. App. Div. 1993), a breach-of-contract claim, a state appellate court enjoined the suspension of a student accused of cheating on an examination; the court took this action because the college had not followed all the elements of its written disciplinary procedure. But in *Ahlum v. Administrators of Tulane Educational Fund,* 617 So. 2d 96 (La. Ct. App. 1993), the appellate court of another state refused to enjoin Tulane University's suspension of a student found guilty of sexual assault. Noting that the proper standard of judicial review of a private college's disciplinary decisions was the "arbitrary and capricious" standard, the court upheld the procedures used and the sufficiency of the factual basis for the suspension. Since the court determined that Tulane's procedures exceeded even the due process protections required in *Goss v. Lopez,* it did not attempt to determine the boundaries of procedural protections appropriate for the disciplinary actions of private colleges and universities.

In *Boehm v. University of Pennsylvania School of Veterinary Medicine,* 573 A.2d 575 (Pa. Super. Ct. 1990), the court, after reviewing case law, legal scholarship, and other sources, concluded that:

> A majority of the courts have characterized the relationship between a private college and its students as contractual in nature. Therefore, students who are being disciplined are entitled only to those procedural safeguards which the school specifically provides. . . . The general rule, therefore, has been that where a private university or college establishes procedures for the suspension or expulsion of its students, substantial compliance with those established procedures must be had before a student can be suspended or expelled [573 A.2d at 579].

Determining that the school had "followed its Code of Rights punctiliously and that the disciplinary proceedings complied with due process and were fundamentally fair" (573 A.2d at 582), the appellate court reversed the trial court's order for a preliminary injunction, viewing that order as "interference with the legitimate authority of the school to sanction students who, after compliance with established procedure, had been found guilty of violating the school's Honor Code" (573 A.2d at 586).

In an opinion extremely deferential to a private institution's disciplinary procedure, and allegedly selective administrative enforcement of the disciplinary code, a federal appellate court refused to rule that Dartmouth College's suspension of several white students violated federal nondiscrimination laws. In *Dartmouth Review v. Dartmouth College,* 889 F.2d 13 (1st Cir. 1989), the students alleged that the college's decision to charge them with disciplinary code violations, and the dean's refusal to help them prepare for the hearing (which was promised in the student handbook), was based on their race. The court disagreed, stating that unfairness or inconsistency of administrative behavior did not equate to racial discrimination, and, since they could not demonstrate a causal link between their race and the administrators' conduct, the students' claims failed.

In reviewing determinations of academic performance, rather than disciplinary misconduct, the courts have crafted lesser procedural requirements. In *Militana v. University of Miami,* 236 So. 2d 162 (Fla. Dist. Ct. App. 1970), for example, the court upheld the dismissal of a medical student, stating flatly that notice and opportunity to be heard, though required in discipline cases, are "not required when the dismissal is for academic failure." Yet even here, the contract theory (see Section 3.2) may provide some lesser procedural protections for students in academic jeopardy at private institutions.

As is also true for public institutions, the line between academic and disciplinary cases may be difficult to draw. In *Napolitano v. Trustees of Princeton University,* 453 A.2d 263 (N.J. Super. Ct., App. Div. 1982), the court reviewed the university's withholding of a degree, for one year, from a student whom a campus committee had found guilty of plagiarizing a term paper. In upholding the university's action, the court determined that the problem was one "involving academic standards and not a case of violation of rules of conduct." In so doing, the court distinguished "academic disciplinary actions" from disciplinary actions involving other types of "misconduct," according greater deference to the institution's decisions in the former context and suggesting that lesser "due process" protection was required. The resulting dichotomy differs from the "academic/disciplinary" dichotomy delineated in Section 7.3.3 and suggests the potential relevance of a third, middle category for "academic disciplinary" cases. (Compare the *Easley* and *Jaksa* cases in Section 7.3.2.2.) Because such cases involve academic standards, courts should be sufficiently deferential to avoid interference with the institution's expert judgments on such matters; however, because such cases may also involve disputed factual issues concerning student conduct, courts should afford greater due process rights than they would in academic cases involving only the evaluation of student performance.

While the doctrinal bases for procedural rights in the public and private sectors are different, and while the law accords private institutions greater deference, some courts may nevertheless encourage a rough similarity of treatment by seeking guidance from public-sector precedents when deciding private-sector cases. The *Slaughter* case above provides a good illustration. So does *Miller v. Hamline University School of Law*, 601 F.2d 970 (8th Cir. 1979), in which the court applied the *Horowitz* due process analysis (Section 7.3.3) to a private school's dismissal of a student for academic deficiency. Such a similarity of treatment may also make good policy sense for many private institutions. It may thus be prudent for private school administrators to use the constitutional due process principles in Sections 7.3.2 and 7.3.3 of this volume as general guides in implementing their own procedural systems. And if a private school makes a conscious policy choice not to use certain procedures that due process would require for public schools, that choice should be clearly reflected in its rules and regulations, so as to inhibit a court from finding such procedures implicit in the rules or in the student-institution relationship.

SELECTED ANNOTATED BIBLIOGRAPHY

Sec. 7.1 (Disciplinary and Grievance Systems)

Beaney, William M., & Cox, Jonathan C. S. "Fairness in University Disciplinary Proceedings," 22 *Case Western L. Rev.* 390 (1971). Legal and policy analyses, and suggested guidelines, concerning the development of fair disciplinary proceedings on campus.

Pavela, Gary. "Limiting the Pursuit of Perfect Justice on Campus: A Proposed Code of Student Conduct," 6 *J. Coll. & Univ. Law* 137 (1980). A well-drafted sample code, including standards of conduct and hearing procedures, with comprehensive annotations explaining particular provisions and cites to relevant authorities. The code represents an alternative to the procedural complexities of the criminal justice model.

Pavela, Gary. "Therapeutic Paternalism and the Misuse of Mandatory Psychiatric Withdrawals on Campus," 9 *J. Coll. & Univ. Law* 101 (1982–83). Analyzes the pitfalls associated with postsecondary institutions' use of "psychiatric withdrawals" of students. Pitfalls include violations of Section 504 (on disability discrimination) and of students' substantive and procedural due process rights. The article concludes with "Policy Considerations," including the limits of psychiatric diagnosis, the danger of substituting a "therapeutic" approach as a solution for disciplinary problems, and the "appropriate uses for a psychiatric withdrawal policy." For a later monograph adapted from this article, with model standards and procedures, hypothetical case studies, and a bibliography, see Gary Pavela, *The Dismissal of Students with Mental Disorders: Legal Issues, Policy Considerations, and Alternative Responses* (College Administration Publications, 1985); and see also Pavela entry for Section 7.3.

Picozzi, James M. "University Disciplinary Process: What's Fair, What's Due, and What You Don't Get," 96 *Yale L.J.* 2132 (1987). Written by a defendant in a student disciplinary case. Provides a critical review of case law and institutional grievance procedures, concluding that the minimal due process protections endorsed by the courts are insufficient to protect students' interests.

Stoner, Edward N., & Cerminara, Kathy L. "Harnessing the 'Spirit of Insubordination': A Model Student Disciplinary Code," 17 *J. Coll. & Univ. L.* (1990). Provides a model student code that includes definitions, judicial authority, proscribed conduct, judicial policies, sanctions, and appeals. Provides commentary on each of these categories.

U.S. District Court, Western District of Missouri (*en banc*). "General Order on Judicial Standards of Procedure and Substance in Review of Student Discipline in Tax-Supported Institutions of Higher Education," 45 *Federal Rules Decisions* 133 (1968). A set of guidelines promulgated for the guidance of the district court in deciding students' rights cases. The guidelines are similarly useful to administrators and counsel seeking to comply with federal legal requirements.

See Brown & Buttolph entry for Section 7.2.

See Folger & Shubert entry for Section 1.1.

Sec. 7.2 (Disciplinary Rules and Regulations)

Brown, Valerie L., & Buttolph, Katherine (eds.). *Student Disciplinary Issues: A Legal Compendium* (National Association of College and University Attorneys, 1993). A collection of law review articles, institutional policies, judicial opinions, and conference outlines related to student disciplinary rules and disciplinary systems. Issues related to both academic and nonacademic misconduct are included. A list of additional resources is also provided.

See the bibliography for Section 7.1.

Sec. 7.3 (Procedures for Suspension, Dismissal, and Other Sanctions)

Dessem, R. Lawrence. "*Board of Curators of the University of Missouri v. Horowitz:* Academic Versus Judicial Expertise," 30 *Ohio State L. J.* 476 (1978). Thoroughly canvasses the ramifications and limitations of the *Horowitz* decision.

Golden, Edward J. "Procedural Due Process for Students at Public Colleges and Universities, " 11 *J. Law & Educ.* 337 (1982). Reviews postsecondary education's response to *Goss v. Lopez,* the leading Supreme Court case on disciplinary procedures, and the later *Horowitz* case on academic procedures. After reviewing *Goss*'s and *Horowitz*'s application to dismissals and long-term suspensions, the author reports results of his survey of procedural protections extended by public colleges and universities to students faced with disciplinary or academic dismissal. Includes data on notice, hearing, evidentiary standards, and other procedural issues.

Jennings, Eileen K., & Strope, John L., Jr. "Procedural Due Process in Academia: *Board of Curators v. Horowitz* Seven Years Later," 28 *West's Educ. Law Rptr.* 973 (1986). Reviews the outcome of *Horowitz* and discusses the required elements of due process in academic dismissals.

Pavela, Gary. *The Dismissal of Students with Mental Disorders* (National Association of College and University Attorneys, 1990). Reviews the protections provided by the Rehabilitation Act of 1973 (Section 504) for students with mental disabilities. Recommends elements of an appropriate policy for psychiatric withdrawal, and provides a checklist for responding to students with mental disorders. Includes a case study about a disruptive student and suggests an appropriate institutional response. For related work by the same author, see Pavela, "Therapeutic Paternalism," entry for Section 7.1.

CHAPTER EIGHT

Students' Freedom of Expression

SEC. 8.1. STUDENT PROTEST AND DEMONSTRATIONS

8.1.1. General Principles

Freedom of expression for students is protected mainly by the free speech and press provisions in the First Amendment of the U.S. Constitution, which applies only to "public" institutions (see Section 1.5.2). In some situations, student freedom of expression may also be protected by state constitutional provisions (see Section 1.3.1.1 and the *Schmid* case in Section 11.5.3), by state statutes (see, for example, Cal. Educ. Code §66301 (public institutions) and §94367 (private institutions)), or by the institution's own bill of rights or other internal rules (see Section 1.3.2.1). These latter sources of law may apply to private as well as public institutions; they may also consciously adopt First Amendment norms that have been developed in the courts and that bind public institutions, so that these norms may sometimes be operative on private as well as public campuses. The following discussion focuses on these First Amendment norms and the case law in which they have been developed.

In a line of cases arising mainly from the campus unrest of the late 1960s and early 1970s, courts have affirmed that students have a right to protest and demonstrate peacefully—a right that public institutions may not infringe. This right stems from the free speech clause of the First Amendment as reinforced by that amendment's protection of "the right of the people peaceably to assemble, and to petition the Government for a redress of grievances." The keystone case is *Tinker v. Des Moines School District,* 393 U.S. 503 (1969). Several high school students had been suspended for wearing black armbands to school to protest the United States' Vietnam War policy. The U.S. Supreme Court ruled that the protest was a nondisruptive exercise of free speech and could not be punished by suspension from school. The Court made clear that "First Amendment rights, applied in light of the special characteristics of the school environment, are available to teachers and students" and that students "are possessed of fundamental rights which the state must respect, just as they themselves must respect their obligations to the state." The Court also made clear that the First Amendment protects more than just words; it also protects certain "symbolic acts" that are performed "for the purpose of expressing certain views."

Though *Tinker* involved secondary school students, the Supreme Court soon applied its principles to postsecondary education in *Healy v. James,* 408 U.S. 169 (1972), discussed further in Section 9.1.1. The *Healy* opinion carefully notes the First Amendment's important place on campus:

> State colleges and universities are not enclaves immune from the sweep of the First Amendment. . . . [T]he precedents of this Court leave no room for the view that . . . First Amendment protections should apply with less force on college campuses than in the community at large. Quite to the contrary, "The vigilant protection of constitutional freedoms is nowhere more vital than in the community of American schools" (*Shelton v. Tucker,* 364 U.S. 479, 487 (1960)). The college classroom with its surrounding environs is peculiarly the "marketplace of ideas," and we break no new constitutional ground in reaffirming this nation's dedication to safeguarding academic freedom [408 U.S. at 180].

The free speech protections for students are at their peak when the speech takes place in a "public forum"—that is, an area of the campus that is, traditionally or by official policy, available to students or the entire campus community for expressive activities. See generally G. Sorenson, "The 'Public Forum Doctrine' and Its Application in School and College Cases," 20 *J. Law & Educ.* 445 (1991). This judicially created concept and its attendant "public forum" analysis (see, for example, *Widmar v. Vincent,* discussed in Section 9.1.4) have become increasingly important in student freedom-of-expression cases. Under the currently employed definitions and guidelines, set out by the U.S. Supreme Court in *Perry Education Assn. v. Perry Local Educators' Assn.,* 460 U.S. 37, 45–46 (1983), expressive activities undertaken in a public forum receive far more protection than expressive activities not undertaken in a public forum.

Although *Tinker, Healy,* and *Widmar* apply the First Amendment to the campus just as fully as it applies to the general community, the cases also make clear that academic communities are "special environments," and that "First Amendment rights . . . [must be] applied in light of the special characteristics of the school environment" (*Tinker* at 506). In this regard, "[a] university differs in significant respects from public forums such as streets or parks or even municipal theaters. A university's mission is education, and decisions of this Court have never denied a university's authority to impose reasonable regulations compatible with that mission upon the use of its campus and facilities" (*Widmar v. Vincent*, 454 U.S. 263, 268 n.5 (1981)). The interests that academic institutions may protect and promote, and the nature of threats to these interests, may thus differ from the interests that may exist for other types of entities and in other contexts. Therefore, although First Amendment principles do apply with full force to the campus, their application may be affected by the unique interests of academic communities.

Moreover, colleges and universities may assert and protect their interests in ways that create limits on student freedom of speech. The *Tinker* opinion recognizes "the need for affirming the comprehensive authority of the states and of school officials, consistent with fundamental constitutional safeguards, to prescribe and control conduct in the schools" (at 507). That case also emphasizes that freedom to protest does not constitute freedom to disrupt: "[C]onduct by the student, in class or out of it, which for any reason—whether it stems from time, place, or type of behavior—materially disrupts classwork or involves substantial disorder or invasion of the rights of others is . . . not immunized by the constitutional guarantee of freedom of speech" (at 513). *Healy* makes the same points.

8.1.2. Regulation of Student Protest

By following the *Tinker/Healy* guidelines above, postsecondary institutions may promulgate rules that prohibit certain types of group or individual demonstrations or protest. Students may be suspended if they violate such rules by actively participating in a disruptive demonstration—for example, entering the stands during a college football game and "by abusive and disorderly acts and conduct" depriving the spectators "of the right to see and enjoy the game in peace and with safety to themselves" (*Barker v. Hardway*, 283 F. Supp. 228 (S.D. W. Va.), *affirmed*, 399 F.2d 638 (4th Cir. 1968)), or physically blocking entrances to campus buildings and preventing personnel or other students from using the buildings (*Buttney v. Smiley*, 281 F. Supp. 280 (D. Colo. 1968)).

The critical problem in prohibiting or punishing disruptive protest activity is determining when the activity has become sufficiently disruptive to lose its protection under *Tinker* and *Healy*. In *Shamloo v. Mississippi State Board of Trustees*, 620 F.2d 516 (5th Cir. 1980), for example, the plaintiffs, Iranian nationals who were students at Jackson State University, had participated in two on-campus demonstrations in support of the regime of Ayatollah Khomeini in Iran. The university disciplined the students for having violated campus regulations that required advance scheduling of demonstrations and other meetings or gatherings. When the students filed suit, claiming that the regulations and the disciplinary action violated their First Amendment rights, the defendant argued that the protests were sufficiently disruptive to lose any protection under the First Amendment. The appellate court asked whether the demonstration had "materially and substantially interfered with the requirements of appropriate discipline in the operation of the school"—the standard developed in an earlier Fifth Circuit case and adopted by the U.S. Supreme Court in *Tinker*. Applying this standard to the facts of the case, the court rejected the defendant's claim:

> There was no testimony by the students or teachers complaining that the demonstration was disrupting and distracting. Shamloo testified that he did not think any of the classes were disrupted. Dr. Johnson testified that the demonstration was quite noisy. Dr. Smith testified that he could hear the chanting from his office and that, in his opinion, classes were being disrupted. The only justification for his conclusion is that there are several buildings within a close proximity of the plaza that students may have been using for purposes of study or for classes. There is no evidence that he received complaints from the occupants of these buildings.
>
> The district court concluded that "the demonstration had a disruptive effect with respect to other students' rights." But this is not enough to conclude that the demonstration was not protected by the First Amendment. The court must also conclude (1) that the disruption was a *material* disruption of classwork or (2) that it involved *substantial* disorder or invasion of the rights of others. It must constitute a *material* and *substantial* interference with discipline. The district court did not make such a conclusion and we certainly cannot, especially in light of the conflicting evidence found in the record. We cannot say that the demonstration did not constitute activity protected under the First Amendment [620 F.2d at 522].

As *Shamloo* suggests, and *Tinker* states expressly, administrators seeking to regulate protest activity on grounds of disruption must base their action on something more substantial than mere suspicion or fear of possible disruption:

> Undifferentiated fear or apprehension of disturbance is not enough to overcome the right to freedom of expression. Any departure from absolute regimentation may cause trouble. Any variation from the majority's opinion may inspire fear. Any word spoken, in class, in the lunchroom, or on the campus, that deviates from the views of another person may start an argument or cause disturbance. But our Constitution says we must take this risk (*Terminiello v. Chicago*, 337 U.S. 1 (1949)); and our history says that it is this sort of hazardous freedom— this kind of openness—that is the basis of our national strength and of the independence and vigor of Americans who grow up and live in this relatively permissive, often disputatious, society [*Tinker* at 508–09].

Yet substantial disruption need not be a fait accompli before administrators can take action. It is sufficient that administrators have actual evidence on which they can "reasonably . . . forecast" (*Tinker* at 514) that substantial disruption is imminent.

The administrator should also determine whether the disruption is created by the protesters themselves or by the onlookers' reaction to their presence. In striking down a regulation limiting off-campus speakers at Mississippi state colleges, the court in *Stacy v. Williams*, 306 F. Supp. 963 (N.D. Miss. 1969), emphasized that "one simply cannot be restrained from speaking, and his audience cannot be prevented from hearing him, unless the feared result is likely to be engendered by what the speaker himself says or does." Either the protesters must themselves engage in conduct that is physically disruptive, as in *Barker* and *Buttney* above, or their words and acts must be "directed to inciting or producing imminent" disruption by others and "likely to produce" such disruption (*Brandenburg v. Ohio*, 395 U.S. 444 (1969)) before an administrator may stop the protest or discipline the protesters. Where the onlookers rather than the protesters have created the disruption, the administrator's proper recourse is against the onlookers.

Besides adopting regulations prohibiting disruptive protest, public institutions may also promulgate "reasonable regulations with respect to the time, the place, and the manner in which student groups conduct their speech-related activities" (*Healy* at 192–93). Students who violate such regulations may be disciplined even if their violation did not create substantial disruption. As applied to speech in the public forum, however, such regulations may cover only those times, places, or manners of expression that are "basically incompatible with the normal activity of a particular place at a particular time" (*Grayned v. Rockford*, 408 U.S. 104, 116 (1972)). Incompatibility must be determined by the physical impact of the speech-related activity on its surroundings and not by the content or viewpoint of the speech (see Section 8.3).

In the *Shamloo* case described earlier, for instance, the court invalidated a campus regulation requiring that "all events sponsored by student organizations, groups, or individual students must be registered with the director of student activities, who, in cooperation with the vice-president for student affairs, approves activities of a wholesome nature." The court reasoned that:

> [R]egulations must be reasonable as limitations on the time, place, and manner of the protected speech and its dissemination (*Papish v. Board of Curators of the University of Missouri*, 410 U.S. 667 . . . (1973); *Healy v. James*, 408 U.S. 169 . . . (1972)). Disciplinary action may not be based on the disapproved *content* of the protected speech (*Papish*, 410 U.S. at 670 . . .).
>
> The reasonableness of a similar university regulation was previously addressed by this court in *Bayless v. Martine*, 430 F.2d 872, 873 (5th Cir. 1970). In *Bayless*,

ten students sought injunctive relief from their suspension for violating a university regulation. The regulation in *Bayless* created a Student Expression Area that could be reserved forty-eight hours in advance for any nonviolent purpose. All demonstrations similar to the one held by the Iranian students were regulated to the extent that they could only be held at the Student Expression Area "between the hours of 12:00 noon to 1:00 P.M. and from 5:00 to 7:00 P.M." but there was no limitation on the content of the speech. This court noted that the requirement of forty-eight hours advance notice was a reasonable method to avoid the problem of simultaneous and competing demonstrations, and it also provided advance warning of the possible need for police protection. This court upheld the validity of the regulation as a valid exercise of the right to adopt and enforce reasonable nondiscriminatory regulations as to the time, place, and manner of a demonstration.

There is one critical distinction between the regulation examined in *Bayless* and the Jackson State regulation. The former made no reference to the *content* of the speech that would be allowed in the Student Expression Area. As long as there was no interference with the flow of traffic, no interruption of the orderly conduct of university affairs, and no obscene material, the students were not limited in what they could say. Apparently, the same cannot be said with respect to the Jackson State regulations, which provide that only "activities of a *wholesome* nature" will be approved. And if a demonstration is not approved, the students participating may be subjected to disciplinary action, including the possibility of dismissal.

Limiting approval of activities only to those of a "wholesome" nature is a regulation of *content* as opposed to a regulation of time, place, and manner. Dr. Johnson testified that he would disapprove a student activity if, in his opinion, the activity was unwholesome. The presence of this language converts what might have otherwise been a reasonable regulation of time, place, and manner into a restriction on the content of speech. Therefore, the regulation appears to be unreasonable on its face [620 F.2d at 522–23].

Clark v. Community for Creative Non-Violence, 468 U.S. 288 (1984), although not a higher education case, has become a leading precedent on the validity of "time, place, and manner" restrictions on protest demonstrations in the public forum. (The case also speaks importantly to the "symbolic acts" or "symbolic speech" issue developed by the *Tinker* case.) In *Clark,* the U.S. Supreme Court upheld National Park Service regulations limiting protests in parks. The Court noted that these regulations were "manner" regulations conforming to this three-part judicial test: "they are justified without reference to the content of the regulated speech, . . . they are narrowly tailored to serve a significant governmental interest, and . . . they leave open ample alternative channels for communication of the information."

Another recent U.S. Supreme Court precedent with important ramifications for "time, place, and manner" regulation of student protests is *Ward v. Rock*

Against Racism, 491 U.S. 781 (1989). The Court affirmed that government has a substantial interest in regulating noise levels to prevent annoyance to persons in adjacent areas and refined the first two parts of the *Clark* test: "'[A] regulation of the time, place, or manner of protected speech must be narrowly tailored to serve the government's legitimate content-neutral interests but . . . need not be the least restrictive or least intrusive means of doing so. Rather, the requirement of narrow tailoring is satisfied so long as the . . . regulation promotes a substantial government interest that would be achieved less effectively absent the regulation'" (quoting *United States v. Albertini,* 472 U.S. 675, 689 (1985)). The overall effect of the *Ward* case, combined with the *Clark* case, is to create a more deferential standard, under which it is more likely that courts will uphold the constitutionality of time, place, and manner regulations of speech.

Postsecondary administrators who are drafting or implementing protest regulations must be attentive not only to the various judicial requirements just discussed but also to the doctrines of "overbreadth" and "vagueness." The overbreadth doctrine provides that regulations of speech must be "narrowly tailored" to avoid sweeping within their coverage speech activities that would be constitutionally protected under the First Amendment. The vagueness doctrine provides that regulations of conduct must be sufficiently clear so that the persons to be regulated can understand what is required or prohibited and conform their conduct accordingly. Vagueness principles apply more stringently when the regulations deal with speech-related activity: "'Stricter standards of permissible statutory vagueness may be applied to a statute having a potentially inhibiting effect on speech; a man may the less be required to act at his peril here, because the dissemination of ideas may be the loser'" (*Hynes v. Mayor and Council of Oradell,* 425 U.S. 610, 620 (1976), quoting *Smith v. California,* 361 U.S. 147, 151 (1959)). In the *Shamloo* case, the court utilized both doctrines in invalidating campus regulations prohibiting demonstrations that are not "of a wholesome nature." Regarding the vagueness doctrine, the court reasoned that:

> The restriction on activities other than those of a "wholesome" nature raises the additional issue that the Jackson State regulation may be void for vagueness. . . . An individual is entitled to fair notice or a warning of what constitutes prohibited activity by specifically enumerating the elements of the offense (*Smith v. Goguen,* 415 U.S. 566 . . . (1974)). The regulation must not be designed so that different officials could attach different meaning to the words in an arbitrary and discriminatory manner (*Smith v. Goguen, supra*). But, of course, we cannot expect "mathematical certainty" from our language (*Grayned v. City of Rockford,* 408 U.S. 104 . . . (1972)). The approach adopted by this court with respect to university regulations is to examine whether the college students would have any "difficulty in understanding what conduct the regulations allow and what conduct they prohibit" (quoting *Jenkins v. Louisiana State Board of Education,* 506 F.2d 992, 1004 (5th Cir. 1975)).

The requirement that an activity be "wholesome" before it is subject to approval is unconstitutionally vague. The testimony revealed that the regulations are enforced or not enforced depending on the purpose of the gathering or demonstration. Dr. Johnson admitted that whether or not something was wholesome was subject to interpretation and that he, as the vice-president of student affairs, and Dr. Jackson, director of student activities, could come to different conclusions as to its meaning. . . . The regulation's reference to wholesome activities is not specific enough to give fair notice and warning. A college student would have great difficulty determining whether or not his activities constitute prohibited unwholesome conduct. The regulation is void for vagueness [620 F.2d at 523–24].

The time, place, and manner tests and the overbreadth and vagueness doctrines, as well as principles concerning "symbolic" speech, all played an important role in another leading case, *Students Against Apartheid Coalition v. O'Neil*, 660 F. Supp. 333 (W.D. Va. 1987), and 671 F. Supp. 1105 (W.D. Va. 1987), *affirmed*, 838 F.2d 735 (4th Cir. 1988). At issue in this case was a University of Virginia regulation prohibiting student demonstrations against university policies on investment in South Africa. In the first phase of the litigation, students challenged the university's policy prohibiting them from constructing shanties—flimsy structures used to protest apartheid conditions in South Africa—on the university's historic central grounds, "the Lawn." The federal district court held that the university's policy created an unconstitutional restriction on symbolic expression in a public forum. Specifically, the court declared that the "current lawn use regulations . . . are vague, are too broad to satisfy the University's legitimate interest in esthetics, and fail to provide the plaintiffs with a meaningful alternative channel for expression."

UVA subsequently revised its policy to tailor it narrowly to the achievement of the university's goals of historic preservation and aesthetic integrity. The students again brought suit to enjoin the enforcement of the new policy on the same constitutional grounds they had asserted in the first suit. The case was heard by the same judge, who this time held in favor of the defendant university and upheld the revised policy. The court determined that the amended policy applied only to "structures," as narrowly defined in the policy; that the policy restricted such structures from only a small section of the Lawn; and that the policy focused solely on concerns of architectural purity. Applying the *Clark* test, the court held that:

[UVA] may regulate the symbolic speech of its students to preserve and protect the Lawn area as an architectural landmark. To be constitutionally permissible, the regulation must be reasonable in time, place and manner. The revised Lawn Use Policy lies within the constitutional boundaries of the first amendment. The new policy is content-neutral, precisely aimed at protecting the University's esthetics concern in architecture, and permits students a wide array of additional modes of communication. The new policy is also sufficiently detailed to inform students as to the types of expression restricted on the Lawn [671 F. Supp. at 1108].

On appeal by the students, the U.S. Court of Appeals for the Fourth Circuit agreed with the reasoning of the district court and affirmed its decision.

The *O'Neil* case, together with the *Shamloo* case, serves to illuminate pitfalls that administrators will wish to avoid in devising and enforcing their own campus's demonstration regulations. The *O'Neil* litigation also provides a good example of how to respond to and resolve problems concerning the validity of campus regulations.

8.1.3. Prior Approval of Protest Activities

Sometimes, institutions have attempted to avoid disruption and disorder on campus by requiring that protest activity be approved in advance and by approving only those activities that will not pose problems. Under this strategy, a protest would be halted or its participants disciplined, not because the protest was in fact disruptive or violated reasonable time, place, and manner requirements but merely because it had not been approved in advance. Administrators at public institutions should be extremely leery of such a strategy. A prior approval system constitutes a "prior restraint" on free expression—that is, a temporary or permanent prohibition of expression imposed before the expression has occurred rather than a punishment imposed afterward. Prior restraints "are the most serious and the least tolerable infringement of First Amendment rights" (*Nebraska Press Assn. v. Stuart*, 427 U. S. 539, 559 (1976)).

Hammond v. South Carolina State College, 272 F. Supp. 947 (D.S.C. 1967), provides a classic example of prior restraint. The defendant college had a rule providing that "the student body is not to celebrate, parade, or demonstrate on the campus at any time without the approval of the office of the president." Several students were expelled for violating this rule after they held a demonstration for which they had not obtained prior approval. The court found the rule to be "on its face a prior restraint on the right to freedom of speech and the right to assemble" and held the rule and the expulsions under it to be invalid.

The courts have not asserted, however, that all prior restraints on expression are invalid. *Healy v. James* (Sections 8.1.1 and 9.1.1) summarizes the current judicial attitude: "While a college has a legitimate interest in preventing disruption on campus, which under circumstances requiring the safeguarding of that interest may justify . . . [a prior] restraint, a 'heavy burden' rests on the college to demonstrate the appropriateness of that action." Although it is difficult to ascertain what restraints would be valid under *Healy,* such restraints probably could be imposed for the limited purpose of ensuring that student protest activities will not violate time, place, or manner regulations meeting the guidelines in Section 8.1.2. In *Auburn Alliance for Peace and Justice v. Martin,* 684 F. Supp. 1072 (M.D. Ala. 1988), *affirmed without opin.,* 853 F.2d 931 (11th Cir. 1988), for instance, the trial and appellate courts upheld the facial validity of Auburn's regulations of a campus public forum and also held that the university's denial of a student-faculty group's request for week-long, round-the-clock use of this forum was an appropriate means of implementing time, place, and manner requirements. Probably a prior approval mechanism could also be used for the limited purpose of determining that protest activities will not cause substantial disruption (see Section 8.1.4). In either case, however, it is questionable whether prior approval requirements would be appropriate if applied to small-scale protests that have no reasonable potential for disruption. Also in either case, prior approval regulations would have to contain a clear definition of the protest activity to which they apply, precise standards to limit the administrator's discretion in making approval decisions, and procedures for ensuring an expeditious and fair decision-making process. Administrators must always assume the burden of proving that the protest activity would violate a reasonable time, place, or manner regulation or would cause substantial disruption. Given these complexities, prior approval requirements may invite substantial legal challenges. Administrators should carefully consider whether and when the prior approval strategy is worth the risk. There are always alternatives: disciplining students who violate regulations prohibiting disruptive protest; disciplining students who violate time, place, or manner requirements; or using injunctive or criminal processes, as set out in Section 7.1.3.

8.1.4. Court Injunctions and Criminal Prosecutions

When administrators are faced with a mass disruption that they cannot end by discussion, negotiation, or threat of disciplinary action, they may want to seek judicial assistance. A court injunction terminating the demonstration is one option. Arrest and criminal prosecution is the other. Although both options involve critical tactical considerations and risks, commentators favor the injunction for most situations, primarily because it provides a more immediate judicial forum for resolving disputes and because it shifts the responsibility for using law enforcement officials from administrators to the court. Injunctions may also be used in some instances to enjoin future disruptive conduct, whereas criminal prosecutions are limited to punishing past conduct. The use of the injunctive process does not legally foreclose the possibility of later criminal prosecutions, and injunctive orders or criminal prosecutions do not legally prevent the institution from initiating student disciplinary proceedings. Under U.S.

Supreme Court precedents, none of these combinations would constitute double jeopardy. (For other problems regarding the relationship between criminal prosecutions and disciplinary proceedings, see Section 7.1.3.)

The legality of injunctions or criminal prosecutions depends on two factors. First, the conduct at issue must be unlawful under state law. To warrant an injunction, the conduct must be an imminent or continuing violation of property rights or personal rights protected by state statutory law or common law; to warrant a criminal arrest and prosecution, the conduct must violate the state criminal code. Second, the conduct at issue must not constitute expression protected by the First Amendment. Both injunctive orders and criminal convictions are restraints on speech-related activity and would be tested by the principles discussed in Section 8.1.2, concerning the regulation of student protest. Since injunctions act to restrain future demonstrations, they may operate as prior restraints on expression and would also be subject to the First Amendment principles described in Section 8.1.3.

When the assistance of the court is requested, public and private institutions are on the same footing. Since the court, rather than the institution, will ultimately impose the restraint, and since the court is clearly a public entity subject to the Constitution, both public and private institutions' use of judicial assistance must comply with First Amendment requirements. Also, for both public and private institutions, judicial assistance depends on the same technical requirements regarding the availability and enforcement of injunctions and the procedural validity of arrests and prosecutions.

SEC. 8.2. STUDENT PRESS

8.2.1. General Perspectives

A public institution's relationships with student newspapers, magazines, and other publications should be viewed in the first instance under the same principles that are applicable to student organizations (see Section 9.1). Student publications are often under the auspices of some student organization (such as the newspaper staff), which may be recognized by the school or funded from mandatory student activity fees. Such organizations can claim the same freedom of association as the organizations discussed in Section 9.1, and a public institution's regulation of such organizations is limited by the principles set out in that section.

However, student publications must also be viewed from an additional perspective, not directly involved in the section on student organizations: the perspective of freedom of the press. As perhaps the most staunchly guarded of all First Amendment rights, the right to a free press protects student publications from virtually all encroachments on their editorial prerogatives by public institutions. In a series of forceful cases, courts have implemented this student press freedom, using First Amendment principles akin to those that would apply to a big-city daily published by a private corporation.[1]

The chief concern of the First Amendment's free press guarantee is censorship. Thus, whenever a public institution seeks to control or coercively influence the content of a student publication, it will have a legal problem on its hands. The problem will be exacerbated if the institution imposes a prior restraint on publication; that is, a prohibition imposed in advance of publication rather than a sanction imposed subsequently (see Section 8.1.3). Conversely, the institution's legal problems will be alleviated if the institution's regulations (concerning, for example, the allocation of office space or limitations on the time, place, or manner of distribution) do not affect the message, ideas, or subject matter of the publication and do not permit prior restraints on publication.

8.2.2. Mandatory Student Fee Allocations for Student Publications

Institutions and objecting students have no more right to prohibit or challenge the allocation of mandatory student fees to student newspapers that express a particular viewpoint than they have to prohibit or challenge such allocations to other student organizations expressing particular viewpoints. In *Arrington v. Taylor*, 380 F. Supp. 1348 (M.D.N.C. 1974), *affirmed*, 526 F.2d 587 (4th Cir. 1975), for example, the court rejected a challenge to the University of North Carolina's use of mandatory fees to subsidize its campus newspaper, the *Daily Tar Heel*. Since the paper did not purport to speak for the entire student body, and its existence did not inhibit students from expressing or supporting opposing viewpoints, the subsidy did not infringe First Amendment rights. Eight years later, the same court reconsidered and reaffirmed *Arrington* in *Kania v. Forham*, 702 F.2d 475 (4th Cir. 1983); and in 1992 another U.S. Court of Appeals (citing *Kania*) reached the same result (*Hays County Guardian v. Supple*, 969 F.2d 111, 123 (5th Cir. 1992)).

A university's attempts to reduce the funding of a student newspaper were struck down in *Stanley v. Magrath*, 719 F.2d 279 (8th Cir. 1983). The University of Minnesota changed the funding mechanism of one of its student newspapers

---

[1]Problems may also arise concerning outside newspapers that are distributed on campus, and the students' rights to obtain such newspapers. In *Hays County Guardian v. Supple*, 969 F.2d 111 (5th Cir. 1992), for example, the court invalidated restrictions on distribution of a free newspaper distributed throughout the county. See generally *City of Cincinnati v. Discovery Network*, 113 S. Ct. 1505 (1993).

by eliminating mandatory student fees and instead allowing students to elect individually whether or not a portion of their fees would go to the *Minnesota Daily*. Institution of this refundable fee system came on the heels of intense criticism from students, faculty, religious groups, and the state legislature over a satirical "Humor Issue" of the paper.

Although the university argued that the change in funding mechanism came in response to student objections about having to fund the paper (which the court assumed *arguendo* was a legitimate motivation), the court pointed to evidence suggesting that, at least in part, the change was impermissibly in retaliation for the content of the "Humor Issue." It then held that the school failed to carry its burden of showing that the permissible motive would have produced the same result even in the absence of the impermissible one and struck down the funding change.

Rosenberger v. Rector and Visitors of the University of Virginia, 115 S. Ct. 2510 (1995) (further discussed in Section 9.1.4), is the first U.S. Supreme Court pronouncement on mandatory student fee allocations for student publications. The case generally confirms the principles from *Arrington* and *Stanley*. But *Rosenberger* also extends the analysis of the earlier cases in two important respects: (1) *Rosenberger* focuses specifically on viewpoint discrimination issues that may arise when a university or its student government decides to fund some student publications but not others; and (2) *Rosenberger* addresses the special situation that arises when a student publication has an editorial policy based on a religious perspective.

The plaintiffs in *Rosenberger* were students who published a magazine titled "Wide Awake: A Christian Perspective at the University of Virginia." As described by the U.S. Supreme Court:

The paper's Christian viewpoint was evident from the first issue, in which its editors wrote that the journal "offers a Christian perspective on both personal and community issues, especially those relevant to college students at the University of Virginia." App. 45. The editors committed the paper to a two-fold mission: "to challenge Christians to live, in word and deed, according to the faith they proclaim and to encourage students to consider what a personal relationship with Jesus Christ means." Ibid. The first issue had articles about racism, crisis pregnancy, stress, prayer, C. S. Lewis' ideas about evil and free will, and reviews of religious music. In the next two issues, Wide Awake featured stories about homosexuality, Christian missionary work, and eating disorders, as well as music reviews and interviews with University professors. Each page of Wide Awake, and the end of each article or review, is marked by a cross. The advertisements carried in Wide Awake also reveal the Christian perspective of the journal. For the most part, the advertisers are churches, centers for Christian study, or Christian bookstores [115 S. Ct. at 2515].

The university's guidelines for student fee allocations ("Guidelines") permitted "student news, information, opinion, entertainment, or academic communications media groups," among other groups, to apply for allocations that the university would then use to pay the group's bills from outside contractors who printed its publication. The Guidelines provided, however, that student groups could not use fee allocations to support "religious activity," defined as activity that "primarily promotes or manifests a particular belief in or about a deity or an ultimate reality." Fifteen student publications received funding, but the Wide Awake publication did not because the Student Council determined that it was a religious activity. Wide Awake's members challenged this denial as a violation of their free speech and press rights under the First Amendment.

The U.S. Supreme Court upheld Wide Awake's claim because the university's action was a kind of censorship based on the publication's viewpoint:

> Vital First Amendment speech principles are at stake here. The first danger to liberty lies in granting the State the power to examine publications to determine whether or not they are based on some ultimate idea and if so for the State to classify them. The second, and corollary, danger is to speech from the chilling of individual thought and expression. That danger is especially real in the University setting, where the State acts against a background and tradition of thought and experiment that is at the center of our intellectual and philosophic tradition. . . . For the University, by regulation, to cast disapproval on particular viewpoints of its students risks the suppression of free speech and creative inquiry in one of the vital centers for the nation's intellectual life, its colleges and university campuses [115 S. Ct. at 2520].

The Court then addressed the additional considerations that arose in the case because Wide Awake published *religious* viewpoints rather than *secular* viewpoints based on politics or culture. Since Wide Awake sought to use public (university) funds to subsidize religious viewpoints, the First Amendment establishment clause also became a focus of the analysis. The Court, however, rejected the argument that funding Wide Awake would violate the establishment clause (see the discussion of the case in section 9.1.4). Concluding that the university funding would be "neutral toward religion," the Court emphasized that this funding was part of a broad program that "support[ed] various student enterprises, including the publication of newspapers, in recognition of the diversity and creativity of student life." The Court also emphasized that the university's Guidelines

> have a separate classification for, and do not make third-party payments on behalf of, "religious organizations," which are those "whose purpose is to practice a devotion to an acknowledged ultimate reality or deity." The category of

support here is for "student news, information, opinion, entertainment, or academic communications media groups," of which Wide Awake was 1 of 15 in the 1990 school year. WAP did not seek a subsidy because of its Christian editorial viewpoint; it sought funding as a student journal, which it was [115 S. Ct. at 2522].

8.2.3. Permissible Scope of Regulation

Joyner v. Whiting, 477 F.2d 456 (4th Cir. 1973), arose after the president of North Carolina Central University permanently terminated university financial support for the campus newspaper. The president asserted that the newspaper had printed articles urging segregation and had advocated the maintenance of an all-black university. The court held that the president's action violated the student staff's First Amendment rights:

> It may well be that a college need not establish a campus newspaper, or, if a paper has been established, the college may permanently discontinue publication for reasons wholly unrelated to the First Amendment. But if a college has a student newspaper, its publication cannot be suppressed because college officials dislike its editorial comment. . . .
>
> The principles reaffirmed in *Healy* [*v. James,* discussed in Section 9.1.1] have been extensively applied to strike down every form of censorship of student publications at state-supported institutions. Censorship of constitutionally protected expression cannot be imposed by suspending the editors, suppressing circulation, requiring imprimatur of controversial articles, excising repugnant materials, withdrawing financial support, or asserting any other form of censorial oversight based on the institution's power of the purse [477 F.2d at 460].

The president had also asserted, as grounds for terminating the paper's support, that the newspaper would employ only blacks and would not accept advertising from white-owned businesses. While such practices were not protected by the First Amendment and could be enjoined, the court held that the permanent cutoff of funds was an inappropriate remedy for such problems because of its broad effect on all future ability to publish.

Bazaar v. Fortune, 476 F.2d 570, *rehearing,* 489 F.2d 225 (5th Cir. 1973), is also illustrative. The University of Mississippi had halted publication of an issue of *Images,* a student literary magazine written and edited with the advice of a professor from the English department, because a university committee had found two stories objectionable on grounds of "taste." While the stories concerned interracial marriage and black pride, the university disclaimed objection on this basis and relied solely on the stories' inclusion of "earthy" language. The university argued that the stories would stir an adverse public reaction, and, since the magazine had a faculty adviser, their publication would reflect badly on the university. The court held that the involvement of a faculty adviser did not enlarge the university's authority over the magazine's content. The university's action violated the First Amendment because "speech cannot be stifled by the state merely because it would perhaps draw an adverse reaction from the majority of people, be they politicians or ordinary citizens, and newspapers. To come forth with such a rule would be to virtually read the First Amendment out of the Constitution and, thus, cost this nation one of its strongest tenets."

Schiff v. Williams, 519 F.2d 257 (5th Cir. 1975), concerned the firing of the editors of the *Atlantic Sun,* the student newspaper of Florida Atlantic University. The university's president based his action on the poor quality of the newspaper and on the editors' failure to respect university guidelines regarding the publication of the paper. The court characterized the president's action as a form of direct control over the paper's content and held that such action violated the First Amendment. Poor quality, even though it "could embarrass, and perhaps bring some element of disrepute to the school," was not a permissible basis on which to limit free speech. The university president in *Schiff* attempted to bolster his case by arguing that the student editors were employees of the state. The court did not give the point the attention it deserved. Presumably, if a public institution chose to operate its own publication (such as an alumni magazine) and hired a student editor, the institution could fire that student if the technical quality of his or her work was inadequate. The situation in *Schiff* did not fit this model, however, because the newspaper was not set up as the university's own publication. Rather, it was recognized by the university as a publication primarily by and for the student body, and the student editors were paid from a special student activities fee fund under the general control of the student government association.

While arrangements such as those in *Schiff* may insulate the student newspaper from university control, it might nevertheless be argued that a newspaper's use of mandatory student fees and university facilities constitutes state action (Section 1.5.2), thus subjecting the student editors themselves to First Amendment restraints when dealing with other students and with outsiders. However, the court rejected a state action argument (over a strong dissent) in *Mississippi Gay Alliance v. Goudelock,* 536 F.2d 1073 (5th Cir. 1976), a suit against a student newspaper that had refused to print an ad for a gay counseling service. And in *Sinn v. The Daily Nebraskan,* 829 F.2d 662 (8th Cir. 1987), the court held that the newspaper was not engaged in state action when it refused to print sexual preferences in classified ads. In *Gay and Lesbian Students Assn. v. Gohn,* 850 F.2d 361 (8th Cir. 1988) (further discussed in Section 9.1.1), however, the court distinguished *Sinn* and found state action in a situation where the student organization's activity was "not free from university control."

Joyner, Bazaar, and *Schiff,* along with the cases in Section 8.2.2, clearly illustrate the very substantial limits on an administrator's authority to control the student press in public institutions. Although each case involves a different regulatory technique and a different rationale for regulation, the administrators lost each time. Yet even these cases suggest grounds on which student publications can be subjected to some regulation. The *Joyner* case indicates that the student press can be prohibited from racial discrimination in its staffing and advertising policies. *Stanley* and *Rosenberger* (Section 8.2.2) suggest that institutions may alter the funding mechanisms for student publications if it does not do so for reasons associated with a publication's content or viewpoint. *Bazaar* indicates that institutions may dissociate themselves from student publications to the extent of requiring or placing a disclaimer on the cover or format of the publication. (The court specifically approved the following disclaimer after it reheard the case: "This is not an official publication of the university.") *Schiff* suggests enigmatically that there may be "special circumstances" where administrators may regulate the press to prevent "significant disruption on the university campus or within its educational processes."

In these and other student press cases, the clear lesson is not "don't regulate" but rather "don't censor." As long as administrators avoid direct or indirect control of content, they may regulate publications by student organizations or individual students in much the same way that they may regulate other organizations (Section 9.1) or students generally (Section 8.1). Even content need not be totally beyond an administrator's concern. A disclaimer requirement can be imposed to avoid confusion about the publication's status within the institution. Content that is illegal under state law because it is obscene or libelous may also be regulated, as the next two subsections suggest. And advertising content in a publication also can be controlled to some extent. In *Pittsburgh Press Co. v. Pittsburgh Commission on Human Relations,* 413 U.S. 376 (1973), for instance, the U.S. Supreme Court upheld a regulation prohibiting newspapers from publishing "help-wanted" advertisements in sex-designated columns. And in *Virginia State Board of Pharmacy v. Virginia Citizens Consumer Council,* 425 U.S. 748 (1976), while invalidating a statutory ban on advertising prescription drug prices, the Court did affirm the state's authority to regulate false or misleading advertising and advertising that proposes illegal transactions.

Issues regarding advertising in student newspapers are considered at length in *Lueth v. St. Clair County Community College,* 732 F. Supp. 1410 (E.D. Mich. 1990). The plaintiff, a former editor of the student newspaper, sued the college because it had prohibited the publication of ads for an off-campus nude-dancing club. Concluding that the advertising was "commercial speech" (Section 11.5.4.1) and that the student-run newspaper was a public forum (Section 8.1.1), the court applied the First Amendment standards for commercial speech set out in *Central Hudson Gas & Electric Corp. v. Public Service Commission*, 447 U.S. 557 (1980), as modified by *Board of Trustees of the State University of New York v. Fox*, 492 U.S. 469 (1989) (both discussed in Section 11.5.4.1). Although the college had substantial interests in not fostering underage drinking or the degradation of women, the court held the advertising prohibition unconstitutional because the college had no advertising guidelines or other limits on its authority to ensure that its regulation of advertising was "narrowly tailored" to achieve its interests. (This case should be of particular interest to institutions considering the regulation of alcohol-related ads in student publications; see S. Dodge, "Many Colleges Move to Restrict Alcohol-Related Ads in Student Papers, Vendors' Sponsorship of Events," *Chron. Higher Educ.*, Feb. 21, 1990, A39.)

8.2.4. Obscenity

It is clear that public institutions may discipline students or student organizations for having published obscene material. Public institutions may even halt the publication of such material if they do so under carefully constructed and conscientiously followed procedural safeguards. A leading case is *Antonelli v. Hammond*, 308 F. Supp. 1329 (D. Mass. 1970), which invalidated a system of prior review and approval by a faculty advisory board, because the system did not place the burden of proving obscenity on the board, or provide for a prompt review and internal appeal of the board's decisions, or provide for a prompt final judicial determination. Clearly, the constitutional requirements for prior review are stringent, and the creation of a constitutionally acceptable system is a very difficult and delicate task.

Moreover, institutional authority extends only to material that is actually obscene, and the definition or identification of obscenity is, at best, an exceedingly difficult proposition. In a leading Supreme Court case, *Papish v. Board of Curators of the University of Missouri*, 410 U.S. 667 (1973), the plaintiff was a graduate student who had been expelled for violating a board of curators bylaw prohibiting distribution of newspapers "containing forms of indecent speech." The newspaper at issue had a political cartoon on its cover that "depicted policemen raping the Statue of Liberty and the Goddess of Justice. The caption under the cartoon read: 'With Liberty and Justice for All.'" The newspaper also "contained an article entitled 'M——— F——— Acquitted,' which discussed the trial and acquittal on an assault charge of a New York City youth who was a member of an organization known as 'Up Against the Wall, M——— F———.'" After being expelled, the student sued the university, alleging a violation of her First Amendment rights. The Court, in a per curiam opinion, ruled in favor of the student:

> We think *Healy* [*v. James,* Section 9.1.1] makes it clear that the mere dissemination of ideas—no matter how offensive to good taste—on a state university cam-

pus may not be shut off in the name alone of "conventions of decency." Other recent precedents of this Court make it equally clear that neither the political cartoon nor the headline story involved in this case can be labeled as constitutionally obscene or otherwise unprotected [410 U.S. at 670].

Obscenity, then, is not definable in terms of an institution's or an administrator's own personal conceptions of taste, decency, or propriety. Obscenity can be defined only in terms of the guidelines that courts have constructed to prevent the concept from being used to choke off controversial social or political dialogue:

> We now confine the permissible scope of . . . regulation [of obscenity] to works which depict or describe sexual conduct. That conduct must be specifically defined by the applicable state law, as written or authoritatively construed. A state offense must also be limited to works which, taken as a whole, appeal to the prurient interest in sex, which portray sexual conduct in a patently offensive way, and which, taken as a whole, do not have serious literary, artistic, political, or scientific value [*Miller v. California*, 413 U.S. 15, 24 (1973)].

Although these guidelines were devised for the general community, the Supreme Court made clear in *Papish* that "the First Amendment leaves no room for the operation of a dual standard in the academic community with respect to the content of speech." Administrators devising campus rules for public institutions are thus bound by the same obscenity guidelines that bind the legislators promulgating obscenity laws. Under these guidelines, the permissible scope of regulation is very narrow, and the drafting or application of rules is a technical exercise that administrators should undertake with the assistance of counsel, if at all.

8.2.5. Libel

As they may for obscenity, institutions may discipline students or organizations that publish libelous matter. Here again, however, the authority of public institutions extends only to matter that is libelous according to technical legal definitions. It is not sufficient that a particular statement be false or misleading. Common law and constitutional doctrines require that (1) the statement be false; (2) the publication serve to identify the particular person libeled; (3) the publication cause at least nominal injury to the person libeled, usually including but not limited to injury to reputation; and (4) the falsehood be attributable to some fault on the part of the person or organization publishing it. The degree of fault depends on the subject of the alleged libel. If the subject is a public official or what the courts call a "public figure," the statement must have been made with "actual malice"; that is, with knowledge of its falsity or with reckless disregard for its truth or falsity. In all other situations governed by the First Amendment, the statement need only have been made negligently. Courts make this distinction in order to give publishers extra breathing space when reporting on certain matters of high public interest.[2]

Given the complexity of the libel concept, administrators should approach it most cautiously. Because of the need to assess both injury and fault, as well as identify the defamatory falsehood, libel may be even more difficult to combat than obscenity. Suppression in advance of publication is particularly perilous, since injury can only be speculated about at that point, and reliable facts concerning fault may not be attainable. Much of the material in campus publications, moreover, may involve public officials or public figures and thus be protected by the higher fault standard of actual malice.

Although these factors might reasonably lead administrators to forgo any regulation of libel, there is a countervailing consideration: institutions or administrators may occasionally be held liable in court for libelous statements in student publications. Such liability could exist where the institution sponsors a publication (such as a paper operated by the journalism department as a training ground for its students), employs the editors of the publication, establishes a formal committee to review material in advance of publication, or otherwise exercises some control (constitutionally or unconstitutionally) over the publication's content. In any case, liability would exist only for statements deemed libelous under the criteria set out above.

Such potential liability, however, need not necessarily prompt increased surveillance of student publications. Increased surveillance would demand regulations that stay within constitutional limits yet are strong enough to weed out all libel—an unlikely combination. And since institutional control of the publication is the predicate to the institution's liability, increased regulation increases the likelihood of liability should a libel be published. Thus, administrators may choose to handle liability problems by lessening rather than enlarging control. The privately incorporated student newspaper operating independently of the institution would be the clearest example of a no-control/no-liability situation.

A 1981 decision by the New York State Court of Claims provides a leading example of libel law's application to student newspapers at public institutions. The court's opinion in the case, *Mazart v. State*, 441 N.Y.S.2d 600 (N.Y. Ct. Cl. 1981), illustrates the basic steps in establishing libel and affirms that institutional control over the newspaper, or lack thereof, is a key to establishing or

---

[2]The U.S. Supreme Court has developed the constitutional boundaries of libel law in a progression of decisions beginning with *New York Times v. Sullivan*, 376 U.S. 254 (1964). See also *Curtis Publishing Co. v. Butts*, 388 U.S. 130 (1967); *Associated Press v. Walker*, 388 U.S. 162 (1967); *Gertz v. Robert Welch, Inc.*, 418 U.S. 323 (1974); and *Time, Inc. v. Firestone*, 424 U.S. 448 (1976).

avoiding institutional liability. The opinion also discusses the question of whether an institution can ever restrain in advance the planned publication of libelous material.

The plaintiffs (claimants) in *Mazart* were two students at the State University of New York–Binghamton who were the targets of an allegedly libelous letter to the editor published in the student newspaper, the *Pipe Dream*. The letter described a prank that had occurred in a male dormitory and characterized it as an act of prejudice against homosexuals. The plaintiffs' names appeared at the end of the letter, although they had not in fact written it, and the body of the letter identified them as "members of the gay community." Applying accepted principles of libel law to the educational context in which the incident occurred, the court determined that this letter was libelous:

> Did the letter in the *Pipe Dream* expose claimants to hatred, contempt, or aversion, or induce an evil or unsavory opinion of them in the minds of a substantial number of the community? The answer to the question is far from simple. In general, the community we are concerned with here was the university community located on a campus outside of the City of Binghamton, Broome County, New York. According to the chairman of the English Department at the university, . . . sexual orientation had no more bearing in the classroom than religious affiliation. The assistant vice president for finance, management, and control of the university opined that the published letter had a "very low, very little effect" on the campus community.
>
> No doubt the impact of the published letter on the collective mind of the university was considerably less than it might have been had the letter been published in a conservative rural American village. Nonetheless, the court finds that an unsavory opinion of the claimants did settle in the minds of a substantial number of persons in the university community. . . . The question of homosexuality was a significant one on the university campus. . . . Both claimants testified that they were accosted by numerous fellow students after the event and queried about their sexual orientation, and the court finds their testimony, in this respect, credible. Deviant sexual intercourse and sodomy were crimes in the state of New York at the time the letter was published (Penal Law, §§130 and 130.38). Certainly those members of the university community who did not personally know the claimants would logically conclude that claimants were homosexual, since the letter identified them as being members of the "gay community." The court finds that a substantial number of the university community would naturally assume that the claimants engaged in homosexual acts from such identification [441 N.Y.S.2d at 603–04].

The court then rejected the state's argument that, even if the letter was libelous, its publication was protected by a qualified privilege because the subject matter was of public concern. Again using commonly accepted libel principles, the court concluded that a privilege did not apply because the editors of the *Pipe Dream* acted in a grossly irresponsible manner by failing to give due consideration to the standards of information gathering and dissemination. It is obvious that authorship of a letter wherein the purported author appears to be libeled should be verified. Not only was the authorship of the letter herein not verified but it appears that the *Pipe Dream,* at least in November of 1977, had no procedures or guidelines with regard to the verification of the authorship of any letters to the editor [441 N.Y.S.2d at 604].

Third, the court held that, although the letter was libelous and not privileged, the university (and thus the state) was not liable for the unlawful acts of the student newspaper. In its analysis, the court considered and rejected two theories of liability: "(1) [that] the state, through the university, may be vicariously liable for the torts of the *Pipe Dream* and its editors on the theory of *respondeat superior* (that is, the university, as principal, might be liable for the torts of its agents, the student paper and editors); and (2) [that] the state, through the university, may have been negligent in failing to provide guidelines to the *Pipe Dream* staff regarding libel generally and, specifically, regarding the need to review and verify letters to the editor."

In rejecting the first theory, the court relied heavily on First Amendment principles:

The state could be held vicariously liable if the university and the *Pipe Dream* staff operated in some form of agency relationship. However, it is characteristic of the relationship of principal and agent that the principal has a right to control the conduct of the agent with respect to matters entrusted to him. While this control need not apply to every detail of an agent's conduct and can be found where there is merely a right held by the principal to make management and policy decisions affecting the agent, there can be no agency relationship where the alleged principal has no right of control over the alleged agent.

There are severe constitutional limitations on the exercise of any form of control by a state university over a student newspaper . . . (*Panarella v. Birenbaum,* 37 A.D.2d 987, 327 N.Y.S.2d 755, *affirmed,* 32 N.Y.2d 108, 343 N.Y.S.2d 333, 296 N.E.2d 238). . . . Censorship or prior restraint of constitutionally protected expression in student publications at state-supported institutions has been uniformly proscribed by the courts. Such censorship or prior restraint cannot be imposed by suspending editors (*Scoville v. Board of Education of Joliet Township High School District 204,* 425 F.2d 10), by suppressing circulation (*Channing Club v. Board of Regents of Texas Tech. University,* 317 F. Supp. 688), by requiring prior approval of controversial articles (*Quarterman v. Byrd,* 453 F.2d 54 (4th Cir.); *Trujillo v. Love,* 322 F. Supp. 1266; *Antonelli v. Hammond,* 308 F. Supp. 1329), by excising or suppressing distasteful material (*Trujillo v. Love, supra; Korn v. Elkins,* 317 F. Supp. 138; *Zucker v. Panitz,* 299 F. Supp. 102), or by withdrawing financial support (*Joyner v. Whiting,* 477 F.2d 456 (4th Cir.); *Antonelli v. Hammond, supra*). Claimants' counsel argues that "the issue of prior restraint has never been extended to libel . . . cases." . . . In fact, in the absence of special circumstances, the publication of libelous material will not be restrained by the courts. . . .

Thus, it appears that a policy of prior approval of items to be published in a student newspaper, even if directed only to restraining the publication of potentially libelous material (cf. *Trujillo v. Love, supra*), would run afoul of *Near v. State of Minnesota, supra,* wherein the Court stated that "liberty of the press, historically considered and taken up by the federal Constitution, has meant, principally although not exclusively, immunity from previous restraints or censorship" (283 U.S. at 716). . . . The court, therefore, finds that the university was powerless to prevent the publication of the letter.

Although claimants' counsel suggests in his argument that the university's involvement with the funding of the *Pipe Dream* might afford it some measure of control, this involvement affords little, if any, actual control over the funding and expenditures of the newspaper . . . and, in any event, it is settled that no form of editorial control over constitutionally protected expression in student publications can be based on the university's power of the purse.

No doubt the university benefits, and did benefit at the time of the publication of the letter, from the existence of the *Pipe Dream.* That the university recognized participation on the newspaper as a form of independent study indicates that it received educational benefits. Furthermore, the *Pipe Dream* served as a means of disseminating information to the university community and as a forum for debate and discussion for members of the university community. However, these factors, which might suggest an agency relationship, are insufficient to overcome the university's lack of control over the newspaper.

The fact that the university created a climate wherein the student newspaper flourished by furnishing office space and janitorial services hardly creates an agency relationship which would permit recovery against the state. Such accouterments are nothing more than a form of financial aid to the newspaper which cannot be traded off in return for editorial control (see *Joyner v. Whiting, supra; Antonelli v. Hammond, supra*).

The court recognizes that the *Pipe Dream* and its staff may be incapable of compensating claimants for any damages flowing from the libel. But, in light of the university's eschewing control, editorial or otherwise, over the paper and the constitutionally imposed barriers to the exercise by the university of any editorial control over the newspaper, the court must reluctantly conclude that the relationship of the university and the *Pipe Dream* is not such as would warrant the imposition of vicarious liability on the state for defamatory material appearing in the student newspaper (see "Tort Liability of a University for Libelous Material in Student Publications," 71 *Michigan L. Rev.* 1061) [441 N.Y.S.2d at 604–06; some citations omitted].

Focusing on the tort law concept of "duty," the court then rejected the claimant's second liability theory:

The second theory . . . involves the question of whether the state university, and therefore the state, can be cast in damages in simple negligence for failing to provide to the student editors guidelines and procedures designed to avoid the publication of libelous material. As discussed above, there are constitutional limitations on the actual exercise of editorial control by the university, but this does not necessarily preclude the existence of a duty on the part of the university to furnish guidance.

In view of the absolute hands-off policy adopted by the university administration, it is clear that no such guidelines were furnished, and from the evidence adduced at trial, it does not appear that student editors verified the authorship of controversial letters to the editor prior to the subject publication. The issue then is whether there was a duty on the part of the university administration. The court concludes that there was not. It is clear from a reading of the published cases dealing with the rights of college students that the courts uniformly regard them as young adults and not children. . . .

Furthermore, the establishment by statute of the minimum voting age (Election Law, §5–102), drinking age (Alcoholic Beverage Control Law, §65), and the age of consent for marriage (Domestic Relations Law, §7) at 18 years, is indicative of a recognition, at least on the part of the legislature, of a substantial degree of maturity in college-aged persons.

. . . [T]he court in *Greenberg v. CBS, Inc.*, 69 A.D.2d 693, 419 N.Y.S.2d 988, stated: "The elementary standards of basic news reporting are common knowledge. News articles and broadcasts must contain the answers to the essential inquiries of who, what, where, when, why, and how" (419 N.Y.S.2d 988). Certainly the need to verify the authorship of a letter wherein the purported author appears to be libeled is rudimentary. A conclusion that the university had a duty to furnish guidance to the *Pipe Dream* concerning libel would in effect be a finding that the *Pipe Dream* editors lacked that degree of maturity and common sense necessary to comprehend the normal procedures for information gathering and dissemination. But surely such a finding would be anomalous since those editors' contemporaries might well be selected to sit on a jury (Judiciary Law, §510(2)), assigned the task of determining, without the aid and guidance of expert testimony, whether a newspaper (the *Pipe Dream* or any other) had failed to adhere to generally followed standards, resulting in the publication of libel. . . .

The court must, therefore, find that the university had no duty to supply news gathering and dissemination guidelines to the *Pipe Dream* editors since they were presumed to already know those guidelines. Admittedly, it appears that the student editors of the *Pipe Dream* in 1977 either did not know or simply ignored common-sense verification guidelines with regard to the publication of the instant letter. But that was not the fault of the university. In either event, there was no duty on the part of the university. The editors' lack of knowledge of or failure to adhere to standards which are common knowledge (*Greenberg v. CBS, Inc., supra)* and ordinarily followed by reasonable persons . . . was not reasonably foreseeable [441 N.Y.S.2d at 606–07].

Mazart v. State is an extensively reasoned precedent in an area where there has been a dearth of precedent. The court's opinion provides much useful guidance for administrators of public institutions. The opinion's reasoning depends, however, on particular circumstances concerning the campus setting in which the libel occurred, the irresponsibility of the student editors, the degree of control the institution exercised over the newspaper, and the foreseeability of the student editors' irresponsible acts. Administrators will therefore want to consult with counsel before attempting to apply the principles in *Mazart* to occurrences on their own campuses.

8.2.6. Obscenity and Libel in Private Institutions

Since the First Amendment does not apply to private institutions that are not engaged in state action (Section 1.5.2), such institutions have a freer hand in regulating obscenity and libel. Yet private institutions should devise their regulatory role cautiously. Regulations broadly construing libel and obscenity based on lay concepts of those terms could stifle the flow of dialogue within the institution, while attempts to avoid this problem with narrow regulations may lead the institution into the same definitional complexities that public institutions face when seeking to comply with the First Amendment. Moreover, in devising their policies on obscenity and libel, private institutions will want to consider the potential impact of state law. Violation of state obscenity or libel law by student publications could subject the responsible students to injunctions, damage actions, and even criminal prosecutions, causing unwanted publicity for the institution. But if the institution regulates the student publications to prevent such problems, it could be held liable along with the students if it exercises sufficient control over the publication (see Sections 2.1 and 8.2.5).

SEC. 8.3. THE SPECIAL PROBLEM OF HATE SPEECH

Since the late 1980s, colleges and universities have increasingly confronted the legal, policy, and political aspects of the "hate speech" problem.[3] Responding to escalating racial, anti-Semitic, homophobic, and sexist incidents on campus, as well as to developments in the courts, institutions have enacted, revised, and sometimes revoked rules of conduct that regulate certain types of harassing or abusive student behavior directed against members of minority groups. Often the harassment or abuse involved in campus incidents or covered by conduct rules has been conveyed by the spoken or written word or by symbolic

---

[3]Portions of this section are extracted and adapted (without further attribution) from W. Kaplin, "A Proposed Process for Managing the First Amendment Aspects of Campus Hate Speech," 63 *J. Higher Educ.* 517 (1992), copyright ©1992 by the Ohio State University Press; and from W. Kaplin, "Hate Speech on the College Campus: Freedom of Speech and Equality at the Crossroads," 27 *Land & Water L. Rev.* 243 (1992), copyright © 1992 by the University of Wyoming.

conduct—thus raising difficult issues concerning students' free speech and press rights and having important implications for both academic freedom and equal educational opportunity for students.

"Hate speech" is an imprecise, catch-all term that generally includes verbal and written words and symbolic acts that convey a grossly negative assessment of particular persons or groups based on their race, gender, ethnicity, religion, sexual orientation, or disability. Hate speech thus is highly derogatory and degrading, and the language is typically coarse. The purpose of the speech is more to humiliate or wound than it is to communicate ideas or information. Common vehicles for such speech include epithets, slurs, insults, taunts, and threats. Because the viewpoints underlying hate speech may be considered "politically incorrect," the debate over hate speech codes has sometimes become intertwined with the political correctness phenomenon on American campuses.

Hate speech is not limited to a face-to-face confrontation or shouts from a crowd. It takes many forms. It may appear on T-shirts, posters, classroom blackboards, bulletin boards, or in flyers and leaflets, phone calls, letters, or electronic mail messages on a computer screen. It may be a cartoon appearing in a student publication or a joke told on a campus radio station or at an after-dinner speech, a skit at a student event, an anonymous note slipped under a dormitory door, or graffiti scribbled on a wall or sidewalk. It may be conveyed through defacement of posters or displays; through symbols such as burning crosses, swastikas, KKK insignia, and Confederate flags; and even through themes for social functions, such as black-face Harlem parties or parties celebrating white history week.

When hate speech is directed at particular individuals, it may cause real psychic harm to those individuals and may also inflict pain on the broader class of persons who belong to the group denigrated by the hate speech. Moreover, the feelings of vulnerability, insecurity, and alienation that repeated incidents of hate speech can engender in the victimized groups may prevent them from taking full advantage of the educational, employment, and social opportunities on the campus and may undermine the conditions necessary for constructive dialogue with other persons or groups. Ultimately, hate speech may degrade the intellectual environment of the campus, thus harming the entire academic community.

Since hate speech regulations may prohibit and punish particular types of messages, pressing constitutional issues arise under the First Amendment, for public institutions (see Section 1.5.2), as well as for private institutions that are subject to state constitutional provisions or statutes employing First Amendment norms (see Section 8.1.1, this volume) or that voluntarily adhere to First Amendment norms. A number of important cases have reached the courts since 1989, some involving university hate speech codes and others involving city ordinances or state statutes that were construed to cover hate speech activities or that enhanced the penalties for conduct undertaken with racist or other biased motivations.

The U.S. Supreme Court's 1992 decision in *R.A.V. v. City of St. Paul,* 112 S. Ct. 2538 (1992), addresses the validity of a city ordinance directed at hate crimes. This ordinance made it a misdemeanor to place on public or private property any symbol or graffiti that one reasonably knew would "arouse anger, alarm or resentment in others on the basis of race, color, creed, religion or gender." R.A.V., a juvenile who had set up and burned a cross in the yard of a black family, challenged the ordinance as overbroad (see this volume, Section 8.1.2). The lower courts upheld the validity of the statute by narrowly construing it to apply only to expression that would be considered fighting words or incitement. The U.S. Supreme Court disagreed and invalidated the ordinance, but the majority opinion by Justice Scalia did not use overbreadth analysis. Instead, it focused on the viewpoint discrimination evident in the ordinance and invalidated the ordinance because its restriction on speech content was too narrow rather than too broad:

> Although the phrase in the ordinance, "arouses anger, alarm or resentment in others," has been limited by the Minnesota Supreme Court's construction to reach only those symbols or displays that amount to "fighting words," the remaining, unmodified terms make clear that the ordinance applies only to "fighting words" that insult, or provoke violence, "on the basis of race, color, creed, religion or gender." Displays containing abusive invective, no matter how vicious or severe, are permissible unless they are addressed to one of the specified disfavored topics. Those who wish to use "fighting words" in connection with other ideas—to express hostility, for example, on the basis of political affiliation, union membership, or homosexuality—are not covered. The First Amendment does not permit St. Paul to impose special prohibitions on those speakers who express views on disfavored subjects [112 S. Ct. at 2547].

The Court did note several narrow exceptions to this requirement of viewpoint neutrality but found that the St. Paul ordinance did not fall into any of these narrow exceptions (112 S. Ct. at 2545–47). The Court also determined that the city could not justify its narrow viewpoint-based ordinance. The city did have a compelling interest in promoting the rights of those who have traditionally been subject to discrimination. But because a broader ordinance without the viewpoint-based restriction would equally serve this interest, the law was not "reasonably necessary" to the advancement of the interest and was thus invalid.

The Supreme Court visited the hate speech problem again in *Wisconsin v. Mitchell,* 113 S. Ct. 2194 (1993). At issue was the constitutionality of a state law that enhanced the punishment for commission of a crime when the victim was intentionally selected because of his "race, religion, color, disability, sexual orientation, national origin or ancestry" (Wis. Stat. §939.645(1)(b)). The state had applied the statute to a defendant who, with several other black males, had seen and discussed a movie that featured a racially motivated beating and thereupon had brutally assaulted a white male. Before the attack, the defendant had said, among other things, "There goes a white boy; go get him." A jury convicted the defendant of aggravated battery, and the court enhanced his sentence because his actions were racially motivated.

The Court unanimously upheld the statute because it focused on the defendant's motive, traditionally a major consideration in sentencing. Unlike the *R.A.V.* case, the actual crime was not the speech or thought itself but the assault—"conduct unprotected by the First Amendment." Moreover, the statute did not permit enhancement of penalties because of "mere disagreement with offenders' beliefs or biases" but rather because "bias-inspired conduct . . . is thought to inflict greater individual and societal harm." The Court did caution, moreover, "that a defendant's abstract beliefs, however obnoxious to most people, may not be taken into consideration by a sentencing judge." Thus, in order for a penalty-enhancing statute to be constitutionally applied, the prosecution must show more than the mere fact that a defendant is, for example, a racist. Such evidence alone would most likely be considered irrelevant and unduly prejudicial by a trial judge. Instead, the prosecution must prove that the defendant's racism motivated him to commit the particular crime; there must be a direct connection between the criminal act and a racial motive. This showing will generally be difficult to make and may necessitate direct evidence such as that in *Mitchell,* where the defendant's own contemporaneous statements indicated a clear and immediate intent to act on racial or other proscribed grounds.

Although no case involving campus hate speech has yet reached the U.S. Supreme Court, there have been several important cases in the lower courts. The first was *Doe v. University of Michigan,* 721 F. Supp. 852 (E.D. Mich. 1989). The plaintiff, a graduate student, challenged the university's hate speech policy, whose central provision prohibited "[a]ny behavior, verbal or physical, that stigmatizes or victimizes an individual on the basis of race, ethnicity, religion, sex, sexual orientation, creed, national origin, ancestry, age, marital status, handicap, or Vietnam-era veteran status." The policy prohibited such behavior if it "[i]nvolves an express or implied threat to" or "[h]as the purpose or reasonably foreseeable effect of interfering with" or "[c]reates an intimidating, hostile, or demeaning environment" for individual pursuits in academics, employment, or extracurricular activities. This prohibition applied to behavior in "educational and academic centers, such as classroom buildings, libraries, research laboratories, recreation and study centers." Focusing on the wording of the policy and the way in which the university interpreted and applied this language, the court held that the policy was unconstitutionally overbroad on its face because its wording swept up and sought to punish substantial amounts of constitutionally protected speech. In addition, the court held the policy to be unconstitutionally vague on its face. This fatal flaw arose primarily from the words "stigmatize" and "victimize" and the phrases "threat to" or "interfering with," as applied to an individual's academic pursuits—language which was so vague that students would not be able to discern what speech would be protected and what would be prohibited.

Similarly, in *UWM Post, Inc. v. Board of Regents of the University of Wisconsin System,* 774 F. Supp. 1168 (E.D. Wis. 1991), the court utilized both overbreadth and vagueness analysis to invalidate a campus hate speech regulation. The regulation applied to "racist or discriminatory comments, epithets, or other expressive behavior directed at an individual" and prohibited any such speech that "intentionally" (1) "demean[s]" the race, sex, or other specified characteristics of the individual, and (2) "create[s] an intimidating, hostile, or demeaning environment for education." The court held this language to be overbroad because it encompassed many types of speech that would not fall within any existing exceptions to the principle that government may not regulate the content of speech. Regarding vagueness, the court rejected the plaintiffs' argument that the phrase "discriminatory comments, epithets, or other expressive behavior" and the word "demean" were vague. But the court nevertheless held the regulation unconstitutionally vague because another of its provisions, juxtaposed against the language quoted above, created confusion as to whether the prohibited speech must actually demean the individual and create a hostile educational environment, or whether the speaker must only *intend* those results and they need not actually occur.

A third case, *Iota Xi Chapter of Sigma Chi Fraternity v. George Mason University,* 993 F.2d 386 (4th Cir. 1993), was decided (unlike the other two) after the U.S. Supreme Court's decision in *R.A.V. v. City of St. Paul.* In this case, a fraternity had staged an "ugly woman contest" in which one member wore black face, used padding and women's clothes, and presented an offensive caricature of a black woman. After receiving numerous complaints about the skit from other students, the university imposed heavy sanctions on the fraternity. The fraternity, relying on the First Amendment, sought an injunction that would force the school to lift the sanctions. The trial court granted summary judgment for the fraternity, and the appellate court affirmed the trial court's ruling.

Determining that the skit was "expressive entertainment" or "expressive conduct" protected by the First Amendment and that the sanctions constituted a content-based restriction on speech, the court applied reasoning similar to that in *R.A.V.:*

The mischief was the University's punishment of those who scoffed at its goals of racial integration and gender neutrality, while permitting, even encouraging, conduct that would further the viewpoint expressed in the University's goals and probably embraced by a majority of society as well. . . .

The University, however, urges us to weigh Sigma Chi's conduct against the substantial interests inherent in educational endeavors. . . . The University certainly has a substantial interest in maintaining an environment free of discrimination and racism, and in providing gender-neutral education. Yet it seems equally apparent that it has available numerous alternatives to imposing punishment on students based on the viewpoints they express. We agree wholeheartedly that it is the University officials' responsibility, even their obligation, to achieve the goals they have set. On the other hand, a public university has many constitutionally permissible means to protect female and minority students. We must emphasize, as have other courts, that "the manner of [its action] cannot consist of selective limitations upon speech." [R.A.V.], 112 S. Ct. at 2548. . . . The First Amendment forbids the government from "restrict[ing] expression because of its message [or] its ideas." *Police Department v. Mosley,* 408 U.S. 92, 95 (1972). The University should have accomplished its goals in some fashion other than silencing speech on the basis of its viewpoint [993 F.2d at 393].[4]

The three campus cases, combined with *R.A.V.,* make clear the exceeding difficulty public institutions face in attempting to promulgate hate speech regulations that would survive First Amendment scrutiny. Read against the backdrop of earlier Supreme Court cases on freedom of speech, the hate speech cases reflect and confirm five major free speech principles, which, together, severely constrain the authority of government to regulate hate speech. Under the first principle, regulations on the content of speech—that is, the speaker's message—are highly suspect. As the U.S. Supreme Court has frequently stated, "[A]bove all else, the First Amendment means that government has no power to restrict expression because of its message, its ideas, its subject matter, or its content. . . . There is an 'equality of status in the field of ideas,' and government must afford all points of view an equal opportunity to be heard" (*Police Department v. Mosley,* 408 U.S. 92, 95–96 (1972), quoting A. Meiklejohn, *Political Freedom: The Constitutional Powers of the People* (1948), 27 (reprinted by Greenwood Press, 1979)).

Under the second free speech principle, the emotional content as well as the cognitive content of speech is protected from government regulation. As the U.S. Supreme Court explained in *Cohen v. California,* 403 U.S. 15 (1971):

---

[4]In a strong concurring opinion, one judge agreed with the decision only because the university had "tacitly approv[ed]" of the skit without giving any indication that the fraternity would be punished, and then imposed sanctions only after the skit had been performed. More generally, the concurring judge asserted that the university had "greater authority to regulate expressive conduct within its confines as a result of the unique nature of the educational forum" (see this volume, Section 8.1.1) and therefore could regulate certain offensive speech that interferes with its ability to "provide the optimum conditions for learning" and thus "runs directly counter to its mission."

[M]uch linguistic expression serves a dual communicative function: it conveys not only ideas capable of relatively precise, detached explication, but otherwise inexpressible emotions as well. In fact, words are often chosen as much for their emotive as their cognitive force. We cannot sanction the view that the Constitution, while solicitous of the cognitive content of individual speech, has little or no regard for that emotive function which, practically speaking, may often be the more important element of the overall message [403 U.S. at 26].

Under the third free speech principle, speech may not be prohibited merely because persons who hear or view it are offended by the message. In a flag-burning case, *Texas v. Johnson,* 491 U.S. 397 (1989), the U.S. Supreme Court reaffirmed that "[i]f there is a bedrock principle underlying the First Amendment, it is that the government may not prohibit the expression of an idea simply because society finds the idea itself offensive or disagreeable."

Under the fourth free speech principle, government may not regulate speech activity with provisions whose language is either overbroad or vague and would thereby create a chilling effect on the exercise of free speech rights. As the U.S. Supreme Court has stated, "Because First Amendment freedoms need breathing space to survive, government may regulate in the area only with narrow specificity" (*NAACP v. Button,* 371 U.S. 415, 433 (1963)).

And under the fifth free speech principle, when government is regulating what is considered an unprotected type of speech—for example, fighting words or obscenity—it generally may not restrict expression of certain topics or viewpoints in that unprotected area without also restricting expressions of other topics and viewpoints within that same area. For example, if government utilizes the "fighting words" rationale for regulation, it must generally regulate all fighting words or none; it cannot selectively regulate only fighting words that convey disfavored messages. This principle, sometimes called the "underbreadth" principle, is a new addition to First Amendment jurisprudence derived from the *R.A.V.* case discussed earlier.

In light of the imposing barriers to regulation erected by these principles, it is critical that institutions (public and private alike) emphasize *nonregulatory* approaches for dealing with hate speech. Such approaches do not rely on the prohibition of certain types of speech or the imposition of involuntary sanctions on transgressors, as do regulatory approaches. Moreover, nonregulatory initiatives may reach or engage a wider range of students than regulatory approaches can. They also may have more influence on student attitudes and values and may be more effective in creating an institutional environment that is inhospitable to hate behavior. Thus, nonregulatory initiatives may have a broader and longer-range impact on the hate speech problem. Nonregulatory initiatives may also be more in harmony with higher education's mission to foster critical examination and dialogue in the search for truth. See generally S. Sherry, "Speaking of Virtue: A Republican Approach to University Regulation of Hate Speech,"

75 *Minn. L. Rev.* 933, 934–36, 942–44 (1991). Nonregulatory initiatives, moreover, do not raise substantial First Amendment issues. For these reasons, institutions should move to regulatory options only if they are certain that nonregulatory initiatives cannot suitably alleviate existing or incipient hate speech problems.

In addition to nonregulatory initiatives, institutions may regulate hate *conduct* or *behavior* (as opposed to speech) on their campuses. Hateful impulses that manifest themselves in such behavior or conduct are not within the constitutional protections accorded speech (that is, the use of words or symbols to convey a message). Examples include kicking, shoving, spitting, throwing objects at persons, trashing rooms, and blocking pathways or entryways. Since such behaviors are not speech, they can be aggressively prohibited and punished in order to alleviate hate problems on campus.

If an institution also deems it necessary to regulate speech itself, either in formulating general policies or in responding to particular incidents, it should first consider the applicability or adaptability of regulations that are already in or could readily be inserted into its general code of student conduct. The question in each instance would be whether a particular type of disciplinary regulation can be applied to some particular type of hate speech without substantially intruding on free speech values and without substantial risk that a court would later find the regulation's application to hate speech unconstitutional. Under this selective incremental approach, much hate speech must remain unregulated because no type of regulation could constitutionally reach it. But some provisions in conduct codes might be applied to some hate speech. The following discussion considers six potential types of such regulations.

First, when hate speech is combined with nonspeech actions in the same course of behavior, institutions may regulate the nonspeech elements of behavior without violating the First Amendment. A campus building may be spray-painted with swastikas; homophobic graffiti may be painted on a campus sidewalk; a KKK insignia may be carved into the door of a dormitory room; a student may be shoved or spit on in the course of enduring verbal abuse. All these behaviors convey a hate message and therefore involve speech; but all also have a nonspeech element characterizable as destruction of property or physical attack. While the institution cannot prohibit particular messages, it can prohibit harmful acts; such acts therefore may be covered under neutral regulations governing such nonspeech matters as destruction and defacement of property or physical assaults of persons.

Second, institutions may regulate the time or place at which hate speech is uttered, or the manner in which it is uttered, as long as they use neutral regulations that do not focus on the content or viewpoint of the speech. For example, an institution could punish the shouting of racial epithets in a dormitory quadrangle in the middle of the night, as long as the applicable regulation would also cover (for example) the shouting of cheers for a local sports team at the same location and time.

Third, institutions may regulate the content of hate speech that falls within one of the various exceptions to the principle forbidding content-based restrictions on speech. Thus, institutions may punish hate speech that constitutes fighting words, obscenity, incitement, or private defamation. Any such regulation, however, must comply with the new "underbreadth" principle announced in the *R.A.V.* case. Under this principle, an institution could not have a specific hate speech code based on (for example) a "fighting words" rationale, but it could have a broader regulation that applies to hate speech constituting fighting words as well as to all other types of fighting words.

Fourth, institutions probably may regulate hate speech in the form of threats or intimidation aimed at particular individuals and creating in them a realistic fear for their physical safety or the security of their property. Speech activities with such effects are analogous to assaults, which typically are punishable under both criminal law and tort law. Such activities, even though carried out in part through speech, may be reached under code provisions dealing generally with physical assaults or other threats of physical harm to person or property. (See *United States v. Hayward*, 6 F.3d 1241, 1249–52 (7th Cir. 1993).)

Fifth, institutions probably may regulate hate speech that occurs on or is projected onto private areas, such as dormitory rooms or library study carrels, and thereby infringes on privacy interests of individuals who legitimately occupy these places. For First Amendment purposes, such private areas are not considered "public forums" open to public dialogue; and the persons occupying such places may be "captive audiences" who cannot guard their privacy by avoiding the hate speech (see *Frisby v. Schultz*, 487 U.S. 474 (1988)). For these two reasons, it is likely that hate speech of this type could be constitutionally reached under provisions dealing generally with unjustified invasions of students' personal privacy.

Sixth, institutions probably may regulate hate speech that furthers a scheme of racial or other discrimination. If a fraternity places a sign in front of its house reading "No blacks allowed here," the speech is itself an act of discrimination, making it unlikely that black students would seek to become members of that fraternity. When such speech is an integral element of a pattern of discriminatory behavior, institutions should be able to cover it and related actions under a code provision prohibiting discrimination on the basis of identifiable group characteristics such as race, sex, or ethnicity. The *R.A.V.* majority opinion itself apparently supports such a rationale when it suggests that the nondiscrimination requirements of Title VII (the federal employment discrimination statute) would not violate the "underbreadth" principle and could constitutionally be applied to sexual harassment accomplished in part through speech.

In addition to these six bases for regulating hate speech, institutions may also—as was suggested earlier—devise enhanced penalties under their conduct codes for hate *behavior* or *conduct* (such as the racially inspired physical attack in *Wisconsin v. Mitchell* above) that does not itself involve speech. An offense that would normally merit a semester of probation, for instance, might be punished by a one-semester suspension upon proof that the act was undertaken for racial reasons. Institutions must proceed most cautiously, however. The delicate inquiry into the perpetrator's motives that penalty enhancement requires is usually the domain of courts, lawyers, and expert witnesses, guided by formal procedures and rules of evidence as well as a body of precedent. An institution should not consider itself equipped to undertake this type of inquiry unless its disciplinary system has well-developed fact-finding processes and substantial assistance from legal counsel or a law-trained judicial officer. Institutions should also assure themselves that the system's "judges" can distinguish between the perpetrator's actual motivation for the offense (which is a permissible basis for the inquiry) and the perpetrator's thoughts or general disposition (which, under *Mitchell,* is an impermissible consideration).

SEC. 8.4. FREE SPEECH ON CAMPUS COMPUTER NETWORKS

Increasingly, free speech on campus is enhanced, and free speech issues are compounded, by the growth of technology. Cable and satellite transmission technologies, for instance, are having such an effect on some campuses. But the clearest and most important example—now and for the foreseeable future—is computer technology. Computer labs, campus LAN's, and Internet gateways have assumed a pervasive presence on most campuses, and are used increasingly by students for e-mail communications, discussion groups, research, access to information on campus activities and services, and entertainment. Students may be both senders (speakers) and receivers (listeners); their purposes may be related to course work or extracurricular activities, or may be purely personal; and their communications may be local (within the institution) or may extend around the world.

As the number, variety, and reach of computer communications have increased, so have the development of institutional computer use policies and other institutional responses to perceived problems. The problems may be of the "traffic cop" variety, occasioning a need for the institution to allocate its limited computer resources by directing traffic to prevent traffic jams. Or the problems may be more controversial, raising computer misuse issues such as defamation, harassment, threats, hate speech, copyright infringement, and academic dishonesty. The latter types of problems may present more difficult legal issues, since institutional regulations attempting to alleviate these problems may be viewed as content-based restrictions on speech.

Public institutions, therefore, must keep a watchful eye on the First Amendment when drafting and enforcing computer use policies. Just as federal and state legislation regulating computer communications may be invalidated under the free speech and press clauses (see Section 12.1.7), particular provisions of campus regulations can be struck as well is they contravene these clauses. Although private institutions are not similarly bound (see Section 1.5.2), they may voluntarily protect student free expression through student codes or bills of rights, or computer use policies themselves, or through campus custom—or may be bound by state statutes or regulations to protect free expression; thus student affairs professionals at private institutions will also need to be keenly aware of First Amendment developments regarding computer speech.

Under existing First Amendment principles (see generally Sections 8.1.1, 8.1.2, and 8.3), administrators should ask four main questions when devising new computer use policies or when reviewing or applying existing policies: (1) Are you seeking to regulate, or do you regulate, the content of computer speech ("cyberspace speech")? (2) If a particular regulation is content-based, does it fit into any First Amendment exceptions that permit content-based regulations— in particular the exceptions for obscenity, child pornography, fraudulent commercial representations, purely private defamation, or "true" threats? (3) (A) Does your institution own the computer hardware or software being used for the computer speech; and (B) if so, has your institution created "forums" for discussion on the computer networks it owns? (4) Are your regulations or proposed regulations clear, specific, and narrow?

For question 1, if a computer use policy regulates the content of speech—the ideas, opinions, or viewpoints expressed—the courts will usually subject the regulation to a two-part standard of "strict scrutiny": (1) Does the content regulation further a "compelling" governmental interest, and (2) Is the regulation "narrowly tailored" and "necessary" to achieve this interest? The institution's need to act in cases of copyright infringement, bribery, blackmail, stalking, or other violations of federal and state law may often be considered compelling interests, as may the need to protect the institution's academic integrity when computers are used for "cheating"; these interests may meet the strict scrutiny standard if the regulations are very carefully drawn. But otherwise, the standard is extremely difficult to meet. In contrast, if a computer regulation served "neutral" government interests not based on the content of speech (for example, routine "traffic cop" regulations), a less stringent and easier-to-meet standard would apply.

Regarding question 2, if the restriction on computer speech is content-based, and thus extremely difficult to justify under the strict scrutiny standard, it could still survive if it falls into one of the First Amendment exceptions. These exceptions are all technical and narrow, however (see, for example, Section 8.2.4), and collectively would cover only a portion of the computer speech that an institution might wish to limit.

Regarding question 3, institutions may be in a stronger regulatory position when they own the computers, computer programs, or networks whose use they are restricting; the First Amendment standards would then be low and would generally permit content-based restrictions of computer speech (regardless of whether they fall into one of the exceptions) other than restrictions based on the particular viewpoint of the speaker. But these lower standards apparently would not apply if the institution had used the computers, programs, or networks it owns to create an open or public "forum" for expression by students or by the campus community. In such circumstances, under the "public forum doctrine," the First Amendment prohibition on content restrictions would continue to apply unless the institution could fit within an exception. See Joseph Beckham and William Schmid, "Forum Analysis in Cyberspace: The Case of Public Sector Higher Education," 98 *West's Education Law Rptr.* 11 (May 18, 1995).

Under question 4, the focus is on the actual wording of each regulatory provision in the institution's computer use policy. Even if a particular provision has been devised in conformance with the First Amendment principles addressed in questions 1–3, it must in addition be drafted with a precision sufficient to meet constitutional standards of narrowness and clarity. If it does not, it will be subject to invalidation under either the "overbreadth" doctrine or the "vagueness" doctrine (see generally Section 7.2.1).

One may fairly ask whether all these existing First Amendment principles should apply to the vast new world of cyberspace. Indeed, scholars and judges are currently debating whether free speech and press law will apply in full to computer technology. See Lawrence Lessig, "The Path of Cyberlaw," 104 *Yale L.J.* 1743 (1995). Although courts are committed to taking account of the unique aspects of each new communications technology, and allowing First Amendment law to grow and adapt in the process, it does not appear likely at present that the basic principles discussed above will be discarded or radically transformed when applied to cyberspace. In fact, in the leading case to date, *American Civil Liberties Union v. Reno* (discussed in Section 12.1.7), all three judges who wrote opinions relied explicitly on the principles addressed in this section under questions 1, 2, and 4; and one of these judges (Dalzell) also dwelt at length on the "forum" aspects of the Internet (question 3). Thus, although administrators will need to follow both legal and technological developments closely in this fast-moving area, for the present they should work from the premise that basic First Amendment principles are their authoritative guides.

SELECTED ANNOTATED BIBLIOGRAPHY

Sec. 8.1   (Student Protest and Demonstrations)

Blasi, Vincent. "Prior Restraints on Demonstrations," 68 *Mich. L. Rev.* 1482 (1970). A comprehensive discussion of First Amendment theory and case law and the specific manner in which the law bears on the various components of a student demonstration.

Herman, Joseph. "Injunctive Control of Disruptive Student Demonstrations," 56 *Va. L. Rev.* 215 (1970). Analyzes strategic, constitutional, and procedural issues concerning the use of injunctions to control disruptive student protest.

Sec. 8.2 (Student Press)

Comment, "Student Editorial Discretion, the First Amendment, and Public Access to the Campus Press," 16 *U. Cal. Davis L. Rev.* 1089 (1983). Reviews the constitutional status of student newspapers under the First Amendment, analyzes the applicability of the state action doctrine to student newspapers on public campuses, and discusses the question of whether noncampus groups have any right to have material published in campus newspapers on public campuses.

Duscha, Julius, & Fischer, Thomas. *The Campus Press: Freedom and Responsibility* (American Association of State Colleges and Universities, 1973). A handbook that provides historical, philosophical, and legal information on college newspapers. Discusses case law that affects the campus press and illustrates the variety of ways the press may be organized on campus and the responsibilities the institution may have for its student publications.

Ingelhart, Louis E. *Student Publications: Legalities, Governance, and Operation* (Iowa State University Press, 1993). An overview of issues regarding publication of student newspapers, yearbooks, and magazines. Aimed primarily at administrators, the book discusses organizational, management, and funding issues as well as censorship and other potential legal problems associated with such publications.

Nichols, John E. "Vulgarity and Obscenity in the Student Press, 10 *J. Law & Educ.* 207 (1981). Examines the legal definitions of vulgarity and obscenity as they apply to higher education and secondary education and reviews the questions these concepts pose for the student press.

Note, "Tort Liability of a University for Libelous Material in Student Publications," 71 *Mich. L. Rev.* 1061 (1973). Provides the reader with a general understanding of libel law and discusses the various theories under which a university may be held liable for the torts of its student press. Author also recommends preventive measures to minimize university liability.

Sec. 8.3 (The Special Problem of Hate Speech)

Byrne, J. Peter. "Racial Insults and Free Speech Within the University," 79 *Georgetown L.J.* 399 (1991). Author argues that, to protect "the intellectual values of academic discourse," universities may regulate racial (and other similar) insults on campuses even if the state could not constitutionally enact and enforce the same type of regulation against society at large. He asserts, however, that public universities may not use such regulations "to punish speakers for advocating any idea in a reasoned manner." Article analyzes the evolution of relevant constitutional law and examines polices enacted at the University of Wisconsin, the University of Michigan, and Stanford University. Author was a member of a committee to formulate a "student speech and expression policy" at Georgetown University.

Kaplin, William. "A Proposed Process for Managing the Free Speech Aspects of Campus Hate Speech," 63 *J. Higher Educ.* 517 (1992). Describes a process for dealing with "hate speech" while preserving individuals' rights to free speech. Identifies key principles of First Amendment law that circumscribe the institution's discretion to deal with hate speech, suggests regulatory options that may be implemented consistent with these principles, and emphasizes the need to consider nonregulatory options prior to considering regulatory options.

Lawrence, Charles R., III. "If He Hollers Let Him Go: Regulating Racist Speech on Campus," 1990 *Duke L.J.* 431 (1990). Develops an argument for the constitutionality of hate speech regulations based on an interpretation of *Brown v. Board of Education,* calls for carefully drafted hate speech regulations on the campuses, explores the injurious nature of hate speech, and criticizes the position of free speech libertarians.

Massaro, Toni M. "Equality and Freedom of Expression: The Hate Speech Dilemma," 32 *William and Mary L. Rev.* 211 (1991). Summarizes theoretical and practical aspects of the hate speech debate; critiques the approaches of "civil liberties theorists," "civil rights theorists," and "accommodationists"; and reviews various narrow approaches to regulating campus hate speech.

Strossen, Nadine. "Regulating Racist Speech on Campus: A Modest Proposal?" 1990 *Duke L.J.* 484 (1990). Reviews the First Amendment principles and doctrines applicable to campus hate speech regulations; responds to Charles Lawrence's advocacy of hate speech regulations (see entry above); and argues that "prohibiting racist speech would not effectively counter, and could even aggravate, the underlying problem of racism," and that "means consistent with the first amendment can promote racial equality more effectively than can censorship." Includes substantial discussion of ACLU policies and activities regarding hate speech.

Sunstein, Cass. "Liberalism, Speech Codes, and Related Problems," 79 *Academe* 14 (July-Aug. 1993). Traces the tension between academic freedom and hate speech and relates hate speech regulation to the "low-value speech" versus "high-value speech" dichotomy developed in U.S. Supreme Court precedents. Author's primary purpose is to "defend the constitutionality of narrowly drawn restrictions on hate speech, arguing in the process against the broader versions that have become popular in some institutions."

Sec. 8.4 (Free Speech on Campus Computer Networks)

Symposium, "Emerging Media Technology and the First Amendment," *104 Yale L. J.* 1613 (1994). Provides various perspectives on the role of freedom of expression in the technological revolution. Contains a foreword by Owen Fiss, "In Search of a New Paradigm," followed by seven commentaries: (1) Jerry Berman and Daniel J. Weitzner, "Abundance and User Control: Renewing the Democratic Heart of the First Amendment in the Age of Interactive Media"; (2) Anne Wells Branscomb, "Anonymity, Autonomy, and Accountability: Challenges to the First Amendment in Cyberspace"; (3) M. Ethan Katsh, "Rights, Camera, Action: Cyberspatial Settings and the First Amendment"; (4) Thomas G. Krattenmaker and L. A. Powe, Jr., "Converging First Amendment Principles for Converging Communications Media"; (5) Lawrence Lessig, "The Path of Cyberlaw"; (6) Cass R. Sunstein, "The First Amendment in Cyberspace"; and (7) Eugene Volokh, "Cheap Speech and What It Will Do."

CHAPTER NINE

Student Organizations

SEC. 9.1. STUDENT ORGANIZATIONS

Student organizations provide college students with the opportunity to learn leadership skills, supplement their formal academic experience, or pursue diverse interests that their academic program may not provide. Although administrators typically view student organizations as an important supplement to classroom learning, colleges may face liability for the actions of student organizations or for decisions to award or deny funding to these organizations. Recognition of a student organization as an "official" college group may lead to claims that the organization is the agent of the college, raising concerns about the institution's potential liability in contract and tort (see Section 2.3).

9.1.1. Right to Organize

Students in public postsecondary institutions have a general right to organize; to be officially recognized whenever the school has a policy of recognizing student groups; and to use meeting rooms, bulletin boards, and similar facilities open to campus groups. Occasionally, a state statute will accord students specific organizational rights (see *Student Assn. of the University of Wisconsin–Milwaukee v. Baum*, 246 N.W.2d 622 (Wis. 1976), discussed in Section 2.2.4). More generally, organizational rights are protected by the freedom-of-association and freedom-of-expression concepts of the First Amendment. However, public institutions retain authority to withhold or revoke recognition in certain instances and to evenhandedly regulate the organizational use of campus facilities. The balance between the organization's rights and the institution's authority was struck in *Healy v. James,* 408 U.S. 169 (1972), the leading case in the field.

Healy arose after a student organization's request for recognition was denied. The request for recognition as a local Students for a Democratic Society (SDS) organization had been approved by the student affairs committee at Central Connecticut State College, but the college's president denied recognition, asserting that the organization's philosophy was antithetical to the college's commitment to academic freedom and that the organization would be a disruptive influence on campus. The denial of recognition had the effect of prohibiting the student group from using campus meeting rooms and campus bulletin boards and from placing announcements in the student newspaper. The U.S. Supreme Court found the president's reasons insufficient under the facts to justify the extreme effects of nonrecognition on the organization's ability to "remain a viable entity" on campus and "participate in the intellectual give and take of campus debate." The Court therefore overruled the president's decision and remanded the case to the lower court, ruling that the college had to recognize the student group if the lower court determined that the group was willing to abide by all reasonable campus rules.

The associational rights recognized in *Healy* are not limited to situations where recognition is the issue. In *Gay Students Organization of the University of New Hampshire v. Bonner,* 509 F.2d 652 (1st Cir. 1974), for instance, the plaintiff (GSO) was an officially recognized campus organization. After it sponsored a dance on campus, the state governor criticized the university's policy regarding GSO; in reaction, the university announced that GSO could no longer hold social functions on campus. GSO filed suit, and the federal appeals court found that the university's new policy violated the students' freedom of association and expression. *Healy* was the controlling precedent, even though GSO had not been denied recognition:

> The Court's analysis in *Healy* focused not on the technical point of recognition or nonrecognition but on the practicalities of human interaction. While the Court concluded that the SDS members' right to further their personal beliefs had been impermissibly burdened by nonrecognition, this conclusion stemmed from a finding that the "primary impediment to free association flowing from nonrecognition is the denial of use of campus facilities for meetings and other appropriate purposes." The ultimate issue at which inquiry must be directed is the effect which a regulation has on organizational and associational activity, not the isolated and for the most part irrelevant issue of recognition per se [509 F.2d at 658–59].

Healy and related cases reveal three broad bases on which administrators may regulate the recognition of student organizations without violating associational rights. First,

a college administrator may impose a requirement . . . that a group seeking official recognition affirm in advance its willingness to adhere to reasonable campus
law. Such a requirement does not impose an impermissible condition on the students' associational rights. Their freedom to speak out, to assemble, or to petition for changes in school rules is in no sense infringed. It merely constitutes
an agreement to conform to reasonable standards respecting conduct. This is a
minimal requirement, in the interest of the entire academic community, of any
group seeking the privilege of official recognition [*Healy* at 193].

Such standards of conduct, of course, must not themselves violate the First
Amendment or other constitutional safeguards. Recognition, for instance, could
not be conditioned on the organization's willingness to abide by a rule prohibiting all peaceful protest demonstrations on campus (see Section 8.1.2) or
requiring all campus newspaper announcements to be approved in advance by
the administration (see Section 8.2.1). But as long as campus rules avoid such
pitfalls, student organizations must comply with them, just as individual students must. If the organization refuses to agree in advance to obey campus law,
recognition may be denied until such time as the organization does agree. If
a recognized organization violates campus law, its recognition may be suspended or withdrawn for a reasonable period of time.

Second, "associational activities need not be tolerated where they . . . interrupt classes . . . or substantially interfere with the opportunity of other students
to obtain an education" (*Healy* at 189). Thus, administrators may also deny recognition to a group that would create substantial disruption on campus, and
they may revoke the recognition of a group that has created such disruption. In
either case, the institution has the burden of demonstrating with reasonable
certainty that substantial disruption will or did in fact result from the organization's actions—a burden that the college failed to meet in *Healy*. This burden
is a heavy one because "denial of recognition . . . [is] a form of prior restraint"
of First Amendment rights (*Healy* at 184).

Third, the institution may act to prevent organizational activity that is itself
illegal under local, state, or federal laws, as well as activity "directed to inciting
or producing imminent lawless action and . . . likely to incite or produce such
action" (*Brandenburg v. Ohio*, 395 U.S. 444, 447 (1969), quoted in *Healy* at
188). While the GSO case specifically supported this basis for regulation, the
court found that the institution had not met its burden of demonstrating that
the group's activities were illegal or inciting. A similar conclusion was reached
in *Gay Lib v. University of Missouri*, 558 F.2d 848 (8th Cir. 1977), *reversing* 416
F. Supp. 1350 (W.D. Mo. 1976). The trial court found, on the basis of the university's expert evidence, that recognition of the student group "would pre-
dictably lead to increased homosexual activities, which include sodomy [a
felony under state law] as one of the most prevalent forms of sexual expression
in homosexuality." Relying on this finding and on the fact that sodomy is an
illegal activity that can be prohibited, the trial court upheld the university's

refusal to recognize the group. Overruling the trial court, the appellate court held that the university's proof was insufficient to demonstrate that the student organization intended to breach university regulations or advocate or incite imminent lawless acts. At most, the group intended peaceably to advocate the repeal of certain criminal laws—expression that constitutionally could not be prohibited. Thus, the appellate court concluded that the university's denial of recognition impermissibly penalized the group's members because of their status rather than their conduct. (To the same effect, see *Gay Activists Alliance v. Board of Regents,* 638 P.2d 1116 (Okla. 1981); and see generally Note, "The Rights of Gay Student Organizations," 10 *J. Coll. & Univ. Law* 397 (1983–84).)

All rules and decisions regarding student organizations should be supportable on one or more of these three regulatory bases. Administrators should apply the rules evenhandedly, carefully avoiding selective applications to particular groups whose philosophy or activities are repugnant to the institution. Decisions under the rules should be based on a sound factual assessment of the impact of the group's activity rather than on speculation or on what the Supreme Court calls "undifferentiated fear or apprehension." Decisions denying organizational privileges should be preceded by "some reasonable opportunity for the organization to meet the university's contentions" or "to eliminate the basis of the denial" (*Wood v. Davison,* 351 F. Supp. 543, 548 (N.D. Ga. 1972)). Keeping these points in mind, administrators can retain substantial yet sensitive authority over the recognition of student groups.

Denial of funding by a public institution to a group because of the views its members espouse is a clear violation of constitutional free speech protections, even if the denial comes from a student government committee rather than from an institutional official. In *Gay and Lesbian Students Assn. v. Gohn,* 850 F.2d 361 (8th Cir. 1988), a committee of the student senate denied funds to an organization that provided education about homosexuality. The court, noting that the administration had upheld the committee's denial of funding, said, "The University need not supply funds to student organizations; but once having done so, it is bound by the First Amendment to act without regard to the content of the ideas being expressed" (850 F.2d at 362). An exception to this principle has been recognized, however, if a public institution refuses to fund certain religiously affiliated organizations because to do so would violate the establishment clause, although a recent decision of the U.S. Supreme Court suggests that establishment clause justifications for refusing to fund such organizations will not be successful (see Section 9.1.4).

Although most challenges to denials of funding or recognition have been against public institutions, a significant case brought against Georgetown University illustrates some of the issues facing private, religiously affiliated institutions. Two student gay rights groups sought official recognition by the university, which refused, citing Catholic doctrine that condemns homosexuality. Denial of recognition meant that the groups could not use the university's facilities or its mailing and labeling services, could not have a mailbox in the student activities office, and could not request university funds. The student group sued under a District of Columbia law (D.C. Code §1–2520) that outlaws discrimination (in the form of denying access to facilities and services) on the basis of (among other characteristics) sexual orientation. The university defended its actions on the grounds of free exercise of religion.

In *Gay Rights Coalition of Georgetown University Law Center v. Georgetown University,* 536 A.2d 1 (D.C. 1987), the court issued seven separate opinions, which—although none attracted a majority of the judges—reached a collective result of not requiring the university to recognize the groups but requiring it to give them access to facilities, services, and funding.

By severing the recognition process from the granting of access to university facilities and funding, the court avoided addressing the university's constitutional claim with regard to recognition. In interpreting the D.C. statute, the court found no requirement that "one private actor . . . 'endorse' another" (536 A.2d at 5). For that reason, Georgetown's denial of recognition to the student groups did not violate the statute. But the statute did require equal treatment, according to the court. And, the court concluded, the District of Columbia's compelling interest in eradicating discrimination based on sexual preference outweighed any burden on the university's freedom of religion that providing equal access would imply. For a critical analysis of this case and the conflicts it embodies, see F. N. Dutile, "God and Gays at Georgetown: Observations on *Gay Rights Coalition of Georgetown University Law Center v. Georgetown University,*" 15 *J. Coll. & Univ. Law* 1 (1988).

In the wake of the *Gay Rights Coalition* case, the U.S. Congress, which has legislative jurisdiction over the District of Columbia, passed The Nation's Capital Religious Liberty and Academic Freedom Act, 102 Stat. 2269 (1988). The law provided that the District government would not receive further appropriations unless it adopted legislation authorizing religiously affiliated institutions to deny endorsement or benefits in a situation like that in the *Gay Rights Coalition* case. The constitutionality of the law was challenged by D.C. City Council members in *Clarke v. United States,* 898 F.2d 162 (D.C. Cir. 1990). Although a panel of the appellate court affirmed a trial court's ruling that the law was an unconstitutional burden on the free speech of City Council members, the *en banc* court vacated the panel opinion as moot in *Clarke v. United States,* 898 F.2d 161 (D.C. Cir. 1990) (*en banc*) because the appropriations act had expired. The next year's appropriations act did not contain a funding limitation because Congress used its power under the District of Columbia Self-Government and Governmental Reorganization Act (Pub. L. No. 93–198 (1973)) to amend the District of Columbia law directly to permit religious institutions to discriminate on the basis of sexual orientation.

The regulations that student organizations themselves may promulgate can be subject to constitutional challenges as well. For example, in *Alabama Student Party v. Student Government Assn. of Alabama*, 867 F.2d 1344 (11th Cir. 1989), students challenged the student government's regulations that severely restricted campaigning for student government offices. The students claimed that these regulations violated their free speech rights. Declaring that the elections were an educational function of the university and deserved great deference, the court upheld the regulations.

9.1.2. Right Not to Organize

The right-to-organize concept has a flip side. Students often are organized into a large campuswide or collegewide association recognized by the institution as a student government or similar representational organization. Mandatory student activities fees sometimes are collected by the institution and channeled to the student association. Where such circumstances pertain at a public institution, may students argue that their constitutional rights are violated—either by a requirement that they be members of the association or by a requirement that their activity fees be used to support the association? Or may a public institution channel funds from a mandatory student activities fee to nonrepresentational, special-purpose organizations (such as minority or foreign student groups, social action groups, and academic or honorary societies) when other students object to supporting those organizations' beliefs or statements?

An early case, *Good v. Associated Students of the University of Washington*, 542 P.2d 762 (Wash. 1975), distinguished between the university's requirement that students be *members* of the ASUW, a nonprofit organization that purported to represent all of the university's students, and the university's ability to impose a mandatory student fee. The court found that the membership requirement was unconstitutional for those students who disagreed with the organization's political viewpoints: "There is no room in the First Amendment for such absolute compulsory support, advocation, and representation" (542 P.2d at 768). With regard to the mandatory fee, however, the court balanced the students' First Amendment rights against the university's interest in providing an environment for diverse ideas. The court concluded that "dissenting students should not have the right to veto every event, speech, or program with which they disagree." Accordingly, student associations like the ASUW may use mandatory fees as long as (1) such use does not "exceed the statutory purposes" for which fees may be spent and (2) the group does not "become the vehicle for the promotion of one particular viewpoint, political, social, economic or religious" (542 P.2d at 769).

A similar approach can be taken toward the validity of mandatory fee allocations to special-purpose organizations. If students have no "right to veto every event, speech, or program" they disagree with, they also should not be able to veto university support for every organization that they disagree with. Thus, unlike broad representational groups such as the ASUW, special-purpose groups can promote a "particular viewpoint." In *Larson v. Board of Regents of the University of Nebraska*, 204 N.W.2d 568 (Neb. 1973), for instance, the court rejected student challenges to mandatory fee allocations for the student newspaper and the visiting-speakers program, whose views the plaintiffs opposed. Because restrictions on the content or purpose of the organization (assuming they are lawful) violate constitutional guarantees, the institution's fee allocations, as a whole, must provide a forum for a broad spectrum of viewpoints rather than selectively supporting particular ones with which the institution feels comfortable.

In a more recent case, the Supreme Court of California considered the question of mandatory student fees. In *Smith v. Regents of California*, 844 P.2d 500 (Cal. 1993), students challenged the regents' authority to impose a mandatory student fee; they also argued that the allocation of these fees to on-campus groups whose political activities these students opposed violated their constitutional rights. The court made short work of the students' first claim, stating that the regents had broad discretion to carry out the university's educational mission. With regard to the constitutional claim, the court characterized the issue as a conflict between the regents' authority in educational matters and the students' right to be free of compelled speech and association:

> The solution to this problem is to set a rational limit on the use of mandatory fees. We can do this by recognizing what is obviously true, namely, that a group's dedication to achieving its political or ideological goals, at some point, begins to outweigh any legitimate claim it may have to be educating students on the University's behalf. To fund such a group through mandatory fees will usually constitute more of a burden on dissenting students' speech and associational rights than is necessary to achieve any significant educational goal. The University can teach civics in other ways that involve a lesser burden on those rights, or no burden at all [844 P.2d at 508].

The court gave the regents a choice. They could develop a system of evaluating student organizations to ensure that only those whose primary purpose was educational rather than political would receive student fees; or, if they chose to continue the present system of recognizing any group of at least four students who wished to establish a student organization, they would have to follow the guidelines laid down by the U.S. Supreme Court in *Chicago Teachers' Union v. Hudson*, 475 U.S. 292 (1986). These guidelines require the regents to ascertain which groups are predominantly educational (eligible for funds) and which are predominantly political and/or ideological (ineligible for funds), and to "offer students the option of deducting a corresponding amount from the mandatory fee" (844 P.2d at 513). Furthermore, students "who disagree with the Regents' calculation of the corresponding deduction will be entitled to the procedural safeguards" set forth in *Hudson* and related cases (844 P.2d at 516).

One judge, strongly dissenting from the outcome in *Smith,* argued that the distinction between "educational" and "ideological" speech was "spurious," and warned that the outcome would expose the regents to protracted litigation. Believing that all campus groups engaged in any form of speech have an educational purpose, the judge would have permitted their funding as long as the funds were allocated in a neutral fashion.

Several courts have addressed student challenges to the allocation of mandatory student fees to outside groups, loosely linked to the institution, that espouse views that some students oppose. In *Galda v. Rutgers, The State University of New Jersey,* 772 F.2d 1060 (3d Cir. 1985), a federal appellate court enjoined the state university from imposing a compulsory fee on students to fund an outside, nonpartisan public interest organization. The students argued that the levy of the fee violated the First Amendment, since the university compelled them to contribute to an organization that espoused and promoted ideological causes they opposed. Rutgers contended that the educational benefits to the students justified university funding. The court concluded that the educational benefits provided students through university funding were incidental to the group's ideological activities and that the university had neither demonstrated a compelling state interest to override the students' First Amendment rights nor attempted any less drastic means of satisfying its educational interests.

In *Carroll v. Blinken,* 957 F.2d 991 (2d Cir. 1992), the court faced a similar set of issues. Students who opposed the activities of the New York Public Interest Research Group (NYPIRG) sued the State University of New York at Albany, arguing that allocating a portion of their mandatory student fees to NYPIRG constituted compelled speech and association in violation of the First Amendment. Although the court agreed that using mandatory fees to support NYPIRG did constitute compelled speech and association, it held that the infringement on the student's First Amendment rights was justified. It pointed out that the university had a strong interest in supporting NYPIRG because the organization promoted extracurricular activities, its activities provided educational experiences for participating students, and it contributed to the exchange of diverse ideas on campus. The court therefore ruled that the university could allocate mandatory fees to a group whose ideas and activities the students opposed, but it also held that the organization must spend at least the equivalent of the students' contributions on campus. Furthermore, said the court, NYPIRG's practice of defining its membership to include all fee-paying students, whether they wished membership status or not, unjustifiably compelled the students' association and thus violated the First Amendment.

The collective outcomes in the cases discussed earlier suggest that, in overseeing student organizations, administrators should avoid imposing compulsory membership requirements. In allocating mandatory student fees, they should develop evenhanded processes devoid of artificial limits on the number or type of viewpoints that may be supported. If the process does include limits on the purposes or groups that may be supported, these limits should be demonstrably consistent with the three bases for regulation set out in Section 9.1.1 or some other substantial and evenly applied educational priority of the institution, and with the special rules regarding discrimination (Section 9.1.3) and religious activities (Section 9.1.4). And, given the outcome in *Smith,* they may wish to consider developing a system that permits students to deduct from their fees an amount equivalent to the proportion of funds allocated to "political or ideological" groups.

9.1.3. Principle of Nondiscrimination

While the law prohibits administrators from imposing certain restrictions on student organizations (as Sections 9.1.1 and 9.1.2 indicate), there are other restrictions that administrators may be required to impose. The primary example concerns discrimination, particularly on the basis of race or sex. Just as the institution usually cannot discriminate on grounds of race or sex, neither can the student organization discriminate—either as the agent of (see generally Section 2.1) or with the substantial support of the institution. The institution has an obligation either to prohibit discrimination by student organizations or to withhold institutional support from those that do discriminate.

In public institutions, student organizations may be subject to constitutional equal protection principles under the state action doctrine (Section 1.5.2) if they act as agents of the institution or make substantial use of institutional facilities, resources, or funds. Thus, in *Joyner v. Whiting,* 477 F.2d 456 (4th Cir. 1973) (also discussed in Section 8.2.3), a black-oriented student newspaper allegedly had a segregationist editorial policy and had discriminated by race in staffing and in accepting advertising. Although the court prohibited the university president from permanently cutting off the paper's funds, because of the restraining effect of such a cutoff on free press, it did hold that the president could and must prohibit the discrimination in staffing and advertising: "The equal protection clause forbids racial discrimination in extracurricular activities of a state-supported institution . . . and freedom of the press furnishes no shield for discrimination."

Uzzell v. Friday, 547 F.2d 801 (4th Cir. 1977), concerned certain rules of student organizations at the University of North Carolina. The Campus Governing Council, legislative branch of the student government, was required under its constitution to have at least two minority students, two males, and two females among its eighteen members. The student Honor Court, under its rules, permitted defendants to demand that a majority of the judges hearing the case be of the same race or the same sex as the defendant. Eschewing the need for any extended analysis, the court invalidated each of the provisions as race discrimination. "Without either reasonable basis or compelling interest, the composition of the council is formulated on the basis of race. This form of constituency blatantly fouls the letter and the spirit of both the Civil Rights Act [42 U.S.C. §2000d] and the Fourteenth Amendment." (The sex discrimination aspects of the provisions were not challenged by the plaintiff students or addressed by the court.) In *Friday v. Uzzell*, 438 U.S. 912 (1978), the U.S. Supreme Court, seeing possible affirmative action issues underlying this use of racial considerations, vacated the appellate court's judgment and remanded the case for further consideration in light of the *Bakke* decision (see Section 4.1.5).

In 1979, the appeals court reconsidered its earlier decision and, by a vote of 4 to 3, again invalidated the rules (*Uzzell v. Friday*, 591 F.2d 997 (4th Cir. 1979) (*en banc*)). The majority held that the rules were contrary to the teaching of *Bakke*:

> The permeating defect in the organization of . . . the governing council is the imposition of an artificial racial structure upon this elective body that bars non-minority students from eligibility for appointment to the council. This resort to race affronts *Bakke*. Although the regulation seeks to provide "protective repre-sentation," its effect is to establish a racial classification, as it relies exclusively on race to preclude nonminority students from enjoying opportunities and benefits available to others [591 F.2d at 998].

The minority, reading *Bakke* more liberally, argued that more facts were neces-sary before the court could ascertain whether the student government rules were invalid race discrimination, on the one hand, or valid affirmative action, on the other. They therefore asserted that the case should be returned to the dis-trict court for a full trial:

> The present record simply does not permit a firm conclusion as to the extent of discrimination at the University of North Carolina and the need for and efficacy of the present regulations. The majority's condemnation of the regulations because they impinge upon the rights of others is simplistic. *Bakke* teaches that as a necessary remedial measure a victimized group may be preferred at the expense of other innocent persons. What cries out for determination in the instant case is whether such preferment is justified under the principles of *Bakke* [591 F.2d at 1001].

In June 1980, the Fourth Circuit recalled its 1979 decision because the *en banc* court that had heard the appeal was improperly constituted: a senior judge sat as a member of the panel—a violation of a federal statute (28 U.S.C. §46) requir-ing that an *en banc* panel consist only of active circuit court judges. The new rehearing *en banc* placed the matter before the appeals court for the third time (*Uzzell v. Friday*, 625 F.2d 1117 (4th Cir. 1980) (*en banc*)). On this occasion, the court ruled 5 to 3 to remand the case to the district court for a full development of the record and reconsideration in light of *Bakke*. In so ruling, the court expressly adopted the dissenting view of the 1979 decision. The majority indicated that racially conscious actions that impinge on one class of persons in order to ameliorate past discrimination against another class are not unlawful per se, and that "the university should have the opportunity to justify its regulations so that the district court can apply the *Bakke* test: Is the classification necessary to the accomplishment of a constitutionally permissible purpose?"

Federal civil rights laws (see Section 12.4) may require private as well as public institutions to ensure, as a condition to receiving federal funds, that student organizations do not discriminate. The Title VI regulations (Section 12.4.2) contain several provisions broad enough to cover student organizations; in particular, 34 C.F.R. §100.3(b)(1) prohibits institutions from discriminating by race, either "directly or through contractual or other arrangements," and 34 C.F.R. §100.3(b)(4) prohibits institutions from discriminating in the provision of services or benefits that are offered "in or through a facility" constructed or operated in whole or part with federal funds. And the Title IX regulations (Section 12.4.3) prohibit institutions from "providing significant assistance" to any organization "which discriminates on the basis of sex in providing any aid, benefit, or service to students" (34 C.F.R. §106.31(b)(7); see also §106.6(c)). Title IX does not apply, however, to the membership practices of tax-exempt social fraternities and sororities (20 U.S.C. §1681(a)6(A)). (For a discussion of the civil rights statutes' application to student organizations and other activities that do not receive federal funds, see this volume, Sections 12.4.7.3 and 12.4.7.4.)

State law may also provide protection against discrimination by student organizations at both public and private institutions. In *Frank v. Ivy Club*, 576 A.2d 241 (N.J. 1990), the court was asked to determine whether two private "eating clubs" affiliated with Princeton University, which at the time admitted only men to membership, were subject to the state's nondiscrimination law as places of public accommodation.

In 1979, Sally Frank, then an undergraduate at Princeton, filed a charge with the New Jersey Division on Civil Rights (the state's human rights agency), asserting that she was denied membership in the clubs on the basis of her gender, and that this denial constituted unlawful discrimination by a place of public accommodation. She also filed a charge against the university, asserting that it was responsible for supervising the clubs and therefore was partially responsible for their discriminatory activities. The clubs characterized themselves as private organizations, and the university asserted that the clubs were private organizations not formally affiliated with the university.

After protracted procedural battles, the Division on Civil Rights asserted jurisdiction over Frank's claim and determined that the clubs were places of public accommodation and thus subject to the nondiscrimination requirements of state law. It also ruled that the clubs enjoyed a "symbiotic relationship" with the university, since the university had assisted them in their business affairs, a majority of upper-division Princeton students took their meals at the clubs (relieving the university of the responsibility of providing meals for them), and the clubs would not have come into being without the existence of the university. From these findings, the Division on Civil Rights concluded that probable cause existed to believe that the clubs had unlawfully discriminated against Frank on the basis of her gender.

After several appeals to intermediate courts and other procedural wrangling, the New Jersey Supreme Court finally considered both the procedural and the substantive issues, affirming the jurisdiction of the Division on Civil Rights and its findings and conclusions that the clubs must cease their discriminatory membership policies. The court reasoned that "where a place of public accommodation [the university] and an organization that deems itself private [the clubs] share a symbiotic relationship, particularly where the allegedly 'private' entity supplies an essential service which is not provided by the public accommodation, the servicing entity loses its private character and becomes subject to laws against discrimination" (576 A.2d at 257). The court also upheld the Division on Civil Rights' ruling that the clubs not be permitted to sever their ties with Princeton, but that they be ordered to obey the law.

While the state court proceedings were in progress, one of the clubs filed a claim in federal court, asserting that the state civil rights agency's assertion of jurisdiction over its activities violated its rights to free association under the First Amendment of the U.S. Constitution. A federal appellate court affirmed a trial court's finding that the club's federal claims were not moot (they had not been addressed in the state proceedings), and that the club would be permitted to litigate its federal claims, although it would be bound by the undisputed stipulations of fact that had been reached in the state proceedings (*Ivy Club v. Edwards*, 943 F.2d 270 (3d Cir. 1991)).

In light of such constitutional and regulatory requirements, it is clear that administrators cannot ignore alleged discrimination by student organizations. In some areas of concern, discrimination being the primary example, administrators must deal affirmatively with the rules and practices of campus student organizations in order to fulfill their institution's obligations under the law.

9.1.4. Religious Activities

In *Widmar v. Vincent,* 454 U.S. 263 (1981), a case involving the University of Missouri-Kansas City (UMKC), the U.S. Supreme Court established important rights for student religious groups at public postsecondary institutions who seek to use the institution's facilities. In 1972, the board of curators of UMKC promulgated a regulation prohibiting the use of university buildings or grounds "for purposes of religious worship or religious teaching." In 1977, UMKC applied this regulation to a student religious group called Cornerstone and denied it permission to continue meeting in university facilities. According to the Court:

Cornerstone is an organization of evangelical Christian students from various
denominational backgrounds. . . . Cornerstone held its on-campus meetings in
classrooms and in the student center. These meetings were open to the public
and attracted up to 125 students. A typical Cornerstone meeting included prayer,
hymns, Bible commentary, and discussion of religious views and experiences
[454 U.S. at 265 n.2].

Following this denial, eleven members of Cornerstone sued the university,
alleging that it had abridged their rights to free exercise of religion and freedom
of speech under the First Amendment. The district court rejected the students'
arguments, holding that UMKC's regulation was necessary to fulfill the university's obligation, under the establishment clause of the First Amendment, to
refrain from supporting religion (*Chess v. Widmar,* 480 F. Supp. 907 (W.D.
Mo. 1979)). The appellate court reversed the district court (635 F.2d 1310 (8th
Cir. 1980)). It determined that the group's activities were protected by the free
speech clause of the First Amendment. Applying a classic free speech analysis,
the appellate court held that the university had violated the students' rights by
placing content-based restrictions on their speech. The Supreme Court agreed
with the appellate court.

For the U.S. Supreme Court, as for the lower courts, the threshold question
was whether the case would be treated as a free speech case. In considering this
question, Justice Powell's opinion for the Court (with Justice White dissenting)
characterized the students' activities as "religious speech," which, like other
speech, is protected by the free speech clause. The university, by making its
facilities generally available to student organizations, had created a "forum"
open to speech activities, which the Court described both as a "limited public
forum" and an "open forum." The free speech clause therefore applied to the
situation. This clause did not require UMKC to establish a forum; once UMKC
had done so, however, the clause required it to justify any exclusion of a student group from this forum because of the content of its activities:

In order to justify discriminatory exclusion from a public forum based on the
religious content of a group's intended speech, the university must satisfy the
standard of review appropriate to content-based exclusions. It must show that
its regulation is necessary to serve a compelling state interest and that it is narrowly drawn to achieve that end [454 U.S. at 269–70].

In attempting to justify its regulation under this standard, UMKC relied on
the First Amendment's establishment clause and on the establishment clause
in the Missouri state constitution. Its argument was that maintaining separation
of church and state, as mandated by these clauses, was a "compelling state
interest," which justified its no-religious-worship regulation under the free
speech clause. Resorting to establishment clause jurisprudence, the Court

rejected this argument. Although the Court agreed that maintaining separation of church and state was a compelling interest, it did not believe that an equal-access policy violated the establishment clause. The Court applied the three-part test of *Lemon v. Kurtzman,* 403 U.S. 602 (1971):

"First, the [governmental policy] must have a secular legislative purpose; second, its principal or primary effect must be one that neither advances nor inhibits religion . . . ; finally, the [policy] must not foster an excessive government entanglement with religion" [403 U.S. at 612–13].

The court then applied the test:

In this case two prongs of the test are clearly met. Both the district court and the court of appeals held that an open-forum policy, including nondiscrimination against religious speech, would have a secular purpose and would avoid entanglement with religion. But the district court concluded, and the university argues here, that allowing religious groups to share the limited public forum would have the "primary effect" of advancing religion.

The university's argument misconceives the nature of this case. The question is not whether the creation of a religious forum would violate the establishment clause. The university has opened its facilities for use by student groups, and the question is whether it can now exclude groups because of the content of their speech (see *Healy v. James,* 408 U.S. 169 . . . (1972)). In this context we are unpersuaded that the primary effect of the public forum, open to all forms of discourse, would be to advance religion.

We are not oblivious to the range of an open forum's likely effects. It is possible—perhaps even foreseeable—that religious groups will benefit from access to university facilities. But this Court has explained that a religious organization's enjoyment of merely "incidental" benefits does not violate the prohibition against the "primary advancement" of religion [citations omitted].

We are satisfied that any religious benefits of an open forum at UMKC would be "incidental" within the meaning of our cases. Two factors are especially relevant.

First, an open forum in a public university does not confer any imprimatur of state approval on religious sects or practices. As the court of appeals quite aptly stated, such a policy "would no more commit the university . . . to religious goals" than it is "now committed to the goals of the Students for a Democratic Society, the Young Socialist Alliance," or any other group eligible to use its facilities (*Chess v. Widmar,* 635 F.2d at 1317).

Second, the forum is available to a broad class of nonreligious as well as religious speakers; there are over 100 recognized student groups at UMKC. The provision of benefits to so broad a spectrum of groups is an important index of secular effect [citations omitted]. If the establishment clause barred the extension of general benefits to religious groups, "a church could not be protected by the police and fire departments, or have its public sidewalk kept in repair"

(*Roemer v. Maryland Public Works Board,* 426 U.S. 736, 747 . . . (1976) (plurality opinion). . . . At least in the absence of empirical evidence that religious groups will dominate UMKC's open forum, we agree with the court of appeals that the advancement of religion would not be the forum's "primary effect" [454 U.S. at 270–75].

With regard to the university's argument that its interest in enforcing the Missouri constitution's prohibition against public support for religious activities outweighed the students' free speech claim, the Court stated:

Our cases have required the most exacting scrutiny in cases in which a state undertakes to regulate speech on the basis of its content (see, for example, *Carey v. Brown,* 447 U.S. 455 . . . (1980); *Police Dept. v. Mosley,* 408 U.S. 92 . . . (1972)). On the other hand, the state interest asserted here—in achieving greater separation of church and state than is already ensured under the establishment clause of the federal Constitution—is limited by the free exercise clause and in this case by the free speech clause as well. In this constitutional context, we are unable to recognize the state's interest as sufficiently "compelling" to justify content-based discrimination against respondents' religious speech [454 U.S. at 276].

Since UMKC could not justify its content-based restriction on access to the forum it had created, the Court declared the university's regulation unconstitutional. The plaintiff students thereby obtained the right to have their religious group hold its meetings in campus facilities generally open to student groups. It follows that other student religious groups at other public postsecondary institutions have the same right to use campus facilities; institutions may not exclude them, whether by written policy or otherwise, on the basis of the religious content of their activities.[1]

Widmar has substantial relevance for public institutions, most of which have created forums similar to the forum at UMKC. The opinion falls far short, however, of requiring institutions to relinquish all authority over student religious groups. There are substantial limits to the opinion's reach:

1. *Widmar* does not require (nor does it permit) institutions to create forums especially for religious groups, or to give them any other preferential treatment. As the Court noted, "Because this case involves a forum already made generally available to student groups, it differs from those cases in which this Court

---

[1]In 1984, Congress passed and the President signed the Equal Access Act, 98 Stat. 377, giving limited statutory recognition to the principles underlying *Widmar.* By its terms, however, the Act extends these principles to, and applies only to, "public secondary schools[s] . . . receiv[ing] federal financial assistance."

has invalidated statutes permitting school facilities to be used for instruction by religious groups but not by others" (454 U.S. at 271 n.10; see also 454 U.S. at 273 n.13).

2. Nor does *Widmar* require institutions to create a forum for student groups generally, or to continue to maintain one, if they choose not to do so. The case applies only to situations where the institution has created and voluntarily continues to maintain a forum for student groups.

3. *Widmar* requires access only to facilities that are part of a forum created by the institution, not to any other facilities. Similarly, *Widmar* requires access only for students: "We have not held . . . that a campus must make all of its facilities equally available to students and nonstudents alike, or that a university must grant free access to all of its grounds or buildings" (454 U.S. at 267 n.5).

4. *Widmar* does not prohibit all regulation of student organizations' use of forum facilities; it prohibits only content-based restrictions on access. Thus, the Court noted that "a university's mission is education, and decisions of this Court have never denied its authority to impose reasonable regulations compatible with that mission upon the use of its campus and facilities" (454 U.S. at 267 n.5). In particular, according to the Court, the *Widmar* opinion "in no way undermines the capacity of the university to establish reasonable time, place, and manner regulations" (454 U.S. at 276) for use of the forum. Such regulations must be imposed on all student groups, however, not just student religious organizations, and must be imposed without regard to the content of the group's speech activities (see *Heffron v. International Society for Krishna Consciousness*, 452 U.S. 640 (1981)). If a student religious group or other student group "violate[s] [such] reasonable campus rules or substantially interfere[s] with the opportunity of other students to obtain an education" (454 U.S. at 277), the institution may prohibit the group from using campus facilities for its activities.

5. *Widmar* does not rule out every possible content-based restriction on access to a forum. The Court's analysis quoted above makes clear that a content-based regulation would be constitutional under the First Amendment if it were "necessary to serve a compelling state interest and . . . narrowly drawn to achieve that end." As *Widmar* and other First Amendment cases demonstrate, this standard is exceedingly difficult to meet. But the *Widmar* opinion suggests at least two possibilities, the contours of which are left for further development should the occasion arise. First, the Court hints that, if there is "empirical evidence that religious groups will dominate . . . [the institution's] open forum" (454 U.S. at 275, also quoted above), the institution apparently may regulate access by these groups to the extent necessary to prevent domination. Second, if the student demand for use of forum facilities exceeds the supply, the institution may "make academic judgments as to how best to allocate scarce resources" (454 U.S. at 276). In making such academic judgments, the institution may apparently prefer the educational content of some group activities over

others and allocate its facilities in accord with these academic preferences. Justice Stevens's opinion concurring in the Court's judgment contains an example for consideration:

> If two groups of twenty-five students requested the use of a room at a particular time—one to view Mickey Mouse cartoons and the other to rehearse an amateur performance of *Hamlet*—the First Amendment would not require that the room be reserved for the group that submitted its application first. . . . A university should be allowed to decide for itself whether a program that illuminates the genius of Walt Disney should be given precedence over one that may duplicate material adequately covered in the classroom. . . . A university legitimately may regard some subjects as more relevant to its educational mission than others. But the university, like the police officer, may not allow its agreement or disagreement with the viewpoint of a particular speaker to determine whether access to a forum will be granted [454 U.S. at 278].

For another example of a content-based restriction that was approved by a federal appellate court subsequent to *Widmar,* see *Chapman v. Thomas,* 743 F.2d 1056 (4th Cir. 1984). In this case, the court ruled that North Carolina State University could prohibit a student from door-to-door canvassing in dormitories to publicize campus Bible study meetings, even though it permitted candidates for top student government offices to campaign door to door.

If a university funds student organizations, may it exclude religious activities or religiously affiliated organizations from eligibility for funding? This question was addressed in *Rosenberger v. Rector and Visitors of the University of Virginia,* 115 S. Ct. 2510 (1995).

The defendant, a public university, had established a mandatory student activities fee, the income from which supported a student activities fund (SAF) used to subsidize a variety of student organizations. All recognized student groups had to achieve the status of a "Contracted Independent Organization" (CIO), after which some groups could then submit certain of their bills to the Student Council for payment from SAF funds. The eligible bills were those from "outside contractors" or "third-party contractors" that provide services or products to the student organization. Disbursement was made directly to the third party; no payments went directly to a student group. The university's SAF guidelines prohibited the use of SAF funds for, *inter alia,* religious activities, defined by the guidelines as an activity that "primarily promotes or manifests a particular belief in or about a deity or an ultimate reality." The guidelines also excluded certain types of organizations from funding, including political and religious organizations.

The *Rosenberger* plaintiffs were student members of Wide Awake Productions (WAP), a CIO established to publish a campus magazine that "offers a Christian perspective on both personal and community issues" (115 S. Ct. at 2515, quoting from the magazine's first issue). WAP applied for SAF funding—funding already provided to fifteen student "media groups"—to be used to pay the printer that published its magazine. The university rejected the request on grounds that WAP's activities were religious. The students challenged this denial of funding as a violation of their First Amendment speech and press rights.

The tension between the free speech and the establishment clause of the First Amendment is clearly illuminated by the sharply divergent majority and dissenting opinions in the U.S. Supreme Court. The majority opinion addresses *Rosenberger* from a free speech standpoint, and finds no establishment clause justification for infringing the rights of a student publication that reports the news from a religious perspective. On the other hand, the dissent characterizes the students' publication as an evangelical magazine directly financed by the state and regards such funding to be a clear example of an establishment clause violation. Justice O'Connor's narrow concurring opinion, tailored specifically to the facts of the case, serves to limit the majority's holding and reduce the gulf between the majority and the dissent.

Explicating the majority's free speech analysis, Justice Kennedy described the Student Activities Fund (SAF) as a forum "more in a metaphysical sense than in a spatial or geographic sense," but nonetheless determined that the SAF, as established and operated by the university, is a "limited public forum" for First Amendment purposes. Having opened the SAF to the university community, the university "must respect the lawful boundaries it has itself set. [It] may not exclude speech where its distinction is not 'reasonable in light of the purpose served by the forum' (citing *Cornelius v. NAACP Legal Defense & Education Fund*, 473 U.S. 788, 804–806 (1985)), nor may it discriminate against speech on the basis of its viewpoint (citing *Lamb's Chapel v. Center Moriches Union Free School District*, 506 U.S. 1032 (1993)" [115 S. Ct. at 2516–17].

The majority then determined that the university had denied funding to WAP because of its perspective, or viewpoint, rather than because it dealt with the general subject matter of religion. Thus, although "it is something of an understatement to speak of religious thought and discussion as just a viewpoint," "viewpoint discrimination is the proper way to interpret the university's objection to Wide Awake":

> By the very terms of the SAF prohibition, the [u]niversity does not exclude religion as a subject matter but selects for disfavored treatment those student journalistic efforts with religious editorial viewpoints. Religion may be a vast area of inquiry, but it also provides, as it did here, a specific premise, a perspective, a standpoint from which a variety of subjects may be discussed and considered. The prohibited perspective, not the general subject matter, resulted in the refusal to make the third-party payments [to the printer], for the subjects discussed were otherwise within the approved category of publications [115 S. Ct. at 2517–18].

Furthermore, the majority rejected the university's contention that "no viewpoint discrimination occurs because the Guidelines discriminate against an entire class of viewpoints." Because of the "complex and multifaceted nature of public discourse . . . [i]t is as objectionable to exclude both a theistic and an atheistic perspective on the debate as it is to exclude one, the other, or yet another political, economic, or social viewpoint" [115 S. Ct. at 2518].

Having determined that the university had violated the students' free speech rights, the majority considered whether providing SAF funds to WAP would nevertheless violate the establishment clause. In order for a government regulation to survive an establishment clause challenge, it must be neutral toward religion (see Section 1.6). Relying on past decisions upholding governmental programs when "the government, following neutral criteria and evenhanded policies, extends benefits to recipients whose ideologies and viewpoints, including religious ones, are broad and diverse," the Court held that the SAF is neutral toward religion:

> There is no suggestion that the university created [the SAF] to advance religion or adopted some ingenious device with the purpose of aiding a religious cause. The object of the SAF is to open a forum for speech and to support various student enterprises, including the publication of newspapers, in recognition of the diversity and creativity of student life. . . . The category of support here is for "student news, information, opinion, entertainment, or academic communications media groups," of which *Wide Awake* was 1 of 15 in the 1990 school year. WAP did not seek a subsidy because of its Christian editorial viewpoint; it sought funding as a student journal, which it was [115 S. Ct. at 2522].

Thus, the WAP application for funding depended not on the religious editorial viewpoint of the publication, nor on WAP being a religious organization, but rather on the neutral factor of its status as a student journal. "Any benefit to religion is incidental to the government's provision of secular services for secular purposes on a religion-neutral basis" (115 S. Ct. at 2524).

In completing its establishment clause analysis, the majority distinguished another line of cases forbidding the use of tax funds to support religious activities and rejected the contention that the mandatory student activities fee is a tax levied for the support of a church or religion. Unlike a tax, which the majority describes as an exaction to support the government and a revenue-raising device, the student activity fee is used for the limited purpose of funding student organizations consistent with the educational purposes of the university. No public funds would flow directly into WAP's coffers; instead, the university would pay printers (third-party contractors) to produce WAP's publications. This method of third-party payment, along with university-required disclaimers stating that the university is not responsible for or represented by the recipient organization, evidenced the attenuated relationship between the university and WAP.

The majority found no difference in "logic or principle, and no difference of constitutional significance, between a school using its funds to operate a facility to which students have access [as in *Widmar*], and a school paying a third-party contractor to operate the facility on its behalf."

Justice O'Connor's important concurring opinion carefully limits her analysis to the facts of the case, emphasizing that "[t]he nature of the dispute does not admit of any categorical answers, nor should any be inferred from the Court's decision today." O'Connor bases her concurrence on four specific considerations that ameliorate the establishment clause concerns that otherwise would arise from government funding of religious messages. First, at the insistence of the university, student organizations such as WAP are separate and distinct from the university. All groups that wish to be considered for SAF funding are required to sign a contract stating that the organization exists and operates independently of the university. Moreover, all publications, contracts, letters, or other written materials distributed by the group must bear a disclaimer acknowledging that, while members of the university faculty and student body may be associated with the group, the organization is independent of the "corporation which is the university and which is not responsible for the organizations' contracts, acts, or omissions."

Second, Justice O'Connor noted that no money is given directly to WAP. By paying a third-party vendor, in this case a printer, to publish WAP's journal, the university is able to ensure that the funding it has granted is being used to "further the University's purpose in maintaining a free and robust marketplace of ideas, from whatever perspective." This method of funding, according to the concurrence, is analogous to a school providing equal access to a generally available physical facility, like a printing press on campus.

Third, because WAP does not exist "in a vacuum," it will not be mistakenly perceived to be university-endorsed. This potential danger is greatly diminished by both the number and variety of other publications receiving SAF funding. O'Connor thus found it illogical to equate university funding of WAP with the endorsement of one particular viewpoint.

Fourth, the mandatory student fee may be susceptible to a free speech clause challenge by a student who objects to paying for speech with which she disagrees (see generally Section 9.1.2), and the remedy in such a situation may be to allow the student to "opt out" of paying a portion of the fee:

> [T]he existence of . . . an opt-out possibility not available to citizens generally . . . provides a potential basis for distinguishing proceeds of the student fees in this case from proceeds of the general assessments in support of religion that lie at the core of the prohibition against religious funding, . . . and from government funds generally. Unlike monies dispensed from state or federal treasuries, the Student Activities Fund is collected from students who themselves administer

the fund and select qualifying recipients only from among those who originally paid the fee. The government neither pays into nor draws out of this common pool, and a fee of this sort appears conducive to granting individual students proportional refunds. The Student Activities Fund, then, represents not government resources, whether derived from tax revenue, sales of assets, or otherwise, but a fund that simply belongs to the students [115 S. Ct. at 2527–28 (O'Connor, J., concurring) (citations omitted)].

Although the first three of Justice O'Connor's distinctions were also relied on by Justice Kennedy, Justice O'Connor states her conclusions more narrowly than Kennedy and limits her reasoning more tightly to the unique facts of the case. O'Connor, unlike Kennedy, also adds the fourth consideration regarding potential opt-out remedies. Since Justice O'Connor provides the critical fifth vote that forms the 5 to 4 majority, her opinion carries unusual significance. To the extent her establishment clause analysis is narrower than Justice Kennedy's, it is her opinion rather than his that apparently provides the current baseline for understanding the establishment clause restrictions on public institutions' funding of student religious groups.

The four dissenting justices disagree with both the majority's free speech clause analysis and its establishment clause analysis. Regarding the former, Justice Souter insisted that the university's refusal to fund WAP was not viewpoint discrimination but rather a "subject-matter distinction," an educational judgment not to fund student dialogue on the particular subject of religion regardless of the viewpoints expressed. Regarding the establishment issue, which he termed the "central question in this case," Justice Souter argued that, because "there is no warrant for distinguishing among public funding sources for purposes of applying the First Amendment's prohibition of religious establishment, . . . the university's refusal to support petitioners' religious activities is compelled by the Establishment Clause." Emphasizing that WAP's publications call on Christians "to live, in word and deed, according to the faith they proclaim . . . and to consider what a personal relationship with Jesus Christ means" (115 S. Ct. at 82, quoting from WAP's first issue), Justice Souter likens the paper to an "evangelist's mission station and pulpit" (115 S. Ct. at 2535). He thus argues that the use of public (SAF) funds for this activity is a "direct subsidization of preaching the word" and a "direct funding of core religious activities by an arm of the State" (115 S. Ct. at 2535).

The majority's reasoning in *Rosenberger* generally parallels the Court's earlier reasoning in *Widmar v. Vincent* and generally affirms the free speech and establishment principles articulated in that case. More important, both Justice Kennedy's and Justice O'Connor's opinions extend student organizations' First Amendment rights beyond access to *facilities* (the issue in *Widmar*) to include access to *services*. Some critics of the majority (such as the four dissenting justices) and some religious interest groups advocating a broad reading of Justice Kennedy's opinion, argue in addition that the majority's reasoning may even extend to access to direct funding for religious activities or religious student organizations.

The Kennedy and O'Connor opinions also refine the *Widmar* free speech analysis by distinguishing between *content*-based restrictions on speech (the issue in *Widmar*) and *viewpoint*-based restrictions (the issue as the Court framed it in *Rosenberger*). The latter type of restriction, sometimes called viewpoint discrimination, is the most suspect of all speech restrictions and the type least likely to be tolerated by the courts. *Widmar* appears to reserve a range of discretion for a higher educational institution to make academic judgments based on the educational *content* of a student organization's activities; *Rosenberger* appears to prohibit any such discretion when the institution's academic judgment is based on consideration of the student group's *viewpoints* (see 115 S. Ct. at 2524–25).

In the wake of *Rosenberger*, public institutions need to reassess their guidelines for funding student activities. Given the Court's determination that a refusal to fund publications because of their religious viewpoint (as opposed to a refusal to fund all religious activity) is unconstitutional, colleges will need to either forego funding for all student activities—an unlikely and unnecessary reaction to *Rosenberger*—or provide funding on a neutral basis that does not take into account the religious viewpoint, or other particular viewpoint, of the organizations receiving funding.

Rosenberger calls into question the earlier decision of *Tipton v. University of Hawaii*, 15 F.3d 922 (9th Cir. 1994), in which another appellate court had upheld the University of Hawaii's decision to deny funding to student organizations whose purpose is to promote a particular religious point of view. The university did, however, permit funding of student religious groups for secular activities. Representatives of several of the religious groups denied funding alleged violations of their First Amendment rights to free speech, free association, and the free exercise of religion, and an equal protection clause violation as well. The appellate court upheld the summary judgment awarded to the university, relying on the U.S. Supreme Court's decision in *Rust v. Sullivan*, 111 S. Ct. 1759 (1991) (see Section 12.3.2), which permitted the government to decline to subsidize certain forms of constitutionally protected activity. The majority in *Rosenberger* rejected any reliance on *Rust*, however, distinguishing between situations in which the government pays private entities to "convey its own message" (as in *Rust*) and situations in which government subsidizes private groups who articulate not the government's message, but their own.

The issues addressed in *Widmar, Rosenberg*, and *Tipton* demonstrate the continuing tension between free speech and establishment clause issues as they relate to the actions of public colleges and universities. Current legal doctrine distinguishes between the responsibility to *recognize* student organizations and the responsibility to *fund* them, although with different results for public colleges (which must recognize and, if they fund, must do so on a neutral basis) than for private colleges (which need not recognize but must sometimes provide equal access to facilities—see Section 9.1.1).

SEC. 9.2. FRATERNITIES AND SORORITIES

Fraternal organizations have been part of campus life at many colleges and universities for over a century. Some, such as Phi Beta Kappa, were founded to recognize academic achievement, while others have a predominantly social focus. Because of their strong ties to colleges and universities, whether because the houses occupied by members are on or near the college's property or because their members are students at the college, the consequences of the individual and group behavior of fraternity and sorority members can involve the college in legal problems.

The legal issues that affect nonfraternal student organizations (see Section 9.1) may also arise with respect to fraternities and sororities. But because fraternal organizations have their own unique histories and traditions, are related to national organizations that may influence their activities, and play a significant social role on many campuses, they may pose unique legal problems for the college with which they are affiliated.

Supporters of fraternal, or "Greek," organizations argue that members perform more service to the college and the community and make larger alumni contributions than nonmembers, and that fraternity houses provide room and board to undergraduate students whom the college would otherwise be required to accommodate. Critics of fraternal organizations argue that they foster "elitism, sexism, racism and in worst instances, criminal activity" (V. L. Brown, "College Fraternities and Sororities: Tort Liability and the Regulatory Authority of Public Institutions of Higher Education," 58 *West's Educ. Law Rptr.* (1990)). Institutions have responded to problems such as hazing, alcohol and drug abuse, sexual harassment and assault, and the death or serious injury of fraternity members in various ways—for instance, by regulating social activities, suspending or expelling individual fraternities, or abolishing the entire Greek system on campus.

Fraternities and sororities may be chapters of a national organization or independent organizations. The local chapters, whether or not they are tied to a national organization, may be either incorporated or unincorporated associations. If the fraternity or sorority provides a house for some of its members, it may be located on land owned by the colleges or it may be off campus. In either case, the college may own the fraternity house, or an alumni organization (sometimes called a "house corporation") may own the house and assume responsibility for its upkeep.

9.2.1. Institutional Recognition and Regulation of Fraternal Organizations

Recognition by a college is significant to fraternal organizations because many national fraternal organizations require such recognition as a condition of the local organization's continued affiliation with the national. The conditions under which recognition is awarded by the college are important because they may determine, or enhance, the college's power to regulate the conduct of the organization or its members.

Some colleges and universities require, as a condition of recognition of fraternal organizations, that each local fraternity sign a "relationship statement." These statements outline the college's regulations and elicit the organization's assurance that it will obtain insurance coverage, adhere to fire and building codes, and comply with the institution's policy on the serving of alcohol. Some of these statements also require members to participate in alcohol awareness programs or community service. Some statements include restrictions on parties and noise, and extend the jurisdiction of the college's student conduct code and disciplinary system to acts that take place where students live, even if they live off campus.

On some campuses, institutional regulation of fraternal organizations extends to their membership practices. Traditionally, fraternities and sororities have limited their membership to one gender, and in the past many of these organizations prohibited membership for nonwhite and non-Christian individuals (see Brown, "College Fraternities" (cited earlier). In recent years, however, several colleges and universities, including Middlebury, Bowdoin, and Trinity (Conn.) Colleges, have required fraternities and sororities to admit members of both sexes (see N. S. Horton, "Traditional Single-Sex Fraternities on College Campuses: Will They Survive in the 1990s?" 18 *J. Coll. & Univ. Law* 419 (1992)) and, in general, to avoid discriminatory practices.

Other colleges have banned fraternities altogether. For example, Colby College, a private liberal arts college, withdrew recognition of all its fraternities and sororities in 1984 because administrators believed that fraternal activities were incompatible with its goals for student residential life. When a group of students continued some of the activities of a banned fraternity, despite numerous attempts by the college's administration to halt them, the president and college dean imposed discipline on the "fraternity" members, ranging from disciplinary probation to one-semester suspensions.

In *Phelps v. President and Trustees of Colby College*, 595 A.2d 403 (Me. 1991), the students sought to enjoin the discipline and the ban on fraternities under

Maine's Civil Rights Act, 5 M.R.S.A. §§4681–4683 (Supp. 1990) and the state constitution's guarantees of free speech and the right to associate. Maine's Supreme Judicial Court rejected the students' claims. It held that the state law, directed against harassment and intimidation, did not apply to the actions of the college because it "stopped short of authorizing Maine courts to mediate disputes between private parties exercising their respective rights of free expression and association" (595 A.2d at 407). The court also held that the actions of private entities, such as the college, were not subject to state constitutional restrictions.

But public colleges and universities face constitutional obstacles to banning fraternities, including the First Amendment's guarantee of the right to associate (see Sections 8.1.1, 8.1.2, and 9.1). Although the University of Colorado surmounted a First Amendment challenge to its imposition of sanctions on a fraternity for race discrimination in membership (*Sigma Chi Fraternity v. Regents of the University of Colorado,* 258 F. Supp. 515 (D. Colo. 1966)), the decision of the U.S. Supreme Court in *Roberts v. United States Jaycees,* 468 U.S. 609 (1983), which established the parameters of constitutionally protected rights of association, could provide the impetus for other constitutional challenges to the banning of one, or all, fraternal organizations at public institutions. For analysis of how *Roberts* may apply to fraternal organizations at public colleges, see J. Harvey, "Fraternities and the Constitution: University-Imposed Relationship Statements May Violate Student Associational Rights," 17 *J. Coll. & Univ. Law* 11 (1990); and see also G. F. Hauser, "Social Fraternities at Public Institutions of Higher Education: Their Rights Under the First and Fourteenth Amendments," 19 *J. Law & Educ.* 433 (1990).

Although a clear articulation of the college's expectations regarding the behavior of fraternity members may provide a deterrent to misconduct, some courts have viewed institutional attempts to regulate the conduct of fraternity members as an assumption of a duty to control their behavior, with a correlative obligation to exercise appropriate restraint over members' conduct. For example, in *Furek v. University of Delaware,* 594 A.2d 506 (Del. 1991), the state's Supreme Court ruled that the university could be found liable for injuries a student received during fraternity hazing, since the university's strict rules against hazing demonstrated that it had assumed a duty to protect students against hazing injuries. (See Section 9.2.2 for further discussion of these liability issues.)

Because of the potential for greater liability when regulation is extensive, some institutions have opted for "recognition" statements such as those used to recognize other student organizations. Although this minimal approach may defeat a claim that the institution has assumed a duty to supervise the activities of fraternity members, it may limit the institution's authority to regulate the activities of the organization, although the institution can still discipline individual student members who violate its code of student conduct.

A study that examined tort liability issues related to fraternal organizations (E. D. Gulland & M. B. Powell, *Colleges, Fraternities and Sororities: A White Paper on Tort Liability Issues* (American Council on Education, 1989), at 14–15) recommends that recognition statements include the following provisions:

1. Description of the limited purpose of recognition (no endorsement, but access to institutional facilities).

2. Specification of the lack of principal-agent relationship between college and fraternity.

3. Acknowledgment that the fraternity is an independently chartered corporation existing under state laws.

4. Confirmation that the college assumes no responsibility for supervision, control, safety, security, or other services.

5. Restrictions on use of the college's name, tax identification number, or other representations that the fraternity is affiliated with the college.

6. Requirement that the fraternity furnish evidence that it carries insurance sufficient to cover its risks.

One area where institutional regulation of fraternal organizations is receiving public—and legislative—attention is the "ritual" of hazing, often included as part of pledging activities. Over thirty states have passed laws outlawing hazing. Illinois's antihazing law (Ill. Rev. Stat. ch. 144, para. 221 (1989)) was upheld against a constitutional challenge in *People v. Anderson*, 591 N.E.2d 461 (Ill. 1992). (See also Mass. Ann. Laws ch. 269, §§17–19 (Supp. 1987); Cal. Educ. Code §32050 (West 1990); and Virginia Hazing, Civil and Criminal Liability, Va. Code Ann. §18.2–56.)

Although an institution may not wish explicitly to assume a duty to supervise the conduct of fraternity members, it does have the power to sanction fraternal organizations and their members if they violate institutional policies against hazing or other dangerous conduct. In *Psi Upsilon v. University of Pennsylvania*, 591 A.2d 755 (Pa. Super. Ct. 1991), a state appellate court refused to enjoin the university's imposition of sanctions against a fraternity whose members kidnapped and terrorized a nonmember as part of a hazing activity. The student filed criminal charges against the twenty students who participated in the prank, and the university held a hearing before imposing sanctions on the fraternity. After the hearing, the university withdrew its recognition of the fraternity for three years, took possession of the fraternity house without compensating the fraternity, and prohibited anyone who took part in the kidnapping from participating in a future reapplication for recognition.

In evaluating the university's authority to impose these sanctions, the court first examined whether the disciplinary procedures met legal requirements. Noting that the university was privately controlled, the court ruled that the students were entitled "'only to those procedural safeguards which the school specifically provides'" (591 A.2d at 758, quoting *Boehm v. University of Pennsylvania School of Veterinary Medicine,* 573 A.2d 575 (Pa. Super. Ct. 1990)). The court then turned to the relationship statement that the fraternity had entered into with the university.

Characterizing the relationship statement as contractual, the court ruled that it gave ample notice to the members that they must assume collective responsibility for the activities of individual members, and that breaching the statement was sufficient grounds for sanctions. After reviewing several claims of unfairness in the conduct of the disciplinary proceeding, the court upheld the trial judge's denial of injunctive relief.

Although institutions may have the authority to sanction fraternities and their members for criminal conduct or violations of the campus conduct code, conduct that may be construed as antisocial, but is not unlawful, may be difficult to sanction. For example, some public institutions have undertaken to prohibit such fraternity activities as theme parties with ethnic or gender overtones or offensive speech. These proscriptions, however, may run afoul of the First Amendment's free speech guarantees. For example, George Mason University sanctioned Sigma Chi fraternity for holding an "ugly woman contest," a fund-raising activity where fraternity members dressed as caricatures of various types of women, including an offensive caricature of a black woman. (For the facts of this case, see Section 8.3.) The fraternity sued the university under 42 U.S.C. §1983 (see this volume, Section 2.3.3), alleging a violation of its rights under the First and Fourteenth Amendments.

Although the university argued forcefully that the racial parody violated its goals of promoting cultural and racial diversity, as well as its affirmative action plan, a trial court granted summary judgment for the fraternity, and a federal appellate court affirmed that ruling in *Iota Xi Chapter of Sigma Chi Fraternity v. George Mason University,* 993 F.2d 386 (4th Cir. 1993). The court acknowledged that the skit was "an exercise in teenage campus excess" and noted that determining whether it deserved First Amendment protection was "all the more difficult because of [the skit's] obvious sophomoric nature" (993 F.2d at 389). The court determined that the skit was protected both as expressive entertainment under *Barnes v. Glen Theatre, Inc.,* 111 S. Ct. 2456 (1991) (which decided that nude dancing is expressive conduct and is protected under the First Amendment) and as expressive conduct under *Texas v. Johnson,* 491 U.S. 397 (1989) (which ruled that burning an American flag is protected expressive conduct). It also cited the prohibitions against content-based suppression of speech described by the Supreme Court in *R.A.V. v. City of St. Paul* (discussed in Section 8.3).

Colleges are limited in their ability to sanction fraternities for offensive speech (or expressive conduct), but they can hold individual student members to the same code of conduct expected of all students, particularly with regard to social activities and the use of alcohol.

9.2.2. Institutional Liability for the Acts of Fraternal Organizations

Despite the fact that fraternal organizations are separate legal entities, colleges and universities have faced legal liability from injured students, parents of students injured or killed as a result of fraternity activity, or victims of violence related to fraternity activities. Because most claims are brought under state tort law theories, the response of the courts has not been completely consistent. The various decisions suggest, however, that colleges and universities can limit their liability in these situations but that fraternities and their members face increased liability, particularly for actions that courts view as intentional or reckless.

As discussed in Section 2.3.1, liability may attach if a judge or jury finds that the college owed an individual a duty of care, then breached that duty, and that the breach was the proximate cause of the injury. Because colleges are legally separate entities from fraternal organizations, the college owes fraternities, their members, and others only the ordinary duty of care to avoid injuring others. But in some cases, courts have found either that a special relationship exists between the college and the injured student or that the college has assumed a duty to protect the student.

In *Furek v. University of Delaware*, 594 A.2d 506 (Del. 1991), the Delaware Supreme Court reversed a directed verdict for the university and ordered a new trial on the issue of liability in a lawsuit by a student injured during a hazing incident. The court noted the following factors in determining that a jury could hold the institution at least partially responsible for the injuries: (1) The university owned the land on which the fraternity house was located, although it did not own the house. The injury occurred in the house. (2) The university prohibited hazing and was aware of earlier hazing incidents by this fraternity. The court stated:

> In view of past hazing incidents involving physical harm to students, the occurrence of the unusual activities preceding fraternity hazing as witnessed by campus security . . . and the common knowledge on campus that hazing occurred, there was sufficient evidence for jury determination on the issue of whether the hazing which caused injury to Furek was foreseeable. . . . The likelihood of injury during fraternity activities occurring on university campuses is greater than the utility of university inaction [594 A.2d at 522–23].

While *Furek* may be an anomaly among the cases in which colleges are sued for negligence (see Section 2.3.1.1), the opinion suggests some of the dangers of institutional attempts to regulate the conduct of fraternities or their members—for instance, by assuming duties of inspecting kitchens or houses, requiring that fraternities have faculty or staff advisers employed by the college, providing police or security services for off-campus houses, or assisting these organizations in dealing with local municipal authorities. Such actions may suggest to juries deliberating a student's negligence claim that the institution had assumed a duty of supervision (see Gulland & Powell, *Colleges, Fraternities and Sororities,* cited in Section 9.2.1).

Colleges and universities have been codefendants with fraternities in several cases. In most of these cases, the institution has escaped liability. For example, in *Thomas v. Lamar University-Beaumont,* 830 S.W.2d 217 (Tex. Ct. App. 1992), the mother of a student who died as a result of pledge hazing sued both the fraternity and the university, which owned the track that was used during the hazing incident. The plaintiff asserted that the university had waived its sovereign immunity because it had failed to supervise those who used its track. The trial court determined that the university had no duty of supervision and awarded summary judgment for the university. The appellate court affirmed.

In *Estate of Hernandez v. Board of Regents,* 838 P.2d 1283 (Ariz. Ct. App. 1991), the personal representative of a man killed in an automobile accident caused by an intoxicated fraternity member sued the University of Arizona and the fraternity. The plaintiff asserted that the university was negligent in continuing to lease the fraternity house to the house corporation when it knew that the fraternity served alcohol to students who were under the legal drinking age of twenty-one.

The plaintiff cited the "Greek Relationship Statement," which required all fraternities to participate in an alcohol awareness educational program, as evidence of the university's assumption of a duty to supervise. The statement also required an upper-division student to be assigned to each fraternal organization to educate its members about responsible conduct relating to alcohol. Furthermore, the university employed a staff member who was responsible for administering its policies on the activities of fraternities and sororities. Despite these attempts to suggest that the university had assumed a duty to supervise the activities of fraternities, the court applied Arizona's social host law, which absolved both the fraternity and the university of liability, and affirmed the trial court's award of summary judgment.

When the student's own behavior is a cause of the injury, the courts have typically refused to hold colleges or fraternities liable for damages. In *Whitlock v. University of Denver,* 744 P.2d 54 (Colo. 1987), the Colorado Supreme Court rejected a student's contention that the university had undertaken to regulate the use of a trampoline in the yard of a fraternity house, even though the university owned the land and had regulated other potentially dangerous activities in the past. Similarly, students injured in social events sponsored by fraternities have not prevailed when the injury was a result of the student's voluntary and intentional action. For example, in *Foster v. Purdue University,* 567 N.E.2d 865 (Ind. Ct. App. 1991), a student who became a quadriplegic after diving headfirst into a fraternity's "water slide" was unsuccessful in his suit against both the university and the fraternity of which he was a member. Similarly, in *Hughes v. Beta Upsilon Building Assn.,* 619 A.2d 525 (Me. 1993), a student who was paralyzed after diving into a muddy field on the fraternity's property at the University of Maine was unsuccessful because the court ruled that the Building Association, landlord for the local fraternity chapter, was not responsible for the chapter's activities.

When, however, the injury is a result of misconduct by *other* fraternity members, individual and organizational liability will attach. Particularly in cases where pledges have been forced to consume large amounts of alcohol as part of a hazing ritual, fraternities and their members have been held responsible for damages. In *Ballou v. Sigma Nu General Fraternity,* 352 S.E.2d 488 (S.C. Ct. App. 1986), a state appellate court found that the *national* fraternity owes a duty of care to initiates not to injure them; the court therefore held that fraternity responsible for damages related to a pledge's wrongful death from alcohol poisoning. A student who sustained serious neurological damage after forced intoxication was similarly successful in a suit against the local chapter, *Quinn v. Sigma Rho Chapter,* 507 N.E.2d 1193 (Ill. App. Ct. 1987), as was the father of a student who died after being forced to drink as part of an initiation ritual for the lacrosse team at Western Illinois University. In that case, the students were found liable as individuals (*Haben v. Anderson,* 597 N.E.2d 655 (Ill. App. Ct. 1993)). For a review of the potential liability of national fraternities for hazing injuries, see Note, "Alcohol and Hazing Risks in College Fraternities: Re-evaluating Vicarious and Custodial Liability of National Fraternities," *Review of Litigation* 191 (1988).

Because of the increasing tendency of plaintiffs to look to national fraternities for damages, several national fraternities have developed risk management information and training programs for local chapters. College administrators responsible for oversight of fraternal organizations should work with national fraternities to advance their mutual interest in minimizing dangerous activity, student injuries, and ensuing legal liability. Given the seriousness of injuries related to misconduct by fraternities and their members, administrators should examine their institutional regulations, their relationship or recognition statements, and their institutional code of student conduct to ascertain the extent of the college's potential liability. Educational programs regarding the responsible use of alcohol, swift disciplinary action for breaches of the code of student conduct, and monitoring (rather than regulation) of the activities of fraternal organizations may reduce the likelihood of harm to students or others and of liability for the college.

SELECTED ANNOTATED BIBLIOGRAPHY

Sec. 9.1 (Student Organizations)

Comment, "'Fee Speech': First Amendment Limitations on Student Fee Expenditures," 20 *Cal. Western L. Rev.* 279 (1984). Focuses on the particular problem of "using mandatory student fees to finance political or ideological activities." Analyzes the constitutional issues raised by this practice, from the perspectives of both the university and the students who object to such uses of mandatory fees; reviews prior cases on student fees as well as on mandatory labor union dues; and proposes a new analytical scheme for determining the constitutionality of particular mandatory student fees.

Sec. 9.2 (Fraternities and Sororities)

Curry, Susan J. "Hazing and the 'Rush' Toward Reform: Responses from Universities, Fraternities, State Legislatures, and the Courts," 16 *J. Coll. & Univ. Law* 93 (1989). Examines the various legal theories used against local and national fraternities, universities, and individual fraternity members to redress injury or death resulting from hazing. Also reviews the response of one university to the hazing death of a pledge and its revised regulation of fraternities. Two state antihazing laws are also discussed.

Lewis, Darryll M. H. "The Criminalization of Fraternity, Non-Fraternity and Non-Collegiate Hazing," 51 *Miss. L.J.* 111 (1991). Describes state laws that make hazing and associated activities subject to criminal penalties.

Walton, Spring J., Bassler, Stephen E., & Cunningham, Robert Briggs. "The High Cost of Partying: Social Host Liability for Fraternities and Colleges," 14 *Whittier L. Rev.* 659 (1993). Discusses the implications of state social host laws for local and national fraternities and for colleges and universities. Concludes that increased regulation of fraternities by colleges may prompt judicial imposition of a duty on colleges to prevent injuries related to fraternity social activity.

CHAPTER TEN

Intramural, Club, and Intercollegiate Athletics

SEC. 10.1. APPLICABLE LAW

10.1.1. General Principles

Athletics, as a subsystem of the postsecondary institution, is governed by the general principles set forth elsewhere in this book. These principles, however, must be applied in light of the particular characteristics and problems of curricular, extracurricular, and intercollegiate athletic programs. A student athlete's eligibility for financial aid, for instance, would be viewed under the general principles in Section 4.2, but aid conditions related to the student's eligibility for or performance in intercollegiate athletics create a special focus for the problem (see Section 10.2). The institution's tort liability for injuries to students would be subject to the general principles in Section 2.3.1, but the circumstances and risks of athletic participation provide a special focus for the problem (see Section 10.6). Similarly, the due process principles in Section 7.3 may apply when a student athlete is disciplined, and the First Amendment principles in Section 8.1 may apply when student athletes engage in protest activities. But in each case, the problem may have a special focus.

Surrounding these special applications of the law to athletics, there are major new legal and policy issues that pertain specifically to the status of "big-time" intercollegiate athletics within the higher education world. In addition to the problem of low graduation rates, the debate has focused on academic entrance requirements for student athletes (see L. Greene, "The New NCAA Rules of the Game: Academic Integrity or Racism?" 28 *St. Louis U. L.J.* 101 (1984)); post-secondary institutions' recruiting practices; alleged doctoring or padding of high school and college transcripts to obtain or maintain athletic eligibility; drug use among athletes and mandatory drug testing (Section 10.5); alleged exploitation of black athletes; improper financial incentives and rewards or improper academic assistance for student athletes; and the authority and practices of the NCAA and athletic conferences (Section 10.7) regarding such matters. The over-arching concern prompted by these issues is one of integrity: the integrity of individual institutions' athletic programs, the integrity of academic standards at institutions emphasizing major intercollegiate competition, the integrity of higher education's mission in an era when athletics has assumed such a substantial role in the operation of the system. See J. Thelin & L. Wiseman, *The Old College Try: Balancing Academics and Athletics in Higher Education* (George Washington University, 1989).

10.1.2. Due Process: Disciplining Athletes

If a student athlete is being disciplined for some infraction, the penalty may be suspension from the team. In such instances, the issue raised is whether the procedural protections accompanying suspension from school are also applicable to suspension from a team. For institutions engaging in state action (see Sections 1.5.2 and 10.7.2), the constitutional issue is whether the student athlete has a "property interest" or "liberty interest" in continued intercollegiate competition sufficient to make suspension of that interest a deprivation of "liberty or property" within the meaning of the due process clause. Several federal court cases have addressed this question. (Parallel "liberty or property" issues also arise in the context of student suspensions and dismissals (Section 7.3.2).)

In *Behagen v. Intercollegiate Conference of Faculty Representatives,* 346 F. Supp. 602 (D. Minn. 1972), a suit brought by University of Minnesota basketball players suspended from the team for participating in an altercation during a game, the court reasoned that participation in intercollegiate athletics has "the potential to bring [student athletes] great economic rewards" and is thus as important as continuing in school. The court therefore held that the students' interests in intercollegiate participation were protected by procedural due process and granted the suspended athletes the protections established in the *Dixon* case (Section 7.3.2). In *Regents of the University of Minnesota v. NCAA,* 422 F. Supp. 1158 (D. Minn. 1976), the same district court reaffirmed and further explained its analysis of student athletes' due process rights. The court reasoned that the opportunity to participate in intercollegiate competition is a property interest entitled to due process protection, not only because of the possible remunerative careers that result but also because such participation is an important part of the student athlete's educational experience.[1] The same court later used much the same analysis in *Hall v. University of Minnesota*, 530 F. Supp. 104 (D. Minn. 1982).

In contrast, the court in *Colorado Seminary v. NCAA*, 417 F. Supp. 885 (D. Colo. 1976), relying on an appellate court's opinion in a case involving high school athletes (*Albach v. Odle*, 531 F.2d 983 (10th Cir. 1976)), held that college athletes have no property or liberty interests in participating in intercollegiate sports, participating in postseason competition, or appearing on television. The appellate court affirmed (570 F.2d 320 (10th Cir. 1978)). (The trial court did suggest, however, that revocation of an athletic scholarship would infringe a student's property or liberty interests and therefore would require due process safeguards (see Section 10.2).) And in *Hawkins v. NCAA*, 652 F. Supp. 602, 609–11 (C.D. Ill. 1987), the court held that student athletes have no property interest in participating in postseason competition. Given this disagreement among the courts, the extent of student athletes' procedural due process protections remains an open question, and administrators should tread cautiously in this area.

10.1.3. First Amendment: Protests by Athletes

When student athletes are participants in a protest or demonstration, their First Amendment rights must be viewed in light of the institution's particular interest in maintaining order and discipline in its athletic programs. An athlete's protest that disrupts an athletic program would no more be protected by the First Amendment than any other student protest that disrupts institutional functions. While the case law regarding athletes' First Amendment rights is even more sparse than that regarding their due process rights, *Williams v. Eaton*, 468 F.2d 1079 (10th Cir. 1972), does specifically apply the *Tinker* case (Section 8.1.1) to a protest by intercollegiate football players. Black football players had been suspended from the team for insisting on wearing black armbands during a game to protest the alleged racial discrimination of the opposing church-related school. The court held that the athletes' protest was unprotected by the First Amendment because it would interfere with the religious freedom rights of the opposing players and their church-related institution. The *Williams* opinion is unusual in that it mixes considerations of free speech and freedom of religion. The court's analysis would have little relevance to situations where religious freedom is not involved. Since the court did not find that the athletes' protest was disruptive, it relied solely on the seldom-used "interference with the rights of others" branch of the *Tinker* case.

---

[1]Although the appellate court reversed this decision, 560 F.2d 352 (8th Cir. 1977), it did so on other grounds and did not question the district court's due process analysis.

More recently, in *Marcum v. Dahl*, 658 F.2d 731 (10th Cir. 1981), the court considered a First Amendment challenge to an institution's nonrenewal of the scholarships of several student athletes. The plaintiffs, basketball players on the University of Oklahoma's women's team, had been involved during the season in a dispute with other players over who should be the team's head coach. At the end of the season, they had announced to the press that they would not play the next year if the current coach was retained. The plaintiffs argued that the institution had refused to renew their scholarships because of this statement to the press and that the statement was constitutionally protected. The trial court and then the appellate court disagreed. Analogizing the scholarship athletes to public employees for First Amendment purposes (see *LHE* 3d, Sections 3.7.1 and 3.7.3), the appellate court held that (1) the dispute about the coach was not a matter of "general public concern" and the plaintiffs' press statement on this subject was therefore not protected by the First Amendment and (2) the plaintiffs' participation in the dispute prior to the press statement, and the resultant disharmony, provided an independent basis for the scholarship nonrenewal.

10.1.4. State and Federal Statutes

State and federal statutory law also has some special applications to an institution's athletes or athletic programs. Questions have arisen, for example, about the eligibility of injured intercollegiate athletes for workers' compensation (see *LHE* 3d, Section 6.5.5). Criminal laws in some states prohibit agents from entering representation agreements with student athletes (see, for example, Mich. Comp. Laws Ann. §750.411e) or from entering into such an agreement without notifying the student's institution (see, for example, Fla. Stat. Ann. §240.537). State antihazing statutes may have applications to the activities of athletic teams and clubs (see, for example, Ill. Rev. Stat. ch. 144, para. 222, as construed and upheld in *People v. Anderson*, 591 N.E.2d 461 (Ill. 1992), a prosecution brought against members of a university lacrosse club). Regarding federal law, the antitrust statutes may have some application to the institution's relations with its student athletes when those relations are governed by athletic association and conference rules (this volume, Section 10.7.3). And the Student Right-to-Know Act, discussed next, contains separate provisions dealing with the low graduation rates of student athletes in certain sports.

The Student Right-to-Know Act (Title I of the Student-Right-to-Know and Campus Security Act), 104 Stat. 2381–2384 (1990), ensures that potential student athletes will have access to data that will help them make informed choices when selecting an institution. Under the Act, an institution of higher education that participates in federal student aid programs and that awards "athletically related student aid" must annually provide the Department of Education with certain information about its student athletes. Athletically related student aid is defined as "any scholarship, grant, or other form of financial assistance the terms of which require the recipient to participate in a program of intercollegiate athletics at an institution of higher education in order to be eligible to receive such assistance" (104 Stat. 2384, 20 U.S.C. §1092(e)(8)).

Institutions must report the following information, broken down by race and gender: (1) the number of students receiving athletically related student aid in basketball, football, baseball, cross country/track, and all other sports combined (20 U.S.C. §1092(e)(1)(A)); (2) the completion or graduation rates of those students (20 U.S.C. §1092(e)(1)(C)); and (3) the average completion or graduation rate for the four most recent classes (20 U.S.C. §1092(e)(1)(E)). The same types of information must be collected on students in general (20 U.S.C. §1092(e)(1)(B, D, & F)). In addition to reporting to the Department of Education, institutions must provide this information to potential student athletes and their parents, guidance counselors, and coaches (20 U.S.C. §1092(e)(2)). Other students may receive the information upon request.[2] The secretary of education may waive the annual reporting requirements if, in his opinion, an institution of higher education is a member of an athletic association or conference that publishes data "substantially comparable" to the information specified in the Act (20 U.S.C. §1092(e)(6)). Regulations implementing the Act are published at 34 C.F.R. Part 668.

SEC. 10.2. ATHLETIC SCHOLARSHIPS

An athletic scholarship will usually be treated in the courts as a contract between the institution and the student. Typically, the institution offers to pay the student's educational expenses in return for the student's promise to participate in a particular sport and maintain athletic eligibility by complying with university, conference, and NCAA regulations (see Section 10.7). Unlike other student-institutional contracts (see Section 3.2), the athletic scholarship contract may be a formal written agreement signed by the student and, if the student is underage, by a parent or guardian. Moreover, the terms of the athletic scholarship may be heavily influenced by athletic conference and NCAA rules regarding scholarships and athletic eligibility.

In NCAA member institutions, a letter-of-intent document is provided to prospective student athletes. The student athlete's signature on this document functions as a promise that the student will attend the institution and participate in intercollegiate athletics in exchange for the institution's promise to pro-

---

[2]This information is in addition to other information that institutions must provide to prospective and enrolled students under 20 U.S.C. §1092. See this volume, Section 4.2.2., and see also Section 12.3.3.3.

vide a scholarship or other financial assistance. Courts have generally not addressed the issue of whether the letter of intent, standing alone, is an enforceable contract that binds the institution and the student athlete to their respective commitments. Instead, courts have viewed the signing of a letter of intent as one among many factors to consider in determining whether a contractual relationship exists. Thus, although the letter of intent serves as additional evidence of a contractual relationship, it does not yet have independent legal status and, in effect, must be coupled with a financial aid offer in order to bind either party. See generally M. Cozzillio, "The Athletic Scholarship and the College National Letter of Intent: A Contract by Any Other Name," 35 *Wayne L. Rev.* 1275 (1989).

Although it is possible for either the institution or the student to breach the scholarship contract and for either party to sue, as a practical matter the cases generally involve students who file suit after the institution terminates or withdraws the scholarship. Such institutional action may occur if the student becomes ineligible for intercollegiate competition, has fraudulently misrepresented information regarding his or her academic credentials or athletic eligibility, has engaged in serious misconduct warranting substantial disciplinary action, or has declined to participate in the sport for personal reasons. The following three cases illustrate how such issues arise and how courts resolve them.

In *Begley v. Corp. of Mercer University,* 367 F. Supp. 908 (E.D. Tenn. 1973), the university withdrew from its agreement to provide an athletic scholarship for Begley after realizing that a university assistant coach had miscalculated Begley's high school GPA, and that his true GPA did not meet the NCAA's minimum requirements. Begley filed suit, asking the court to award money damages for the university's breach of contract. The court dismissed the suit, holding that the university was justified in not performing its part of the agreement, since the agreement also required Begley to abide by all NCAA rules and regulations. Because Begley, from the outset, did not have the minimum GPA, he was unable to perform his part of the agreement. Thus, the court based its decision on the fundamental principle of contract law that "'where one party is unable to perform his part of the contract, he cannot be entitled to the performance of the contract by the other party'" (quoting 17 Am. Jur. 2d at 791–92, *Contracts,* §355).

In *Taylor v. Wake Forest University,* 191 S.E.2d 379 (N.C. Ct. App. 1972), the university terminated the student's scholarship after he refused to participate in the football program. Originally, the student had withdrawn from the team to concentrate on academics when his grades fell below the minimum that the university required for athletic participation. Even after he raised his GPA above the minimum, however, the student continued his refusal to participate. The student alleged that the university's termination of his athletic scholarship was a breach and asked the court to award money damages equal to the costs incurred in completing his degree. He argued that, in case of conflict between his educational achievement and his athletic involvement, the scholarship terms allowed him to curtail his participation in the football program in order to "assure reasonable academic progress." He also argued that he was to be the judge of "reasonable academic progress." The court rejected the student's argument and granted summary judgment for the university. According to the court, permitting the student to be his own judge of his academic progress would be a "strange construction of the contract." Further, by accepting the scholarship, the student was obligated to "maintain his athletic eligibility . . . both physically and scholastically. . . . When he refused to [participate] in the absence of any injury or excuse other than to devote more time to his studies, he was not complying with his contractual agreements."

In *Conard v. University of Washington*, 814 P.2d 1242 (Wash. Ct. App. 1991), after three years of providing financial aid, the university declined to renew the scholarships of two student athletes for a fourth year because of the students' "serious misconduct." Although the scholarship agreement stipulated a one-year award of aid that would be considered for renewal under certain conditions, the students argued that it was their expectation, and the university's practice, that the scholarship would be automatically renewed for at least four years. The appellate court did not accept the students' evidence to this effect because the agreement, by its "clear terms," lasted only one academic year and provided only for the *consideration* of renewal. The university's withdrawal of aid, therefore, was not a breach of the contract.

Due process issues may also arise if an institution terminates or withdraws an athletic scholarship. The contract itself may specify certain procedural steps that the institution must take before withdrawal or termination. Conference or NCAA rules may contain other procedural requirements. And for public institutions, the federal Constitution's Fourteenth Amendment (or comparable state constitutional provision) may sometimes superimpose other procedural obligations upon those contained in the contract and rules. In the *Conard* case discussed earlier, for example, the Washington Court of Appeals held that the students had a "legitimate claim of entitlement" to the renewal of their scholarships because each scholarship was "issued under the representation that it would be renewed subject to certain conditions," and because it was the university's practice to renew athletic scholarships for at least four years. Since this "entitlement" constituted a property interest under the Fourteenth Amendment, the court held that any deprivation of this entitlement "warrants the protection of due process" (see Section 10.1.2).

The Washington Supreme Court reversed the court of appeals on the due process issue (834 P.2d 17 (Wash. 1992)). The students' primary contention was that a "mutually explicit understanding" had been created by "the language of their contracts and the common understanding, based upon the surrounding circumstances and the conduct of the parties." The court rejected this argument, stating that "the language of the offers and the NCAA regulations are not sufficiently certain to support a mutually explicit understanding, [and] the fact that scholarships are, in fact, normally renewed does not create a 'common law' of renewal, absent other consistent and supportive [university] policies or rules." Consequently, the court held that the students had no legitimate claim of entitlement to renewal of the scholarships, and that the university thus had no obligation to extend them due process protections prior to nonrenewal.

Although the Washington Court of Appeals' decision in *Conard* is no longer good law, it is illustrative of the types of due process safeguards a court would require in a misconduct case if it found that a particular scholarship agreement created a protected property interest in renewal:

> Clearly, at least notice and an opportunity to be heard are required. In addition, the student athlete who faces nonrenewal of his or her scholarship based on misconduct must be given a written copy of any information on which the nonrenewal recommendation is based in time to prepare to address that information at the hearing. The student should be given the opportunity to present and rebut evidence, and the hearing must be conducted by an objective decisionmaker. The student has a right to be represented by counsel and to have a record made of the hearing for review purposes. Finally, the student has the right to a written decision from the hearing board setting forth its determination of contested facts and the basis for its decision [814 P.2d at 1246].

Apparently, a court would also require the same protections in a situation where the institution had terminated a multiyear athletic scholarship.

Occasionally, student athletes have sued their institutions even when the institution has not terminated or withdrawn the athlete's scholarship. Such cases are likely to involve alleged exploitation or abuse of the athlete, and may present not only breach-of-contract issues paralleling those in the cases above but also more innovative tort law issues. The leading case, highly publicized in its day, is *Ross v. Creighton University*, 957 F.2d 410 (7th Cir. 1992). The plaintiff in this case had been awarded a basketball scholarship from Creighton, even though his academic credentials were substantially below those of the average Creighton student. The plaintiff alleged that the university knew of his academic limitations but nevertheless lured him to Creighton with assurances that it would provide sufficient academic support so that he would "receive a meaningful education." While at Creighton, the plaintiff maintained a D average; and, on the advice of the athletic department, his curriculum consisted largely of courses such as "Theory of Basketball." After four years, he "had the overall language skills of a fourth grader and the reading skills of a seventh grader."

The plaintiff based his suit on three tort theories and a breach-of-contract theory. The trial court originally dismissed all four claims. The appellate court agreed with the trial court on the tort claims but reversed the trial court and allowed the plaintiff to proceed to trial on the breach-of-contract claim. The plaintiff's first tort claim was a claim of "educational malpractice" based on Creighton's not providing him with "a meaningful education [or] preparing him for employment after college." The court refused to recognize educational malpractice as a cause of action, listing four policy concerns supporting its decision: (1) the inability of a court to fashion "a satisfactory standard of care by which to evaluate" instruction; (2) its inability to determine the cause and nature of damage to the student; (3) the potential flood of litigation that would divert institutions' attention from their primary mission; and (4) the threat of involving courts in the oversight of daily institutional operations. The plaintiff's second claim was that Creighton had committed "negligent admission" because it owed a duty to "recruit and enroll only those students reasonably qualified to and able to academically perform at CREIGHTON." The court rejected this novel theory because of similar problems in identifying a standard of care by which to judge the institution's admissions decisions. The court also noted that, if institutions were subjected to such claims, they would admit only exceptional students, thus severely limiting the opportunities for marginal students. The plaintiff's last tort claim was negligent infliction of emotional distress. The court quickly rejected this claim because its rejection of the first two claims left no basis for proving that the defendant had been negligent in undertaking the actions that may have distressed the plaintiff.

Although the court rejected all the plaintiff's negligence claims, it did embrace his breach-of-contract claim. In order to discourage "any attempt to repackage an educational malpractice claim as a contract claim," however, the court required the plaintiff to "do more than simply allege that the education was not good enough. Instead, he must point to an identifiable contractual promise that the defendant failed to honor. . . . [T]he essence of the plaintiff's complaint would not be that the institution failed to perform adequately a promised educational service, but rather that it failed to perform that service at all." Judicial consideration of such a claim is therefore not an inquiry "into the nuances of educational processes and theories, but rather an objective assessment of whether the institution made a good faith effort to perform on its promise."

Following this approach, the court reviewed the plaintiff's allegations that the university failed (1) to provide adequate tutoring; (2) to require that the plaintiff attend tutoring sessions; (3) to allow the plaintiff to "red-shirt" for one year to concentrate on his studies; and (4) to afford the plaintiff a reasonable opportunity to take advantage of tutoring services. The court concluded that these allegations were sufficient to warrant further proceedings and therefore remanded the case to the trial court. (Soon thereafter, the parties settled the case.)

The court's disposition of the tort claims in *Ross* does not mean that student athletes can never succeed with such claims. In a similar case, *Jackson v. Drake University*, 778 F. Supp. 1490 (S.D. Iowa 1991), the court did recognize two tort claims—negligent misrepresentation and fraud—brought by a former student athlete. After rejecting an educational malpractice claim for reasons similar to those in *Ross*, the court allowed the plaintiff to proceed with his claims that "Drake did not exercise reasonable care in making representations [about its commitment to academic excellence] and had no intention of providing the support services it had promised." The court reasoned that the policy concerns "do not weigh as heavily in favor of precluding the claims for negligent misrepresentation and fraud as in the claim for [educational malpractice]."

SEC. 10.3. SEX DISCRIMINATION

Sex discrimination remains a major issue in athletics programs. Before the passage of Title IX (20 U.S.C. §1681 *et seq.*) (see Section 12.4.3), the legal aspects of this controversy centered on the Fourteenth Amendment's equal protection clause. As in earlier admissions cases (Section 4.1.4.2), courts searched for an appropriate analysis by which to ascertain the constitutionality of sex-based classifications in athletics. Since the implementation in 1975 of the Title IX regulations (34 C.F.R. Part 106), the equal protection aspects of sex discrimination in high school and college athletics have played second fiddle to Title IX. Title IX applies to both public and private institutions receiving federal aid and thus has a broader reach than equal protection, which applies only to public institutions (see Section 1.5.2). Title IX also has several provisions on athletics that establish requirements more extensive than anything devised under the banner of equal protection. And Title IX is supported by enforcement mechanisms beyond those available for the equal protection clause (see Sections 12.4.8 and 12.4.9).

In addition to Title IX, state law (including state equal rights amendments) also has significant applications to college athletics. In *Blair v. Washington State University*, 740 P.2d 1379 (Wash. 1987), for example, women athletes and coaches at Washington State University used the state's equal rights amendment and the state nondiscrimination law to challenge the institution's funding for women's athletic programs. The trial court had ruled against the university, saying that funding for women's athletic programs should be based on the percentage of women enrolled as undergraduates. In calculating the formula, however, the trial court had excluded football revenues. The Washington Supreme Court reversed on that point, declaring that the state's equal rights amendment "contains no exception for football." It remanded the case to the trial court for revision of the funding formula. See "Comment: *Blair v. Washington State University:*

Making State ERA's a Potent Remedy for Sex Discrimination in Athletics," 14 *J. Coll. & Univ. Law* 575 (1988).

Although the regulations interpreting Title IX with regard to athletics were effective in 1975, they were not appreciably enforced at the postsecondary level until the late 1980s—partly because the U.S. Supreme Court, in *Grove City College v. Bell* (discussed in Section 12.4.7.3), had held that Title IX's nondiscrimination provisions applied only to programs that were direct recipients of federal aid. Congress reversed the result in *Grove City* in the Civil Rights Restoration Act of 1987, making it clear that Title IX applies to all activities of colleges and universities that receive federal funds.

Section 106.41 of the Title IX regulations is the primary provision on athletics; it establishes various equal opportunity requirements applicable to "interscholastic, intercollegiate, club, or intramural athletics." Section 106.37(c) establishes equal opportunity requirements regarding the availability of athletic scholarships. Physical education classes are covered by Section 106.34, and extracurricular activities related to athletics, such as cheerleading and booster clubs, are covered generally under Section 106.31. The regulations impose nondiscrimination requirements on these activities whether or not they are directly subsidized by federal funds (see this volume, Section 12.4.7.4), and they do not exempt revenue-generating sports, such as men's football or basketball, from the calculation of funds available for the institution's athletic programs.

One of the greatest controversies stirred by Title IX concerns the choice of sex-segregated versus unitary (integrated) athletic teams. The regulations develop a compromise approach to this issue, which roughly parallels the equal protection principles that emerged from the earlier court cases.[3]

Under Section 106.41(b):

[An institution] may operate or sponsor separate teams for members of each sex where selection for such teams is based upon competitive skill or the activity involved is a contact sport. However, where a recipient operates or sponsors a team in a particular sport for members of one sex but operates or sponsors no

---

[3]It is still somewhat an open question whether Title IX's athletic regulations fully comply with constitutional equal protection and due process requirements. There is some basis for arguing that the Title IX regulations do not fully meet the equal protection requirements that courts have constructed or will construct in this area (see W. Kaplin and S. Marmur, "Validity of the 'Separate but Equal' Policy of the Title IX Regulations on Athletics," a memorandum reprinted in 121 *Congressional Record* 1090, 94th Cong., 1st Sess. (1975)). One court has ruled on the question, holding Section 86.41 (b) (now 106.41(b)) of the Title IX regulations unconstitutional as applied to exclude physically qualified girls from competing with boys in contact sports (*Yellow Springs Exempted Village School District v. Ohio High School Athletic Association,* 443 F. Supp. 753 (S.D. Ohio 1978)). On appeal, however, a U.S. Court of Appeals reversed the district court's ruling (647 F.2d 651 (6th Cir. 1981)) because, given the posture of the case and the absence of evidence in the record, "we believe it inappropriate for this court to make any ruling on the matter at this time."

such team for members of the other sex, and athletic opportunities for members of that sex have previously been limited, members of the excluded sex must be allowed to try out for the team offered unless the sport involved is a contact sport. For the purposes of this part, contact sports include boxing, wrestling, rugby, ice hockey, football, basketball, and other sports the purpose or major activity of which involves bodily contact.

This regulation requires institutions to operate unitary teams only for non-contact sports where selection is not competitive. Otherwise, the institution may operate either unitary or separate teams and may even operate a team for one sex without having any team in the sport for the opposite sex, as long as the institution's overall athletic program "effectively accommodate[s] the interests and abilities of members of both sexes" (34 C.F.R. §106.41(c)(1)). In a noncontact sport, however, if an institution operates only one competitively selected team, it must be open to both sexes whenever the "athletic opportunities" of the traditionally excluded sex "have previously been limited" (34 C.F.R. §106.41(b)).

Regardless of whether its teams are separate or unitary, the institution must "provide equal athletic opportunity for members of both sexes" (34 C.F.R. §106.41(c)). While equality of opportunity does not require either equality of "aggregate expenditures for members of each sex" or equality of "expenditures for male and female teams," an institution's "failure to provide necessary funds for teams for one sex" is a relevant factor in determining compliance (34 C.F.R. §106.41(c)). Postsecondary administrators grappling with this slippery equal opportunity concept will be helped by Section 106.41(c)'s list of ten nonexclusive factors by which to measure overall equality:

1. Whether the selection of sports and levels of competition effectively accommodate the interests and abilities of members of both sexes.

2. The provision of equipment and supplies.

3. Scheduling of games and practice time.

4. Travel and per diem allowance.

5. Opportunity to receive coaching and academic tutoring.

6. Assignment and compensation of coaches and tutors.

7. Provision of locker rooms, practice and competitive facilities.

8. Provision of medical and training facilities and services.

9. Provision of housing and dining facilities and services.

10. Publicity.

The equal opportunity focus of the regulations also applies to athletic scholarships. Institutions must "provide reasonable opportunities for such awards for members of each sex in proportion to the number of each sex participating in . . . intercollegiate athletics" (34 C.F.R. §106.37(c)(1)). If the institution operates separate teams for each sex (as permitted in §106.41), it may allocate athletic scholarships on the basis of sex to implement its separate-team philosophy, as long as the overall allocation achieves equal opportunity.

In 1979, after a period of substantial controversy, the Department of Health, Education and Welfare (now Department of Education) issued a lengthy Policy Interpretation of its Title IX regulations as they apply to intercollegiate athletics (44 Fed. Reg. 71413 (Dec. 11, 1979)). This Policy Interpretation is still considered authoritative and is currently used by federal courts reviewing allegations of Title IX violations. It addresses each of the ten factors listed in Section 106.41(c) of the regulations, providing examples of information the Department of Education will use to determine whether an institution has complied with Title IX. For example, "opportunity to receive coaching and academic tutoring" would include the availability of full-time and part-time coaches for male and female athletes, the relative availability of graduate assistants, and the availability of tutors for male and female athletes. "Compensation of coaches" includes attention to the rates of compensation, conditions relating to contract renewal, nature of coaching duties performed, and working conditions of coaches for male and female teams (44 Fed. Reg. at 71416). Further elucidation of the ten factors is found in the *Title IX Athletics Investigator's Manual* published by and available from the ED's Office for Civil Rights (which enforces Title IX).[4]

Most Title IX disputes have involved complaints to the Office for Civil Rights. In the past, this office has been criticized for its "lax" enforcement efforts and for permitting institutions to remain out of compliance with Title IX (*Gender Equity in Intercollegiate Athletics: The Inadequacy of Title IX Enforcement by the U.S. Office for Civil Rights* (Lyndon B. Johnson School of Public Affairs, University of Texas, 1993)). Perhaps partly for this reason, women athletes in recent years have often chosen to litigate their claims in the courts.

Although the first major court challenge to an institution's funding for intercollegiate athletics ended with a settlement rather than a court order (*Haffer v. Temple University*, 678 F. Supp. 517 (E.D. Pa. 1987)), this case set the tone for subsequent litigation. In *Haffer* a federal trial judge certified a class of "all current women students at Temple University who participate, or who are or have been deterred from participating because of sex discrimination[,] in Temple's intercollegiate athletic program." Although the case was settled, with the university agreeing to various changes in scholarships and support for women ath-

---

[4]As with all government publications providing guidance on compliance, administrators and counsel should obtain the most current version of this manual to use in assessing their institution's Title IX compliance. To review OCR's web site that includes a list of current publications, enter http://www.ed.gov/offices/OCR.

letes, it encouraged women students at other colleges and universities to challenge the revenues allocated to women's and men's sports. For discussion see "Comment: *Haffer v. Temple University:* A Reawakening of Gender Discrimination in Intercollegiate Athletics," 16 *J. Coll. & Univ. Law* 137 (1989).

The leading case to date on Title IX's application to intercollegiate athletics is *Cohen v. Brown University,* 991 F.2d 888 (1st Cir. 1993). In that case, a U.S. Court of Appeals upheld a district court's preliminary injunction ordering Brown University to reinstate its women's gymnastics and women's volleyball programs to full varsity status pending the trial of a Title IX claim. Until 1971, Brown had been an all-male university. At that time, it merged with a women's college and, over the next six years, upgraded the women's athletic program to include fourteen varsity teams. It later added one other such team. It thus had fifteen women's varsity teams as compared to sixteen men's varsity teams; the women had 36.7 percent of all the varsity athletic opportunities available at the university, and the men had 63.3 percent. (Brown's student population is approximately 48 percent women.) In 1991, however, the university cut four varsity teams: two men's teams (for a savings of $15,795) and two women's teams (for a savings of $62,028). These cuts disproportionately reduced the budgeted funds for women, but they did not significantly change the ratio of athletic opportunities, since women retained 36.6 percent of the available slots.

In upholding the district court's injunction, the appellate court first noted that an institution would not be found in violation of Title IX merely because there was a statistical disparity between the percentage of women and the percentage of men in its athletic programs. The court then focused on the ten factors listed in Section 106.41(c) of the Title IX regulations (shown earlier) and noted that the district court based its injunction on the first of these factors: "Brown's failure effectively to accommodate the interests and abilities of female students in the selection and level of sports." To be in compliance with this factor, a university must satisfy at least one of three tests set out in the Title IX Policy Interpretation:

> (1) Whether intercollegiate level participation opportunities for male and female students are provided in numbers substantially proportionate to their respective enrollments; or
>
> (2) Where the members of one sex have been and are underrepresented among intercollegiate athletes, whether the institution can show a history and continuing practice of program expansion which is demonstrably responsive to the developing interest and abilities of the members of that sex; or
>
> (3) Where the members of one sex have been and are underrepresented among intercollegiate athletes, and the institution cannot show a continuing practice of program expansion such as that cited above, whether it can be demonstrated that the interests and abilities of the members of that sex have been fully and effectively accommodated by the present program [44 Fed. Reg. at 71418].

The appellate court agreed with the district court that Brown clearly did not fall within the first option. Further, the district court did not abuse its discretion in deciding that, although the university had made a large burst of improvements between 1971 and 1977, the lack of continuing expansion efforts precluded the university from satisfying the second option. Thus, since the university could not comply with either of the first two options, "it must comply with the third benchmark. To do so, the school must fully and effectively accommodate the underrepresented gender's interests and abilities, even if that requires it to give the underrepresented gender . . . what amounts to a larger slice of a shrinking athletic-opportunity pie." The appellate court then focused on the word "fully" in the third option, interpreting it literally to mean that the underrepresented sex must be "fully" accommodated, not merely proportionately accommodated as in the first option. Since Brown's cuts in the women's athletic programs had created a demand for athletic opportunities for women that was not filled, women were not "fully" accommodated. Thus, since Brown could meet none of the three options specified in the Policy Interpretation, the court concluded that the university had likely violated Title IX, and it therefore affirmed the district court's entry of the preliminary injunction.

Holding that the plaintiffs had made their required showing and that Brown had not, the court turned to the issue of remedy. Although the appellate court upheld the preliminary injunction, it noted the need to balance the institution's academic freedom with the need for an effective remedy for the Title IX violation. The appellate court stated that, since the lower court had not yet held a trial on the merits, its order that Brown maintain women's varsity volleyball and gymnastics teams pending trial was within its discretion. The appellate court noted, however, that a more appropriate post-trial remedy, assuming that a Title IX violation was established, would be for Brown to propose a program for compliance. In balancing academic freedom against Title IX's regulatory scheme, the court noted:

This litigation presents an array of complicated and important issues at a crossroads of the law that few courts have explored. The beacon by which we must steer is Congress's unmistakably clear mandate that educational institutions not use federal monies to perpetuate gender-based discrimination. At the same time, we must remain sensitive to the fact that suits of this genre implicate the discretion of universities to pursue their missions free from governmental interference and, in the bargain, to deploy increasingly scarce resources in the most advantageous way [991 F.2d at 907].

See also *Roberts v. Colorado State Board of Agriculture*, 998 F.2d 824, 833–34 (10th Cir. 1993), which includes a contrasting discussion of remedies; and see generally B. Kramer, *Title IX in Intercollegiate Athletics: Litigation Risks Facing Colleges and Universities*, Public Policy Series no. 93–2 (Association of Governing Boards, 1993).

After the appellate court in *Cohen* remanded the case to the district court, that court held a full trial on the merits, after which it ruled again in favor of the plaintiffs and ordered Brown to submit a plan for achieving full compliance with Title IX. When the district court found Brown's plan to be inadequate and entered its own order specifying that Brown must remedy its Title IX violation by elevating four women's teams to full varsity status, Brown appealed again. In late 1996, the First Circuit issued another ruling in what is called "*Cohen* IV" (*Cohen* II being its earlier 1993 ruling, and *Cohen* I and *Cohen* III being the district court rulings that preceded *Cohen* II and *Cohen* IV). By a 2–to–1 vote in *Cohen* IV, 101 F. 3d 155 (1st Cir. 1996), the appellate court affirmed the district court's ruling that Brown was in violation of Title IX. In so doing, the court explicitly relied upon, and refused to reconsider, its legal analysis from *Cohen* II. The *Cohen* II reasoning, as further explicated in *Cohen* IV, thus remains the law in the First Circuit and the leading example of how courts will apply Title IX to the claims of women athletes.

One of Brown's major arguments in *Cohen* IV was that

the significant disparity in athletics opportunities for men and women at Brown is the result of a gender-based differential in the level of interest in sports and that the district court's [ruling] requires universities to provide athletics opportunities for women to an extent that exceeds their relative interests and abilities in sports [101 F. 3d at 178].

The court viewed this argument "with great suspicion" and rejected it:

Thus, there exists the danger that, rather than providing a true measure of women's interest in sports, statistical evidence purporting to reflect women's interest instead provides only a measure of the very discrimination that is and has been the basis for women's lack of opportunity to participate in sports. . . . [E]ven if it can be empirically demonstrated that, at a particular time, women have less interest in sports than do men, such evidence, standing alone, cannot justify providing fewer athletics opportunities for women than for men. Furthermore, such evidence is completely irrelevant where, as here, viable and successful women's varsity teams have been demoted or eliminated [101 F. 3d at 179–180].

Regarding Brown's obligation to remedy its Title IX violation, however, the *Cohen* IV court overruled the district court because that court "erred in substituting its own specific relief in place of Brown's statutorily permissible proposal to comply with Title IX by cutting men's teams until substantial proportionality was achieved." The appellate court "agree[d] with the district court that Brown's proposed plan fell short of a good faith effort to meet the requirements of Title IX as explicated by this court in *Cohen* II and as applied by the district court on remand." Nevertheless, it determined that cutting men's teams "is a permissible means of effectuating compliance with the statute," and that Brown should have the opportunity to submit another plan to the district court. This disposition, said the court, was driven by "our respect for academic freedom and reluctance to interject ourselves into the conduct of university affairs."

Both in the *Cohen* and the *Roberts* case, the courts appeared to serve warning on institutions that do not provide equivalent intercollegiate athletic opportunities for men and women, and that have either a stringently limited athletic budget or one that must be cut. For such institutions, compliance with Title IX can occur only if the institution downgrades by reducing opportunities for men's sports to the level available for women's sports, or reduces men's opportunities to a lesser degree and uses the savings to enhance women's opportunities. Both appellate opinions deferred to the institution's right to determine for itself how it will structure its athletic programs, but once the institution was out of Title IX compliance, these courts did not hesitate to require a remedy. Financial problems did not exempt the institutions from Title IX compliance.

SEC. 10.4. DISCRIMINATION ON THE BASIS OF DISABILITY

Under Section 504 of the Rehabilitation Act of 1973 and its implementing regulations (see Section 12.4.4), institutions must afford disabled students an equal opportunity to participate in physical education and in athletic and recreational programs. Like Title IX, Section 504 applies to athletic activities even if they are not directly subsidized by federal funds (see Section 12.4.7.4). The Department of Education's regulations set forth the basic requirement:

(1) In providing physical education courses and athletics and similar programs and activities to any of its students, a recipient to which this subpart applies may not discriminate on the basis of handicap. A recipient that offers physical education courses or that operates or sponsors intercollegiate, club, or intramural athletics shall provide to qualified handicapped students an equal opportunity for participation in these activities.

(2) A recipient may offer to handicapped students physical education and athletic activities that are separate or different from those offered to nonhandicapped students only if separation or differentiation is consistent with the requirements . . . [that the programs and activities be operated in "the most integrated setting appropriate"] and only if no qualified handicapped student is denied the opportunity to compete for teams or to participate in courses that are not separate or different [34 C.F.R. §104.47(a)].

By these regulations, a student in a wheelchair could be eligible to participate in a regular archery program, for instance, or a deaf student on a regular wrestling team (34 C.F.R. Part 104 Appendix A), because they would retain full capacity to play those sports despite their disabilities. In these and other situations, however, questions may arise concerning whether the student's skill level would qualify him to participate in the program or allow him to succeed in the competition required for selection to intercollegiate teams.

The case law on Section 504's application to disabled athletes is sparse. In the first major case, *Wright v. Columbia University*, 520 F. Supp. 789 (E.D. Pa. 1981), the court relied on Section 504 to protect a disabled student's right to participate in intercollegiate football. The student had been blind in one eye since infancy; because of the potential danger to his "good" eye, the institution had denied him permission to participate. In issuing a temporary restraining order against the university, the court accepted (pending trial) the student's argument that the institution's decision was discriminatory within the meaning of Section 504 because the student was qualified to play football despite his disability and was capable of making his own decisions about "his health and well-being."

In a more recent case, *Pahulu v. University of Kansas*, 897 F. Supp. 1387 (D. Kan. 1995), the court reached the opposite result. The plaintiff, a football player, had sustained a blow to the head during scrimmage and consequently experienced tingling and numbness in his arms and legs. After the team physician and a consulting neurosurgeon diagnosed the symptoms as transient quadriplegia caused by a congenitally narrow cervical cord, they recommended that the student be disqualified from play for his senior year, even though he obtained the opinions of three other specialists who concluded he was fit to play. The student then sought a preliminary injunction, claiming that the university's decision violated Section 504. The court disagreed, holding on the basis of questionable reasoning that the plaintiff: (a) was not disabled within the meaning of Section 504, and (b) was not "otherwise qualified" to play football even if he was disabled. As to (a), the court reasoned that the plaintiff's physical impairment did not "substantially limit" the "major life activity" of learning, since he still retained his athletic scholarship, continued to have the same access to educational opportunities and academic resources, and could participate in the football program in some other capacity. As to (b), the court reasoned that the plaintiff did not meet the "technical standards" of the football program because he had failed to obtain medical clearance, and that:

> the conclusion of the KU physicians, although conservative, is reasonable and rational. Thus the defendants' decision regarding disqualification has a rational and reasonable basis and is supported by substantial competent evidence for which the court is unwilling to substitute its judgment.

A late 1996 case, *Knapp v. Northwestern University*, 101 F.3d 473 (7th Cir. 1996), uses reasoning similar to—but more fully developed than—that in *Pahulu* to deny relief to a basketball player who had been declared ineligible due to a heart problem. Applying the Section 504 definition of disability, the court ruled that: (a) playing intercollegiate basketball is not itself a "major life activit[y], nor is it an integral part of "learning," which the Section 504 regulations do acknowledge to be a major life activity; (b) the plaintiff's heart problem only precludes him from performing "a particular function" and does not otherwise "substantially limit" his major life activity of learning at the university; and (c) consequently, the plaintiff is not disabled within the meaning of Section 504 and cannot claim its protections. The court also ruled that the plaintiff could not claim Section 504 protection because he was not "otherwise qualified": "Even if we were inclined to find Knapp disabled [under Section 504], he would still come up short because we also hold as a matter of law that he is not, under the statute, 'otherwise qualified' to play intercollegiate basketball at Northwestern." In reaching this conclusion, the court deferred to the university's judgment regarding the substantiality of risk and the severity of harm to the plaintiff: "[M]edical determinations of this sort are best left to team doctors and universities as long as they are made with reason and rationality and with full regard to possible and reasonable accommodations."

In addition to Section 504, the Americans with Disabilities Act (see Section 12.1.6, this volume) may also provide some protections for student athletes subjected to discrimination on the basis of a disability in institutional athletic programs. Title II of the Act (public services) (42 U.S.C. §§12131–12134) would apply to students in public institutions, and Title III (public accommodations) (42 U.S.C. §§12181–12189) would apply to students in private institutions. See generally C. Jones, "College Athletes: Illness or Injury and the Decision to Return to Play," 40 *Buffalo L. Rev.* 113, 189–97 (1992).

SEC. 10.5. DRUG TESTING

Drug testing of athletes has become a focus of controversy in both amateur and professional sports. Intercollegiate athletics is no exception. Legal issues may arise under the federal Constitution's Fourth Amendment search-and-seizure clause and its Fourteenth Amendment due process clause; under search-and-seizure, due process, or right-to-privacy clauses of state constitutions; under various state civil rights statutes; under state tort law (see generally Section 2.3.1); or under the institution's own regulations, including statements of students' rights. Public institutions may be subject to challenges based on any of these sources; private institutions generally are subject only to challenges based on tort law, their own regulations, civil rights statutes applicable to private action, and (in some states) state constitutional provisions limiting private as well as public action (see generally Section 1.5).

For public institutions, the primary concern is the Fourth Amendment of the federal Constitution, which protects individuals against unreasonable searches and seizures, and parallel state constitutional provisions that may provide similar (and sometimes greater) protections. In *Skinner v. Railway Labor Executives Assn.*, 489 U.S. 602, 619 (1989), the U.S. Supreme Court held that the collection of urine or blood for drug testing constitutes a search within the meaning of the Fourth Amendment and that the validity of such a search is determined by a reasonableness test:

> What is reasonable . . . "depends on all of the circumstances surrounding the search or seizure and the nature of the search or seizure itself." . . . Thus, the permissibility of a particular practice "is judged by balancing its intrusion on the individual's Fourth Amendment interests against its promotion of legitimate governmental interests" [quoting *United States v. Montoya de Hernandez*, 473 U.S. 531, 537 (1985); citations omitted].

Derdeyn v. University of Colorado, 832 P.2d 1031 (Colo. Ct. App. 1991), *affirmed*, 863 P.2d 929 (Colo. 1993), provides an example of a university drug-testing program held to be unreasonable under the *Skinner* standard. The university initiated a program for testing its student athletes when it had a "reasonable suspicion" that they were using drugs. As a condition to participation in intercollegiate athletics, all athletes were asked to sign a form consenting to such tests. The university initiated the program "because of a desire to prepare its athletes for drug testing in NCAA sanctioned sporting events, a concern for athletes' health, an interest in promoting its image, and a desire to ensure fair competition" (832 P.2d at 1032). In a class action suit, student athletes challenged this program on several grounds. The Supreme Court of Colorado held that the program violated both the federal Constitution's Fourth Amendment and a similar provision of the Colorado constitution. Applying the *Skinner* reasonableness test, the court determined, "based on a balancing of the privacy interests of the student athletes and the governmental interests of CU, that CU's drug-testing program is unconstitutional" (863 P.2d at 946). In addition, the court held that the university's consent form was not sufficient to waive the athletes' constitutional rights. The university bore the burden of proof in showing that the waiver was signed voluntarily. Relying on the trial testimony of several athletes, which "revealed that, because of economic or other commitments the students had made to the University, [the students] were not faced with an unfettered choice in regard to signing the consent" (832 P.2d at 1035), the Colorado Supreme Court invalidated the university's program and prohibited its continuation.

Subsequent to *Derdeyn*, the U.S. Supreme Court again faced Fourth Amendment drug testing issues in *Vernonia School District 47J v. Acton*, 115 S.Ct. 2386 (1995), when it considered the constitutionality of a public school district's *random* drug testing of student athletes. Seventh grader James Acton and his parents sued the school district after James had been barred from the school football team because he and his parents refused to sign a form consenting to random urinalysis drug testing. In an attempt to control a "sharp increase" in drug use among students, the district had implemented a policy requiring that all student athletes be tested at the beginning of each season for their sport and that thereafter 10 percent of the athletes be chosen at random for testing each week of the season. In a 6–to–3 decision, the U.S. Supreme Court overruled the U.S. Court of Appeals for the Ninth Circuit (23 F. 3d 1514 (9th Cir. 1994)) and upheld the policy.

The majority opinion by Justice Scalia relied on *Skinner* to conclude that the collection of urine samples from students is a search that must be analyzed under the reasonableness test. The majority then examined three factors to determine the reasonableness of the search: (1) "the nature of the privacy interest upon which the search . . . intrudes;" (2) "the character of the intrusion that is complained of;" and (3) "the nature and immediacy of the governmental concern at issue . . . , and the efficacy of [the drug test in] meeting it." Regarding the first factor, the Court emphasized that "particularly with regard to medical examinations and procedures," student athletes have even less an expectation of privacy than students in general due to the "communal" nature of locker rooms and the additional regulations student athletes are subject to on matters such as preseason physicals, insurance coverage, and training rules.

Regarding the second factor, the Court stated that urinalysis drug testing is not a significant invasion of the student's privacy because the process for collecting urine samples is "nearly identical to those [conditions] typically encountered in restrooms;" the information revealed by the urinalysis (what drugs, if any, are present in the student's urine) is negligible; the test results are confidential and available only to specific personnel; and the results are not turned over to law enforcement officials. And regarding the third factor, the Court determined that the school district has an "important, indeed perhaps compelling," interest in deterring schoolchildren from drug use as well as a more particular interest in protecting athletes from physical harm that could result from competing in events under the influence of drugs; that there was evidence of a crisis of disciplinary actions and "rebellion . . . being fueled by alcohol and drug abuse," which underscored the immediacy of the district's concerns; and that the drug testing policy "effectively addressed" these concerns. The plaintiffs had argued that the district could fulfill its interests by testing when it had reason to suspect a particular athlete of drug use, and that this would be a less intrusive means of effectuating the interests. The Court rejected this proposal, arguing that it

> brings the risk that teachers will impose testing arbitrarily upon troublesome but not drug-likely students. It generates the expense of defending lawsuits that charge such arbitrary imposition, or that simply demand greater process before

accusatory drug testing is imposed. And not least of all, it adds to the ever-expanding diversionary duties of schoolteachers the new function of spotting and bringing to account drug abuse, a task for which they are ill prepared, and which is not readily compatible with their vocation. . . . In many respects, we think, testing based on "suspicion" of drug use would not be better, but worse [115 S.Ct. at 2396].

Although *Vernonia* is an elementary and secondary school case, its reasonableness test and the three factors for applying it will also likely guide analysis of Fourth Amendment challenges to drug testing of student athletes at colleges and universities. Some of the considerations relevant to application of the three factors would differ for higher education, however, so it is unclear whether the balance would tip in favor of drug testing plans as it did in *Vernonia*. The Court itself takes pains to limit its holding to public elementary and secondary education:

We caution against the assumption that suspicionless drug testing will readily pass constitutional muster in other contexts. The most significant element in this case is the first we discussed: that the Policy was undertaken in furtherance of the government's responsibilities, under a public school system, as guardian and tutor of children entrusted to its care. [W]hen the government acts as guardian and tutor the relevant question is whether the search is one that a reasonable guardian and tutor might undertake [115 S.Ct. at 2396].

While the state constitution was only a secondary consideration in *Derdeyn* and *Vernonia*, it was the primary focus in *Hill v. NCAA*, 273 Cal. Rptr. 402 (Cal. Ct. App. 1990), *reversed*, 865 P.2d 633 (Cal. 1994), a case in which Stanford University student athletes challenged the university's implementation of the NCAA's required drug-testing program. The constitutional clause at issue was not a search-and-seizure clause as such but rather a right-to-privacy guarantee (Cal. Const. Art. I, §1). Both the intermediate appellate court and the Supreme Court of California determined that this guarantee covered drug testing, an activity designed to gather and preserve private information about individuals. Further, both courts determined that the privacy clause limited the information-gathering activities of private as well as public entities, since the language revealed that privacy was an "inalienable right" that no one may violate. Although the private entity designated as the defendant in the *Hill* case was an athletic conference (the NCAA) rather than a private university, the courts' reasoning would apply to the latter as well.

In *Hill*, the intermediate appellate court's privacy analysis differed from the Fourth Amendment balancing test of *Skinner* because the court required the NCAA "to show a compelling interest before it can invade a fundamental privacy right"—a test that places a heavier burden of justification on the alleged violator than does the Fourth Amendment balancing test. The Supreme Court of California disagreed on this point, holding that the correct approach "requires that privacy interests be specifically identified and carefully compared with competing or countervailing privacy and nonprivacy interests in a 'balancing test'" (865 P.2d at 655). Under this approach, "[i]nvasion of a privacy interest is not a violation of the state constitutional right to privacy if the invasion is justified by a legitimate and important competing interest" (865 P.2d at 655–56), rather than a compelling interest, as the lower court had specified. Using this balancing test, the California Supreme Court concluded that "the NCAA's decision to enforce a ban on the use of drugs by means of a drug testing program is reasonably calculated to further its legitimate interest in maintaining the integrity of intercollegiate athletic competition" and therefore does not violate the California constitution's privacy guarantee.

In addition to its illustration of state privacy concepts, the *Hill* case also demonstrates the precarious position of institutions that are subject to NCAA or conference drug-testing requirements. As the intermediate appellate court indicated, Stanford, the institution that the *Hill* plaintiffs attended, was in a dilemma. "As an NCAA member institution, if it refused to enforce the consent provision, it could be sanctioned, but if it did enforce the program, either by requiring students to sign or withholding them from competition, it could be sued." To help resolve the dilemma, Stanford intervened in the litigation and sought its own declaratory and injunctive relief. These are the same issues and choices that other institutions will continue to face until the various legal issues concerning drug testing have finally been resolved.

In *Bally v. Northeastern University,* 532 N.E.2d 49 (Mass. 1989), a state civil rights law provided the basis for a challenge to a private institution's drug-testing program. The defendant, Northeastern University, required all students participating in intercollegiate athletics to sign an NCAA student athlete statement that includes a drug-testing consent form. The institution's program called for testing of each athlete once a year as well as other random testing throughout the school year. When a member of the cross-country and track teams refused to sign the consent form, the institution declared him ineligible. The student claimed that this action breached his contract with the institution and violated his rights under both the Massachusetts Civil Rights Act and a state right-to-privacy statute. A lower court granted summary judgment for Northeastern on the contract claim and for the student on the civil rights and privacy claims.

The Massachusetts Supreme Court reversed the lower court's judgment for the student. To prevail on the civil rights claim, according to the statute, the student had to prove that the institution had interfered with rights secured by the Constitution or laws of the United States or the Commonwealth and that such interference was by "threats, intimidation, or coercion." Although the court assumed *arguendo* that the drug-testing program interfered with the student's rights to be free from unreasonable searches and seizures and from invasions of reasonable expectations of privacy, it nevertheless denied his claim because he had made no showing of "threats, intimidation, or coercion." Similarly, the court denied the student's claim under the privacy statute because "[t]he majority of our opinions involving a claim of an invasion of privacy concern the public dissemination of information," and the student had made no showing of any public dissemination of the drug-testing results. In addition, because the student was not an employee, state case law precedents regarding employee privacy, on which the student had relied, did not apply.

Since the courts have not spoken definitively, it is not clear what drug-testing programs and procedures will be valid. In the meantime, institutions (and athletic conferences) that wish to engage in drug testing of student athletes may follow these minimum suggestions, which are likely to enhance their program's capacity to survive challenge under the various sources of law listed at the beginning of this section:

1. Articulate *and document* both the strong institutional interests that would be compromised by student athletes' drug use and the institution's basis for believing that such drug use is occurring in one or more of its athletic programs.

2. Limit drug testing to those athletic programs where drug use is occurring and is interfering with institutional interests.

3. Develop evenhanded and objective criteria for determining who will be tested and in what circumstances.

4. Specify the substances whose use is banned and for which athletes will be tested, limiting the named substances to those whose use would compromise important institutional interests.

5. Develop detailed and specific protocols for testing of individuals and lab analysis of specimens, limiting the monitoring of specimen collection to that which is necessary to ensure the integrity of the collection process, and limiting the lab analyses to those necessary to detect the banned substances (rather than to discover other personal information about the athlete).

6. Develop procedures for protecting the confidentiality and accuracy of the testing process and the laboratory results.

7. Embody all the above considerations into a clear written policy that is made available to student athletes before they accept athletic scholarships or join a team.

SEC. 10.6. TORT LIABILITY FOR ATHLETIC INJURIES

Tort law (see Sections 2.3.1 and 2.4.1) poses special problems for athletic programs and departments. Because of the physical nature of athletics and because athletic activities often require travel to other locations, the danger of injury to students and the possibilities for institutional liability are greater than those resulting from other institutional functions. In *Scott v. State*, 158 N.Y.S.2d 617 (N.Y. Ct. Cl. 1956), for instance, a student collided with a flagpole while chasing a fly ball during an intercollegiate baseball game; the student was awarded $12,000 in damages because the school had negligently maintained the playing field in a dangerous condition, and the student had not assumed the risk of such danger.

When negligence is alleged against a public institution (as in the case just discussed), the general principles of tort immunity may also apply. In *Lowe v. Texas Tech University*, 530 S.W.2d 337 (Tex. Civ. App. 1975), for instance, a varsity football player with a knee injury had his damages suit dismissed by the intermediate appellate court because the university had sovereign immunity; but on further appeal, the suit was reinstituted because it fell within a specific statutory waiver of immunity (540 S.W.2d 297 (1976)).

Several recent cases have focused on whether a university can be held liable for its failure to prepare adequately for emergency medical situations. In *Kleinknecht v. Gettysburg College*, 989 F.2d 1360 (3d Cir. 1993), parents of a student athlete sued the college for the wrongful death of their son, who had died from a heart attack suffered during a practice session of the intercollegiate lacrosse team. The student had no medical history that would indicate any danger of such an occurrence. No trainers were present when he was stricken, and no plan prescribing steps to take in medical emergencies was in effect. Students and coaches reacted as quickly as they could to reach the nearest phone, over two hundred yards away, and call an ambulance. The parents sued the college for negligence (see generally Section 2.3.1.1), alleging that the college owed a duty to its student athletes to have measures in place to provide prompt medical attention in emergencies. They contended that the delay in securing an ambulance, caused by the college's failure to have an emergency plan in effect, resulted in their son's death. The federal district court, applying Pennsylvania law, granted summary judgment for the college, holding that the college owed no duty to the plaintiffs' son in the circumstances of this case and that, even if a duty were owed, the actions of the college's employees were reasonable and did not breach the duty.

The appellate court reversed the district court's judgment and remanded the case for a jury trial, stressing that

> Drew [the athlete] was not engaged in his own private affairs as a student at
> Gettysburg College. Instead, he was participating in a scheduled athletic practice

for an intercollegiate team sponsored by the College under the supervision of College employees. On these facts we believe that [under the law of Pennsylvania] a special relationship existed between the College and Drew that was sufficient to impose a duty of reasonable care on the College [989 F.2d at 1367].

Having determined the existence of a duty of reasonable care, the court then delineated the specific demands that that duty placed on the college in the circumstances of this case. Since it was generally foreseeable that a life-threatening injury could occur during sports activities such as lacrosse, and given the magnitude of such a risk and its consequences, "the College owed a duty to Drew to have measures in place at the lacrosse team's practice . . . to provide prompt treatment in the event that he or any other members of the lacrosse team suffered a life-threatening injury." However, "the determination whether the College has breached this duty at all is a question of fact for the jury."

Even when the institution does or may owe a duty to the student athlete in a particular case, the student athlete will have no cause of action against the institution if its breach of duty was not the cause of the harm suffered. In *Hanson v. Kynast*, 494 N.E.2d 1091 (Ohio 1986), for example, the court avoided the issue of whether the defendant university owed a duty to a student athlete to provide for a proper emergency plan, because the delay in treating the athlete, allegedly caused by the university's negligent failure to have such a plan, caused the athlete no further harm. The athlete had suffered a broken neck in a lacrosse game and was rendered a quadriplegic; the evidence made it clear that, even if medical help had arrived sooner, nothing could have been done to lessen the injuries. In other words, the full extent of these injuries had been determined before any alleged negligence by the university could have come into play.

As the *Kleinknecht* court's reasoning suggests, the scope of the institution's duty to protect student athletes in emergencies and otherwise may depend on a number of factors, including whether the activity is intercollegiate (versus a club team) or an extracurricular activity, whether the particular activity was officially scheduled or sponsored, and perhaps whether the athlete was recruited or not. The institution's duty will also differ if the student athlete is a member of a visiting team rather than the institution's own team. In general, there is no special relationship such as that in *Kleinknecht* between the institution and a visiting athlete; there is only the relationship arising from the visiting student's status as an invitee of the institution (see generally Section 2.3.1.1). In *Fox v. Board of Supervisors of Louisiana State University and Agricultural and Mechanical College*, 576 So. 2d 978 (La. 1991), for example, a visiting rugby player from St. Olaf's club team was severely injured when he missed a tackle during a tournament held at LSU. The court determined that the injured player had no cause of action against LSU based on the institution's own actions or omissions. The only possible direct liability claim he could have had would have been based on a theory that the playing field onto which he had been invited was unsafe for play, a contention completely unsupported by the evidence.

In addition to the institution's liability for its own negligent acts, there are also issues concerning the institution's possible vicarious liability for the acts of its student athletes or its athletic clubs. In the *Fox* case discussed earlier, the visiting athlete also claimed that the university was vicariously liable for negligent actions of its rugby club in holding a cocktail party the night before the tournament, in scheduling teams to play more than one game per day (the athlete was injured in his second match of the day), and in failing to ensure that visiting clubs were properly trained and coached. His theory was that these actions had resulted in fatigued athletes playing when they should not have, thus becoming more susceptible to injury. The appellate court held that LSU could not be vicariously liable for the actions of its rugby club. Although LSU provided its rugby team with some offices, finances, and supervision, and a playing field for the tournament, LSU offered such support to its rugby club (and other student clubs) only to enrich students' overall educational experience by providing increased opportunities for personal growth. The university did not recruit students for the club, and it did not control the club's activities. The club therefore was not an agent of the university and could not bind LSU by its actions.

The same conclusion was reached in *Hanson v. Kynast* (cited above), which concerned a university's vicarious liability for a student's actions. During an intercollegiate lacrosse game, Kynast body-checked and taunted a player on the opposing team. When Hanson (another opposing team player) grabbed Kynast, Kynast threw Hanson to the ground, breaking his neck. Hanson sued Kynast and Ashland University, the team for which Kynast was playing when the incident occurred. The court held that Ashland University, which Kynast attended, was not liable for his actions because he received no scholarship, joined the team voluntarily, used his own playing equipment, and was guided but not controlled by the coach. In essence, the court held that Kynast was operating as an individual, voluntarily playing on the team, not as an agent of the university. (See also *Townsend v. State,* 237 Cal. Rptr. 146 (Cal. Ct. App. 1987), in which the court, relying on state statutes, similarly refused to hold a university vicariously liable for a nonscholarship varsity basketball player's assault on another team's player.)

A similar result would also likely pertain when a student is injured in an informal recreational sports activity. In *Swanson v. Wabash College,* 504 N.E. 2d 327 (Ind. Ct. App. 1987), for example, a student injured in a recreational basketball game sued the college for negligence. The court ruled that the college had no legal duty to supervise a recreational activity among adult students, and that the student who had organized the game was neither an agent nor an employee of the college, so *respondeat superior* liability did not attach.

SEC. 10.7. ATHLETIC ASSOCIATIONS AND CONFERENCES

Various associations and conferences have a hand in regulating intercollegiate athletics. Most institutions with intercollegiate programs are members of both a national association (for example, the National Collegiate Athletic Association (NCAA)) and a conference (for example, the Atlantic Coast Conference (ACC)).

The NCAA is the largest and most influential of the athletic associations. It is an unincorporated association composed of over nine hundred public and private colleges and universities. It has a constitution that sets forth the association's fundamental law, and it has enacted extensive bylaws that govern its operations. The constitution and bylaws are published in the *NCAA Manual,* which is updated periodically. To preserve the amateur nature of college athletics, and the fairness of competition, the NCAA includes in its bylaws a complex set of rules regarding recruiting, academic eligibility, and the like. Regarding eligibility, for instance, the NCAA has requirements on minimum grade point average and SAT or ACT scores for incoming freshman student athletes; requirements regarding satisfactory academic progress for student athletes; restrictions on transfers from one school to another; rules on "redshirting" and longevity as a player; limitations on financial aid, compensation, and employment, and limitations regarding professional contracts and players' agents (see generally G. Wong, *Essentials of Amateur Sports Law* (2d ed., Praeger, 1994), 239–284). (The NCAA has different rules for its different divisions, and the various conferences affiliated with the NCAA may also have rules on such matters, as long as they meet the minimum requirements of the NCAA.) To enforce these rules, the NCAA has an enforcement program that includes compliance audits, self-reporting, investigations, and official inquiries, culminating in a range of penalties that the NCAA can impose against its member institutions but not against the institutions' employees.

Legal issues often arise as a result of the rule-making and enforcement activities of these associations and conferences. Individual institutions have become involved in such legal issues in two ways. Coaches and student athletes penalized for violating conference or association rules have sued their institutions as well as the conference or association to contest the enforcement of these rules. And institutions themselves have sued conferences or associations over their rules, policies, or decisions. The majority of such disputes have involved the NCAA, since it is the primary regulator of intercollegiate athletics in the United States. The resulting litigation frequently presents a difficult threshold problem of determining what legal principles should apply to resolution of the dispute.

10.7.1. Federal Constitutional Constraints

In a series of cases, courts have considered whether the NCAA, as an institutional membership association for both public and private colleges and universities, is engaged in state action (see Section 1.5.2) and thus is subject to the constraints of the U.S. Constitution, such as due process and equal protection. In an early leading case, *Parish v. NCAA*, 506 F.2d 1028 (5th Cir. 1975), for example, several basketball players at Centenary College, later joined by the college, challenged the constitutionality of an NCAA academic requirement then known as the "1.600 rule." Using first the "government contacts" theory and then the "public function" theory (both are explained in Section 1.5.2), the court held that the NCAA was engaged in state action. It then proceeded to examine the NCAA's rule under constitutional due process and equal protection principles, holding the rule valid in both respects.

Subsequent to the decision in *Parish* and other similar decisions in NCAA cases, the U.S. Supreme Court issued several opinions that narrowed the circumstances under which courts will find state action (see especially *Rendell-Baker v. Kohn*, discussed in Section 1.5.2). In *Arlosoroff v. NCAA*, 746 F.2d 1019 (4th Cir. 1984), the court relied on these Supreme Court opinions to reach a result contrary to the *Parish* line of cases. The plaintiff was a varsity tennis player at Duke University (a private institution) whom the NCAA had declared ineligible for further competition because he had participated in amateur competition for several years before enrolling at Duke. He claimed that the bylaw under which the NCAA had acted was invalid under the due process and equal protection clauses. Determining that the NCAA's promulgation and enforcement of the bylaw did not fit within either the government contacts or the public function theory, the court held that the NCAA was not engaged in state action and therefore was not subject to constitutional constraints.

In 1988, the U.S. Supreme Court came down on the *Arlosoroff* side of the debate in a 5-to-4 split decision in *NCAA v. Tarkanian*, 488 U.S. 179 (1988). The NCAA had opened an official inquiry into the basketball program at the University of Nevada, Las Vegas (UNLV). UNLV conducted its own investigation into the NCAA's allegations and reported its findings to the NCAA's Committee on Infractions. The committee then charged UNLV with thirty-eight infractions, including ten infractions concerning the alleged failure of its highly successful, towel-chewing basketball coach, Jerry Tarkanian, to cooperate with an NCAA investigation. As a result, the NCAA placed UNLV's basketball team on a two-year probation and ordered UNLV to show cause why further penalties should not be imposed "unless UNLV severed all ties during the probation between its intercollegiate program and Tarkanian." Reluctantly, after holding a hearing, UNLV suspended Tarkanian in 1977. Tarkanian sued both the university and the NCAA, alleging that they had deprived him of his property interest in the position of basketball coach without first affording him procedural due process protections. The trial court agreed and granted the coach injunctive relief and attorney's fees. The Nevada Supreme Court upheld the trial court's ruling, agreeing that Tarkanian's constitutional due process rights had been violated. This court regarded the NCAA's regulatory activities as state action because "many NCAA member institutions were either public or government supported" and because the NCAA had participated in the dismissal of a public employee, traditionally a function reserved to the state (*Tarkanian v. NCAA,* 741 P.2d 1345 (Nev. 1987)).

The U.S. Supreme Court, analyzing the NCAA's role and its relationship with UNLV and the state, disagreed with the Nevada courts and held that the NCAA was not a state actor. The Court noted that UNLV, clearly a state actor, had actually suspended Tarkanian and that the issue therefore was "whether UNLV's actions in compliance with the NCAA rules and recommendations fumed the NCAA's conduct into state action." Defining state action as action engaged in by those "'who carry a badge of authority of a State and represent it in some capacity, whether they act in accordance with their authority or misuse it'" (488 U.S. at 191; quoting *Monroe v. Pape,* 365 U.S. 167, 172 (1961)), the Court concluded that "the source of the legislation adopted by the NCAA is not Nevada but the collective membership, speaking through an organization that is independent of any particular State." It further noted that the majority of the NCAA's membership consisted of private institutions (488 U.S. at 193 n.13).

The Court also rejected arguments that the NCAA was a state actor because UNLV had delegated its state power to the NCAA. While such a delegation of power could serve to transform a private party into a state actor, no such delegation had occurred. Tarkanian was suspended by UNLV, not by the NCAA; the NCAA could only enforce sanctions against the institution as a whole, not against specific employees. Moreover, UNLV could have taken other paths of action, albeit unpleasant ones, in lieu of suspending the coach: it could have withdrawn from the NCAA or accepted additional sanctions while still remaining a member. Further, although UNLV, as a representative of the state of Nevada, did contribute to the development of NCAA policy, in reality it was the full membership of the organization that promulgated the rules leading to Tarkanian's suspension, not the state of Nevada.

The Court also found that UNLV had not delegated state investigatory authority to the NCAA. Moreover, UNLV had not formed a partnership with the NCAA simply because it decided to adhere to the NCAA's recommendation regarding Tarkanian. The interests of UNLV and the NCAA were in fact hostile to one another:

> During the several years that the NCAA investigated the alleged violations, the NCAA and UNLV acted much more like adversaries than like partners engaged in a dispassionate search for the truth. The NCAA cannot be regarded as an agent of UNLV for purposes of that proceeding. It is more correctly characterized

as an agent of its remaining members which, as competitors of UNLV, had an interest in the effective and evenhanded enforcement of the NCAA's recruitment standards [488 U.S. at 196].

Disagreeing with the U.S. Supreme court majority, the four dissenting justices argued that UNLV and the NCAA had acted jointly in disciplining Tarkanian; that the NCAA, which had no subpoena power and no direct power to sanction Tarkanian, could have acted only through the state; and that the NCAA was therefore engaged in state action.

The *Tarkanian* case does not foreclose all possibilities for finding that an athletic association or conference is engaged in state action. As the Supreme Court itself recognized, state action may be present "if the membership consist[s] entirely of institutions located within the same State, many of them public institutions created by [that State]" (488 U.S. at 193 n.13). Even if the member institutions were not all located in the same state, state action might exist if the conference were composed entirely of state institutions. For example, in *Stanley v. Big Eight Conference,* 463 F. Supp. 920 (D. Mo. 1978), a case preceding *Tarkanian,* the court applied the Fourteenth Amendment's due process clause to the defendant conference because all its members were state universities. Even if a conference were like the NCAA, with both public and private members located in different states, courts might distinguish *Tarkanian* and find state action in a particular case where there was clear evidence that the conference and a state institution had genuinely mutual interests and were acting jointly to take adverse action against a particular student or coach. Finally, even if there were no basis for finding that a particular conference is engaged in state action, courts would still be able to find an individual *state institution* to be engaged in state action (see Section 1.5.2) when it directed the enforcement of conference rules, and suit could therefore be brought against the institution rather than the conference. In *Spath v. NCAA,* 728 F.2d 25 (1st Cir. 1984), for example, the court held that the University of Lowell, also a defendant, was a state actor even if the NCAA was not and therefore proceeded to the merits of the plaintiff's equal protection and due process claims. See also *Barbay v. NCAA and Louisiana State University,* 1987 Westlaw 5619 (E.D. La. 1987).

Moreover, even if federal state action arguments will not work and the federal Constitution therefore does not apply, athletic associations and conferences may occasionally be suable under state constitutions for violations of state constitutional rights (see generally Section 1.3.1.1). In *Hill v. NCAA,* 865 P.2d 633 (Cal. 1994) (this volume, Section 10.5), for example, the California Supreme Court held that the right-to-privacy guarantee of the California constitution could be applied to the NCAA, even though it is a private organization.

10.7.2. State Statutes Regulating Athletic Associations' Enforcement Activities

Partially in response to the *Tarkanian* litigation and NCAA investigations in other states, and to protect in-state institutions as well as their athletic personnel and student athletes, a number of states have passed or considered "due process" statutes (see Fla. Stat. §§240.5339 to 240.5349 (1991); Ill. Ann. Stat., ch. 144, paras. 2901 to 2913 (1991); Nev. Rev. Stat. §§85–1202 to 85–1210 (1990); Nev. Rev. Stat. §398.005 *et seq.*). Such statutes require national athletic associations to extend certain due process protections to those accused in any enforcement proceeding. The second Nevada statute referred to above, for example, requires that each accused be given the opportunity to confront all witnesses, that an impartial entity be empaneled to adjudicate the proceeding, and that all proceedings be made public (Nev. Rev. Stat. §§398.155 to 398.255). The state courts may issue injunctions against an association that violates the statute's requirements, and the persons harmed may also obtain damages under some of the statutes (for example, Nev. Rev. Stat. §398.245). Many of the statutes' protections are not included in the NCAA's own enforcement regulations (see Comment, "Home Court Advantage: Florida Joins States Mandating Due Process in NCAA Proceedings," 20 *Fla. State L. Rev.* 871, 889–900 (1993)).

The NCAA challenged the Nevada statute in *NCAA v. Miller, Governor, State of Nevada,* 795 F. Supp. 1476 (D. Nev. 1992), *affirmed,* 10 F.3d 633 (9th Cir. 1993). The lower court held the statute unconstitutional as both an invalid restraint on interstate commerce and an invalid interference with the NCAA's contract with its members. First, the court found that the NCAA and its member institutions are heavily involved in interstate commerce through their athletic programs, and that the statute restrained that commerce by curtailing the NCAA's capacity to establish uniform rules for all of its members throughout the United States, thus violating the federal Constitution's commerce clause (Article I, Section 8, clause 3). Second, the court agreed that Nevada's statute "substantially impair[ed] existing contractual relations between itself and the Nevada member institutions[,] in violation of the Contracts Clause of Article I, Section 10 of the United States Constitution." Since the Nevada law would give Nevada schools an unfair advantage over other schools, it would undermine the basic purpose of the NCAA's agreement with its members and destroy the NCAA's goal of administering a uniform system for all its members.

In affirming, the appellate court focused only on the commerce clause problem. The court held that the statute directly regulated interstate commerce:

> It is clear that the Statute is directed at interstate commerce and only interstate commerce. By its terms, it regulates only interstate organizations, *i.e.,* national collegiate athletic associations which have member institutions in 40 or more

states. Nev. Rev. Stat. 398.055. Moreover, courts have consistently held that the NCAA, which seems to be the only organization regulated by the Statute, is engaged in interstate commerce in numerous ways. It markets interstate intercollegiate athletic competition, . . . [it] schedules events that call for transportation of teams across state lines and it governs nationwide amateur athlete recruiting and controls bids for lucrative national and regional television broadcasting of college athletics [10 F.3d at 638].

According to the court, the statute would "have a profound effect" on the NCAA's interstate activities. Since the NCAA must apply its enforcement procedures "even-handedly and uniformly on a national basis" in order to maintain integrity in accomplishing its goals, it would have to apply Nevada's procedures in every other state as well. Thus, "the practical effect of [Nevada's] regulation is to control conduct beyond the boundaries of the State." Moreover, since other states had enacted or might enact procedural statutes that differed from Nevada's, the NCAA would be subjected to the potentially conflicting requirements of various states. In both respects, the Nevada statute created an unconstitutional restraint on interstate commerce.

The Nevada litigation should not be interpreted as casting doubt on all state statutes that regulate athletic associations and conferences. Not all statutes will have a substantial adverse effect on the association's activities in *other* states, and thus not all state statutes will work to restrain interstate commerce or to impair an association's contractual relations with its members. Various other types of regulatory statutes, and even some types of due process statutes, could be distinguishable from *Miller* in this respect. With such statutes, however, other legal issues may arise. In *Kneeland v. NCAA*, 850 F.2d 224 (5th Cir. 1988), for instance, the court refused to apply the Texas Open Records Act to the NCAA and the Southwest Athletic Conference, because they could not be considered governmental bodies subject to the Act.

10.7.3. Antitrust Laws

Federal and state antitrust laws will apply to athletic associations and conferences in some circumstances. Such laws may be used to challenge the membership rules of the associations and conferences, their eligibility rules for student athletes, and other joint or concerted activities of the members that allegedly have anticompetitive or monopolistic effects. Most cases thus far have been brought against the NCAA, either by a member institution or by a student athlete. Member institutions could also become defendants in such lawsuits, however, since they are the parties that would be engaging in the joint or concerted activity under auspices of the conference or association.

The leading case, *NCAA v. Board of Regents of the University of Oklahoma*, 468 U.S. 85 (1984), concerned an NCAA plan for regulating the televising of college football games by its member institutions. The U.S. Supreme Court held that the NCAA's enforcement of the plan violated Section 1 of the Sherman Antitrust Act (15 U.S.C. §1) and was therefore invalid. In its salient features, the challenged television plan was mandatory for all NCAA members; it limited the total number of games a member institution could have televised; it fixed prices at which each institution could sell the broadcast rights to its games; and it prohibited member institutions from selling the broadcast rights to their games unless those games were included in the NCAA's television package agreed upon with the networks. The plan was challenged by schools desiring to negotiate their own television contracts free from the set prices and output limitations imposed on them by the NCAA plan.

Although acknowledging from the outset that the NCAA plan was "perhaps the paradigm of an unreasonable restraint of trade," the Court held that it was not a per se violation of the Sherman Act. The Court reasoned that in the "industry" of college football, such "restraints on competition are essential if the product is to be available at all" (468 U.S. at 99). In order to ensure the integrity of intercollegiate athletic competition, participating schools must act jointly through the NCAA. Through its regulatory activities in this field, the NCAA enables institutions to preserve "the character of college football" and thus "enables a product to be marketed which might otherwise be unavailable" (468 U.S. at 102). The Court thus found that, by maintaining the existence of college football in its traditional form, as opposed to allowing it to die out or become professionalized, the NCAA's actions as a whole "widen consumer choice—not only the choices available to sports fans but also those available to athletes—and hence can be viewed as procompetitive" (468 U.S. at 102).

Having rejected a rule of per se invalidity, the Court then analyzed the case under the "rule of reason," considering both the plan's anticompetitive impact and its procompetitive impact. In a lengthy discussion, the Court found that the NCAA television plan restricted individual institutions from negotiating their own television contracts and had a significant adverse impact on member institutions' ability to compete openly in the sports broadcasting market. The Court also found that the NCAA wields market power in this market. The Court then turned to the NCAA's alleged justifications for the plan, to determine whether they should take precedence over the plan's anticompetitive impact.

The NCAA argued that, if individual institutions were permitted to negotiate their own television contracts, the market could become saturated, and the prices that networks would pay for college football games would decrease as a result. The Court disagreed with this premise, noting that the NCAA's television plan was not "necessary to enable the NCAA to penetrate the market through an attractive package sale. Since broadcasting rights to college football constitute a unique product for which there is no ready substitute, there is no need for collective action in order to enable the product to compete against its nonexistent competitors" (468 U.S. at 115). The NCAA also argued that, if there was too much college football on television, fewer people would attend live games, thereby decreasing ticket sales, and its television plan was therefore needed to protect gate attendance. The Court rejected this argument as well, because such protection—through collective action—of what was presumed to be an inferior product was itself "inconsistent with the basic policy of the Sherman [Antitrust] Act" (468 U.S. at 116).

Under the rule of reason, therefore, the Court held that the NCAA's enforcement of its television plan was a clear restraint of trade in violation of Section I of the Sherman Act. See B. Gregory & J. C. Busey, "Alternative Broadcasting Arrangements After NCAA," 61 *Indiana L.J.* 65 (1985).

In a subsequent case, *McCormack v. NCAA*, 845 F.2d 1338 (5th Cir. 1988), the court considered the legality of the NCAA's eligibility rules, holding that they do not violate the Sherman Act. Alumni, football players, and cheerleaders of Southern Methodist University (SMU) sued the NCAA after it had suspended and imposed sanctions on the school's football program for violating the restrictions on compensation given to student athletes. Assuming without deciding that the football players had standing to sue, the court upheld the dismissal of the claim. It found that, under the rule of reason as used in the *University of Oklahoma* case, the NCAA's eligibility rules were a reasonable means of promoting the amateurism of college football. Unlike the regulations regarding the television plan in the *University of Oklahoma* case, the court found that "[i]t is reasonable to assume that most of the regulatory controls of the NCAA are justifiable means of fostering competition among amateur athletic teams and intercollegiate athletics" (845 F.2d at 1344).

More recently, two other important cases have also upheld NCAA eligibility regulations against antitrust challenges, each case employing different reasoning. In both cases, a football player with one year of intercollegiate eligibility remaining entered himself in the professional football draft and used the services of an agent. Neither of the players was drafted, and each then attempted to rejoin his college—despite NCAA "no-draft" rules, which at that time prohibited players who had entered the draft or obtained an agent from returning to play. When the NCAA refused to let them play, each player sued the NCAA and their schools, challenging the no-draft rule as well as the no-agent rule under the Sherman Act.

In one of these cases, *Banks v. NCAA*, 746 F. Supp. 850 (N.D. Ind. 1990), *affirmed*, 977 F.2d 1081 (7th Cir. 1992)), the player filed suit under Section I of the Sherman Act (15 U.S.C. §1). Although acknowledging that the rule of reason was the appropriate standard for the case, the district court nevertheless rejected Banks's request for injunctive relief, because he had alleged no anticompetitive effect of the NCAA's rules, even though there was clear evidence of a procompetitive effect of upholding the amateur nature of college football. The appellate court affirmed:

> Banks' allegation that the no-draft rule restrains trade is absurd. None of the NCAA rules affecting college football eligibility restrain trade in the market for college players because the NCAA does not exist as a minor league training ground for future NFL players but rather to provide an opportunity for competition among amateur students pursuing a collegiate education. . . . [T]he regulations of the NCAA are designed to preserve the honesty and integrity of intercollegiate athletics and foster fair competition among the participating amateur college students [977 F.2d at 1089–90; footnotes and citations omitted].

In the other case, *Gaines v. NCAA*, 746 F. Supp. 738 (M.D. Tenn. 1990), the student football player filed suit under Section 2 of the Sherman Act (15 U.S.C. §2) and sought an injunction against the NCAA and Vanderbilt University to reinstate his eligibility to play football. Unlike the court in *Banks*, the *Gaines* court accepted the NCAA's argument that its eligibility rules "are not subject to antitrust analysis because they are not designed to generate profits in a commercial activity but to preserve amateurism by assuring that the recruitment of student athletes does not become a commercial activity." The court distinguished the *University of Oklahoma* case by stressing that the rules involved there had commercial objectives (generation of broadcasting profits), whereas the no-draft and no-agent rules did not. The court also held that, even if the antitrust laws did apply to the NCAA's rules, these rules did not violate Section 2 of the Sherman Act, because the NCAA's no-agent and no-draft rules were justified by legitimate business reasons. (See generally Note, "An End Run Around the Sherman Act? *Banks v. NCAA* and *Gaines v. NCAA*," 19 *J. Coll. & Univ. Law* 295 (1993).)

These antitrust cases beginning with *University of Oklahoma* clearly establish that the NCAA and other athletic associations and conferences are subject to antitrust laws, at least when their actions have some commercial purpose or impact. But their rules, even when they have anticompetitive effects, will generally not be considered per se violations of the Sherman Antitrust Act. They can be upheld under Section I if they are reasonable and if their procompetitive impact offsets their anticompetitive impact, and they can be upheld under Section 2 if they have legitimate business justifications.

10.7.4. Common Law Principles

Even if the courts refrain from applying the Constitution to most activities of athletic associations and conferences, and even if state statutes and antitrust laws have only a narrow range of applications, associations and conferences are still limited in an important way by another relevant body of legal principles: the common law of "voluntary private associations." See Note, "Judicial Review of Disputes Between Athletes and the National Collegiate Athletic Association," 24 *Stanford L. Rev.* 903, 909–916 (1972). Primarily, these principles would require the NCAA and other conferences and associations to adhere to their own rules and procedures, fairly and in good faith, in their relations with their member institutions. *California State University, Hayward v. NCAA,* 121 Cal. Rptr. 85 (Cal. Ct. App. 1975), for instance, arose after the NCAA had declared the university's athletic teams indefinitely ineligible for postseason play. The university argued that the NCAA's decision was contrary to the NCAA's own constitution and bylaws. The appellate court affirmed the trial court's issuance of a preliminary injunction against the NCAA, holding the following principle applicable to the NCAA:

> Courts will intervene in the internal affairs of associations where the action by the association is in violation of its own bylaws or constitution. "It is true that courts will not interfere with the disciplining or expelling of members of such associations where the action is taken in good faith and in accordance its laws or rules, or it is not authorized by the bylaws of the association, a court may review the ruling of the board and direct the reinstatement of the member" [quoting another case] [121 Cal. Rptr. at 88, 89].

The case then went back to the lower court for a trial on the merits. The lower court again held in favor of the university and made its injunction against the NCAA permanent. In a second appeal, under the name *Trustees of State Colleges and Universities v. NCAA,* 147 Cal. Rptr. 187 (Cal. Ct. App. 1978), the appellate court again affirmed the lower court, holding that the NCAA had not complied with its constitution and bylaws in imposing a penalty on the institution. The appellate court also held that, even if the institution had violated NCAA rules, under the facts of the case the NCAA was estopped from imposing a penalty on the institution. (The *Hayward* case is extensively discussed in J. D. Dickerson & M. Chapman, "Contract Law, Due Process, and the NCAA," 5 *J. Coll. & Univ. Law* 197 (1978–79).)

As *Hayward* in particular demonstrates, postsecondary institutions do have legal weapons to use in disputes with the NCAA and other athletic associations or conferences. The common law clearly applies to such disputes. Antitrust law also has some applicability; some role may still be found for state regulatory statutes more narrowly crafted than the state of Nevada's; and the U.S. Constitution may also still have some application in a narrow range of cases. Administrators should be aware, however, that these weapons are two-edged: student athletes may also use them against the institution when the institution and the athletic association are jointly engaged in enforcing athletic rules against the student. In such circumstances, the institution may be so aligned with the athletic association that it is subject to the same legal principles that bind the association. Moreover, if the institution is public, the U.S. Constitution may apply to the situation even if the courts do not consider the association itself to be engaged in state action.

SELECTED ANNOTATED BIBLIOGRAPHY

Sec. 10.1 (Applicable Law)

Berry, Robert C., & Wong, Glenn M. *Law and Business of the Sports Industries: Common Issues in Amateur and Professional Sports* (2d ed., Greenwood Press, 1993). The second volume of a comprehensive, two-volume overview of the law applicable to athletics. Most of the discussion either focuses on or has direct application to intercollegiate sports. The twelve chapters cover such topics as "The Amateur Athlete," "Sex Discrimination in Athletics," "Application of Tort Law," "Drug Testing," and "Criminal Law and Its Relationship to Sports." Includes numerous descriptions or edited versions of leading cases, set off from and used to illustrate the textual analysis.

"On Collegiate Athletics," 60 *Educ. Record* no. 4 (Fall 1979). A symposium with articles and other material, including Elaine H. El-Khawas, "Self-Regulation and Collegiate Athletics"; Cym H. Lowell, "The Law and Collegiate Athletics in Public Institutions"; and "Responsibilities in the Conduct of Collegiate Athletic Programs: American Council on Education Policy Statements" (three policy statements, directed respectively to institutional trustees, presidents, and athletic directors, developed by ACE and its Commission on Collegiate Athletics).

"Symposium on Athletics in Higher Education," 8 *J. Coll. & Univ. Law* 291 (198182). Contains the following lead articles: Ann V. Thomas & Jan Sheldon Wildgen, "Women in Athletics: Winning the Game but Losing the Support"; Larry R. Thompson & J. Timothy Young, "Taxing the Sale of Broadcast Rights to College Athletics—An Unrelated Trade or Business?"; Robert H. Ruxin, "Unsportsmanlike Conduct: The Student Athlete, the NCAA, and Agents"; and Edward Branchfield & Melinda Grier, "*Aiken v. Lieuallen* and *Peterson v. Oregon State University*—Defining Equity in Athletics" (includes a conciliation agreement settling the *Peterson* case).

"Symposium on Postsecondary Athletics and the Law," 5 *J. Coll. & Univ. Law* nos. 1 and 2 (1978–79). Contains numerous articles, including Anne M. C. Hermann, "Sports and the Handicapped: Section 504 of the Rehabilitation Act of 1973 and Curricular, Intramural, Club, and Intercollegiate Athletic Programs in Postsecondary Educational Institutions"; Philip R. Hochberg, "The Four Horsemen Ride Again: Cable Communications and Collegiate Athletics"; Stephen Horn, "Intercollegiate Athletics: Waning Amateurism and Rising Professionalism"; Cym H. Lowell, "Judicial Review of Rule-Making in Amateur Athletics"; John C. Weistart, "Antitrust Issues in the Regulation of College Sports"; and Harvey L. Zuckman, "Throw 'Em to the Lions (or Bengals): The Decline and Fall of Sports Civilization as Seen Through the Eyes of a United States District Court." Also includes a bibliography on postsecondary athletics and the law by Edmund Edmonds.

Weistart, John C., & Lowell, Cym H. *The Law of Sports* (Michie, 1979, with 1985 supp.). A reference work, with comprehensive citations to authorities, treating the legal issues concerning sports. Of particular relevance to postsecondary institutions are the chapters on "Regulation of Amateur Athletics," "Public Regulation of Sports Activities," and "Liability for Injuries in Sports Activities."

Wong, Glenn M. *Essentials of Amateur Sports Law* (2d ed., Praeger, 1994). Provides background information and a quick reference guide on sports law issues. Covers contract and tort law problems, sex discrimination in athletics, broadcasting, trademark law, drug testing, and various matters regarding athletic associations and athletic eligibility. Also includes detailed descriptions of the NCAA; sample forms for athletic contracts, financial aid agreements, and releases of liability; and a glossary of legal and sports terms. Of particular interest to nonlawyers such as athletic directors, coaches, and student athletes.

Sec. 10.2 (Athletic Scholarships)

Cross, Harry M. "The College Athlete and the Institution," 38 *Law & Contemporary Problems* 151 (1973). A legal analysis of the student athlete's status within the institution. Discusses admissions, recruitment, athletic eligibility, and the athlete's status as a member of the student body. Written by a law professor and former NCAA president.

Davis, Timothy. "An Absence of Good Faith: Defining a University's Educational Obligation to Student Athletes," 28 *Houston L. Rev.* 743 (1991), examines the relationship between the student athlete and the university, the potential exploitation of the student athlete, and the resulting compromise of academic integrity. Author argues that the good-faith doctrine of contract law should be used to define the university's obligation, so that the contract will be breached if the university "obstructs or fails to further the student-athlete's educational opportunity."

Sec. 10.3 (Sex Discrimination)

Gaal, John, DiLorenzo, Louis P., & Evans, Thomas S. "HEW's Final Policy Interpretation on Title IX and Intercollegiate Athletics," 6 *J. Coll. & Univ. Law* 345 (1980). A critical analysis of the Department of Education's (then HEW's) final guidelines on how Title IX applies to postsecondary athletic programs. The article should be read together with John Gaal and Louis P. DiLorenzo, "The Legality and Requirements of HEW's Proposed Policy Interpretation of Title IX and Intercollegiate Athletics," 6 *J. Coll. & Univ. Law* 161 (1979–80), an earlier article on the proposed guidelines and the underlying Title IX regulations.

Sec. 10.4 (Discrimination on the Basis of Disability)

Jones, Cathy J. "College Athletes: Illness or Injury and the Decision to Return to Play," 40 *Buffalo L. Rev.* 113 (1992). Discusses the rights and liabilities in situations where a student athlete seeks to play or return to play after being diagnosed with a medical condition that could cause injury or death. Analyzes the rights of the athletes under the U.S. Constitution, Section 504 of the Rehabilitation Act of 1973, and the Americans with Disabilities Act of 1990. Suggests that athletes' autonomy must be respected and that "[l]iability on the part of the institution and its employees should be judged by a reasonableness standard."

Mitten, Matthew. "Amateur Athletes with Handicaps or Physical Abnormalities: Who Makes the Participation Decision?" 71 *Neb. L. Rev.* 987 (1992). Discusses the circumstances under which athletes with disabilities may participate in competitive sports. Outlines the problem from the perspectives of the athletic associations, the athlete, the team physician, and university administrators. Traces the rights and obligations of the parties under state statutory law, federal constitutional law, and Section 504 of the Rehabilitation Act. Does not discuss the ramifications of the Americans with Disabilities Act.

Sec. 10.5 (Drug Testing)

Ranney, James T. "The Constitutionality of Drug Testing of College Athletes: A Brandeis Brief for a Narrowly-Intrusive Approach," 16 *J. Coll. & Univ. Law* 397 (1990). Identifies the legal and policy issues that institutions should consider in developing a drug-testing program. Author concludes that the threat of "performance-enhancing drugs" justifies random warrantless searches while the threat of "street drugs" only justifies searches based on reasonable suspicion or probable cause. Article also discusses procedural safeguards to guarantee the reliability of the testing and protect the athletes' due process rights.

See Burling entry for Section 2.5.

Sec. 10.6 (Tort Liability for Athletic Injuries)

Langerman, Samuel, & Fidel, Noel. "Sports Injury—Negligence," 15 *Proof of Facts 2d* 1 (American Jurisprudence, 1978, with periodic supp.). A thorough examination of the issues involved in this increasingly litigated area of the law. Covers "Duty of Administrator of Sports Program," "Unsafe Facilities or Equipment," "Inadequate Coaching or Supervision," "Effect of Age and Experience of Plaintiff," "Contributory Negligence," "Assumption of Risk," and other topics. Includes "Practice Comments" of the authors and model question-and-answer dialogues with expert witnesses. Primarily for lawyers.

Sec. 10.7 (Athletic Associations and Conferences)

Weistart, John C. "Antitrust Issues in the Regulation of College Sports," 5 *J. Coll. & Univ. Law* 77 (1979). A systematic treatment of antitrust law's particular applications to intercollegiate athletics. Reviews issues facing the NCAA regional conferences and particular schools.

Weistart, John C. "Legal Accountability and the NCAA," 10 *J. Coll. & Univ. Law* 167 (1983–84). An essay exploring the unique status and role of the NCAA in intercollegiate athletics. Reviews structural deficiencies, such as the NCAA's alleged failure to accommodate the interests of student athletes in its governance structure; and suggests that the NCAA should be considered to have a fiduciary relationship to its member institutions. Also examines the role of judicial supervision of NCAA activities and its effect on the NCAA's regulatory objectives.

Young, Sherry. "The NCAA Enforcement Program and Due Process: The Case for Internal Reform," 43 *Syracuse L. Rev.* 747 (1992). Outlines complaints about NCAA rules enforcement, traces case law challenging NCAA procedures, explains and critiques the current enforcement program, and calls for further amendment of the NCAA's enforcement procedures.

See Berry & Wong entry and Wong entry for Section 10.1.

CHAPTER ELEVEN

The College and Local and State Governments

SEC. 11.1. GENERAL PRINCIPLES

Postsecondary institutions are typically subject to the regulatory authority of one or more local government entities, such as a city, village, town, or county government. Some local regulations—fire and safety codes, for example—are relatively noncontroversial. Others may be highly controversial. Controversies have arisen, for instance, over local governments' attempts to regulate or prohibit genetic experimentation, nuclear weapons research or the production or storage of nuclear weapons components or radioactive materials, and the use of animals in laboratory experiments. Examples of controversial ordinances include ordinances that require permits for large-group gatherings at which alcohol will be served, restrict smoking in the workplace, and control rents. Land use regulations and zoning board rulings are also frequently controversial, as Section 11.2 will illustrate. In dealing with ordinances and issues such as these, postsecondary administrators must be aware of the extent of, and limits on, each local government's regulatory authority.

A local government has only the authority delegated to it by state law. When a local government has been delegated "home rule" powers, its authority will usually be broadly interpreted; otherwise, its authority will usually be narrowly construed. Even where a local body has general authority, it cannot exercise that authority in a way that conflicts with state law, which generally prevails over local law in case of conflict. Nor can a local government regulate matters that the state otherwise has "preempted" by its own extensive regulation of the field, or matters that are considered protected by the state's sovereign immunity. Nor, of course, can local governments regulate in a way that violates the federal Constitution.

Although these principles apply to regulation and taxation of both public and private institutions, public institutions are more likely than private institutions to escape the local government's net. Since public institutions are more heavily regulated by the states, for instance, they are more likely in particular cases to have preemption defenses. Public institutions may also defend against local regulation by asserting sovereign immunity, a defense not available to private institutions or to many municipal or county community colleges.

Unlike the federal government and local governments, state governments have general rather than limited powers and can claim all power that is not denied them by the federal Constitution or their own state constitution, or that has not been preempted by federal law. Thus, the states have the greatest reservoir of legal authority over postsecondary education, although the extent to which this source is tapped varies greatly from state to state.

The states' functions in matters concerning postsecondary education include regulating, funding, planning, and coordinating. States also have emerging responsibilities for assessing and ensuring the accountability of institutional programs. These functions are performed through myriad agencies, such as boards of regents, statewide planning or coordinating boards, departments of education or higher education, institutional licensure boards or commissions, and State Approval Agencies (SAAs), which operate under contract to the federal Veterans Administration to approve courses for which veterans' benefits may be expended. New agencies called State Postsecondary Review Entities (SPREs), created by the Higher Education Amendments of 1992 (106 Stat. 637 *et seq.*, 20 U.S.C. §1099a–3), monitor certain institutions that participate in Title IV student aid programs; states may create a new agency to be the SPRE, assign the SPRE function to an existing state agency, or form a consortium with other states. In addition, various professional and occupational licensure boards indirectly regulate postsecondary education by evaluating programs of study and establishing educational prerequisites for taking licensure examinations. Other state agencies whose primary function is not education (such as workers' compensation boards, labor boards, ethics boards, or environmental quality agencies) may also regulate postsecondary education as part of a broader class of covered institutions, corporations, or government agencies.

SEC. 11.2. ZONING OFF-CAMPUS HOUSING

Zoning and land use regulations of local (and sometimes state) governments can influence the operation of postsecondary institutions in many ways. For student affairs professionals, probably the most pertinent area of concern is the zoning of off-campus student housing.

Zoning ordinances that prevent groups of college students from living together in residential areas may create particular problems for institutions that depend on housing opportunities in the community to help meet student housing needs. Some communities have enacted ordinances that specify the number of unrelated individuals who may live in the same residential dwelling, and many of these ordinances have survived constitutional challenge (see, for example, *Village of Belle Terre v. Boraas,* 416 U.S. 1 (1974), where the Court rejected the argument that such a restriction violated the residents' freedom-of-association rights).

In *Borough of Glassboro v. Vallorosi,* 568 A.2d 888 (N.J. 1990), the borough had sought an injunction against the leasing of a house in a residential district to ten unrelated male college students. The borough had recently amended its zoning ordinance to limit "use and occupancy" in the residential districts to "families" only. The ordinance defined "family" as "one or more persons occupying a dwelling unit as a single nonprofit housekeeping unit, who are living together as a stable and permanent living unit, being a traditional family unit or the functional equivalency [sic] thereof."

Tracking the ordinance's language, the court determined that the ten students constituted a "single housekeeping unit," which was a "stable and permanent living unit" (568 A.2d at 894). The court relied particularly on the fact that the students planned to live together for three years and that they "ate together, shared household chores, and paid expenses from a common fund" (568 A.2d at 894). The court also cautioned that zoning ordinances are not the most appropriate means for dealing with problems of noise, traffic congestion, and disruptive behavior.

Another type of restriction on off-campus housing was invalidated in *Kirsch v. Prince Georges County,* 626 A.2d 372 (Md. 1993). Prince Georges County, Maryland, had enacted a "mini-dorm" ordinance that regulated the rental of residential property to students attending college. Homeowners and the students they wished to rent to brought an equal protection claim against the county. The ordinance defined a "mini-dormitory" as

[a]n off-campus residence, located in a building that is, or was originally constructed as[,] a one-family, two-family, or three-family dwelling which houses at least three (3), but not more than five (5), individuals, *all or part of whom are unrelated to one another by blood, adoption or marriage and who are registered full-time or part-time students at an institution of higher learning* [§27–107.1(a) (150.1), cited in 626 A.2d at 373–74; emphasis added].

For each mini-dorm, the ordinance specified a certain square footage per person for bedrooms, one parking space per resident, and various other requirements.

The ordinance also prohibited local zoning boards from granting variances for mini-dorms, from approving departures from the required number of parking spaces, and from permitting nonconforming existing uses.

The court determined that Maryland's constitution provides equal protection guarantees similar to those of the U.S. Constitution's Fourteenth Amendment. Relying on *City of Cleburne v. Cleburne Living Center*, 473 U.S. 432 (1985), as the source of a strengthened "rational basis" test to use for Fourteenth Amendment challenges to restrictive zoning laws, the court determined that this test was the appropriate one to evaluate whether the mini-dorm ordinance was "rationally related to a legitimate governmental purpose." The court then examined the purpose of the ordinance:

> The stated purpose of the Prince Georges County "mini-dorm" ordinance is to "prevent or control detrimental effects upon neighboring properties, such as illegal parking and saturation of available parking by residents of minidormitories, litter, and noise." . . . At argument, the County Attorney conceded that the ordinance was passed to address complaints regarding noise, litter, and parking problems from residents of the College Park area, the site of the principal campus of the University of Maryland. . . . Notwithstanding the county-wide effect of the ordinance, the County failed to identify any other neighborhoods in the County where similar off-campus student housing created noise, litter, or parking problems [626 A.2d at 380].

The court was careful to distinguish the *Boraas* case (above), on which the county had relied in its defense of the ordinance:

> Unlike the zoning ordinance analyzed in *Boraas*, the Prince Georges County "mini-dorm" ordinance does not differentiate based on the nature of the use of the property, such as a fraternity house or a lodging house, but rather on the occupation of the persons who would dwell therein. Therefore, under the ordinance a landlord of a building . . . is permitted to rent the same for occupancy by three to five unrelated persons so long as they are not pursuing a higher education without incurring the burdens of complying with the arduous requirements of the ordinance [626 A.2d at 381].

Noting that the problems the ordinance sought to avoid would occur irrespective of whether the tenants were students, the court held that the ordinance "creat[ed] more strenuous zoning requirements for some [residential tenant classes] and less for others based solely on the occupation which the tenant pursues away from that residence," thus establishing an irrational classification forbidden by both the federal and the state constitutions.

SEC. 11.3. STUDENT VOTING: ON-CAMPUS CANVASSING AND REGISTRATION

The passage of the Twenty-Sixth Amendment to the U.S. Constitution in 1971, which lowered the voting age to eighteen, created several new problems for postsecondary administrators. On some voting issues, administrators may at most play an intermediary or advocate role in disputes between students and the community. Other issues require positive action by administrators to establish guidelines for voting activities on campus.

The regulation of voter canvassing and registration on campus is the voting issue most likely to require the direct involvement of college and university administrators. Any regulation must accommodate the First Amendment rights of the canvassers; the First Amendment rights of the students, faculty, and staff who may be potential listeners; the privacy interests of those who may not wish to be canvassed; the requirements of local election law; and the institution's interests in order and safety. Not all of these considerations have been explored in litigation.

James v. Nelson, 349 F. Supp. 1061 (N.D. Ill. 1972), illustrates one type of challenge to a campus canvassing regulation. Northern Illinois University had for some time prohibited all canvassing in student living areas. After receiving requests to modify this prohibition, the university proposed a new regulation that would have permitted canvassing under specified conditions. Before the new regulation could go into effect, however, it had to be adopted in a referendum by two-thirds of the students in each dormitory, after which individual floors could implement it by a two-thirds vote. The court held that this referendum requirement unconstitutionally infringed the freedom-of-association and freedom-of-speech rights of the students who wished to canvas or to be canvassed. The basis for the *James* decision is difficult to discern. The court emphasized that the proposed canvassing regulation was not "in any way unreasonable or beyond the powers of the university administration to impose in the interests of good order and the safety and comfort of the student body." If the proposed regulation was constitutional, a referendum adopting it would not infringe anyone's constitutional rights. The court's implicit ruling must be that the university's blanket prohibition on canvassing was an infringement of First Amendment rights, and a requirement that this prohibition could be removed only by a two-thirds vote of the students in each dormitory and each floor was also an infringement on the rights of those students who would desire a liberalized canvassing policy.

National Movement for the Student Vote v. Regents of the University of California, 123 Cal. Rptr. 141 (Cal. Ct. App. 1975), was decided on statutory grounds.

A local statute permitted registrars to register voters at their residence. University policy, uniformly enforced, did not allow canvassing in student living areas. Registrars were permitted to canvass in public areas of the campus and in the lobbies of the dormitories. The court held that the privacy interest of the students limited the registrars' right to canvass to reasonable times and places and that the limitations imposed by the university were reasonable and in compliance with the law. In determining reasonableness, the court emphasized the following facts:

> There were evidence and findings to the effect that dining and other facilities of the dormitories are on the main floor; the private rooms of the students are on the upper floors; the rooms do not contain kitchen, washing, or toilet facilities; each student must walk from his or her room to restroom facilities in the halls of the upper floors in order to bathe or use the toilet facilities; defendants, in order to "recognize and enhance the privacy" of the students and to minimize assaults upon them and thefts of their property, have maintained a policy and regulations prohibiting solicitation, distribution of materials, and recruitment of students in the upper-floor rooms; students in the upper rooms complained to university officials about persons coming to their rooms and canvassing them and seeking their registrations; defendants permitted signs regarding the election to be posted throughout the dormitories and permitted deputy registrars to maintain tables and stands in the main lobby of each dormitory for registration of students; students in each dormitory had to pass through the main lobby thereof in order to go to and from their rooms; a sign encouraging registration to vote was at each table, and students registered to vote at the tables [123 Cal. Rptr. at 146].

Although the *National Movement v. Regents* decision is based on a statute, the court's language suggests that it would use similar principles and factors in considering the constitutionality of a public institution's canvassing regulations under the First Amendment. In a later case, *Harrell v. Southern Illinois University*, 457 N.E.2d 971 (Ill. App. Ct. 1983), the court did use similar reasoning in upholding, against a First Amendment challenge, a university policy that prohibited political candidates from canvassing dormitory rooms except during designated hours in the weeks preceding elections. The court also indicated that the First Amendment (as well as that state's election law) would permit similar restrictions on canvassing by voter registrars. Thus, although public institutions may not completely prohibit voter canvassing on campus, they may impose reasonable restrictions on the "time, place, and manner" of canvassing in dormitories and other such "private" locations on campus. (See also Section 11.5.4.2.)

SEC. 11.4. RELATIONS WITH LOCAL POLICE

Since the academic community is part of the surrounding community, it will generally be within the geographical jurisdiction of one or more local (town, village, city, county) police forces. The circumstances under which local police may and will come onto the campus, and their authority once on campus, are thus of concern to every administrator. Their role on campus depends on a mixture of considerations: the state and local law of the jurisdiction, federal constitutional limitations on police powers, the adequacy of the institution's own security services, and the terms of any explicit or implicit understanding between local police and campus authorities.

If the institution has its own uniformed security officers, administrators must decide what working relationships these officers will have with local police. This decision will depend partly on the extent of the security officers' authority, especially regarding arrests, searches, and seizures—authority that should also be carefully delineated (see generally Section 5.2.1). Similarly, administrators must understand the relationship between arrest and prosecution in local courts, on the one hand, and campus disciplinary proceedings on the other (see Section 7.1.3). Although administrators cannot make crime an internal affair by hiding evidence of crime from local police, they may be able to assist local law enforcement officials in determining prosecution priorities. Campus and local officials may also be able to cooperate in determining whether a campus proceeding should be stayed pending the outcome of a court proceeding, or vice versa.

The powers of local police are circumscribed by various federal constitutional provisions, particularly the Fourth Amendment strictures on arrests, searches, and seizures. These provisions limit local police authority on both public and private campuses. Under the Fourth Amendment, local police usually must obtain a warrant before arresting or searching a member of the academic community or searching or seizing any private property on the campus (see Section 5.1.2). On a private institution's campus, nearly all the property may be private, and local police may need a warrant or the consent of whoever effectively controls the property before entering most areas of the campus. On a public institution's campus, it is more difficult to determine which property would be considered public and which private, and thus more difficult to determine when local police must have a warrant or consent prior to entry. In general, for both public and private institutions, police will need a warrant or consent before entering any area in which members of the academic community have a "reasonable expectation of privacy" (see generally *Katz v. United States,* 389 U.S. 347 (1967)). The constitutional rules and concepts are especially complex in this area, however, and administrators should consult counsel whenever questions arise concerning the authority of local police on campus.

In *People v. Dickson,* 154 Cal. Rptr. 116 (Cal. Ct. App. 1979), the court considered the validity of a warrantless search of a chemistry laboratory conducted by local police and campus security officers at the Bakersfield campus of California State University. The search uncovered samples of an illegal drug and materials used in its manufacture—evidence that led to the arrest and conviction of the defendant, a chemistry professor who used the laboratory. The court upheld the search and the conviction because, under the facts of the case (particularly facts indicating ready access to the laboratory by many persons, including campus police), the professor had no "objectively reasonable expectation of privacy" in his laboratory.

Under a similar rationale, a Pennsylvania appellate court rejected the argument that undercover police were required to obtain a search warrant before they entered a fraternity party. In *Commonwealth v. Tau Kappa Epsilon,* 560 A.2d 786 (Pa. Super. Ct. 1989), *reversed on other grounds,* 609 A.2d 791 (Pa. 1992), two undercover officers, recent graduates of Pennsylvania State University, entered parties at eleven fraternities and observed the serving of beer to minors. The fraternities were convicted of serving beer to minors, and they appealed their convictions, arguing that the police officers' warrantless entry violated the Fourth Amendment. The court disagreed:

> Security was so lax as to be virtually nonexistent; a person could enter and be furnished beverages almost at will. Under these circumstances, the fraternities could be found to have consented to the entry of [the police] and to have surrendered any reasonable expectation of privacy with respect to the events occurring in their houses [560 A.2d at 791].

That these particular searches were upheld even though the officers did not procure a warrant, however, does not mean that the practice of obtaining warrants can be routinely dispensed with. When there is time to do so, procuring a warrant or the consent of the person whose expectation of privacy may be invaded is still the surest policy.

In 1980, Congress enacted legislation that limits police search-and-seizure activities on college campuses. The legislation, the Privacy Protection Act of 1980 (42 U.S.C. §2000aa *et seq.*), was passed in part to counter the U.S. Supreme Court's decision in *Zurcher v. Stanford Daily,* 436 U.S. 547 (1978). In *Zurcher,* the Palo Alto, California, Police Department had obtained a warrant to search the files of the *Stanford Daily,* a student newspaper, for photographs of participants in a demonstration during which several police officers had been assaulted. The lower court found probable cause to believe that the *Stanford Daily*'s files did contain such photographs but no probable cause to believe that the newspaper itself was engaged in any wrongdoing. The U.S. Supreme Court held that the *Stanford Daily,* even though an innocent third party and even though engaged in publication activities, had no First or Fourth Amendment rights to assert against the search warrant.

The Privacy Protection Act's coverage is not confined to newspapers, the subject of the *Zurcher* case. As its legislative history makes clear, the Act also protects scholars and other persons engaged in "public communication"—that is, the "flow of information to the public" (see S. Rep. No. 874, 96th Cong., 2d Sess., in 4 *U.S. Code Cong. & Admin. News* 3950, 3956 (1980)).

Section 101(a) of the Act pertains to the "work product materials" of individuals intending "to disseminate to the public a newspaper, book, broadcast, or other similar form of public communication." The section prohibits the searching for or seizure of the work product of such individuals by any "government officer or employee [acting] in connection with the investigation or prosecution of a criminal offense." There are several exceptions, however, to the general prohibition in Section 101(a). Search and seizure of work-product material is permitted (1) where "there is probable cause to believe that the person possessing such materials has committed or is committing the criminal offense to which the materials relate" and this offense does not consist of "the receipt, possession, communication, or withholding of such materials"; (2) where there is probable cause to believe that the possessor has committed or is committing an offense consisting "of the receipt, possession, or communication of information relating to the national defense, classified information, or restricted data" prohibited under specified provisions of national security laws; and (3) where "there is reason to believe that the immediate seizure of such materials is necessary to prevent the death of, or serious bodily injury to, a human being."

Section 101(b) of the Act covers "documentary materials, other than work product materials." The section prohibits search and seizure of such materials in the same way that Section 101(a) prohibits search and seizure of work product. The same exceptions to the general prohibition also apply. There are also two additional exceptions unique to Section 101(b), under which search and seizure of documentary materials is permitted if:

(3) there is reason to believe that the giving of notice pursuant to a subpoena duces tecum would result in the destruction, alteration, or concealment of such materials; or

(4) such materials have not been produced in response to a court order directing compliance with a subpoena duces tecum, and—

(A) all appellate remedies have been exhausted; or

(B) there is reason to believe that the delay in an investigation or trial occasioned by further proceedings relating to the subpoena would threaten the interests of justice.

Section 106 of the Act authorizes a civil suit for damages for any person subjected to a search or seizure that is illegal under Section 101(a) or 101(b).

The Act's language and legislative history clearly indicate that the Act applies to local and state, as well as federal, government officers and employees. It thus limits the authority of city, town, and county police officers both on campus and in off-campus investigations of campus scholars or journalists. The Act limits police officers and other government officials, however, only when they are investigating criminal, as opposed to civil, offenses. Scholars and journalists thus are not protected, for example, from the seizure of property to satisfy outstanding tax debts or from the regulatory inspections or compliance reviews conducted by government agencies administering civil laws. Moreover, the Act's legislative history makes clear that traditional subpoena powers and limitations are untouched by the Act (see S. Rep. No. 874, 96th Cong., 2d Sess., in 4 *U.S. Code Cong. & Admin. News* 3950, 3956–60 (1980)).

Different problems arise when local police enter a campus not to make an arrest or conduct a search but to engage in surveillance of members of the institutional community. In *White v. Davis,* 533 P.2d 222 (Cal. 1975), a history professor at UCLA sued the Los Angeles police chief to enjoin the use of undercover police agents for generalized surveillance in the university. Unidentified police agents had registered at the university and compiled dossiers on students and professors based on information obtained during classes and public meetings. The California Supreme Court held that such action was a prima facie violation of students' and faculty members' First Amendment freedoms of speech, assembly, and association, as well as the "right-to-privacy" provision of the California constitution. The case was returned to the trial court to determine whether the police were acting on any compelling state interest that would justify the infringement of constitutional rights.

The court's opinion differentiates the First Amendment surveillance problem from the more traditional Fourth Amendment search-and-seizure problem:

> Our analysis of the limits imposed by the First Amendment upon police surveillance activities must begin with the recognition that with respect to First Amendment freedoms "the Constitution's protection is not limited to direct interference with fundamental rights" (*Healy v. James* (1972) 408 U.S. 169, 183 . . .). Thus, although police surveillance of university classrooms and organizations' meetings may not constitute a direct prohibition of speech or association, such surveillance may still run afoul of the constitutional guarantee if the effect of such activity is to chill constitutionally protected activity. . . .
>
> As a practical matter, the presence in a university classroom of undercover officers taking notes to be preserved in police dossiers must inevitably inhibit the exercise of free speech both by professors and students [533 P.2d at 228–29].

The court also emphasized the special danger that police surveillance poses for academic freedom:

> The police investigatory conduct at issue unquestionably poses . . . [a] debilitating . . . threat to academic freedom. . . . According to the allegations of the complaint, which for purposes of this appeal must be accepted as true, the Los Angeles Police Department has established a network of undercover agents which keeps regular check on discussions occurring in various university classes. Because the identity of such police officers is unknown, no professor

or student can be confident that whatever opinion he may express in class will not find its way into a police file. . . . The crucible of new thought is the university classroom; the campus is the sacred ground of free discussion. Once we expose the teacher or the student to possible future prosecution for the ideas he may express, we forfeit the security that nourishes change and advancement. The censorship of totalitarian regimes that so often condemns developments in art, science, and politics is but a step removed from the inchoate surveillance of free discussion in the university; such intrusion stifles creativity and to a large degree shackles democracy [533 P.2d at 229–31].

The principles of *White v. Davis* would apply equally to local police surveillance at a private institution. As an agency of government, the police are prohibited from violating any person's freedom of expression or right to privacy, whether on a public campus or a private one.

SEC. 11.5. COMMUNITY ACCESS TO INSTITUTIONAL PROPERTY

11.5.1. Public Versus Private Institutions

Postsecondary institutions have often been locations for many types of events that attract people from the surrounding community and sometimes from other parts of the state, country, or world. Because of their capacity for large audiences and the sheer numbers of students and faculty and staff members on campus every day, postsecondary institutions provide an excellent forum for speakers, conferences, and exhibits, as well as for pamphleteering and for other kinds of information exchanges. In addition, cultural, entertainment, and sporting events attract large numbers of outside persons. The potential commercial market presented by concentrations of student consumers may also attract entrepreneurs to the campus, and the potential labor pool that these students represent may also attract employment recruiters. Whether public or private, postsecondary institutions have considerable authority to determine how and when their property will be used for such events and activities and to regulate access by outside persons. Although a public institution's authority is more limited than that of a private institution, the case of *State v. Schmid*, 423 A.2d 615 (N.J. 1980) (discussed in Section 11.5.3), diminishes the distinction between public and private institutions' authority to deny access to outsiders who want to engage in expressional activities.

Both private and public institutions customarily have ownership or leasehold interests in their campuses and buildings—interests protected by the property law of the state. Subject to this statutory and common law, both types of institution have authority to regulate how and by whom their property is used. Typically, an institution's authority to regulate use by its students and faculty members is limited by the contractual commitments it has made to these groups (see Section 3.2). Thus, for instance, students may have contractual rights to the reasonable use of dormitory rooms and the public areas of residence halls or of campus libraries and study rooms; and faculty members may have contractual rights to the reasonable use of office space or classrooms. For the outside community, however, such contractual rights usually do not exist.

A public institution's authority to regulate the use of its property is further limited by the federal Constitution, in particular the First Amendment (see, for example, *Lamb's Chapel v. Center Moriches Union Free School District,* 113 S. Ct. 2141 (1993)), and may also be affected by state statutes or regulations applicable to state property in general or specifically to the property of state educational institutions. Unlike contract law limitations, these limitations on institutional authority may provide rights of access and use not only to faculty members and students (see, for example, Sections 8.1.1, 8.1.2, and 9.1.1 on the First Amendment usage rights of students) but also to the outside community.

Sections 11.5.2 to 11.5.4 explore various statutes, regulations, and constitutional considerations that affect outsiders' access to the property of postsecondary institutions.

11.5.2. Speaker Bans

Administrators may seek to exclude particular speakers or events from campus in order to avoid campus disruption, hate mongering, or other perceived harms. Such attempts inevitably precipitate clashes, not only with the participants but also with those on campus who demand the right to hear the speaker or attend the event. These clashes have sometimes resulted in litigation. Most of the cases on access to campus facilities have involved regulations on off-campus speakers, commonly referred to as "speaker bans."

Since rules regulating off-campus speakers provide a convenient target for a First Amendment attack, such rules should be drafted with extreme care. Much of the law that has developed concerning faculty members' and students' free speech rights on campus also applies to the issue of off-campus speakers (see Sections 8.1 and 8.3).

Under the First Amendment, administrators of public institutions may reasonably regulate the time, place, and manner of speeches and other communicative activities engaged in by on- or off-campus persons. Problems arise when these basic rules of order are expanded to include regulations under which speakers can be banned because of the content of their speech or their political affiliation or persuasion. Such regulations are particularly susceptible to judicial invalidation because they are prior restraints on speech (see Section 8.1.3). *Stacy v. Williams,* 306 F. Supp. 963 (N.D. Miss. 1969), is a leading example. The board of trustees of the Institutions of Higher Learning of the State of Mississippi promulgated rules providing, in part, that "all speakers invited to the campus of any of the state institutions of higher learning must first be investigated and approved by the head of the institution involved and when invited the names of such speakers must be filed with the executive secretary of the board of trustees." The regulations were amended several times to prohibit "speakers who will do violence to the academic atmosphere," "persons in disrepute from whence they come," persons "charged with crime or other moral wrongs," any person "who advocates a philosophy of the overthrow of the United States," and any person "who has been announced as a political candidate or any person who wishes to speak on behalf of a political candidate." In addition, political or sectarian meetings sponsored by any outside organization were prohibited.

Under the authority of these regulations, the board prevented political activists Aaron Henry and Charles Evers from speaking on any Mississippi state campus. Students at several schools joined faculty members and other persons as plaintiffs in an action to invalidate the regulations. The court struck down the regulations because they created a prior restraint on the students' and faculties' First Amendment right to hear speakers. Not all speaker bans, however, are unconstitutional under the court's opinion. When the speech "presents a 'clear and present danger' of resulting in serious substantive evil," a ban would not violate the First Amendment:

> For purpose of illustration, we have no doubt that the college or university authority may deny an invitation to a guest speaker requested by a campus group if it reasonably appears that such person would, in the course of his speech, advocate (1) violent overthrow of the government of the United States, the state of Mississippi, or any political subdivision thereof; (2) willful destruction or seizure of the institution's buildings or other property; (3) disruption or impairment, by force, of the institution's regularly scheduled classes or other educational functions; (4) physical harm, coercion, or intimidation or other invasion of lawful rights of the institution's officials, faculty members, or students; or (5) other campus disorder of violent nature. In drafting a regulation so providing, it must be made clear that the "advocacy" prohibited must be of the kind which prepares the group addressed for imminent action and steels it to such action, as opposed to the abstract espousal of the moral propriety of a course of action by resort to force; and there must be not only advocacy to action but also a reasonable apprehension of imminent danger to the essential functions and purposes of the institution, including the safety of its property and the protection of its officials, faculty members, and students [306 F. Supp. at 973–74].

The court also promulgated a set of "Uniform Regulations for Off-Campus Speakers," which, in its view, complied with the First Amendment (306 F. Supp. at 979–80). These regulations provide that all speaker requests come from a recognized student or faculty group, thus precluding any outsider's insistence on using the campus as a forum. This approach accords with the court's basis for invalidating the regulations: the rights of students or faculty members to hear a speaker.

Besides meeting a "clear and present danger" or incitement test, speaker ban regulations must use language that is sufficiently clear and precise to be understood by the average reader. Ambiguous or vague regulations run the risk of being struck down under the First and Fourteenth Amendments as "void for vagueness" (see Sections 7.1.2, 7.2.1, and 8.1.2). In *Dickson v. Sitterson*, 280 F. Supp. 486 (M.D.N.C. 1968), the court relied on this ground to invalidate a state statute and regulations prohibiting a person from speaking at state colleges or universities if he was a "known member of the Communist party," was "known to advocate the overthrow of the Constitution of the United States or the state of North Carolina," or had "pleaded the Fifth Amendment" in response to questions relating to the Communist party or other subversive organizations.

The absence of rules can be just as risky as poorly drafted ones, since either situation leaves administrators and affected persons with insufficient guidance. *Brooks v. Auburn University,* 412 F.2d 1171 (5th Cir. 1969), is illustrative. A student organization, the Human Rights Forum, had requested that the Reverend William Sloan Coffin speak on campus. After the request was approved by the Public Affairs Seminar Board, the president of Auburn overruled the decision because the Reverend Coffin was "a convicted felon and because he might advocate breaking the law." Students and faculty members filed suit contesting the president's action, and the U.S. Court of Appeals upheld their First Amendment claim:

> Attributing the highest good faith to Dr. Philpott in his action, it nevertheless is clear under the prior restraint doctrine that the right of the faculty and students to hear a speaker, selected as was the speaker here, cannot be left to the discretion of the university president on a pick and choose basis. As stated, Auburn had no rules or regulations as to who might or might not speak and thus no question of a compliance with or a departure from such rules or regulations is presented. This left the matter as a pure First Amendment question; hence the basis for prior restraint. Such a situation of no rules or regulations may be equated with a licensing system to speak or hear and this has been long prohibited.
>
> It is strenuously urged on behalf of Auburn that the president was authorized in any event to bar a convicted felon or one advocating lawlessness from the campus. This again depends upon the right of the faculty and students to hear. We do not hold that Dr. Philpott could not bar a speaker under any circumstances. Here there was no claim that the Reverend Coffin's appearance would lead to violence or disorder or that the university would be otherwise disrupted. There is no claim that Dr. Philpott could not regulate the time or place of the speech or the manner in which it was to be delivered. The most recent state-

ment of the applicable rule by the Supreme Court, perhaps its outer limits, is contained in the case of *Brandenburg v. Ohio*, [395 U.S. 444]: . . . "[T]he constitutional guarantees of free speech and free press do not permit a state to forbid or proscribe advocacy of the use of force or of law violation except where such advocacy is directed to inciting or producing imminent lawless action and is likely to incite or produce such action." . . . There was no claim that the Coffin speech would fall into the category of this exception [412 F.2d at 1172–73].

Under these cases, regulations concerning off-campus speakers present sensitive legal and policy issues for public institutions. If such regulations are determined to be necessary, they should be drafted with the aid of counsel. The cases clearly permit reasonable regulation of "the time or place of the speech or the manner in which it . . . [is] delivered," as the *Brooks* opinion notes. But regulating a speech because of its content is permissible only in the narrowest of circumstances, such as those set out in *Stacy* and in *Brooks.* The regulations promulgated by the court in *Stacy* provide useful guidance in drafting legally sound regulations. The five First Amendment principles set out in Section 8.3 of this volume will also be helpful.

11.5.3. Trespass Statutes and Ordinances

States and local governments often have trespass or unlawful-entry laws that limit the use of a postsecondary institution's facilities by outsiders. Such statutes or ordinances typically provide that offenders are subject to ejection from the campus and that violation of an order to leave, made by an authorized person, is punishable as a misdemeanor. Counsel for institutions should carefully examine these laws, and the court decisions interpreting them, to determine each law's particular coverage. Some laws may cover all types of property; others may cover only educational institutions. Some laws may cover all postsecondary institutions, public or private; others may apply only to public or only to private institutions. Some laws may be broad enough to restrict members of the campus community under some circumstances; others may be applicable only to outsiders. There may also be technical differences in the standards for determining what acts will be considered a trespass or when an institution's actions will constitute implied consent to entry. (For an illustrative case, see *People v. Leonard,* 405 N.E.2d 831 (N.Y. 1984), in which the court reviewed the applicability of state trespass law to the exclusion of a sometime student from the SUNY-Binghamton campus.)

A number of reported cases have dealt with the federal and state constitutional limitations on a state or local government's authority to apply trespass laws to the campus setting. *Braxton v. Municipal Court,* 514 P.2d 697 (Cal. 1973), is a leading example. Several individuals had demonstrated on the San Francisco State campus against the publication of campus newspaper articles that they considered "racist and chauvinistic." A college employee notified the protestors that they were temporarily barred from campus. When they disobeyed this order, they were arrested and charged under Section 626.4 of the California Penal Code. This statute authorized "the chief administrative officer of a campus or other facility of a community college, state college, or state university or his designate" to temporarily bar a person from the campus if there was "reasonable cause to believe that such person has wilfully [*sic*] disrupted the orderly operation of such campus or facility." The protestors argued that the state trespass statute was unconstitutional for reasons of overbreadth and vagueness (see Sections 7.2.1, 8.1.2, and 8.3).

The California Supreme Court rejected the protestors' argument. Regarding overbreadth, the court concluded:

> Without a narrowing construction, section 626.4 would suffer First Amendment overbreadth. For example, reasoned appeals for a student strike to protest the escalation of a war, or the firing of the football coach, might "disrupt" the "orderly operation" of a campus; so, too, might calls for the dismissal of the college president or for a cafeteria boycott to protest employment policies or the use of nonunion products. Yet neither the "content" of speech nor freedom of association can be restricted merely because such expression or association disrupts the tranquillity of a campus or offends the tastes of school administrators or the public. Protest may disrupt the placidity of the vacant mind just as a stone dropped in a still pool may disturb the tranquillity of the surface waters, but the courts have never held that such "disruption" falls outside the boundaries of the First Amendment. . . .
>
> Without a narrowing construction, section 626.4 would also suffer overbreadth by unnecessarily restricting conduct enmeshed with First Amendment activities. Although conduct entwined with speech may be regulated if it is completely incompatible with the peaceful functioning of the campus, section 626.4 on its face fails to distinguish between protected activity such as peaceful picketing or assembly and unprotected conduct that is violent, physically obstructive, or otherwise coercive. . . .
>
> In order to avoid the constitutional overbreadth that a literal construction of section 626.4 would entail, we interpret the statute to prohibit only incitement to violence or conduct physically incompatible with the peaceful functioning of the campus. We agree with the Attorney General in his statement: "The word 'disrupt' is commonly understood to mean a physical or forcible interference, interruption, or obstruction. In the campus context, disrupt means a *physical* or *forcible* interference with normal college activities."
>
> The disruption must also constitute "a substantial and material threat" to the orderly operation of the campus or facility (*Tinker v. Des Moines School District*, 393 U.S. 503, 514 (1969)). The words "substantial and material" appear in the portion of the statute which authorizes reinstatement of permission to come onto the campus (Penal Code §626.4(c)). Accordingly, we read those words

as expressing the legislature's intent as to the whole function of the statute; we thus construe section 626.4 to permit exclusion from the campus only of one whose conduct or words are such as to constitute, or incite to, a substantial and material physical disruption incompatible with the peaceful functioning of the academic institution and of those upon its campus. Such a substantial and material disruption creates an emergency situation justifying the statute's provision for summary, but temporary, exclusion [514 P.2d at 701, 703–05].

The court then also rejected the vagueness claim:

Petitioners point out that even though the test of substantial and material physical disruption by acts of incitement of violence constitutes an acceptable constitutional standard for preventing overbroad applications of the statute in specific cases, the enactment still fails to provide the precision normally required in criminal legislation. Thus, for example, persons subject to summary banishment must guess at *what* must be disrupted (i.e., classes or the attendance lines for athletic events), and *how* the disruption must take place (by picketing or by a single zealous shout in a classroom or by a sustained sit-in barring use of a classroom for several days).

Our examination of the legislative history and purposes of section 626.4 reveals, however, that the Legislature intended to authorize the extraordinary remedy of summary banishment only when the person excluded has committed acts illegal under other statutes; since these statutes provide ascertainable standards for persons seeking to avoid the embrace of section 626.4, the instant enactment is not void for vagueness [514 P.2d at 705].

In *Kirstel v. State,* 284 A.2d 12 (Md. Ct. Spec. App. 1971), another court upheld a similar state statute against constitutional attack. This Maryland statute (since recodified as Md. Code Ann., Educ. §26–102) authorized the "highest official or governing body" of each public college or university to deny campus access to individuals "who have no lawful business to pursue at the institution, or who are acting in a manner disruptive or disturbing to the normal educational functions of the institution." Like the litigants in *Braxton,* Kirstel argued that the statute was vague and overbroad, asserting in particular the vagueness of the "no lawful business" language in the statute. Also like *Braxton,* the court had to work hard to clarify and thus justify a statute that would not win any awards for precision. By equating the phrase "lawful business" with the similarly vague and technical phrase "constitutionally protected" activity, however, the *Kirstel* opinion adds little to an understanding of the Maryland statute.

One case that does strike down a trespass statute is *Grody v. State,* 278 N.E.2d 280 (Ind. 1972), where the law at issue provided:

It shall be a misdemeanor for any person to refuse to leave the premises of any institution established for the purpose of the education of students enrolled therein when so requested, regardless of the reason, by the duly constituted officials of any such institution [Ind. Code Ann. §10–4533].

The court held that the law was void on its face owing to vagueness and overbreadth in violation of the First and Fourteenth Amendments:

> This statute attempts to grant to some undefined school "official" the power to order cessation of *any* kind of activity whatsoever, by *any* person whatsoever, and the official does not need to have any special reason for the order. The official's power extends to teachers, employees, students, and visitors and is in no way confined to suppressing activities that are interfering with the orderly use of the premises. This statute empowers the official to order any person off the premises because he does not approve of his looks, his opinions, his behavior, no matter how peaceful, or *for no reason at all.* Since there are no limitations on the reason for such an order, the official can request a person to leave the premises solely because the person is engaging in expressive conduct even though that conduct may be clearly protected by the First Amendment. If the person chooses to continue the First Amendment activity, he can be prosecuted for a crime under §10–4533. This statute is clearly overbroad [278 N.E.2d at 282–83].

Even if a regulation or statute is neither vague nor overbroad, it may be vulnerable to a procedural due process attack. There is authority for the proposition that notice and a hearing are sometimes required before a noncampus person can be excluded from a public campus. The court in the *Braxton* case, for example, having narrowly construed the California statute to avoid vagueness and overbreadth, then declared:

> We recognize, likewise, that the statute must be construed so as not to violate the precepts of procedural due process; hence, we interpret section 626.4 to require notice and a hearing on alleged misconduct before the issuance of any exclusion order unless the campus administrator reasonably finds that the situation is such an exigent one that the continued presence on the campus of the person from whom consent to remain is withdrawn constitutes a substantial and material threat of significant injury to persons or property (§626.4(c)). Even when an exclusion order issues without a hearing, a postexclusion hearing must be held as soon as reasonably possible not later than seven days following a request by the person excluded [514 P.2d at 700].

Similarly, in *Dunkel v. Elkins,* 325 F. Supp. 1235 (D. Md. 1971), the court construed the Maryland statute upheld in *Kirstel* to require that the institution provide notice and an opportunity for a hearing before excluding an outsider from campus. If a prior hearing is not feasible because of emergency conditions, then a prompt hearing must be held after the expulsion. The burden of proof is on the institution to establish that the person to be excluded fell within the terms of the statute.

A notice and a hearing were also required in *Watson v. Board of Regents of the University of Colorado*, 512 P.2d 1162 (Colo. 1973). The plaintiff was a consultant to the University of Colorado Black Student Alliance with substantial ties to the campus. The university had rejected his application for admission. Believing that a particular admissions committee member had made the decision to reject him, the plaintiff threatened his safety. The university president then notified the plaintiff in writing that he would no longer be allowed on campus. Nevertheless, the plaintiff returned to campus and was arrested for trespass. Relying on *Dunkel v. Elkins,* the court agreed that the exclusion violated procedural due process:

> Where students have been subjected to disciplinary action by university officials, courts have recognized that procedural due process requires—prior to imposition of the disciplinary action—adequate notice of the charges, reasonable opportunity to prepare to meet the charges, an orderly administrative hearing adapted to the nature of the case, and a fair and impartial decision. . . . The same protection must be afforded nonstudents who may be permanently denied access to university functions and facilities.
>
> As part of a valid Regents' regulation of this type, in addition to providing for a hearing, there should be a provision for the person or persons who will act as adjudicator(s).
>
> In the present posture of this matter we should not attempt to "spell out" all proper elements of such a regulation. This task should be undertaken first by the regents. We should say, however, that when a genuine emergency appears to exist and it is impractical for university officials to grant a prior hearing, the right of nonstudents to access to the university may be suspended without a prior hearing, so long as a hearing is thereafter provided with reasonable promptness [512 P.2d at 1165].

Most trespass litigation concerning postsecondary education, such as the cases described, has probed federal constitutional and state statutory limits on public institutions' authority. The debate has been extended to private institutions, however, by the litigation in *State v. Schmid*, 423 A.2d 615 (N.J. 1980), sometimes known as the *Princeton University* case.

Chris Schmid, a nonstudent and a member of the United States Labor Party, was arrested and convicted of trespass for attempting to distribute political materials on the campus of Princeton University. Princeton's regulations required nonstudents and non-university-affiliated organizations to obtain permission to distribute materials on campus. No such requirement applied to students or campus organizations. The regulations did not include any provisions indicating when permission would be granted or what times, manners, or places of expression were appropriate. Schmid claimed that the regulations violated his rights to freedom of expression under both the federal Constitution and the New Jersey state constitution.

First addressing the federal constitutional claim under the First Amendment, the court acknowledged that the "state action" requirement (this volume, Section 1.5.2), a predicate to the application of the First Amendment, "is not readily met in the case of a private educational institution." Reviewing the various theories on which state action has been grounded, the court extensively analyzed their applicability to the case but declined to hold that Princeton's exclusion of Schmid constituted state action under any of the theories.

Although, in the absence of a state action finding, the First Amendment could not apply to Schmid's claim, the court did not find itself similarly constrained in applying the state constitution. Addressing Schmid's state constitutional claim, the court determined that the state constitutional provisions protecting freedom of expression (even though similar to the First Amendment provision) could be construed more expansively than the First Amendment so as to reach Princeton's actions. The court reaffirmed that state constitutions are independent sources of individual rights; that state constitutional protections may surpass the protections of the federal Constitution; and that this greater expansiveness could exist even if the state provision is identical to the federal provision, because state constitutional rights are not intended to be simply mirror images of federal rights (see this volume, Section 1.3.1.1).

In determining whether the more expansive state constitutional protections did protect Schmid against the trespass claim, the court attempted to balance the "legitimate interests in private property with individual freedoms of speech and assembly":

> The state constitutional equipoise between expressional rights and property rights must be . . . gauged on a scale measuring the nature and extent of the public's use of such property. Thus, even as against the exercise of important rights of speech, assembly, petition, and the like, private property itself remains protected under due process standards from untoward interferences with or confiscatory restrictions upon its reasonable use. . . .
>
> On the other hand, it is also clear that private property may be subjected by the state, within constitutional bounds, to reasonable restrictions upon its use in order to serve the public welfare. . . .
>
> We are thus constrained to achieve the optimal balance between the protections to be accorded private property and those to be given to expressional freedoms exercised upon such property [423 A.2d at 629].

To strike the required balance, the court announced a "test" encompassing several "elements" and other "considerations":

> We now hold that, under the state constitution, the test to be applied to ascertain the parameters of the rights of speech and assembly upon privately owned

property and the extent to which such property reasonably can be restricted to accommodate these rights involves several elements. This standard must take into account (1) the nature, purposes, and primary use of such private property, generally, its "normal" use, (2) the extent and nature of the public's invitation to use that property, and (3) the purpose of the expressional activity undertaken upon such property in relation to both the private and public use of the property. This is a multifaceted test which must be applied to ascertain whether in a given case owners of private property may be required to permit, subject to suitable restrictions, the reasonable exercise by individuals of the constitutional freedoms of speech and assembly.

Even when an owner of private property is constitutionally obligated under such a standard to honor speech and assembly rights of others, private property rights themselves must nonetheless be protected. The owner of such private property, therefore, is entitled to fashion reasonable rules to control the mode, opportunity, and site for the individual exercise of expressional rights upon his property. It is at this level of analysis—assessing the reasonableness of such restrictions—that weight may be given to whether there exist convenient and feasible alternative means to individuals to engage in substantially the same expressional activity. While the presence of such alternatives will not eliminate the constitutional duty, it may lighten the obligations upon the private property owner to accommodate the expressional rights of others and may also serve to condition the content of any regulations governing the time, place, and manner for the exercise of such expressional rights [423 A.2d at 630].

Applying each of the three elements in its test to the particular facts concerning Princeton's campus and Schmid's activity on it, the court concluded that Schmid did have state constitutional speech and assembly rights, which Princeton was obligated to honor:

The application of the appropriate standard in this case must commence with an examination of the primary use of the private property, namely, the campus and facilities of Princeton University. Princeton University itself has furnished the answer to this inquiry [in its university regulations] in expansively expressing its overriding educational goals, viz:

The central purposes of a university are the pursuit of truth, the discovery of new knowledge through scholarship and research, the teaching and general development of students, and the transmission of knowledge and learning to society at large. Free inquiry and free expression within the academic community are indispensable to the achievement of these goals. The freedom to teach and to learn depends upon the creation of appropriate conditions and opportunities on the campus as a whole as well as in classrooms and lecture halls. All members of the academic community share the responsibility for securing and sustaining the general conditions conducive to this freedom. . . .

Free speech and peaceable assembly are basic requirements of the university as a center for free inquiry and the search for knowledge and insight.

No one questions that Princeton University has honored this grand ideal and has in fact dedicated its facilities and property to achieve the educational goals expounded in this compelling statement.

In examining next the extent and nature of a public invitation to use its property, we note that a public presence within Princeton University is entirely consonant with the university's expressed educational mission. Princeton University, as a private institution of higher education, clearly seeks to encourage both a wide and continuous exchange of opinions and ideas and to foster a policy of openness and freedom with respect to the use of its facilities. The commitment of its property, facilities, and resources to educational purposes contemplates substantial public involvement and participation in the academic life of the university. The university itself has endorsed the educational value of an open campus and the full exposure of the college community to the "outside world"—that is, the public at large. Princeton University has indeed invited such public uses of its resources in fulfillment of its broader educational ideas and objectives.

The further question is whether the expressional activities undertaken by the defendant in this case are discordant in any sense with both the private and public uses of the campus and facilities of the university. There is nothing in the record to suggest that Schmid was evicted because the purpose of his activities, distributing political literature, offended the university's educational policies. The reasonable and normal inference thus to be extracted from the record in the instant case is that defendant's attempt to disseminate political material was not incompatible with either Princeton University's professed educational goals or the university's overall use of its property for educational purposes. Further, there is no indication that, even under the terms of the university's own regulations, Schmid's activities . . . directly or demonstrably "disrupt[ed] the regular and essential operations of the university" or that, in either the time, the place, or the manner of Schmid's distribution of the political materials, he "significantly infringed on the rights of others" or caused any interference or inconvenience with respect to the normal use of university property and the normal routine and activities of the college community [423 A.2d at 630–31].

Princeton, however, invoked the other considerations included in the court's test. It argued that in order to protect its private property rights as an owner and its academic freedom as a higher education institution, it had to require that outsiders have permission to enter its campus and that its regulations reasonably implemented this necessary requirement. The court did not disagree with the first premise of Princeton's argument, but it did disagree that Princeton's regulations were a reasonable means of protecting its interests:

In addressing this argument, we must give substantial deference to the importance of institutional integrity and independence. Private educational institutions perform an essential social function and have a fundamental responsibility to assure the academic and general well-being of their communities of students, teachers, and related personnel. At a minimum, these needs, implicating academic freedom and development, justify an educational institution in controlling those who seek to enter its domain. The singular need to achieve essential educational goals and regulate activities that impact upon these efforts has been acknowledged even with respect to public educational institutions (see, for example, *Healy v. James,* 408 U.S. at 180 . . . *Tinker v. Des Moines Indep. Community School Dist.,* 393 U.S. 503, 513–14 . . . (1969)). Hence, private colleges and universities must be accorded a generous measure of autonomy and self-governance if they are to fulfill their paramount role as vehicles of education and enlightenment.

In this case, however, the university regulations that were applied to Schmid . . . contained no standards, aside from the requirement for invitation and permission, for governing the actual exercise of expressional freedom. Indeed, there were no standards extant regulating the granting or withholding of such authorization, nor did the regulations deal adequately with the time, place, or manner for individuals to exercise their rights of speech and assembly. Regulations thus devoid of reasonable standards designed to protect both the legitimate interests of the university as an institution of higher education and the individual exercise of expressional freedom cannot constitutionally be invoked to prohibit the otherwise noninjurious and reasonable exercise of such freedoms. . . .

In these circumstances, given the absence of adequate reasonable regulations, the required accommodation of Schmid's expressional and associational rights, otherwise reasonably exercised, would not constitute an unconstitutional abridgment of Princeton University's property rights. . . . It follows that, in the absence of a reasonable regulatory scheme, Princeton University did in fact violate defendant's state constitutional rights of expression in evicting him and securing his arrest for distributing political literature upon its campus [423 A.2d at 632–33].

The court thus reversed Schmid's conviction for trespass.

Princeton sought U.S. Supreme Court review of the New Jersey court's decision. The university argued that the court's interpretation of *state* constitutional law violated its rights under *federal* law. Specifically, it claimed a First Amendment right to institutional academic freedom (see Section 6.4.1) and a Fifth Amendment right to protect its property from infringement by government (here, the New Jersey court). In a per curiam opinion, the Supreme Court declined to address the merits of Princeton's arguments, declaring the appeal moot because Princeton had changed its regulations since the time of Schmid's conviction (*Princeton University and State of New Jersey v. Schmid,* 455 U.S. 100 (1982)). Although the Supreme Court therefore dismissed the appeal, the dismissal had no negative effect on the New Jersey court's opinion, which stands as authoritative law for that state.

The New Jersey Supreme Court's reasoning was subsequently approved and followed by the Pennsylvania Supreme Court in *Pennsylvania v. Tate,* 432 A.2d

1382 (Pa. 1981). The defendants had been arrested for trespassing at Muhlenberg College, a private institution, when they distributed leaflets on campus announcing a community-sponsored lecture by the then FBI director. The Pennsylvania court developed an analysis similar to the New Jersey court's and invoked the free expression guarantees of the Pennsylvania state constitution. The standardless nature of the college's regulations was again a crucial factor rendering the trespass conviction a violation of state constitutional rights.

State v. Schmid is a landmark case—the first to impose constitutional limitations on the authority of private institutions to exclude outsiders from their campuses. *Schmid* does not, however, create a new nationwide rule. The applicability of its analysis to private campuses in states other than New Jersey and Pennsylvania will vary, depending on the particular individual rights clauses in a state's constitution, the existing precedents construing their application to private entities, and the receptivity of a state's judges to the New Jersey court's view of the nature and use of private campuses. Even in New Jersey and Pennsylvania, the *Schmid* and *Tate* precedents do not create the same access rights to all private campuses; as *Schmid* emphasizes, the degree of access required depends on the primary use for which the institution dedicates its campus property and the scope of the public invitation to use that particular property. Administrators dealing with access of outsiders should consult counsel concerning their own state's law and their institution's status under it.

Nor does *Schmid* prohibit private institutions from regulating the activity of outsiders to whom they must permit entry. Institutions may still adopt regulatory standards that impose reasonable time, place, and manner restrictions on access. Indeed, the new regulations adopted by Princeton after Schmid's arrest were cited favorably by the New Jersey court. Although they were not at issue in the case, since they were not the basis of the trespass charge, the court noted that "these current amended regulations exemplify the approaches open to private educational entities seeking to protect their institutional integrity while at the same time recognizing individual rights of speech and assembly and accommodating the public whose presence nurtures academic inquiry and growth." The new Princeton regulations, which are set out in full in the court's opinion (423 A.2d at 617–18 n.2), thus provide substantial guidance for institutions that are subject to state law such as New Jersey's or that as a matter of educational policy desire to change their access regulations.

11.5.4. Soliciting and Canvassing

The university campus may be an attractive marketplace not only for speakers, pamphleteers, and canvassers conveying social, political, or religious messages but also for companies selling merchandise to college students. Whether the enterprising outsider wishes to develop a market for ideas or for commodities, the public institution's authority to restrict contact with its students is limited by the First Amendment. As in other circumstances, because of the First Amendment's applicability, a public institution's authority to regulate soliciting and canvassing is more limited than that of a private institution.

Historically, litigation and discussion of free speech have focused on rights attending the communication of political or social thought. Although the U.S. Supreme Court's opinion in *Virginia State Board of Pharmacy v. Virginia Citizens Consumer Council*, 425 U.S. 748 (1976), made clear that the protection of the First Amendment likewise extends to purely "commercial speech," even when the communication is simply "I will sell you X at Y price," the degree of protection afforded commercial speech is less than that afforded noncommercial speech.

The Supreme Court has consistently approved time, place, and manner restrictions on speech where they (1) are not based on the speech's "content or subject matter," (2) "serve a significant governmental interest," and (3) "leave open ample alternative channels for communication of the information" (*Heffron v. International Society for Krishna Consciousness*, 452 U.S. 640 (1981); see also *Clark v. Community for Creative Non-Violence*, discussed in Section 8.1.2). Within these guidelines, public institutions may subject both noncommercial and commercial speech to reasonable regulation of the time, place, and manner of delivery, although somewhat more flexible guidelines exist for commercial speech (see the *Central Hudson* case discussed later in this chapter). In addition, public institutions may regulate the content of commercial speech in ways that would not be permissible for other types of speech.

11.5.4.1. Commercial solicitation. Several court decisions involving American Future Systems, Inc., a corporation specializing in the sale of china and crystal, address the regulation of commercial speech by a public university. In *American Future Systems v. Pennsylvania State University*, 618 F.2d 252 (3d Cir. 1980) (*American Future Systems I*), the plaintiff corporation challenged the defendant university's regulations on commercial activities in campus residence halls. The regulations in question barred "the conducting of any business enterprise for profit" in student residence halls except where an individual student invites the salesperson to his or her room for the purpose of conducting business only with that student. No rules prevented businesses from placing advertisements in student newspapers or on student radio, or from making sales attempts by telephone or mail.

American Future Systems (AFS) scheduled a number of sales demonstrations in Penn State residence halls in the fall of 1977. When Penn State officials attempted to stop the sales demonstrations, AFS argued that such action violated its First Amendment "commercial speech" rights. At this point, Penn State informed AFS "that it would be permitted to conduct the demonstration portion of its show if no attempts were made to sell merchandise to the students during the presentation" (618 F.2d at 254). Claiming that the sales transactions were essential to its presentation, AFS ceased its activity and commenced its lawsuit. AFS based its argument on the *Virginia State Board of Pharmacy* case (cited earlier), but the appellate court did not find it controlling:

> *Virginia Pharmacy Board* . . . by itself, does not resolve the issue presented by this case, however. The statutory scheme discussed in *Virginia Pharmacy Board* effectively suppressed all dissemination of price information throughout the state. The case at hand presents a dramatically different fact situation, implicating many different concerns.
>
> Penn State argues that it can restrict the use of its residence halls to purposes which further the educational function of the institution. It urges that transacting sales with groups of students in the dormitories does not further the educational goals of the university and, therefore, can be lawfully prohibited. It emphasizes that AFS seeks a ruling that its sales and demonstrations be permitted in the residence halls, areas which are not open to the general public. In light of all the facts of this case, we believe Penn State is correct [618 F.2d at 255].

In reaching its conclusion, the court inquired whether Penn State had established a "public forum" for free speech activity (see *Widmar v. Vincent*, this volume, Section 9.1.4) in the residence halls:

> When the state restricts speech in some way, the court must look to the special interests of the government in regulating speech in the particular location. The focus of the court's inquiry must be whether there is a basic incompatibility between the communication and the primary activity of an area. . . .
>
> As discussed above, members of the general public do not have unrestricted access to Penn State residence halls. "No Trespassing" signs are posted near the entrances to all the residence halls. Although nonresidents of the halls may enter the lobbies, they may not proceed freely to the private living areas. We believe that these facts demonstrate that the arena at issue here, the residence halls at Penn State, does not constitute a "public forum" under the First Amendment [618 F.2d at 256].

The court then inquired whether, despite the absence of a public forum, AFS could still claim First Amendment protection for solicitation and sales activities occurring in the residence halls. According to the court, such a claim depends on whether the activity impinges on the primary business for which the area in question is used:

> We recognize that the absence of a "public forum" from this case does not end our inquiry, however. There are some "non-public-forum" areas where the communication does not significantly impinge upon the primary business carried on there. Penn State asserts that the AFS group sales do impinge significantly on

the primary activities of a college dormitory. Penn State argues that its residence halls are "exclusively dedicated to providing a living environment which is conducive to activities associated with being a student and succeeding academically." It contends that group sales activities within the residence halls would disrupt the proper study atmosphere and the privacy of the students. It reiterates that there is no history of allowing group commercial transactions to take place in the dormitories. We conclude that Penn State has articulated legitimate interests which support its ban on group sales activity in the dormitories. We also conclude that these interests are furthered by the proscription against commercial transactions [618 F.2d at 256–57].

Completing its analysis, the court addressed and rejected a final argument made by AFS—that Penn State cannot distinguish between commercial and noncommercial speech in making rules for its residence halls and that, since Penn State permits political and other noncommercial group activities, it must permit commercial activities as well. The court replied:

As noted above, Penn State has advanced reasonable objectives to support its ban on group commercial activity in the residence halls. Further, it has emphasized that traditionally there has been an absence of such activity in the halls. This places commercial speech in a quite different category from activities historically associated with college life, such as political meetings or football rallies. We cannot say that the record in this case reveals any arbitrary, capricious, or invidious distinction between commercial and noncommercial speech. We therefore conclude that AFS is incorrect in its assertion that the Penn State policy violates the First Amendment because it treats noncommercial speech differently from commercial speech [618 F.2d at 257–59].

Having determined that AFS's activities were commercial speech entitled to First Amendment protection but that Penn State's regulations complied with First Amendment requirements applicable to such speech, the court in *American Future Systems I* upheld the regulations and affirmed the lower court's judgment for Penn State.

Soon, however, a second generation of litigation was born. In accordance with its understanding of the appellate court's opinion in the first lawsuit, AFS requested Penn State to allow group demonstrations that would not include consummation of sales and would take place only in residence hall common areas. AFS provided the university with a copy of its "script" for these demonstrations, a series of seventy-six cue cards. Penn State responded that AFS could use certain cue cards with information the university considered to have "educational value" but not cue cards with "price guarantee and payment plan information," which the university considered "an outright group commercial solicitation." AFS sued again, along with several Penn State students, arguing that Penn State's censorship of its cue cards violated its right to commercial speech and contradicted the court's opinion in *American Future Systems I*. After losing again in the trial court, AFS finally gained a victory when the appellate court ruled in its favor (*American Future Systems v. Pennsylvania State University*, 688 F.2d 907 (3d Cir. 1982) (*American Future Systems II*)).

The appellate court carefully distinguished this litigation from the prior litigation in *American Future Systems I*. The only issue in this second case, said the court, was whether Penn State could lawfully censor the content of AFS's commercial speech. In resolving this issue, the court applied the test for ascertaining the validity of commercial speech regulations that the U.S. Supreme Court had established in *Central Hudson Gas & Electric Corp. v. Public Service Commission*, 447 U.S. 557 (1980):

> For commercial speech to come within [the First Amendment], it at least must concern lawful activity and not be misleading. Next, we ask whether the asserted governmental interest is substantial. If both inquiries yield positive answers, we must determine whether the regulation directly advances the government interest asserted and whether it is not more extensive than is necessary to serve that interest [688 F.2d at 913; quoting *Central Hudson* at 566].

Applying this test, the court determined that Penn State's prohibition of AFS's demonstration violated AFS's First Amendment rights. The only interest that Penn State had articulated, said the court, was the maintenance of "the proper study atmosphere" in its dormitories. But Penn State allowed noncommercial activity to take place in the common areas of residence; thus, its policy differentiating between commercial and noncommercial activity was not sufficiently substantial to justify outlawing the commercial content of AFS's presentation. The court therefore reversed the lower court's entry of summary judgment for Penn State and remanded the case for trial.

Several students were also plaintiffs in *American Future Systems II*. They claimed that the university had violated their First Amendment rights to make purchases in group settings in the residence hall common areas and to host and participate in sales demonstrations in the private rooms of residence halls. The students argued that these rights are not aspects of commercial speech, as AFS's rights are, but are noncommercial speech, as well as freedom of association and due process, rights that deserve higher protection. The appellate court determined that the lower court's record was not sufficiently developed on these points and remanded the students' claims to the lower court for further consideration—thus leaving these arguments unresolved.

In further proceedings, after remand to the trial court, the plaintiff students and American Future Systems, Inc. obtained a preliminary injunction against Penn State's ban on group sales demonstrations in individual students' rooms (*American Future Systems v. Pennsylvania State University*, 553 F. Supp. 1268 (M.D. Pa. 1982)); and subsequently the court entered a permanent injunction against this policy (*American Future Systems v. Pennsylvania State University*, 568 F. Supp. 666 (M.D. Pa. 1983)). The court emphasized the students' own rights to receive information and, from that perspective, did not consider the speech at issue to be subject to the lower standards applicable to commercial speech. On appeal by the university, however, the U.S. Court of Appeals for the Third Circuit disagreed, considering the speech to be commercial and overruling the district court (*American Future Systems, Inc. v. Pennsylvania State University*, 752 F.2d 854 (3d Cir. 1985) (*American Future Systems III*)).

The appellate court decided that a state university's substantial interest as a property owner and educator in preserving dormitories for their intended study-oriented use and in preventing them from becoming "rent-free merchandise marts," was sufficient to overcome both the commercial vendor's free speech rights to make group sales presentations in students' dormitory rooms and the students' free speech rights to join with others to hear and discuss this information. In applying the *Central Hudson* standards discussed earlier, the court found that, although the sales activities involved were lawful, the state university's substantial interests justified a narrowly drawn regulation prohibiting group demonstrations in students' dormitory rooms.

Subsequent to *American Future Systems III*, students on another campus brought a similar issue to court in another case involving American Future Systems' group demonstrations. The subject of this suit was the defendant's regulation prohibiting "private commercial enterprises" from operating on SUNY campuses or facilities. The defendant had used this resolution to bar AFS from holding group demonstrations in students' dormitory rooms. This case made it to the U.S. Supreme Court in *Board of Trustees of the State University of New York v. Fox*, 492 U.S. 469 (1989). The Court used the occasion to restate the last part of the *Central Hudson* test ("whether [the regulation] is not more extensive than necessary to serve [the government] interest"); as restated, it now requires only that the regulation be "narrowly tailored" to achieve the government's interest, or that there be a "reasonable fit" between the regulation and the government interest. This restatement makes the standard governing commercial speech more lenient, allowing courts to be more deferential to institutional interests when campus commercial activities are at issue. The Court remanded the case to the lower courts for reconsideration in accordance with this more deferential test. The Court also remanded the question whether the university's regulation was unconstitutionally overbroad on its face because it applied to and limited noncommercial speech (that is, more highly protected speech) as well as commercial speech.

The three appellate court opinions in the complex *American Future Systems* litigation, supplemented by the Supreme Court's decision in the *Fox* case, provide guidance for administrators concerned with commercial activity in public institutions. A public institution clearly has considerable authority to place restrictions on outsiders' access to its campus for such purposes. The institution may reasonably restrict the "time, place, and manner" of commercial activity—for instance, by limiting the places where group demonstrations may be held in residence halls, prohibiting the consummation of sales during group demonstrations, or prohibiting commercial solicitations in libraries or classrooms. The institution may also regulate the content of commercial activity to ensure that it is not fraudulent or misleading and does not propose illegal transactions. Other content restrictions—namely, restrictions that directly advance a substantial institutional interest and are narrowly tailored to achieve that interest—are also permissible.

Administrators cannot comfortably assume, however, that this authority is broad enough to validate every regulation of commercial activity. Regulations that censor or sharply curtail all dissemination of commercial information may infringe the First Amendment. *American Future Systems II* is a leading example. Similarly, a regulation prohibiting all in-person, one-on-one contacts with students, even when the representative does not attempt to close a deal or when the student has initiated the contact, may be invalid. In some locations, moreover, the institution's interest in regulating may be sufficiently weak that it cannot justify bans or sharp restrictions at these locations. Possible examples include orderly solicitations in the common areas of student unions or other less private or studious places on campus; solicitations of an individual student conducted in the student's own room by prior arrangement; and solicitations at the request of student organizations in locations customarily used by such organizations, when such solicitations involve no deceptive practices and propose no illegal or hazardous activity.

It is also clear from U.S. Supreme Court precedents (see, for example, *Consolidated Edison Co. v. Public Service Commission,* 447 U.S. 530 (1980)), that not all speech activity of commercial entrepreneurs is "commercial" speech. Activity whose purpose is not to propose or close a commercial transaction— for example, an educational seminar or a statement on political, economic, or other issues of public interest—may fall within First Amendment protections higher than those accorded commercial speech. Administrators should also be guided by this distinction when regulating, since their authority to limit access to campus and their authority to restrict the content of what is said will be narrower when entrepreneurs wish to engage in "public-interest" rather than "commercial" speech. While this distinction may become blurred when an entrepreneur combines both types of speech in the same activity, there are discussions in both *American Future Systems III* (752 F.2d at 862) and *Fox* (492 U.S. at 481) that will provide guidance in this circumstance.

11.5.4.2. Noncommercial canvassing. As discussed in Sections 11.5.4 and 11.5.4.1, noncommercial speech is afforded greater protection under the First

Amendment than commercial speech. Consequently, a public institution's authority to regulate political canvassing, charitable solicitations, public opinion polling, and other types of noncommercial speech is more limited than its authority to regulate commercial sales and solicitations.

In *Brush v. Pennsylvania State University*, 414 A.2d 48 (Pa. 1980), students at Penn State challenged university restrictions on canvassing in residence halls. The regulations permitted canvassing (defined as "any attempt to influence student opinion, gain support, or promote a particular cause or interest") by registered individuals in the living areas of a dormitory if the residents of that building had voted in favor of open canvassing. A majority vote to ban canvassing precluded access to living areas by canvassers unless they were specifically invited in advance by a resident. All canvassers remained free, however, to reach students by mail or telephone and to contact residents in the dining halls, lobbies, and conference rooms of each dormitory.

The Supreme Court of Pennsylvania upheld these regulations. It determined that the university had substantial interests in protecting the privacy of its students, preventing breaches of security, and promoting quiet study conditions. The regulations reasonably restricted the time, place, and manner of speech in furtherance of these government interests. Additionally, insofar as the regulations did not eliminate effective alternatives to canvassing inside the living areas, the university had afforded canvassers ample opportunity to reach hall residents.

On the basis of *Brush*, public institutions can confidently exclude canvassers from the actual living quarters of student residence facilities when a majority of the residents have voted to preclude such access. Similar restrictions applied to dining halls, student unions, sidewalks, or other less private areas, however, may violate the First Amendment rights of the speakers and of the potential listeners who are not in favor of the restriction. No-canvassing rules imposed on student living areas with separate living units, such as married students' garden apartments or town houses, may also be unconstitutional; in such circumstances the institution's interests in security and study conditions may be weaker, and the students' (or student family's) interest in controlling their individual living space is greater. See generally *Schaumburg v. Citizens for Better Environment*, 444 U.S. 620 (1980).

Whether rules such as Penn State's would be valid if imposed directly by the administration and not decided by the student vote is not addressed in *Brush*. But given the strong institutional interests in security and in preserving conditions appropriate for study, it is likely that narrowly drawn no-canvassing rules limited to living areas of dormitories and other similar spaces would be constitutional even without approval by student vote. In *Chapman v. Thomas*, 743 F.2d 1056 (4th Cir. 1984), the court upheld such a restriction, calling the dormitory living area a "nonpublic forum" (see *Perry Education Assn. v. Perry Local*

Educators' Assn., 460 U.S. 37 (1983)), to which the institution may prohibit or selectively regulate access. For the same reason, no-canvassing rules would probably be constitutional, even without student vote, as applied to study halls, library stacks and reading rooms, laboratories, and similar restricted areas.

A later case, *Glover v. Cole*, 762 F.2d 1197 (4th Cir. 1985), provides further support for the validity of such content-neutral restrictions on noncommercial solicitation and also illustrates a different type of regulation that may be constitutionally employed to restrict such activity. The plaintiffs, members of a socialist political party, had sought to solicit donations and sell political publications on campus. The president of West Virginia State College (the defendant in the case) had prohibited this activity by invoking a systemwide policy prohibiting sales and fund-raising activities anywhere on campus by groups that were not sponsored by the students. The court determined that the plaintiffs' activities were "political advocacy" rather than commercial speech and thus highly protected by the First Amendment. Nevertheless, the regulation was valid because it was a content-neutral regulation of the *manner* of speech in a "limited public forum" and met the constitutional standards applicable to such regulations (see Section 8.1.2):

> There has been no direct infringement on Glover's and Measel's expressive activity, simply a prohibition against sales and fund raising on campus. Since the campus area is generally open for all debate and expressive conduct, we do not find that first amendment interests seriously are damaged by the administration's decision to limit the use of its property through uniform application of a sensible "manner" restriction. Plaintiffs' activities may be at the core of the first amendment, but the college has a right to preserve the campus for its intended purpose and to protect college students from the pressures of solicitation. In so ruling, we note that plaintiffs have more than ample alternative channels available to tap the student market for fund raising. The literature itself sets out in plain English requests for donations for the cause. Anyone interested enough to peruse the material learns that the preparation of the materials costs something and that the group is in need of financial (as well as moral and political) support. In addition, if the campus is plaintiffs' key market, they can organize a student group or obtain a student sponsor to raise funds on campus [762 F.2d at 1203].

The features noted by the court are important to the validity of all campus regulations of noncommercial solicitation. First of all, the regulation was narrow—limited to sales and fund raising—and left other "more than ample" channels for on-campus expression open to outsiders such as the plaintiffs. In addition, the regulation applied neutrally and uniformly to all outside groups, without reference to the beliefs of the group or the viewpoints its members would express on campus. Finally, the university could demonstrate that the regulation was tailored to the protection of significant institutional interests that would be impeded if outsiders could raise funds and sell items on campus. Campus regulation of noncommercial solicitation will not always be supported by such interests. In *Hays County Guardian v. Supple*, 969 F.2d 111 (5th Cir. 1992), for example, Southwest Texas State University had a regulation prohibiting the in-person distribution on campus of free newspapers containing advertisements. The plaintiffs—the publishers of a free newspaper distributed countywide, joined by university students—challenged the regulation's application. The court invalidated the regulation because the university did not demonstrate any significant interest that the regulation was "narrowly tailored" to protect.

For discussion of the related topic of voter canvassing and registration, see Section 11.3.

SEC. 11.6. STATE OPEN-MEETINGS AND OPEN-RECORDS LAWS

11.6.1. Open Meetings and Public Disclosure

Open-meetings laws provide a particularly good illustration of the controversy and litigation that can be occasioned when a general state law is applied to the particular circumstances of postsecondary education. In an era of skepticism about public officials and institutions, public postsecondary administrators must be especially sensitive to laws whose purpose is to promote openness and accountability in government. As state entities, public postsecondary institutions are often subject to open-meetings laws and similar legislation, and the growing body of legal actions under such laws indicates that the public intends to make sure that public institutions comply.

Litigation to enforce or to clarify the effect of open-meetings laws on public institutions has been initiated by the media, faculty members, students, education associations, and members of the general public. In *Arkansas Gazette Co. v. Pickens*, 522 S.W.2d 350 (Ark. 1975), for instance, a newspaper and one of its reporters argued that committees of the University of Arkansas board of trustees, not just the full board itself, were subject to the Arkansas Freedom of Information Act. The reporter had been excluded from a committee meeting on a proposed rule change that would have allowed students of legal age to possess and consume intoxicating beverages in university-controlled facilities at the Fayetteville campus. The Arkansas Freedom of Information Act provided in part that "public business be performed in an open and public manner so that the electors shall be advised of the performance of public officials and of the decisions that are reached in public activity and in making public policy" (Ark. Code Ann. §12–2802, now Ark. Code Ann. §25–19–102). The board of trustees contended, and the lower court agreed, that meetings of the board's committees were not "public meetings" within the meaning of the Act. The Arkansas Supreme Court reversed, reasoning that the "intent of the legislature, as so emphatically set forth in its statement of policy, [was] that public business be performed in an open and public manner" (522 S.W.2d at 353). The court could find no distinction between the board's business and that of its committees and thus applied the open-meetings requirement to both.

Wood v. Marston, 442 So. 2d 934 (Fla. 1983), concerned the application of Florida's open-meetings law to a University of Florida search-and-screen committee formed to recommend candidates for dean of the law school. The Florida statute stated that (with certain specified exceptions) "all meetings of any board or commission of any state agency . . . at which official acts are to be taken are declared to be public meetings open to the public at all times" (Fla. Stat. Ann. §286.011). The plaintiffs, members of the local news media, sought to enjoin the search-and-screen committee from meeting in private session. Under existing Florida case law, committees that performed only advisory or "fact-gathering" functions, as distinguished from "decision-making" functions, did not perform "official acts" within the statute's meaning and thus were not covered by the statute. The defendants argued that, because the search-and-screen committee's decisions were subject to further review, the committee should be considered an advisory body exempted from the statute. The court rejected this claim:

> The search-and-screen committee had an admitted "fact-gathering" role in the solicitation and compilation of applications. It had an equally undisputed decision-making function in screening the applicants. In deciding which of the applicants to reject from further consideration, the committee performed a policy-based, decision-making function delegated to it by the president of the university through the faculty as a whole. Nor does the fact that the results were submitted to the faculty as a whole, which had the authority to review the work of the screening committee, render the committee's function any less policy based or decision making [442 So. 2d at 938–39].

Not all cases, however, have been resolved in favor of openness. In *Donahue v. State,* 474 N.W.2d 537 (Iowa 1991), an associate professor denied promotion asserted that the meeting of the faculty appeals panel should have been open under Iowa's open-meetings law. The court ruled that the panel was an advisory board without policy-making power, and thus did not fit the statutory definition of "government body" contemplated by the statute. And in *The Missoulian v. Board of Regents of Higher Education,* 675 P.2d 962 (Mont. 1984), the court rejected a Montana newspaper's claim that the state's open-meetings law applied to the board of regents' periodic review of Montana state college presidents. Adopting a balancing test that weighed the individual's right to privacy against the public's right to know, the court held that the right to privacy prevailed under the particular facts of the case.

In a case of particular concern to student affairs professionals, Georgia's highest court ruled that the proceedings of the student disciplinary board of the University of Georgia were subject to the state's open-meetings and open-records laws. In *Red and Black Publishing Co. v. Board of Regents,* 427 S.E.2d 257 (Ga. 1993), the university's student newspaper had sought access to the Student Organization Court's records and proceedings involving discipline for hazing charges against two fraternities. Although the law provided that meetings of the "governing body" of any state agency must be open to the public, the law also covered the meetings of committees created by the governing body at which official action is taken. The court found that the judicial board was a vehicle through which the university took official action, in that it enforced the university's code of student conduct. Thus, the court ruled that the university must permit members of the public, including the media, to attend the disciplinary board's hearings.

State open-meetings laws have changed the way boards and committees at some public institutions conduct their business. Administrators at public colleges should seek legal advice to ensure compliance with these laws.

11.6.2. Open-Records Laws

As cousins of open-meetings laws, state public document acts and freedom-of-information laws also have had an important impact on postsecondary education. In *Redding v. Brady,* 606 P.2d 1 193 (Utah 1980), the editor of the student newspaper at Weber State College sued under the Utah Information Practices Act and the state's Public and Private Writings Act to compel the release of salary figures for all Weber State employees. When the court decided in Redding's favor, the legislature responded by enacting the Publication of Higher Education Salary Data Act, which authorized limited disclosure of salaries of groups of employees but generally forbade the disclosure of "personally identifiable salary data." Redding then sued a second time, arguing that both the Utah state constitution and the federal Constitution's First Amendment created a public right of access to documents such as those he sought and that accordingly the legislation was unconstitutional.

In the second suit, *Redding v. Jacobsen,* 638 P.2d 503 (Utah 1981), the Utah Supreme Court agreed that there was an emerging right of access to government documents under recent First Amendment decisions of the U.S. Supreme Court. This emerging right, however, had to be balanced against employees' rights of privacy, which the state legislation sought to protect. Determining that the right to gather news should not prevail, in this particular instance, over a right to privacy which the legislature had deemed paramount, the court upheld the legislation's constitutionality.

Privacy may, however, take a back seat under some state open-records laws. In *Denver Publishing Co. v. University of Colorado,* 812 P.2d 682 (Colo. Ct. App. 1991), the court held that the state's open-records law required the university to disclose the settlement it had reached with a former chancellor. Although the court said that documents implicating the privacy of individuals would be protected from disclosure, the court did not view either the settlement agreement with the former chancellor, who had disputed his termination, or a letter agreement between another chancellor and the university as implicating protected privacy rights.

In *Red and Black Publishing Co. v. Board of Regents* (discussed in Section 11.6.1), the Georgia Supreme Court also ruled that the state's open-records law applied to the records of the student disciplinary board. Although the university argued that releasing the records would violate the Family Educational Rights and Privacy Act (FERPA), the state's high court disagreed. (The FERPA regulations have since been changed to permit the disclosure of disciplinary records to certain parties; see Section 3.3.1). In contrast to the breadth of the Georgia court's interpretation of its open-records law, Connecticut's Supreme Court, in *University of Connecticut v. Freedom of Information Commission,* 585 A.2d 690 (Conn. 1991), ruled that Connecticut's open-records law did not require disclosure of names of students who worked for the university's police force.

Several courts have been asked to determine whether nonprofit foundations incorporated separately from a public college or university but formed to raise funds for the institution are subject to state open-records laws. In *State ex rel. Toledo Blade Co. v. University of Toledo Foundation,* 602 N.E.2d 1159 (Ohio 1992), Ohio's Supreme Court determined that the state's public records disclosure statute encompassed the foundation as a "public office." The newspaper had sought the names of donors to the foundation, and the court ruled that these names must be disclosed. In contrast, in *State ex rel. Guste v. Nicholls College Foundation,* 592 So. 2d 419 (La. Ct. App. 1991), *affirmed,* 593 So. 2d 651 (La. 1992), (further discussed in Section 2.2.4), the court found that the foundation, a private nonprofit corporation linked to a state college, was not a public body, although it said that the state had the authority to inspect records of *public* funds received by the foundation.

Inquiries related to college athletics have spawned litigation over the application of state open-records laws. For example, in *University of Kentucky v. Courier-Journal,* 830 S.W.2d 373 (Ky. 1992), the University of Kentucky was required to disclose its response to an NCAA investigation of alleged rules violations. Although the university argued that appendices to the report, including documents and transcripts of interviews, came within the law's exception for "preliminary materials," the court disagreed, ruling that the entire report was a public document. In *Cremins v. Atlanta Journal,* 405 S.E.2d 675 (Ga. 1991), the *Atlanta Journal* succeeded in gaining information about outside income of some university coaches. And in *Milwaukee Journal v. Board of Regents of the University of Wisconsin System,* 472 N.W.2d 607 (Wis. Ct. App. 1991), the court ruled that the University of Wisconsin must disclose the names of applicants for the positions of football coach and athletic director.

In some states, curriculum materials at a public institution may be considered a "public record" subject to inspection by the public. In *Russo v. Nassau County Community College*, 603 N.Y.S.2d 294 (N.Y. 1993), an individual filed a request under the state's Freedom of Information Act for class materials used in a college sex education course. Although a state appellate court denied the request, stating that the materials were not "records" under the law's definition, the state's high court reversed and granted access to the materials.

As these cases demonstrate, the general problem created by open-records statutes and similar laws is how to balance the public's right to know with an individual's right to privacy or an institution's need for confidentiality. Administrators must consider the complex interplay of all these interests. Sometimes, the legislation provides guidelines or rules for striking this balance. Even in the absence of such provisions, some courts have narrowly construed open-records laws to avoid intrusion on compelling interests of privacy or confidentiality. The trend, however, appears to be in the direction of openness and public access, even when the institution considers the information sensitive or private.

SELECTED ANNOTATED BIBLIOGRAPHY

Sec. 11.1 (General Principles)

Reynolds, Osborne M. *Handbook of Local Government Law* (West, 1982 plus periodic pocket part). A comprehensive, well-documented review of local government law. Divided into twenty-two chapters, including "Limits on State Control of Municipalities," "Relationship of Municipalities to Federal Government," "Powers of Municipalities," "Finances of Local Government," "Local Control of the Use of Property," and "Local Regulation of Trade, Business, and Other Enterprises."

Sec. 11.2 (Zoning Off-Campus Housing)

Tracy, JoAnn. "Comment: Single-Family Zoning Ordinances: The Constitutionality of Suburban Barriers Against Nontraditional Households," 31 *St. Louis U. L.J.* 1023 (1987). Reviews decisions of the Supreme Court and other courts on the definition of "family" for zoning purposes. Discusses Fourteenth Amendment implications of restrictions on relationships between residents, and suggests alternatives to marriage, blood, or adoption for limiting the number of occupants of single-family homes.

Sec. 11.4 (Relations with Local Police)

Bickel, Robert. "The Relationship Between the University and Local Law Enforcement Agencies in Their Response to the Problem of Drug Abuse on the Campus," in D. Parker Young (ed.), *Higher Education: The Law and Campus Issues* (Institute of Higher Education, University of Georgia, 1973), 17–27. A practical discussion of the general principles of search and seizure, double jeopardy, and confidentiality in the campus drug abuse context; also discusses the necessity of administrators' having the advice of counsel.

Cowen, Lindsay. "The Campus and the Community: Problems of Dual Jurisdiction," in D. Parker Young (ed.), *Proceedings of a Conference on Higher Education: The Law and Student Protest* (Institute of Higher Education, University of Georgia, 1970), 28–32. A brief discussion of the policy considerations governing the division of authority between the institution and local law enforcement agencies.

Kalaidjian, Ed. "Problems of Dual Jurisdiction of Campus and Community," in G. Holmes (ed.), *Student Protest and the Law* (Institute of Continuing Legal Education, University of Michigan, 1969), 131–48. Addresses issues arising out of concurrent criminal and disciplinary proceedings and police entry onto campus.

Sec. 11.5 (Community Access to Institutional Property)

Finkin, Matthew. "On 'Institutional' Academic Freedom," 61 *Tex. L. Rev.* 817 (1983). Considers the collapse of the distinction between institutional autonomy and academic freedom and applies this discussion to *State v. Schmid*, the Princeton University case.

Sec. 11.6 (State Open-Meetings and Open-Records Laws)

Cleveland, Harlan. *The Costs and Benefits of Openness: Sunshine Laws and Higher Education* (Association of Governing Boards of Universities and Colleges, 1985). A research report that reviews state open-meeting laws and the court decisions and state attorney general opinions construing these laws. Compares the various state laws, using a list of twenty-three characteristics relating to openness. Author analyzes the costs and benefits of openness under these laws, concluding that the costs generally outweigh the benefits. Report includes an appendix of attorney general opinions and a bibliography. Reprinted in 12 *J. Coll & Univ. Law* 127 (1985).

CHAPTER TWELVE

The College and the Federal Government

SEC. 12.1. FEDERAL REGULATION OF POSTSECONDARY EDUCATION

12.1.1. Overview

The federal government is a government of limited powers; it has only those powers that are expressly conferred by the U.S. Constitution or can reasonably be implied from those conferred. The remaining powers are, under the Tenth Amendment, "reserved to the states respectively, or to the People." Although the Constitution does not mention education, let alone delegate power over it to the federal government, it does not follow that the Tenth Amendment reserves all authority over education to the states or the people; see *Case v. Bowles,* 327 U.S. 92 (1946). Many federal constitutional powers—particularly the spending power, the taxing power, the commerce power, and the civil rights enforcement powers—are broad enough to extend to many matters concerning education. Whenever an activity falls within the scope of one of these federal powers, the federal government has authority over it.

When Congress passes a law pursuant to its federal constitutional powers, that law will "preempt" or supersede any state and local laws that impinge on the effectuation of Congress's powers. The application of this federal "preemption doctrine" to postsecondary education is illustrated by *United States v. City of Philadelphia,* 798 F.2d 81 (3d Cir. 1986), where the court held that military recruiting laws and policies, passed pursuant to Congress's constitutional powers to raise and support armies, preempted a local civil rights ordinance prohibiting discrimination against homosexuals. However, when it passes federal laws pursuant to its constitutional powers, Congress may not always enforce the law directly against the states by abrogating their Eleventh Amendment immunity from suit; see *Seminole Tribe of Florida v. Florida,* 116 S. Ct. 1114 (1996).

In recent times, the federal government has used its constitutional powers extensively to regulate and fund higher education. Despite the attempts of institutions and their national associations to limit the impact of federal regulations and federal funding conditions, the federal presence on campus continues to increase. Although mandated self-regulation is still used in some areas of federal regulation such as restrictions on the use of human subjects or research on animals, self-regulatory actions by institutions have been criticized as insufficient or self-serving.

In the following sections, the regulatory issues with the broadest application to postsecondary student affairs are analyzed. In addition to those discussed, other federal statutes may also become important in particular circumstances. The federal bankruptcy law (11 U.S.C. §101 *et seq.*), for instance, is important when a student loan recipient declares bankruptcy (see Section 4.2.7.1) and when an institution encounters severe financial distress. The Military Selective Service Act (50 U.S.C. §451 *et seq.*) is important when the federal government seeks to prohibit nonregistrants from receiving federal student aid (see Section 4.2.2). The Communications Act of 1934, as amended (47 U.S.C. §151 *et seq.*), is important when a postsecondary institution seeks or holds a Federal Communications Commission license to operate an instructional television channel or other broadcasting license. Even the federal election laws may affect campus activities, since the Federal Elections Commission has proposed a ban on campaigning on college campuses.

Furthermore, many of the targets of federal regulation are also regulated by state law. The interplay between state and federal law can be complex and, occasionally, divisive. For example, public institutions in states that have banned discrimination on the basis of sexual orientation face a dilemma when military recruiters ask to conduct their activities on campus (see generally Comment, "Exclusion of Military Recruiters from Public School Campuses: The Case Against Federal Preemption," 39 *UCLA L. Rev.* 941 (1992)). The sections following can only hint at the scope and complexity of regulation in these areas; the assistance of expert counsel is recommended if issues arise in these or related areas.

12.1.2. Fair Labor Standards Act

The Fair Labor Standards Act (FLSA) (29 U.S.C. §201 *et seq.*) establishes the minimum hourly wage and the piecework rates as well as overtime pay requirements for certain nonsupervisory employees. The law does not apply to independent contractors. The law also requires that records be kept of the hours worked by nonexempt employees and the compensation paid therefor.

The FLSA is enforced by the Wage and Hour Division of the U.S. Department of Labor; no private right of action is available. The secretary of labor has two years from the date of the violation to file an enforcement action, but the statute provides that if the violation is "willful," the limitations period is extended to three years (29 U.S.C. §255(a)). A violation is "willful" if the employer "knew or showed reckless disregard for the matter of whether its conduct was prohibited by the FLSA" (*McLaughlin v. Richland Shoe Co.*, 486 U.S. 128 (1988)).

In situations where an applicable state law establishes a minimum wage rate that conflicts with the federal standard, the higher rate must prevail (29 U.S.C. §218).

The FLSA issue most pertinent to student affairs professionals concerns the status of student assistants who serve in a capacity such as residence hall adviser. In *Marshall v. Regis Educational Corp.*, 666 F.2d 1324 (10th Cir. 1981), the secretary of labor contended that the college's student residence hall assistants (RAs) were "employees" within the meaning of the Act and therefore must be paid the prescribed minimum wage. The college argued that its RAs were not employees and that, even if they were, application of the Act to these RAs would violate the college's academic freedom protected by the First Amendment. Affirming the district court, the appellate court accepted the college's first argument and declined to consider the second. The court's opinion focuses on the unique circumstances of academic life:

> RAs resided in the dormitories where they assisted the residence directors and actively participated in the development and implementation of programs designed to enhance the quality of resident-hall living.
>
> Although RAs did not work a specified number of hours per day, they were generally available in the halls for an estimated twenty hours a week. In order to keep their status as RAs they were required to maintain a specified grade point average. In exchange for the performance of these duties, RAs received a reduced rate on their rooms, the use of a free telephone, and a $1,000 tuition credit. . . .
>
> The government contends that RAs were "employees" because they received compensation and the college enjoyed an immediate economic benefit from their services. The government emphasizes that RAs displaced employees whom Regis would otherwise have been required to hire. Regis counters that the primary purpose of the RA program was educational, that RAs at Regis were not "employees," but student recipients of financial aid. The college rejects the argument that RAs displace other employees, stressing that the peer counseling and educational aspects of the resident assistant program would be lost if it were operated without students. . . . In *Rutherford Food Corp. v. McComb*, 331 U.S. 722 (1947), . . . the Supreme Court declared that the determination of employment

under the FLSA ought not depend on isolated factors but upon the "circumstances of the whole activity" (331 U.S. at 730). This test is controlling in the case at bar.

Our holding that RAs are not employees does not require the conclusion that no student working at the college would be within the scope of the FLSA. No such inference should be drawn. There are undoubtedly campus positions which can be filled by students and which require compliance with the FLSA. Students working in the bookstore selling books, working with maintenance, painting walls, etc., could arguably be "employees." . . .

The record shows that student athletes who receive tuition grants are required to maintain a specified academic average and to fulfill certain duties with respect to training programs and to participate in sports events on campus; student leaders in the student government associations are similarly situated. Selected student leaders have specified duties and responsibilities and receive tuition credits. . . .

We agree with the district court (considering the totality of the circumstances) in finding that RAs at Regis were legally indistinguishable from athletes and leaders in student government who received financial aid. We therefore hold that the RAs at Regis College were not "employees" within the meaning of the Act, but student recipients of financial aid [666 F.2d at 1326–28].

In *Alabama A&M University v. King,* 1 Wage and Hour Cases 2d 1608 (Ala. Ct. Civ. App. 1994), however, the court held that residence hall counselors at Alabama A&M are employees and also ruled that they are eligible for overtime payments if they work more than forty hours per week.

12.1.3. Employment Discrimination Laws

Aside from the nondiscrimination requirements that it imposes as conditions on federal spending (see Section 12.4), the federal government also directly regulates employment discrimination under several other statutes. Primary among them is Title VII of the Civil Rights Act of 1964 (42 U.S.C. §2000e *et seq.*), as amended by the Civil Rights Act of 1991. These statutes are discussed briefly in Section 2.2.2 of this volume.

Courts have often been deferential to higher education institutions when considering employment discrimination claims brought against them. Usually, however, courts have displayed this deference in cases where the institution's refusal to hire, renew, or tenure a faculty member is alleged to be discriminatory. In such cases, the reluctance of courts to intervene may stem from a recognition of the limits of their competence to second-guess decisions resulting from a peer review process that emphasizes subjective evaluation of scholarly work or teaching ability. Such considerations are usually absent in cases brought by administrators or staff personnel in positions without faculty status. Since the justifications for according deference to higher education institutions do not apply with the same force to these nonfaculty cases, courts may be more activist in applying federal nondiscrimination laws to them.

In addition to the differing degrees of deference, employment decisions regarding administrators and staff may raise different types of issues under federal nondiscrimination laws than do employment decisions regarding faculty. Two cases, both decided under the Age Discrimination in Employment Act, illustrate two such issues. In *EEOC v. University of Texas Health Science Center*, 710 F.2d 1091 (5th Cir. 1983), the court considered the ADEA's application to a campus security force. The plaintiff had been refused employment because he exceeded the force's maximum hiring age of forty-five. The center argued that age was a bona fide occupational qualification (BFOQ) for the position of security officer, not subject to the Act's prohibition, because the job demanded an exceptional level of physical fitness. The court held in favor of the center—but only because it was able to present "consistent testimony at trial that physical strength, agility, and stamina are important to the training and performance of campus policemen." In *EEOC v. Board of Trustees of Wayne County Community College*, 723 F.2d 509 (6th Cir. 1983), the court considered the applicability, to a community college president, of an ADEA provision excluding high-level public appointees in policy-making positions from the Act's protections. The EEOC argued that, because the college's board of trustees exercised broad policy-making powers, the president did not fall within the exclusion and was therefore protected by the Act. The court rejected this argument, reasoning that "shared, overlapping, and complementary authority [is] no less capable of being denominated policy making than is exclusive authority."

Federal law also prohibits discrimination against individuals on the basis of eligibility for military service and provides reemployment rights for individuals who must leave their jobs to serve on active duty in the military. The Veterans Readjustment Benefits Act (Pub. L. No. 89–358 (1966)), amended by the Vietnam Era Veterans' Readjustment Assistance Act of 1974 (Pub. L. No. 93–508, codified at 38 U.S.C. §4212 *et seq.*), requires that employers who receive $10,000 or more in federal contracts "shall take affirmative action to employ and advance in employment qualified special disabled veterans and veterans of the Vietnam era," 38 U.S.C. sec. 4212(a). Another law, first enacted in 1954 and modified, retitled, and recodified several times since then, is now entitled "Employment and Reemployment Rights of Members of the Uniformed Services" (38 U.S.C. 4301 *et seq.*). This law requires that all employers (defined as "any person, institution, organization, or other entity that pays salary or wages for work performed . . ." as well as the state and federal governments) 38 U.S.C. sec. 4303(4) (A) (I)) may not discriminate against any applicant or employee who has performed or has an obligation to perform military service, and employers to restore individuals covered by these laws to their previous position or a similar one unless the employer can demonstrate that such restoration is impossible or unreasonable. Amendments added in 1991 (Pub. L. No. 102–25) require the employer to retrain returning veterans for their previous positions, if necessary; the amendments also regulate the provision of employer-offered health insurance for such individuals. In *King v. St. Vincent's Hospital,* 112 S. Ct. 570 (1991), the U.S. Supreme Court ruled unanimously that the Veterans' Reemployment Rights Act does not limit the amount of time individuals may serve on active duty before they lose the right to be restored to their former position; there is no requirement that the length of active duty be "reasonable," and reemployment rights apparently do not expire as long as there is a position available for the veterans and they are qualified or are able to become requalified. However, Congress amended this law in 1994 to limit the reinstatement protections to those veterans absent from their jobs for five years or less (38 U.S.C. sec. 4312, added by P.L. 103–353, 108 Stat. 3153, October 13, 1994).

Sexual harassment (discussed briefly in Section 2.2.2) can also pose a serious problem for nonfaculty employees and students (harassment of students is discussed in Sections 6.2 and 12.4.3). Even if the harasser is not a university employee, the university may face legal liability if the harassment can be linked to the victim's job responsibilities. The development of the "reasonable woman" standard (*Ellison v. Brady,* 924 F.2d 872 (9th Cir. 1991)) and the remedies of compensatory and punitive damages now available under the Civil Rights Act of 1991 make it more likely that charges of sexual harassment will be filed; the right to a jury trial and recent judicial willingness to hold employers strictly accountable for proven harassment suggest that institutions should educate their staff and faculty about this issue and pursue complaints with the same attention they devote to other allegedly illegal behavior.

12.1.4. Immigration Laws

Many citizens of foreign countries come to the United States to study, teach, lecture, or do research at American higher education institutions. The conditions under which such foreign nationals may enter and remain in the United States are governed by a complex set of federal statutes codified in Title 8 of the *United States Code* and by regulations promulgated and administered primarily by the U.S. Department of State and the Immigration and Naturalization Service (INS) of the U.S. Department of Justice. The statutes and regulations establish numerous categories and subcategories for aliens entering the United States, with differing eligibility requirements and conditions of stay attaching to each.

Under the Immigration and Nationality Act and its various amendments (codified at 8 U.S.C. §1101 *et seq.*), aliens may enter the United States either as immigrants or as nonimmigrants. Immigrants are admitted for permanent residence in the country (resident aliens). Nonimmigrants are admitted only for limited time periods to engage in narrowly defined types of activities (nonresident aliens).

Eligibility for the immigrant class is subject to various numerical limitations and various priorities or preferences for certain categories of aliens (8 U.S.C. §§1151–1159). The nonimmigrant class is usually not limited numerically, but it is subdivided into eighteen specific categories (A through R), which define, and thus serve to limit, eligibility for nonimmigrant status. Of the two classes, the nonimmigrant is the greater source of problems for postsecondary institutions and is the focus for the remainder of this section.

Through a series of foreign policy crises—beginning with the Iranian crisis in 1979–80, when the federal government imposed new restrictions on foreign students from Iran—higher education institutions have been sensitized anew to immigration law's potential impact on the campuses. Aside from the need to adapt to such political crises, higher education institutions have a general interest in knowing the immigration status of each foreign national whom they enroll as a student, hire for a staff or faculty position, or invite to the campus as a temporary guest, and in helping these foreign nationals adapt to this country and maintain their legal status for the term of their stay. In these situations, administrators and counsel will need a sound grasp of the federal laws and regulations governing immigration.

The immigration status of foreign students has been of increasing concern to higher education as the proportion of applicants and students from foreign countries has grown. In 1980, there were approximately 305,000 nonresident alien students on American campuses. Over the decade, this figure grew steadily, reaching 397,000 nonresident alien students in 1990 (*Digest of Education Statistics* (U.S. National Center for Education Statistics, 1992), 174). (For further statistical data, see the Institute of International Education's comprehensive annual census of foreign students, published under the title *Open Doors*.)

In recent years, three new laws passed by Congress have extensively revised the Immigration and Nationality Act of 1952: the Immigration Reform and Control Act of 1986 (Pub. L. No. 99–603, 100 Stat. 3359 (1986)) (IRCA); the Immigration Act of 1990 (Pub. L. No. 101–649, 104 Stat. 4978 (1990)) (IMMACT '90); and the Miscellaneous and Technical Immigration and Naturalization Amendments of 1991 (Pub. L. No. 102–232, 105 Stat. 1733 (1991)) (MTINA). IRCA requires employers to verify that all individuals hired after November 6, 1982, are legally entitled to work in the United States. The law provides penalties for noncompliance and establishes an opportunity for all undocumented aliens who entered the United States before January 1, 1982, to apply for legalization without fear of deportation (8 U.S.C. §§1324a and 1324b). IRCA also includes important new protections against discrimination on the basis of alienage and national origin. The 1990 Act is the most comprehensive of the new laws. It amends the preference system for admission into the United States, revises the nonimmigrant categories, and repeals certain exclusions from admission. MTINA, as its name implies, further refines the changes made by the 1990 Act.

After the new legislation, nonimmigrant students continue to qualify for admission to the United States under one of three categories: "academic" student (8 U.S.C. §1101(a)(15)(F)), "vocational" or "nonacademic" student (8 U.S.C. §1101(a)(15)(M)), or "exchange visitor" (8 U.S.C. §1101(a)(15)(J)). In each category, the statute provides that the "alien spouse and minor children" of the student may also qualify for admission "if accompanying him or following to join him."

The first of the three student categories is for aliens in the United States "temporarily and solely for the purpose of pursuing [a full] course of study at an established college, university, seminary, conservatory, . . . or other academic institution or in a language training program" (8 U.S.C. §1101(a)(15)(F)(i)). The second category is for aliens in the United States "temporarily and solely for the purpose of pursuing a full course of study at an established vocational or other recognized nonacademic institution (other than a language training program)" (8 U.S.C. §1101(a)(15)(M)(i)). The former category is called "F-l" and the included students are "F-1's"; the latter category is called "M-1" and the students are "M-1's." The spouses and children of these students are called "F-2's" and "M-2's," respectively. The third category, exchange visitor, is known as the "J" category. It includes any alien (and the family of any alien) "who is a bona fide student, scholar, trainee, teacher, professor, research assistant, specialist, or leader in a field of specialized knowledge or skill, or other person of similar description, who is coming temporarily to the United States as a participant in a program designated by the Director of the United States Information Agency, for the purpose of teaching, instructing or lecturing, studying, observing, conducting research, consulting, demonstrating special skills, or receiving training" (8 U.S.C. §1101(a)(15)(J)). Exchange visitors who will attend medical school, and the institutions they will attend, are subject to additional requirements under 8 U.S.C. §1182(j). Another provision of the statute, 8 U.S.C. §1182(e), establishes the conditions under which an alien who has been an exchange visitor may remain in or return to the United States, after returning to his or her country of nationality, for purposes of employment.

The Department of State's role in regulating foreign students is shaped by its power to grant or deny visas to persons applying to enter the United States. Consular officials verify whether an applicant alien has met the requirements under one of the pertinent statutory categories and the corresponding requirements established by State Department regulations. The State Department's regulations for academic and nonacademic or vocational student visas are in 22 C.F.R. §41.61. Requirements for exchange visitor status are in 22 C.F.R. §41.62.

The Immigration and Naturalization Service has authority to approve the schools that foreign students may attend and for which they may obtain F-1 or M-1 visas from the State Department (8 C.F.R. §214.3). The INS is also responsible for ensuring that foreign students do not violate the conditions of their visas once they enter the United States. In particular, the INS must determine that holders of F–1 and M–1 student visas are making satisfactory progress toward the degree or other academic objective they are pursuing. The regulations under which the INS fulfills this responsibility are now located in 8 C.F.R. §214.2(f) for academic students and 8 C.F.R. §214.2(m) for vocational students. These regulations specify the periods of time for which foreign students may be admitted into the country and the circumstances that will constitute a "full course of study." In addition, the regulations establish the ground rules for on-campus employment of foreign students, off-campus employment (much more restricted than on-campus employment), transfers to another school, temporary absences from the country, and extensions of stay beyond the period of initial admission. Another regulation, 8 C.F.R. §248, establishes the ground rules for changing nonimmigrant status from a student category to a nonstudent category and vice versa. There are substantial differences in the regulatory provisions applicable to F–1 students and those applicable to M–1's.

A third federal government agency, the United States Information Agency, also has responsibilities regarding foreign students. It operates the exchange visitor program (see 22 C.F.R. §514.1 *et seq.*). This agency's regulations implementing the program are codified in 22 C.F.R. Part 514. Section 514.4(a) defines the status of "student" for purposes of these regulations. Sections 514.20 to 514.23 govern the roles of postsecondary institutions, professors, research scholars, trainees, and students that participate in exchange visitor programs.

In addition to its impact on enrollment of foreign students, immigration law also circumscribes the postsecondary institution's decisions on employing aliens in staff or faculty positions and inviting aliens to campus to lecture or otherwise participate in campus life. Again, three nonimmigrant categories are particularly important: "exchange visitor" (8 U.S.C. §1101(a)(15)(J)), "temporary visitor" (8 U.S.C. §1101(a)(15)(B)), and "temporary worker" (8 U.S.C. §1101(a)(15)(H)). For the first and third, but not the second, of these categories, the statute also provides that the "alien spouse and minor children" of the alien may qualify for admission "if accompanying him or following to join him."

The first category, exchange visitor, is the "J" category already discussed with reference to students. The statutory definition, quoted earlier, is broad enough to include some types of employees as well. The second or "B" category is for aliens "visiting the United States temporarily for business or temporarily for pleasure," except those "coming for the purpose of study or of performing skilled or unskilled labor or as a representative of foreign press, radio, film, or other foreign information media coming to engage in such vocation" (8 U.S.C. §1101a)(15) (B)). Visitors for business are B–1's, and visitors for pleasure are B–2's.

After IMMACT '90 and MTINA, the third, or "H," category includes three substantially revised subcategories of temporary alien workers: nurses, fashion models, and specialized workers (H–1's); other workers who will "perform temporary service or labor" when such services or labor are agricultural in nature or when "unemployed persons capable of performing such service or labor cannot be found in this country" (H–2's); and workers who will act as trainees (H–3's) (8 U.S.C. §1101(a)(15)(H)(i)-(iii)). For each subcategory, the statute prescribes more limited rules for alien medical school graduates.

The Immigration Act of 1990 also created three new categories that are important to higher education institutions. The "O" visa is for nonimmigrant visitors who have extraordinary ability in the areas of arts, sciences, education, business, or athletics and are to be employed for a specific project or event such as an academic-year appointment or a lecture tour (8 U.S.C. §1101(a)(15)(O)). The "P" visa is for performing artists and (after 1991, when MTINA was enacted) athletes at an internationally recognized level of performance who seek to enter the United States as nonimmigrant visitors to perform, teach, or coach (8 U.S.C. §1101(a)(15)(P)). The "Q" visa is designated for international cultural exchange visitors "coming temporarily (for a period not to exceed fifteen months) to the United States as a participant in an international cultural exchange program approved by the attorney general for the purpose of providing practical training, employment, and the sharing of the history, culture, and traditions of the country of the alien's nationality" (8 U.S.C. §1101(a)(15)(Q)).

The INS publishes a guide entitled *Handbook for Employers* (INS Pub. No. M–274) that explains the law and regulations regarding visitors and foreign workers, and directs employers to the correct forms. See also R. Hopper, "College Hiring After the Immigration Act of 1990—Immigrant Employment Categories and Procedures," IHELG Monograph 91–9 (Institute for Higher Education Law and Governance, University of Houston, 1991).

The State Department and the INS have the same authority over these employment and visitor categories as they do over the foreign student categories. Pertinent State Department regulations are in 22 C.F.R. §41.31 (temporary visitors) and 22 C.F.R. §41.53 (temporary workers and trainees). Pertinent INS regulations are in 8 C.F.R. §214.2(b) (temporary visitors) and 8 C.F.R. §214.2(h) (temporary workers).

The federal government may exclude certain classes of aliens, even though they fit within one of the immigrant or nonimmigrant categories. The Immigration Act of 1990 radically revised the classes of excludable aliens, most notably eliminating the exclusions based on publications, teachings, affiliations, and beliefs incompatible with our system of government. The exclusions based on sexual behavior and mental disabilities were also eliminated. The health, crime, and security-related grounds for exclusion were revised to reflect growing societal concerns such as AIDS, illicit drug use, and terrorist activities. The ideology-based exclusions were also amended. Although the statute still bars aliens who are members of communist or totalitarian parties, the attorney general may now grant exceptions when membership was involuntary or when membership was terminated a certain length of time prior to application for admission.

As amended by IMMACT '90, Section 1182 of Title 8 (8 U.S.C. §1182) now codifies the classes of aliens subject to exclusion. Subsections (a)(1) and (a)(3)(A), (C), and (D) have particular application to postsecondary education. Section 1182(a)(1) excludes certain aliens from admission into the United States on health-related grounds. Generally, an alien is inadmissible if his or her physical or mental health poses a threat to society or if he or she has a communicable disease of public health significance. In January 1991, the Department of Health and Human Services (HHS) proposed that infectious tuberculosis be the only disease on the list, thereby eliminating all sexually transmitted diseases (STDs), including acquired immune deficiency syndrome (AIDS) (Notice of Proposed Rulemaking, 56 Fed. Reg. 2486 (January 23, 1991)). After receiving over 40,000 comments about this notice, HHS stayed any changes to the list pending further review (Interim Final Rule, 56 Fed. Reg. 25000 (May 31, 1991)), thus leaving intact for the time being the list published at 42 C.F.R. §34.2.

Section 1182(a)(3)(A) permits exclusion of aliens "who a consular officer or the Attorney General knows, or has reasonable ground to believe, seeks to enter the United States to engage solely, principally, or incidentally in . . . any unlawful activity." Section 1182(a)(3)(D) excludes aliens affiliated with a communist or totalitarian group unless the association was involuntary or has terminated (as discussed above). Section 1182(a)(3)(C) permits exclusion of aliens whom "the Secretary of State has reasonable ground to believe would have potentially serious adverse foreign policy consequences for the United States." There are, however, two important exceptions to this exclusion. One is for foreign officials (§1182(a)(3)(c)(ii)). The other is for aliens whose "past, current, or expected beliefs, statements, or associations" might otherwise raise foreign policy concerns but are "lawful within the United States" (§1182(a)(3)(c)(iii)). The second exception may be overridden "if the Secretary of State personally determines that the alien's admission would compromise a compelling United States foreign policy interest."

The ideology-based exclusions were the subject of a major U.S. Supreme Court case involving higher education. *Kleindienst v. Mandel*, 408 U.S. 753 (1976), concerned a Belgian citizen (Mandel) who was editor of a Belgian Left Socialist weekly and had authored a two-volume work entitled *Marxist Economic Theory*. In 1969, he applied for a nonimmigrant visa to enter the United States to give an address at Stanford University. When Mandel's planned visit became known, other higher education institutions invited him to address their groups. The theme of one conference was to be "Revolutionary Strategy in Imperialist Countries." The American Consulate in Brussels refused Mandel a visa because, among other reasons, his published views rendered him inadmissible under two provisions covering writings on communism and totalitarianism (8 U.S.C. §§1182(a)(28)(D) and 1182(a)(28)(G)(v), since repealed by IMMACT '90, as discussed above). Although the State Department subsequently did recommend that Mandel be admitted, the INS, acting on behalf of the attorney general, denied temporary admission. Mandel then brought suit along with eight other plaintiffs, all of whom were United States citizens and university professors in various social science fields. These plaintiffs asserted that their plans to participate with Mandel in various public forums had been disrupted by the visa denial. Thus, the plaintiffs argued, their First Amendment right to receive information had been abridged.

The Court held that Congress had plenary authority to enact legislation excluding aliens with certain political affiliations and beliefs; that the State Department and the attorney general's office acted within this authority in excluding Mandel; that Mandel, as an unadmitted and nonresident alien, had no constitutional right of entry to the United States but that the remaining plaintiffs did possess First Amendment rights to receive information from Mandel; and that Congress's authority to exclude aliens and the Executive's discretion in exercising this authority prevailed over the First Amendment claims. Displaying extensive deference to congressional and Executive judgments regarding aliens, the Court stated it would uphold exclusion policies if they were supported by a "facially legitimate and bona fide reason" (408 U.S. at 769–70). The Court made it clear that it was not addressing First Amendment issues but only the validity of the State Department's exclusion policies.

The *Mandel* case and other controversies (see, for example, *Abourezk v. Reagan*, 785 F.2d 1043 (D.C. Cir. 1986)) underscore the practical impact of congressional power and Executive discretion to regulate the entry of foreign visitors. Administrators or faculty members who invite foreign visitors to their campuses or to their professional meetings should be sensitive to this power and discretion, under which the federal government may totally exclude certain scholars from visiting the United States or drastically curtail their activities when here. Administrators and faculty should also take careful note, however, of the new freedom-of-expression protections (8 U.S.C. §1182(a)(3)(c)(iii)) created by IMMACT '90 that would now statutorily protect foreign scholars and journalists such as the plaintiff in *Kleindienst v. Mandel*.

Similarly, administrators should be aware that the federal government's treatment of visitors, as well as other foreign nationals within or seeking to enter the United States, may depend on contemporary trends in U.S. foreign policy. Two pieces of legislation in 1992 illustrate the use of immigration laws to effectuate current foreign policy goals. The Soviet Scientists Immigration Act of 1992 (Pub. L. No. 102–509, 106 Stat. 3316, codified at 8 U.S.C. §1153) allows admission into the United States of highly specialized scientists of the independent states of the former Soviet Union and the Baltic States. Interim rules related to this law can be found at 58 Fed. Reg. 30699 (1993). The Chinese Student Protection Act of 1992 (Pub. L. No. 102–404, 106 Stat. 1969, codified at 8 U.S.C. §1255), passed in response to the Tiananmen Square incident, allows Chinese nationals already admitted into this country to automatically adjust status under the immigration laws to lawful permanent resident status. Interim rules may be found at 58 Fed. Reg. 35832 (1993).

A case arising from the Iranian crisis also graphically illustrates the intertwining of foreign policy crises and immigration law. *Narenji v. Civiletti*, 617 F.2d 745 (D.C. Cir. 1979), arose as a challenge to presidential actions in the wake of the seizure of the United States Embassy in Iran. As part of the Executive's response to the crisis, the attorney general's office published a regulation governing nonimmigrant students from Iran residing in the United States. The regulation required all Iranian nonimmigrant postsecondary students to report to a local INS office or campus representative to "provide information as to residence and maintenance of nonimmigrant status" (617 F.2d at 746). Failure to comply with the regulation subjected the student to deportation proceedings. Iranian students challenged this regulation as both beyond the scope of the attorney general's authority and violative of the constitutional guarantee of equal protection. The trial court agreed in a lengthy opinion (481 F. Supp. 1132 (D.D.C. 1979)), but the U.S. Court of Appeals reversed, holding that the attorney general possessed statutory authority to act as he did. It also held that Congress and the Executive have broad discretion to draw distinctions on the basis of nationality when dealing with immigration matters, and courts will sustain these distinctions unless they are found to be totally irrational. Applying this "rational basis" test to the challenged regulation, the appellate court found that it was rationally related to the Executive's efforts to resolve the crisis generated by the embassy takeover.

As the foregoing discussion indicates, the immigration laws present a host of thorny problems for postsecondary administrators. Some of the questions that arise will be unforeseeable. Some will be dependent on the conduct of foreign affairs. Others will require detailed knowledge of the law's technicalities. Institutions that have been or expect to be confronted by a substantial number of immigration problems should consider having on staff an administrator or legal counsel (or both) knowledgeable about INS and State Department requirements and the paperwork necessary for handling this complex regulatory area.

12.1.5. Copyright Laws

12.1.5.1. Overview. The basis for all copyright law is Article I, Section 8, Clause 8 of the U.S. Constitution, which authorizes Congress "to promote the progress of science and useful arts, by securing for limited times to authors and inventors the exclusive right to their respective writings and discoveries." In 1976, after many years of effort inside and outside government, Congress revised the federal copyright law. Effective as of January 1, 1978, the General Revision of the Copyright Law (17 U.S.C. §101 *et seq.*) has particular relevance to educational institutions, because it specifies what kinds of copying of copyrighted materials may be done for teaching and scholarship. This question, previously governed by the judicially created "fair use" doctrine, is now governed by the codification of that doctrine in Section 107 of the Act. Another section that is particularly important to educational institutions, Section 108, deals with copying by libraries and archives. And a third pertinent section, Section 117 (added in 1980; 94 Stat. 3028), deals with copying of computer programs.

In 1990, Congress passed the Copyright Remedy Clarification Act (Pub. L. No. 101–553, 104 Stat. 2749), which allows copyright holders to collect damages from public colleges and universities. Prior to the amendment, several federal appellate courts had ruled that the Eleventh Amendment prohibited the application of the Copyright Act's damages provisions to state agencies. The enforceability of this law is unclear, however, because the U.S. Supreme Court ruled in *Seminole Tribe of Florida v. Florida,* 116 S. Ct. 1114 (1996), that state agencies in states that had not waived sovereign immunity against federal court litigation could not be sued by private parties. Since federal copyright law is the exclusive remedy for copyright violations, *Seminole* suggests that public colleges and universities that are protected by the sovereign immunity doctrine (see Section 2.3.3) may be immune from this litigation. Administrators should consult counsel for further developments in this regard.

Another series of amendments to the copyright law also were enacted in 1990. These amendments (the Visual Artists' Rights Act of 1990 (104 Stat. 5128), the Architectural Works Copyright Protection Act of 1990 (104 Stat. 5133), and the Computer Software Rental Amendments Act of 1990 (104 Stat. 5134)) are part of the Judicial Improvements Act (Pub. L. No. 101–650). These Acts extend copyright protection to a wider array of works than were previously protected. The Visual Artists Rights Act amends Section 101 of 17 U.S.C. by adding visual art productions to the list of objects that receive copyright protection; it also lists objects excluded from the category of protected "visual arts." This law took effect on June 1, 1990. The Architectural Works Copyright Protection Act of 1990 adds architectural works as a category of protection under Section 101 of Title 17; it took effect on December 1, 1990. The Computer Software Rental Amendments Act of 1990 amends Section 109(b) of Title 17, and prohibits the owner of a record, tape, or software program from lending, selling, or renting these for direct or indirect commercial advantage; this law also took effect on December 1, 1990.

12.1.5.2. The fair use doctrine. Section 107 of the Act states that "the fair use of a copyrighted work . . . for purposes such as criticism, comment, news reporting, teaching (including multiple copies for classroom use), scholarship, or research is not an infringement of copyright." The section lists four factors that one must consider in determining whether a particular "use" is "fair": "(1) the purpose and character of the use, including whether such use is of a commercial nature or is for nonprofit educational purposes; (2) the nature of the copyrighted work; (3) the amount and substantiality of the portion used in relation to the copyrighted work as a whole; and (4) the effect of the use upon the potential market for or value of the copyrighted work."

Application of these rather vague standards to individual cases is left to the courts. Some guidance on their meaning may be found, however, in a document included in the legislative history of the revised Copyright Act: the "Agreement on Guidelines for Classroom Copying in Not-for-Profit Educational Institutions" (in H.R. Rep. No. 94–1476, 94th Cong., 2d Sess. (1976)). A second document in the legislative history, the "Guidelines for the Proviso of Subsection 108(g)(2)" (Conf. Rep. No. 94–1733, 94th Cong., 2d Sess. (1976)), provides comparable guidance on the provision within Section 108 dealing with copying for purposes of interlibrary loans. The "Guidelines for Classroom Copying" were adopted by thirty-eight educational organizations and the publishing industry to set minimum standards of educational fair use under Section 107 of the Act. Guidelines are established for "Single Copying for Teaching" (for example, a chapter from a book may be copied for the individual teacher's use in scholarly research, class preparation, or teaching) as well as for "Multiple Copies for Classroom Use" (for example, one copy per pupil in one course may be made, provided that the copying meets several tests; these tests, set out in the House Report, concern the brevity of the excerpt to be copied, the spontaneity of the use, and the cumulative effect of multiple copying in classes within the institution).

The guidelines were cited by a federal appeals court in *Marcus v. Rowley*, 695 F.2d 1171 (9th Cir. 1983). The case involved a public school teacher who reproduced approximately half of a copyrighted booklet and included it in course materials she distributed to her students at no charge. The court ruled that the teacher's use of the copyrighted material did not constitute fair use. The opinion emphasizes that a person need not have sold or profited from copying in order to violate the Copyright Act: "The first factor to be considered in determining the applicability of the doctrine of fair use is the purpose and character of the use, and specifically whether the use is of a commercial nature or is for a nonprofit educational purpose. . . . Nevertheless, a finding of a nonprofit educational purpose does not automatically compel a finding of fair use."

In another copyright case, *Addison-Wesley Publishing Co. v. New York University,* filed in December 1982 in federal district court (Civil Action No. 82 Civ. 8333, S.D.N.Y.), the Association of American Publishers coordinated a suit on behalf of nine publishing companies against NYU, nine of its faculty members, and a photocopying shop near the campus. The plaintiffs' complaint listed thirteen instances of alleged unlawful photocopying and sought a permanent injunction against further unlawful copying and an award of damages for the copyright owners. The suit was reportedly the first of its kind involving a university and its faculty members.

In April 1983, the parties reached an out-of-court settlement of the case. In return for the plaintiffs' withdrawal of their claims, NYU agreed to: adopt and implement a copyright policy corresponding to the "Guidelines for Classroom Copying"; publish its policy in the faculty handbook and publicize it to the faculty periodically by other means; post notices about its copyright policy at all campus copying facilities; and investigate alleged incidents of copyright violation and take appropriate action against faculty members "consistent with remedial and disciplinary actions taken in respect of violations of other university policies." The full texts of the settlement and of the NYU photocopying policy were published in 13 *Coll. Law Dig.* 258, printed in *West's Educ. Law Rptr.*, June 2, 1983 (Special NACUA Pamphlet). (See also D. Edwards, "University of North Carolina Copyright Guidelines on Photocopying," 14 *Coll. Law Dig.* 121, printed in *West's Educ. Law Rptr.*, Jan. 12, 1984 (Special NACUA Pamphlet), which critiques the NYU settlement and provides guidelines to help faculty and staff comply with the copyright law.)

The first higher education copyright case resulting in a judicial opinion is *Basic Books v. Kinko's Graphics Corp.*, 758 F. Supp. 1522 (S.D.N.Y. 1991). A group of publishers brought a copyright infringement action against a chain of copying shops for copying excerpts from their books without permission, compiling those excerpts into packets, and selling them to college students. Kinko's argued that its actions fit within the "fair use" doctrine of Section 107 of the Copyright Act. According to the court, "The search for a coherent, predictable interpretation applicable to all cases remains elusive. This is so particularly because any common law interpretation proceeds on a case-by-case basis" (758 F. Supp at 1530).

Using the four factors in the statute, as well as the "Agreement on Guidelines" promulgated as part of the NYU settlement, the court ruled that (1) Kinko's was merely repackaging the material for its own commercial purposes; (2) the material in the books was factual (which would suggest a lower level of protection under the fair use doctrine); (3) Kinko's had copied a substantial proportion of the work, and whether the book was out of print or not was irrelevant because copyright fees are the only "profits" available to the publisher once the book is unavailable. The court also found that even one chapter is a "substantial" portion if that chapter is meant to stand alone; and (4) Kinko's copying reduced the market for textbooks. Furthermore, the court ruled that, for an entire compilation to avoid violating the Act, *each* item in the compilation must pass the fair use test. The judge awarded the plaintiffs $510,000 in statutory damages plus legal fees. Kinko's decided not to appeal the decision, and settled the case in October 1991 for $1.875 million in combined damages and legal fees.

The Association of American Publishers "has mapped out a long-range program to monitor and seek compliance with the copyright law" ("Publishers Welcome Agreement Ending Kinko's Suit," reprinted in 22 *Coll. Law Dig.* 74 (Nov. 7, 1991)). Given the potential cost of such litigation, seeking permission to copy or use copyrighted material is imperative. Individuals seeking permission may find useful the AAP's publication, "How to Request Copyright Permissions" (reprinted in 22 *Coll. Law Dig.* 75 (Nov. 7, 1991)), as well as "Use of Photocopied Anthologies for Courses Snarled by Delays and Costs of Copyright-Permission Process," *Chron. Higher Educ.*, Sept. 11, 1991, A19. The latter article describes the Copyright Clearance Center that will, for a modest fee, handle copyright requests for over 250 publishers.

The existence of the Copyright Clearance Center may make it difficult for defendants in copyright infringement cases to argue that making copies without paying a royalty was justified. In *American Geophysical Union v. Texaco, Inc.*, 802 F. Supp. 1 (S.D.N.Y. 1992), a federal trial judge found that Texaco had infringed the copyrights of several scientific journals by making multiple copies of scientific articles for its scientists and researchers to keep in their files. The judge noted that Texaco could have obtained a license that permits unlimited copying of the journals affiliated with the Copyright Clearance Center, and found that Texaco's actions violated three elements of the fair use test. The U.S. Court of Appeals for the Second Circuit affirmed this holding (60 F.3d 913 (2d Cir. 1994)).

Copyright laws also apply to the authors of published works. Unless authors specifically retain the copyright, they must seek permission from the copyright holder (usually the publisher) to reproduce their own material. For a discussion of the fair use doctrine in the higher education context, see R. Kasunic, "Fair Use and the Educator's Right to Photocopy Copyrighted Material for Classroom Use," 19 *J. Coll. & Univ. Law* 271 (1993).

12.1.5.3. Use of unpublished material. The copyright laws cover unpublished as well as published material, a fact that many faculty (and administrators) are unaware of. And although the unauthorized use of unpublished material would ordinarily result in liability for the researcher rather than the institution, the college or university could face liability if the research were funded by an external grant made to the institution or if the faculty member argued that the institution shared liability for some other reason.

In a pair of cases, a federal appeals court ruled that unpublished material enjoys the same protection as published material and that the fair use doctrine applies to both types of material. In *New Era Publications International v. Henry Holt and Co.*, 873 F.2d 576 (2d Cir. 1989), the publishing company that owns the rights to the unpublished papers of L. Ron Hubbard, who founded the Church of Scientology, sued Henry Holt and Company, which was about to publish *Bare-Faced Messiah*, Russell Miller's biography of Hubbard. Miller had quoted from Hubbard's unpublished writings, and New Era alleged that doing so without its permission violated the Act. Although the court refused to stop publication of the book, the majority ruled that the Act had been infringed. The opinion says that the fair use doctrine bars virtually all use of unpublished sources without permission of the copyright holder.

Two years earlier, judges in the same circuit upheld a trial judge's ruling that Random House not publish a biography of J. D. Salinger until the author, Ian Hamilton, had removed all quotations from Salinger's unpublished letters (*Salinger v. Random House*, 811 F.2d 90 (2d Cir. 1987)). Hamilton had quoted from letters to Salinger's correspondents, which they had placed in university archives.

Legal scholars, including one of the Second Circuit judges, have criticized this pair of decisions, saying that privacy law provides an appropriate remedy if the authors of unpublished materials object to their publication and that copyright law was not designed to protect material not intended for publication. Congress reacted to these cases by passing the Copyright Amendments Act in late 1992 (Pub. L. No. 102–492, 106 Stat. 3145). The law amends Section 107 of Title 17 (the fair use doctrine) by adding: "The fact that a work is unpublished shall not itself bar a finding of fair use if such finding is made upon consideration of all the above factors."

12.1.5.4. Other forms of copyright protection. An issue that may not have been contemplated by the drafters of the Copyright Act (and that certainly was not an issue for the framers of the Constitution) is the application of copyright protection to computer software. Unless it has been placed in the public domain, computer software is protected by copyright law (17 U.S.C. §117), and duplication or distribution, even without charge, of copyrighted software violates the law. Both the content and the structure of the software program are protected (see *Whelan Associates, Inc. v. Jaslow Dental Laboratory, Inc.*, 797 F.2d 1222 (3d Cir. 1986). Institutions have entered license agreements with software companies, particularly where multiple copies of software are used or a computer network is in place. For an analysis of institutional liability for copyright violations involving software, see M. Gemignani, "A College's Liability for Unauthorized Copying of Microcomputer Software by Students," 15 *J. Law & Educ.* 421 (1986).

For a useful summary of the fair use doctrine and the application of copyright law to videotapes, software, performances, and music, as well as written material, see T. Hemnes & A. Pyle, *A Guide to Copyright Issues in Higher Education* (National Association of College and University Attorneys, 1991). Advances in computer technology, and the spread of "electrocopying" through computerized databases, prompted Congress to enact amendments entitled "Criminal Penalties for Copyright Infringement" (Pub. L. No. 102–561, 106 Stat. 4233) in 1992. These amendments to the criminal code make certain types of copyright infringement a felony (18 U.S.C. §2319 (b)). They provide that violations of 18 U.S.C. §2319(a) shall result in imprisonment for not more than five years or fines in the amount set forth in the criminal law, or both, if the offense consists of reproduction or distribution or both during any 180-day period of at least ten copies or records of one or more copyrighted works with a retail value of over $2,500. Stiffer penalties are prescribed for second and subsequent violations. The sharing of information gained from computerized databases through interlibrary loan, the circulation of copyrighted material on networked computers, and other dissemination of protected material have resulted in sometimes restrictive contracts between producers of information and institutional libraries or other users. They have also resulted in litigation.

Given the courts' strict interpretation of the fair use doctrine and the opportunities provided by computer networks and other technology for violation of the copyright laws, colleges and universities can expect publishers to pursue their rights aggressively. University counsel can expect more change in this area of copyright law as new technology makes information sharing easier and more difficult to detect through conventional means.

Copyright also applies to music. In 1988, several higher education associations entered an agreement with the American Society of Composers, Authors, and Publishers (ASCAP) and Broadcast Music, Inc. (BMI) on five-year music licenses. Institutions will pay blanket royalty fees for all copyrighted music in the ASCAP/BMI repertory that is publicly performed at their institutions. The agreement is reprinted in 18 *Coll. Law Dig.* 210 (Mar. 31, 1988).

In light of developments in copyright law, postsecondary institutions should thoroughly review their policies and practices on photocopying and other means of reproducing copyrighted works, with special attention to the copying of computer software. Institutions may wish to consider providing faculty and staff with explicit guidelines on the use of copyrighted material, particularly unpublished material, computer software, and music. The institution's copying policy should be published for staff and students as well as faculty members, and a notice apprising users of the policy's existence, and the places where it is published or available for distribution, should be posted at campus photocopying and computer facilities.

12.1.5.5. The "work made for hire" doctrine. Although the Copyright Act's "work made for hire" doctrine has seldom been applied in the higher education context, a Supreme Court decision clarifying the doctrine merits a brief discussion. The "work made for hire" doctrine is an exception to the Act's presumption that the author of a work also holds its copyright. In a "work made for hire," the employer is considered the "author" and owns the copyright unless the parties enter a written agreement that gives the copyright to the employee. A work is made "for hire" if (1) it is done by an employee within the scope of his or her employment, or (2) it is part of a larger work (such as a motion picture, a compilation, a text, or an atlas) and the parties agree in writing that it is made for hire.

In *Community for Creative Non-Violence v. Reid*, 490 U.S. 104 (1989), the Court was asked to decide who owned a statue commissioned by CCNV, an organization devoted to helping homeless people, for display at a Christmas pageant. Both Reid, the sculptor, and CCNV filed competing copyright registrations. The Court decided that the "work made for hire" doctrine did not apply to Reid because he was an independent contractor and not an employee of CCNV. The Court did rule, however, that CCNV might be a "coauthor" because of the suggestions that CCNV employees had made to the sculptor during the creation of the statue; it remanded that question to the trial court for such a determination.

The Court stated that the controlling issue is whether the author is an "employee," listing the factors relevant to such a determination. Because the Court found that Reid was an independent contractor, it did not define further the phrase "within the scope of employment." Thus, it is not clear whether an institution could, if it wished to, assert copyright ownership of a book, article, software program, or musical composition that was produced as the result of an agreement by the institution to give a faculty or staff member a reduced workload (or a paid leave) in return for the production of that specific work.

The "work made for hire" doctrine also has potential relevance for copyright of materials prepared under the auspices of an external funding agent. Although some funding agreements specify whether the funding source will have superior rights to any inventions, discoveries, or other products of the research, other agreements are silent on this issue.

12.1.5.6. Copyright and standardized tests. One further issue in copyright law of interest to colleges and universities, and most particularly to the testing agencies, is whether states can require disclosure of test questions, answers, and other copyrighted information under "truth-in-testing" laws. New York's Standardized Testing Act (N.Y. Educ. Law §§340–348) requires developers of standardized tests to disclose to test takers and to the public test questions, answers, answer sheets, and related research reports. In *Assn. of American Medical Colleges v. Carey*, 728 F. Supp. 873 (N.D.N.Y. 1990), the AAMC, which develops the Medical College Admissions Test, sought a declaratory judgment that the Copyright Act preempted such disclosure. A federal trial court issued a permanent injunction barring enforcement of Sections 341, 341(a), and 342 of the law. The state argued that two of the Copyright Act's exemptions permitted disclosure of the test materials (the "fair use" exemption and the "archives" exemption). The U.S. Court of Appeals for the Second Circuit vacated the permanent injunction and reversed and remanded the case for trial, stating that genuine issues of fact were unresolved concerning the effect of disclosure of test questions and answers on reuse of the test (the fourth, or "market impact," test under the fair use doctrine) (*Assn. of American Medical Colleges v. Cuomo*, 928 F.2d 519 (2d Cir. 1991)).

12.1.6. Americans with Disabilities Act

The Americans with Disabilities Act of 1990 (ADA) (Pub. L. No. 101–336, codified at 42 U.S.C. §12101 *et seq.*) provides broad protections for individuals with disabilities in five areas: employment, public accommodations (see Section 4.1.4.3), state and local government services, transportation, and telecommunications. Similar in intent to Section 504 of the Rehabilitation Act (Section 12.4.4), the ADA provides broader protection, since a larger number of entities are subject to it (they need not be recipients of federal funds), and a larger number of activities are encompassed by it.

The law protects an "individual with a disability." Disability is defined as "a physical or mental impairment that substantially limits one or more major life activities" of the individual, "a record of such impairment," or "being regarded as having such impairment" (42 U.S.C. §12102). This definition, while covering current disabilities, also would prohibit discrimination against an individual based on a past disability that no longer exists, or a perceived disability that does not, in fact, exist. The definition of "impairment" includes contagious diseases, learning disabilities, HIV (whether symptomatic or asymptomatic), drug addiction, and alcoholism (36 C.F.R. §104), although the employment provisions exclude current abusers of controlled substances from the law's protections.

Title I of the ADA covers employment; Title II requires nondiscrimination on the part of state and local government, a category that specifically includes state colleges and universities. Title II provides that "no qualified individual with a disability shall, by reason of such disability[,] be excluded from participation in or be denied the benefits of the services, programs, or activities of a public entity, or be subjected to discrimination by any such entity" (42 U.S.C. §12132). For purposes of Title II, an individual with a disability is "qualified" when "with or without reasonable modification to rules, policies, or practices, the removal of architectural, communication, or transportation barriers, or the provision of auxiliary aids and services, [the individual] meets the essential eligibility requirements for the receipt of services or his participation in programs or activities provided by a public entity" (42 U.S.C. §12131). Title II also incorporates the provisions of Titles I and III (public accommodations), making them applicable to public institutions. The U.S. Department of Justice has the responsibility for providing technical assistance for, and for enforcing, Titles II and III of the ADA. Regulations interpreting Title II appear at 28 C.F.R. Part 35.

Title III extends the nondiscrimination provisions to places of public accommodation, whose definition includes colleges and universities, whether public or private, if they "affect commerce" (42 U.S.C. §12181). Title III focuses on ten areas of institutional activity:

1. Eligibility criteria for the services provided by colleges and universities (28 C.F.R. §36.301)

2. Modifications in policies, practices, or procedures (such as rules and regulations for parking or the policies of libraries) (28 C.F.R. §36.302)

3. Auxiliary aids and services (such as interpreters or assistive technology) (28 C.F.R. §36.303)

4. Removal of architectural barriers (28 C.F.R. §36.304)

5. Alternatives to barrier removal (if removal is not readily achievable) (28 C.F.R. §36.305)

6. Personal devices and services, which the law does not require the public accommodation to provide (28 C.F.R. §36.306)

7. Conditions under which the public accommodation must provide accessible or special goods upon request (28 C.F.R. §36.307)

8. Accessible seating in assembly areas (28 C.F.R. §36.308)

9. Accessibility to and alternatives for examinations and courses that reflect the individual's ability rather than the individual's impairment (28 C.F.R. §36.309)

10. Accessible transportation (28 C.F.R. §36.310)

Title III imposes a wide range of requirements on colleges and universities, from admissions policies to residence hall and classroom accessibility to the actions of individual faculty (who may, for instance, be required to modify examinations or to use special technology in the classroom). The regulations also affect the college's planning for public performances, such as plays, concerts, or athletic events, and provide detailed guidelines for making buildings accessible during their renovation or construction. The implications of the ADA for a college's responsibility to provide auxiliary aids and services is discussed in Section 5.3.1. Public telephones must also be made accessible to individuals with disabilities, including those with hearing impairments. For an overview of some of the implications of the ADA for institutions of higher education, see F. Thrasher, "The Impact of Titles II and III of the Americans with Disabilities Act of 1990 on Academic and Student Services at Colleges, Universities, and Proprietary Schools," 22 *Coll. Law Dig.* 257 (June 18, 1992).

12.1.7. Regulation of Computer Network Communications

Under the Communications Act of 1934 (see this volume, Section 12.1.1), as recently amended by the Telecommunications Act of 1996 (110 Stat. 56), the federal government is the primary regulator of radio, television, and telephone communications. As new communication technologies have evolved, the federal government has also included them within its regulatory reach. The newest focus of regulatory activity, and of legal and policy concerns, is computer technology and the Internet.

The first major federal legislation regarding computers was passed in 1986. In that year, Congress passed the Computer Fraud and Abuse Act of 1986 (18 U.S.C. §1030 *et seq.*) and the Electronic Communications Privacy Act of 1986 (18 U.S. C. §2510 *et seq.* and §2701 *et seq.*). The former act prohibits the intentional and knowing accessing of a "federal interest computer" without prior government authorization. The latter act creates limited privacy rights for computer users by prohibiting the *interception* of private computer communications and the *disclosure* of intercepted communications. This prohibition applies to colleges and universities as systems operators as well as to individual faculty, students, and staff members. There are various important exceptions, however, that permit system operators to intercept or disclose in certain circumstances (18 U.S.C. §2511). Under Section 2511(2)(a)(I), for instance, the operator may intercept when it is necessary to view the content in order to forward the message; and under Section 2511(3)(b)(IV), the operator may disclose a message to law enforcement officials if it appears related to the commission of a crime.

Most recently, Congress passed the Communications Decency Act of 1996 ("CDA") (110 Stat. 56, 133 135, 47 U.S.C. §223 (a) to (h)), which was enacted as Title V of the Telecommunications Act of 1996. The CDA regulates the content of computer communications. Section 223(a) (47 U.S.C. §223(a))—called the "indecency" provision—applies criminal penalties to anyone who:

> 1) in interstate or foreign communications . . .
>
> (B) by means of a telecommunications device *knowingly—*
>
> (i) makes, creates, or solicits, and
>
> (ii) initiates the transmission of, any comment, request, suggestion, proposal, image, or other *communication which is obscene or indecent,* knowing that the recipient of the communication is *under 18 years of age,* regardless of whether the maker of such communication placed the call or initiated the communication;
>
> . . . or
>
> 2) *knowingly permits* any telecommunications facility *under his control* to be used for any activity prohibited by paragraph (1) with the *intent* that it be used for such activity . . . [emphasis added].

Section 223(d)—called the "patently offensive" provision—applies criminal penalties to anyone who:

> (1) in interstate or foreign communications knowingly—
>
> (A) uses an interactive computer service to send to a specific person or persons *under 18 years of age,* or

(B) uses any interactive computer service to display *in a manner available to a person under 18 years of age,* any comment, request, suggestion, proposal, image or other *communication that, in context, depicts or describes, in terms patently offensive as measured by contemporary community standards, sexual or excretory activities or organs,* regardless of whether the user of such service placed the call or initiated the communication; or

(2) *knowingly permits* any telecommunications facility *under such person's control* to be used for an activity prohibited by paragraph (1) with the *intent* that it be used for such activity . . . [emphasis added].

These provisions were challenged in court as soon as the president had signed the Act, and the ensuing court decisions provide the best guidance to date on how the First Amendment will apply to, and limit, Congress's authority to regulate the content of computer communications.

In *American Civil Liberties Union v. Reno,* 929 F. Supp. 824 (E. D. Pa. 1996), a three-judge panel of the United States District Court for the Eastern District of Pennsylvania granted a preliminary injunction against enforcement of both Section 223(a) and Section 223(d) of the Communications Decency Act. The plaintiffs had claimed that both Section 223(a) and Section 223(d) violated the free speech and press clauses of the First Amendment, as well as the Fifth Amendment due process clause. Although the court's decision was unanimous, each of the judges wrote a separate opinion. Chief Judge Sloviter determined that Sections 223(a) and (d) were government-imposed, content-based restrictions on speech that failed to meet standards of strict scrutiny. Judge Buckwalter determined that these provisions were both unconstitutionally overbroad and unconstitutionally vague. And Judge Dalzell determined that, although the provisions were not unconstitutionally vague in his view, they were overbroad content-based restrictions and were unconstitutional for that reason.

Specifically, Chief Judge Sloviter held that the CDA is subject to review under a strict scrutiny standard because it is a "government-imposed content-based restriction on speech and the speech at issue is entitled to constitutional protection." Under the strict scrutiny standard, a regulation of speech will be upheld only if the government can show that it furthers a compelling governmental interest by the least restrictive means possible. If the government's means of regulation "sweep[s] more broadly than necessary and thereby chills the expression of adults," the regulation will violate the First Amendment even if the interest being furthered is compelling. The Chief Judge agreed that "it is evident beyond the need for elaboration that a State's interest in safeguarding the physical and psychological well-being of a minor is compelling," and "this interest extends to shielding minors from the influence of literature that is not obscene by adult standards." But she did not agree that the CDA furthers this interest in the least restrictive (or the narrowest) way. It is "either technologically impossible or economically prohibitive for many of the plaintiffs to comply with the CDA without seriously impeding their posting of online material which adults have a constitutional right to access." Thus, Sloviter stated, "I conclude inexorably from the foregoing that the CDA reaches speech subject to the full protection of the First Amendment at least for adults. . . . Moreover, there is no effective way for many Internet content providers to limit the effective reach of the CDA to adults because there is no realistic way for many providers to ascertain the age of those accessing their materials."

Judge Buckwalter based his decision on the fact that the "statute is overbroad and does not meet the strict scrutiny standard." In addition, he asserted that the word *indecent* in Section 223(a) is unconstitutionally vague and that the terms *in context* and *patently offensive* in Section 223(d) also are unconstitutionally vague. He did note, however, that it is too early in the development of this new medium to conclude that other attempts to regulate protected speech within this medium will also fail.

In supporting his conclusions, Judge Buckwalter reasoned that "the CDA does not define the term 'indecent,' and the FCC has not promulgated regulations defining indecency in the medium of cyberspace. . . . Indecent in this statute is an undefined word which, standing alone, offers no guidelines whatsoever as to its parameters." He emphasized that, "[i]n statutes that break into relatively new areas the need for definition is greater, because even commonly understood terms may have different connotations or parameters in this new context." Moreover,

> the unique nature of the medium cannot be overemphasized in discussing and determining the vagueness issue. This is not to suggest that new technology should drive constitutional law. To the contrary, I remain of the belief that our fundamental constitutional principles can accommodate any technological achievements, even those which, presently, seem to many to be in the nature of a miracle such as the Internet [921 F. Supp. at 865 note 9].

The third member of the three-judge panel, Judge Dalzell, emphasized that this case is not about obscenity or child pornography, which the government could completely ban from the Internet, but rather "is about 'indecency' as that word has come to be understood" in the U.S. Supreme Court's First Amendment jurisprudence. The CDA's regulation of indecent speech, being a content-based regulation, is subject to strict scrutiny. Although Dalzell does not agree that the provisions are unconstitutionally vague, he does agree with Judge Buckwalter that they are overbroad. The provisions are not vague, in Judge Dalzell's view, because Congress intended that the phrase "indecent" in Section 223(a) would be defined with reference to the "longer description" of patently offensive speech in Section 223(d), which is a definition consistent with earlier Supreme Court cases.

To analyze the overbreadth of the CDA provisions, Judge Dalzell engaged in what he called a "medium specific approach to mass communication." A medium-specific analysis allows the court to determine the "proper fit" between First Amendment concerns and other competing interests by considering the special qualities of the computer network medium. Relying on the court's extensive findings of fact (929 F. Supp. at 830–849), he concluded not only that the CDA is unconstitutional but also:

> [F]rom the Supreme Court's many decisions regulating the different media differently, I conclude that we cannot simply assume that the Government has the power to regulate protected speech over the Internet, devoting our attention solely to the issue of whether the CDA is a constitutional exercise of that power. Rather, we must also decide the validity of the underlying assumption as well, to wit, whether the Government has the power to regulate protected speech at all. That decision must take into account the underlying technology, and the actual and potential reach, of that medium [929 F. Supp. at 877].

In concluding that "Congress may not regulate indecency on the Internet at all," Judge Dalzell cited four specific characteristics of the Internet:

> Four related characteristics of Internet communication have a transcendent importance to our shared holding that the CDA is unconstitutional on its face. . . . First, the Internet presents very low barriers to entry. Second, these barriers to entry are identical for both speakers and listeners. Third, as a result of these low barriers, astoundingly diverse content is available on the Internet. Fourth, the Internet provides significant access to all who wish to speak in the medium, and even creates a relative parity among speakers [929 F. Supp. at 877].

Thus,

> [t]he Internet may be fairly regarded as a never-ending worldwide conversation. The Government may not, through the CDA, interrupt that conversation. As the most participatory form of mass speech yet developed, the Internet deserves the highest protection from governmental intrusion. It is no exaggeration to conclude that the Internet has achieved, and continues to achieve, the most participatory market place of mass speech that this country—and indeed the world—has yet seen [929 F. Supp. at 883].

Under the CDA, according to Judge Dalzell, the "speech enhancing" benefits that have resulted from the utilization and development of the Internet would be undermined; barriers to entry for speakers subject to the CDA would skyrocket; the diversity of the content would diminish; and the relative parity among speakers that now exists would be altered. Moreover, although the government has a compelling interest in protecting children from pornography, the government can do so through enforcement of already existing laws that criminalize obscenity and child pornography.

Based on the careful individual analyses of the three judges, the court granted the plaintiffs' motion for a preliminary injunction and enjoined the Government from "enforcing, prosecuting, investigating or reviewing any matter premised upon" Sections 223(a)(1)(B) and 223(a)(2) of the CDA "to the extent that such enforcement, prosecution, investigation, or review are based upon allegations other than obscenity or child pornography. . . ."[1] On December 6, 1996, the U.S. Supreme Court announced that it will review the U.S. District Court's judgment in this case; see 65 U.S.L.W 3295.

SEC. 12.2. FEDERAL TAXATION OF POSTSECONDARY EDUCATION

Federal tax laws impose various filing, reporting, disclosure, withholding, and payment requirements on postsecondary institutions. This section briefly discusses the tax laws that have the most important applications to student affairs in postsecondary education. These laws are based on Congress's taxing power. Federal tax law is highly technical and complex; to deal effectively with its many requirements, postsecondary institutions will need ready access to expert accounting and auditing services and the regular advice of counsel expert in taxation.

12.2.1. Taxation of Student Financial Assistance

Income tax provisions exert substantial influences on postsecondary institutions and their staffs and students. For instance, Section 117 of the Internal Revenue Code governs the taxability of scholarships, fellowships, assistantship awards, and other forms of financial aid. In general, if the recipient obtains financial aid in return for providing services that benefit the institution, the aid is considered to be compensation and is taxable to the student; if no such strings are attached, the aid is treated as a gift, and the recipient may exclude it from taxable income (see *Bingler v. Johnson*, 394 U.S. 741 (1969)). The distinction is important not only for the student receiving the aid but also for the institution—which must determine whether to withhold employment taxes from the student's award.

In the Tax Reform Act of 1986 (Pub. L. No. 99–514, 100 Stat. 2085), Congress amended Section 117 in three ways. First, only students who are degree candidates may exclude scholarships or fellowships from their gross income. Other students, such as postdoctoral students, must pay taxes on all such grants they receive. Second, the amount of any scholarship or fellowship is excludable from gross income only to the extent used for tuition, course-required fees, books,

---

[1] In a later case, *Shea v. Reno*, 930 F. Supp. 916 (S.D.N.Y. 1996), another plaintiff challenged the patently offensive provision of the CDA. The court did not accept the argument that this provision was unconstitutionally vague but did invalidate it on grounds of overbreadth.

supplies, and equipment. Amounts used for expenses such as room and board are not excludable from income. Third, Congress explicitly affirmed that no portion of a scholarship or fellowship award that represents compensation for teaching, research, or other services is excludable from income. In 1988, in the Technical and Miscellaneous Revenue Act, Congress again amended Section 117 by adding a new paragraph, (d)(5), on tuition-reduction plans. This paragraph authorizes graduate students engaged in teaching and research to exclude from gross income a reduction in tuition that is not compensation for their teaching and research. The Treasury regulations implementing Section 117 are in 26 C.F.R. §1.117–1 *et seq.*

12.2.2. Coverage of Student Employees Under Social Security

The laws establishing the Social Security system are found in two different titles of the *United States Code.* Title 42 (§401 *et seq.*) establishes the "Federal Old Age and Survivors Insurance Trust Fund and Federal Disability Insurance Trust Fund" and sets the requirements on eligibility for benefits. Title 26 (§3101 *et seq.*), the Federal Insurance Contributions Act (FICA), defines which employers and employees are subject to taxation and levies the appropriate tax. The postsecondary education community's exposure to these laws was enhanced by the Social Security Amendments of 1983 (97 Stat. 65), which affected the tax liability of postsecondary institutions in two ways. First, Section 102(b)(1)(C) of the amendments (97 Stat. 70) deleted the language from 26 U.S.C. §3121(b)(8)(B) that had previously provided an exemption from the system for "service performed in the employ of a religious, charitable, educational, or other organization" as defined in 26 U.S.C. §501(c)(3). Thus, private institutions in that category can no longer claim such an exemption. Second, Section 103(a) of the amendments modified 42 U.S.C. §418 *et seq.*, which had allowed states voluntarily to enter into agreements with the U.S. secretary of health and human services for the coverage of state and local employees under the Social Security system. As amended, this provision forbids states that have entered such agreements from withdrawing from them, thus locking into the system states that are participating under voluntary agreements. The constitutionality of this provision was upheld in *Bowen v. Public Agencies Opposed to Social Security Entrapment,* 477 U.S. 41 (1986). Public postsecondary institutions covered by such an agreement thus have no option of dropping out.

Congress again broadened the applicability of FICA to public postsecondary institutions and their employees in the Omnibus Budget Reconciliation Act of 1990 (104 Stat. 1388). This Act added a new section (26 U.S.C. §3121(b)(7)(F)) to the Code, which brought within FICA state employees and the employees of state political subdivisions and instrumentalities who are not members of a state retirement system or that of a subdivision or instrumentality. Regulations implementing this provision are in 26 C.F.R. §31.3121(b)(7).

Although the 1983 and 1990 Acts constricted the number of institutions and employees exempt from the Social Security tax, they left intact exemptions for several classes of employees common to postsecondary institutions. Among the classes still exempt from coverage are (1) students "enrolled and regularly attending classes" who are also employees of the institution (see Revenue Ruling 78 17, 1978–1 C.B. 306), except for student employees at public institutions that are covered by, and include such students in, voluntary agreements between the state and the secretary of health and human services (26 U.S.C. §3121(b) (10)); (2) students "enrolled and . . . regularly attending classes" who perform domestic services at college clubs, sororities, or fraternities (26 U.S.C. §3121(b) (2)); and (3) student nurses "enrolled and . . . regularly attending classes" at a state-approved nurses' training school who are employed at a "hospital or a nurses' training school" (26 U.S.C. §3121(b)(13)). For these student categories, controversy has arisen over the meaning of the phrase "regularly attending classes" as it applies to part-time students.

The exemption for student nurses was at issue in *Johnson City Medical Center Hospital v. United States*, 999 F.2d 973 (6th Cir. 1993). Relying on the statutory exemption and the IRS regulation implementing it (26 C.F.R. §31.3121(b) (13)–1), the hospital sought a refund of FICA taxes paid with respect to employees who were registered students at a nearby nursing school at East Tennessee State University. The United States relied on a revenue ruling interpreting the statutory exemption (Revenue Ruling 85–74, 1985–1 C.B. 331). That ruling set out three requirements the employer must meet to obtain the exemption: "(1) [t]he employment is substantially less than full time, (2) [t]he total amount of earnings is nominal, and (3) [t]he only services performed by the student nurse for the employer are incidental parts of the student nurse's training toward a [nursing] degree." The court determined that this ruling reflected Congress's intent for the exemption and upheld the ruling's validity. Then, applying the ruling to the facts of the case, the court held that the university did not meet two of the three requirements. It did meet the first requirement, because the student nurses worked no more than forty hours over a two-week period. However, because the student nurses earned the regular, and not a reduced, rate of pay for their services, their earnings were not nominal as provided in the second requirement; and because the work was not formally part of a nurses' training program, the hospital did not meet the third requirement. The employment of the student nurses therefore did not fall within the exemption, and the court denied the hospital's request for a refund.

SEC. 12.3. FEDERAL AID-TO-EDUCATION PROGRAMS

12.3.1. Overview

The federal government's major function regarding postsecondary education is to establish national priorities and objectives for federal spending on education and to provide funds in accordance with those decisions. To implement its priorities and objectives, the federal government attaches a wide and varied range of conditions to the funds it makes available under its spending power and enforces these conditions against postsecondary institutions and other aid recipients. Some of these conditions are specific to the program for which funds are given. Others, called "cross-cutting" conditions, apply across a range of programs; they will be discussed in Section 12.3.3. Cumulatively, these conditions exert a substantial influence on postsecondary institutions, often leading to institutional cries of economic coercion and federal control. In light of such criticisms, the federal role in funding postsecondary education has for many years been a major political and policy issue. The particular national goals to be achieved through funding and fund conditions, and the delivery and compliance mechanisms best suited to achieving these goals, will likely remain subjects of debate for the foreseeable future.

Federal spending for postsecondary education has a long history. Shortly after the founding of the United States, the federal government began endowing public higher education institutions with public lands. In 1862, Congress passed the first Morrill Act, providing grants of land or land scrip to the states for the support of agricultural and mechanical colleges, and later provided continuing appropriations for these colleges. The second Morrill Act, providing money grants for instruction in various branches of higher education, was passed in 1890. In 1944, Congress enacted the first GI Bill, which was followed in later years by successive programs providing funds to veterans to further their education. The National Defense Education Act, passed in 1958 after Congress was spurred by Russia's launching of *Sputnik,* included a large-scale program of low-interest loans for students in institutions of higher education. The Higher Education Facilities Act of 1963 authorized grants and low-interest loans to public and private nonprofit institutions of higher education for constructing and improving various educational facilities. Then, in 1965, Congress finally jumped broadly into supporting higher education with the passage of the Higher Education Act of 1965 (20 U.S.C. §1001 *et seq.*). The Act's various titles authorized federal support for a range of postsecondary education activities, including community educational services; resources, training, and research for college libraries and personnel; strengthening of developing institutions; and student financial aid programs (see Section 4.2.2). The Act has been frequently amended since 1965 and continues to be the primary authorizing legislation for federal higher education spending.

Funds provided under the Higher Education Act and other aid programs should be sharply distinguished from funds provided under federal procurement programs. Many federal agencies, such as the U.S. Department of Defense, enter into procurement contracts with postsecondary institutions or consortia, the primary purpose of which is to obtain research or other services that meet the government's own needs. True aid-to-education programs, in contrast, directly serve the needs of institutions, their students and faculty, or the education community in general, rather than the government's own needs for goods or services. The two systems—assistance and procurement—operate independently of one another, with different statutory bases and different regulations, and often with different agency officials in charge. Guidelines for differentiating the two systems are set out in Chapter 63 of Subtitle V of 41 U.S.C.: "Using Procurement Contracts and Grant and Cooperative Agreements."

12.3.2. Legal Structure of Aid Programs

Federal aid for postsecondary education is disbursed by a number of federal agencies. The five most important are the U.S. Department of Education, the U.S. Department of Health and Human Services, the National Foundation of Arts and Humanities (comprising the National Endowment for the Humanities, the National Endowment for the Arts, and the Institute of Museum Services), the National Science Foundation, and (at least with respect to student aid) the Department of Veterans Affairs. The U.S. Department of Education was created in 1979 by the Department of Education Organization Act (93 Stat. 668, 20 U.S.C. §3401 *et seq.*). The Act transferred functions of the then U.S. Office of Education (a constituent unit of the then U.S. Department of Health, Education, and Welfare), the National Institute of Education, and several other federal agencies to the new department, which formally came into existence on May 4, 1980, in accordance with the Act and Executive Order 12212 (45 Fed. Reg. 29557 (May 2, 1980)). (For general information about the Department, see http://www.ed.gov). The Act also redesignated the remainder of the then U.S. Department of Health, Education, and Welfare (HEW) as the new U.S. Department of Health and Human Services (HHS). (The Public Health Service, previously a constituent agency of HEW and now of HHS, administers aid programs for students in medical, dental, pharmacy, nursing, and other health education programs (see 42 C.F.R. Part 57).)

The Department of Veterans Affairs administers the various veterans' educational benefits programs, authorized in 38 U.S.C. §3011 *et seq.*, 38 U.S.C. §3451 *et seq.*, and 10 U.S.C. §2131 *et seq.* (See *Max Cleland, Administrator of VA v. National College of Business*, 435 U.S. 213 (1978), upholding various federal statutory requirements regarding veterans' use of VA benefits.) The DVA contracts with State Approving Agencies, which review courses and determine whether to approve them as courses for which veterans can expend veterans' benefits. The State Approving Agencies, and the institutions seeking approval for their courses, must follow criteria and procedures for such approvals that are set out in 38 U.S.C. §3675 *et seq.* (see Section 4.2.2 of this volume). Regulations implementing the veterans' benefits programs are published in 38 C.F.R. Part 21.

Federal aid to postsecondary education is dispensed in a variety of ways. Depending on the program involved, federal agencies may: award grants or make loans directly to individual students; guarantee loans made to individual students by third parties; award grants directly to faculty or staff members; make grants or loans to postsecondary institutions; enter "cooperative agreements" (as opposed to procurement contracts) with postsecondary institutions; or award grants, make loans, or enter agreements with state agencies, which in turn provide aid to institutions or their students or faculty. Whether an institution is eligible to receive federal aid, either directly from the federal agency or a state agency or indirectly through its student recipients, depends on the requirements of the particular aid program. Typically, however, the institution must be accredited by a recognized accrediting agency or demonstrate compliance with one of the few statutorily prescribed substitutes for accreditation.

The "rules of the game" regarding eligibility, application procedures, the selection of recipients, allowable expenditures, conditions on spending, records and reports requirements, compliance reviews, and other federal aid requirements are set out in a variety of sources. Postsecondary administrators will want to be familiar with these sources in order to maximize their institution's ability to obtain and effectively utilize federal money.

The starting point is the statute that authorizes the particular federal aid program, along with the statute's legislative history. Occasionally, the appropriations legislation funding the program for a particular fiscal year will also contain requirements applicable to the expenditure of the appropriated funds. The next source, adding specificity to the statutory base, is the set of regulations for the program. These regulations, which are published in the *Federal Register* (Fed. Reg.) and then codified in the *Code of Federal Regulations* (C.F.R.), are the primary source of the administering agency's program requirements. Title 34 of the *Code of Federal Regulations* is the Education title, the location of the U.S. Department of Education's regulations.

Published regulations have the force of law and bind the government, the aid recipients, and all the outside parties. In addition, agencies may supplement their regulations with program manuals, program guidelines, policy guidance or memoranda, agency interpretations, and "dear colleague" letters. These materials generally do not have the status of law; although they may sometimes be binding on recipients who had actual notice of them before receiving federal funds, more often they are treated as agency suggestions that do not bind anyone (see 5 U.S.C. §552(a)(1); 20 U.S.C. §1232). Additional requirements or suggestions may be found in the grant award documents or agreements under which the agency dispenses the aid, or in agency grant and contract manuals that establish general agency policy.

There is also a federal statute, the General Education Provisions Act (20 U.S.C. §1221 *et seq.*), that applies specifically and only to the U.S. Department of Education, placing additional restrictions on its rules of the game. The Act (GEPA) establishes numerous organizational, administrative, and other requirements applicable to ED spending programs. For instance, the Act establishes procedures that ED must follow when proposing program regulations (20 U.S.C.

§1232). The GEPA provisions on enforcement of conditions attached to federal funds do not apply, however, to Higher Education Act programs (20 U.S.C. §1234i(2)). To supplement GEPA, the Department of Education has promulgated extensive general regulations published at 34 C.F.R. Parts 74–81. These "Education Department General Administrative Regulations" (EDGAR) establish uniform policies for all ED grant programs. The applicability of Part 74 of these regulations to higher education institutions is specified at 34 C.F.R. §§74.1 (a), 74.4(b), and 81.2. Running to 150 pages in the *Code of Federal Regulations,* EDGAR offers comprehensive coverage of the legal requirements for obtaining and administering ED grants.

Other funding agencies have general regulations that set certain conditions applicable to a range of their aid programs. The Public Health Service of HHS, for example, has published a final rule governing the investigation and reporting of scientific misconduct (codified at 42 C.F.R. Part 50, subpart A). The rule defines scientific misconduct and requires institutions receiving financial assistance to develop an administrative process for responding to a report of suspected misconduct. The institution must make an immediate inquiry to determine whether an investigation is needed; if so, the institution must advise the Office of Scientific Integrity (OSI) (now the Office of Research Integrity (ORI); see 57 Fed. Reg. 24262 (June 8, 1992)) that an investigation is warranted. The investigation must begin no later than thirty days after the inquiry has been completed. A full report on the progress and outcome of the investigation must be made to OSI. (The National Science Foundation has a similar scientific misconduct rule published at 45 C.F.R. Part 689.1 *et seq.*)

12.3.3. "Cross-Cutting" Aid Conditions

In addition to the programmatic and fiscal requirements discussed in Section 12.3.2, various statutes and agency regulations establish requirements that are not specific to any particular aid program but implement broader federal policy objectives that "cut across" a range of programs or agencies. The civil rights statutes and regulations discussed in Section 12.4 are a prominent example. Others are the requirements concerning the privacy of student records (discussed in Section 3.3.1) and campus security (discussed in Section 5.2). Other leading examples are discussed in Sections 12.3.3.1 to 12.3.3.3, which follow. The growth and increasing variety of these cross-cutting requirements mark what is perhaps the most significant contemporary trend regarding federal involvement in postsecondary education.

12.3.3.1. Drug-Free Workplace Act of 1988. The Drug-Free Workplace Act of 1988 (41 U.S.C. §§701–702) applies to institutions of higher education that contract with a federal agency to provide services or property worth at least $25,000 or that receive a grant from a federal agency for any amount. To qualify for such a contract or grant, an applicant institution must certify to the contracting or granting agency that it will undertake various activities to provide a drug-free workplace. Grantees' activities must include:

(A) publishing a statement notifying employees that the unlawful manufacture, distribution, dispensation, possession, or use of a controlled substance is prohibited in the grantee's workplace and specifying the actions that will be taken against employees for violations of such prohibition;

(B) establishing a drug-free awareness program to inform employees about—

   (i) the dangers of drug abuse in the workplace;

   (ii) the grantee's policy of maintaining a drug-free workplace;

   (iii) any available drug counseling, rehabilitation, and employee assistance programs; and

   (iv) the penalties that may be imposed upon employees for drug abuse violations;

(C) making it a requirement that each employee to be engaged in the performance of such grant be given a copy of the statement required by subparagraph (A);

(D) notifying the employee in the statement required by subparagraph (A), that as a condition of employment on such grant, the employee will—

   (i) abide by the terms of the statement; and

   (ii) notify the employer of any criminal drug statute conviction for a violation occurring in the workplace no later than 5 days after such conviction;

(E) notifying the granting agency within 10 days after receiving notice of a conviction under subparagraph (D)(ii) from an employee or otherwise receiving actual notice of such conviction;

(F) imposing a sanction on, or requiring the satisfactory participation in a drug abuse assistance or rehabilitation program by, any employee who is so convicted, as required by section 7033 of this title; and

(G) making a good faith effort to continue to maintain a drug-free workplace through implementation of subparagraphs (A), (B), (C), (D), (E), and (F) [41 U.S.C. §702(a)(1)].

The requirements for contractors, contained in Section 701(a)(1), are virtually identical. Section 706(2) of the Act defines "employee" as any employee of the grantee or contractor "directly engaged in the performance of work pursuant to the provisions of the grant or contract."

The Act also applies to individuals who receive a grant from a federal agency or who contract with a federal agency for any amount. Such individuals must certify that they "will not engage in the unlawful manufacture, distribution, dispensation, possession, or use of a controlled substance" in conducting grant activities or performing the contract (41 U.S.C. §§701(a)(2) and 702(a)(2)). Recipients of Pell Grants (see Section 4.2.2) are not considered to be individual grantees for purposes of this section (20 U.S.C. §1070a(I)).

See generally L. White, *Complying with "Drug-Free Workplace" Laws on College and University Campuses* (National Association of College and University Attorneys, 1989).

12.3.3.2. Drug-Free Schools and Communities Act Amendments. The Drug-Free Schools and Communities Act Amendments of 1989 (103 Stat. 1928, 20 U.S.C. §1145g) require institutions receiving federal financial assistance to establish drug and alcohol programs for both students and employees. Specifically, the Act requires institutions to distribute the following materials annually to all students and employees:

    (1)(A) standards of conduct that clearly prohibit, at a minimum, the unlawful possession, use, or distribution of illicit drugs and alcohol by students and employees on its property or as a part of any of its activities;

    (B) a description of the applicable legal sanctions under local, State, or Federal law for the unlawful possession or distribution of illicit drugs and alcohol;

    (C) a description of the health risks associated with the use of illicit drugs and the abuse of alcohol;

    (D) a description of any drug or alcohol counseling, treatment, or rehabilitation or re-entry programs that are available to employees or students; and

    (E) a clear statement that the institution will impose sanctions on students and employees (consistent with local, State, and Federal law), and a description of those sanctions, up to and including expulsion or termination of employment and referral for prosecution, for violations of the standards of conduct required by paragraph (1)(A) [20 U.S.C. §1145g(a)(1)].

In addition, institutions must biennially review their programs to determine their effectiveness, to implement changes if needed, and to ensure that the required sanctions are being carried out. Upon request, institutions must provide to the secretary of education or to the public a copy of all materials they are required to distribute to students and employees and a copy of the report from the biennial review.

The statute does not require institutions to conduct drug tests or to identify students or employees who abuse alcohol. However, if an institution has notice that a student or an employee has violated one of the standards of conduct promulgated under the statute, it must enforce its published sanctions. The statute also does not require institutions to operate treatment programs; institutions must, however, notify students of counseling and treatment programs that are available to them.

In enforcing the standards of conduct and sanctions required by the statute, institutions should of course comply with the requirements of constitutional due process (this volume, Sections 2.2.2 and 7.3.2; see also Section 1.5.2) as well as the record-keeping requirements of the Buckley Amendment (Section 3.3.1).

Final regulations implementing the Drug-Free Schools and Communities Act Amendments were published in 55 Fed. Reg. 33580 (Aug. 16, 1990) and are codified in 34 C.F.R. Part 86.

12.3.3.3. Student Right-to-Know Act. The Student Right-to-Know Act (Title I of the Student-Right-to-Know and Campus Security Act) (104 Stat. 2381–2384 (1990)) amends Section 485 of the Higher Education Act (20 U.S.C. §1092) to impose new information-sharing requirements on higher education institutions that participate in federal student aid programs. Section 103 (20 U.S.C. §1092 (a)(1)(L)) requires such institutions to compile and disclose "the completion or graduation rate of certificate-or-degree-seeking, full-time students" entering the institutions. Disclosure must be made both to current students and to prospective students. Section 104 of the Act (20 U.S.C. §1092(e)) includes additional compilation and disclosure requirements applicable to those institutions that are "attended by students receiving athletically related student aid." These requirements are discussed in Section 10.1.4 of this volume.

12.3.4. Enforcing Compliance with Aid Conditions

The federal government has several methods for enforcing compliance with its various aid requirements. The responsible agency may periodically audit the institution's expenditures of federal money (see, for example, 20 U.S.C. §1094(c) (1)(A)) and may take an "audit exception" for funds not spent in compliance with program requirements. The institution then owes the federal government the amount specified in the audit exception. In addition to audit exceptions, the agency may suspend or terminate the institution's funding under the program or programs in which noncompliance is found (see 34 C.F.R. §§74.113 to 74.115, and 34 C.F.R. §§75.901 and 75.903). Special provisions have been developed for the "limitation, suspension, or termination" of an institution's eligibility to participate in the Department of Education's major student aid programs (see 20 U.S.C. §1094(c)(1)(D)). In addition, agencies are sometimes authorized to impose civil monetary penalties on institutions that fail to comply with program requirements (see, for example, 20 U.S.C. §1094(c)(2)(B)).

Federal funding agencies also apparently have implied authority to sue institutions in court to obtain compliance with grant and contract conditions, although they seldom exercise this power. Furthermore, the federal government may also bring both civil suits and criminal prosecutions, under statutes such as the False Claims Act (31 U.S.C. §3729), against institutions or institutional employees who have engaged in fraudulent activities relating to federal grant or contract funds. When such suits arise from allegations initially made by an employee of the institution that is the subject of the suit (or when an employee makes such allegations even if they are not followed by any lawsuit), the employee will often be protected from retaliation by a federal or state "whistle-blower" statute (see P. Burling & K. A. Matthews, *Responding to Whistleblowers: An Analysis of Whistleblower Protection Acts and Their Consequences* (National Association of College and University Attorneys, 1992)).

In some circumstances, private parties may also be able to sue institutions to enforce federal grant or contract conditions. For example, courts permit persons harmed by institutional noncompliance to bring a "private cause of action" to enforce the nondiscrimination requirements imposed on federal aid recipients under the civil rights spending statutes (see Section 12.4.9). For other types of requirements, however, courts have been less willing to permit such implied causes of action. Student borrowers, for example, usually have not been able to sue their institutions to enforce aid conditions imposed upon the institution by the Higher Education Act (see Section 4.2.2). In other circumstances, statutes occasionally create express private causes of action whereby private parties can sue institutions in the name of the federal government to protect federal interests. Under the False Claims Act, for example, private individuals are expressly authorized to bring "qui tam" suits (suits by an individual "informer" on behalf of himself and the government) for monetary awards against federal fund recipients that have engaged in fraud (31 U.S.C. §3730).

In addition to all these means of enforcement, Executive Order 12549 requires that departments and agencies in the executive branch participate in a government-wide system for debarment and suspension from eligibility for nonprocurement federal assistance. The Office of Management and Budget has promulgated debarment and suspension guidelines, as provided in Section 6 of the executive order, and individual agencies have promulgated their own agency regulations implementing the executive order and OMB guidelines. The Department of Education's regulations are published at 34 C.F.R. Part 85, subparts A–E. These regulations "apply to all persons who have participated, are currently participating or may reasonably be expected to participate in transactions under Federal nonprocurement programs" (§85.110(a)). Section 85.305 sets out the specific bases upon which ED may debar a person or entity from further participation in aid programs. Section 85.201 contains special provisions concerning the effect of debarment or suspension on an educational institution's participation in student aid programs under Title IV of the Higher Education Act.

SEC. 12.4. CIVIL RIGHTS COMPLIANCE

12.4.1. General Considerations

Postsecondary institutions receiving assistance under federal aid programs are obligated to follow not only the programmatic and technical requirements of each program under which aid is received (see Section 12.3) but also various civil rights requirements that apply generally to federal aid programs. These requirements are a major focus of federal spending policy, importing substantial social goals into education policy and making equality of educational opportunity a clear national priority in education. The implementation and enforcement of civil rights have often been steeped in controversy. Some argue that the federal role is too great, and some say that it is too small; some argue that the federal government proceeds too fast, and some insist that it is too slow; others argue that the compliance process is too cumbersome or costly for the affected institutions. Despite the controversy, it is clear that these federal civil rights efforts, over time, have provided a major force for social change in America.

As conditions on spending, the civil rights requirements represent an exercise of Congress's spending power implemented through delegating authority to the various federal departments and agencies that administer federal aid programs. As nondiscrimination principles promoting equal opportunity, the civil rights requirements may also be justifiable as exercises of Congress's power to enforce the Fourteenth Amendment's equal protection clause.

Four different federal statutes prohibit discrimination in educational programs receiving federal financial assistance. Title VI of the Civil Rights Act of 1964 prohibits discrimination on the basis of race, color, or national origin. Title IX of the Education Amendments of 1972 prohibits discrimination on the basis of sex. Section 504 of the Rehabilitation Act of 1973, as amended in 1974, prohibits discrimination against individuals with disabilities. The Age Discrimination Act of 1975 prohibits discrimination on the basis of age. Title IX is specifically limited to educational programs receiving federal financial assistance, while Title VI, Section 504, and the Age Discrimination Act apply to all programs receiving such assistance.

Each statute delegates enforcement responsibilities to each of the federal agencies disbursing federal financial assistance. Postsecondary institutions may thus be subject to the civil rights regulations of several federal agencies, the most important one being the Department of Education, created in 1979, which has assumed the functions of the former HEW Office for Civil Rights with respect to all educational programs transferred from HEW's Office of Education. ED has its own Office for Civil Rights under an assistant secretary for civil rights. The HEW civil rights regulations, formerly published in Volume 45 of the *Code of Federal Regulations* (C.F.R.), were redesignated as ED regulations and republished in 34 C.F.R. Parts 100–106.

Although the language of the four statutes is similar, each statute protects a different group of beneficiaries, and an act that constitutes discrimination against one group does not necessarily constitute discrimination if directed against another group. "Separate but equal" treatment of the sexes is sometimes permissible under Title IX, for instance, but such treatment of the races is never permissible under Title VI. Administrative regulations have considerably fleshed out the meaning of the statutes. Since 1978, HEW's (now ED's) Office for Civil Rights has also published policy interpretations of its regulations in the *Federal Register*. Judicial decisions contribute additional interpretive gloss on major points, but the administrative regulations remain the primary source for understanding the civil rights requirements.

Damages available under these four laws vary, in that Title VI, Title IX, and Section 504 of the Rehabilitation Act have been interpreted to permit compensatory damages, while the Age Discrimination Act has not. Equitable remedies and debarment from future federal contracts are available under all four laws.

12.4.2. Title VI

Title VI of the Civil Rights Act of 1964 (42 U.S.C. §2000d) declares:

> No person in the United States shall, on the ground of race, color, or national origin, be excluded from participation in, be denied the benefits of, or be subjected to discrimination under any program or activity receiving federal financial assistance.

Courts have generally held that Title VI incorporates the same standards for identifying unlawful racial discrimination as have been developed under the Fourteenth Amendment's equal protection clause (see the discussion of the *Bakke* case in Section 4.1.5, and see generally Section 4.1.4.1). But courts have also held that the Department of Education and other federal agencies implementing Title VI may impose nondiscrimination requirements on recipients beyond those developed under the equal protection clause (see *Guardians Assn. v. Civil Service Commission of the City of New York*, 463 U.S. 582 (1983), discussed in Section 12.4.7.2).

Section 100.3(b) of the Education Department's regulations provides the basic, and most specific, reference point for determining what actions are unlawful under Title VI and/or its implementing regulations:

> (b) Specific discriminatory actions prohibited.
>
> (1) A recipient under any program to which this part applies may not directly or through contractual or other arrangements, on ground of race, color, or national origin:
>
> > (i) Deny an individual any service, financial aid, or other benefit provided under the program;

(ii) Provide any service, financial aid, or other benefit to an individual which is different, or is provided in a different manner, from that provided to others under the program;

(iii) Subject an individual to segregation or separate treatment in any matter related to his receipt of any service, financial aid, or other benefit under the program;

(iv) Restrict an individual in any way in the enjoyment of any advantage or privilege enjoyed by others receiving any service, financial aid, or other benefit under the program;

(v) Treat an individual differently from others in determining whether he satisfies any admission, enrollment, quota, eligibility, membership, or other requirement or condition which individuals must meet in order to be provided any service, financial aid, or other benefit provided under the program;

(vi) Deny an individual an opportunity to participate in the program through the provision of services or otherwise or afford him an opportunity to do so which is different from that afforded others under the program (including the opportunity to participate in the program as an employee but only to the extent set forth in paragraph (C) of this section);

(vii) Deny a person the opportunity to participate as a member of a planning or advisory body which is an integral part of the program.

(2) A recipient, in determining the types of services, financial aid, or other benefits, or facilities which will be provided under any such program, or the class of individuals to whom, or the situations in which, such services, financial aid, other benefits, or facilities will be provided under any such program, or the class of individuals to be afforded an opportunity to participate in any such program, may not, directly or through contractual or other arrangements, utilize criteria or methods of administration which have the effect of subjecting individuals to discrimination because of their race, color, or national origin, or have the effect of defeating or substantially impairing accomplishment of the objectives of the program as respect individuals of a particular race, color, or national origin.

(3) In determining the site or location of facilities, an applicant or recipient may not make selections with the effect of excluding individuals from, denying them the benefits of, or subjecting them to discrimination under any programs to which this regulation applies, on the ground of race, color, or national origin; or with the purpose or effect of defeating or substantially impairing the accomplishment of the objectives of the Act or this regulation [34 C.F.R. §100.3(6)].

To supplement these regulations, the Department of Education has also developed criteria (discussed later in this chapter) that deal specifically with the problem of desegregating statewide systems of postsecondary education.

The dismantling of the formerly *de jure* segregated systems of higher education has given rise to considerable litigation over more than two decades. Although most of the litigation has attacked continued segregation in the higher education system of one state, the lengthiest lawsuit involved the alleged failure of the federal government to enforce Title VI in ten states. This litigation—begun in 1970 as *Adams v. Richardson,* continuing with various Education Department secretaries as defendants until it became *Adams v. Bell* in the 1980s, and culminating as *Women's Equity Action League v. Cavazos* in 1990—focused on the responsibilities of the Department of Health, Education, and Welfare, and later the Education Department, to enforce Title VI, rather than examining the standards applicable to state higher education officials. The U.S. District Court ordered HEW to initiate enforcement proceedings against these states (*Adams v. Richardson,* 356 F. Supp. 92 (D.D.C. 1973)), and the U.S. Court of Appeals affirmed the decision (480 F.2d 1159 (D.C. Cir. 1973)). (See the further discussion of the case in Section 12.4.8.) In subsequent proceedings in the case, the district judge ordered HEW to revoke its acceptance of desegregation plans submitted by several states after the 1973 court opinions and to devise criteria for reviewing new desegregation plans to be submitted by the states that were the subject of the case (see *Adams v. Califano,* 430 F. Supp. 118 (D.D.C. 1977)). Finally, in 1990 the U.S. Court of Appeals for the D.C. Circuit ruled that no private right of action against government enforcement agencies existed under Title VI, and the court dismissed the case for lack of jurisdiction (*Women's Equity Action League v. Cavazos,* 906 F.2d 742 (D.C. Cir. 1990)).

After developing the criteria (42 Fed. Reg. 40780 (Aug. 11, 1977)), HEW revised and republished them (43 Fed. Reg. 6658 (Feb. 15, 1978)) as criteria applicable to all states having a history of *de jure* segregation in public higher education. These "Revised Criteria Specifying the Ingredients of Acceptable Plans to Desegregate State Systems of Public Higher Education" require the affected states to take various affirmative steps, such as enhancing the quality of black, state-supported colleges and universities, placing new "high-demand" programs on traditionally black campuses, eliminating unnecessary program duplication between black and white institutions, increasing the percentage of black academic employees in the system, and increasing the enrollment of blacks at traditionally white public colleges. The revised criteria are analyzed in J. Godard, *Educational Factors Related to Federal Criteria for the Desegregation of Public Postsecondary Education* (Southern Regional Education Board, 1980).

Litigation alleging continued *de jure* segregation by state higher education officials has resulted in federal appellate court opinions in four states; the U.S. Supreme Court has ruled in one of these cases. Despite the amount of litigation and the many years of litigation, settlement, or conciliation attempts, the standards imposed by the equal protection clause of the Fourteenth Amendment and by Title VI are still unclear. These cases—brought by private plaintiffs, with the United States acting as intervener—have been brought under both the equal protection clause (by the private plaintiffs and the United States) and Title VI (by the United States); judicial analysis generally uses the equal protection clause standard. Although the U.S. Supreme Court's opinion in *United States v. Fordice*, 112 S. Ct. 2727 (1992), is controlling, an examination of prior federal litigation is useful and establishes a context for analyzing *Fordice*.

Fordice and other recent federal court opinions must be read in the context of Supreme Court precedent in cases related to desegregating the public elementary and secondary schools. It is clear under the Fourteenth Amendment's equal protection clause that, in the absence of a "compelling" state interest (see Section 4.1.5), no public institution may treat students differently on the basis of race. The leading case, of course, is *Brown v. Board of Education*, 347 U.S. 483 (1954). Though *Brown* concerned elementary and secondary schools, the precedent clearly applies to postsecondary education as well, as the Supreme Court affirmed in *Florida ex rel. Hawkins v. Board of Control*, 350 U.S. 413 (1956).

The crux of the legal debate in the higher education desegregation cases has been whether the equal protection clause and Title VI require the state to enact race-neutral policies, or whether the state must go beyond race neutrality to ensure that any remaining vestige of the formerly segregated system (for example, racially identifiable institutions or concentrations of minority students in less prestigious or less well-funded institutions) is removed. Unlike elementary and secondary students, college students select the institution they wish to attend (assuming they meet the admission standards); and the remedies used in elementary and secondary school desegregation, such as busing and race-conscious assignment practices, are unavailable to colleges and universities. But just how the courts should weigh the "student choice" argument against the clear mandate of the Fourteenth Amendment was sharply debated by several federal courts prior to *Fordice*.

In *Geier v. University of Tennessee*, 597 F.2d 1056 (6th Cir. 1979), *cert. denied*, 444 U.S. 886 (1979), the court ordered the merger of two Tennessee universities, despite the state's claim that the racial imbalances at the schools were created by the students' exercise of free choice. The state had proposed expanding its programming at predominantly white University of Tennessee–Nashville; this action, the plaintiffs argued, would negatively affect the ability of Tennessee A&I State University, a predominantly black institution in Nashville, to desegregate its faculty and student body. Applying the reasoning of *Brown* and other elementary and secondary cases, the court ruled that the state's adoption of an "open-admissions" policy had not effectively dismantled the state's dual system of higher education, and the court ordered state officials to submit a plan for desegregating public higher education in Tennessee. In a separate decision, *Richardson v. Blanton*, 597 F.2d 1078 (6th Cir. 1979), the same court upheld the district court's approval of the state's desegregation plan.

In affirming the district court's decision in *Geier,* the appellate court noted that the merger order was based on a finding that the state's failure to "dismantle a statewide dual system, the 'heart' of which was an all-black TSU," was a continuing constitutional violation. The fact that the state had not been found guilty of practicing discrimination at the schools in the recent past was irrelevant. The Sixth Circuit rejected the state's argument that elementary/secondary desegregation precedent, most specifically *Green v. County School Board,* 391 U.S. 430 (1968), did not apply to higher education. "We agree," said the court, "that the 'state's duty is as exacting' to eliminate the vestiges of state-imposed segregation in higher education as in elementary and secondary school systems; it is only the means of eliminating segregation which differ" (597 F.2d at 1065).

Seven years later, the parties were back before the Sixth Circuit. The United States Department of Justice intervened in the case in order to object, on equal protection grounds, to a provision of the consent decree approved by the district court. The provision required the state to assist seventy-five black preprofessional students, through an affirmative action program, so that they could prepare for and be admitted to professional schools in Tennessee. Citing *Bazemore v. Friday,* 478 U.S. 385 (1986), the Justice Department argued that a race-specific remedy was inappropriate because of the voluntary nature of higher education. In *Bazemore,* the Court had ruled that the state's affirmative attempts to desegregate North Carolina's 4–H clubs and establish race-neutral admissions policies constituted an adequate defense to a discrimination claim. When a voluntary activity, such as a 4–H club, was at issue, the Court had ruled, the state's efforts to disestablish a segregated dual system were the crux of the issue, regardless of whether those efforts were completely successful.

The Sixth Circuit, in *Geier v. Alexander,* 801 F.2d 799 (6th Cir. 1986) (*Geier II*), rejected the Department of Justice's interpretation of *Bazemore,* saying, "[I]t appears fallacious to extend *Bazemore* to any level of education" because, no matter how valuable the 4–H experience, "it cannot be compared to the value of an advanced education" (801 F.2d at 805).

Geier was cited in subsequent higher education desegregation cases, sometimes with approval and sometimes with criticism. Desegregation cases brought in Mississippi and Louisiana, both within the jurisdiction of the U.S. Court of Appeals for the Fifth Circuit, show the complexities of these issues and the sharply differing interpretations of the equal protection clause and Title VI. These cases proceeded through the judicial system at the same time, and, considered together, they illustrate the significance of the U.S. Supreme Court's pronouncements in *Fordice.*

The case that culminated in the Supreme Court's *Fordice* opinion began in 1975, when Jake Ayers and other private plaintiffs sued the governor of Mississippi and other state officials for maintaining the vestiges of a *de jure* segregated system. Although HEW had begun Title VI enforcement proceedings against

Mississippi in 1969, it had rejected both desegregation plans submitted by the state, and this private litigation ensued. The United States intervened, and the parties attempted to conciliate the dispute for twelve years. They were unable to do so, and the trial ensued in 1987.

Mississippi had designated three categories of public higher education institutions: comprehensive universities (three historically white, none historically black); one urban institution (black); and four regional institutions (two white, two black). Admission standards differed both between categories and within categories, with the lowest admission standards at the historically black regional institutions. The plaintiffs argued, inter alia, that the state's admission standards, institutional classification and mission designations, duplication of programs, faculty and staff hiring and assignments, and funding perpetuated the prior segregated system of higher education; among other data, they cited the concentration of black students at the black institutions (over 95 percent of the students at each of the three black institutions were black, whereas blacks made up less than 10 percent of the students at the three white universities and 13 percent at both white regional institutions). The state asserted that the existence of racially identifiable universities was permissible, since students could choose which institution to attend, and that the state's higher education policies and practices were race-neutral in intent.

Although the district court acknowledged that the state had an affirmative duty to desegregate its higher education system, it rejected the *Green* precedent as inapplicable to higher education systems and followed the Court's ruling in *Bazemore*, described earlier. The district court said:

> [T]he affirmative duty to desegregate does not contemplate either restricting choice or the achievement of any degree of racial balance. . . . [W]hile student enrollment and faculty and staff hiring patterns are to be examined, greater emphasis should instead be placed on current state higher education policies and practices in order to insure that such policies and practices are racially neutral, developed and implemented in good faith, and do not substantially contribute to the continued racial identifiability of individual institutions [*Ayers v. Allain*, 674 F. Supp. 1523, 1553–54 (N.D. Miss. 1987)].

Applying this standard to the state's actions, and relying on the voluntariness of student choice under *Bazemore*, the court found no violation of law. It concluded that "current actions on the part of the defendants demonstrate conclusively that the defendants are fulfilling their affirmative duty to disestablish the former *de jure* segregated system of higher education" (674 F. Supp. at 1564).

A three-judge panel of the U.S. Court of Appeals for the Fifth Circuit initially did not view *Bazemore* as controlling, and overruled the district court. Because the plaintiffs in *Ayers* had alleged *de jure* segregation (*Bazemore* involved de facto segregation), the court ruled that the correct standard was that of *Geier v.*

Alexander (discussed earlier in this section). The panel cited lower admission standards for predominantly black institutions, the small number of black faculty at white colleges, program duplication at nearby black and white institutions, and continued underfunding of black institutions as evidence of an illegal dual system (*Ayers v. Allain,* 893 F.2d 732 (5th Cir. 1990)). The state petitioned the Fifth Circuit for a rehearing *en banc,* which was granted. The *en banc* court reversed the panel, reinstating the decision of the district court (914 F.2d 676 (5th Cir. 1990)).

The *en banc* court relied on a case decided two decades earlier, *Alabama State Teachers Assn. v. Alabama Public School and College Authority,* 289 F. Supp. 784 (M.D. Ala. 1968), *affirmed per curiam,* 393 U.S. 400 (1969), which held that the scope of the state's duty to dismantle a racially dual system of higher education differed from, and was less strict than, its duty to desegregate public elementary and secondary school systems. The court noted that higher education is neither free nor compulsory (characteristics of public elementary and secondary education); that college students have a diversity of options generally unavailable to elementary and secondary school students; and that it was therefore inappropriate for a court to intervene in policy decisions, such as funding priorities and location of institutions, which were the province of the legislature.

The *en banc* court said that *Green* did not apply to the desegregation of higher education and that the standard articulated in *Bazemore* should have been applied in this case. Furthermore, it saw no conflict between *Green* and *Bazemore,* stating that *Green* had not outlawed all "freedom-of-choice" desegregation plans outside elementary and secondary education. The opinion in *Geier,* on which the earlier panel opinion had relied, received sharp criticism as an over-reading of *Bazemore.* The court implied strongly that the remedies contemplated by the panel's decision would reduce freedom of choice for all students, including minorities, by imposing racial quotas for admission to segregated institutions. And it concluded that differences in funding, expenditures per student, admission standards, and program mix resulted from differences in institutional mission, not from racially motivated discrimination.

Despite its conclusion that the state's conduct did not violate the equal protection clause (and, without specifically addressing it, Title VI), the court did find some present effects of the former *de jure* segregation. The majority wrote:

> The district court incorrectly concluded that the disparities among the institutions were not reminiscent of the former de jure segregated system. *Ayers I,* 674 F. Supp. at 1560. On the contrary, the disparities are very much reminiscent of the prior system. The inequalities among the institutions largely follow the mission designations, and the mission designations to some degree follow the historical racial assignments. But this does not mean the plaintiff class is denied equal educational opportunity or equal protection of law. The defendants have adopted good-faith, race-neutral policies and procedures and have fulfilled or

exceeded their duty to open Mississippi universities to all citizens regardless of race. Their policies toward institutions are not racially motivated [914 F.2d at 692].

Clearly, the *en banc* majority interpreted the legal standard to require affirmative efforts but not to mandate equivalent funding, admission standards, enrollment patterns, or program allocation. The plaintiffs appealed the *en banc* court's ruling to the U.S. Supreme Court.

At the same time, similar litigation was in progress in Louisiana. In 1974, the U.S. Department of Justice sued the state of Louisiana under both the equal protection clause and Title VI, asserting that the state had established and maintained a racially segregated higher education system. The Justice Department cited duplicate programs at contiguous black and white institutions and the existence of three systems of public higher education as examples of continuing racial segregation. After seven years of pretrial conferences, the parties agreed to a consent decree, which was approved by a district court judge in 1981. Six years later, the United States charged that the state had not implemented the consent decree and that almost all of the state's institutions of higher education were still racially identifiable. The state argued that its good-faith efforts to desegregate higher education were sufficient.

In *United States v. Louisiana*, 692 F. Supp. 642 (E.D. La. 1988), a federal district judge granted summary judgment for the United States, agreeing that the state's actions had been insufficient to dismantle the segregated system. In later opinions (718 F. Supp. 499 (E.D. La. 1989), 718 F. Supp. 525 (E.D. La. 1989)), the judge ordered Louisiana to merge its three systems of public higher education, create a community college system, and reduce unwarranted duplicate programs, especially in legal education. Specifically, the court said, the law schools of Southern University and Louisiana State University, both of which are in Baton Rouge, should be merged. Appeals to the Supreme Court followed from all parties,[2] but the U.S. Supreme Court denied review for want of jurisdiction (*Louisiana, ex rel. Guste v. United States*, 110 S. Ct. 708 (1990)).

Despite the flurry of appeals, the district court continued to seek a remedy in this case. It adopted the report of a special master, which recommended that a single governing board be created, that the board classify each institution by mission, and that the graduate programs at the state's comprehensive institutions be evaluated for possible termination. The court also ordered the state to abolish its open-admissions policy and to use new admissions criteria consisting of a combination of high school grades, rank, courses, recommendations,

---

[2]For a description of the litigation history of this case, see Note, "Realizing the Dream: *U.S. v. State of Louisiana*," 50 *La. L. Rev.* 583 (1990).

extracurricular activities, and essays in addition to test scores (751 F. Supp. 621 (E.D. La. 1990)). After the Fifth Circuit's *en banc* opinion in *Ayers v. Allain* was issued, however, the district court judge vacated his earlier summary judgment, stating that although he disagreed with the Fifth Circuit's ruling, he had no choice but to follow it (*United States v. Louisiana,* 751 F. Supp. 606 (E.D. La. 1990)). The governor of Louisiana appealed this ruling, but the judge stayed both the appeal and the remedies he had ordered, pending the Supreme Court's opinion in *Ayers v. Allain,* now titled *United States v. Fordice.*[3]

The U.S. Supreme Court was faced with the issue addressed in *Geier:* which Supreme Court precedents control equal protection and Title VI jurisprudence in higher education desegregation—*Bazemore* or *Green?* In *United States v. Fordice,* 112 S. Ct. 2727 (1992), the Court reversed the decision of the Fifth Circuit's *en banc* majority, sharply criticizing the lower court's reasoning and the legal standard it had applied. First, the Court refused to choose between the two precedents. Justice White, writing for the eight-justice majority, rejected the Fifth Circuit's argument that *Bazemore* limited *Green* to segregation in elementary/secondary education:

> [*Bazemore*] neither requires nor justifies the conclusions reached by the two courts below. . . . *Bazemore* plainly does not excuse inquiry into whether Mississippi has left in place certain aspects of its prior dual system that perpetuate the racially segregated higher education system. If the State perpetuates policies and practices traceable to its prior system that continue to have segregative effects— whether by influencing student enrollment decisions or by fostering segregation in other facets of the university system—and such policies are without sound educational justification and can be practicably eliminated, the State has not satisfied its burden of proving that it has dismantled its prior system [112 S. Ct. at 2737].

The Court also criticized the lower courts for their interpretation of the *Alabama State Teachers Association* case: "Respondents are incorrect to suppose that

---

[3]In proceedings subsequent to the Supreme Court's opinion in *Fordice,* the legal skirmishes in Louisiana continued. After *Fordice* was announced, the Fifth Circuit vacated the district court's summary judgment for the state and remanded the case for further proceedings in light of *Fordice.* The district court then ordered the parties to show cause why the 1988 liability determination and remedy should not be reinstated. It also reinstated its earlier liability finding and entered a new remedial order at 811 F. Supp. 1151 (E.D. La. 1993). By the end of 1993, the U.S. Court of Appeals for the Fifth Circuit had overturned a district court's order to create a single higher education system for the state's public colleges, to create new admissions criteria for state colleges, to create a community college system, and to eliminate duplicative programs in adjacent racially identifiable state institutions (*United States v. Louisiana,* 9 E.3d 1159 (5th Cir. 1993)). The case was remanded to the trial court for resolution of disputed facts and determination of whether program duplication violated *Fordice.*

ASTA validates policies traceable to the *de jure* system regardless of whether or not they are educationally justifiable or can be practicably altered to reduce their segregative effects" (112 S. Ct. at 2737).

White's opinion articulated a standard that appears to be much closer to *Green* than to *Bazemore*, despite his insistence that *Bazemore* can be read to require the outcome in *Fordice.* White wrote:

> [W]e do not disagree with the Court of Appeals' observation that a state university system is quite different in very relevant respects from primary and secondary schools. [The Court then detailed several of the differences, including noncompulsory attendance, differing institutional missions, and the inappropriateness of desegregation remedies such as mandatory assignment of students or busing.] . . . We do not agree with the Court of Appeals or the District Court, however, that the adoption and implementation of race-neutral policies alone suffice to demonstrate that the State has completely abandoned its prior dual system. That college attendance is by choice and not by assignment does not mean that a race-neutral admissions policy cures the constitutional violation of a dual system. In a system based on choice, student attendance is determined not simply by admission policies, but also by many other factors. Although some of these factors clearly cannot be attributed to State policies, many can be. Thus, even after a State dismantles its segregative *admissions* policy, there may still be state action that is traceable to the State's prior *de jure* segregation and that continues to foster segregation. The Equal Protection Clause is offended by "sophisticated as well as simple-minded modes of discrimination" *Lane v. Wilson,* 307 U.S. 268, 275 . . . (1939). If policies traceable to the *de jure* system are still in force and have discriminatory effects, those policies too must be reformed to the extent practicable and consistent with sound educational practices [112 S. Ct. at 2736].

The Court asserted that "there are several surviving aspects of Mississippi's prior dual system which are constitutionally suspect" (at 2738). Although it refused to list all these elements, it discussed four policies that, in particular, appeared to perpetuate the effects of prior *de jure* discrimination: admission policies (for discussion of this portion of the case, see Section 4.1.4.1), the duplication of programs at nearby white and black colleges, the state's "mission classification," and the fact that Mississippi operates eight public institutions. For each category, the court noted the foundations of state policy in previous *de jure* segregation and a failure to alter that policy when *de jure* segregation officially ended. Furthermore, the Court took the lower courts to task for their failure to consider that state policies in each of these areas had influenced student access to higher education and had perpetuated segregation.

The Court emphasized that it was not calling for racial quotas; in its view, the fact "that an institution is predominantly white or black does not in itself make out a constitutional violation" (at 2743). It also refused the plaintiffs' invitation to order the state to provide equal funding for the three traditionally black institutions:

> If we understand private petitioners to press us to order the upgrading of Jackson State, Alcorn State, and Mississippi Valley *solely* so that they may be publicly financed, exclusively black enclaves by private choice, we reject that request. The State provides these facilities for *all* its citizens [112 S. Ct. at 2743].

The Court remanded the case so that the lower court could determine whether the state had "met its affirmative obligation to dismantle its prior dual system" under the standards of the equal protection clause and Title VI.

Although they joined the Court's opinion, two justices provided concurring opinions, articulating concerns they believed were not adequately addressed in the majority opinion. Justice O'Connor reminded the Court that only in the most "narrow" of circumstances should a state be permitted to "maintain a policy or practice traceable to *de jure* segregation that has segregative effects" (at 2743). O'Connor wrote, "Where the State can accomplish legitimate educational objectives through less segregative means, the courts may infer lack of good faith." Even if the state could demonstrate that "maintenance of certain remnants of its prior system is essential to accomplish its legitimate goals," O'Connor added, "it still must prove that it has counteracted and minimized the segregative impact of such policies to the extent possible. Only by eliminating a remnant that unnecessarily continues to foster segregation or by negating insofar as possible its segregative impact can the State satisfy its constitutional obligation to dismantle the discriminatory system that should, by now, be only a distant memory" (112 S. Ct. at 2746). O'Connor's approach would appear to preclude a state from arguing that certain policies which had continued segregative effects were justified by "sound educational policy."

Justice Thomas's concurrence articulates a concern expressed by many proponents of historically black colleges, who worry that the Court's opinion might result in the destruction of black colleges. Because the black colleges could be considered "vestiges of a segregated system" and thus vulnerable under the Court's interpretation of the equal protection clause and Title VI, Thomas wanted to stress that the *Fordice* ruling did *not* require the dismantling of traditionally black colleges. Thomas wrote:

> Today, we hold that "[i]f policies traceable to the *de jure* system are still in force and have discriminatory effects, those policies too must be reformed to the extent practicable and consistent with sound educational policies." . . . I agree that this statement defines the appropriate standard to apply in the higher-education context. I write separately to emphasize that this standard is far different from the one adopted to govern the grade-school context in *Green v. New Kent County*. . . . In particular, because it does not compel the elimination of all

observed racial imbalance, it portends neither the destruction of historically black colleges nor the severing of those institutions from their distinctive histories and traditions [112 S. Ct. at 2744].

The majority opinion, Thomas noted, focused on the state's policies, not on the racial imbalances they had caused. He suggested that, as a result of the ruling in this case, district courts "will spend their time determining whether such policies have been adequately justified—a far narrower, more manageable task than that imposed under *Green*" (at 2745). Thomas emphasized the majority opinion's use of "sound educational practices" as a touchstone for determining whether a state's actions are justifiable:

> Quite obviously, one compelling need to be considered is the *educational* need of the present and future *students* in the Mississippi university system, for whose benefit the remedies will be crafted.
>
> In particular, we do not foreclose the possibility that there exists "sound educational justification" for maintaining historically black colleges *as such*. . . .
>
> I think it indisputable that these institutions have succeeded in part because of their distinctive histories and traditions. . . . Obviously, a State cannot maintain such traditions by closing particular institutions, historically white or historically black, to particular racial groups. . . . Although I agree that a State is not constitutionally *required to* maintain its historically black institutions as such . . . I do not understand our opinion to hold that a State is *forbidden* from doing so. It would be ironic, to say the least, if the institutions that sustained blacks during segregation were themselves destroyed in an effort to combat its vestiges [112 S. Ct. at 2746–47; emphasis in original].

Thomas's concurrence articulates the concerns of some of the parties in the Louisiana and Mississippi cases—namely, that desegregation remedies would fundamentally change or even destroy the distinctive character of historically black colleges, instead of raising their funding to the level enjoyed by the public white institutions in those states.

Justice Scalia wrote a blistering dissent, criticizing the "effectively unsustainable burden the Court imposes on Mississippi, and all States that formerly operated segregated universities" and stating unequivocally that *Green* "has no proper application in the context of higher education, provides no genuine guidance to States and lower courts, and is as likely to subvert as to promote the interests of those citizens on whose behalf the present suit was brought" (at 2746–47).

In Scalia's view, the Court's tests for ascertaining compliance with *Brown* were confusing and vague. He questioned how one would measure whether policies that perpetuate segregation have been eliminated to the extent "practicable" and consistent with "sound educational" practices (at 2747). Scalia also

noted the differences in intensity of the words used by White to describe unlawful policies: those that "substantially restrict a person's choice of which institution to enter," "interfere" with a person's choice, "limit" choice, or "affect"
choice: "If words have any meaning, in this last stage of decrepitude the requirement is so frail that almost anything will overcome it" (at 2747). Scalia asserted:

> [O]ne must conclude that the Court is essentially applying to universities the
> amorphous standard adopted for primary and secondary schools in *Green*. . . .
> [T]oday's opinion requires state university administrators to prove that racially
> identifiable schools are *not* the consequence of any practice or practices . . . held
> over from the prior *de jure* regime. This will imperil virtually any practice or pro-
> gram plaintiffs decide to challenge—just as *Green* has—so long as racial imbal-
> ance remains. And just as under *Green,* so also under today's decision, the only
> practicable way of disproving that "existing racial identifiability is attributable to
> the State," *ante* at 2735, *is to eliminate extant segregation, i.e., to assure racial
> proportionality in the schools* [112 S. Ct. at 2748].

According to Scalia, "*Bazemore's* standard for dismantling a dual system
ought to control here: discontinuation of discriminatory practices and adoption
of a neutral admissions policy. . . . Only one aspect of an historically segregated
university system need be eliminated: discriminatory admissions standards"
(at 2750, 2751). In this regard, Scalia agreed with the majority opinion that the
state's sole reliance on standardized admission tests appeared to have a racially
exclusionary purpose and was not evidence of a neutral admissions process.

Scalia then argued that the majority opinion would harm traditionally black
colleges because it did not require equal funding of black and white institutions.
Equal funding, he noted, would encourage students to attend their own-race
institutions without "paying a penalty in the quality of education" (at 2752).
"What the Court's test is designed to achieve is the elimination of predominantly black institutions. . . . There is nothing unconstitutional about a 'black'
school in the sense, not of a school that blacks *must* attend and that whites *cannot,* but of a school that, as a consequence of private choice in residence or in
school selection, contains, and has long contained, a large black majority" (at
2752). Despite Scalia's criticism, the opinion makes it clear that, although many
elementary/secondary school desegregation remedies are unavailable to higher
education, *Green* controls a district court judge's analysis of whether a state has
eliminated the vestiges of a *de jure* segregated system of higher education.

The cases pending in Louisiana, as well as in Alabama, have already been
influenced by *Fordice*. For example, in *United States v. Alabama*, 787 F. Supp.
1030 (N.D. Ala. 1991), a case that began in 1983, the plaintiffs, a group of black
citizens that had joined the Justice Department's litigation, had argued that the
state's allocation of "missions" to predominantly white and black public colleges perpetuated racial segregation because the black colleges received few

funds for research or graduate education. They also argued that the white colleges' refusal to teach subjects related to race, such as black culture or history, had a discriminatory effect on black students.

A trial court had found, prior to *Fordice*, that the public system of higher education perpetuated earlier *de jure* segregation, but it had ruled against the plaintiffs on the curriculum issue. Both parties appealed. The state argued that its policies were race-neutral and that public universities had a constitutionally protected right of academic freedom to determine what programs and courses would be offered to students, and the plaintiffs took issue with the academic freedom defense. A federal appellate court affirmed the trial court in part (14 F.3d 1534 (11th Cir. 1994)) and applied *Fordice's* teachings to the actions of the state. The court held that, simply because the state could demonstrate legitimate, race-neutral reasons for continuing its past practice of limiting the types of programs and degrees offered by historically black colleges, it was not excused from its obligation to redress the continuing segregative effects of such a policy. But the appellate court differed with the trial court on the curriculum issue, stating that the First Amendment did not limit the court's power to order white colleges and universities to modify their programs and curricula to redress the continuing effects of prior discrimination. The court remanded the case to the trial court to determine whether the state's allocation of research missions to predominantly white colleges perpetuates segregation, and, if so, to determine "whether such effects can be remedied in a manner that is practicable and educationally sound" (14 F.3d at 1556). The results in *Fordice* and in the Alabama litigation may prompt efforts in many southern and border states to reopen desegregation cases that have been closed for several years.

Fordice leaves many questions unanswered, however. Supporters of black colleges argue that the opinion could motivate state officials to merge black and white colleges or even to close the black colleges, limiting access for black students and reducing their educational choices. Historically black colleges, their supporters point out, provide a nurturing environment and more role models for black students than do predominantly white institutions; they have special services for underprepared students; and they have played and continue to play a critical role in the education of blacks. Others argue, however, that single-race institutions, even historically black colleges, are contrary to the intent of the law and that segregating blacks in their own institutions disserves both blacks and whites.

The *Fordice* opinion has been criticized by individuals of all races and political affiliations as insufficiently clear to provide appropriate guidance to states as they attempt to apply its outcome to desegregation of the still racially identifiable public institutions in many states. For a discussion of some of the unresolved issues, see S. Jaschik, "Whither Desegregation?" *Chron. Higher Educ.*, Jan. 26, 1991, A33.

As the history of the last two decades of Title VI litigation makes clear, the desegregation of higher education is very much an unfinished business. Its completion poses knotty legal, policy, and administrative enforcement problems and requires a sensitive appreciation of the differing missions and histories of traditionally black and traditionally white institutions. The challenge is for lawyers, administrators, government officials, and the judiciary to work together to fashion solutions that will be consonant with the law's requirement to desegregate but will increase rather than limit the opportunities available to minority students and faculty.

For analyses of public policy issues and strategies regarding desegregation, see S. L. Myers (ed.), *Desegregation in Higher Education* (University Press of America, 1989), and J. Williams (ed.), *Desegregating America's Colleges and Universities: Title VI Regulation of Higher Education* (Teachers College Press, 1987). For a historical perspective and demonstration of history's continuing relevance to current concerns, see G. Kujovich, "Equal Opportunity in Higher Education and the Black Public College: The End of Separate but Equal," 72 *Minn. L. Rev.* 29 (1987), and L. Ware, "Will There Be a 'Different World' After *Fordice?*" 80 *Academe* 6 (May–June 1994).

12.4.3. Title IX

The central provision of Title IX of the Education Amendments of 1972 (20 U.S.C. §1681 *et seq.*) declares:

(a) No person in the United States shall, on the basis of sex, be excluded from participation in, be denied the benefits of, or be subjected to discrimination under any education program or activity receiving federal financial assistance, except that:

(1) in regard to admissions to educational institutions, this section shall apply only to institutions of vocational education, professional education, and graduate higher education, and to public institutions of undergraduate higher education;

(2) in regard to admissions to educational institutions, this section shall not apply (A) for one year from June 23, 1972, nor for six years after June 23, 1972, in the case of an educational institution which has begun the process of changing from being an institution which admits only students of one sex to being an institution which admits students of both sexes, but only if it is carrying out a plan for such a change which is approved by the secretary of education or (B) for seven years from the date an educational institution begins the process of changing from being an institution which admits only students of only one sex to being an institution which admits students of both sexes, but only if it is carrying out a plan for such a change which is approved by the secretary of education, whichever is the later;

(3) this section shall not apply to an educational institution which is controlled by a religious organization if the application of this subsection would not be consistent with the religious tenets of such organization;

(4) this section shall not apply to an educational institution whose primary purpose is the training of individuals for the military services of the United States, or the merchant marine;

(5) in regard to admissions, this section shall not apply to any public institution of undergraduate higher education which is an institution that traditionally and continually from its establishment has had a policy of admitting only students of one sex.

Title IX also excludes from its coverage the membership practices of tax-exempt social fraternities and sororities (20 U.S.C. §1681(a)(6)(A)); the membership practices of the YMCA, YWCA, Girl Scouts, Boy Scouts, Campfire Girls, and other tax-exempt, traditionally single-sex "youth service organizations" (20 U.S.C. §1681(a)(6)(B)); American Legion, Boys State, Boys Nation, Girls State, and Girls Nation activities (20 U.S.C. §1681(a)(7)); and father-son and mother-daughter activities if provided on a reasonably comparable basis for students of both sexes (20 U.S.C. §1681(a)(8)).

The Department of Education's regulations implementing Title IX (34 C.F.R. Part 106) include provisions paralleling the language of the previously quoted Title VI regulations (see 34 C.F.R. §106.31). Additional Title IX regulations specify in much greater detail the acts of discrimination prohibited in programs and activities receiving federal financial aid. Educational institutions may not discriminate on the basis of sex in admissions and recruitment (with certain exceptions) (see this volume, Section 4.1.4.2); in awarding financial assistance (Section 4.2.3); in athletic programs (Section 10.3); or in the employment of faculty and staff members (Section 2.2.2) or students (see 34 C.F.R. §106.38). Section 106.32 of the regulations prohibits sex discrimination in housing accommodations with respect to fees, services, or benefits, but does not prohibit separate housing by sex (see Section 5.1.1). Section 106.33 requires that separate facilities for toilets, locker rooms, and shower rooms be comparable. Section 106.34 prohibits sex discrimination in student access to course offerings. Sections 106.36 and 106.38 require that counseling services and employment placement services be offered to students in such a way that there is no discrimination on the basis of sex. Section 106.39 prohibits sex discrimination in health and insurance benefits and services, including any medical, hospital, accident, or life insurance policy or plan that the recipient offers to its students. Under Section 106.40, an institution may not "apply any rule concerning a student's actual or potential parental, family, or marital status" that would have the effect of discrimination on the basis of sex, nor may the recipient discriminate against any student on the basis of pregnancy or childbirth.

Litigation brought under Title IX has addressed alleged sex discrimination in the funding of women's athletics (see Section 10.3), the employment of women faculty and staff, and sexual harassment of women faculty and students. In *Franklin v. Gwinnett County Public Schools,* 112 S. Ct. 1028 (1992) (also discussed in Section 12.4.9), the Supreme Court ruled unanimously that plaintiffs suing under Title IX were not limited to equitable relief but could claim monetary damages as well. The case settled a conflict among the federal appellate courts: the lower court in *Franklin* had ruled that monetary damages were not available, whereas the U.S. Court of Appeals for the Third Circuit had ruled that they were (*Pfeiffer v. Marion Center Area School District,* 917 F.2d 779 (3d Cir. 1990)). As a result of this 1992 ruling, it is likely that an increasing number of both students and faculty will use Title IX to challenge alleged discrimination.

The type of damages available to plaintiffs under Title IX is particularly significant for students. Typical equitable remedies (back pay and orders requiring the school to refrain from future discriminatory behavior) are of little use to students, since they are usually due no back pay and are likely to have graduated or left school before the litigation has been completed.

In *Franklin,* the plaintiff, a high school student at North Gwinnett High School in Gwinnett County, Georgia, sued her school board under Title IX and sought relief from both hostile environment and quid pro quo sexual harassment by a teacher. Her complaint alleged that the teacher, also a sports coach, had harassed her continually beginning in the fall of her sophomore year. Franklin accused the teacher of engaging her in sexually oriented conversations, forcibly kissing her on the mouth on school property, telephoning her at home, and asking her to see him socially. She also alleged that during her junior year, the teacher went to Franklin's class, asked the teacher to excuse her, and then took her to a private office where he raped her. According to Franklin's complaint, school officials and teachers were aware of these occurrences. Although the school investigated them, it took no action to stop the harassment and agreed to let the teacher resign in return for dropping all harassment charges.

Franklin first filed a complaint with the U.S. Office of Civil Rights, which investigated her charges. OCR determined that the school district had violated Franklin's Title IX rights and that verbal and physical sexual harassment had occurred. It also found that the district had interfered with her right to complain about the unlawful conduct. But, OCR concluded, because the teacher and the school principal had resigned and because the school had implemented a grievance procedure, the district was now in compliance with Title IX.

The U.S. Supreme Court ruled in Franklin's favor, but it did so on relatively narrow grounds. (The Court's reasoning and legal analysis are discussed in Section 12.4.9.) Franklin had alleged that the district, in failing to stop the harassment, had intentionally discriminated against her. The Court's discussion of the availability of damages in Title IX causes of action discusses only claims of intentional discrimination; the opinion does not discuss whether damages are available in claims of unintentional discrimination.

Several important issues are left unresolved by the Court's *Franklin* opinion. First is the issue of when, and under what theories, the school or college will be found liable under Title IX for sexual harassment by a teacher or other employee. In *Franklin*, the school administrators had actual knowledge of the teacher's misconduct. The Supreme Court did not address whether the school could be found liable because it had actual knowledge of the misconduct but failed to stop it, or whether the school could be liable even absent such knowledge because the teacher's or employee's intentional discrimination may be imputed to the school. (Under agency law, the employer may be held responsible for the unlawful conduct of its agent, even if the employer does not have actual knowledge of the conduct; see Section 2.3.1.) If courts apply agency principles to Title IX sexual harassment claims, it may be easier to hold colleges liable for harassment by their employees because plaintiffs will not need to show intentional discrimination *on the part of the college.*

The second unresolved issue is whether plaintiffs must always show that the discrimination (the sexual harassment) was intentional or whether unintentional discrimination may also be actionable upon a showing of either discriminatory *effect* (see Section 12.4.7.2) or employer negligence. Although *Franklin* does not address this issue, federal district courts in cases subsequent to *Franklin* have required that plaintiffs demonstrate intentional discrimination. See, for example, *R.L.R. v. Prague Public School District I–103*, 838 F. Supp. 1526 (W.D. Okla. 1993). This issue is particularly important in cases where the alleged harasser is a student rather than the agent of the college; see G. Sorenson, "Peer Sexual Harassment: Remedies and Guidelines Under Federal Law," 92 *Ed. Law Rptr.* 1 (1994).

The *Franklin* opinion also does not resolve whether Title VII jurisprudence (which requires a showing of intent for disparate treatment claims but not for impact claims) applies to sexual harassment claims brought under Title IX. If Title VII precedents were to be transposed to Title IX, they would provide guidance on the issues discussed. For example, in a Title VII case, *Karibian v. Columbia University*, 14 F.3d 773 (2d Cir. 1994), a federal appellate court applied agency principles to hold the university liable for a supervisor's harassment of an employee. If the supervisor uses his actual or apparent authority to further the harassment, said the court, the university will be liable, whether or not the target of the harassment had notified the university. If the harasser is not a supervisor, then liability will not attach unless the employer provided no reasonable complaint process or knew of the harassment but did nothing about it, according to the *Karibian* court. Thus, if *Karibian* were applied in Title IX cases, it would provide important guidance on issues—such as whether colleges should permit counselors, residence hall advisers, or other staff to promise individuals who report harassment in confidence that college officials will not be notified, particularly if the accused harasser is a faculty member or an administrator who could be regarded as a supervisor.

Despite these unanswered questions, *Franklin* has enormous significance for colleges and universities because it greatly increases the incentives for students and faculty to challenge sex discrimination and sexual harassment in court. It also may persuade individuals considering litigation over alleged employment discrimination to use Title IX instead of Title VII because of the greater availability of money damages. For analysis of *Franklin v. Gwinnett County* and its implications for colleges and universities, see E. J. Vargyas, "*Franklin v. Gwinnett County Public Schools* and Its Impact on Title IX Enforcement," 19 *J. Coll. & Univ. Law* 373 (1993).

Where a student is an employee and the harassment occurs in that context, the student could seek remedies under either Title IX, Title VII, or similar state laws prohibiting sex discrimination. Although some courts have refused to permit employees to file claims of sex discrimination under Title IX (see, for example, *Storey v. Board of Regents of the University of Wisconsin System,* 600 F. Supp. 838 (W.D. Wis. 1985)) because of the availability of remedies under Title VII, a federal appeals court has made the distinctions between the two laws less significant. This court applied the standards for evaluating a sexual harassment case brought under Title VII to the same type of case brought under Title IX by a student employee.

In *Lipsett v. University of Puerto Rico,* 864 F.2d 881 (1st Cir. 1988), a medical resident who was dismissed from the medical school charged the school with hostile environment sexual harassment under Title IX, Section 1983, and the Fifth Amendment's due process clause. Lipsett charged that her fellow students sexually harassed her verbally and that senior residents, her supervisors, refused to assign her appropriate responsibilities because of her sex. She also charged that her supervisors and professors refused to intervene in her behalf after she had notified them of the harassment. Under the deferential standard of review developed in *University of Michigan v. Ewing* (see Section 6.1.1), the trial court had awarded summary judgment for the university because of alleged academic misconduct on the part of the plaintiff.

The First Circuit, however, applied the sexual harassment analysis developed under Title VII, referring in particular to the U.S. Supreme Court's decision in *Meritor Savings Bank v. Vinson* (see Section 2.2.2), which recognized a claim for hostile environment harassment under Title VII, as well as quid pro quo harassment by a supervisor. Noting that the resident had a mixed status as both employee and student, the court ruled that the disparate treatment standard developed under Title VII, which requires the plaintiff to prove intentional discrimination, should also apply to Title IX sexual harassment claims filed by students who are also employees: "[O]ur present holding—that the Title VII standard for proving discriminatory treatment should apply to claims of sex discrimination arising under Title IX—is limited to the context of employment discrimination" (864 F.2d at 897).

Although the individuals accused of sexual harassment were student employees rather than faculty, the court ruled that the university could be held liable for their actions under Title VII precedent:

> We therefore hold, following *Meritor,* that in a Title IX case, an educational institution is liable upon a finding of hostile environment sexual harassment perpetrated by its supervisors upon employees if an official representing that institution knew, or in the exercise of reasonable care, should have known, of the harassment's occurrence, *unless* that official can show that he or she took appropriate steps to halt it. . . . We further hold that this standard also applies to situations in which the hostile environment harassment is perpetrated by the plaintiff's coworkers. . . . [For claims of quid pro quo harassment], an educational institution is absolutely liable for such acts "whether or not [it] knew, should have known, or approved of the supervisor's actions" [864 F.2d at 901].

The plaintiff also sued university officials under Section 1983 (see this volume, Section 2.3.3); the court held that

> a state official, sued under section 1983 in his or her individual capacity, can be held liable for the behavior of his or her subordinates if (1) the behavior of such subordinates results in a constitutional violation and (2) the official's action or inaction was "affirmative[ly] link[ed]," *Oklahoma City v. Tuttle,* 471 U.S. 808 . . . (1985), to that behavior in the sense that it could be characterized as "supervisory encouragement, condonation, or acquiescence" *or* "gross negligence amounting to deliberate indifference" [864 F.2d at 902].

Since the plaintiff had discussed the harassment numerous times with the dean, the director of surgery, and the director of the surgical residency program, the court concluded that "supervisory encouragement" could be found and that liability could attach.

Although *Lipsett* places harassment of student employees within the *Meritor* framework, federal courts initially were unwilling to permit a student who was not also an employee to attack hostile environment sexual harassment under Title IX. In *Yale v. Alexander,* 631 F.2d 178 (2d Cir. 1980), the court affirmed the trial court's dismissal of all the plaintiffs' claims, because they had not proved that they had suffered a "distinct and palpable injury"; the mere presence of unwelcome sexual attention, according to the court, was insufficient to establish such an injury. (The U.S. Supreme Court subsequently declared that unwelcome sexual behavior was sexual harassment (under Title VII) whether or not the target could demonstrate actual injury (*Harris v. Forklift Systems;* see Section 2.2.2).) In *Alexander,* the court used analogies from the employment context to justify its application of Title IX to sexual harassment.

Since *Alexander* was decided prior to the U.S. Supreme Court's opinion in *Meritor,* it might be misleading to suggest that *Alexander* precludes claims of hostile environment harassment by students. In a later case, a trial court found that Title IX encompasses *both* forms of harassment (*Moire v. Temple University School of Medicine,* 613 F. Supp. 1360 (D. Pa. 1985), *affirmed without opin.,* 800 F.2d 1136 (3d Cir. 1986)). The trial judge wrote, "Temple might be liable under Title IX to the extent it condoned or ratified any individually discriminatory conduct of [the professors]" (613 F. Supp. at 1366). In a footnote, the judge discussed both quid pro quo and hostile environment sexual harassment, noting that "the sexual harassment 'doctrine' has generally developed in the context of Title VII" but that "these guidelines seem equally applicable to Title IX" (613 F. Supp. at 1367, n.2). This approach has also been used in sexual harassment cases brought by children against public school systems; in a recent case, a trial court held that Title IX encompasses claims of hostile environment harassment (*Patricia H. v. Berkeley Unified School District,* 830 F. Supp. 1288 (N.D. Cal. 1993)).

Whether Title IX forbids hostile environment sexual harassment of a student by a fellow student (when the target is not an employee) is a more complicated issue, given the opinion of the U.S. Supreme Court in *R.A.V. v. City of St. Paul, Minn.,* 112 S. Ct. 2538 (1992), and the apparent invalidity of most campus codes prohibiting hate speech (see Section 8.3). In an opinion striking the University of Wisconsin's rule against "hate speech" as violative of the First Amendment, a federal trial judge asserted that *Meritor* had no relevance for hostile environment harassment of one student by another. In *UWM Post v. Board of Regents, University of Wisconsin System,* 774 F. Supp. 1163 (E.D. Wis. 1991), the judge offered three reasons for rejecting the university's claim that Title VII's hostile environment prohibitions should be applied to student speech. First, said the judge, Title VII concerns itself with employment, not education. Second, *Meritor* does not apply because students are not agents of the university, and liability in *Meritor* was based on agency theory. And third, Title VII is a statute, which cannot abrogate the protections of the Constitution (774 F. Supp. at 1177). Similarly, as one commentator has concluded, Title IX does not provide students with a remedy against the college or university for assaults or other sexually oriented misconduct committed by a fellow student unless that student was in a supervisory relationship with the student (for example, a graduate student supervising an undergraduate) or a coworker, and the student victim was also an employee (see T. Steinberg, "Rape on College Campuses: Reform Through Title IX," 18 *J. Coll. & Univ. Law* 39, 58 (1991)).

In public institutions—and also in private colleges and universities in states whose constitutions contain free speech provisions that have been applied to conduct by private parties (see, for example, *State v. Schmid,* discussed in Sections 1.5.3 and 11.5.3)—administrators may find it difficult to discipline students for hostile environment sexual harassment of other students. Conversely, the Supreme Court's ruling in *Franklin* raises the financial stakes in Title IX litigation if the perpetrator of the sexual harassment, whether of the quid pro quo or the hostile environment variety, is a faculty member, an administrator, a fellow student in a supervisory role, or some other "agent" of the college or university.

Absent the student's ability to establish an agency relationship between the harasser and the institution, potential plaintiffs' remedies for peer sexual harassment may be limited. The language of Title IX may provide some assistance in this regard, however, if plaintiffs argue that the harassment "denies them the benefits of . . . an education program" (20 U.S.C. §1681(a)).

Given the result in *Franklin,* colleges and universities may wish to review their policies on sexual harassment of students by faculty and other employees. And although consensual sexual relationships between faculty and students do not violate Title IX (as long as the student is beyond the statutory age of consent), some institutions have issued policies forbidding consensual sexual relationships between faculty and students because of the conflict of interest and potential for abuse of the professor's power over the student's academic record. For a defense of such policies, see P. DeChiara, "The Need for Universities to Have Rules on Consensual Sexual Relationships Between Faculty Members and Students," 21 *Columbia J. Law & Social Problems* 137 (1988); for a criticism of such policies, see E. Keller, "Consensual Amorous Relationships Between Faculty and Students: The Constitutional Right to Privacy," 15 *J. Coll. & Univ. Law* 21 (1988). For a comprehensive collection of relevant articles, EEOC policy guidance on sexual harassment issues, and model institutional policies, see E. Cole (ed.), *Sexual Harassment on Campus: A Legal Compendium* (2d ed., National Association of College and University Attorneys, 1990).

12.4.4. Section 504

Section 504 of the Rehabilitation Act of 1973, as amended (29 U.S.C. §794) states:

> No otherwise qualified individual with a disability in the United States . . . shall, solely by reason of his disability, be excluded from the participation in, be denied the benefits of, or be subjected to discrimination under any program or activity receiving federal financial assistance.

The Department of Education's regulations on Section 504 (34 C.F.R. Part 104) contain specific provisions that establish standards for postsecondary institutions to follow in their dealings with "qualified" students and applicants with disabilities; "qualified" employees and applicants for employment; and members of the public with disabilities who are seeking to take advantage of institutional programs and activities open to the public. A "qualified individual with a disability" is "any person who (i) has a physical or mental impairment which substantially limits one or more major life activities, (ii) has a record of such an impairment, or (iii) is regarded as having such an impairment" (34 C.F.R. §104.3(j)). In the context of postsecondary and vocational education services, a "qualified" person with a disability is someone who "meets the academic and technical standards requisite to admission or participation in the recipient's education program or activity" (34 C.F.R. §104.3(k)(3)). Whether an individual with a disability is "qualified" in other situations depends on different criteria. In the context of employment, a qualified individual with a disability is one who, "with reasonable accommodation, can perform the essential functions of the job in question" (34 C.F.R. §104.3(k)(1)). With regard to other services, a qualified individual with a disability is someone who "meets the essential eligibility requirements for the receipt of such services" (34 C.F.R. §104.3(k)(4)).

Although the Section 504 regulations resemble those for Title VI and Title IX in the types of programs and activities considered, they differ in some of the means used for achieving nondiscrimination. The reason for these differences is that "different or special treatment of handicapped persons, because of their handicaps, may be necessary in a number of contexts in order to ensure equal opportunity" (42 Fed. Reg. 22676 (May 4, 1977)). Institutions receiving federal funds may not discriminate on the basis of disability in admission and recruitment of students (see Section 4.1.4.3); in providing financial assistance (Section 4.2.3); in athletic programs (Section 10.4); in housing accommodations (Section 5.1.1); or in the employment of faculty and staff members (Section 2.2.2) or students (see 34 C.F.R. §104.46(c)). The regulations also prohibit discrimination on the basis of disability in a number of other programs and activities of postsecondary institutions.

Section 104.43 requires nondiscriminatory "treatment" of students in general. Besides prohibiting discrimination in the institution's own programs and activities, this section requires that, when an institution places students in an educational program or activity not wholly under its control, the institution "shall assure itself that the other education program or activity, as a whole, provides an equal opportunity for the participation of qualified handicapped persons." In a student-teaching program, for example, the "as a whole" concept allows the institution to make use of a particular external activity even though it discriminates, provided that the institution's entire student-teaching program, taken as a whole, offers student teachers with disabilities "the same range and quality of choice in student-teaching assignments afforded nonhandicapped students" (42 Fed. Reg. at 22692 (comment 30)). Furthermore, the institution must operate its programs and activities in "the most integrated setting appropriate," that is, by integrating disabled persons with nondisabled persons to the maximum extent appropriate (34 C.F.R. §104.43(d)).

The Education Department's regulations recognize that certain academic adjustment may be necessary to protect against discrimination on the basis of disability:

(a) *Academic requirements.* A recipient to which this subpart applies shall make such modifications to its academic requirements as are necessary to ensure that such requirements do not discriminate or have the effect of discriminating, on the basis of handicap, against a qualified handicapped applicant or student. Academic requirements that the recipient can demonstrate are essential to the program of instruction being pursued by such student or to any directly related licensing requirement will not be regarded as discriminatory within the meaning of this section. Modifications may include changes in the length of time permitted for the completion of degree requirements, substitution of specific courses required for the completion of degree requirements, and adaptation of the manner in which specific courses are conducted.

(b) *Other rules.* A recipient to which this subpart applies may not impose upon handicapped students other rules, such as the prohibition of tape recorders in classrooms or of dog guides in campus buildings, that have the effect of limiting the participation of handicapped students in the recipient's education program or activity.

(c) *Course examination.* In its course examinations or other procedures for evaluating students' academic achievement in its program, a recipient to which this subpart applies shall provide such methods for evaluating the achievement of students who have a handicap that impairs sensory, manual, or speaking skills as will best ensure that the results of the evaluation represent the student's achievement in the course, rather than reflecting the student's impaired sensory, manual, or speaking skills (except where such skills are the factors that the test purports to measure).

(d) *Auxiliary aids.* (1) A recipient to which this subpart applies shall take such steps as are necessary to ensure that no handicapped student is denied the benefits of, excluded from participation in, or otherwise subjected to discrimination under the education program or activity operated by the recipient because of the absence of educational auxiliary aids for students with impaired sensory, manual, or speaking skills. (2) Auxiliary aids may include taped texts, interpreters, or other effective methods of making orally delivered materials available to students with hearing impairments, readers in libraries for students with visual impairments, classroom equipment adapted for use by students with manual impairments, and other similar services and actions. Recipients need not provide attendants, individually prescribed devices, readers for personal use or study, or other devices or services of a personal nature [34 C.F.R. §104.44].

Section 104.47(b) provides that counseling and placement services be offered on the same basis to disabled and nondisabled students. The institution is specifically charged with ensuring that job counseling is not more restrictive for disabled students. Under Section 104.47(c), an institution that supplies significant assistance to student social organizations must determine that these organizations do not discriminate against disabled students in their membership practices.

The institution's programs or activities—"when viewed in their entirety"—must be physically accessible to students with disabilities, and the institution's facilities must be usable by them. The regulations applicable to existing facilities differ from those applied to new construction:

> (a) *Program accessibility.* A recipient shall operate each program or activity to which this part applies so that the program or activity, when viewed in its entirety, is readily accessible to handicapped persons. This paragraph does not require a recipient to make each of its existing facilities or every part of a facility accessible to and usable by handicapped persons.
>
> (b) *Methods.* A recipient may comply with the requirements of paragraph (a) of this section through such means as redesign of equipment, reassignment of classes or other services to accessible buildings, assignment of aides to beneficiaries, home visits, delivery of health, welfare, or other social services at alternate accessible sites, alteration of existing facilities and construction of new facilities in conformance with the requirements of §104.23, or any other methods that result in making its program or activity accessible to handicapped persons. A recipient is not required to make structural changes in existing facilities where other methods are effective in achieving compliance with paragraph (a) of this section. In choosing among available methods for meeting the requirement of paragraph (a) of this section, a recipient shall give priority to those methods that offer programs and activities to handicapped persons in the most integrated setting appropriate [34 C.F.R. §104 22; see also policy interpretations of this regulation at 43 Fed. Reg. 36034 and 36035 (1978)].

If structural changes in existing facilities—that is, facilities existing in June 1977, when the regulations became effective—were necessary to make a program or an activity accessible, they must have been completed by June 1980. All new construction must be readily accessible when it is completed.

In *Southeastern Community College v. Davis,* 442 U.S. 397 (1979), set forth in Section 4.1.4.3, the U.S. Supreme Court added some important interpretive gloss to the regulation on academic adjustments and assistance for disabled students (34 C.F.R. §104.44). The Court quoted but did not question the validity of the regulation's requirement that an institution provide "auxiliary aids"—such as interpreters, taped texts, or braille materials—for students with sensory impairments. It made very clear, however, that the law does not require "major" or "substantial" modifications in an institution's curriculum or academic standards to accommodate disabled students. To require such modifications, the Court said, would be to read into Section 504 an "affirmative action obligation" not warranted by its "language, purpose, [or] history." Moreover, if the regulations were to be interpreted to impose such obligation, they would to that extent be invalid.

The Court acknowledged, however, that the line between discrimination and a lawful refusal to take affirmative action is not always clear. Thus, in some instances programmatic changes may be required where they would not fundamentally alter the program itself. In determining where this line is to be drawn, the Court would apparently extend considerable deference to postsecondary institutions' legitimate educational judgments respecting academic standards and course requirements. Davis had argued that Southeastern's insistence that its students be capable of performing all the functions of a professional nurse was discriminatory, since North Carolina law did not require as much from applicants for a license to practice. In a footnote to its opinion, the Court rejected this claim: "Respondent's argument misses the point. Southeastern's program, structured to train persons who will be able to perform all normal roles of a registered nurse, represents a legitimate academic policy, and is accepted by the state. In effect, it seeks to ensure that no graduate will pose a danger to the public in any professional role [that] he or she might be cast [in]. Even if the licensing requirements of North Carolina or some other state are less demanding, nothing in the Act requires an educational institution to lower its standards."

While *Davis* thus limits postsecondary institutions' legal obligation to modify their academic programs to accommodate disabled students, the opinion does not limit an institution's obligation to make its facilities physically accessible to qualified students with disabilities, as required by the regulations (34 C.F.R. §104.22)—even when doing so involves major expense. In *Davis,* the Court found that, because of her hearing disability, the plaintiff was not "otherwise qualified" for admission to the nursing program. When a person with a disability is qualified and has been admitted, however, Section 104.22 requires that facilities as a whole be "readily accessible" to that person.

The U.S. Supreme Court spoke a second time on the significance of Section 504—this time with regard to whether individuals with contagious diseases are protected by Section 504. In *School Board of Nassau County v. Arline,* 480 U.S. 273 (1987), the Court held that a teacher with tuberculosis was protected by Section 504 and that her employer was required to determine whether a reasonable accommodation could be made for her. Subsequent to *Arline,* Congress, in amendments to Section 504 (42 U.S.C. §706 (8)(D)), and the EEOC, in regulations interpreting the employment provisions of the Americans with Disabilities Act (29 C.F.R. §1630.2(r)), provided other statutory protections for students and staff with contagious diseases. For a discussion of the relevant legal principles under Section 504 in a case where a university dismissed a dental student suffering from AIDS, see *Doe v. Washington University,* 780 F. Supp. 628 (E.D. Mo. 1991).

The availability of compensatory damages under Section 504 was addressed in *Tanberg v. Weld County Sheriff,* 787 F. Supp. 970 (D. Colo. 1992). Citing

Franklin v. Gwinnett County Public Schools (Section 12.4.9), the federal trial judge ruled that a plaintiff who proves intentional discrimination under Section 504 can be entitled to compensatory damages.

The significance of *Davis* may be limited for an additional reason, in that the Americans with Disabilities Act affords broader rights of access and accommodation to students, employees, and, in some cases, the general public than contemplated by *Davis*. ADA remedies are broader than those provided for by Section 504 and will now apply to all colleges and universities, whether or not they receive federal funds. For a comparison of Section 504 and the ADA with regard to access to colleges and universities for students with disabilities, see H. Kaufman, *Access to Institutions of Higher Education for Students with Disabilities* (National Association of College and University Attorneys, 1991). See also Note, "Americans with Disabilities Act of 1990: Significant Overlap with Section 504 for Colleges and Universities," 18 *J. Coll. & Univ. Law* 389 (1992).

12.4.5. Age Discrimination Act

The Age Discrimination Act of 1975 (42 U.S.C. §6101 *et seq.*) contains a general prohibition on age discrimination in federally funded programs and activities. Under the Age Discrimination Act's original statement-of-purpose clause, the prohibition applied only to "unreasonable" discrimination—a limitation not found in the Title VI, Title IX, or Section 504 civil rights statutes. Congress postponed the Act's effective date, however, and directed the U.S. Commission on Civil Rights to study age discrimination in federally assisted programs. After considering the commission's report, submitted in January 1978, Congress amended the Age Discrimination Act in October 1978 (Pub. L. No. 95–478) to strike the word "unreasonable" from the statement-of-purpose clause, thus removing a critical restriction on the Act's scope.

In 1979, the U.S. Department of Health, Education, and Welfare issued final regulations under the Age Discrimination Act (44 Fed. Reg. 33768 (June 12, 1979)). These regulations, now codified in 45 C.F.R. Part 90, "state general, government-wide rules" for implementing this law (45 C.F.R. §90.2(a)). Every federal agency administering federal aid programs must implement its own specific regulations consistent with HEW's (now HHS's) general regulations.

The general regulations, together with the extensive commentary that accompanies them (44 Fed. Reg. 33768–33775, 33780–33787), provide a detailed explanation of the Age Discrimination Act. The regulations are divided into several subparts. Subpart A explains the purpose and coverage of the Act and regulations and defines some of the regulatory terminology. Subpart B of the regulations explains the ADA's prohibition against age discrimination in programs covered by the Act and also lists the exceptions to this prohibition. Section 90.12 sets out the specific prohibition as follows:

(b) *Specific rules:* A recipient may not, in any program or activity receiving federal financial assistance, directly or through contractual, licensing, or other arrangements, use age distinctions or take any other actions which have the effect, on the basis of age, of:

(1) excluding individuals from, denying them the benefits of, or subjecting them to discrimination under, a program or activity receiving federal financial assistance, or

(2) denying or limiting individuals in their opportunity to participate in any program or activity receiving federal financial assistance.

Sections 90.14 and 90.15 of the regulations set out the exceptions to Section 90.12. Explanatory commentary accompanying the regulations makes it clear that recipients can never justify exceptions to the general prohibition on the basis of cost-benefit considerations alone; they must meet the specific tests in Sections 90.14 and 90.15 of the regulations (44 Fed. Reg. 33774, 33783).

Although the regulations and commentary add considerable particularity to the brief provisions of the Act, the full import of the Act for postsecondary institutions can be ascertained only by a study of the specific regulations that agencies have promulgated or will promulgate to fulfill the mandate of the general regulations. The HHS specific regulations, for example, are codified in 45 C.F.R. Part 91.

The Education Department published final rules to interpret the Age Discrimination Act as it applies to the department's financial assistance programs (most notably, the student financial assistance programs) at 34 C.F.R. Part 110 (56 Fed. Reg. 40194). The Education Department's regulations track the general regulations in many respects, and they require institutions to provide the same type of assurance of compliance that they must provide under Titles IV and IX and Section 504. The regulations establish a procedure for filing a complaint with the department under the Age Discrimination Act (34 C.F.R. §110.31), provide for mediation of disputes under the Act by the Federal Mediation and Conciliation Service (34 C.F.R. §110.32), and describe the department's investigation process if mediation fails to resolve the complaint (34 C.F.R. §110.33). Penalties for violations of the Act, including termination of funding or debarment from future funding, are contained at 34 C.F.R. §110.35. A person filing a complaint under the Act must exhaust the administrative remedies provided by the regulations before filing a civil complaint in court (34 C.F.R. §110.39).

12.4.6. Affirmative Action

Affirmative action poses a special problem under the federal civil rights statutes. The Department of Education's Title VI regulations both require and permit affirmative action under certain circumstances:

(i) In administering a program regarding which the recipient has previously discriminated against persons on the ground of race, color, or national origin, the recipient must take affirmative action to overcome the effects of prior discrimination.

(ii) Even in the absence of such prior discrimination, a recipient in administering a program may take affirmative action to overcome the effects of conditions which resulted in limiting participation by persons of a particular race, color, or national origin [34 C.F.R. §100.3(b)(6)].

The Title IX regulations also permit affirmative action for voluntary correction of conditions that resulted in limited participation by the members of one sex in the institution's programs and activities (34 C.F.R. §106.3(b)). However, both the Title IX and the Section 504 regulations require a recipient to engage in "remedial action" rather than "affirmative action" to overcome the effects of its own prior discrimination (34 C.F.R. §106.3(a); 34 C.F.R. §104.6(a)). In addition, the Section 504 regulations suggest that the recipient take only "voluntary action" rather than "affirmative action" to correct conditions that resulted in limited participation by the handicapped (34 C.F.R. §104.6(b)). But none of the regulations define "affirmative action," "remedial action," or "voluntary action," or set out the limits of permissible action.

One federal district court has ruled that in a Title VI case, some "affirmative action" may itself constitute a Title VI violation. In *Flanagan v. President and Directors of Georgetown College*, 417 F. Supp. 377 (D.D.C. 1976), the issue was that Georgetown Law Center had allocated 60 percent of its scholarship funds to minority students, who constituted only 11 percent of the class. The university claimed that the program was permissible under Section 100.3(b)(6)(ii) of the Title VI regulations. The court disagreed, holding that the scholarship program was not administered on a "racially neutral basis" and was "reverse discrimination on the basis of race, which cannot be justified by a claim of affirmative action." Subsequently, in *Regents of University of California v. Bakke*, 438 U.S. 265 (1978) (see Section 4.1.5), the first U.S. Supreme Court case on affirmative action under Title VI, a 5-to-4 majority of the Court agreed that Title VI did not require complete racial neutrality in affirmative action. But no majority of justices could agree on the extent to which Title VI and its regulations permit racial or ethnic preferences to be used as one part of an affirmative action program.

Like the Title VI, Title IX, and Section 504 regulations, the HHS general regulations under the Age Discrimination Act of 1975 (see Section 12.4.5) also include a provision on affirmative action:

(a) Where a recipient is found to have discriminated on the basis of age, the recipient shall take any remedial action which the agency may require to overcome the effects of the discrimination. If another recipient exercises control over the recipient that has discriminated, both recipients may be required to take remedial action.

(b) Even in the absence of a finding of discrimination, a recipient may take affirmative action to overcome the effects of conditions that resulted in limited participation in the recipient's program or activity on the basis of age.

(c) If a recipient operating a program which serves the elderly or children, in addition to persons of other ages, provides special benefits to the elderly or to children, the provision of those benefits shall be presumed to be voluntary affirmative action provided that it does not have the effect of excluding otherwise eligible persons from participation in the program [45 C.F.R. §90.49].

Paralleling the other civil rights regulations, this regulation distinguishes between required (subsection (a)) and permitted (subsection (b)) actions and, like Title IX and Section 504, uses the term "remedial action" to describe the former. Also like the Title IX and Section 504 regulations, this regulation specifies that "remedial action" is permitted only when the recipient has discriminated in the past against the class of persons whom the regulations protect. In addition, the Age Discrimination Act regulation contains a unique provision (subsection (c)), which, under certain circumstances, brings the provision of special benefits to two age groups—the elderly and children—under the protective umbrella of "voluntary affirmative action." The Act's regulations do not include explanatory commentary on Section 90.49. Nor, in common with the other civil rights regulations, do they define "remedial action" or "affirmative action" or (except for subsection (c)) the scope of permissible action.

Thus, the federal regulations give postsecondary administrators little guidance concerning the affirmative or remedial actions they must take to maintain compliance, or may take without jeopardizing compliance. Insufficient guidance, however, is not a justification for avoiding affirmative action when it is required by the regulations, nor should it deter administrators from taking voluntary action when it is their institution's policy to do so. Rather, administrators should proceed carefully, seeking the assistance of legal counsel and keeping abreast of the developing case law and agency policy interpretations on affirmative action.

12.4.7. Scope and Coverage Problems

In recent years, the scope and coverage of the civil rights statutes have been the subject of intense debate, considerable litigation, and several congressional bills. The following subsections review the most complex and controversial of the scope and coverage issues.

The administrative regulations implementing the civil rights statutes (particularly the regulations of the Department of Education) provide the initial guidance on these issues. Courts have sometimes reviewed the regulations to determine whether they are authorized by the statute being implemented. Where there are gaps in the regulations or the statutes, courts have also stepped in to provide answers. And in one instance, after a controversial U.S. Supreme Court decision (in *Grove City College v. Bell)*, Congress passed a law (the Civil Rights Restoration Act) that overturned a Court decision (see Section 12.4.7.4).

As the volume of litigation has increased, it has become apparent that the similarities of statutory language under the four civil rights statutes give rise to similar scope and coverage issues. Answers to an issue under one statute will thus provide guidance in answering comparable issues under another statute. There are some critical differences, however, in the statutory language and implementing regulations for each statute (for example, as explained in Section 12.4.7.1, Title VI and the Age Discrimination Act have provisions limiting their applicability to employment discrimination, whereas Title IX and Section 504 do not), and each statute has its own unique legislative history. Therefore, to gain a fine-tuned view of further developments, administrators and counsel should approach each statute and each scope and coverage issue separately, taking account of both their similarities to and their differences from the other statutes and other issues.

12.4.7.1. Coverage of employment discrimination.

One question concerning scope and coverage is whether the civil rights statutes prohibit discrimination not only against students but also against employees. Both Title VI and the Age Discrimination Act contain provisions that permit coverage of discrimination against employees only when a "primary objective" of the federal aid is "to provide employment" (42 U.S.C. §2000d–3; 42 U.S.C. §6103(c)). Title IX and Section 504 do not contain any such express limitation. Consistent with the apparent open-endedness of the latter two statutes, both the Title IX and the Section 504 regulations have provisions comprehensively covering discrimination against employees, while the Title VI and the Age Discrimination Act regulations cover employment discrimination only in narrow circumstances (34 C.F.R. §§100.2 and 100.3(c); 45 C.F.R. §90.3(b)(2)).

The first major U.S. Supreme Court case on scope and coverage—*North Haven Board of Education v. Bell,* 456 U.S. 512 (1982)—concerned employment. In that case, the Court considered two questions: (1) whether the Title IX statute applies to the employment practices of educational institutions; and (2) if it does, whether the scope and coverage of the Title IX employment regulations are consistent with the Title IX statute.

Looking to the wording of the statute, the statute's legislative history, and the statute's "postenactment history" in Congress and at HEW (now ED), the Court (with three dissenters) answered both questions in the affirmative.

In a later case, *Consolidated Rail Corp. v. Darrone,* 465 U.S. 624 (1984), the Court also upheld Section 504's applicability to discrimination against employees.

12.4.7.2. Coverage of unintentional discriminatory acts. None of the four statutes explicitly state whether they prohibit actions whose effects are discriminatory (that is, actions that have a disproportionate or disparate impact on the class of persons protected) or whether such actions are prohibited only if taken with a discriminatory intent or motive. The regulations for Title VI and the Age Discrimination Act, however, contain provisions that apparently prohibit actions with discriminatory effects, even if those actions are not intentionally discriminatory (34 C.F.R. §100.3(b)(2); 45 C.F.R. §90.12), and the Section 504 regulations prohibit actions that have the effect of subjecting a qualified individual to discrimination on the basis of disability (34 C.F.R. §104.4 (b)(4) and (5)). Title IX's regulations prohibit testing or evaluation of skill that has a discriminatory effect on the basis of sex (34 C.F.R. §§106.21(b)(2) and 106.34), and they also prohibit certain employment practices with discriminatory effects (34 C.F.R. §106.51(a)(3)).

The leading U.S. Supreme Court case on the intent issue is *Guardians Assn. v. Civil Service Commission of the City of New York,* 463 U.S. 582 (1983). The justices issued six opinions in the case, none of which commanded a majority and which, according to Justice Powell, "further confuse rather than guide." The Court's basic difficulty was reconciling *Lau v. Nichols,* 414 U.S. 563 (1974), which held that Title VI and HEW's regulations prohibit actions with discriminatory effects, and *Regents of the University of California v. Bakke,* 438 U.S. 265 (1978), which indicated that Title VI reaches no further than the Fourteenth Amendment's equal protection clause, which prohibits only intentional discrimination.

Although the Court could not agree on the import of these two cases or on the analysis to adopt in the case before it, one can extract some meaning from *Guardians* by pooling the views expressed in the various opinions. A majority of the justices did hold that the intent standard is a necessary component of the Title VI statute. A different majority, however, held that, even though the statute embodies an intent test, the ED regulations that adopt an effects test are nevertheless valid. In his opinion, Justice White tallied the differing views of the justices on these points (463 U.S. at 584 n.2, and 607 n.27). He then rationalized these seemingly contradictory conclusions by explaining that "the language of Title VI on its face is ambiguous; the word 'discrimination' is inherently so." The statute should therefore be amenable to a broader construction by ED, "at least to the extent of permitting, if not requiring, regulations that reach" discriminatory effects (463 U.S. at 592; see also 463 U.S. at 643–45 (opinion of Justice Stevens)).

The result of this confusing melange of opinions is to validate the Education Department's regulations extending Title VI coverage to actions with discriminatory effects. At the same time, however, the *Guardians* opinions suggest that, if the department were to change its regulations so as to adopt an intent test, such a change would also be valid. Any such change, though, would in turn be subject to invalidation by Congress, which could amend the Title VI statute (or other statutes under which the issue arose) to replace its intent standard with an effects test. Such legislation would apparently be constitutional.

In *Alexander v. Choate*, 469 U.S. 287 (1985), the Court also considered the intent issue under Section 504. After reviewing the various opinions in the *Guardians* case on Title VI, the Court determined that that case does not control the intent issue under Section 504 because Section 504 raises considerations different from those raised by Title VI. In particular:

> Discrimination against the handicapped was perceived by Congress to be most often the product not of invidious animus, but rather of thoughtlessness and indifference—of benign neglect. . . . Federal agencies and commentators on the plight of the handicapped similarly have found that discrimination against the handicapped is primarily the result of apathetic attitudes rather than affirmative animus.
>
> In addition, much of the conduct that Congress sought to alter in passing the Rehabilitation Act would be difficult if not impossible to reach were the Act construed to proscribe only conduct fueled by a discriminatory intent. For example, elimination of architectural barriers was one of the central aims of the Act (see, for example, S. Rep. No. 93–318, p. 4 (1973), U.S. Code Cong. & Admin. News 1973, pp. 2076, 2080), yet such barriers were clearly not erected with the aim or intent of excluding the handicapped [469 U.S. at 295–97].

Although these considerations suggest that discriminatory intent need not be a requirement under Section 504, the Court also noted some countervailing considerations:

> At the same time, the position urged by respondents—that we interpret Section 504 to reach all action disparately affecting the handicapped—is also troubling. Because the handicapped typically are not similarly situated to the nonhandicapped, respondents' position would in essence require each recipient of federal funds first to evaluate the effects on the handicapped of every proposed action that might touch the interests of the handicapped, and then to consider alternatives for achieving the same objectives with less severe disadvantage to the handicapped. The formalization and policing of this process could lead to a wholly unwieldy administrative and adjudicative burden [469 U.S. at 298].

Faced with these difficulties, the Court declined to hold that one group of considerations would always have priority over the other. "While we reject the boundless notion that all disparate-impact showings constitute prima facie cases under Section 504, we assume without deciding that Section 504 reaches at least some conduct that has an unjustifiable disparate impact upon the handicapped."

Thus "splitting the difference," the Court left for another day the specification of what types of Section 504 cases will not require evidence of a discriminatory intent.

A related, but different, issue involves the showing that plaintiffs must make to obtain compensatory damages under Title VI. In *Craft v. Board of Trustees of the University of Illinois,* 793 F.2d 140 (7th Cir. 1986), the court, reading together *Guardians* and *Alexander v. Choate,* held that the plaintiffs must show intentional discrimination to obtain *compensatory* damages under Title VI but need show only a disparate impact to obtain *equitable* (injunctive) relief. This distinction between compensatory and equitable relief had been suggested in both Justice White's and Justice Rehnquist's opinions in *Guardians.*

12.4.7.3. Scope of the phrase "receiving federal financial assistance." Each of the four civil rights statutes prohibits discrimination in (1) "a program or activity" that is (2) "receiving federal financial assistance." Uncertainty about the definitions of these two terms, and their interrelation, has created substantial questions about the scope of the civil rights statutes. The first term is discussed in Section 12.4.7.4; the second is discussed here. The major question regarding the second term is whether indirect or student-based aid, such as Pell Grants or veterans' education benefits, is "federal financial assistance" that would trigger the protections of the civil rights statutes.

The statutes do not define the phrase "federal financial assistance." But the Education Department's regulations for each statute contain a broad definition. Under Title IX, for instance, "federal financial assistance" includes, inter alia, grants or loans for construction, student assistance, grants of real or personal property, services of federal personnel, and "any other contract, agreement, or arrangement" that provides assistance to an "education program or activity" (34 C.F.R. §106.2(g)). The definitions in the Title VI (34 C.F.R. §100.13), Section 504 (34 C.F.R. §104.3(h)(i)), and ADA (45 C.F.R. §90.4) regulations are similar.

The leading case addressing the definition of federal financial assistance is *Grove City College v. Bell,* 465 U.S. 555 (1984). The college, a private liberal arts institution, received no direct federal or state financial assistance. Many of the college's students, however, did receive Basic Educational Opportunity Grants (now Pell Grants), which they used to defray their educational costs at the college. The Education Department determined that Grove City was a recipient of "federal financial assistance" under 34 C.F.R. §106.2(g)(1) and advised the college to execute an Assurance of Compliance (a form certifying that the college will comply with Title IX) as required by 34 C.F.R. §106.4. The college refused, arguing that the indirect aid received by its students did not constitute federal financial assistance to the college.

The U.S. Supreme Court unanimously held that the student aid constituted aid to the college and that, if the college did not execute an Assurance of Compliance, the Education Department could terminate the student aid. The Court rejected the college's distinction between federal aid that was given directly to the college and "indirect" federal aid that was channeled to students, stating that the statute made no distinction, and thus neither would the Court.

12.4.7.4. Scope of the phrase "program or activity." The civil rights statutes proscribe discrimination in a "program or activity" that is "receiving" federal aid. Thus, besides determining that the aid involved fits the definition of "federal financial assistance," prior to 1988 it was not clear whether the entire institution or just those programs actually receiving funding from the federal government were subject to the dictates of these civil rights statutes. The Title VI regulations did contain a comprehensive definition of "program," however, that included within it the concept of "activity" (34 C.F.R. §100.13(g)). The Title IX, Section 504, and Age Discrimination Act regulations had only sketchy references to these terms (34 C.F.R. §106.31(a); 34 C.F.R. §104.43(a); 45 C.F.R. §90.3(a)).

Numerous questions about the "program or activity" concept arose in litigation prior to 1988. The most controversial was the question of how to apply this concept to indirect or student-based aid, such as Pell Grants or veterans' education benefits. Did all the institution's programs "receive" this aid, or was the institution itself the "program," thus binding the entire institution to the nondiscrimination requirement? Or was only the institution's financial aid office or some lesser portion of the institution bound?

Another set of questions related to both indirect student-based aid and direct (or earmarked) institution-based aid, such as construction grants. If a program or an activity in an institution did not directly receive federal funds but benefited from the receipt of funds by other institutional programs or activities, was it subject to nondiscrimination requirements? (See *Haffer v. Temple University*, 688 F.2d 14 (3d Cir. 1982), applying the "benefit theory" for extending the scope of a civil rights statute.) Or if a program or an activity did not directly receive federal funds but engaged in discriminatory practices that "infected" programs or activities that did directly receive funds, was it subject to nondiscrimination requirements? (See *Iron Arrow Honor Society v. Heckler*, 702 F.2d 549 (5th Cir. 1983), *vacated as moot*, 464 U.S. 67 (1983), adopting the "infection theory" for extending the scope of a civil rights statute.) Although the passage of the Civil Rights Restoration Act of 1987 (which became effective in March 1988) has eliminated the uncertainty about these issues, a long road of litigation led to the Act's passage and is worthy of summary.

The U.S. Supreme Court first addressed the "program or activity" concept in *North Haven Board of Education v. Bell*, 456 U.S. 512 (1982), discussed in Section 12.4.7.1. In considering the validity of the Education Department's Title IX regulations on employment (Subpart E), the Court noted the "'program-specific' nature of the [Title IX] statute" and indicated that, to be valid, the regulations must be "consistent with the Act's program specificity." To support this conclusion, the Court cited Section 901(a) of Title IX (20 U.S.C. §1681(a)), prohibiting sex discrimination in a "program or activity" receiving federal funding; Section 902 (20 U.S.C. §1682), authorizing federal agencies to implement regulations regarding any "program or activity" for which it provides funds; and another provision in Section 902—called the "pinpoint" provision—requiring that any fund termination by a federal agency "be limited in its effect to the particular program, or part thereof, in which . . . noncompliance has been . . . found."

Although holding that Title IX is limited in its scope to particular programs and activities, the Court in *North Haven* declined to define "program," the key term giving life to the concept of program specificity. Two years later, however, the Court again confronted this definitional issue in *Grove City College v. Bell*, 465 U.S. 555 (1984), discussed in Section 12.4.7.3. Having unanimously agreed that the students' receipt of Basic Educational Opportunity Grants (BEOGs) constituted "federal financial assistance" for the college, the justices then faced the problem of identifying the program or activity that received this assistance and was therefore subject to Title IX. With three of the justices dissenting, the Court held that the program or activity was not the entire institution (as the appellate court had determined) but only the college's financial aid program.

The *Grove City* analysis of the "program or activity" issue proved to be highly controversial. Members of Congress criticized the analysis as being inconsistent with congressional intent. Civil rights groups and other interested parties criticized the decision's narrowing effect on federal enforcement of civil rights—not only under Title IX but also under the other three civil rights statutes using the same "program or activity" language, and not only for federal aid to education but for other types of federal assistance as well.

Between 1984 and 1987, several bills were introduced in Congress to overturn the *Grove City* decision, but none of them could muster sufficient support for passage. In 1987, the Civil Rights Restoration Act (CRRA) of 1987 (Pub. L. No. 100–259, 102 Stat. 28) was passed over the veto of President Reagan and became effective on March 22, 1988. The CRRA amends the four civil rights laws (Title VI, Title IX, Section 504, and the Age Discrimination Act) by defining "program or activity" as:

> all the operations of . . . a college, university, or other postsecondary institution . . . any part of which is extended federal financial assistance [20 U.S.C. §1687].

This language clearly indicates that colleges will be covered in their entirety by these laws if any part of their operations is extended federal aid—although special language in Title IX, which does not appear in the other three laws, exempts religious organizations if the law's requirements are inconsistent with their religious tenets (20 U.S.C. §1687).

12.4.8. Administrative Enforcement

Compliance with each of the four civil rights statutes is enforced through a complex system of procedures and mechanisms administered by the federal agencies that provide financial assistance. Postsecondary administrators should develop a sound understanding of this enforcement process so that they can satisfactorily pursue both the rights and the responsibilities of their institutions should compliance problems arise.

The Title VI statute delegates enforcement responsibility to the various federal funding agencies. Under Executive Order 12250, 45 Fed. Reg. 72995 (1980), the U.S. attorney general is responsible for coordinating agency enforcement efforts. The attorney general has implemented enforcement regulations (28 C.F.R. Part 42) as well as "Guidelines for the Enforcement of Title VI" (28 C.F.R. §50.3), which impose various requirements on agencies responsible for enforcement. Each agency, for instance, must issue guidelines or regulations on Title VI for all programs under which it provides federal financial assistance (28 C.F.R. §42.404). These regulations and guidelines must be available to the public (28 C.F.R. §42.405). The Justice Department's regulations require the agencies to collect sufficient data on such items as the racial composition of the population eligible for the program and the location of facilities in order to determine compliance (28 C.F.R. §42.406). All Title VI compliance decisions must be made by, or be subject to the review of, the agency's civil rights office. Programs found to be complying must be reviewed periodically to ensure continued compliance. A finding of probable noncompliance must be reported to the attorney general (28 C.F.R. §42.407). Each agency must establish complaint procedures and publish them in its guidelines. All Title VI complaints must be logged in the agency records (28 C.F.R. §42.408). If a finding of probable noncompliance is made, enforcement procedures shall be instituted after a "reasonable period" of negotiation. If negotiations continue for more than sixty days after the finding of noncompliance, the agency must notify the attorney general (28 C.F.R. §42.411). If several agencies provide federal financial assistance to a substantial number of the same recipients for similar or related purposes, the agencies must coordinate Title VI enforcement efforts. The agencies shall designate one agency as the lead agency for Title VI compliance (28 C.F.R. §42.413). Each agency must develop a written enforcement plan, specifying priorities, timetables, and procedures, which shall be available to the public (28 C.F.R. §42.415).

Under the Department of Education's Title VI regulations, fund recipients must file assurances with ED that their programs comply with Title VI (34 C.F.R. §100.4) and must submit "timely, complete, and accurate compliance reports at such times, and in such form and containing such information, as the responsible Department official or his designee may determine to be necessary to enable him to ascertain whether the recipient has complied or is complying" with Title VI (34 C.F.R. §100.6(b)). ED may make periodic compliance reviews and must accept and respond to individual complaints from persons who believe that they are victims of discrimination (34 C.F.R. §100.7). If an investigation reveals a violation that cannot be resolved by negotiation and voluntary compliance (34 C.F.R. §100.7(d)), ED may refer the case to the Justice Department for prosecution (see this volume, Section 12.4.9) or commence administrative proceedings for fund termination (34 C.F.R. §100.8). Any termination of funds must be "limited in its effect to the particular program, or part thereof, in which . . . noncompliance has been . . . found" (42 U.S.C. §2000d–1; 34 C.F.R. §100.8(c)). The regulations specify the procedural safeguards that must be observed in the fund termination proceedings: notice, the right to counsel, a written decision, an appeal to a reviewing authority, and a discretionary appeal to the secretary of education (34 C.F.R. §§100.9 and 100.10).

Like Title VI, Title IX enforcement is coordinated by the attorney general under Executive Order 12250. Title IX also includes the same limit as Title VI on the scope of fund termination (20 U.S.C. §1682) and utilizes the same procedures for fund termination (34 C.F.R. §106.71). An institution subject to Title IX must appoint at least one employee to coordinate its compliance efforts and must establish a grievance procedure for handling gender discrimination complaints within the institution (34 C.F.R. §106.8).

Section 504 is also subject to Executive Order 12250, and funding agencies' enforcement efforts are thus also coordinated by the attorney general. The attorney general's coordination regulations, setting forth enforcement responsibilities of federal agencies for nondiscrimination on the basis of disability, are published in 28 C.F.R. Part 41. The Section 504 statute also establishes an Interagency Coordinating Council for Section 504 enforcement, the membership of which includes, among others, the attorney general and the secretary of education (29 U.S.C. §794c). ED's Section 504 regulations for its own programs impose compliance responsibilities similar to those under Title IX. However, recipients with fewer than fifteen employees need not conform to certain requirements: (1) having a copy of the remedial plan available for inspection (34 C.F.R. §104.6(c)(2)); (2) appointing an agency employee to coordinate the compliance effort (34 C.F.R. §104.7(a)); and (3) establishing a grievance procedure for handling discrimination complaints (34 C.F.R. §104.7(b)). Most postsecondary educational institutions are not excepted from these requirements, since most have more than the minimum number of employees. Section 504 also adopts the Title VI procedural regulations concerning fund terminations.

Under the Age Discrimination Act, federal funding agencies must propose implementing regulations and submit them to the secretary of health and human services for review; all such agency regulations must be consistent with HHS's "general regulations" (42 U.S.C. §6103(a)(4); 45 C.F.R. §90.31). Each agency must hold "compliance reviews" and other investigations to determine adherence to ADA requirements (45 C.F.R. §90.44(a)). Each agency must also follow specified procedures when undertaking to terminate a recipient's funding (45 C.F.R. §90.47). Termination of funds is limited to the "particular program or activity, or part of such program or activity, with respect to which [a] finding [of discrimination] has been made," and may not be based "in whole or in part on any finding with respect to any program or activity which does not receive Federal financial assistance" (42 U.S.C. §6104(b)). The ADA contains a number of substantive exceptions to coverage, more expansive than the exceptions to the ether civil rights statutes (see Section 12.4.5).

The federal courts exercise a limited review of federal agencies' enforcement efforts. If a federal agency terminates an institution's funding, the institution may appeal that decision to the courts once it has exhausted administrative review procedures within the agency. In addition, if a federal agency abuses its enforcement authority during enforcement proceedings and before a final decision, an affected educational institution may also seek injunctive relief from such improper enforcement efforts.

Different questions are presented when judicial review of federal agency enforcement is sought not by postsecondary institutions but by the victims of the institutions' alleged discrimination. Such victims may seek judicial orders requiring a federal agency to fulfill its statutory duty to enforce the civil rights statutes; or, on a smaller scale, an alleged victim may challenge in court an agency's failure or refusal to act on a complaint that he or she had filed with an agency responsible for enforcing the civil rights statutes. The case law indicates that courts will not be receptive to such requests for judicial intervention in administrative enforcement activities—at least not unless Congress itself authorizes victims to seek such redress from the courts.

In *Adams v. Richardson*, 356 F. Supp. 92 (D.D.C. 1973), *affirmed*, 480 F.2d 1159 (D.C. Cir. 1973), some victims of unlawful discrimination sought judicial intervention to compel enforcement of Title VI. The plaintiffs accused HEW of failure to enforce Title VI in the southern states. In the part of the case dealing with higher education, HEW had found the higher education systems of ten states out of compliance with Title VI and had requested each state to submit a desegregation plan within four months. Three years later, after the lawsuit had been filed and the court was ready to rule, five states still had not submitted any plan and five had submitted plans that did not remedy the violations. HEW had not commenced administrative enforcement efforts or referred the cases to the Justice Department for prosecution. The district court ordered HEW to commence enforcement proceedings.

The appellate court agreed with the district court's conclusion, but, noting that HEW had not issued desegregation guidelines for colleges and universities and thus was ill-equipped to move quickly, modified the terms of the district court's injunction so that HEW would be given more time to initiate enforcement proceedings.

After the appellate court's decision, the district court maintained jurisdiction over the case in order to supervise compliance with its injunction. The judge issued a number of other decisions after 1973, some of which were reviewed by the appellate court. In April 1977, the district court revoked HEW's approval of several states' higher education desegregation plans and ordered HEW to devise criteria (see Section 12.4.2) by which it would evaluate new plans to be submitted by these states. In March 1983, the court entered another order requiring HEW (by then ED) to obtain new plans from five states that had defaulted on plans previously accepted by HEW. This order established time limits by which ED was required to initiate formal enforcement proceedings against these states, and several others whose plans had never been approved, if they had not submitted new, acceptable plans. The order also required ED to report systematically to the plaintiffs on enforcement activities regarding the states subject to the suit.

On the government's appeal of the district court's 1983 order, the appellate court remanded the case to the district court for a determination of whether the plaintiffs continued to have the legal "standing" (see Section 1.4.2) necessary to maintain the lawsuit and justify judicial enforcement of the order (*Women's Equity Action League v. Bell* and *Adams v. Bell,* 743 F.2d 42 (D.C. Cir. 1984)). In 1987, the district court dismissed the case, ruling that the plaintiffs lacked standing to pursue the litigation (*Adams v. Bennett,* 675 F. Supp. 668 (D.D.C. 1987)). The district judge reasoned that ED's Office for Civil Rights had not caused the segregation that the plaintiffs were subjected to, and that the degree to which ED's continued monitoring of state acts would redress this segregation was "speculative."

Although initially the appellate court reversed the district court, ordering additional hearings on what remedies should be granted to desegregate the dual systems, in 1990 it decided to dismiss the case, by then titled *Women's Equity Action League v. Cavazos* (906 F.2d 742 (D.C. Cir. 1990)). In the opinion, Judge Ruth Bader Ginsburg said, "Congress has not explicitly or implicitly authorized the grand scale action plaintiffs delineate" and called the plaintiffs' action an attempt to make the trial court a "nationwide overseer or pacer of procedures government agencies use to enforce civil rights prescriptions controlling educational institutions that receive federal funds" (906 F.2d at 744). If suits directly against a discriminating entity (for which a private right of action does exist under Title VI; see Section 12.4.9) are adequate to redress injuries, "federal courts will not oversee the overseer" (906 F.2d at 748, quoting *Coker v. Sullivan,* 902 F.2d 84, 89 (D.C. Cir. 1990)). Only if Congress creates such a private right of action, said the court, may plaintiffs file claims directly against the government agency charged with enforcing the law.

Two other cases have reached similar results when an individual victim has challenged an agency's enforcement activities. In *Marlow v. United States Department of Education*, 820 F.2d 581 (2d Cir. 1987), the court dismissed a lawsuit challenging ED's decision to take no action on an administrative complaint the plaintiff had filed under Section 504. The court held that there is no statutory or implied right of action against the federal funding agency for individual complainants who seek only judicial review of the agency's disposition of a particular complaint. Another federal appeals court reached the same conclusion in a similar suit, and held as well that an individual complainant cannot enjoin ED from continuing to fund the institution against which the complaint was made (*Salvador v. Bennett*, 800 F.2d 97 (7th Cir. 1986)).

12.4.9. Other Enforcement Remedies

Administrative negotiation and fund termination are not the only means federal agencies have for enforcing the civil rights statutes. In some cases, the responsible federal agency may also go to court to enforce the civil rights obligations that educational institutions have assumed by accepting federal funds. Title VI authorizes agencies to enforce compliance not only by fund termination but also by "any other means authorized by law" (42 U.S.C. §2000d–1). ED's Title VI regulations explain that "such other means may include, but are not limited to, (1) a reference to the Department of Justice with a recommendation that appropriate proceedings be brought to enforce any rights of the United States under any law of the United States (including other titles of the Act), or any assurance or other contractual undertaking, and (2) any applicable proceeding under state or local law" (34 C.F.R. §100.9(a)). ED may not pursue these alternatives, however, "until (1) the responsible department official has determined that compliance cannot be secured by voluntary means, (2) the recipient or other person has been notified of its failure to comply and of the action to be taken to effect compliance, and (3) the expiration of at least ten days from the mailing of such notice to the recipient or other person" (34 C.F.R. §100.9(d)). Similar enforcement alternatives and procedural limitations apply to enforcement of Title IX, Section 504, and the Age Discrimination Act.

Besides administrative agency enforcement by fund termination or court suit, educational institutions may also be subject to private lawsuits brought by individuals who have allegedly been discriminated against in violation of the civil rights statutes or regulations. In legal terminology, the issue is whether the civil rights statutes afford these victims of discrimination a "private cause of action" against the institution that is allegedly discriminating.

The basic requisites for a private cause of action are outlined in *Cort v. Ash*, 422 U.S. 66 (1975). "In determining whether a private remedy is implicit in a statute not expressly providing one, several factors are relevant. First, is the plaintiff one of the class for whose *especial* benefit the statute was enacted—that is, does the statute create a federal right in favor of the plaintiff? Second, is there any indication of legislative intent, explicit or implicit, either to create such a remedy or to deny one? Third, is it consistent with the underlying purposes of the legislative scheme to imply such a remedy for the plaintiff? And finally, is the cause of action one traditionally relegated to state law, in an area basically the concern of the states, so that it would be inappropriate to infer a cause of action based solely on federal law?" (422 U.S. at 78; citations omitted).

If an individual can meet these requirements, three related issues may then arise: whether the individual must "exhaust" any available "administrative remedies" before bringing a private suit; whether the individual may obtain monetary damages, in addition to or instead of injunctive relief, if successful in the private suit; and whether the individual may obtain attorney's fees from the defendant if successful in the suit.

For many years, courts and commentators disagreed on whether the civil rights statutes could be enforced by private causes of action. Developments since the late 1970s, however, have established a strong basis for acceptance of private causes of action under all four statutes. The 1979 case of *Cannon v. University of Chicago*, 441 U.S. 677 (1979), arising under Title IX, is illustrative.

The plaintiff in *Cannon* had been denied admission to the medical schools of the University of Chicago and Northwestern University. She sued both institutions, claiming that they had rejected her applications because of her sex and that such action violated Title IX. The U.S. Court of Appeals for the Seventh Circuit held that individuals cannot institute private suits to enforce Title IX. The U.S. Supreme Court reversed. While acknowledging that the statute does not expressly authorize a private cause of action, the Court held that one can be implied into the statute under the principles of *Cort v. Ash*. In applying the four considerations specified in that case, the Court in *Cannon* concluded, "Not only the words and history of Title IX, but also its subject matter and underlying purposes, counsel application of a cause of action in favor of private victims of discrimination."

The discussion of the third consideration in *Cort*—whether a private cause of action would frustrate the statute's underlying purposes—is particularly illuminating. The Court identified two purposes of Title IX: to avoid the use of federal funds to support sex discrimination and to give individual citizens effective protection against such practices. While the first purpose is served by the statutory procedure for fund termination (see Section 12.4.8 of this chapter), the Court determined that a private remedy would be appropriate if the violation were insufficient to trigger fund termination, a finding that would leave the individual without relief.

In a statement of particular interest to postsecondary administrators, the Court in *Cannon* also addressed and rejected the universities' argument that private suits would unduly interfere with their institutional autonomy, calling the argument speculative and unsupported.

Subsequently, in the case of *Guardians Assn. v. Civil Service Commission of the City of New York,* 463 U.S. 582 (1983), the Supreme Court affirmed the availability of private causes of action under Title VI. The Court issued no majority opinion, however, so the case's teaching on the issue is limited and can be gleaned only from tallying the views of those justices who accepted private causes of action under Title VI. A year after *Guardians,* and relying in part on that case, the Supreme Court also finally held that individuals may bring private lawsuits to enforce Section 504 (*Consolidated Rail Corp. v. Darrone,* 465 U.S. 624 (1984)).

Another development, illustrating legislative rather than judicial resolution of the "private cause of action" issue, occurred with passage of the 1978 amendments to the Age Discrimination Act. Congress added a new section to the Act, authorizing private suits by "any interested person" in federal district courts "to enjoin a violation of this Act by any program or activity receiving federal financial assistance" (42 U.S.C. §6104(e)).

Courts permitting private enforcement suits under the civil rights statutes usually have not required the complainants to exhaust administrative remedies before filing suit. The exception to this trend is the Age Discrimination Act, for which Congress itself has provided an exhaustion requirement. In the 1978 ADA amendments, the provision authorizing private suits also prohibits bringing such suits "if administrative remedies have not been exhausted" (42 U.S.C. §6104 (e)(2)(B)). Section 6104(f) of the amendments and the general ADA regulations (45 C.F.R. §90.50) indicate when such exhaustion shall be deemed to have occurred.

Authorization of private causes of action, even when exhaustion has occurred or is not required, does not necessarily mean that a complainant may obtain every kind of remedy ordinarily available in civil lawsuits. *Cannon* did not itself resolve the remedies question, and in the wake of *Cannon,* a number of lower courts ruled that private causes of action under Title IX were limited to injunctive relief and that money damages were not available (see, for example, *Lieberman v. University of Chicago,* 660 F.2d 1185 (7th Cir. 1985)). In *Guardians,* however, a tally of the individual justices' views indicates that a majority would permit a damages remedy under Title VI if the plaintiff could prove that the defendant had discriminated *intentionally* (463 U.S. at 607 n.27; see also Section 12.4.7.2 of this chapter). And in *Darrone,* although the Court declined to determine "the extent to which money damages are available" in a Section 504 case, it did authorize back-pay awards (a type of equitable relief) for victims of intentional discrimination.

In early 1992, the Supreme Court alleviated much of the uncertainty concerning remedies and resolved some conflicts among lower courts, at least with respect to Title IX. In a case discussed in Section 12.4.3—*Franklin v. Gwinnett County Public Schools,* 112 S. Ct. 1028 (1992)—a student brought an action under

Title IX seeking compensatory damages for alleged intentional sex discrimination—in particular, sexual harassment by a coach-teacher at her high school. The school administration failed to protect her from this harassment, despite having knowledge of it. The school district agreed to close its investigation in return for the teacher's resignation. Although the U.S. Department of Education investigated and determined that the school district had violated the student's Title IX rights, the department terminated the investigation after the school and the school district came into compliance with Title IX. The student then filed her cause of action for damages, which was rejected by the lower courts.

Reversing, the Supreme Court stated three bases for holding that money damages is a permissible remedy under Title IX: first, the firmly established principle that, once a cause of action exists, the courts may use all appropriate remedies to enforce the plaintiff's rights unless Congress has expressly indicated otherwise; second, the *Cannon* Court's reliance on Congress's awareness that, in the decade immediately preceding enactment of Title IX, the Court had accepted implied rights of action in six cases and permitted damage remedies in three of them; and third, the enactment, subsequent to *Cannon,* of the Civil Rights Remedies Equalization Amendment of 1986 (42 U.S.C. §2000d–7) (discussed later in this section), and the Civil Rights Restoration Act of 1987 (see Section 12.4.7.4), which the Court regarded as implicit congressional acknowledgments that private remedies, including money damages, are available under Title IX. Although confessing that the multiple opinions in *Guardians Association* had made it difficult to determine the Court's viewpoint on damage remedies, the *Gwinnett* Court noted that "a clear majority [in *Guardians Association*] expressed the view that damages were available under Title VI in an action seeking remedies for an intentional violation, and no Justice challenged the traditional presumption in favor of a federal court's power to award appropriate relief in a cognizable cause of action."

The *Gwinnett* case, permitting compensatory damages under Title IX, also serves to reinforce the availability of such damages under Title VI—as the Court indicated by its reliance on the prior *Guardians Association* case. The *Gwinnett* reasoning will apparently apply to Section 504 as well; see, for example, *Wood v. President and Trustees of Spring Hill College,* 978 F.2d 1214 (11th Cir. 1992). The *Gwinnett* analysis does not extend to the Age Discrimination Act, however, since that statute expressly provides only for suits "to enjoin a violation of this Act" (42 U.S.C. §6104(e)), thus indicating that injunctive relief (and not money damages) is the only permissible remedy.

While *Gwinnett,* read against the backdrop of *Guardians Association* and *Darrone,* thus settles many of the questions concerning remedies available in private causes of action, it is still unclear whether awarding punitive damages (as opposed to compensatory damages) is an available remedy under Title IX, Title VI, or Section 504. It is also not clear that the Court would extend the availability of money damages under these statutes to cases where the plaintiff can prove only unintentional discrimination (see Section 12.4.7.2).

An additional complexity may arise when a private suit for money damages is brought against a state college or university. Such institutions may be considered arms of the state and, as such, may claim Eleventh Amendment immunity from suit in federal court (see Section 2.3.3). In *Atascadero State Hospital v. Scanlon*, 473 U.S. 234 (1985), the U.S. Supreme Court highlighted this point by holding that, in enacting Section 504, Congress did not abrogate the states' Eleventh Amendment immunity. Subsequently, however, Congress enacted the Civil Rights Remedies Equalization Amendment of 1986 (100 Stat. 1845, 42 U.S.C. §2000d–7). This new statute specifically declares that states are not immune under the Eleventh Amendment from federal court suits alleging violations of Section 504, Title IX, Title VI, the Age Discrimination Act, or any other federal statute prohibiting discrimination by recipients of federal financial assistance.

The final issue regarding private causes of action concerns attorney's fees. When a plaintiff successfully invokes one of the civil rights statutes against an institution, the institution may be liable for the plaintiff's attorney's fees. Under the Civil Rights Attorney's Fees Awards Act of 1976 (42 U.S.C. §1988), courts have discretion to award "a reasonable attorney's fee" to "the prevailing party" in actions under Title IX, Title VI, and several other civil rights statutes. Although this Act does not apply to Section 504 suits or ADA suits, the omission is inconsequential because both Section 504 and the ADA have their own comparable provisions authorizing the award of attorney's fees (29 U.S.C. §794a(b); 42 U.S.C. §6104(e)(1)).

SEC. 12.5. DEALING WITH THE FEDERAL GOVERNMENT

12.5.1. Handling Federal Rule Making and Regulations

Administrative agencies write regulations both to implement legislation and to formalize their own housekeeping functions. To prepare such regulations, agencies typically engage in a process of rule making, which includes an opportunity for the public to comment on regulatory proposals. Information on particular agencies' rule-making activities is published in the *Federal Register*. Final regulations (along with summaries of public comment on proposed drafts) are also published in the *Federal Register*, and these regulations are then codified in the *Code of Federal Regulations*.

Postsecondary administrators have long complained that the multitude of federal regulations applying to the programs and practices of postsecondary institutions create financial and administrative burdens for their institutions. These burdens can be decreased as postsecondary administrators and legal counsel take more active roles in the process by which the federal government makes and enforces rules. The following suggestions outline a strategy for active involvement that an institution may undertake by itself, in conjunction with other similarly situated institutions, or through educational associations to which it belongs. (See generally C. Saunders, "Regulating the Regulators," *Chron. Higher Educ.*, Mar. 22, 1976, A32, which includes suggestions similar to some of those following.)

1. Appoint someone to be responsible for monitoring the *Federal Register* and other publications for announcements and information on regulatory proposals and regulations that will affect postsecondary education. Each agency periodically prepares an agenda of all regulations it expects to propose, promulgate, or review in the near future and publishes this agenda in the *Federal Register*. The *Federal Register* also publishes "Notice(s) of Intent" to publish rules (NOIs) (sometimes called "Advance Notice(s) of Proposed Rulemaking" (ANPRs)) and "Notice(s) of Proposed Rulemaking" (NPRMs), the latter of which are drafts of proposed regulations along with invitations for comments from interested parties. Notices of the establishment of a *committee* to negotiate rule making on a subject or proposed rule are also published in the *Federal Register*. If further information on a particular rule-making process or a particular regulatory proposal would be useful, have institutional personnel ask the agency for the pertinent information. Some agencies may have policies that make draft regulations or summaries available for review before the proposed form is published.

2. File comments and deliver testimony in response to NOIs and NPRMs when the rules would have a likely impact on institutional operations. Support these comments with specific explanations and data showing how the proposed regulations would have a negative impact on the institution. Have legal counsel review the proposed rules for legal and interpretive problems, and include legal questions or objections with your comments when appropriate. Consider filing comments in conjunction with other institutions that would be similarly affected by the proposed regulations. In addition, when negotiated rule making is provided, participate in the negotiation process if your institution is eligible to do so.

3. Keep federal agencies informed of your views on and experiences with particular federal regulations. Compile data concerning the regulations' impact on your institution, and present these data to the responsible agency. Continue to communicate complaints and difficulties with final regulations to the responsible agency, even if the regulations were promulgated months or years ago. In addition, determine whether any federal advisory committee has been appointed for the agency or the issues that are of concern to your institution. (The Federal Advisory Committee Act, 5 U.S.C. App. §1, regulates the formation and operation of such committees.) If so, also keep the committee informed of your views and experience regarding particular regulations.

4. When the institution desires guidance concerning ambiguities or gaps in particular regulations, consider submitting questions to the administering agency. Make the questions specific and, if the institution has a particular viewpoint on how the ambiguity or gap should be resolved, forcefully argue that

view. Legal counsel should be involved in this process. Once questions are submitted, press the agency for answers.

5. Be concerned not only with the substance of regulations but also with the adequacy of the rule-making and rule-enforcing procedures. Be prepared to object whenever institutions are given insufficient notice of an agency's plans to make rules, too few opportunities to participate in rule making, or inadequate opportunities to criticize or receive guidance on already implemented regulations.

6. Develop an effective process for institutional self-regulation. With other institutions, develop criteria and data to use in determining the circumstances in which self-regulation is more effective than government regulation. Use a record of institutional success at self-regulation, combined with developed rationales for self-regulation, to argue in selected situations that government regulation is unnecessary.

7. When an agency passes a particular regulation that your institution (and presumably others) believes will have an ill-advised impact on higher education interests, consider obtaining a review of the regulation's legality. One of the most important considerations is whether the regulation is "ultra vires"—that is, whether, in promulgating the regulation, the agency has exceeded the scope of authority Congress has delegated to it. Such issues may be the basis for a court challenge of agency regulations. Such legal issues may also be raised during the rule-making process itself, to bolster policy reasons for opposing particular regulations.

Several pieces of legislation enacted since the early 1980s provide new assistance for postsecondary institutions that do involve themselves in the federal regulatory process. One statute, the Regulatory Flexibility Act (5 U.S.C. §601 *et seq.*), adds a new Chapter VI to the federal Administrative Procedure Act. Another statute, the Negotiated Rulemaking Act of 1990 (5 U.S.C. §§561 *et seq.*), adds a new subchapter III to the Administrative Procedure Act. A third statute, the Equal Access to Justice Act (28 U.S.C. §2412), amends Chapter V of the Administrative Procedure Act.

The Regulatory Flexibility Act benefits three types of "small entities," each of which is defined in Section 601: the "small business," the "small organization," and the "small governmental jurisdiction." The Act's purpose is "to establish as a principle of regulatory issuance that [federal administrative] agencies shall endeavor . . . to fit regulatory and informational requirements to the scale of the businesses, organizations, and governmental jurisdictions subject to regulation" (96 Stat. 1164 §2(b)). To implement this principle, the Act provides that (1) in October and April of every year, agencies must publish a "regulatory flexibility agenda," which describes and explains any forthcoming regulations that are "likely to have a significant economic impact on a substantial number of small entities" (5 U.S.C. §602); (2) agencies proposing new regulations must provide, for public comment, an "initial regulatory flexibility analysis" containing a description of "the impact of the proposed rule on small entities" and a description of "alternatives to the proposed rule" that would lessen its economic impact on small entities (§603); (3) agencies promulgating final regulations must issue a "final regulatory flexibility analysis" containing a summary of comments on the initial analysis and, where regulatory alternatives were rejected, an explanation of why they were rejected (§604); (4) for any regulation "which will have a significant economic impact on a substantial number of small entities," agencies must "assure that small entities have been given an opportunity to participate in the rulemaking" (§609); and (5) agencies must periodically review and, where appropriate, revise their regulations with an eye to reducing their economic impact on small entities (§610).

The key issue for postsecondary institutions under the Regulatory Flexibility Act is one of definition: To what extent will postsecondary institutions be considered to be within the definition for one of the three groups of "small entities" protected by the Act? The first definition, for the "small business" (§601(3)), is unlikely to apply, except to some proprietary institutions. The second definition, for the "small organization" (§601(4)), will apply to many, but not necessarily all, private nonprofit institutions. And the third definition, for the "small governmental jurisdiction" (§601(5)), will apparently apply to some, but relatively few, public institutions—primarily community colleges. Thus, not every postsecondary institution will be within the Act's protected classes.

The second statute, the Negotiated Rulemaking Act of 1990 (104 Stat. 4969 (1990), codified at 5 U.S.C. §§561–570), was enacted to encourage agencies to use negotiations among interested parties as part of their rule-making process. Through an agency-established committee (5 U.S.C. §565), agencies may informally negotiate a proposed rule that accommodates the varying interests of groups participating in the process and represents a consensus on the subject for which the committee was established. The rationale is that greater involvement and face-to-face discussion of opposing viewpoints will yield a proposed rule that may be formally adopted and enforced more quickly than would occur under more formal rule-making procedures (5 U.S.C. §561 note).

The third new statute, the Equal Access to Justice Act, was originally promulgated in 1980 (Pub. L. No. 96–481, 94 Stat. 2321 (1980)), and then was amended and permanently renewed in 1985 (Pub. L. No. 99–80, 99 Stat. 183 (1985)). By authorizing courts to award attorney's fees and other expenses to certain parties that prevail in a civil action brought against or by a federal administrative agency, this Act assists institutions that must litigate with the federal government over procedural defects in rule making, substantive defects in regulations that were not resolved during the rule-making process, or interpretive issues regarding the application of regulations. If an institution prevails in such litigation, it may receive attorney's fees unless the agency shows that its position in the suit was "substantially justified" (28 U.S.C. §2412(d)(1)(A)). Like the Regulatory Flexibility Act, this Act's application to postsecondary education is limited by its definitions: apparently, to be a "party" eligible for attorney's fees, a postsecondary institution must have no more than five hundred employees and, unless it is a 501(c)(3) organization, must have a net worth of not more than $7 million (28 U.S.C. §241 2(d)(2)(B)). Moreover, state colleges and universities do not appear to be within the definition of "party," which includes a "unit of local government" but makes no reference to state-level agencies and entities. Individual agencies must publish their own regulations implementing the Act; the Department of Education's regulations, for example, are in 34 C.F.R. Part 21.

Another recent development that will help postsecondary institutions cope with the federal regulatory process is Executive Order 12866, issued by President Clinton on September 30, 1993 (58 Fed. Reg. 51725). The executive order sets out twelve principles of regulation for federal administrative agencies, including the requirement that each agency "shall identify and assess available alternatives to direct regulation" (§1(b)(3)), "shall assess both the costs and the benefits of the intended regulation" (§1(b)(6)), and "shall seek views of appropriate state, local, and tribal officials before imposing regulatory requirements" on those entities (§1(b)(9)). The order also establishes a number of procedural requirements—for example, requiring each agency periodically to "prepare an agenda of all regulations under development or review" (§4(b) and (c)), periodically to "review its existing significant regulations to determine whether any such regulations should be modified or eliminated so as to make the agency's regulatory program more effective [and] less burdensome" (§5(a)), and to "provide the public with meaningful participation in the regulatory process" and "afford the public a meaningful opportunity to comment" on any proposed regulation (§6(a)(1)). In addition, the order addresses various structural matters. For example, it assigns to the Office of Information and Regulatory Affairs (OIRA) within the Office of Management and Budget (§2(b)) various responsibilities for monitoring the regulatory processes of each agency (see, for example, §4(e)), and it requires that each agency appoint a regulatory policy officer "to foster the development of effective, innovative, and least burdensome regulations and to further the principles" in Section l(b) of the order (§6(a)(2)).

12.5.2. Obtaining Information

Information will often be an indispensable key to a postsecondary institution's ability to deal effectively with the federal government, in rule-making processes or otherwise. Critical information sometimes will be within the control of the institution—for example, information about its own operations and the effect of federal programs on these operations. At other times, critical information will be under the government's control—for example, data collected by the government itself or information on competing policy considerations being weighed internally by an agency as it formulates regulatory proposals. When the latter type of information is needed, it may sometimes be obtained during the course of a rule-making proceeding (see Section 12.5.1). In addition, the following legislation may help institutional administrators and legal counsel: the Freedom of Information Act (FOIA) Amendments of 1974; the Privacy Act of 1974; the Government in the Sunshine Act of 1976; and the Government Printing Office Electronic Information Access Enhancement Act of 1993 (Pub. L. No. 103–40, 107 Stat. 112 (1993)), an Act facilitating electronic access to government data. Executive Orders 12866 and 12356 and successor government orders may also be of help.

The Freedom of Information Act Amendments (5 U.S.C. §552) afford the public access to information from federal government files that is not specifically exempted from disclosure by the legislation. Nine categories of information are exempted from disclosure under Section 552(b), the most relevant to postsecondary institutions being national security information, federal agencies' internal personnel rules and practices, interagency or intra-agency memoranda or letters that would not be available except in litigation, and investigatory files compiled for law enforcement purposes.

The FOIA is useful when an institution believes that the government holds information that would be helpful in a certain situation, but informal requests have not yielded the necessary materials. By making an FOIA request, an institution can obtain agency information that may help the institution understand agency policy initiatives; or document a claim, process a grievance, or prepare a lawsuit against the government or some third party; or determine what information the government has that it could use against the institution—for example, in a threatened fund termination proceeding. Specific procedures to follow in requesting such information are set out in the statute and in each agency's own policies on FOIA requests. Persons or institutions whose requests are denied by the agency may file a suit against the agency in a U.S. District Court. The burden of proof is on the agency to support its reasons for denial. (See A. Adler, *Using the Freedom of Information Act: A Step-by-Step Guide* (American Civil Liberties Union Foundation, 1990).)

The Privacy Act (codified in part at 5 U.S.C. §552a) is discussed in Section 3.3.3 of this volume with regard to student records. The point to be made here is that someone who requests certain information under the FOIA may find an obstacle in the Privacy Act. The FOIA itself exempts "personnel and medical files and similar files the disclosure of which would constitute a clearly unwarranted invasion of personal privacy" (5 U.S.C. §552(b)(6)). The Privacy Act provides an even broader protection for information whose release would infringe privacy interests. While the Act thus may foil someone who requests information, it may also protect a postsecondary institution and its employees and students when the federal government has information concerning them in its files. Individual agencies each publish their own regulations implementing the Privacy Act. The Department of Education's regulations are published in 34 C.F.R. §5b.1 *et seq.*

The Government in the Sunshine Act (5 U.S.C. §552b) assures the public that "meetings of multimember federal agencies shall be open with the exception of discussions of several narrowly defined areas" (H.R. Rep. No. 880, 94th Cong., 2d Sess. (1976), at 2, reprinted in 3 *U.S. Code Cong. & Admin. News* 2184 (1976)). Institutions can individually or collectively make use of this Act by sending a representative to observe and report on agency decision making that is expected to have a substantial impact on their operations.

Executive Order 12866 (also discussed in Section 12.5.1) requires agencies to do various cost-benefit assessments of proposed regulations and to make this information available to the public after the regulations are published (§6(1) (3)(E)(I)). The order also provides that OIRA (see Section 12.5.1) will "maintain a publicly available log" containing information about the status of regulatory actions and the oral and written communications received from outsiders regarding regulatory matters (§6(b)(4)(C)).

Executive Order 12356 (47 Fed. Reg. 27836 (Apr. 6, 1982)) establishes the necessary procedures and the schedule for classifying and declassifying government documents related to national security. This order, signed by President Reagan in April 1982, revoked prior Executive Order 12065, which had been signed by President Carter in June 1978. Although this executive order is still in effect, President Clinton has convened a task force to propose changes to the classification system and draft a new executive order (58 Fed. Reg. 29480 (1993)).

The 1982 executive order has the same function as its predecessors, establishing standards and procedures for classifying and declassifying government documents related to national security. But the 1982 order appears more restrictive than the 1978 order, since it added additional materials to the list of what can be classified; broadened the concept of "national security"; switched, for borderline cases, from a presumption against to a presumption in favor of classification; and deleted procedures for declassification of material after a set number of years. It remains to be seen whether a new executive order by President Clinton will alter these aspects of the 1982 order.

SELECTED ANNOTATED BIBLIOGRAPHY

General

Gaffney, Edward M., & Moots, Philip R. *Government and Campus: Federal Regulation of Religiously Affiliated Higher Education* (University of Notre Dame Press, 1982). Analyzes various aspects of federal regulation of religiously affiliated colleges and universities. Chapters treat religious preference in employment; student admissions and discipline policies; restrictions on the use of federal funds; accommodation to the needs of disabled persons, including reformed alcoholics and drug abusers; tax problems; labor law problems; and sexual segregation of on- and off-campus student housing. Each chapter offers recommendations for regulatory changes that would reduce church-state tension. See also these authors' earlier work, *Church and Campus*, listed in the Chapter One bibliography for this volume (Section 1.6).

Sec. 12.1 (Federal Regulation of Postsecondary Education)

Ansell, Edward O. (ed.). *Intellectual Property in Academe: A Legal Compendium* (National Association of College and University Attorneys, 1991). A collection of journal articles, conference outlines, and other materials on patent, trademark, and copyright law. Articles discuss the fair use doctrine and its implications for faculty research and teaching; the ownership and use of computer software; and expected future issues in the area of copyright, patent, and trademark law. An extensive selected bibliography is also included.

Bedrosian, Alex (ed.). *Advisor's Manual of Federal Regulations Affecting Foreign Students and Scholars* (rev. ed., National Association for Foreign Student Affairs, 1993). A practical guide covering all the federal regulations that are important to administrators and counsel who deal with foreign students, employees, or visitors. Discusses both nonimmigrant and immigrant status, with special emphasis on the F, M, H, and J nonimmigrant categories. Includes an appendix of sample forms.

Bender, David. *Computer Law: Software Protection and Litigation* (Matthew Bender, 1988). Applies traditional copyright law to the evolving area of the ownership and use of computer software. Practice aids and litigation suggestions are provided.

Crews, Kenneth D. *Copyright, Fair Use, and the Challenge for Universities: Promoting the Progress of Higher Education* (University of Chicago Press, 1993). Provides background on copyright law and discusses the fair use doctrine. Includes a survey of copyright policies at ninety-eight research universities and describes how universities have responded to legislation and litigation related to copyright. Guidelines for the development of institutional copyright policy are provided, and the *Basic Books v. Kinko's Graphics* case is discussed.

Ginsberg, Gilbert J., & Abrams, Daniel B. *Fair Labor Standards Handbook for States, Local Government and Schools* (Thompson Publishing Group, 1986). A loose-leaf service, updated monthly, that discusses the application of the FLSA to public employees. The sections covering exempt employees, overtime provisions, special rules for police and firefighters, record keeping, and enforcement are of particular significance for administrators at public colleges and universities. The statute, regulations, administrative rulings, and judicial interpretations are included in appendices.

Gordon, Charles, & Gordon, Ellen G. *Immigration and Nationality Law* (Matthew Bender, 1981, and periodic supp.). An abridgment, in loose-leaf form, of the eight-volume treatise *Immigration Law and Procedure*. Divided into two parts, the first on "Immigration" and the second on "Nationality and Citizenship." Of particular use to postsecondary administrators and counsel are Chapter 1, "General Survey";

Chapter 2, "What Aliens May Enter the United States"; and Chapter 3, "Procedure for Entering the United States."

Government Affairs Bulletin (National Association for Foreign Student Affairs). A periodic newsletter reporting on immigration and naturalization issues of current importance to institutions of higher education. Tracks legislation, regulations, and policy formulation in the legislative and executive branches. Also includes grant announcements and instructions for completing INS forms.

Interpreter Releases and *Immigration Briefings* (Federal Publications, Inc.). Immigration law research resources published weekly and monthly, respectively. *Interpreter Releases* gives capsule summaries that track judicial and administrative decisions, legislation, and other actions and rulings of government agencies. Its sister publication, *Immigration Briefings,* gives an in-depth analysis of one particular area of immigration law of current importance.

Kaufman, Hattie. *Access to Institutions of Higher Education for Students with Disabilities* (National Association of College and University Attorneys, 1991). Discusses institutional responsibilities to provide access to and accommodation for disabled students under both the Rehabilitation Act and the Americans with Disabilities Act. Adjustments to academic programs, auxiliary aids, student housing, participation in athletic activities, transportation, and student activities are discussed. Portions of the regulations specific to colleges are included as an appendix.

Kurzban, Ira. *Kurzban's Immigration Law Sourcebook* (4th ed., American Immigration Law Association, 1993). A reference tool detailing the statutory law, regulations, administrative decisions, and judicial precedents relating to immigration. These chapters will be particularly helpful to higher education administrators and counsel: Chapter 5 (Nonimmigrant Visas), Chapter 7 (Employment Based Immigration and Labor Certification), and Chapter 12 (Employer Sanctions, Unfair Immigration Related Employment Practices and Legalization). Includes discussion of the Immigration Act of 1990.

Rothstein, Laura F. *Disabilities and the Law* (Shepard's/McGraw-Hill, 1992). A reference guide designed for lawyers, educators, and medical professionals. Includes chapters on the Americans with Disabilities Act, the Rehabilitation Act, and federal and state laws related to disability discrimination, among others. The chapter on higher education discusses admissions, programs and services (including academic modifications and auxiliary services), athletics, health insurance, physical facilities, confidentiality requirements, learning-disabled students, and mentally impaired students. Updated annually.

Yale-Loehr, Stephen (ed.). *Understanding the Immigration Act of 1990* (Federal Publications, 1991). A descriptive and analytical review of the 1990 legislation and its comprehensive overhaul of U.S. immigration law. Each of the thirteen chapters is aimed at a major aspect of the new law. Chapters 3 (employment-based immigrants), 5 (F–1 nonimmigrants), and 6 (H–1B nonimmigrants) will be particularly helpful to higher education institutions. Also includes the full text of the 1990 Act.

See "Symposium" entry for Section 8.4.

Sec. 12.2 (Federal Taxation of Postsecondary Education)

Ashford, Deborah, & Frank, Robert. *Lobbying and the Law: A Guide to Federal Tax Law Limitations on Legislative and Political Activities by Nonprofit Organizations* (2d ed., Hogan & Hartson/Frank & Company, 1990). Covers participation in political campaigns, direct and grass-roots lobbying, mass media communications, and activities excluded from the definition of lobbying. An appendix includes an overview of the lobbying laws of every state.

Harding, Bertrand, Jr., & Peterson, Norm. *U.S. Taxation of International Students and Scholars: A Manual for Advisers and Administrators* (rev. ed., National Association for Foreign Student Affairs, 1993). Practical advice on the taxability of scholarships, fellowships, living allowances, and travel grants for foreign students and scholars, as well as the withholding and reporting requirements imposed on their institutions. A related work by the same publisher—Deborah Vance, *U.S. Federal Income Tax Guide for International Students and Scholars* (rev. ed., National Association for Foreign Student Affairs, 1994)—provides a layperson's guide to U.S. taxation and filing requirements for foreign students and scholars.

Hopkins, Bruce. *The Law of Tax-Exempt Organizations* (6th ed., Wiley, 1992, and periodic supp.). A reference volume, for managers and administrators as well as counsel, that examines the pertinent federal law affecting the different types of nonprofit organizations, including colleges and universities. Emphasis is on how to obtain and maintain tax-exempt status. Contains citations to Internal Revenue Code provisions, Treasury Department revenue rulings, and court decisions.

Kaplan, Richard L. "Intercollegiate Athletics and the Unrelated Business Income Tax," 80 *Columbia L. Rev.* 1430 (1980). Reviews the unrelated business income tax as it affects the postsecondary institution's athletic program. Author argues that many schools' intercollegiate athletic programs have taken on the appearance of business activities unrelated to the institution's educational mission, and thus may be liable to taxation. Article also includes broader discussion of the unrelated business income tax in the higher education context.

Kelly, Marci. "Financing Higher Education: Federal Income-Tax Consequences," 17 *J. Coll. & Univ. L.* 307 (1991). Discusses federal tax law as it applies to the financing of education through scholarships, prizes, loans, and student employment. Provides guidance for administrators in counseling students, structuring new financial aid programs, and administering existing programs.

Sec. 12.3 (Federal Aid-to-Education Programs)

Advisory Commission on Intergovernmental Relations. *The Evolution of a Problematic Partnership: The Feds and Higher Education* (Advisory Commission on Intergovernmental Relations, 1981). Examines the history and growth of the federal government's involvement in higher education. Chapters include "The Scope of Federal Involvement in Higher Education," "The Evolution of a Federal Role: 1787–1958," "Beginnings of a New Federal Role in Higher Education: The National Defense Education Act," "A Direct Federal Role Established: The Higher Education Acts of 1963 and 1965," "Equal Opportunity Preeminent: The 1972 Higher Education Amendments," and "A Growing Regulatory Presence." Contains various figures, graphs, and tables charting major developments in the relationship between the federal government and higher education.

Cappalli, Richard. *Rights and Remedies Under Federal Grants* (Bureau of National Affairs, 1979). A systematic treatment of the federal grants system. Contains sections on "The Theory and Structure of Grants," including analyses of types and purposes of federal grants and constitutional supports for the grant system; "Agency Enforcement of Grant Conditions"; "Expanding Bases of Judicial Intervention"; "Due Process and Federal Grants"; "Grantee Hearing Rights: Withholding of Entitlements"; "Termination of Competitive Grants"; "Grant Suspensions"; "Rights of Applicants for Federal Funds"; "Subgrantees"; "Guideposts for Reform"; and other topics. Author has also published a lengthier treatment of this topic and related topics in a three-volume treatise, *Federal Grants and Cooperative Agreements: Law, Policy, and Practice* (Clark Boardman Callaghan, 1982).

Green, Deirdre (ed.). *College and University Business Administration* (5th ed., National Association of College and University Business Officers, 1992). Includes two chapters of particular relevance to institutional administration of federal grants and contracts: Chapter 15 ("Auditing," by Warren Spruill), which includes discussion of both internal audits and external audits by federal government auditors; and Chapter 21 ("Research and Sponsored Programs" by Julie Norris), which discusses report and record-keeping requirements, allowability of costs, and certifications and assurances required by federal agencies (for example, Drug-Free Workplace, debarment and suspension, and lobbying certifications).

Palmer, Carolyn, & Gehring, Donald (eds.). *A Handbook for Complying with the Program & Review Requirements of the 1989 Amendments to the Drug-Free Schools and Communities Act* (College Administration Publications, 1992). A how-to manual for college administrators who are setting up or reviewing on-campus drug and alcohol programs in accordance with federal law. The handbook also provides a guide, supplemented by a comprehensive appendix, to federal and private funding sources, research and studies on the subject, organizations concerned with drug-free education, and model standards and guidelines.

Whitehead, Kenneth D. *Catholic Colleges and Federal Funding* (Ignatius Press, 1988). Examines the question whether religiously affiliated colleges and universities must safeguard "academic freedom" and have "institutional autonomy" in order to be eligible for federal aid. Discusses eligibility requirements (such as accreditation), accrediting agencies' policies, the current understanding of academic freedom and the role of the AAUP, and parallel issues regarding state (rather than federal) aid for religiously affiliated institutions. Written by the then deputy assistant secretary for higher education programs in the U.S. Department of Education.

Sec. 12.4 (Civil Rights Compliance)

Baxter, Felix V. "The Affirmative Duty to Desegregate Institutions of Higher Education—Defining the Role of the Traditionally Black College," 11 *J. Law & Educ.* 1 (1982). Provides "an analytical framework to assess, in a consistent fashion, the role which [black] institutions should play in a unitary system." Reviews various legal strategies to deflect the "very real threat to black efforts to desegregate state systems of higher education."

Bell, Derrick A., Jr. "Black Colleges and the Desegregation Dilemma," 28 *Emory L. J.* 949 (1979). Reviews the development of desegregation law and its impact on black colleges. Author argues that black colleges continue to provide a special service to black Americans and that litigation and legislation should be tailored to accommodate and promote this service.

Campbell, Nancy Duff, et al. *Sex Discrimination in Education: Legal Rights and Remedies* (National Women's Law Center, 1983). A detailed, two-volume analysis of Title IX. Volume I examines such questions as Title IX's impact on admissions, campus health programs, and sexual harassment, and reviews litigation problems and strategies under Title IX. Volume II is a document sourcebook that includes the legislative history of Title IX, administrative regulations and guidelines, and various court and settlement documents.

Handicapped Requirements Handbook (Federal Programs Advisory Service, 1978, and periodic supp.). A comprehensive, practical guide to complying with Section 504 of the Rehabilitation Act of 1973. Includes Section 504 agency regulations and interpretations, summaries of court decisions, a self-evaluation questionnaire, and a glossary of terms.

Preer, Jean. "Lawyers v. Educators: Changing Perceptions of Desegregation in Public Higher Education," 1 *N.C. Central L.J.* 74 (1979), reprinted in 53 *J. Higher Educ.* 119 (1982). Examines the tension between lawyers' and educators' perceptions of desegregation in public universities and colleges. Discusses three historical examples: the Morrill Act of 1890, "the reactions of civil rights lawyers and educators to the regional educational compact of the 1940s," and the "legal and educational paradoxes" of *Adams v. Richardson* (see Sections 12.4.2 and 12.4.8). Author concludes that "both lawyers and educators need to expand their vision." An extended version of these themes appears in Jean Preer, *Lawyers v. Educators: Black Colleges and Desegregation in Public Higher Education* (Greenwood Press, 1982), especially rich in historical materials.

Williams, John B., IV (ed.). *Desegregating America's Colleges and Universities: Title VI Regulation of Higher Education* (Teachers College Press, 1987). Offers a range of policy proposals aimed at increasing the proportion of blacks among college students and faculty. Authors—including Barbara Newell, Larry Leslie, James Blackwood, Charles Willie, and Edgar Epps—discuss trends in black enrollment and degree attainment at the undergraduate and graduate levels, financial inequities in previously segregated systems of public postsecondary education, achievement of black and white students in predominantly white and predominantly black institutions, and the future of Title VI enforcement. The book is intended for administrators, faculty, policy makers, and researchers.

Wilson, Reginald (ed.). *Race and Equity in Higher Education* (American Council on Education, 1983). Contains five essays produced by the American Council on Education-Aspen Institute Seminar on the Desegregation of Higher Education. Essays (by J. Egerton, J. E. Blackwell, J. L. Prestage, P. R. Dimond, and A. L. Berrian) examine the history and politics of higher education desegregation, provide data on demographic changes in recent decades, analyze constitutional standards and remedies, evaluate desegregation plans of states involved in *Adams v. Richardson* (see Sections 12.4.2 and 12.4.8) litigation, and propose new policies and agendas.

Sec. 12.5 (Dealing with the Federal Government)

Adler, Allan R. (ed.). *Litigation Under the Federal Open Government Laws: The Freedom of Information Act, the Privacy Act, the Government in the Sunshine Act, the Federal Advisory Committee Act* (18th ed., American Civil Liberties Union Foundation, 1993). Provides analysis, practical advice, and trial strategies for obtaining information from federal government agencies. Updated annually.

Administrative Conference of the United States. *Federal Administrative Procedure Sourcebook: Statutes and Related Materials* (2d ed., Office of the Chairman, Administrative Conference, 1992). A handy guide that collects together materials on the Administrative Procedure Act, Equal Access to Justice Act, Federal Advisory Committee Act, Freedom of Information Act, Negotiated Rulemaking Act, Privacy Act, Regulatory Flexibility Act, and other legislation regarding the administrative process. Includes texts of the Acts, legislative histories, an overview of each Act, agency regulations and executive orders, citations and bibliographies, and materials on judicial review of federal agency decisions.

Bouchard, Robert F., & Franklin, Justin D. (eds.). *Guidebook to the Freedom of Information and Privacy Acts* (2d ed., Clark Boardman Callaghan, 1986). A compilation of materials that explain the FOIA and the Privacy Act and provide guidance on how to obtain information under them.

Brademus, John. *The Politics of Education* (University of Oklahoma Press, 1987). Discusses the federal role in education, the legislative process with reference to education, contemporary themes and concerns regarding education policy, and the relationship between education and democracy. Written "from a highly personal perspective" by a former congressman who became president of a large private university after leaving Congress.

Clune, William, III. *The Deregulation Critique of the Federal Role in Education,* Project Report no. 82–A11 (Institute for Research on Educational Finance and Governance, Stanford University, 1982). Analyzes the theoretical basis for deregulation, the criticisms of then current federal regulatory efforts, and the benefits and disadvantages of deregulation.

Mintz, Benjamin, & Miller, Nancy. *A Guide to Federal Agency Rulemaking* (2d ed., Office of the Chairman, Administrative Conference of the United States, 1991). Provides comprehensive explanation and analysis of federal agency rule-making processes, including judicial review of rule making. Includes discussion of the Administrative Flexibility Act, the Negotiated Rulemaking Act of 1990, and the Paperwork Reduction Act.

Saunders, Charles B. "How to Keep Government from Playing the Featured Role," 59 *Educ. Record* 61 (1978). Author asserts that the federal presence on campus is permanent and proposes a strategy for coping with this presence. He suggests that both the government and postsecondary administrators adopt a "test of necessity" for determining when a new federal regulation may be needed, and that administrators commit themselves to "developing a system of self-regulation."

STATUTE INDEX

CASE INDEX

SUBJECT INDEX

organizations, 81–82; of captive and affiliated organizations, 82–88; express, 68, 69; implied, 68, 69; inherent, 68–69; and legal consequences, 69–71; and liability, 71; sources of, 67–68, 71–88, 132–134; of staff, 75–81; subdelegation of, 72; types of, 68–69

Auxiliary aids: and admissions, 172–173; for disabled students, 266–268, 568, 569

Auxiliary enterprises: administering, 278, 280; and contract law, 273–275; growth of, 272–273; and state noncompetition statutes, 275–278

Ayers, J., 549–551

B

Baida, A. H., 222
Bakaly, C. G., Jr., 132
Bakken, G. M., 63
Balancing test, in academic freedom, 306–307
Bankruptcy law, and debt collection, 231–235
Barmore Zucker, L. S., 261
Basic Educational Opportunity Grants, 578, 580
Bassler, S. E., 427
Baxter, F. V., 599–600
Bazluke, F. T., 121, 134
Beach, J. A., 61
Beaney, W. M., 356
Beckham, J., 394
Bedrosian, A., 596
Bell, D. A., Jr., 243, 600
Bender, D., 596
Bender, L. W., 11
Berman, D., 255
Berman, J., 396
Berman, P., 321n
Berrian, A. L., 601
Berry, R. C., 465
Bess, J. L., 132
Beta Upsilon, and liability, 426
Bickel, R. D., 59, 65–66, 134, 505–506
Birth control services, 269–271
Blackmun, H. A., 186, 189
Blackwell, J. E., 601
Blackwood, J., 600
Blasi, V., 243, 394
Block, D. J., 66
Bok, D., 61
Bookman, M., 134
Borowsky, P., 133
Bouchard, R. F., 601
Brademus, J., 601
Branchfield, E., 465
Branscomb, A. W., 396

Brawer, F. B., 12
Brechner, J., 59
Brennan, W. J., Jr., 186, 189, 191–195, 201–202
Broadcast Music, Inc., 525
Brown, L. M., 66
Brown, R. S., 324
Brown, V. L., 357–358, 419, 420
Buckwalter, R. L., 530, 531
Bunting, E., 157
Burdens of proof, and standards of review, 30–33
Bureau of National Affairs, 61
Burger, W. E., 186
Burling, P., 134, 136, 333, 543
Busey, J. C., 462
Bush, G.H.W., 222
Buss, W. G., 350
Butler, B. B., 211n, 243
Buttolph, K., 357–358
Byrne, J. P., 323, 395

C

Cage, M. C., 11
Calamari, J. D., 275, 280
California: academic freedom in, 308, 313–318; admissions in, 158, 178–179, 205; affirmative action in, 184–186, 189–195, 200, 202, 203; alcohol consumption in, 100; athletics in, 449–450, 454, 458, 464; authority in, 68–69, 81; birth control services in, 269–270; canvassing in, 473–474; case law in, 21; child care services in, 268–269; constitutional rights in, 112; contracts in, 141; debt collection in, 235, 236; degree revocation in, 293–294; disciplinary process in, 332; financial aid in, 229–231; housing in, 249; obscenity in, 377; personal liability in, 119–120; police relations in, 475–476, 478–479; privacy in, 148; protests in, 365; qualified privilege in, 29; searches and seizures in, 254; security on, 256–257, 260–261, 263; sexual harassment in, 298, 565; speech in, 388–389; standards of review in, 33; state constitutional rights in, 48–49; student organizations in 403–404, 422; tort liability in, 91; trespass in, 483–485, 486

Campbell, N. D., 600
Campus common law, 18–19, 63
Canvassing: noncommercial, 498–501; of student voters, 473–474
Cappalli, R., 599
Carmona, J., 210
Carnegie Council on Policy Studies in Higher Education, 9